Richard S. Moore Family
1811-1998

The Genealogy of the Moore Family
By Audrey Hopkins

Table of Contents

Acknowledgments 3

The Family Reunion 4

Moore Coat of Arms 5

Descendants of Richard S. Moore 6

Family Group Sheets 76

Index 428

Copyright © 1999
All rights reserved.
Publishing Rights: Turner Publishing Company

This book or any part thereof may not be reproduced by any means, mechanical or electronic, without the written consent of the Author and Publisher, except for personal family historical research.

The information contained in this publication was produced from available materials. The Publisher is not responsible for errors or omissions.

ISBN: 978-1-68162-242-2

Acknowledgments

I want to thank everyone for helping provide the information I needed to create this book. Especially my wonderful sister and her husband, Janice and Orval Bair. Also Elwood Moore, Willa Mae Case and June Gerlode. Without their help, none of this would have been possible. Also to Alva Moore for being understanding when I was gone from home.

My sincere appreciation to the personnel of each county courthouse, library, and funeral homes in the United States for their courtesy, kindness and sincere help in this project.

We apologize for any errors if there is any. To all of you many thanks and hope you will enjoy this book as much as I have enjoyed putting it together. We love you all and may the Good Lord be with you all.

The author

Audrey F. Hopkins

The Family Reunion

From miles and miles away they came
   to see their precious beloved ones.
They talk and cry; they laugh and sing
   of every little happening.

Their hearts are joyful as they can be,
And, yet, they weep for the lost
   they cannot see.

The childlike frolics, they come to mind
As they share and remember what's left behind.

Oh, their hearts are aflutter with days gone by,
And, for a time, they have left today by the wayside.
But, all too soon, the hours have past;
They have questioned and pondered to the very last.

The good-byes are at hand.
Their hearts crumble, you see,
As they tuck away every precious memory.

They laugh, and they hold everything in their heart,
As they say their good-byes, and, then, do they part.

                        Ronda L. Bair
                        June 5, 1988

The surname MOORE has two possible sources of origin, one from the Old French more, - 'swarthy' and the other from the Old English mor, - 'marsh.'

Once everyone was known by a single name but this led to confusion and so an extra name was adopted. Thus, a man named John who was of swarthy complexion might be known as 'John (the) Moore,' and William who dwelt near a marsh as 'William (of the) Moore,' the additional name eventually becoming hereditary as a surname.

Early records mention William de More of Suffolk in the Domesday Book of 1086; Johannes Fitius More of Lincolnshire in the records of the Templars (1185) and Simon atte Moore in the 1296 Subsidy Rolls of Sussex.

Sir John Moore (1761-1809) was a famous British General who died at Coruna after defeating the French army.

Among early emigrants from England to America was John Moore who is recorded in Massachusetts in 1631. Benjamin Moore (1748-1816) was celebrated American protestant Episcopal clergyman.

The arms illustrated may be described heraldically as: Azure, on a chief Moor's head proper wreathed about the temples; and for Motto: 'Vis Unita Fortior'. Writers of the past have attributed symbolism to the tinctures and charges of heraldry-thus, azure (blue) is said to denote Loyalty; or (gold), Generosity; and gules (red), Magnanimity. The crest obviously is intended as a pun on the surname, and the motto may be translated as "Strength united is the powerful."

Descendants of Richard S Moore

Generation No. I

1. RICHARD S^1 MOORE was born 1811 in VA. He married REBECCA OWEN 1832, daughter of ARCHIBALD OWEN and NANCY JUDD.

Notes for RICHARD S MOORE:
Listed on the 1840-60 census Illinois, then 1870-80 census Kansas, no record after that.

More about RICHARD S MOORE:
Census: Bet. 1840-60, Little Rock Twp, Kendall County, IL
Occupation: Mason-Farmer.

More about REBECCA OWEN:
Occupation: Housewife.

Children of RICHARD MOORE and REBECCA OWEN are:

- 2. i. WILLIAM H^2 MOORE, b. 1833, Illinois.
- 3. ii. REUBEN MOORE, b. November 29, 1834, Kendall County, IL; d. March 08, 1884, Elgin, Chautauqua County, KS.
- 4. iii. SENY MOORE, b. August 17, 1836, Aurora, Kane County, IL; d. November 15, 1908, Inglewood, Los Angeles County, CA.
- 5. iv. MATILDA JANE MOORE, b. March 11, 1837, Plano, Kendall County, IL; d. April 24, 1926, Jefferson, Greene County, IA.
- v. THOMAS S MOORE, b. 1840, Illinois; d. 1939; m. ADELINE ISABELL, January 08, 1863, Kendall County, IL.

    Marriage notes for THOMAS MOORE and ADELINE ISABELL:
    Copy of marriage license.

- 6. vi. JAMES F MOORE, b. March 04, 1843, Kendall County, IL; d. December 18, 1915, Lincolin Twp, Madison County, IA.
- 7. vii. CALVIN W MOORE, b, February 1845, Illinois.
- viii. MARTHA MOORE, b. 1847; m. THOMAS BASCOM.
- 8. ix. CHARLOTTE M MOORE, b. 1849, Illinois.
- 9. x. PHOEBE C MOORE, b. 1852, Illinois.
- 10. xi. MARION M MOORE, b. 1854, Illinois.
- 11. xii. SUSAN N MOORE, b. October 03, 1855, Putman County, IL; d. August 24, 1939, Jay, Delaware County, OK.
- xiii. ANDREW J MOORE, b. 1858, m. AMANDA PAUL, September 17, 1880, Eldorado, Butler County, KS.

    Marriage notes for ANDREW MOORE and AMANDA PAUL:
    Copy of marriage license.

- xiv. GEORGE MOORE.

Generation No. 2

2. WILLIAM H[2] MOORE (RICHARD S[1]) was born 1833 in Illinois.

Children of WILLIAM H MOORE are:
- i. CLARENCE[3] MOORE.
- ii. JOSEPHINE MOORE.

3. REUBEN[2] MOORE (RICHARD S[1]) was born November 29, 1834 in Kendall County, IL, and died March 08, 1884 in Elgin, Chautauqua County, KS. He married (1) MELVINA BARBARA PAUL August 23, 1851 in Pennfield, Kendall County, IL. He married (2) ELIZABETH A PITTS June 26, 1883 in Sedan, Chautauqua County, KS.

Notes for REUBEN MOORE:
Copy of military discharge, pension papers.

More about REUBEN MOORE:
Buried Location: Oak Grove Cemetery, Chautauqua County, KS.
Fact 2: Helped the Negro slaves to escape on their way North.
Military: Private, Co 5, 15th Regt Kansas Cav Vols.
Occupation: Farmer.
Property: March 04, 1874, Land Application No 2153.

More about MELVINA BARBARA PAUL:
Buried Location: Oak Grove Cemetery, Chautauqua County, KS.
Occupation: Housewife.

Marriage notes for REUBEN MOORE and MELVINA PAUL:
Copy of marriage registration, certificate of marriage, married by Justice of Peace Josiah Lehman.

Notes for ELIZABETH A PITTS:
Copies of warranty deeds, deed records.

Marriage notes for REUBEN MOORE and ELIZABETH PITTS:
Copy of marriage license; married by Justice of Peace Joseph Layman.

Children of REUBEN MOORE and MELVINA PAUL are:
- 12. i. WILLIAM OSCAR[3] MOORE, b. May 31, 1852, Kendall County, IL; d. September 17, 1921, Whitewater, Butler County, KS.

- ii. RICHARD EDGAR MOORE, b. July 03, 1854, Iowa; d. January 21, 1934; m. EUNICE ELECTA ADAMS, January 1, 1882, Cariboo, Butler County, KS.

    Notes for RICHARD EDGAR MOORE:
    Copy of deed record.

    More about EUNICE ELECTA ADAMS:
    Cause of death was child birth.

    Marriage notes for RICHARD MOORE and EUNICE ADAMS:
    Copy of marriage license.

- iii. JOHN EDWARD MOORE, b. August 1, 1857, Chautauqua, Chautauqua County, KS; d. September 22, 1869, Potwin, Butler County, KS.

    More about JOHN EDWARD MOORE:
    Buried Location: Shaffer Cemetery, Butler County, KS.

- 13. iv. JAMES MONROE MOORE, b. October 26, 1859, Lawrence, Douglas County, KS; d. July 20, 1954, Chautauqua, Chautauqua County, KS.
- v. MINNIE MOORE, b. 1860, Kansas.
- 14. vi. MELISSA REBECCA MOORE, b. December 19, 1862, Douglas County, KS; d. April 30, 1923, Berryville, Carroll County, AR.
- 15. vii. SARAH LOUISE MOORE, b. July 06, 1867, Chautauqua, Chautauqua County, KS; d. January 12, 1889.
- 16. viii. ETTA ELLEN MOORE, b. October 27, 1874, Butler County, KS; d. October 3, 1945, Dewey, Washington County, OK.

4. SENY[2] MOORE (RICHARD S[1]), b. August 17, 1836 in Aurora, Kane County, IL; d. November 15, 1908 in Inglewood, Los Angeles County, CA; m. EDMUND HALL, May 07, 1856 in Kendall County, IL, son of DAVID HALL and SARAH JENNER.

More about SENY MOORE:
Buried Location: Shaffer Cemetery, Butler County, KS.

More about EDMUND HALL:
Buried Location: August 27, 1894, Shaffer Cemetery, Butler County, KS.
Occupation: Farmer.

Children of SENY MOORE and EDMUND HALL are:

17. i. HARRIETT EL NORA[3] HALL, b. December 15, 1857, Plano, Kendall County, IL; d. May 29, 1947, El Dorado, Butler County, KS.
18. ii. FRANCIS LEATON HALL, b. May 18, 1859, Plano, Kendall County, IL; d. January 24, 1936, Kaw City, Kaw County, OK.
19. iii. OWEN ARCHEBALD HALL, b. July 09, 1862, Plano, Kendall County, IL; d. July 14, 1950, Butler County, KS
20. iv. ELMER ELWOOD HALL, b. November 14, 1863, Chicago, Cook County, IL; d. June 06, 1942, El Dorado, Butler County, KS.
21. v. AMERICA SENY HALL, b. January 17, 1865, Aurora, Kane County, IL; d. March 15, 1909, Long Beach, Los Angeles County, CA.
    vi. DAVID R HALL, b. January 29, 1866, IA; d. February 05, 1881, KS.

    More about DAVID R HALL:
    Buried Location: February 1881, Shaffer Cemetery, Butler County, KS.

22. vii. VERNE REUBEN HALL, b. December 15, 1868, Potwin, Butler County, KS; d. January 19, 1939, El Dorado, Butler County, KS.
23. viii. FLORENCE ANN HALL, b. February 2, 1873, Potwin, Butler County, KS; d. May 22, 1947, Potwin, Butler County, KS.
    ix. ROBERT E HALL, b. January 23, 1874, KS; d. January 20, 1907, Potwin, Butler County, KS.

    Notes for ROBERT E HALL:
    As was told to me, Janice (Hall) Bair, by Aunt Celia Miller. Robert died of a slit throat by a jealous boyfriend of the school teacher. One day Robert drove out to see his ex-girlfriend, who was the school teacher, and while they were talking, her boyfriend arrived and became very angry. The boyfriend then killed the teacher and slit Robert's throat. Robert was able to drive the wagon back home, where he lived for three days before dying.
    This story was written by a neighbor boy by the name of Don Wilson. I do not know at what age he was when he wrote this story, but I do have a copy (page 4 and 5) that I take as being from a journal that he had typed up.
    This incident, perhaps, should not be in this story as it is too gruesome but it was a happening in my early lifetime. I was 15 years old.
    One cold winter night, it was January 16, 1907, Mother and I were at home. A knock sounded at the door. It was our neighbor from 1/2 mile away east. When mother opened the door, the man could hardly speak and almost fell. "Oh! Mrs Wilson, someone has almost killed Bob!"
    Mother was always one to help so she bundled us up and we walked to the neighbors, the Halls. We were the first neighbors to get there. The family was too shocked to do anything. Mother took over and tried to dress the wounds in his neck as best she could. The noise of his breathing I can almost still hear. Mother had Mose Hall, a brother, go to Potwin for Dr. Stalman. That was almost five miles. There were no telephones then of course. It was about midnight.
    We had no idea what had happened. Finally Dr. Stalman came. Bob was still bleeding very bad. To stop the bleeding the doctor put formaldehyde on the wounds. This was good at the time as it cooked the flesh.
    Still no one knew for sure just what had happened. Next morning someone found Bob's horse and buggy at the barn. The buggy was all bloody and the lap robe was stiff with frozen blood. Next, someone went to the Whitewater school house and there they found Mary H (Myrtle) Glass on the floor, dead! Blood was all over the inside of the room where she had tried to get away.
    Soon it was known that Bob Hall had killed his sweetheart, Myrt Glass, because of jealousy over another man, then Bob tried to commit suicide.
    Bob sorta recovered but in three or four days the flesh at his throat began to give way and the blood started to run. Bob bled to death on the morning of January 20, 1907. There had been an outsider at the home all the time C.D. was there and a couple family members, and it took all four of them to hold Bob on the bed as he died. He was a large man.
    If Bob Hall had walked out of that house there would have been a public lynching, even though the Halls and the Glasses were the "salt of the Earth." Tis best things went as they did!
    To me at that time it didn't seem like much of a thing but as the years go by, as they do, one will look back and can't help but think of the Higher Power that guides our destiny, Very few see such as this but it did happen!

    More about ROBERT E HALL:
    Buried Location: Shaffer Cemetery, Butler County, KS.

24. x. EUSEBA ELMIRA HALL, b. April 23, 1877, KS; d. May 04, 1954, Port Angeles, WI.
25. xi. ALMEDA MAUDE HALL, b. August 17, 1880, Potwin, Butler County, KS; d. December 26, 1969, El Dorado, Butler County, KS.
26. xii. MARY ELMIRA HALL, b. May 05, 1883, Kansas; d. 1963.

5. MATILDA JANE^2 MOORE (RICHARD S^1) was born March 11, 1837 in Plano, Kendall County, IL; d. April 24, 1926 in Jefferson, Greene County, IA; m. HARVEY I GREENFIELD October 23, 1856 in Kendall County, IL.

    Notes for MATILDA JANE MOORE:
Copy of death certificate.
No stone marker.

    More about MATILDA JANE MOORE:
Buried Location: April 26, 1926, Pleasant Hill Cemetery, IA.

    Notes for HARVEY I GREENFIELD:
No stone marker.

    Marriage notes for MATILDA MOORE and HARVEY GREENFIELD:
Copy of marriage license.

Children of MATILDA MOORE and HARVEY GREENFIELD are:

27.   i. SARAH REBECCA^3 GREENFIELD, b. January 29, 1858, Plano, Kendall County, IL; d. January 03, 1937, Martensdale, Warren County, IA.
    ii. EMMA JANE GREENFIELD, b. January 16, 1860, Plano, Kendall County, IL; d. 1860, Plano, Kendall County, IL.
    iii. GEORGE ELMER GREENFIELD, b. March 11, 1862, Plano, Kendall County, IL; d. March 28, 1941, Amaka, Greene County, IA, m. EFFIE FOSHER.

    More about GEORGE ELMER GREENFIELD:
Buried Location: March 30, 1941, Cooper, Greene County, IA.

    iv. JAMES IRA GREENFIELD, b. December 20, 1863, Milbrook, Kendall County, IL; d. April 18, 1947, University Park, Mahaska County, IA; m. MARY ELLEN WILSON, November 24, 1887, Winterset, Madison County, IA.

    More about JAMES IRA GREENFIELD:
Buried Location: April 20, 1947, University Park, Mahaska County, IA.

    v. CHARLOTTE GREENFIELD, b. March 13, 1870, Massilon, Cedar County, IA.
    vi. LILLY MAE GREENFIELD, b. March 13, 1870, Massilon, Cedar County, IA; m. WILLIAM E ATCHISON, July 04, 1887, Madison County, IA.

    Notes for LILLY MAE GREENFIELD:
Called Mary.

    Notes for WILLIAM E ATCHISON:
Called Will.

6. JAMES F^2 MOORE, (RICHARD S^1), b. March 04, 1843, Kendall County, IL; d. December 18, 1915 in Lincolin Twp, Madison County, IA; m. MARTHA M SHEARER December 31, 1868 in Madison County, IA.

More about JAMES F MOORE:
Buried Location: Peru Cemetery, IA.

More about MARTHA M SHEARER:
Buried Location: Peru Cemetery, IA.

Marriage notes for JAMES MOORE and MARTHA SHEARER:
Copy of marriage license.

Children of JAMES MOORE and MARTHA SHEARER are:
    i. IRA AUSTIN^3 MOORE, b. October 01, 1869, Iowa; d. June 07, 1938, Iowa; m. MARY ROSE APPLEGATE, September 04, 1894, Madison County, IA.

    More about IRA AUSTIN MOORE:
Buried Location: Winterset, Madison County, IA.

    Notes for MARY ROSE APPLEGATE:
Called Minnie.

28.   ii. WILLIAM H MOORE, b. February 01, 1871, Iowa; d. November 02, 1938, Madison County, IA.
    iii. NETTIE M MOORE, b. April 12, 1872, Iowa; d. June 28, 1937, Madison County, IA; m. ELWOOD C HUSKEY, October 02, 1892, Madison County, IA.

    More about NETTIE M MOORE:
Buried Location: July 02, 1937, Barney, IA.

iv. MARY MOORE, b. 1875, Iowa; d. 1890, Iowa.

> More about MARY MOORE:
> Buried Location: Peru, IA.

v. MYRTLE E MOORE, b. December 12, 1877, Iowa; d. June 12, 1946, Madison County, IA.

> More about MYRTLE E MOORE:
> Buried Location: June 14, 1946, Peru, IA.

vi. JAMES CLARENCE MOORE, b. January 21, 1879, Iowa; d. September 16, 1936, Iowa.

> More about JAMES CLARENCE MOORE:
> Buried Location: September 19, 1936, Peru, IA.

vii. HERBERT L MOORE, b. May 28, 1881, Iowa; d. November 21, 1950, Iowa; m. EDITH BEECROFT, August 13, 1906, Madison County, IA.

> More about HERBERT L MOORE:
> Buried Location: Peru, IA.

viii. ELIZABETH ANN MOORE, b. August 31, 1886, Peru, Madison County, IA; d. November 12, 1938, Murray, Clarke County, IA; m. GEORGE CLIFTON, November 15, 1903, Winterset, Madison County, IA.

7. CALVIN W^2 MOORE (RICHARD S^1), b. February 1845 in Illinois; m. CARINDA ??? 1873.

Children of CALVIN MOORE and CARINDA ??? are:
i. ADA^3 MOORE, b. May 1872, KS; m. (1) LEWIS BYRAN, 1894; m. (2) J E WOLFE, March 25, 1912, Bartlesville, Washington County, OK.

> Marriage notes for ADA MOORE and J WOLFE:
> Copy marriage license.

ii. MINNIE MOORE, b. 1876, Iowa.
iii. GEORGE MOORE, b. October 1884, Kansas.

8. CHARLOTTE M^2 MOORE (RICHARD S^1), b. 1849 in IL; m. THOMAS GARRITY March 01, 1876 in Madison County, IA.

Marriage notes for CHARLOTTE MOORE and THOMAS GARRITY:
Copy of marriage record

Children of CHARLOTTE MOORE and THOMAS GARRITY are:
i. JULIE E^3 GARRITY, b. 1877, Iowa.
ii. SARAH W GARRITY, b. 1879, Iowa.

9. PHOEBE C^2 MOORE (RICHARD S^1), b. 1852 in Illinois. She married JAMES H COLLEY October 12, 1869 in Butler County, KS.

Marriage notes for PHOEBE MOORE and JAMES COLLEY:
Copy of marriage license.

Children of PHOEBE MOORE and JAMES COLLEY are:
i. LAURA F^3 COLLEY, b. 1870, KS; m. JOHN E SUELTHAUS, June 30, 1892, Sedgwick County, Kansas.
ii. MAUDE COLLEY, b. 1872, Kansas.
iii. LELIA COLLEY, b. 1874, Kansas.
iv. EMMA COLLEY, b. 1878, Kansas.
v. WALTER COLLEY, b. March 27, 1881, Kansas; d. November 29, 1894, Kansas.

> More about WALTER COLLEY:
> Buried Location: Greenwood Cemetery, KS

vi. GEORGE COLLEY, b. 1885, Kansas; d. 1885, Kansas.

10. MARION M^2 MOORE (RICHARD S^1), was born 1854 in Illinois; married ??? DANE.

Children of MARION MOORE and ??? DANE:
i. WILLIAM^3 MOORE.
ii. HELEN MOORE.

11. SUSAN N² MOORE (RICHARD S¹) was born October 03, 1855 in Putman County, IL, and died August 24, 1939 in Jay, Delaware County, OK. She married (1) ??? MAYS. She married (2) SAMUEL R ATKINSON October 26, 1872 in Eldorado Twp, Butler County, KS, son of WILLIAM ATKINSON and CATHERINE FAUL.

Notes for SUSAN N MOORE:
Copy of death certificate.

More about SUSAN N MOORE:
Buried Location: August 26, 1939, Mt Hope Cemetery, Independence, KS.
Occupation: Housewife.

Notes for SAMUEL R ATKINSON:
Copy of pension claim.

More about SAMUEL R ATKINSON:
Buried Location: Mt Hope Cemetery, Independence, KS.
Fact 1: Civil War, Co. F Regt KS. Cav. Vols.
Occupation: Farmer.

Marriage notes for SUSAN MOORE and SAMUEL ATKINSON:
Copy of marriage license.

Children of SUSAN MOORE and SAMUEL ATKINSON are:

    i. CHARLES A³ ATKINSON, b. October 17, 1873, Potwin, Butler County, KS; d. September 16, 1874, Potwin, Butler County, KS.

    More about CHARLES A ATKINSON:
    Buried Location: Shaffer Cemetery, Butler County, KS.

    ii. ROBERT ATKINSON, b. September 13, 1875, Potwin, Butler County, KS; d. November 07, 1875, Potwin, Butler County, KS.

    More about ROBERT ATKINSON:
    Buried Location: Shaffer Cemetery, Butler County, KS.

29.   iii. ADA FRANCIS ATKINSON, b. April 12, 1876, Butler County, KS; d. July 24, 1959, Drumright, Creek County, OK.

    iv. WILLIAM R ATKINSON, b. August 20, 1878, Butler County, KS; m. CLEMMIE JENNINGS August 06, 1902, Howard, Elk County, KS.

    Marriage notes for WILLIAM ATKINSON and CLEMMIE JENNINGS:
    Copy of marriage license.

    v. ALPHARD M ATKINSON, b. December 28, 1880.
    vi. EFFIE E ATKINSON, b. February 24, 1883; m. JOSEPH GARRISON, July 18, 1900, Howard, Elk County, KS.
    vii. FRED L ATKINSON, b. May 25, 1887.
    vii. MINNIE M ATKINSON, b. June 29, 1891.
30.   ix. JOHN C ATKINSON, b. March 12, 1899.

Generation No. 3

12. WILLIAM OSCAR³ MOORE (REUBEN², RICHARD S¹), was born May 31, 1852 in Kendall County, IL; died September 17, 1921 in Whitewater, Butler County, KS; married LOUISA M ADAMS April 16, 1876 in Towanda, Butler County, KS, daughter of DAVID ADAMS and SARAH WAIT.

Notes for WILLIAM OSCAR MOORE:
Copy of probate papers, newspaper obit and car accident report.
Never filed for birth certificate.
Was made guardian over Etta Ellen Moore when her parents died, but never raised her.

More about WILLIAM OSCAR MOORE:
Buried Location: Shaffer Cemetery, Butler County, KS.
Occupation: Farmer.

More about LOUISA M ADAMS:
Buried Location: February 28, 1953, Shaffer Cemetery, Butler County, KS.
Occupation: Housewife.

Marriage notes for WILLIAM MOORE and LOUISA ADAMS:
Copy of marriage license.

Children of WILLIAM MOORE and LOUISA ADAMS are:
- 31. i. OLIVE⁴ MOORE, b. Potwin, Butler County, KS.
-     ii. E WILLIAM MOORE, b. 1877, Potwin, Butler County, KS; d. 1894, Kansas.

More about E WILLIAM MOORE:
Buried Location: Shaffer Cemetery, Butler County, KS.
Fact 1: 17 yrs old when died.

- 32. iii. EFFIE, SARAH MOORE, b. June 27, 1879, Potwin, Butler County, KS; d. August 1977. Boise, Ada County, ID.
- 33. iv. LEON ARTHUR MOORE, b. October 11, 1883, Potwin, Butler County, KS; d. October 18, 1969, Wichita, Sedgwick County, KS.
- 34. v. REUBEN DAVID MOORE, b. November 21, 1886, Murdock Twp, Butler County, KS; d. April 14, 1963, El Dorado, Butler County, KS.
- 35. vi. ORIN EGAR MOORE, b. November 29, 1888. Potwin, Butler County, KS; d. August 09, 1982, Newton, Harvey County, KS.
-     vii. ELMER MOORE b. 1891, Potwin, Butler County, KS; d. Potwin, Butler County, KS.

    More about ELMER MOORE:
    Buried Location: Shaffer Cemetery, Butler County, KS

-     viii. RUTH MOORE, b. 1893, Potwin, Butler County, KS; d. 1900, Potwin, Butler County, KS.

    More about RUTH MOORE:
    Buried Location: Shaffer Cemetery, Butler County, KS.

- 36. ix. RAYMOND I MOORE, b. April 03, 1896, Potwin, Butler County, KS; d. December 18, 1979, Newton, Harvey County, KS.
-     x. INFANT MOORE, b. 1899, Potwin, Butler County, KS; d. 1899, Potwin, Butler County, KS.

    More about INFANT MOORE:
    Buried Location: Shaffer Cemetery, Butler County, KS.

13. JAMES MONROE³ MOORE (REUBEN², RICHARD S¹) was born October 26, 1859 in Lawrence, Douglas County, KS, and died July 20, 1954 in Chautauqua, Chautauqua County, KS. He married JULIA BELL SMITH August 16, 1884 in Elgin, Chautauqua County, KS, daughter of THOMAS SMITH and MARY DALE.

More about JAMES MONROE MOORE:
Buried Location: Oak Grove Cemetery, Chautauqua County, KS.
Occupation: Farmer/Santa Fe Railroad.

More about JULIA BELL SMITH:
Occupation: Housewife.

Marriage notes for JAMES MOORE and JULIA SMITH:
Copy of marriage license.

Children of JAMES MOORE and JULIA SMITH are:
- 37. i. DELLA M⁴ MOORE, b. April 15, 1885, Chautauqua, Chautauqua County, KS; d. 1918.
-     ii. INFANT TWIN MOORE, b. April 15, 1885, Chautauqua, Chautauqua County, KS; d. April 15, 1885, Chautauqua, Chautauqua County, KS.

More about INFANT TWIN MOORE:
Fact 1: twin to Della

38. iii. ROSA L MOORE, b. September 08, 1887, Chautauqua, Chautauqua County, KS.
39. iv. EVA V MOORE, b. November 14, 1889, Osage County, KS.
40. v. CLARA S MOORE, b. February 20, 1892, Chautauqua, Chautauqua County, KS; d. September 09, 1926, OK.
    vi. LESTER L MOORE, b. 1894; m. LIDA L CARRIKIER, February 25, 1920, Sedan, Chautauqua County, KS.

    Marriage notes for LESTER MOORE and LIDA CARRIKIER:
    Copy of marriage license.

41. vii. CLYDE EARL MOORE, b. July 31, 1896, Oklahoma; d. August 26, 1981, Sedan, Chautauqua County, KS.

14. MELISSA REBECCA^3 **MOORE** (REUBEN^2, RICHARD S^1) was born December 19, 1862 in Douglas County, KS, and died April 30, 1923 in Berryville, Carroll County, AR. She married JOHN IRA TAYLOR July 04, 1881 in Butler County, KS, son of ROBERT TAYLOR and JENNIE WEIR.

Notes for MELISSA REBECCA MOORE:
Raised Etta Ellen Moore when her parents died.

More about MELISSA REBECCA MOORE:
Buried Location: Altoona, Wilson County, KS.
Occupation: Housewife.

More about JOHN IRA TAYLOR:
Buried Location: Altoona, Wilson County, KS.
Occupation: Blacksmith.

Children of MELISSA MOORE and JOHN TAYLOR are:
42. i. MELVINA JANE^4 TAYLOR, b. May 10, 1882, Elgin, Chautauqua County, KS; d. February 06, 1945.
43. ii. CARL WILLIAM TAYLOR, b. June 16, 1884, Butler County, KS; d. February 22, 1972, Mesa, Maricopa County, AZ.
44. iii. MABEL BLANCHE, TAYLOR, b. December 19, 1886, Butler County, KS; d. April 23, 1960, Eureka, Greenwood County, KS.
45. iv. JAMES ORCEN TAYLOR, b. October 19, 1890, Altoona, Wilson County, KS; d. May 1964, Newkirk, Kay County, OK.
46. v. GLADYS HAZEL TAYLOR, b. November 14, 1895, Newkirk, Kay County, OK; d. February 20, 1977, Pratt, Pratt County, KS.
    vi. JOHN HAROLD TAYLOR, b. March 20, 1898, Chanute, Neosho County, KS; d. February 04, 1949.
47. vii. GEORGE LACKEY TAYLOR, b. December 08, 1901, Butler County, KS; d. February 1957, Bethal, Oxford County. ME.

15. SARAH LOUISE^3 **MOORE** (REUBEN^2, RICHARD S^1) was born July 06, 1867 in Chautauqua, Chautauqua County, KS, and died January 12, 1889. She married (1) WILLIAM THOMPSON SMITH, son of THOMAS SMITH and MARY DALE. She married (2) CLAUDE M THURMAN in Bartlesville, Washington County, OK.

Notes for SARAH LOUISE MOORE:
Picture of tombstone.

More about SARAH LOUISE MOORE:
Burial: Oak Grove Cemetery, Chautauqua County, KS.

Notes for WILLIAM THOMPSON SMITH:
Picture of tombstone, copy of funeral home record.

More about WILLIAM THOMPSON SMITH:
Burial: December 08, 1946, McGill Cemetery, Butler County, KS.
Cause of Death: Fracture 3rd cervical vertebra auto accident.
Occupation: Farmer.

Marriage notes for SARAH MOORE and CLAUDE THURMAN:
Copy of marriage license

Children of SARAH MOORE and WILLIAM SMITH are:
48. i. OSCAR L^4 SMITH, b. February 1886, Kansas; d. 1963.
49. ii. BERTHA M SMITH, b. March 1888, Kansas; d. 1966.

16. ETTA ELLEN^3 **MOORE** (REUBEN^2, RICHARD S^1) was born October 27, 1874 in Butler County, KS, and died October 03, 1945 in Dewey, Washington County, OK. She married GEORGE ALLEN WILEY March 19, 1893 in Altoona, Wilson County, KS.

Notes for ETTA ELLEN MOORE:
Copy of newspaper obit.

More about ETTA ELLEN MOORE:
Buried Location: October 06, 1945, Altoona, Wilson County, KS.

Notes for GEORGE ALLEN WILEY:
Copy of newspaper obit.

More about GEORGE ALLEN WILEY:
Buried Location: Altoona, Wilson County, KS.
Occupation: Banker/Post Office/Dewey Portland Cement Co.

Marriage notes for ETTA MOORE and GEORGE WILEY:
Copy of marriage license.

Children of ETTA MOORE and GEORGE WILEY are:

50.   i.   STELLA ADALINE[4] WILEY, b. January 13, 1894, Altoona, Wilson County, KS; d. November 01, 1986, Dewey Washington County, OK.

      ii.   WALTER GEORGE WILEY, b. May 27, 1895, Altoona, Wilson County, KS; d. June 18, 1941, Newton, Harvey County, KS; m. IRENE SULLIVAN.

        Notes for WALTER GEORGE WILEY:
        Copy of newspaper obit.

        More about WALTER GEORGE WILEY:
        Cause of Death: Auto accident.

        Notes for IRENE SULLIVAN:
        Copy of newspaper obit.

        More about IRENE SULLIVAN:
        Buried Location: Dewey Cemetery, Dewey, OK.

      iii.   REUBEN WILLIAM WILEY, b. March 04, 1899, Altoona, Wilson County, KS; d. May 28, 1904, Harrison County, AR.

        More about REUBEN WILLIAM WILEY:
        Buried Location: Altoona, Wilson County, KS.
        Cause of Death: Rheumatic fever.

      iv.   JOHN MOORE WILEY, b. October 23, 1904, Altoona, Wilson County, KS; d. March 14, 1934, Oklahoma City, Oklahoma County, OK; m. IRMA ROGERS WILLAMS.

        Notes for JOHN MOORE WILEY:
        Copy of newspaper obit and funeral register.

        More about JOHN MOORE WILEY:
        Buried Location: March 16, 1934, Altoona, Wilson County, KS.
        Fact 1: Killed at work. Occupation: Gauger for Wolverine Oil Co.

17. HARRIETT EL NORA[3] HALL (SENY[2] MOORE, RICHARD S[1]), b. December 15, 1857 in Plano, Kendall County, IL; d. May 29, 1947 in El Dorado, Butler County, KS; m. ROBERT J KELLY October 24, 1890 in El Dorado, Butler County, KS.

Notes for HARRIETT EL NORA HALL:
Was called Nora.
Copy of obituary and funeral home record.

More about HARRIETT EL NORA HALL:
Buried Location: June 01, 1947, McGill Cemetery, Potwin, Butler County, KS.
Cause of death: Myocarditis.

More about ROBERT J KELLY:
Buried Location: McGill Cemetery, Potwin, Butler County, KS.

Marriage notes for HARRIETT HALL and ROBERT KELLY:
Copy of marriage license.

Children of HARRIETT HALL and ROBERT KELLY are:
      i.   MOSE[4] KELLY.
      ii.   ROBERT E KELLY.
      iii.   ROMONA KELLY.

18. FRANCIS LEATON[3] HALL (SENY[2] MOORE, RICHARD S[1]), b. May 18, 1859 in Plano, Kendall County, IL; d. January 24, 1936 in Kaw City, Kaw County, OK; m. RACHEL CAROLINE PAUL January 06, 1881 in El Dorado, Butler County, KS, daughter of WILLIAM PAUL and ELIZA CHASE.

More about FRANCIS LEATON HALL:
Buried Location: Shaffer Cemetery, Butler County, KS.
Fact 1: Arrived in Potwin, KS in 1867.

More about RACHEL CAROLINE PAUL:
Buried Location: Shaffer Cemetery, Butler County, KS.

Marriage notes for FRANCIS HALL and RACHEL PAUL:
Copy of marriage license.

Children of FRANCIS HALL and RACHEL PAUL are:
51. i.   GRACE MAUDE[4] HALL, b. July 27, 1881, Potwin, Butler County, KS; d. September 28, 1962, El Dorado, Butler County, KS.
52. ii.   ROY LUTRELL HALL, b. August 03, 1882, Potwin, Butler County, KS; d. July 12, 1959, Elko, Elko County, NV.
53. iii. ALICE ELIZA HALL, b. March 20, 1884, Potwin, Butler County, KS; d. November 08, 1930, Newton, Harvey County, KS.
54. iv.   LULU SENY HALL, b. November 07, 1886, Potwin, Butler County, KS; d. 1982, Sweeny, Matagorda County, TX.
     v.   JAMES EDMUND HALL, b. January 17, 1888, Oak Valley, Elk County, KS; d. February 02, 1960; m. EMMA MOSSMAN.

           Notes for JAMES EDMUND HALL:
           Was called Ed.

55. vi.   IRA EMMUTT HALL, b. November 05, 1890, Potwin, Butler County, KS; d. August 28, 1974, La Habra, Orange County, CA.
56. vii. GUY CHRISTIAN HALL, b. January 03, 1894, Potwin, Butler County, KS; d. January 08, 1961, Newton, Harvey County, KS.
57. viii. CELIA LAVERNA HALL, b. December 29, 1895, Potwin, Butler County, KS; d. July 11, 1987, Buena Vista, Chaffee County, CO.
58. ix.   ZACHARY HURSHEL HALL, b. December 20, 1900, Potwin, Butler County, KS; d, June 02, 1979, Newton, Harvey County, KS.

19. OWEN ARCHEBALD[3] HALL (SENY[2] MOORE, RICHARD S[1]), b. July 09, 1862 in Plano, Kendall County, IL; d. July 14, 1950 in Butler County, KS; m. FRANCES EMMA LETZKUS October 21, 1896 in El Dorado, Butler County, KS.

More about OWEN ARCHEBALD HALL:
Buried Location: McGill Cemetery, Potwin, Butler County, KS.

Notes for FRANCES EMMA LETZKUS:
Also known as Aunt Doll.

More about FRANCES EMMA LETZKUS:
Buried Location: McGill Cemetery, Potwin, Butler County, KS.

Marriage notes for OWEN HALL and FRANCES LETZKUS:
Copy of marriage license.

Children of OWEN HALL and FRANCES LETZKUS are:
     i.   MABEL INEZ[4] HALL, b. December 21, 1896, El Dorado, Butler County, KS; d. May 31, 1933, Potwin, Butler County, KS; m. CECIL HAROLD POE, June 23, 1915, El Dorado, Butler County, KS.

           Notes for MABEL INEZ HALL:
           Copy of funeral home record.

           More about MABEL INEZ HALL:
           Buried Location: June 02, 1933, McGill Cemetery, Potwin, Butler County, KS.
           Cause of death: Strychnine poisoning.

           Notes for CECIL HAROLD POE:
           Copy of funeral home record.

           More about CECIL HAROLD POE:
           Buried Location: McGill Cemetery, Potwin, Butler County, KS.
           SSAN: 511-07-3020.

           Marriage notes for MABEL HALL and CECIL POE:
           Copy of marriage license.

     ii.   VIRGIL H HALL, b. April 21, 1910, Holly, Prowers County, CO; d. November 03, 1980, Paramount, Los Angles County, CA; m. THERESIE ROBERTS, August 09, 1934.

           More about VIRGIL H HALL:
           Buried Location: November 06, 1980, Rose Hills Memorial Park, Whittier, CA.
           Cause of death: Cardiac arrest from cerebral thrombosis.
           SSAN: 512-09-5260.

More about THERESIE ROBERTS:
Buried Location: Rose Hills Memorial Park, Whittier, CA.

20. ELMER ELWOOD[3] HALL (SENY[2] MOORE, RICHARD S[1]), b. November 14, 1863 in Chicago, Cook County, IL; d. June 06, 1942 in El Dorado, Butler County, KS; m. SARAH FRANCES MAXWELL November 28, 1885 in El Dorado, Butler County, KS.

Notes for ELMER ELWOOD HALL:
Copy of funeral home record.

More about ELMER ELWOOD HALL:
Buried Location: June 08, 1942, Towanda, Butler County, KS.
Cause of death: Coronary artery des arteriorclerosis.

Notes for SARAH FRANCES MAXWELL:
Called Sallie.

More about SARAH FRANCES MAXWELL:
Buried Location: Towanda, Butler County, KS.

Marriage notes for ELMER HALL and SARAH MAXWELL:
Copy of marriage license.

Children of ELMER HALL and SARAH MAXWELL are:
- i. ART[4] HALL, m. VIRGILENE ???.
- ii. BLANCHE HALL, m. WILLIAM W SCRIBNER, September 02, 1912, El Dorado, Butler County, KS.

Marriage notes for BLANCHE HALL and WILLIAM SCRIBNER:
Copy of marriage license.

- iii. NELL HALL, m. ELWOOD WHEELER.
- iv. LYNN MERLE HALL.
- v. INES HALL.
- vi. BABY BOY HALL.

21. AMERICA SENY[3] HALL (SENY[2] MOORE, RICHARD S[1]), b. January 17, 1865 in Aurora, Kane County, IL; d. March 15, 1909 in Long Beach, Los Angeles County, CA; m. JAMES RILEY KELLEY August 01, 1881 in Augusta, Butler County, KS.

Notes for AMERICA SENY HALL:
Copy of death certificate.
Also known as Metta.

More about AMERICA SENY HALL:
Buried Location: March 16, 1909, Sunnyside Cemetery, Long Beach, CA

More about JAMES RILEY KELLEY:
Buried Location: December 04, 1928, Mountainview Cemetery, Pasadina, CA.

Marriage notes for AMERICA HALL and JAMES KELLEY:
Copy of marriage license.

Children of AMERICA HALL and JAMES KELLEY are:
- i. GLADYS IRENE[4] KELLEY, b. August 01, 1889, Newton, Harvey County, KS; d. February 09, 1963.

  More about GLADYS IRENE KELLEY:
  SSAN: 545-12-0834.

- ii. DAPHNE K KELLEY, b. April 25, 1893, Newton, Harvey County, KS; d. August 04, 1980, California; m. WILLIAM BROWN, April 13, 1927.

  More about DAPHNE K KELLEY:
  Buried Location: California.
  SSAN: 568-09-4233.

  More about WILLIAM BROWN:
  Buried Location: California.
  SSAN: 553-16-1055.

- 59. iii. SAMUEL MALCOM KELLEY, b. June 17, 1895, Newton, Harvey County, KS; d. December 05, 1979, Lascaster, Kern County, CA.
- 60. iv. SIDNEY EDMUND KELLEY, b. February 14, 1897. Newton, Harvey County, KS; d. January 31, 1978.

- v. SEBA VERA KELLEY, b. January 21, 1899, Newton, Harvey County, KS; d. January 26, 1985, Calimesa, Riverside County, CA; m. FRANK ALBERT SCHELLING.

    More about SEBA VERA KELLEY:
    Buried Location: California.
    SSAN: 570-60-5101.

- vi. LESLIE CALVIN KELLEY, b. July 02, 1900, Newton, Harvey County, KS; d. June 1967, Amarillo, Potter County, TX.

    More about LESLIE CALVIN KELLEY:
    Buried Location: Amarillo, Potter County, TX.
    SSAN: 566-07-0807.

- vii. THELMA DORIS KELLEY, b. August 29, 1905, Long Beach, Los Angeles County, CA; d. August 21, 1967; m. ELMER EVERTT BRACE.

22. VERNE REUBEN[3] HALL (SENY[2] MOORE, RICHARD S[1]), b. December 15, 1868 in Potwin, Butler County, KS; d. January 19, 1939 in El Dorado, Butler County, KS; m. ELLA BARNES November 30, 1897 in El Dorado, Butler County, KS.

More about VERNE REUBEN HALL:
Buried Location: Shaffer Cemetery, Butler County, KS.

Children of VERNE HALL and ELLA BARNES are:
- i. EDWINA[4] HALL.
- ii. MILO HALL, d. 1979; m. RUTH PORTER HUNT, January 07, 1914, El Dorado, Butler County, KS.
- iii. CLARENE HALL.

23. FLORENCE ANN[3] HALL (SENY[2] MOORE, RICHARD S[1]), b. February 02, 1873 in Potwin, Butler County, KS; d. May 22, 1947 in Potwin, Butler County, KS; m. CHARLES REUBEN JACOBS November 13, 1893 in El Dorado, Butler County, KS, son of CHRISTIAN JACOBS and ELIZABETH FRANZ.

Children of FLORENCE HALL and CHARLES JACOBS are:
- i. BABY UNKNOWN[4] JACOBS.
- 61. ii. ENUICE MARJORIE JACOBS, b. October 02, 1894, Potwin, Butler County, KS; d. July 12, 1982, Elk City, Montgomery County, KS.
- iii. NITA F JACOBS, b. December 04, 1896, Potwin, Butler County, KS; d. January 1979, Meridian, Ada County, ID; m. ARCHIE D SCRIVNER, February 01, 1915, Wichita, Sedgwick County, KS.

    More about ARCHIE D SCRIVNER:
    SSAN: 519-32-9040.

- 62. iv. HOMER JACOBS, b. January 18, 1899, Potwin, Butler County, KS, d. December 26, 1995, El Dorado, Butler County, KS.
- 63. v. LESTON LYLE JACOBS, b. April 30, 1902, Potwin, Butler County, KS; d. March 19, 1965.
- vi. CLARICE JACOBS, b. 1913; d. 1924.

24. EUSEBA ELMIRA[3] HALL (SENY[2] MOORE, RICHARD S[1]), b. April 23, 1877 in Kansas; d. May 04, 1954 in Port Angeles, WI; m. (1) ??? BROADHURST; m. (2) CHARLES BENJAMIN SOWARD January 08, 1910.

Notes for EUSEBA ELMIRA HALL:
Also known as Aunt Seba.

More about EUSEBA ELMIRA HALL:
Buried Location: Wichita, KS.

Children of EUSEBA HALL and ??? BROADHURST are:
- i. HOPE[4] BROADHURST.
- ii. HALEY BROADHURST.
- iii. RUTH BROADHURST m. DEWEY BRYANT.
- iv. DEWEY BRYANT BROADHURST.

Children of EUSEBA HALL and CHARLES SOWARD are:
- v. RAYMOND MARTIN[4] SOWARD.
- vi. GARY SOWARD.
- vii. SONDRA SOWARD.
- viii. RICHARD SOWARD.
- 64. ix. LUCILLE SOWARD.

25. ALMEDA MAUDE[3] HALL (SENY[2] MOORE, RICHARD S[1]), b. August 17, 1880 in Potwin, Butler County, KS; d. December 26, 1969 in El Dorado, Butler County, KS; m. GEORGE ROY MAXWELL December 26, 1896 in El Dorado, Butler County, KS.

Notes for ALMEDA MAUDE HALL:
Also known as Maude.

More about ALMEDA MAUDE HALL:
Fact 1: 16 years old when she got married.

Marriage notes for ALMEDA HALL and GEORGE MAXWELL:
Copy of marriage license.

Children of ALMEDA HALL and GEORGE MAXWELL are:
- i. ETNA[4] MAXWELL, m. ??? ARNOLD.
- ii. LEONARD BILL BAILY MAXWELL, b. December 08, 1897; d. September 14, 1916; m. CECIL ???.

    More about LEONARD BILL BAILY MAXWELL:
    Buried Location: Burden, Cowley County, KS.

    More about CECIL ???:
    Buried Location: Burden, Cowley County, KS.

26. MARY ELMIRA[3] HALL (SENY[2] MOORE, RICHARD S[1]), b. May 05, 1883 in Kansas; d. 1963; m. JOSEPH R MILLER.

Notes for MARY ELMIRA HALL:
Also known as Molly.

More about MARY ELMIRA HALL:
Buried Location: Winfield, KS.

Children of MARY HALL and JOSEPH MILLER are:
- i. HOWARD[4] MILLER.
- ii. EDMOND MILLER.
- iii. IVA MILLER.
- iv. ANNONA MILLER.
- v. KALLEY MILLER.

27. SARAH REBECCA[3] GREENFIELD (MATILDA JANE[2] MOORE, RICHARD S[1]), b. January 29, 1858 in Plano, Kendall County, IL; d. January 03, 1937 in Martensdale, Warren County, IA; m. BENJAMIN THORNBURG January 04, 1880 in Madison County, IA, son of ABSOLEM THORNBURG and DELILAH MILLER.

Notes for SARAH REBECCA GREENFIFLD:
Called Gettie.
Copy of newspaper obit.

More about SARAH REBECCA GREENFIELD:
Buried Location: January 04, 1937, Wick Cemetery, Martensdale, IA.

More about BENJAMIN THORNBURG:
Buried Location: Wick Cemetery, Martensdale, IA.

Child of SARAH GREENFIELD and BENJAMIN THORNBURG is:
65.   i. ALMA DELILAH[4] THORNBURG, b. October 27, 1880, Winterset, Madison County, IA; d. October 31, 1974, Indianola, Warren County, IA.

28. WILLIAM H[3] MOORE (JAMES F[2], RICHARD S[1]), b. February 01, 1871 in Iowa; d. November 02, 1938 in Madison County, IA; m. DELILAH M HOYT October 08, 1902 in Madison County, IA.

More about WILLIAM H MOORE:
Buried Location: November 05, 1938, Peru, IA.

Child of WILLIAM MOORE and DELILAH HOYT is:
- i. AUSTIN[4] MOORE.

29. ADA FRANCIS[3] ATKINSON (SUSAN N[2] MOORE, RICHARD S[1]), b. April 12, 1876 in Butler County, KS; d. July 24, 1959 in Drumright, Creek County, OK; m. (1) WILL COPELAND; m. (2) JACOB HENRY COPELAND October 28, 1894 in Howard, Elk County, KS; m. (3) J E WOLFE March 25, 1912 in Bartlesville, Washington County, OK.

Notes for JACOB HENRY COPELAND:
Copy of funeral home record.

More about JACOB HENRY COPELAND:
Buried Location: December 26, 1949, Kilgore Cemetery, Kilgore, TX.
Occupation: Carpenter.

Marriage notes for ADA ATKINSON and JACOB COPELAND:
Copy of marriage license.

Children of ADA ATKINSON and JACOB COPELAND are:
- i. IVIL GLADYS[4] COPELAND, b. August 17, 1895, Kansas; d. April 23, 1897, Kansas.
- ii. WILLIAM CARL COPELAND, b. December 07, 1897, Kansas; d. June 16, 1898, Kansas.
- iii. VERA BEATRICE COPELAND, b. March 07, 1903, Independence, Montgomery County, KS; d. January 02, 1983, Drumwright, Creek County, OK; m. JOE KILPATRICK, October 28, 1920, Bartlesville, Washington County, OK.

    Marriage notes for VERA COPELAND and JOE KILPATRICK:
    Copy of marriage license.

66. iv. PHYLLIS USEBA MAE COPELAND, b. January 26, 1906, Independence, Montgomery County, KS; d. October 08, 1979, Bartlesville, Washington County, OK.

67. v. LEONA BELLE COPELAND, b. November 14, 1915, Independence, Montgomery County, KS; d. October 20, 1992, Pampa, Gray County, TX.

30. JOHN C[3] ATKINSON (SUSAN N[2] MOORE, RICHARD S[1]), b. March 12, 1899; m. JOSEPHINE LOVELACE.

Children of JOHN ATKINSON and JOSEPHINE LOVELACE are:
- i. GERALD[4] ATKINSON. ii. WILBUR ATKINSON.
- iii. WALTER ATKINSON, m. MABLE ROBINSON, January 18, 1936, Hominy, Osage County, OK.

    Marriage notes for WALTER ATKINSON and MABLE ROBINSON:
    Copy of marriage license.

- iv. CLAUDE ATKINSON.

Generation No. 4

31. OLIVE⁴ MOORE (WILLIAM OSCAR³, REUBEN², RICHARD S¹⁾), b. in Potwin, Butler County, KS; m. ??? NECOMB.

More about OLIVE MOORE:
Cause of death: child birth.
Medical Information: Died at child birth.

Child of OLIVE MOORE and ??? NECOMB is:
    i. HAZEL⁵ NECOMB, m. ??? WITT.

32. EFFIE SARAH⁴ MOORE (WILLIAM OSCCAR³, REUBEN², RICHARD S¹), b. June 27, 1879 in Potwin, Butler County, KS; d. August 1977 in Boise, Ada County, ID; m. (1) ROBERT COURTER; m. (2) GEORGE PICKRELL; m. (3) WILLIAM T FOSTER September 09, 1903 in Winfield, Cowley County, KS.

More about ROBERT COURTER:
Occupation: Lumberman.

Marriage notes for EFFIE MOORE and WILLLAM FOSTER:
Copy of marriage license.

Children of EFFIE MOORE and ROBERT COURTER are:
    i. CECIL⁵ COURTER, b. July 27, 1898; d. August 27, 1990.

    More about CECIL COURTER:
    SSAN: 556-10-6533.

68. ii. CLARENCE COURTER, b. January 07, 1900, Enid, Garfield County, OK; d. October 26, 1980, Santa Rosa, Sonoma County, CA.
    iii. FREDA COURTER.
    iv. KENNETH COURTER, b. December 25, 1905; d. December 1981, Roseburg, Douglas County, OR.

    More about KENNETH COURTER:
    SSAN: 553-07-1520.

33. LEON ARTHUR⁴ MOORE (WILLIAM OSCAR³, REUBEN², RICHARD S¹), b. October 11, 1883 in Potwin, Butler County, KS; d. October 18, 1969 in Wichita, Sedgwick County, KS; m. NELLIE MAE METZ, daughter of BEN METZ and HETTIE MAIN.

Notes for LEON ARTHUR MOORE:
Copy of funeral home record.

More about LEON ARTHUR MOORE:
Buried Location: October 16, 1969, Rose Hill Cemetery, South Haven, KS.
Occupation: Farmer.
SSAN: 510-30-6531.

More about NELLIE MAE METZ:
Buried Location: Rose Hill Cemetery, South Haven, KS.
Occupation: Housewife.

Children of LEON MOORE and NELLIE METZ are:
    i. RAYMOND⁵ MOORE.
    ii. ARLENE MOORE, b. December 04, 1925, Wichita, Sedgwick County, KS; d. September 10, 1934, Wichita, Sedgwick County, KS.

    Notes for ARLENE MOORE:
    Arlene was riding in a trailer that her parents were pulling on 13th Street in Wichita, KS. The trailer came unhooked and Arlene was killed when a vehicle then hit the trailer. This came from a typed note of the Leon Family Tree.
    Copy of funeral record.

    More about ARLENE MOORE:
    Buried Location: September 12, 1934, South Haven, Sumner County, KS.
    Cause of death: Car accident.

69. iii. FLOYD VIRGIL MOORE, b. April 29, 1906, Potwin, Butler County, KS; d. June 05, 1995, Wichita, Sedgwick County, KS.
70. iv. ZELMA ELVA MOORE, b. November 08, 1908, Syracuse, Hamilton County, KS, d. February 22, 1998, Clearwater, Sedgwick County, KS.

71. v. RICHARD DONALD MOORE, b. September 01, 1913, Whitewater, Butler County, KS.

34. REUBEN DAVID[4] MOORE (WILLIAM OSCAR[3], REUBEN[2], RICHARD S[1]), b. November 21, 1886 in Murdock Twp, Butler County, KS; d. April 14, 1963 in El Dorado, Butler County, KS; m. EDITH LEONA TAYLOR February 12, 1908 in Potwin, Butler County, KS, daughter of WILLIAM TAYLOR and SARAH LIGGETT.

Notes for REUBEN DAVID MOORE:
Copy funeral home record.

More about REUBEN DAVID MOORE:
Buried Location: April 17, 1963, Towanda, Butler County, KS.
Occupation: Farmer.
SSAN: 511-32-7161.

Notes for EDITH LEONA TAYLOR:
Copy of funeral home record and death certificate.

More about EDITH LEONA TAYLOR:
Buried Location: January 28, 1975, Towanda, Butler County, KS.
Occupation: Housewife.
SSAN: 511-68-3859.

Marriage notes for REUBEN MOORE and EDITH TAYLOR:
Copy of marriage license.

Children of REUBEN MOORE, and EDITH TAYLOR are:
72. i. WILLIAM REUBEN[5] MOORE, b. January 08, 1909, Benton, Butler County, KS; d. April 05, 1987, Wichita, Sedgwick County, KS.
73. ii. VIOLET MARIE MOORE, b. July 15, 1911, Benton, Butler County, KS; d. July 09, 1996, US 54, Butler County, KS.
74. iii. GLENN LEON MOORE, b. March 02, 1913, Potwin, Butler County, KS.
75. iv. LLOYD MERLE MOORE, b. June 18, 1915, Whitewater, Butler County, KS.
76. v. RUTH B MOORE, b. November 04, 1917, Benton, Butler County, KS.
77. vi. OPAL MARIAN MOORE, b. August 08, 1922, Murduck Twp, Butler County, KS.
78. vii. ALVA DANIEL MOORE, b. November 28, 1927, Potwin, Butler County, KS.
79. viii. VEDA MAE MOORE, b. July 22, 1930, Potwin, Butler County, KS.

35. ORIN EGAR[4] MOORE (WILLIAM OSCAR[3], REUBEN[2], RICHARD S[1]), b. November 29, 1888 in Potwin, Butler County, KS; d. August 09, 1982 in Newton, Harvey County, KS; m. SUSAN MAY KEYS March 05, 1913 in Potwin, Butler County, KS, daughter of JOHN KEYS and EVA SULLIVAN.

Notes for ORIN EGAR MOORE:
Copy of funeral home record,
In memory of, military certificate of commission and discharge papers, and also a copy of war risk insurance payment statement.

More about ORIN EGAR MOORE:
Buried Location: August 12, 1982, Whitewater Cemetery, Butler County, KS.
Cause of death: Cancer of colon.
Fact 1: WWI.
Occupation: Farmer.
SSAN: 509-40-5865-A.

Notes for SUSAN MAY KEYS:
Copy of funeral home record, in memory of and death certificate.

More about SUSAN MAY KEYS:
Buried Location: January 21, 1975, Whitewater Cemetery Butler County, KS.
Cause of death: Cerebral vascular hemorrhage.
Medical Information: Hypertensive cardiovascular disease.
Occupation: Housewife.
SSAN: 510-68-1338.

Marriage notes for ORIN MOORE and SUSAN KEYS:
Copy of marriage license and wedding picture.

Children of ORIN MOORE and SUSAN KEYS are:
80. i. ELWOOD ORIN[5] MOORE, b. November 12, 1913, Whitewater, Butler County, KS.
81. ii. HELEN MAE MOORE, b. March 02, 1916, Milton Twp, Butler County, KS.
82. iii. MELVIN E MOORE, d, October 14, 1993, Albuquerque, Bernalillo County, NM.
     iv. JOHN WILLIAM MOORE, b. December 15, 1923, Whitewater, Butler County, KS; d. November 10, 1994, Wichita, Sedgwick County, KS.

Notes for JOHN WILLIAM MOORE:
Copy of birth certificate and newspaper obit.

More about JOHN WILLIAM MOORE:
Buried Location: November 14, 1994, Whitewater Cemetery, Butler County, KS.
Fact 1: WWII PFC Army.
Occupation: Music teacher.

36. RAYMOND I[4] MOORE (WILLIAM OSCAR[3], REUBEN[2], RICHARD S[1]), b. April 03, 1896 in Potwin, Butler County, KS; d. December 18, 1979 in Newton, Harvey County, KS; m. VIDA M MAXWELL July 10, 1917 in Whitewater, Butler County, KS, daughter of Guy MAXWELL and MIMA MCGILL.

Notes for RAYMOND I MOORE:
Copy of funeral home record.

More about RAYMOND I MOORE:
Buried Location: December 21, 1979, McGill Cemetery, Potwin, Butler County, KS.
Occupation: Carpenter.
SSAN: 515-20-2386.

Notes for VIDA M MAXWELL:
Copy of vital information form from Newton Presbyterian Manor.

More about VIDA M MAXWELL: Buried Location: McGill Cemetery, Potwin, Butler County, KS.
Occupation: Housewife.
SSAN: 509-14-6787.

Marriage notes for RAYMOND MOORE and VIDA MAXWELL:
Copy of marriage license.

Child of RAYMOND MOORE and VIDA MAXWELL is:
    i.   DOROTHY[5] MOORE.

37. DELLA M[4] MOORE (JAMES MONROE[3], REUBEN[2], RICHARD S[1]) was born April 15, 1885 in Chautauqua, Chautauqua County, KS, and died 1918. She married (1) ERNEST FITTRO; married (2) GEORGE HAFFAKER March 06, 1904 in Sedan, Chautauqua County, KS.

More about DELLA M MOORE:
Cause of death: Flu.

Marriage notes for DELLA MOORE and GOERGE HAFFAKER:
Copy of marriage license.

Child of DELLA MOORE and ERNEST FITTRO is:
    i.   OTIS[5] FITTRO.

Children of DELLA MOORE and GEORGE HAFFAKER are:
    ii.   GLADYS[5] HAFFAKER.
    iii.   LAWRENCE HAFFAKER.
    iv.   HAZEL HAFFAKER, b. 1905; d. 1909.

38. ROSA L[4] MOORE (JAMES MONROE[3], REUBEN[2], RICHARD S[1]) b. September 08, 1887 in Chautauqua, Chautauqua County, KS; m. (1) JESS CRAWFORD; m. (2) RUBEN B SPRINELL June 04, 1882 in Rosalia, Butler County, KS; m. (3) MARSH ECKER 1903 in Sedan, Chautauqua County, KS.

Marriage notes for ROSA MOORE and RUBEN SPRINELL:
Copy of marriage license.

Children of ROSA MOORE and JESS CRAWFORD are:
    i.   LEROY[5] CRAWFORD.
    ii.   LILLIE CRAWFORD.
    iii.   INFANT CRAWFORD.
    iv.   JULIA BELL CRAWFORD.
    v.   JERRY CRAWFORD.
    vi.   J O CRAWFORD.

Children of ROSA MOORE and MARSH ECKER are:
    vii.   MARGARIE[5] ECKER.
    viii.   GEORGE ECKER.

39. EVA V[4] MOORE (JAMES MONROE[3], REUBEN[2], RICHARD S[1]) was born November 14, 1889 in Osage County, KS. She married E HARVEY RILEY September 28, 1904 in Sedan, Chautauqua County, KS.

Marriage notes for EVA MOORE and E RILEY:
Copy of marriage license.

Child of EVA MOORE and E RILEY is:
83.   i.   STELLA[5] RILEY, b. 1906, KS.

40. CLARA S[4] MOORE (JAMES MONROE[3], REUBEN[2], RICHARD S[1]) was born February 20, 1892 in Chautauqua, Chautauqua County, KS; died September 09, 1926 in Oklahoma; married (1) GUY JOHNSON; married (2) E VIRGE RECTOR February 26, 1913 in Sedan, Chautauqua County, KS.

Marriage notes for CLARA MOORE and E RECTOR:
Copy of marriage license.

Child of CLARA MOORE and Guy JOHNSON is:
   i.   MAXINE[5] JOHNSON.

Children of CLARA MOORE and E RECTOR are:
   ii.   LOUISE[5] RECTOR.
   iii. T MARIE RECTOR.
   iv.   VIRGIE BELL RECTOR.

41. CLYDE EARL[4] MOORE (JAMES MONROE[3], REUBEN[2], RICHARD S[1]), born July 31, 1896 in Oklahoma; died August 26, 1981 in Sedan, Chautauqua County, KS; married RHODA R CARRIKIER December 27, 1922 in Sedan, Chautauqua County, KS, daughter of PAUL CARRIKIER and LUCINDA KNOTT.

Notes for CLYDE EARL MOORE:
Copy of death certificate and funeral home record.

More about CLYDE EARL MOORE:
Buried Location: Oak Hill Cemetery, Chautauqua, KS.
Cause of death: cardio vascular accident.
Medical Information: Hypertension, Emphysema.
Occupation: Farmer.
SSAN: 511-22-7414.

Notes for RHODA R CARRIKIER:
Copy of death certificate.

More about RHODA R CARRIKIER:
Buried Location: June 15, 1982, Oak Hill Cemetery, Chatauqua, KS.
Occupation: Housewife.
SSAN: 510-68-7368.

Marriage notes for CLYDE MOORE and RHODA CARRIKIER:
Copy of marriage license.

Children of CLYDE MOORE and RHODA CARRIKIER are:
   i.   PAULINE[5] MOORE, b. Kansas; m. WOODROW TALLEY, May 05, 1953, Lancaster County, NE.

Marriage notes for PAULINE MOORE and WOODROW TALLEY:
Copy of marriage license.

   ii.   PAUL MOORE, m. MARGARET KIRCHNER, May 18, 1946, Chautauqua, Chautauqua County, KS.

Marriage notes for PAUL MOORE and MARGARET KIRCHNER:
Copy of marriage license.

   iii. ALLEN MOORE.

42. MELVINA JANE[4] TAYLOR (MELISSA REBECCA[3] MOORE, REUBEN[2], RICHARD S[1]), born May 10, 1882 in Elgin, Chautauqua County, KS; died February 06, 1945; married BERNARD N HAGSTROM August 31, 1907 in Fredonia, Wilson County, KS.

Children of MELVINA TAYLOR and BERNARD HAGSTROM are:
   i.   BERTHA[5] HAGSTROM, m. ??? PINKSTON.
   ii.   BEULAH HAGSTROM, m. ??? DONOVAN.
   iii. EMANUEL HAGSTROM.
   iv.   MARJIE HAGSTROM.
   v.   ORVILLE HAGSTROM.
   vi.   PERMELIA HAGSTROM, m. ??? CARTER.
   vii. THEODORE HAGSTROM.

- viii. GLADYS HAGSTROM, b. 1910; d. 1910.
- ix. BESSIE HAGSTROM, b. 1917; d. 1921.
- x. OSCAR HAGSTROM, b. 1920; d. 1929.

43. CARL WILLIAM[4] TAYLOR (MELISSA REBECCA[3] MOORE, REUBEN[2], RICHARD S[1]), born June 16, 1884 in Butler County, KS; died February 22, 1972 in Mesa, Maricopa County, AZ; married ELIZABETH JOHNSON May 02, 1906 in Fredonia, Wilson County, KS, daughter of HENRY JOHNSON and EVELINE TURNER.

Notes for CARL WILLIAM TAYLOR:
Copy of death certificate.

More about CARL WILLIAM TAYLOR:
Buried Location: February 24, 1972, East Resthaven, Phoenix, AZ.
Occupation: Farmer.
SSAN: 512-07-2249.

Notes for ELIZABETH JOHNSON:
Called Lizzie.

More about ELIZABETH JOHNSON:
Burial: May 26, 1962, East Rest Haven Cemetery, Chandler, AZ.
Moved: 1938, Toronto, KS to Chandler, AZ.
Occupation: Housewife.

Children of CARL TAYLOR and ELIZABETH JOHNSON are:
- i. CLEO TURNER[5] TAYLOR, m. ??? O'LEAR.
- ii. NELLIE TAYLOR, m. OSCAR POWERS.
- iii. GERALDINE TAYLOR.
- iv. FERN TAYLOR, m. WESLEY LIVINGSTON.
- v. HARVEY TAYLOR.
- vi. CECIL TAYLOR.
- vii. GLEN TAYLOR.

44. MABEL BLANCHE[4] TAYLOR (MELISSA REBECCA[3] MOORE, REUBEN[2], RICHARD S[1]), born December 19, 1886 in Butler County, KS; died April 23, 1960 in Eureka, Greenwood County, KS; married JOHN IRA CROSSFIELD April 11, 1906 in Altoona, Wilson County, KS, son of FRANCIS CROSSFIELD and ALICE STARK.

Notes for MABEL BLANCHE TAYLOR:
Copy of funeral home report.

More about MABEL BLANCHE, TAYLOR:
Buried Location: April 26, 1960, Altoona, Wilson County, KS.
Occupation: Housewife.

Notes for JOHN IRA CROSSFIELD:
Copy of newspaper obituary and funeral; In memory of.

More about JOHN IRA CROSSFIELD:
Buried Location: September 14, 1964, Altoona, Wilson County, KS.

Children of MABEL TAYLOR and JOHN CROSSFIELD are:
- i. EDITH MARIE[5] CROSSFIELD, b. January 26, 1907, Altoona, Wilson County, KS; d. October 17, 1907, Altoona, Wilson County, KS.
- ii. INFANT SON CROSSFIELD, b. February 02, 1908; d. February 02, 1908.
- 84. iii. LEWIS IRA CROSSFIELD, b. January 22, 1909, Altoona, Wilson County, KS; d. July 25, 1972, Toronto, Woodson County, KS.
- iv. HAZEL LOUISE CROSSFIELD, b. July 02, 1912; d. April 11, 1918.
- 85. v. LELAND FRANCIS CROSSFIELD, b. August 19, 1917, Toronto, Woodson County, KS; d. April 29, 1981, Wichita, Sedgwick County, KS.

45. JAMES ORCEN[4] TAYLOR (MELISSA REBECCA[3] MOORE, REUBEN[2], RICHARD S[1]), born October 19, 1890 in Altoona, Wilson County, KS; died May 1964 in Newkirk, Kay County, OK; married UNKNOWN ???.

More about JAMES ORCEN TAYLOR:
SSAN: 443-03-8981.

Children of JAMES TAYLOR and UNKNOWN ??? are:
- i. JOHN[5] TAYLOR.
- ii. GEORGE TAYLOR.
- iii. WILDA MAE TAYLOR.

46. GLADYS HAZEL[4] TAYLOR (MELISSA REBECCA[3] MOORE, REUBEN[2], RICHARD S[1]) was born November 14, 1895 in Newkirk, Kay County, OK, and died February 20, 1977 in Pratt, Pratt County, KS. She married AZEL COFFLAND SHARITS August 25, 1915 in Toronto, Woodson County, KS, son of CHARLES SHARITS and MARY COFFLAND.

Notes for GLADYS HAZEL TAYLOR:
Copy of newspaper obituary and funeral home record

More about GLADYS HAZEL TAYLOR:
Buried Location: February 22, 1977, Stafford Cemetery, Stafford, KS.
Cause of death: Adenacarcinoma of rectum.
SSAN: 509-22-2385.

Notes for AZEL COFFLAND SHARITS:
Copy of newspaper obituary, funeral home record and in memory of.

More about AZEL COFFLAND SHARITS:
Buried Location: November 18, 1978, Stafford Cemetery, Stafford, KS.
Occupation: Railroad.
SSAN: 702-16-7381.

Marriage notes for GLADYS TAYLOR and AZEL SHARITS:
Copy of newspaper clipping.

Child of GLADYS TAYLOR and AZEL SHARITS is:
86. i. ELOISE[5] SHARITS.

47. GEORGE LACKEY[4] TAYLOR (MELISSA REBECCA[3] MOORE, REUBEN[2], RICHARD S[1]), born December 08, 1901 in Butler County, KS; died February 1957 in Bethal, Oxford County, ME; married FAYE ???.

Children of GEORGE TAYLOR and FAYE ??? are:
  i. KENT[5] TAYLOR.
  ii. BRUCE TAYLOR.

48. OSCAR L[4] SMITH (SARAH LOUISE[3] MOORE, REUBEN[2], RICHARD S[1]), born February 1886 in Kansas; died 1963; married MARY CATHARINE STEVENS.

Child of OSCAR SMITH and MARY STEVENS is:
  i. LAVERNA[5] SMITH.

49. BERTHA M[4] SMITH (SARAH LOUISE[3] MOORE, REUBEN[2], RICHARD S[1]), born March 1888 in Kansas; died 1966; married FRED PETTY December 29, 1904.

Notes for BERTHA M SMITH:
Picture of tombstone.

Notes for FRED PETTY:
Picture of tombstone.

Children of BERTHA SMITH and FRED PETTY are:
  i. JUNE LEOTA FERN[5] PETTY, b. 1918; d. 1922.

      Notes for JUNE LEOTA FERN PETTY:
      Picture of tombstone.

  ii. FRED PETTY.
  iii. ROY PETTY.
  iv. DEAN PETTY.
  v. ALVIN PETTY.
  vi. OLA PETTY.
  vii. NORA PETTY.
  vii. EULA PETTY.
  ix. IRENE PETTY.

50. STELLA ADALINE[4] WILEY (ETTA ELLEN[3] MOORE, REUBEN[2], RICHARD S[1]), born January 13, 1894 in Altoona, Wilson County, KS; died November 01, 1986 in Dewey Washington County, OK; married JOHN EVERETT ELLER April 22, 1911 in Altoona, Wilson County, KS, son of JOHN ELLER and ELIZA ROUTH.

Notes for STELLA ADALINE WILEY:
Copy of funeral home record.

More about STELLA ADALINE WILEY:
Buried Location: November 05, 1986, Dewey Cemetery, Dewey, OK.
Ethnicity/Relig: Christian Church.
Occupation: Housewife.
SSAN: 441-64-2750.

More about JOHN EVERETT ELLER:
Buried Location: November 28, 1975, Dewey Cemetery, Dewey, OK.
Ethnicity/Relig: Christian Church.
Occupation: Electrician/ farmer.

Marriage notes for STELLA WILEY and JOHN ELLER:
Copy of marriage license.

Children of STELLA WILEY and JOHN ELLER are:
- 87. i. HELEN LOUISE[5] ELLER, b. November 08, 1911, Altoona, Wilson County, KS; d. September 09, 1991, Oklahoma City, Oklahoma County, OK.
- 88. ii. GEORGE EVERETT ELLER, b. January 29, 1915. Altoona, Wilson County, KS; d. April 10, 1998.
- 89. iii. JAMES WILKERSON ELLER, b. July 08, 1918, Dewey, Washington County, OK; d. September 12, 1995, Ochelata, Washington County, OK.
- 90. iv. WILLA MAE ELLER, b. November 19, 1922, Dewey, Washington County, OK.
- 91. v. ELIZABETH IRENE ELLER, b. April 12, 1926, Dewey Washington County, OK.
- 92. vi. BARBARA LEDORA ELLER, b. March 20, 1929, Dewey, Washington County, OK.

51. GRACE MAUDE[4] HALL (FRANCIS LEATON[3], SENY[2] MOORE, RICHARD S[1]), born July 27, 1881 in Potwin, Butler County, KS; died September 28, 1962 in El Dorado, Butler County, KS; married JOHN ISAAC DEXTER February 25, 1904 in Joplin, Jasper County, MO, son of CHARLES DEXTER and JANE BALLARD.

Notes for GRACE MAUDE HALL:
Copy of obituary.

More about GRACE MAUDE HALL:
Cause of death: Cancer.

Notes for JOHN ISAAC DEXTER: Copy of funeral home record; newspaper obts.

More about JOHN ISAAC DEXTER:
Buried Location: September 30, 1962, McGill Cemetery, Potwin, Butler County, KS.
Cause of death: Acute circulatory failure.
Occupation: Retired gasoline plant operator.
SSAN: 443-01-4133.

Marriage notes for GRACE HALL and JOHN DEXTER:
Copy of marriage license.

Children of GRACE HALL and JOHN DEXTER are:
- 93. i. ZORA DOUTHARD[5] DEXTER, b. December 15, 1904, Longton, Elk County, KS.
- 94. ii. VIOLA G DEXTER, b. May 14, 1906.
- 95. iii. JUANITA FAYE DEXTER, b. January 22, 1908, Longton, Elk County, KS; d. February 21, 1994, Wichita, Sedgwick County, KS.

52. ROY LUTRELL[4] HALL (FRANCIS LEATON[3], SENY[2] MOORE, RICHARD S[1]), born August 03, 1882 in Potwin, Butler County, KS; died July 12, 1959 in Elko, Elko County, NV; married (1) WINNIFRED MOSSMAN; married (2) ELENER PEDERREN December 14, 1902.

Children of ROY HALL and WINNIFRED MOSSMAN are:
- i. LESTER MILTON[5] HALL, b. May 20, 1913; d. October 1986, Cleveland, Bradley County, TX.
- 96. ii. KENNETH J HALL, b. April 08, 1916, Independence, Montgomery County, KS; d. February 09, 1994, Portland, Multnomah County, OR.

53. ALICE, ELIZA[4] HALL (FRANCIS LEATON[3], SENY[2] MOORE, RICHARD S[1]), born March 20, 1884 in Potwin, Butler County, KS; died November 08, 1930 in Newton, Harvey County, KS; married CHARLES MARTIN BRENNER April 17, 1901 in Potwin, Butler County, KS, son of CLERMONT BRENNER and JULIA JACOBS.

Notes for ALICE ELIZA HALL:
Copy of funeral home record.

More about ALICE ELIZA HALL:
Buried Location: November 10, 1930, McGill Cemetery, Potwin, Butler County, KS.
Cause of death: Carcinoma of stomach.
Occupation: Housewife.

Notes for CHARLES MARTIN BRENNER:
Copy of funeral home record.

More about CHARLES MARTIN BRENNER:
Buried Location: May 30, 1947, McGill Cemetery, Potwin, Butler County, KS.
Cause of death: Heart attack.
Occupation: Farmer.

Marriage notes for ALICE HALL and CHARLES BRENNER:
Copy of marriage license.

Children of ALICE HALL and CHARLES BRENNER are:
    i.   HAROLD F^5 BRENNER, b. January 30, 1902, Potwin, Butler County, KS; d. July 08, 1968, Kansas.

Notes for HAROLD F BRENNER:
Copy of funeral handout and newspaper obituary.

More about HAROLD F BRENNER:
Buried Location: McGill Cemetery, Potwin, Butler County, KS.
Occupation: Oil field production worker.
SSAN: 509-03-0706.

97.   ii.   GEORGE LEROY BRENNER, b. January 09, 1908, Longton, Butler County, KS; d. June 12, 1983, El Dorado, Butler County, KS.

98.   iii.   VERL W BRENNER, b. January 14, 1911, Potwin. Butler County, KS; d. October 08, 1955, Newton, Harvey County, KS.

54. LULU SENY^4 HALL (FRANCIS LEATON^3, SENY^2 MOORE, RICHARD S^1), born November 07, 1886 in Potwin, Butler County, KS; died 1982 in Sweeny, Matagorda County, TX; married LEONARD J SEXTON November 28, 1907 in Longton, Elk County, KS.

More about LULU SENY HALL:
Buried Location: Texas.

More about LEONARD J SEXTON:
Buried Location: Longton, Elk County, KS.

Marriage notes for LULU HALL and LEONARD SEXTON:
Copy of marriage license.

Child of LULU HALL and LEONARD SEXTON is:
    i.   VIRGINIA^5 SEXTON, m. ??? TURB0R.

55. IRA EMMUTT^4 HALL (FRANCIS LEATON^3, SENY^2 MOORE, RICHARD S^1), born November 05, 1890 in Potwin, Butler County, KS; died August 28, 1974 in La Habra, Orange County, CA; married BERTHA ALPHA SMITH December 24, 1912 in El Dorado, Butler County, KS.

Notes for IRA EMMUTT HALL:
Copy of death certificate.

More about IRA EMMUTT HALL:
Buried Location: August 30, 1974, Rose Hills Memorial Park, Whittier, CA.
SSAN: 545-12-1525.

Notes for BERTHA ALPHA SMITH:
Copy of death certificate.

More about BERTHA ALPHA SMITH:
Buried Location: August 27, 1982, Rose Hills Memorial Park, Whittier, CA.
SSAN: 568-26-4867.

Marriage notes for IRA HALL and BERTHA SMITH:
Copy of marriage license.

Children of IRA HALL and BERTHA SMITH are:
    i.   BUELL^5 HALL.
99.   ii.   CECIL LORNE HALL, b. January 28, 1915.

56. GUY CHRISTIAN^4 HALL (FRANCIS LEATON^3, SENY^2 MOORE, RICHARD S^1), born January 03, 1894 in Potwin, Butler County, KS; died January 08, 1961 in Newton, Harvey County, KS; married NAOMI ESTELLEE GAINES August 08, 1919 in Newton, Harvey County, KS, daughter of SAMUEL GAINES and MARY SIMPSON.

Notes for GUY CHRISTIAN HALL:
Copy of family Bible register, funeral home record, newspaper obituary, funeral remembrance and death certificate.

More about GUY CHRISTIAN HALL:
Buried Location: January 11, 1961, Whitewater Cemetery, Butler County, KS.
Cause of death: Carcinoma of stomach, metastatic of liver.
Occupation: Retired inspector ATSF Railroad.
SSAN: 710-01-2131.

Notes for NAOMI ESTELLEE GAINES:
Copy of family Bible register, funeral record, funeral home remembrance, newspaper obituary and death certificate.

More about NAOMI ESTELLEE GAINES:
Buried Location: June 24, 1971, Whitewater Cemetery, Butler County, KS.
Cause of death: Metastatic carcenora of brain and kidney.
Occupation: Housewife.

Marriage notes for GUY HALL and NAOMI GAINES:
Copy of marriage license.

Children of GUY HALL and NAOMI GAINES are:
- 100. i. DORIS MAXINE[5] HALL, b. April 15, 1921, Whitewater, Butler County, KS.
- 101. ii. DUANE DELOISE HALL, b. September 01, 1922, Potwin, Butler County, KS.
- 102. iii. CLAYTON OAKLEY HALL, b. April 24, 1924, Whitewater, Butler County, KS.
- iv. NEWELL VIVIAN HALL, b. February 02, 1926, Fairmount Twp, Butler County, KS; d. December 14, 1926, Summit Twp, Marion County, KS.

    Notes for NEWELL VIVIAN HALL:
    Copy of newspaper obituary and funeral home record.

    More about NEWELL VIVIAN HALL:
    Buried Location: Shaffer Cemetery, Butler County, KS.
    Cause of death: Bronchial pneumonia.

- 103. v. WANDA MARLENE HALL, b. May 11, 1928, Newton, Harvey County, KS.
- 104. vi. AUDREY FAYE HALL, b. July 17, 1931, Newton, Harvey County, KS.
- 105. vii. NANCY ANN HALL, b. April 06, 1934, Newton, Harvey County, KS.
- 106. viii. CLARA MAY HALL, b. February 28, 1936, Newton, Harvey County, KS.
- ix. CLIFFORD GAINES HALL, b. February 22, 1938, Newton, Harvey County, KS; d. November 09, 1974, Newton, Harvey County, KS; m. MARY LOU SCHUESSLER, October 06, 1958, Newton, Harvey County, KS.

    Notes for CLIFFORD GAINES HALL:
    Copy of funeral home record.

    More about CLIFFORD GAINES HALL:
    Buried Location: November 13, 1974, Green Valley Cemetery, Furley, KS.
    Cause of death: Suicide hung himself.
    Fact 1: Army Ser. #17575041.
    SSAN: 513-32-4752.

    Marriage notes for CLIFFORD HALL and MARY SCHUESSLER:
    Copy of marriage license.

- 107. x. JANICE DE LOIS HALL, b. November 06, 1942, Newton, Harvey County, KS.

57. CELIA LAVERNA[4] HALL (FRANCIS LEATON[3], SENY[2] MOORE, RICHARD S[1]), born December 29, 1895 in Potwin, Butler County, KS; died July 11, 1987 in Buena Vista, Chaffee County, CO; married FRANK JOSEPH MILLER June 02, 1915 in El Dorado, Butler County, KS, son of FRED MILLER and ANNA UNULL.

Notes for CELIA LAVERNA HALL:
Copy of delayed birth certificate, death certificate.

More About CELIA LAVERNA HALL:
Burial: July 15, 1987, Mt Olivet Cemetery, Buena Vista, CO.
Cause of death: Congestive heart failure/hypertensive cardiovascular disease.
Occupation: Cooks helper.
SSAN: 523-40-2966.

Notes for FRANK JOSEPH MILLER:
Copy of death certificate.

More about FRANK JOSEPH MILLER:
Burial: April 26, 1952, Mt View Cemetery, Pueblo, CO
Cause of death: Coronary occlusion.
Occupation: Steam fitter.
SSAN: 443-03-8323.

Marriage notes for CELIA HALL and FRANK MILLER:
Copy of marriage license.

Children of CELIA HALL and FRANK MILLER are:
- 108. i. BLENDENA CAROLINE^5 MILLER, b. June 30, 1916.
- ii. MARIAN FRANCES MILLER, b. October 03, 1918.
- iii. PEGGY JEAN MILLER, b. November 24, 1921.
- 109. iv. BONNIE LOU MILLER, b. November 08, 1927.

58. ZACHARY HURSHEL^4 HALL (FRANCIS LEATON^3, SENY^2 MOORE, RICHARD S^1), born December 20, 1900 in Potwin, Butler County, KS; died June 02, 1979 in Newton, Harvey County, KS; married MAUDE DELLA FOWLER January 10, 1921 in Newton, Harvey County, KS.

Notes for ZACHARY HURSHEL HALL:
Copy of funeral record.

More about ZACHARY HURSHEL HALL:
Buried Location: June 05, 1979, McGill Cemetery, Potwin, Butler County, KS.
SSAN: 512-03-3166.

Notes for MAUDE DELLA FOWLER:
Copy of funeral record.

More about MAUDE DELLA FOWLER:
Buried Location: April 22, 1978, McGill Cemetery, Potwin, Butler County, KS.
SSAN: 509-48-0273.

Marriage notes for ZACHARY HALL and MAUDE FOWLER:
Copy of marriage license.

Children of ZACHARY HALL and MAUDE FOWLER are:
- 110. i. LOIS^5 HALL.
- 111. ii. CALVIN HALL.

59. SAMUEL MALCOM^4 KELLEY (AMERICA SENY^3 HALL, SENY^2 MOORE, RICHARD S^1), born June 17, 1895 in Newton, Harvey County, KS; died December 05, 1979 in Lascaster, Kern County, CA; married (1) BLANCE LA VON BROWN; married (2) DOROTHY MAY PINKERTON July 06, 1918 in Santa Ana, Orange County, CA, daughter of HENRY PINKERTON and AUGUSTA HINN.

Notes for SAMUEL MALCOM KELLEY:
Called Shelby.

More about SAMUEL MALCOM KELLEY:
Buried Location: Corrine, Box Elder, UT.
SSAN: 569-12-6358.

More about BLANCE LAVON BROWN:
Buried Location: California.
SSAN: 553-16-1055.

More about DOROTHY MAY PINKERTON:
Buried Location: Oakland, Alameda County, CA.

Marriage notes for SAMUEL KELLEY and DOROTHY PINKERTON:
Copy of marriage license.

Children of SAMUEL KELLEY and DOROTHY PINKERTON are:
- i. EUGENE SHELBY^5 KELLEY, b. May 10, 1919, Berkely, Alameda County, CA; m. VIENNA DURFEY, July 17, 1940.
- ii. HENRY JAMES KELLEY, b. January 05, 1922, Mecca, Riverside County, CA; m. BETTY VERO BRACE, March 06, 1943.

60. SIDNEY EDMUND^4 KELLEY (AMERICA SENY^3 HALL, SENY^2 MOORE, RICHARD S^1), born February 14, 1897 in Newton, Harvey County, KS; died January 31, 1978; married DAISY BERRYLINE CAMPBELL May 23, 1922 in Potwin, Butler County, KS.

More about SIDNEY EDMUND KELLEY:
SSAN: 571-01-0881.

More about DAISY BERRYLINE CAMPBELL:
SSAN: 557-30-1208.

Children of SIDNEY KELLEY and DAISY CAMPBELL are:
- i. SIDNEY EDMOND[5] KELLEY JR, b. March 01, 1923.
- ii. HELEN ELIZABETH KELLEY, b. May 13, 1924.
- iii. KATHLEEN SENA KELLEY, b. December 27, 1925.
- iv. PATRICIA ANN KELLEY, b. March 19, 1927.
- v. WOODEST MARION KELLEY, b. October 02, 1928.
- vi. LEOTA SEBA KELLEY, b. November 24, 1930.
- vii. ABEATA DAISY KELLEY, b. April 20, 1938.
- vii. MARILYN JOAN KELLEY, b. March 01, 1941.

61. ENUICE MARJORIE[4] JACOBS (FLORENCE ANN[3] HALL, SENY[2] MOORE, RICHARD S[1]) was born October 02, 1894 in Potwin, Butler County, KS, and died July 12, 1982 in Elk City, Montgomery County, KS. She married HENRY CARL PENNER JR February 29, 1916 in Potwin, Butler County, KS.

Marriage notes for ENUICE JACOBS and HENRY PENNER:
Copy of marriage license.

Children of ENUICE JACOBS and HENRY PENNER are:
- 112. i. ROGER THAINE[5] PENNER, b. January 06, 1917, Potwin, Butler County, KS.
- 113. ii. MARGARET ELNORA PENNER, b. November 15, 1918, Potwin, Butler County, KS; d. May 11, 1967, CA.
- iii. EVELYN RUTH PENNER, b. February 18, 1921.
- 114. iv. IVAN DALE PENNER, b. May 22, 1922, Newton, Harvey County, KS.
- v. BABY BOY PENNER, b. August 08, 1923, Potwin, Butler County, KS; d. August 08, 1923, Potwin, Butler County, KS.
- 115. vi. EDNA MAXINE PENNER, b. August 30, 1924, Potwin, Butler County, KS.
- vii. ELIZABETH ANNA PENNER, b. February 08, 1926.
- 116. viii. NORMA FRANCES PENNER, b. July 17, 1928, Potwin, Butler County, KS.
- ix. GEORGE ROSCUE PENNER, b. April 09, 1932.
- x. RICHARD LEE PENNER, b. August 28, 1933.
- xi. RALPH CARL PENNER, b. July 07, 1938.

62. HOMER[4] JACOBS (FLORENCE ANN[3] HALL, SENY[2] MOORE, RICHARD S[1]), born January 18, 1899 in Potwin, Butler County, KS; died December 26, 1995 in El Dorado, Butler County, KS; married LILA ELLEN LAIRD May 23, 1921 in Newton, Harvey County, KS, daughter of C LAIRD and ELLA ???.

Notes for HOMER JACOBS:
Copy of funeral home record.

More about HOMER JACOBS:
SSAN: 512-12-7585.

Children of HOMER JACOBS and LILA LAIRD are:
- 117. i. CHARLES FORREST[5] JACOBS, b. May 12, 1922, Newton, Harvey County, KS.
- 118. ii. JOAN JACOBS, b. January 15, 1928, Newton, Harvey County, KS.
- 119. iii. JIM LAIRD JACOBS, b. September 23, 1932, El Dorado, Butler County, KS.

63. LESTON LYLE[4] JACOBS (FLORENCE ANN[3] HALL, SENY[2] MOORE, RICHARD S[1]), born April 30, 1902 in Potwin, Butler County, KS; died March 19, 1965; married RUTH DONA RUTHERFORD June 08, 1927 in Newton, Harvey County, KS.

Notes for LESTON LYLE JACOBS:
Also known as Lester.

More about LESTON LYLE JACOBS:
Buried Location: McGill Cemetery, Potwin, Butler County, KS.
SSAN: 512-12-7586.

More about RUTH DONA RUTHERFORD:
Buried Location: February 17, 1972, McGill Cemetery, Potwin, Butler County, KS.

Marriage notes for LESTON JACOBS and RUTH RUTHERFORD:
Copy of marriage license.

Children of LESTON JACOBS and RUTH RUTHERFORD are:
- i. CURTIS[5] JACOBS, b. 1935; d. 1935.
- ii. LANE JACOBS.
- 120. iii. CHARLES RAY JACOBS, b. June 29, 1938, Wichita, Sedgwick County, KS.

64. LUCILLE[4] SOWARD (EUSEBA ELMIRA[3] HALL, SENY[2] MOORE, RICHARD S[1]). She married MONROE HARPER.

Child of LUCILLE SOWARD and MONROE HARPER is:
    i.   CHARLES[5] HARPER.

65. ALMA DELILAH[4] THORNBURG (SARAH REBECCA[3] GREENFIELD, MATILDA JANE[2] MOORE, RICHARD S[1]), born October 27, 1880 in Winterset, Madison County, IA; died October 31, 1974 in Indianola, Warren County, IA; married DAVID NICHOLL October 05, 1898 in Lincolin Twp, Madison County, IA.

More about ALMA DELILAH THORNBURG:
Buried Location: November 1974, Wick Cemetery, Martensdale, IA.

More about DAVID NICHOLL:
Buried Location: Wick Cemetery, Martensdale, IA.
Occupation: Farmer.

Children of ALMA THORNBURG and DAVID NICHOLL are:
    i.   RUBY[5] NICHOLL, b. January 03, 1901, Iowa; d. February 09, 1913, St Marys, Warren County, IA.

        More about RUBY NICHOLL:
        Buried Location: Wick Cemetery, Martensdale, IA.

    ii.   CLAUDE NICHOLL, b. May 02, 1903, Iowa; d. October 29, 1914, St Marys, Warren County, IA.

        More about CLAUDE NICHOLL:
        Buried Location: November 1914, Wick Cemetery, Martensdale, IA.

    iii.   DONALD MERLE NICHOLL, b. April 23, 1908, Indianola, Warren County, IA; d. April 06, 1979, Des Moines, Polk County, IA; m. OPAL GERTRUDE LAMB.
    iv.   HAZEL LEOTA NICHOLL, b. November 23, 1910, St Marys, Warren County, IA; m. (1) ORVILLE WAGNER; m. (2) FLOYD WILLIAM LAMB, December 12, 1928.
121.   v.   CARL RUSSELL NICHOLL, b. April 11, 1916, Wick, Warren County, IA; d. February 12, 1971, Denver, Arapahoe County, CO.

66. PHYLLIS USEBA MAE[4] COPELAND (ADA FRANCIS[3] ATKINSON, SUSAN N[2] MOORE, RICHARD S[1]), born January 26, 1906 in Independence, Montgomery County, KS; died October 08, 1979 in Bartlesville Washington County, OK; married (1) GERALD ORLANDO SEARS April 05, 1922 in Independence, Montgomery County, KS; married (2) FRANCES GIBSON ARTHUR January 20, 1935 in Springfield, Greene County, MO, son of LOREN ARTHUR and LELA GIBSON.

Notes for PHYLLIS USEBA MAE COPELAND:
Copy of newspaper obits and death certificate.

More about PHYLLIS USEBA MAE COPELAND:
Buried Location: October 10, 1979, Dewey Cemetery, Dewey, OK.
Occupation: Housewife.
SSAN: 443-14-5814.

Notes for GERALD ORLANDO SEARS:
Copy of newspaper obits.

More about GERALD ORLANDO SEARS:
Buried Location: February 03, 1975, Memorial Park Cemetery, Bartlesville, OK.
Fact 1: US Army.
Occupation: Carpenter.

Marriage notes for PHYLLIS COPELAND and GERALD SEARS:
Copy of marriage license.

Notes for FRANCES GIBSON ARTHUR:
Called Gib.
Copy of newspaper obit.

More about FRANCES GIBSON ARTHUR:
Buried Location: Dewey Cemetery, Dewey, OK.
Occupation: Sales.

Child of PHYLLIS COPELAND and GERALD SEARS is:
122.   i.   GERALD ORLANDO[5] SEARS JR, b. March 28, 1923, Bartlesville, Washington County, OK.

67. LEONA BELLE[4] COPELAND (ADA FRANCIS[3] ATKINSON, SUSAN N[2] MOORE, RICHARD S[1]), born November 14, 1915 in Independence, Montgomery County, KS; died October 20, 1992 in Pampa, Gray County, TX; married DAVID PIOUS SMITHHISLER January 25, 1931 in Shidler, Osage County, OK, son of CHARLES SMITHHISLER and JENNIE BRADLEY.

Notes for LEONA BELLE COPELAND:
Copy of funeral home report; birth registration sheet.

More about LEONA BELLE COPELAND:
Buried Location: October 23, 1992, Memory Gardens, Pampa, TX.
SSAN: 443-14-6629.

Notes for DAVID PIOUS SMITHHISLER:
Copy of funeral home report.

More about DAVID PIOUS SMITHHISLER:
Buried Location: June 05, 1995, Memory Gardens, Pampa, TX.
Ethnicity/Relig: Catholic.
Occupation: Retired pumper from Kewanee Oil Co.
SSAN: 441-01-2666.

Child of LEONA COPELAND and DAVID SMITHHISLER is:
123.   i.   JAN^5 SMITHHISLER

Generation No. 5

68. CLARENCE[5] COURTER (EFFIE SARAH[4] MOORE, WILLIAM OSCAR[3], REUBEN[2], RICHARD S[1]), born January 07, 1900 in Enid, Garfield County, OK; died October 26, 1980 in Santa Rosa, Sonoma County, CA; married EDNA G SMART 1923 in Enid, Garfield County, OK.

More about CLARENCE COURTER:
Occupation: Lumberman.
SSAN: 545-28-3488.

More about EDNA G SMART:
Occupation: Teacher.

Children of CLARENCE COURTER and EDNA SMART are:
124.   i.   MAX[6] COURTER, b. 1924, Enid, Garfield County, OK.
        ii.   DORIS LEA COURTER, b. 1927, Enid, Garfield County, OK; m. BRUCE WILSON, 1950.

69. FLOYD VIRGIL[5] MOORE (LEON ARTHUR[4], WILLIAM OSCAR[3], REUBEN[2, Richard] S[1]), born April 29, 1906 in Potwin, Butler County, KS; died June 05, 1995 in Wichita, Sedgwick County, KS; married FRANCES ETHLYN WHITNEY June 06, 1935 in Wichita, Sedgwick County, KS, daughter of HERBERT WHITNEY and LULA THOMAS.

Notes for FLOYD VIRGIL MOORE:
Copy of funeral home record.

More about FLOYD VIRGIL MOORE:
Buried Location: June 08, 1995, Jamesburg Park Cemetery, Sedgwick County, KS.
Occupation: Teacher administrator.
SSAN: 510-30-6584.

More about FRANCES ETHLYN WHITNEY:
Occupation: Housewife.

Marriage notes for FLOYD MOORE and FRANCES WHITNEY:
Copy of marriage license.

Children of FLOYD MOORE and FRANCES WHITNEY are:
125.   i.   ALAN ARTHUR[6] MOORE, b. August 05, 1939, Wichita, Sedgwick County, KS; d. February 01, 1996, Minneapolis, Hennepin County, MN.
126.   ii.   WAYNE VIRGIL MOORE, b. May 03, 1942, Wichita, Sedgwick County, KS.

70. ZELMA ELVA[5] MOORE (LEON ARTHUR[4], WILLIAM OSCAR[3], REUBEN[2], RICHARD S[1]), born November 08, 1908 in Syracuse, Hamilton County, KS; died February 22, 1998 in Clearwater, Sedgwick County, KS; married WILLIAM HENRY MYERS June 08, 1935 in Wichita, Sedgwick County, KS.

More about ZELMA ELVA MOORE:
Occupation: Teacher.

Notes for WILLIAM HENRY MYERS:
Called Bill.

More about WILLIAM HENRY MYERS:
Buried Location: November 06, 1991.
Occupation: Boeing.
SSAN: 441-05-8559.

Marriage notes for ZELMA MOORE and WILLIAM MYERS:
Copy of marriage license.

Children of ZELMA MOORE and WILLIAM MYERS are:
        i.   WILLIAM HAROLD[6] MYERS, b. November 13, 1938, Ada, Pontotoc County, OK.
127.   ii.   CAROLYN JUNE, MYERS, b. October 31, 1942. Houston, Harris County, TX.
        iii.   ROBERT GLEN MYERS, b, September 01, 1944, Wichita, Sedgwick County, KS.

            Notes for ROBERT GLEN MYERS:
            Called Bob.
            Copy of birth registration.

71. RICHARD DONALD[5] MOORE (LEON ARTHUR[4], WILLIAM OSCAR[3], REUBEN[2], RICHARD S[1]), born September 01, 1913 in Whitewater, Butler County, KS. He married ERMA LUCILE KIBBE August 27, 1938 in Douglas, Butler County, KS, daughter of WALTER KIBBE and HALLIE WILSON.

Notes for RICHARD DONALD MOORE:
Called Dick.
Copy of birth certificate.

More about RICHARD DONALD MOORE:
Ethnicity/Relig: Christian Church.
Occupation: Boeing and Cessna aircraft.

More about ERMA LUCILE KIBBE:
Buried Location: July 26, 1997, Garden of the Last Supper.
Occupation: Southwestern Bell operator.

Children of RICHARD MOORE and ERMA KIBBE are:
    i.   DONALD JAY⁶ MOORE, b. April 07, 1942, Wichita, Sedgwick County, KS; m. SUZANNE ELIZABETH SCHABELL.

        Notes for DONALD JAY MOORE:
        Called Don.

128.   ii.   JUDITH DIANE MOORE, b. May 09, 1944, Wichita, Sedgwick County, KS.

129.   iii.   KAREN SUE MOORE, b. August 24, 1950, Wichita, Sedgwick County, KS.

72. WILLIAM REUBEN⁵ MOORE (REUBEN DAVID⁴, WILLIAM OSCAR³, REUBEN², RICHARD S¹) was born January 08, 1909 in Benton, Butler County, KS, and died April 05, 1987 in Wichita, Sedgwick County, KS. He married WANDA LUCINA PICKENS June 25, 1932 in Wichita, Sedgwick County, KS, daughter of HOMER PICKENS and MAUDE ANDERSON.

Notes for WILLIAM REUBEN MOORE:
Called Billy.
Copy of birth certificate, death certificate and funeral home record.

More about WILLIAM REUBEN MOORE:
Buried Location: April 08, 1987, Council Hill Cemetery, Peck, KS.
Cause of Death: Cardiac arrest.
SSAN: 512-10-0678.

Marriage notes for WILLIAM MOORE and WANDA PICKENS:
Copy of marriage certificate.

Children of WILLIAM MOORE and WANDA PICKENS are:
130.   i.   MIRIAM ANN⁶ MOORE, b. May 04, 1933, Wichita, Sedgwick County, KS.
131.   ii.   WLLIA PAULINE MOORE, b. April 05, 1935, Butler County, KS.
132.   iii.   HOWARD RAY MOORE, b. November 27, 1936, Wichita, Sedgwick County, KS.
133.   iv.   JAMES REUBEN MOORE, b. June 20, 1942, Wichita, Sedgwick County, KS.

73. VIOLET MARIE⁵ MOORE (REUBEN DAVID⁴, WILLIAM OSCAR3, REUBEN², RICHARD S¹) was born July 15, 1911 in Benton, Butler County, KS; died July 09, 1996 in US 54, Butler County, KS; married CHARLES WESLEY TALLMAN July 31, 1932 in Potwin, Butler County, KS.

Notes for VIOLET MARIE MOORE:
Copy of funeral home record.

More about VIOLET MARIE MOORE:
Buried Location: July 13, 1996, Towanda, Butler County, KS.
Cause of Death: Auto accident.
SSAN: 509-58-0281.

Marriage notes for VIOLET MOORE and CHARLES TALLMAN:
Copy marriage license.

Children of VIOLET MOORE and CHARLES TALLMAN are:
134.   i.   VELMA RUTH⁶ TALLMAN, b. June 11, 1933, Benton, Butler County, KS; d. May 18, 1998. Wichita, Sedgwick County, KS.
135.   ii.   THELMA ELIZABETH TALLMAN, b. September 28, 1934, Benton, Butler County, KS.
        iii.   ROGER DENNIE TALLMAN, b. June 10, 1938, Benton, Butler County, KS; m. NANCY LOU EDWARDS, February 26, 1965, Furley, Sedgwick County, KS.

        More about ROGER DENNIE TALLMAN:
        Fact 1: US Army #US 55 713 761.

        iv.   GLENN EDWARD TALLMAN, b. November 04, 1940, Benton, Butler County, KS; d. December 01, 1995, El Dorado, Butler County, KS; m. SHERRY TAYLOR.

More about GLENN EDWARD TALLMAN:
Buried Location: December 05, 1995, Fairview Cemetery, El Dorado, KS.
Fact 1: SP4 US Army Vietnam War.

74. GLENN LEON[5] MOORE (REUBEN DAVID[4], WILLIAM OSCAR[3], REUBEN[2], RICHARD S[1]) was born March 02, 1913 in Potwin, Butler County, KS. He married EMILY FRANCES WEISKER October 17, 1943 in Sacramento, Sacramento County, CA, daughter of WILLIAM WEISKER and GEORGIA BUNCH.

More about GLENN LEON MOORE:
Fact 1: Army.

Marriage notes for GLENN MOORE and EMILY WEISKER:
Copy of marriage license.

Children of GLENN MOORE and EMILY WEISKER are:
- 136. i. ARTHUR LEON[6] MOORE, b. April 25, 1947.
- 137. ii. WILLIAM DAVID MOORE, b. April 06, 1950.
- iii. NANCY ANN MOORE, b. March 24, 1954, Sacramento, Sacramento County, CA; m. RAYMOND HOAGLAND, August 30, 1984, Sacramento, Sacramento County, CA.

75. LLOYD MERLE[5] MOORE (REUBEN DAVID[4], WILLIAM OSCAR[3], REUBEN[2], RICHARD S[1]) was born June 18, 1915 in Whitewater, Butler County, KS. He married (1) NAOMI HAZEL ULLUM September 10, 1934 in El Dorado, Butler County, KS, daughter of RANDOLPH ULLUM and GERTRUDE STOLTZ. He married (2) MELBA MARIE ELLIS January 22, 1983 in Independence, Montgomery County, KS.

More about LLOYD MERLE MOORE:
Occupation: Oil refinery.

Marriage notes for LLOYD MOORE and NAOMI ULLUM:
Copy of marriage license,

Children of LLOYD MOORE and NAOMI ULLUM are:
- 138. i. GARY LLOYD[6] MOORE, b. December 06, 1935, Potwin, Butler County, KS; d. January 18, 1993, Augusta, Butler County, KS.
- 139. ii. TONY BRENT MOORE, b. April 04, 1942, Potwin, Butler County, KS.

76. RUTH B[5] MOORE (REUBEN DAVID[4], WILLIAM OSCAR[3], REUBEN[2], RICHARD S[1]) was born November 04, 1917 in Benton, Butler County, KS. She married JOHN HAROLD TURNER SR December 21, 1940 in Potwin, Butler County, KS, son of LEE TURNER and FAYE ADAMS.

Notes for JOHN HAROLD TURNER SR:
Died June 10, 1969.
Copy of funeral home record.

More about JOHN HAROLD TURNER SR:
Cause of Death: Auto accident.
Buried Location: June 14, 1969, Towanda, Butler County, KS.
Military: WWII, US Navy, Pipefitter 3/c.
Occupation: Gauger for Vickers Oil Refinery, Potwin, KS.
SSAN: 511-07-2715.

Marriage notes for RUTH B. MOORE and JOHN TURNER SR:
Copy of marriage license.

Children of RUTH B. MOORE and JOHN TURNER SR are:
- 140. i. JOHN HAROLD[6] TURNER JR, b. March 12, 1942, Newton, Harvey County, KS; d. May 20, 1968, Vietnam.
- ii. DAVID P. TURNER, b. October 1, 1944, Newton, Harvey County, KS.

77. OPAL MARIAN[5] MOORE (REUBEN DAVID[4], WILLIAM OSCAR[3], REUBEN[2], RICHARD S[1]) was born August 08, 1922 in Murduck Twp, Butler County, KS. She married MERLE DEAN HARLAN September 20, 1942 in El Dorado, Butler County, KS, son of PAY HARLAN and MAE DUBY.

More about OPAL MARIAN MOORE:
Occupation: secretary/housewife.

More about MERLE DEAN HARLAN:
Occupation: farmer/welder.

Children of OPAL MOORE and MERLE HARLAN are:
- 141. i. JANICE KAY[6] HARLAN, b. November 15, 1943, Wichita, Sedgwick County, KS.
- ii. MERVIN JAY HARLAN, b. August 21, 1946, Wichita, Sedgwick County, KS.
- 142. iii. BARBARA LOUISE HARLAN, b. July 24, 1953, Emporia, Lyon County, KS.

78. ALVA DANIEL⁵ MOORE (REUBEN DAVID⁴, WILLIAM OSCAR³, REUBEN², RICHARD S¹) was born November 28, 1927 in Potwin, Butler County, KS, He married LOIS VALETTE BACHELDER October 23, 1946 in Benton, Butler County, KS.

Notes for ALVA DANIEL MOORE:
Copy of birth certificate.

More about ALVA DANIEL MOORE:
Occupation: farmer/real estate/car salesman.

More about LOIS VALETTE BACHELDER:
Occupation: housewife/real estate.

Children of ALVA MOORE and LOIS BACHELDER are:
- 143. i. EDITH VALETTA⁶ MOORE, b. June 26, 1948, Wichita, Sedgwick County, KS.
- 144. ii. ALAN DEE MOORE, b. 1950, Wichita, Sedgwick County, KS.
- iii. SUE ANN MOORE, b. January 26, 1951, Wichita, Sedgwick County, KS; d. February 15, 1975, Winfield, Cowley County, KS.

    Notes for SUE ANN MOORE:
    Copy of birth certificate, funeral home record and death certificate.

    More about SUE ANN MOORE:
    Buried Location: February 19, 1975, Winfield State Hospital Cemetery, Winfield, KS.
    Cause of Death: Cardiac arrest, hepatic coma.
    Medical Information: Monolism, profound mental retardation.
    SSAN: 515-70-9645.

- 145. iv. AVA LYNNE MOORE, b. October 23, 1954, Wichita, Sedgwick County, KS.
- v. THOMAS HERBERT MOORE, b. July 22, 1962, Eureka, Greenwood County, KS; m. FAYE ANN WICKHAM, June 28, 1997, El Dorado, Butler County, KS.

    Marriage notes for THOMAS MOORE and FAYE WICKHAM:
    Copy of marriage license and invitation.

- 146. vi. ROSE ANNETTE MOORE, b. September 24, 1960, Wichita, Sedgwick County, KS.

79. VEDA MAE⁵ MOORE (REUBEN DAVID⁴, WILLIAM OSCAR³, REUBEN², RICHARD S¹) was born July 22, 1930 in Potwin, Butler County, KS. She married HOWARD MILTON BALZER December 29, 1950 in Potwin, Butler County, KS, son of ABE BALZER.

Marriage notes for VEDA MOORE and HOWARD BALZER:
Copy of marriage license.

Children of VEDA MOORE, and HOWARD BALZER are:
- 147. i. LAVONNE ELAINE⁶ BALZER, b. June 20, 1952, Newton, Harvey County, KS.
- 148. ii. JO ANN BALZER, b. February 17, 1956, Newton, Harvey County, KS.
- iii. SARAH KATHERINE BALZER, b. November 16, 1961, Newton, Harvey County, KS.

    More about SARAH KATHERINE BALZER:
    Occupation: Sales.

- 149. iv. MILTON LEE BALZER. b. February 27, 1964, Newton, Harvey County, KS.
- 150. v. MOREY HOWARD BALZER, b. February 27, 1964, Newton, Harvey County, KS.

80. ELWOOD ORIN⁵ MOORE (ORIN EGAR⁴, WILLIAM OSCAR³, REUBEN², RICHARD S¹) was born November 12, 1913 in Whitewater, Butler County, KS. He married (1) ROSE MARGARET ANDREWS July 01, 1935 in Whitewater, Butler County, KS. He married (2) DELPHIA MAXINE BAXTER June 10, 1939 in Wichita, Sedgwick County, KS, daughter of OTTO BAXTER and FLOY PIERCY.

Marriage notes for ELWOOD MOORE and ROSE ANDREWS:
Copy of marriage license.

Marriage notes for ELWOOD MOORE and DELPHIA BAXTER:
Copy of marriage license.

Child of ELWOOD MOORE and DELPHIA BAXTER is:
- 151. i. LARRY JO⁶ MOORE, b. December 13, 1940, Wichita, Sedgwick County, KS.

81. HELEN MAE⁵ MOORE (ORIN EGAR⁴, WILLIAM OSCAR³, REUBEN², RICHARD S¹) was born March 02, 1916 in Milton Twp, Butler County, KS. She married ELDON JAY MAYHEW August 03, 1938 in Hutchinson, Reno County, KS, son of ALLEN MAYHEW and MARY WOOD.

Marriage notes for HELEN MOORE and ELDON MAYHEW:
Copy of marriage license and marriage certificate.

Children of HELEN MOORE and ELDON MAYHEW are:
- i. JOHN DARYL[6] MAYHEW, b. January 13, 1943, Moab, Grand County, UT; m. CAROL ANN CURFMAN.
- ii. ROBERT JAY MAYHEW, b. July 14, 1947, Pasadena, Los Angeles County, CA; m. JULIE ???.
- iii. ALLEN EDWARD MAYHEW, b. September 30, 1949, Pasadena, Los Angeles County, CA; m. DONNA MICHELLE BORG.

82. MELVIN E[5] MOORE (ORIN EGAR[4], WILLIAM OSCAR[3], REUBEN[2], RICHARD S[1]) died October 14, 1993 in Albuquerque, Bernalillo County, NM. He married JAYNE ???.

More about MELVIN E MOORE:
Buried Location: October 18, 1993, Albuquerque, Bernalillo County, NM.

Children of MELVIN MOORE and JAYNE ??? are:
- i. MIKE[6] MOORE.
- ii. SUSANNE MOORE, m. ??? HENRY.
- iii. SALLY MOORE, m. ??? COLLINS.

83. STELLA[5] RILEY (EVA V[4] MOORE, JAMES MONROE[3], REUBEN[2], RICHARD S[1]) was born 1906 in KS. She married (1) L NEWTON MAYO 1924. She married (2) FRANK SCHISLER 1947.

Children of STELLA RILEY and L MAYO are:
- i. WILLIAM ROY[6] MAYO, b. 1925; m. NORMA LEE CHAPLIN, January 08, 1944, Arkansas City, Cowley County, KS.

    Marriage notes for WILLIAM MAYO and NORMA CHAPLIN:
    Copy of marriage license.

- ii. RICHARD D MAYO, b. 1928; m. GEORGIA IRENE EDMONDS, October 13, 1945, Winfield, Cowley County, KS.

    Marriage notes for RICHARD MAYO and GEORGIA EDMONDS:
    Copy of marriage license.

- iii. EMOGENE E MAYO, b. 1929.
- iv. CHARLES LEO MAYO, b. 1934.

Children of STELLA RILEY and FRANK SCHISLER are:
- v. EDWARD[6] SCHISLER.
- vi. RALPH SCHISLER.
- vii. CORA SCHISLER.
- viii. NELA SCHISLER.
- ix. GILBERT SCHISLER.

84. LEWIS IRA[5] CROSSFIELD (MABEL BLANCHE[4] TAYLOR, MELISSA REBECCA[3] MOORE, REUBEN[2], RICHARD S[1]) was born January 22, 1909 in Altoona, Wilson County, KS, and died July 25, 1972 in Toronto, Woodson County, KS. He married BERNICE E SCHLINLOFF April 17, 1941 in Toronto, Woodson County, KS.

Notes for LEWIS IRA CROSSFIELD:
Copy of newspaper obits.

More about LEWIS IRA CROSSFIELD:
Buried Location: July 27, 1972, Toronto Cemetery, Woodson County, KS.

Children of LEWIS CROSSFIELD and BERNICE SCHLINLOFF are:
- i. CARROL LEW[6] CROSSFIELD.

    Notes for CARROL LEW CROSSFIELD:
    Was saved by a resuscitator when infant failed to breathe properly at birth.
    Copy of newspaper article.

- 152. ii. HELEN CROSSFIELD.
- iii. KAY CROSSFIELD, m. THEODORE BANKS.

    Notes for THEODORE BANKS:
    Called Teddy.

85. LELAND FRANCIS[5] CROSSFIELD (MABEL BLANCHE[4] TAYLOR, MELISSA REBECCA[3] MOORE, REUBEN[2], RICHARD S[1]) was born August 19, 1917 in Toronto, Woodson County, KS, and died April 29, 1981 in Wichita, Sedgwick County, KS. He married (1) BEULAH FRANCES SOWDER May 27, 1941 in Gallup, Mc Kinley County, NM, daughter of FRANKLIN SOWDER and ADDIE ???. He married (2) VIVIAN LEE NIELSON August 18, 1979 in Yates Center, Woodson County, KS.

Notes for LELAND FRANCIS CROSSFIELD:
Copy of newspaper obits.

Notes for BEULAH FRANCES SOWDER:
Copy of newspaper obits.

Children of LELAND CROSSFIELD and BEULAH SOWDER are:
- i. LARRY LEE[6] CROSSFIELD.
- 153. ii. ANN ELIZABETH CROSSFIELD.

86. ELOISE[5] SHARITS (GLADYS HAZEL[4] TAYLOR, MELISSA REBECCA[3] MOORE, REUBEN[2], RICHARD S[1]) She married W.B. AMERINE.

Notes for W.B. AMERINE:
Called Brownie.

Children of ELOISE SHARITS and W. AMERINE are:
- i. WILLIAM[6] AMERINE.

    Notes for WILLIAM AMERINE:
    Called Bill.

- 154. ii. VICKI AMERINE.
- iii. YVONNE ELOISE AMERINE, m. ??? NITZSCHE.

87. HELEN LOUISE[5] ELLER (STELLA ADALINE[4] WILEY, ETTA ELLEN[3] MOORE, REUBEN[2], RICHARD S[1]) was born November 08, 1911 in Altoona, Wilson County, KS, and died September 09, 1991 in Oklahoma City, Oklahoma County, OK. She married GLEN CLIFFORD BARTLETT February 03, 1931 in Bartlesville, Washington County, OK, son of DON BARTLETT and BESSIE HEALD.

More about HELEN LOUISE ELLER:
Buried Location: September 12, 1991, Mt Olive Cemetery, Pauls Valley, OK.
Occupation: Bookkeeper, Housewife.

More about GLEN CLIFFORD BARTLETT:
Buried Location: November 26, 1988, Mt Olive Cemetery, Pauls Valley, OK.
Occupation: Telegraph operator, engineer-Sinclair Arco Oil Co.

Marriage notes for HELEN ELLER and GLEN BARTLETT:
Copy of marriage license.

Children of HELEN ELLER and GLEN BARTLETT are:
- 155. i. WAYNE IRVIN[6] BARTLETT, b. September 04, 1931, Dewey Washington County, OK.
- 156. ii. STELLA MAE BARTLETT, b. February 28, 1934. Dewey Washington County. OK.
- iii. JOHN CARL BARTLETT, b. December 04, 1936, Dewey, Washington County, OK, m. CAROL STEPHENSON, June 03, 1963, Pawhuska, Osage County, OK.

    More about JOHN CARL BARTLETT:
    Fact 1: Green Berets March 16, 1956-March 05, 1959 Sp 4.
    Occupation: Tracker, rancher.

    Marriage notes for JOHN BARTLETT and CAROL STEPHENSON:
    Copy of marriage license.

- 157. iv. NORMA JEAN BARTLETT, b. August 23, 1938, Dewey Washington County, OK.

88. GEORGE EVERETT[5] ELLER (STELLA ADALINE[4] WILEY, ETTA ELLEN[3] MOORE, REUBEN[2], RICHARD S[1]) was born January 29, 1915 in Altoona, Wilson County, KS, and died April 10, 1998, He married (1) WAYNETA ORPHA WOODY August 15, 1936 in Bartlesville, Washington County, OK, daughter of JAMES WOODY and ROSIE COKE. He married (2) KATIE ANDERSON June 30, 1994.

Notes for GEORGE EVERETT ELLER:
Copy of military separation papers.

More about GEORGE EVERETT ELLER:
Fact 1: U.S. Navy WWII 1942-45
Occupation: Welder, inspector Continental Oil Co.

Notes for WAYNETA ORPHA WOODY:
Copy of funeral home record.

More about WAYNETA ORPHA WOODY:
Buried Location: August 15, 1990, Dewey Cemetery, Dewey, OK.
Occupation: Housewife.
SSAN: 443-14-2848.

Children of GEORGE ELLER and WAYNETA WOODY are:
    i.   GEORGE KENNETH[6] ELLER, b. November 29, 1938, Dewey, Washington County, OK; d. November 29, 1938, Dewey, Washington County, OK.

More about GEORGE KENNETH ELLER:
Buried Location: Dewey Cemetery, Dewey, OK.

158.   ii.   NITA JO ELLER: b. November 21, 1947, McAllen, Hildago County, TX.

89. JAMES WILKERSON[5] ELLER (STELLA ADALINE[4] WILEY, ETTA ELLEN[3] MOORE, REUBEN[2], RICHARD S[1]) was born July 08, 1918 in Dewey, Washington County, OK, and died September 12, 1995 in Ochelata, Washington County, OK. He married (1) MARGARET MONTGOMERY December 12, 1939 in Independence, Montgomery County, KS. He married (2) ALICE, MELROSE LUSTER November 14, 1952 in Nowata, Nowata County, OK, daughter of CHARLIE LUSTER and GOLDIE ST CLAIR.

Notes for JAMES WILKERSON ELLER:
Copy of funeral home record.

More about JAMES WILKERSON ELLER:
Buried Location: September 18, 1995, Ramona Cemetery, Ramona, OK.
Fact 1: WWII U.S. Army.
Occupation: Mechanic.
SSAN: 442-20-9954.

Marriage notes for JAMES ELLER and MARGARET MONTGOMERY:
Copy of marriage license.

More about ALICE MELROSE LUSTER:
Buried Location: January 08, 1996, Ramona Cemetery, OK.

Children of JAMES ELLER and MARGARET MONTGOMERY are:
159.   i.   BARBARA ELOUISE[6] ELLER, b. September 24, 1941, Dewey, Washington County, OK.
160.   ii.   SONYA LOU ELLER, b. May 26, 1943, Bartlesville, Washington County, OK.

Children of JAMES ELLER and ALICE LUSTER are:
    iii.   ALMA MAE[6] ELLER, b. July 25, 1953, Bartlesville, Nowata County, OK; d. July 28, 1953, Bartlesville, Nowata County, OK.

        More about ALMA MAE ELLER:
        Buried Location: July 28, 1953, Dewey Cemetery, Dewey, OK.

161.   iv.   ALICE MARIE ELLER, b. July 25, 1953, Bartlesville, Washington County, OK.

90. WILLA MAE[5] ELLER (STELLA ADALINE[4] WILEY, ETTA ELLEN[3] MOORE, REUBEN[2], RICHARD S[1]) was born November 19, 1922 in Dewey Washington County, OK. She married BERNAL LAVERN CASE June 29, 1940 in Dewey Washington County, OK, son of ERVIN CASE and RICKIE SCHERE.

Notes for WILLA MAE ELLER:
Copy of birth certificate.

Notes for BERNAL LAVERN CASE:
Called Bud.
Copy of birth certificate and death certificate.

More About BERNAL LAVERN CASE:
Buried Location: October 04, 1991, Dewey Cemetery, Dewey, OK.
Cause of Death: Metastate Oderoca of the colon.
Occupation: Mechanic, owner auto repair.

Marriage notes for WILLA ELLER and BERNAL CASE:
Copy of marriage license.

Children of WILLA ELLER and BERNAL CASE are:
162.   i.   LARRY ERVIN[6] CASE, b. December 08, 1941, Dewey Washington County, OK.
    ii.   DAVIE LAVERNE CASE, b. May 01, 1946, Bartlesville, Washington County, OK; d. July 08, 1946, Bartlesville, Washington County, OK.

        Notes for DAVIE LAVERNE CASE:
        Copy of birth certificate, hospital certificate and funeral home record.

        More about DAVIE LAVERNE CASE:
        Buried Location: July 10, 1946, Dewey Cemetery, Washington County, OK.
        Cause of Death: Blue baby.

163.   iii.   GERALD ALLEN CASE, b. August 26, 1948, Bartlesville, Washington County, OK.

91. ELIZABETH IRENE⁵ ELLER (STELLA ADALINE⁴ WILEY, ETTA ELLEN³ MOORE, REUBEN², RICHARD S¹) was born April 12, 1926 in Dewey Washington County, OK. She married BOBBY ARNO BROCKHOUSE October 31, 1949 in Kansas City, Jackson County, MO, son of CECIL BROCKHOUSE and IRMA ROACH.

Notes for ELIZABETH IRENE ELLER:
Called Betty.
Copy of birth certificate.

Notes for BOBBY ARNO BROCKHOUSE:
Copy of birth certificate and military papers.

More about BOBBY ARNO BROCKHOUSE:
Buried Location: Oak Ridge Memory Gardens, Kansas City, MO.
Ethnicity/Relig: Christian Church.
Fact 1: U.S. Air Force and Navy WWII 1942-67: Was also in the Army.

Marriage notes for ELIZABETH ELLER and BOBBY BROCKHOUSE:
Copy of marriage license.

Children of ELIZABETH ELLER and BOBBY BROCKHOUSE are:
164.   i.   MICHAEL WAYNE⁶ BROCKHOUSE, b. November 12, 1951, Jacksonville, Duval County, FL.
165.   ii.   MADELINE EILEEN BROCKHOUSE, b. July 30, 1953, Kansas City, Jackson County, MO.

92. BARBARA LEDORA⁵ ELLER (STELLA ADALINE⁴ WILEY, ETTA ELLEN³ MOORE, REUBEN², RICHARD S¹) was born March 20, 1929 in Dewey, Washington County, OK. She married (1) RONALD DEANE BUTTS June 01, 1947 in Dewey, Washington County, OK. She married (2) JOE ANDERSON June 27, 1992 in Champaign, Champaign County, IL.

More About RONALD DEANE BUTTS:
Ethnicity/Relig: Christian Church
Fact 1: WWII.
Occupation: Railroad.

Children of BARBARA ELLER and RONALD BUTTS are:
          i.   DONNA SUE⁶ BUTTS, b. January 05, 1952, Champaign, Champaign County, IL; m. (1) MAX EUGENE BREWER JR, August 23, 1969, Champaign, Champaign County, IL, m. (2) ROGER SKINNER, September 1972, Urbana, Champaign County, IL,

               More about DONNA SUE BUTTS:
               Occupation: RN.

               More about MAX EUGENE BREWER JR:
               Occupation: Postal Clerk.

               Marriage notes for DONNA BUTTS and MAX BREWER:
               Copy of marriage license.

               More about ROGER SKINNER:
               Occupation: RN computer service.

166.   ii.   DARLENE SUE BUTTS, b. December 04, 1954, Champaign, Champaign County, IL.
167.   iii. DIANE SUE BUTTS, b. November 01, 1956, Champaign, Champaign County, IL.
168.   iv.   DEBRA SUE BUTTS, b. November 27, 1958, Champaign, Champaign County, IL.
169.   v.   RONALD EUGENE BUTTS, b. July 11, 1960, Champaign, Champaign County, IL.

93. ZORA DOUTHARD⁵ DEXTER (GRACE MAUDE⁴ HALL, FRANCIS LEATON³, SENY² MOORE, RICHARD S¹) was born December 15, 1904 in Longton, Elk County, KS. She married WILLARD MCCONEGHY October 14, 1922 in El Dorado, Butler County, KS.

Children of ZORA DEXTER and WILLARD MCCONEGHY are:
          i.   ARLENE⁶ MCCONEGHY, b. July 18, 1925, Newton, Harvey County, KS, d. 1977, Wichita, Sedgwick County, KS; m. EDRIE HOWE, 1959.

More about ARLENE MCCONEGHY:
          Buried Location: Wichita, Sedgwick County, KS.

170.   ii.   FRED JOHN MCCONEGHY, b. June 10, 1927, Elbing, Butler County, KS.

94. VIOLA G⁵ DEXTER (GRACE MAUDE⁴ HALL, FRANCIS LEATON³, SENY² MOORE, RICHARD S¹) was born May 14, 1906. She married WILLIAM V ADAMSON June 17, 1929 in Hutchinson, Reno County, KS.

Notes for WILLIAM V ADAMSON:
Called Bill.

More about WILLIAM V ADAMSON:
Buried Location: McGill Cemetery, Potwin, Butler County, KS.

Marriage notes for VIOLA DEXTER and WILLIAM ADAMSON:
Copy of abstract of marriage record.

Children of VIOLA DEXTER and WILLIAM ADAMSON are:
- i. BILLY LEE[6] ADAMSON, b. May 14, 1931; d. November 16, 1991; m. NEVA BELLE KAUFMAN, March 28, 1953, Newton, Harvey County, KS.

    Marriage notes for BILLY ADAMSON and NEVA KAUFMAN:
    Copy of marriage license.

- ii. BOBBY JO ADAMSON, b. October 21, 1932; m. THELMA ROZELLA CAIN, September 05, 1952, Bonner Springs, Butler County, KS.
- 171. iii. MARILYN SUE BROYLES, b. August 06, 1941; foster child.

95. JUANITA FAYE[5] DEXTER (GRACE MAUDE[4] HALL, FRANCIS LEATON[3], SENY[2] MOORE, RICHARD S[1]) was born January 22, 1908 in Longton, Elk County, KS, and died February 21, 1994 in Wichita, Sedgwick County, KS. She married KENNETH WAYNE MCLAIN February 25, 1926 in Potwin, Butler County, KS.

Notes for JUANITA FAYE DEXTER:
Copy of funeral home record.

More about JUANITA FAYE DEXTER:
Buried Location: February 24, 1994, Mission Chapel Mausoleum, Wichita, KS.
SSAN: 496-22-3379.

Notes for KENNETH WAYNE MCLAIN:
Copy of funeral home record.

More about KENNETH WAYNE MCLAIN:
Buried Location: April 18, 1987, Mission Chapel Mausoleum, Wichita, KS.
SSAN: 163-09-3647.

Marriage notes for JUANITA DEXTER and KENNETH MCLAIN:
Copy of marriage license.

Children of JUANITA DEXTER and KENNETH MCLAIN are:
- i. DARLENE[6] MCLAIN, m. ??? WILLIAMS
- ii. JOANN MCLAIN.
- iii. JAMES W MCLAIN SR.

Notes for JAMES W MCLAIN SR:
Called Jimmie.

96. KENNETH J[5] HALL (ROY LUTRELL[4], FRANCIS LEATON[3], SENY[2] MOORE, RICHARD S[1]) was born April 08, 1916 in Independence, Montgomery County, KS, and died February 09, 1994 in Portland, Multnomah County, OR. He married MARIA KATHLEEN ???.

Notes for KENNETH J HALL:
Copy of record of birth, newspaper obts, funeral home record.

More about KENNETH J HALL:
Buried Location: February 14, 1994, Williamette National Cemetery, Portland, OR.
Fact 1: U.S. Coast Guard
Occupation: Merchant seaman; Union Pacific RR.
SSAN: 543-03-2341.

Children of KENNETH HALL and MARIA ??? are:
- i. SHEILA L[6] HALL.
- ii. SHERRY L HALL.
- iii. TERRY JEAN HALL.
- iv. ANNA M INGELMAN, stepchild.
- v. JERRY R DAVIS, stepchild.

97. GEORGE LEROY[5] BRENNER (ALICE ELIZA[4] HALL, FRANCIS LEATON[3], SENY[2] MOORE, RICHARD S[1]) was born January 09, 1908 in Longton, Butler County, KS, and died June 12, 1983 in El Dorado, Butler County, KS. He married NEVA IONA RUSSELL June 26, 1929 in El Dorado, Butler County, KS, daughter of ELISA RUSSELL and RITTA ???.

More about GEORGE LEROY BRENNER:
Buried Location: McGill Cemetery, Potwin, Butler County, KS.
Occupation: Oil field pumper.
SSAN: 509-03-0525.

More about NEVA IONA RUSSELL:
Buried Location: McGill Cemetery, Potwin, Butler County, KS.
SSAN: 515-20-2841.

Marriage notes for GEORGE BRENNER and NEVA RUSSELL:
Copy of marriage license.

Children of GEORGE BRENNER and NEVA RUSSELL are:
  i. VIRGINIA[6] BRENNER, b. 1933; d. 1933.
  ii. GWIN LEE BRENNER, b. July 25, 1933, Newton, Harvey County, KS; d. July 25, 1933, Newton, Harvey County, KS.

    More about GWIN LEE BRENNER:
    Buried Location: July 25, 1933, McGill Cemetery, Potwin, Butler County, KS.
    Cause of Death: Stillborn.

98. VERL W[5] BRENNER (ALICE ELIZA[4] HALL, FRANCIS LEATON[3], SENY[2] MOORE, RICHARD S[1]) was born January 14, 1911 in Potwin, Butler County, KS, and died October 08, 1955 in Newton, Harvey County, KS. He married (1) MARGARET LOUISE GRIMMET March 12, 1936 in Wichita, Sedgwick County, KS, daughter of ORVILLE GRIMMET and IVA BUTCHER. He married (2) WILMA LORENA SCHROLL June 21, 1950 in Colorado Springs, El Paso County, CO, daughter of WILLIAM SCHROLL and LORENA EILERTS.

Notes for VERL W BRENNER:
Copy of funeral home report.

More about VERL W BRENNER:
Buried Location: October 11, 1955, Whitewater Cemetery, Whitewater, KS.
Cause of Death: Coronary Thrombosis-Acute.
Occupation: Vickers Petroleum.
SSAN: 512-03-6976.

Notes for MARGARET LOUISE GRIMMET:
Copy of funeral home report and newspaper obituaries.

More about MARGARET LOUISE GRIMMET:
Buried Location: January 24, 1948, Mcgill Cemetery, Potwin, Butler County, KS.

Cause of Death: Heart attack.
SSAN: 344-12-1709.

Marriage notes for VERL BRENNER and MARGARET GRIMMET:
Copy of marriage license.

Notes for WILMA LORENA SCHROLL:
Copy of funeral home record.

More about WILMA LORENA SCHROLL:
Buried Location: October 04, 1982, Whitewater Cemetery, Butler County, KS.
Cause of Death: Bronchial pneumonia.
Occupation: Telephone operator.
SSAN: 509-09-4885.

Children of VERL BRENNER and MARGARET GRIMMET are:
172. i. RODONNA SUE[6] BRENNER, b. August 21, 1945.
173. ii. IVA JO BRENNER, b. July 08, 1946.

99. CECIL LORNE[5] HALL (IRA EMMUTT[4], FRANCIS LEATON[3], SENY[2] MOORE, RICHARD S[1]) was born January 28, 1915. He married (1) LOIS REVES August 07, 1934. He married (2) JESSIE GENEVA LAWTON November 23, 1968.

More about JESSIE GENEVA LAWTON:
Buried Location: Memory Gardens, CA.

Child of CECIL HALL and LOIS REVES is:
174. i. JOAN ANN[6] HALL, b. August 11, 1946, CA.

100. DORIS MAXINE[5] HALL (Guy CHRISTIAN[4], FRANCIS LEATON[3], SENY[2] MOORE, RICHARD S[1]) was born April 15, 1921 in Whitewater, Butler County, KS. She married LEVERNE NEIL KENNEDY July 22, 1940 in Valley Center, Sedgwick County, KS, son of PAUL KENNEDY and IRENE KIMBERLIN.

Notes for DORIS MAXINE HALL:
Copy of birth certificate.

Notes for LEVERNE NEIL KENNEDY:
Copy of birth certificate and military discharge.

Children of DORIS HALL and LEVERNE KENNEDY are:

      i.   LEVERNE PAUL^6 KENNEDY, b. January 06, 1941, Newton, Harvey County, KS; d. January 06, 1941, Newton, Harvey County, KS.

      Notes for LEVERNE PAUL KENNEDY:
      Copy of birth certificate.

      More about LEVERNE PAUL KENNEDY:
      Buried Location: Shaffer Cemetery, Butler County, KS.

      ii.   BOY KENNEDY, b. April 1941, Newton, Harvey County, KS; d. April 1941, Newton, Harvey County, KS.

175.   iii.   MARY ESTHER KENNEDY, b. May 13, 1942, Newton, Harvey County, KS.
176.   iv.   MARCELLA JEAN KENNEDY, b. March 09, 1946, Newton, Harvey County, KS; d. July 09, 1993, Iola, Allen County, KS.
177.   v.   CHARLENE WILMA KENNEDY, b. August 30, 1947, Eureka, Greenwood County, KS.

101. DUANE DELOISE^5 HALL (Guy CHRISTIAN^4, FRANCIS LEATON^3, SENY^2 MOORE, RICHARD S^1) was born September 01, 1922 in Potwin, Butler County, KS. He married MARY ALICE WEEDMAN May 29, 1945 in Pascagoula, Jackson County, MS.

Notes for DUANE DELOISE HALL:
Copy of military separation papers.

More about DUANE DELOISE HALL:
Fact 1: USCG Ser #572-497 Served 22 Oct 42 - 1 Dec 45

Marriage notes for DUANE HALL and MARY WEEDMAN:
Copy of marriage license.

Children of DUANE HALL and MARY WEEDMAN are:
178.   i.   DIANA KAY^6 HALL, b. September 29, 1946, Shawnee, Potowatomee County, OK.
179.   ii.   MARTHA MAY HALL, b. April 29, 1947; adopted child.

102. CLAYTON OAKLEY^5 HALL (GUY CHRISTIAN^4, FRANCIS LEATON^3, SENY^2 MOORE, RICHARD S^1) was born April 24, 1924 in Whitewater, Butler County, KS. He married EMILY HOPE BIEWENER August 22, 1948 in Newton, Harvey County, KS.

Notes for CLAYTON OAKLEY HALL:
Copy of military separation paper.

More about CLAYTON OAKLEY HALL:
Fact 1: USMC Ser #864287 Active duty 18 Jun 43 - 30 Mar 46.

Marriage notes for CLAYTON HALL and EMILY BIEWENER:
Copy of marriage license.

Children of CLAYTON HALL, and EMILY BIEWENER are:
180.   i.   NAOMI LEE^6 HALL, b. June 10, 1952, Newton, Harvey County, KS.
181.   ii.   CATHERINE ANN HALL, b. July 15, 1954, Newton, Harvey County, KS.

103. WANDA MARLENE^5 HALL (GUY CHRISTIAN^4, FRANCIS LEATON^3, SENY^2 MOORE, RICHARD S^1) was born May 11, 1928 in Newton, Harvey County, KS. She married VICTOR HERBERT COSENTINO August 08, 1949 in Enid, Garfield County, OK.

Marriage notes for WANDA HALL and VICTOR COSENTINO:
Copy of marriage license.

Children of WANDA HALL and VICTOR COSENTINO are:
182.   i.   VERNON LEROY^6 COSENTINO, b. August 13, 1950, Newton, Harvey County, KS.
183.   ii.   GUY VINCENT COSENTINO, b. June 29, 1951, Newton, Harvey County, KS.
184.   iii.   JAMES HALL COSENTINO, b. June 07, 1955, Tucson, Pina County, AZ

104. AUDREY FAYE^5 HALL (GUY CHRISTIAN^4, FRANCIS LEATON^3, SENY^2 MOORE, RICHARD S^1) was born July 17, 1931 in Newton, Harvey County, KS. She married (1) THEODORE HOPKINS JR January 08, 1952 in Wellington, Sumner County, KS. She married (2) BILL J R LUEKENGA June 20, 1975 in Sedgwick, Harvey County, KS. She married (3) ORLIE EUGENE BEER May 06, 1977 in Wichita, Sedgwick County, KS.

Notes for AUDREY FAYE HALL:
Copy of birth certificate.

Marriage notes for AUDREY HALL and THEODORE HOPKINS:
Copy of marriage license.

Notes for BILL J R LUEKENGA:
Copy of death certificate and military separation papers.

More about BILL J R LUEKENGA:
Buried Location: October 27, 1975, Wichita, Sedgwick County, KS.
Cause of Death: Auto accident.
SSAN: 443-30-0101.

Marriage notes for AUDREY HALL and BILL LUEKENGA:
Copy of marriage license.

Marriage notes for AUDREY HALL and ORLIE BEER:
Copy of marriage license.

Children of AUDREY HALL and THEODORE HOPKINS are:
185.   i.   SONDRA SUE^6 HOPKINS, b. April 20, 1952, Newton, Harvey County, KS.
186.   ii. PAMELA KAY HOPKINS, b. January 18, 1954, Newton, Harvey County, KS.
187.   iii. BRUCE LYNN HOPKINS, b. May 04, 1955, Newton, Harvey County, KS.
188.   iv. BRENDA JO HOPKINS, b. September 26, 1957, Newton, Harvey County, KS.
189.   v.   VEDA LOU HOPKINS, b. January 08, 1959, Hutchinson, Reno County, KS.

105. NANCY ANN^5 HALL (GUY CHRISTIAN^4, FRANCIS^5 LEATON^3, SENY^2 MOORE, RICHARD S^1) was born April 06, 1934 in Newton, Harvey County, KS. She married (1) DUANE FRANCIS MCGINN May 28, 1952 in Halstead, Harvey County, KS. She married (2) VICTOR STEFFEN February 14, 1998 in Hutchinson, Reno County, KS.

Marriage notes for NANCY HALL and DUANE MCGINN:
Copy of marriage license.

Children of NANCY HALL and DUANE MCGINN are:
190.   i.   CYNTHIA LOU^6 MCGINN, b. May 28, 1953, Newton, Harvey County, KS.
       ii. KURT FRANCIS MCGINN, b. May 18, 1956, Newton, Harvey County, KS; m. JANICE ANN HOLT GARDNER, April 08, 1995, Wichita, Sedgwick County, KS.
       iii. JILL MARIE MCGINN, b. September 23, 1962, Newton, Harvey County, KS; m. EDMOND JACK JOHNSON, August 13, 1988, Halstead, Harvey County, KS.

   Marriage notes for JILL MCGINN and EDMOND JOHNSON:
   Copy of marriage license.

       iv. KAREN SUE MCGINN, b. June 21, 1968, Newton, Harvey County, KS.

106. CLARA MAY^5 HALL (GUY CHRISTIAN^4, FRANCIS LEATON^3, SENY^2 MOORE, RICHARD S^1) was born February 28, 1936 in Newton, Harvey County, KS. She married DONALD KEITH DEHAVEN May 29, 1954 in Newton, Harvey County, KS.

Notes for CLARA MAY HALL:
Copy of birth certificate.

Notes for DONALD KEITH DEHAVEN:
Copy of birth certificate.

Marriage notes for CLARA HALL and DONALD DEHAVEN:
Copy of Church Holy Matrimony Certificate.

Children of CLARA HALL and DONALD DEHAVEN are:
191.   i.   KIMBERLY SUE^6 DEHAVEN, b. August 08, 1956, Newton, Harvey County, KS.
192.   ii. JEFFREY LYNN DEHAVEN, b. April 25, 1959, Newton, Harvey County, KS.

107. JANICE DE LOIS^5 HALL (GUY CHRISTIAN^4, FRANCIS LEATON^3, SENY^2 MOORE, RICHARD S^1) was born November 06, 1942 in Newton, Harvey County, KS. She married ORVAL ALTON BAIR JR December 11, 1960 in Newton, Harvey County, KS.

More about ORVAL ALTON BAIR JR:
Fact 1: USAF Ser # AF17519446.
Fact 2: Served Feb 5, 1958 - Dec 13, 1977 TDRL 50% disability.
Fact 3: September 1978 - VA declared 100% disability.
Fact 4: Final discharge January 1982 with 60% disability.

Medical Information: Has MS.
Occupation: Aircraft Radio Tech/Instructor in Electronics & ATC Maint Management.

Children of JANICE HALL and ORVAL BAIR are:
- 193. i. RHONDA LEIGH[6] BAIR, b. November 24, 1961, Forbes AFB, Shawnee County, KS.
- 194. ii. TERESA RENEA BAIR, b. September 24, 1962, Port Lyautey NAS, Morocco.
- iii. ROY WILLIAM BAIR, b. July 05, 1964, Otis AFB, Barnstable County, MA; m. MELLISSA JANE MCDOUGHALL, May 05, 1998, Aiea, Oahu, Hl.

108. BLENDENA CAROLINE[5] MILLER (CELIA LAVERNA[4] HALL, FRANCIS LEATON[3], SENY[2] MOORE, RICHARD S[1]) was born June 30, 1916. She married CECIL G CRAIN April 13, 1935 in Pawhuska, Osage County, OK.

Marriage notes for BLENDENA MILLER and CECIL CRAIN:
Copy of marriage license.

Child of BLENDENA MILLER and CECIL CRAIN is:
- i. DEWEY BEN[6] CRAIN, b. November 22, 1936.

109. BONNIE LOU[5] MILLER (CELIA LAVERNA[4] HALL, FRANCIS LEATON[3], SENY[2] MOORE, RICHARD S[1]) was born November 08, 1927. She married AXEL C SWANSON August 09, 1946.

Children of BONNIE MILLER and AXEL SWANSON are:
- i. SUSAN LAVERN[6] SWANSON, b. January 10, 1948.
- ii. PATRICIA HOPE SWANSON, b. September 09, 1950.
- iii. BECKY JO SWANSON, b. February 17, 1958.

110. LOIS[5] HALL (ZACHARY HURSHEL[4], FRANCIS LEATON[3], SENY[2] MOORE, RICHARD S[1]). She married MARION L KIRCHMER September 01, 1943 in Newton, Harvey County, KS, son of CARL KIRCHMER and PEARL BUTLER.

Notes for MARION L KIRCHMER:
Copy of enlisted record and funeral record.

More about MARION L KIRCHMER:
Buried Location: April 28, 1992, Restlawn Gardens of Memory.
SSAN: 511-09-2189.

Children of Lois HALL and MARION KIRCHMER are:
- i. LARRY GENE[6] KIRCHMER, m. VALERIE ABBOTT, July 24, 1965, Newton, Harvey County, KS.

    Marriage notes for LARRY KIRCHMER and VALERIE ABBOTT:
    Copy of marriage license.

- ii. GALEN KIRCHMER.
- iii. TERESA KIRCHMER, m. ??? MILLER.

111. CALVIN[5] HALL (ZACHARY HURSHEL[4], FRANCIS LEATON[3], SENY[2] MOORE, RICHARD S[1]). He married ESTA ??? June 21, 1947 in El Dorado, Butler County, KS.

Notes for CALVIN HALL:
Copy of newspaper article about 50th wedding anniversary.

Children of CALVIN HALL and ESTA ??? are:
- i. SHELDON[6] HALL, m. REBECCA ???.
- ii. BRIAN HALL, m. PAMUELA ???.
- iii. TIM HALL, m. JAN ???.
- iv. LAURIE HALL.
- v. CINDY HALL, m. JEFFREY JACKSON.

112. ROGER THAINE[5] PENNER (ENUICE MARJORIE[4] JACOBS, FLORENCE ANN[3] HALL, SENY[2] MOORE, RICHARD S[1]) was born January 06, 1917 in Potwin, Butler County, KS. He married JESSIE PETTERGILL June 15, 1946.

Child of ROGER PENNER and JESSIE PETTERGILL is:
- i. DARRELL LEE[6] PENNER, b. November 21, 1962.

113. MARGARET ELNORA[5] PENNER (ENUICE MARJORIE[4] JACOBS, FLORENCE ANN[3] HALL, SENY[2] MOORE, RICHARD S[1]) was born November 15, 1918 in Potwin, Butler County, KS, and died May 11, 1967 in California. She married ENNIS CLAUDE DUNCAN.

Children of MARGARET PENNER and ENNIS DUNCAN are:

195.	i.	JOYCE ANN[6] DUNCAN, b. July 28, 1944, California.
196.	ii.	FAITH EILEEN DUNCAN, b. January 14, 1948, California.
197.	iii.	DAVID ROBERT DUNCAN, b. February 05, 1951, California.

114. IVAN DALE[5] PENNER (ENUICE MARJORIE JACOBS, FLORENCE ANN[3] HALL, SENY[2] MOORE, RICHARD S[1]) was born May 22, 1922 in Newton, Harvey County, KS. He married MAXINE DUNBIN March 03, 1957.

Children of IVAN PENNER and MAXINE DUNBIN are:
  i. MICHAEL DALE[6] PENNER, b. December 31, 1957, Denver, Arapahoe County, CO.
  ii. GARY IVAN PENNER, b. April 17, 1960, Denver, Arapahoe County, CO.

115. EDNA MAXINE[5] PENNER (ENUICE MARJORIE[4] JACOBS, FLORENCE ANN[3] HALL, SENY[2] MOORE, RICHARD S[1]) was born August 30, 1924 in Potwin, Butler County, KS. She married (1) WILLIE EARL BEITER June 05, 1945 in Independence, Montgomery County, KS. She married (2) LESLIE ELMER KEHOE November 21, 1965.

Marriage notes for EDNA PENNER and WILLIE BEITER:
Copy of marriage license.

Children of EDNA PENNER and WILLIE BEITER are:
  i. RODNEY EARL[6] BEITER, b. December 14, 1947; m. LINDA LEE PARKER, October 17, 1971.
  ii. TERRY LYNN BEITER, b. December 19, 1949; m. KATHERYN MYERS, November 06, 1972.
  iii. KATHY ANNETTE BEITER, b. October 11, 1953; m. ART REAGAN.

116. NORMA FRANCES[5] PENNER (ENUICE MARJORIE[4] JACOBS, FLORENCE ANN[3] HALL, SENY[2] MOORE, RICHARD S[1]) was bor July 17, 1928 in Potwin, Butler County, KS. She married IVAN ROBERT MORSE January 16, 1949 in Howard, Elk County, KS.

More about IVAN ROBERT MORSE:
Buried Location: April 02, 1996, Longton, Elk County, KS.
Fact 1: Navy WWII.
SSAN: 513-14-3717.

Marriage notes for NORMA PENNER and IVAN MORSE:
Copy of marriage license.

Children of NORMA PENNER and IVAN MORSE are:
198.	i.	ROBERT STEVEN[6] MORSE, b. September 28, 1947, Wichita, Sedgwick County, KS.
199.	ii.	TERESA ANNE MORSE. b. January 19, 1950, Independence, Montgomery County, KS.
200.	iii.	CONNIE ARLENE MORSE, b. July 13, 1952, Eureka, Greenwood County, KS.
	iv.	MARK EDWIN MORSE, b. June 22, 1954, Eureka, Greenwood County, KS; m. CONNIE SUE DORISE.
	v.	GORDON RUSSELL MORSE, b. September 06, 1955, Eureka, Greenwood County, KS, m. RITA ???.
201.	vi.	REX ELDON MORSE, b, December 09, 1956, Eureka, Greenwood County, KS.

117. CHARLES FORREST[5] JACOBS (HOMER[4], FLORENCE ANN[3] HALL, SENY[2] MOORE, RICHARD S[1]) was born May 12, 1922 in Newton, Harvey County, KS. He married WINIFRED TABOR DUGAN September 23, 1944 in Potwin, Butler County, KS.

Marriage notes for CHARLES JACOBS and WINIFRED DUGAN:
Copy of marriage license.

Children of CHARLES JACOBS and WINIFRED DUGAN are:
202.	i.	Joy SUE[6] JACOBS, b. September 22, 1945, El Dorado, Butler County, KS.
203.	ii.	JOHN ERIC JACOBS, b. November 27, 1947, Manhattan, Pottawatomie County, KS.
204.	iii.	JANICE ALLENE JACOBS, b. November 13, 1949, El Dorado, Butler County, KS.
205.	iv.	GARY FORREST JACOBS, b. December 05, 1954, Wichita, Sedgwick County, KS.

118. JOAN[5] JACOBS (HOMER[4], FLORENCE ANN[3] HALL, SENY[2] MOORE, RICHARD S[1]) was born January 15, 1928 in Newton, Harvey County, KS. She married WILLIAM CARL LONG May 01, 1955 in Oxford, Cowley County, KS.

Marriage notes for JOAN JACOBS and WILLIAM LONG.

Copy of marriage license.

Children of JOAN JACOBS and WILLIAM LONG are:
	i.	WILLIAM CARL[6] LONG JR, b. July 18, 1956, Atchison, Atchison County, KS.
206.	ii.	Jim C LONG, b. July 11, 1957, Liberal, Seward County, KS.
207.	iii.	ANNE E LONG, b. August 21, 1958, Hutchinson, Reno County, KS.
208.	iv.	SCOTT JACOBS LONG, b. October 08, 1962, Hutchinson, Reno County, KS.

119. JIM LAIRD[5] JACOBS (HOMER[4], FLORENCE ANN[3] HALL, SENY[2] MOORE, RICHARD S[1]) was born September 23, 1932 in El Dorado, Butler County, KS. He married MARY LOU VOGELMAN June 02, 1957 in Potwin, Butler County, KS, daughter of RAYMOND VOGELMAN and THELMA ???.

Marriage notes for JIM JACOBS and MARY VOGELMAN:
Copy of marriage license.

Children of JIM JACOBS and MARY VOGELMAN are:
- i. PATRICK MARTY[6] JACOBS, b. March 20, 1958, Farmington, San Juan County, NM.
- ii. THOMAS CARL JACOBS, b. May 18, 1960, Albuquerque, Bernalillo County, NM; d. June 20, 1981, Silverton, San Juan County, CO.

    Notes for THOMAS CARL JACOBS:
    Copy of obituary.

    More about THOMAS CARL JACOBS:
    SSAN: 525-19-3092.

- iii. JEFFREY HOMER JACOBS, b. September 02, 1961, Farmington, San Juan County, NM.
- iv. MELANIE DAWN JACOBS, b. January 20, 1964, Farmington, San Juan County, NM; m. HERSHEL PATRIC SPURLIN, July 02, 1982, Farmington, San Juan County, NM.
- v. LUCY SUSANNE JACOBS, b. July 31, 1969, Farmington, San Juan County, NM; m. ANDY HILL, September 02, 1991, Farmington, San Juan County, NM.

120. CHARLES RAY[5] JACOBS (LESTON LYLE[4], FLORENCE ANN[3] HALL, SENY MOORE, RICHARD S[1]) was born June 29, 1938 in Wichita, Sedgwick County, KS. He married JUDITH BERNADINE KNAAK 1961, daughter of EARL KNAAK and ROMANA KOESTER.

Children of CHARLES JACOBS and JUDITH KNAAK are:
- 209. i. ANGELA RAE[6] JACOBS, b. October 22, 1964, Wichita, Sedgwick County, KS.
- ii. KENNETH LYLE JACOBS, b. April 15, 1966, Wichita, Sedgwick County, KS.   iii. MONICA JACOBS, b. July 03, 1970, Wichita, Sedgwick County, KS.

121. CARL RUSSELL[5] NICHOLL (ALMA DELILAH[4] THORNBURG, SARAH REBECCA[3] GREENFIELD, MATILDA JANE[2] MOORE, RICHARD S[1]) was born April 11, 1916 in Wick, Warren County, IA, and died February 12, 1971 in Denver, Arapahoe County, CO. He married (1)EDITH HATAWAY. He married (2) EVELYN ELLEN NICOLLE June 08, 1939 in Missouri, daughter of EARLE NICOLLE and RUTH CLARKE.

More about CARL RUSSELL NICHOLL:
Buried Location: February 16, 1971, Fairmount Cemetery, Denver, CO.
Occupation: Auto supply.

More about EVELYN ELLEN NICOLLE:
Occupation: Telephone operator.

Children of CARL NICHOLL and EVELYN NICOLLE are:
- i. R JUNE[6] NICHOLL, b. November 26, 1939, Martensdale, Warren County, IA, m. KENNETH DAVID GERBODE, February 14, 1959, Aurora, Buchanan County, CO.
- ii. JIMMIE DUANE NICHOLL, b. January 20, 1941, Martensdale, Warren County, IA; m. DELORES GOODE, December 29, 1969, Denver, Arapahoe County, CO.
- iii. DOROTHY KAY NICHOLL, b. June 13, 1949, Osceola, Clarke County, IA; m. (1) DEAN KNOWLES; m. (2) ROBERT OSBORN, February 16, 1968; m. (3) TERRY KELLY, April 30, 1977.

122. GERALD ORLANDO[5] SEARS JR (PHYLIIS USEBA MAE[4] COPELAND, ADA FRANCIS[3] ATKINSON, SUSAN N[2] MOORE, RICHARD S[1]) was born March 28, 1923 in Bartlesville, Washington County, OK. He married NEVA MARIE FIELDS.

Notes for GERALD ORLANDO SEARS JR:
Copy of birth certificate.

Children of GERALD SEARS and NEVA FIELDS are:
- 210. i. MICHAEL ERNEST[6] SEARS, b. March 28, 1946, Vinita, Craig County, OK.
- ii. PATRICK THOMAS SEARS, b. December 28, 1948, Vinita, Craig County, OK; m. DIANE MARIE STAMBECK, August 21, 1976, Kebs, Pittsburg County, OK.
- 211. iii. JANET SUE SEARS, b. December 24, 1955, Bartlesville, Washington County, OK.

123. JAN[5] SMITHHISLER (LEONA BELLE[4] COPELAND, ADA FRANCIS[3] ATKINSON, SUSAN N[2] MOORE, RICHARD S[1]). She married JIM HAWKINS.

Child of JAN SMITHHISLER and JIM HAWKINS is:
- 212. i. DEBBIE[6] HAWKINS.

Generation No. 6

124. MAX[6] COURTER (CLARENCE[5], EFFIE SARAH[4] MOORE, WILLIAM OSCAR[3], REUBEN[2], RICHARD S[1]) was born 1924 in Enid, Garfield County, OK. He married DOROTHY MEHLING in 1949, daughter of CONRAD MEHLING and MARGARET SEILER.

More about MAX COURTER:
Military: Bet. 1942-1945, U.S. Army
Occupation: Lumberman.

Children of MAX COURTER and DOROTHY MEHLING are:
  i. DENISE[7] COURTER, b. 1950, Heraldsburg, Sonoma County, CA; m. DENNIS SCOTT.
  ii. SUSAN COURTER, b. 1952, Heraldsburg, Sonoma County, CA; m. JOHN WERTZ.
  iii. ROSS COURTER, b. 1960, Santa Rosa, Sonoma County, CA; m. RENEE EBEJER.

125. ALAN ARTHUR[6] MOORE (FLOYD VIRGIL[5], LEON ARTHUR[4], WILLIAM OSCAR[3], REUBEN[2], RICHARD S[1]) was born August 05, 1939 in Wichita, Sedgwick County, KS, and died February 01, 1996 in Minneapolis, Hennepin County, MN. He married DELLA JEAN TURPIN August 28, 1963.

More about ALAN ARTHUR MOORE:
Buried Location: February 04, 1996, Park Rapids, Hubbard County, MN.

Children of ALAN MOORE and DELLA TURPIN are:
  i. CADE[7] MOORE.
  ii. MARISSA MOORE.
  iii. GINGER MOORE.

126. WAYNE VIRGIL[6] MOORE (FLOYD VIRGIL[5], LEON ARTHUR[4], WILLIAM OSCAR[3], REUBEN[2], RICHARD S[1]) was born May 03, 1942 in Wichita, Sedgwick County, KS. He married PEGGY CHARLINE EDMINSTER August 10, 1963 in Wichita, Sedgwick County, KS, daughter of LEICHESTFR EDMINSTER and WINIFRED CLARK.

More about WAYNE VIRGIL MOORE:.
Fact 1: 1972-74 Navy Lt Col.
Occupation: Physician.

More about PEGGY CHARLINE EDMINSTER:
Occupation: Minister.

Marriage notes for WAYNE MOORE and PEGGY EDMINSTER:
Copy of marriage license.

Children of WAYNE MOORE and PEGGY EDMINSTER are:
  i. KIRSTEN LEI[7] MOORE, b. May 14, 1967, Minneapolis, Hennepin County, MN; m. PAT SHARTZER, 1989, Kansas.
  ii. KARI COZETTE MOORE, b. December 23, 1969, Minneapolis, Hennepin County, MN.

127. CAROLYN JUNE[6] MYERS (ZELMA ELVA[5] MOORE, LEON ARTHUR[4], WILLIAM OSCAR[3], REUBEN[2], RICHARD S[1]) was born October 31, 1942 in Houston, Harris County, TX She married ROBERT GORDON WAINSCOTT July 06, 1963 in Wichita, Sedgwick County, KS, son of GORDON WAINSCOTT and MAXINE MOUTRY.

Notes for CAROLYN JUNE MYERS:
Copy of birth certificate.

Notes for ROBERT GORDON WAINSCOTT:
Copy of birth certificate.

More about ROBERT GORDON WAINSCOTT:
Occupation: Engineer for Mobil Oil Company.

Marriage notes for CAROLYN MYERS and ROBERT WAINSCOTT:
Copy of marriage license.

Children of CAROLYN MYERS and ROBERT WAINSCOTT are:
  i. JODI LYNN[7] WAINSCOTT, b. March 30, 1963, Wichita, Sedgwick County, KS; m. DAVID BUCHANAN, October 22, 1988, Spring, Harris County, TX.
  ii. STEVE LEE WAINSCOTT, b. September 23, 1967, Wichita, Sedgwick County, KS.

  Notes for STEVE LEE WAINSCOTT:
  Copy of birth certificate.

  iii. DAVID SHAWN WAINSCOTT, b. December 02, 1971, Garland, Dallas County, TX.

  Notes for DAVID SHAWN WAINSCOTT:
  Copy of birth certificate.

128. JUDITH DIANE[6] MOORE (RICHARD DONALD[5], LEON ARTHUR[4], WILLIAM OSCAR[3], REUBEN[2], RICHARD S[1]) was born May 09, 1944 in Wichita, Sedgwick County, KS. She married LLOYD EUGENE KRASE, August 28, 1964 in Wichita, Sedgwick County, KS, son of LLOYD KRASE and ELIZABETH HART.

Notes for JUDITH DIANE MOORE:
Called Judy.
Copy birth certificate.
Graduated from Goddard High School, Goddard, KS.
One year, Emporia State University, Emporia, KS.

1. Janice D (Hall) Bair, received all information about the Krause family from Judy Diane (Moore) Krause.

Notes for LLOYD EUGENE KRASE: Called Gene.
Copy of birth certificate.
Graduated from Cheney rural High School, Cheney, KS.
Bachelor's of business administration (accounting/economics), Wichita State University, Wichita, KS.
Master of science (public administration, Shippensburg University, Shippensburg, PA.

Marriage notes for JUDITH MOORE and LLOYD KRASE:
Copy of marriage certificate.

Children of JUDITH MOORE and LLOYD KRASE are:
- i. SHELLY ANNE^7 KRASE, b. January 06, 1968, Wichita, Sedgwick County, KS; m. (1) ??? ABBELFAZI; m (2)   KENNETH JAMES SAVOY, May 27, 1990, Topeka, Shawnee County, KS.

  Notes for SHELLY ANNE KRASE:
  Graduated from Leavenworth High School, Leavenworth, KS.
  Bachelor's in business administration (economics), Wichita State University, Wichita, KS.
  Bachelor's of science (French), Wichita State University, Wichita, KS.
  Master's of science (economics), Wichita State University, Wichita, KS.

  Notes for KENNETH JAMES SAVOY:
  Graduated from Leavenworth High School, Leavenworth, KS.
  Bachelor's of science (electrical engineering) Wichita State University, Wichita, KS.
  Master's of science (electrical engineering), Wichita State University, Wichita, KS.
  Currently pursuing master's of business administration, University of Missouri, St. Louis, MO.

  Marriage notes for SHELLEY KRASE and KENNETH SAVOY:
  Copy of wedding invitation.

- ii. JILL DIANE KRASE, b. February 20, 1972, Wichita, Sedgwick County, KS; m. SCOTT EDWARD SPRADLIN, June 27, 1992, Wichita, Sedgwick County, KS.

  Notes for JILL DIANE KRASE:
  Graduated from Shawnee Heights High School, Wichita, KS.
  Bachelor's of science (psychology), Kansas State University, Manhattan, KS.
  Currently pursing master's/doctorate (psychology), George Fox University, Newburg, OR.

  Notes for SCOTT EDWARD SPRADLIN:
  Graduated Northwest High School, Wichita, KS.
  Bachelor's of art (Bible and family), Manhattan Christian College, Manhattan, KS.
  Master's of science (counseling) Covenant Theological Seminary, St. Louis, MO.

  Marriage Notes for JILL KRASE and SCOTT SPRADLIN:
  Copy of wedding invitation.

129. KAREN SUE^6 MOORE (RICHARD DONALD^5, LEON ARTHUR^4, WILLIAM OSCAR^3, REUBEN^2, RICHARD S^1) was born August 24, 1950 in Wichita, Sedgwick County, KS. She married PAUL RICHARD HOLLIDAY May 18, 1991 in Wichita, Sedgwick County, KS, son of MYRON HOLLIDAY and MARJORIE IMM.

Notes for KAREN SUE MOORE:
Copy of birth certificate.

Notes for PAUL RICHARD HOLLIDAY:
Graduated Long Island High School.
Graduated Fort Hayes State w/master's in physical education.

More about PAUL RICHARD HOLLIDAY:
Occupation: Farmer.

Marriage notes for KAREN MOORE and PAUL HOLLIDAY:
Copy of marriage license.

Children of KAREN MOORE and PAUL HOLLIDAY are:
- i. HEATH RAY^7 HOLLIDAY, b. September 17, 1977, Ulysses, Grant County, KS; stepchild.

    ii. ADAM BLAIR HOLLIDAY, b. March 28, 1990, Ulysses, Grant County, KS; stepchild.
    iii. EMIE LEA HOLLIDAY, b. October 25, 1993, Ulysses, Grant County, KS; stepchild.
    iv. SETH MYRON HOLLIDAY, b. August 01, 1993, Garden City, Finney County, KS.

    Notes for SETH MYRON HOLLIDAY:
    Copy of birth certificate.

130. MIRIAM ANN[6] MOORE (WILLIAM REUBEN[5], REUBEN DAVID[4], WILLIAM OSCAR[3], REUBEN[2], RICHARD S[1]) was born May 04, 1933 in Wichita, Sedgwick County, KS. She married ROBERT LEE DENNETT November 02, 1952 in Mulvane, Sumner County, KS, son of LEO DENNETT and ELEANA SHARON.

Children of MIRAM MOORE and ROBERT DENNETT are:
    i. CARL LELAND[7] DENNETT, b. January 21, 1956, Wichita, Sedgwick County, KS.

    More about CARL LELAND DENNETT:
    Fact 1: Navy.
    Occupation: Electronic technician.

213.   ii. DIANA LEEANN DENNETT, b. November 23, 1957, Wichita, Sedgwick County, KS.

131. WLLIA PAULINE[6] MOORE (WILLIAM REUBEN[5], REUBEN DAVID[4], WILLIAM 0SCAR[3], REUBEN[2], RICHARD S[1]) was born April 05, 1935 in Butler County, KS. She married (1) RICHARD NHEIL ALLISON January 18, 1954 in Butler County, KS. She married (2) JAMES ELVYN WULZ October 14, 1961.

Notes for JAMES ELVYN WULZ:
James adopted Willa's two sons on October 11, 1964.

Children of WLLIA MOORE and RICHARD ALLISON are:
    i. RICHARD NHEIL[7] ALLISON, b. January 19, 1955.
    ii. RONALD RAY ALLISON, b. May 18, 1957.

Children of WLLIA MOORE and JAMES WULZ are:
214.   iii. RICHARD NHEIL ALLISON[7] WULZ, b. January 19, 1955, McConnell AFB, Sedgwick County, KS.
215.   iv. RONALD RAY ALLISON WULZ, b. May 18, 1957, Winfield, Cowley County, KS.
    v. SUSAN RENE WULZ, b. February 03, 1965, KS; d. February 05, 1965, KS.

132. HOWARD RAY[6] MOORE (WILLIAM REUBEN[5], REUBEN DAVID[4], WILLIAM OSCAR[3], REUBEN[2], RICHARD S[1]) was born November 27, 1936 in Wichita, Sedgwick County, KS. He married MARGARET ANN HORNECKER February 26, 1960 in Wichita, Sedgwick County, KS, daughter of CHARLES HORNECKER and LAVERNE DIXON.

Marriage notes for HOWARD MOORE and MARGARET HORNECKER:
Copy of marriage license.

Children of HOWARD MOORE and MARGARET HORNECKER are:
    i. TROY DOUGLAS[7] MOORE, b. December 28, 1960, Wichita, Sedgwick County, KS; m. JACQUELINE NICOLE GUAJARDO, December 30, 1995, San Diego, San Diego County, CA.
    ii. MICHAEL ALAN MOORE, b. December 03, 1965, Wichita, Sedgwick County, KS; m. JOAN MAE COVERT, August 14, 1993, East Liverpool, Columbiana County, OH.

    Notes for JOAN MAE COVERT:
    Called Joni.

    iii. SHERYL ANN MOORE, b. February 03, 1975.

133. JAMES REUBEN[6] MOORE (WILLIAM REUBEN[5], REUBEN DAVID[4], WILLIAM OSCAR[3], REUBEN[2], RICHARD S[1]) was born June 20, 1942 in Wichita, Sedgwick County, KS. He married JUDY ARLENE HAYES July 07, 1963 in Mulvane, Sumner County, KS, daughter of RALPH HAYES and HELEN SHIP.

Marriage notes for JAMES MOORE and JUDY HAYES:
Copy of marriage license.

Children of JAMES MOORE and JUDY HAYES are:
216.   i. TAMMY RAE[7] MOORE, b. August 21, 1965, Wichita, Sedgwick County, KS.
217.   ii. WESLEY WAYNE MOORE. b. May 04, 1968, Wichita, Sedgwick County, KS.

134. VELMA RUTH[6] TALLMAN (VIOLET MARIE[5] MOORE, REUBEN DAVID[4], WILLIAM OSCAR[3], REUBEN[2], RICHARD S[1]) was born June 11, 1933 in Benton, Butler County, KS, and died May 18, 1998 in Wichita, Sedgwick County, KS. She married (1) ??? RAY. She married (2) HARRY RUSSELL CAIN November 30, 1956 in Newton, Harvey County, KS.

Notes for VELMA RUTH TALLMAN:
Copy of funeral home information sheet, In Loving Memory Card.

More about VELMA RUTH TALLMAN:
Buried Location: May 20, 1998, McGill Cemetery, Potwin, Butler County, KS.
Occupation: Housewife.
SSAN: 509-30-0024.

More about HARRY RUSSELL CAIN:
Occupation: Farmer.

Marriage notes for VELMA TALLMAN and HARRY CAIN:
Copy of marriage license.

Child of VELMA TALLMAN and ??? RAY is:
218.   i.   CINDY D[7] RAY, b. August 28, 1954, Wichita, Sedgwick County, KS.

Children of VELMA TALLMAN and HARRY CAIN are:
219.   ii.   CINDY D[7] CAIN, b. August 28, 1954, Wichita, Sedwick County, KS,
      iii.   HARRY CAIN, b. September 13, 1957, Newton, Harvey County, KS; d. January 03, 1991.
220.   iv.   DANNY J CAIN, b. December 23, 1958, El Dorado, Butler County, KS.
      v.   JERRY D CAIN, b. May 18, 1961, El Dorado, Butler County, KS.
      vi.   BONNIE LOU CAIN, b. February 26, 1963, El Dorado, Butler County, KS; m. CRAIG LAVAN STEPHENS, November 10, 1984, Benton, Butler County, KS.

        Notes for BONNIE LOU CAIN:
        Copy of hospital birth certificate.

        Marriage notes for BONNIE CAIN and CRAIG STEPHENS:
        Copy of marriage license.

135. THELMA ELIZABETH[6] TALLMAN (VIOLET MARIE[5] MOORE, REUBEN DAVID[4], WILLIAM OSCAR[3], REUBEN[2], RICHARD S[1]) was born September 28, 1934 in Benton, Butler County, KS. She married RICHARD DALE EDRIS January 18, 1955 in Potwin, Butler County, KS, son of CHARLES EDRIS and EMMA BROCKWAY.

Notes for THELMA ELIZABETH TALLMAN:
Called Jeep.

More about THELMA ELIZABETH TALLMAN:
Occupation: Food service.

Notes for RICHARD DALE EDRIS:
Copy of newspaper obituary.

More about RICHARD DALE EDRIS:
Buried Location: June 03, 1998, Whitewater Cemetery, Butler County, KS.
Occupation: Milling Cargil.

Marriage notes for THELMA TALLMAN and RICHARD EDRIS:
Copy of marriage license.

Children of THELMA TALLMAN and RICHARD EDRIS are:
221.   i.   CHARLES RICHARD[7] EDRIS, b. May 30, 1955, Newton, Harvey County, KS.
      ii.   HARRY L EDRIS.
222.   iii.   DENNIS LEE EDRIS, b. December 25, 1958, Newton, Harvey County, KS.
223.   iv.   BRUCE LEON EDRIS, b. March 01, 1960, Newton, Harvey County, KS.
224.   v.   SUE CHARLENE EDRIS, b. July 12, 1962, Newton, Harvey County, KS.
225.   vi.   TINA MARIE EDRIS, b. November 17, 1965, Newton, Harvey County, KS.

136. ARTHUR LEON[6] MOORE (GLENN, LEON[5], REUBEN DAVID[4], WILLIAM OSCAR[3], REUBEN[2], RICHARD S[1]) was born April 25, 1947. He married MEG ANN DELAHANTY July 07, 1984 in San Francisco, San Francisco County, CA.

Children of ARTHUR MOORE and MEG DELAHANTY are:

      i.   GEORGE ARTHUR[7] MOORE.
      ii.   CHELACEN MOORE.
      iii.   SAMUEL WILLIAM MOORE.
      iv.   ROSEMARY EMILY MOORE.

137. WILLIAM DAVID[6] MOORE (GLENN LEON[5], REUBEN DAVID[4], WILLIAM OSCAR[3], REUBEN[2], RICHARD S[1]) was born April 06, 1950. He married MARY TERESA GOEBEL in Sacramento, Sacramento County, CA.

Children of WILLIAM MOORE and MARY GOEBEL are:
      i.   BRIAN[7] MOORE, adopted child.

ii. CHRISTOPHER MOORE, adopted child.
iii. KARIN ANN MOORE.
iv. KYLE WILLIAM MOORE.

138. GARY LLOYD[6] MOORE (LLOYD MERLE[5], REUBEN DAVID[4], WILLIAM OSCAR[3], REUBEN[2], RICHARD S[1]) was born December 06, 1935 in Potwin, Butler County, KS, and died January 18, 1993 in Augusta, Butler County, KS. He married BEVERLY TYLER August 29, 1954 in Augusta, Butler County, KS, daughter of IRA C TYLER.

More about GARY LLOYD MOORE:
Buried Location: January 21, 1993, Augusta, Butler County, KS.
Occupation: meat cutter.
SSAN: 515-28-4749.

Marriage notes for GARY MOORE and BEVERLY TYLER:
Copy of marriage license.

Children of GARY MOORE and BEVERLY TYLER are:
i. VALERIE JEAN[7] MOORE, b. September 06, 1955, Augusta, Butler County, KS; m. MARK SMITH, September 07, 1973, Augusta, Butler County, KS.
ii. ANGELA DENISE MOORE, b. February 14, 1958.
iii. MICHAEL B MOORE, b. August 24, 1959; d. February 23, 1960.

More about MICHAEL B MOORE:
Buried Location: Augusta, Butler County, KS.

iv. BRENDA SUE MOORE, b. December 27, 1960; m. (1) CORY DUKE, m. (2) BILL LANTZ.
v. GARY LLOYD MOORE, JR, b. December 22, 1962; m. CATHRYN KAY VALLE, December 11, 1982, Augusta, Butler County, KS.
vi. STEPHEN SCOTT MOORE, b. January 20, 1964.

139. TONY BRENT[6] MOORE (LLOYD MERLE[5], REUBEN DAVID[4], WILLIAM OSCAR[3], REUBEN[2], RICHARD S[1]) was born April 04, 1942 in Potwin, Butler County, KS. He married KAREN JEAN LACKEY January 08, 1963 in El Dorado, Butler County, KS, daughter of FLOYD LACKEY.

More about TONY BRENT MOORE:
Ethnicity/Relig: First Christian.
Occupation: Oil refinery.

More about KAREN JEAN LACKEY:
Ethnicity/Relig: Baptist.
Occupation: Bank clerk.

Marriage notes for TONY MOORE and KAREN LACKEY:
Copy of marriage license.

Children of TONY MOORE and KAREN LACKEY are:
i. LAVINA JEAN[7] MOORE, b. September 03, 1963, Augusta, Butler County, KS; m. ROBERT BLAKE, Augusta, Butler County, KS.
ii. RICK DEAN MOORE, b. August 26, 1964, Augusta, Butler County, KS; m. ANDEE THOMAS.
iii. PAULA LYNN MOORE, b. June 29, 1967, Augusta, Butler County, KS; m. (1) DUKE BRANDT; m. (2) ALLEN BARG.

140. JOHN HAROLD[6] TURNER JR (RUTH B[5] MOORE, REUBEN DAVID[4], WILLIAM OSCAR[3], REUBEN[2], RICHARD S[1]) was born March 12, 1942 in Newton, Harvey County, KS, and died May 20, 1968 in Vietnam. He married SUZANNE PRINCE KEISEL August 15, 1964 in San Rafael, Marion County, CA, daughter of WALTER KEISEL and OTILA SHIELDS.

Notes for JOHN HAROLD TURNER, JR:
Copy of funeral home record.

More about JOHN HAROLD TURNER JR:
Burial: June 02, 1968, Towanda Cemetery, Towanda, KS.
Education: Ponca City Military Academy.
Military: U.S. Army RA 17629987 Co A, Staff Sergeant.

More about SUZANNE PRINCE KEISEL:
Occupation: Bank clerk.

Marriage notes for JOHN TURNER and SUZANNE KEISEL:
Copy of marriage license.

Child of JOHN TURNER and SUZANNE KEISEL is:
i. SUZANNE KEISEL[7] TURNER, b. April 2, 1965, San Diego, San Diego County, CA.

141. JANICE KAY[6] **HARLAN** (OPAL MARIAN[5] MOORE, REUBEN DAVID[4], WILLIAM OSCAR[3], REUBEN[2], RICHARD S[1]) was born November 15, 1943 in Wichita, Sedgwick County, KS. She married (1) ALAN STEINBACK 1960. She married (2) RONALD HIRAM SHEETS February 17, 1963 in Madison, Greenwood County, KS.

Marriage notes for JANICE HARLAN and RONALD SHEETS:
Copy of marriage license.

Children of JANICE HARLAN and RONALD SHEETS are:
- i. MICHELLE RENE[7] SHEETS, m. HARRY EDWARD GIFFORD, August 03, 1985, Emporia, Lyon County, KS.
- ii. STEPHEN RAY SHEETS, b. September 28, 1965, Madison, Greenwood County, KS, m. DENYS SUZANNE MUSCH, March 30, 1991, Madison, Greenwood County, KS.

    Marriage notes for STEPHEN SHEETS and DENYS MUSCH:
    Copy of marriage license.

142. BARBARA LOUISE[6] **HARLAN** (OPAL MARIAN[5] MOORE, REUBEN DAVID4, WILLIAM OSCAR3, REUBEN2, RICHARD S1) was born July 24, 1953 in Emporia, Lyon County, KS. She married DUANE T SCHROEDER November 19, 1976 in Madison, Greenwood County, KS.

Marriage notes for BARBARA HARLAN and DUANE SCHROEDER: Copy of marriage license.

Children of BARBARA HARLAN and DUANE SCHROEDER are:
- i. MELANIE[7] SCHROEDER.
- ii. MATTHEW SCHROEDER.
- iii. SHAWNA MARIE SCHROEDER.

143. EDITH VALETTA[6] **MOORE** (ALVA DANIEL[5], REUBEN DAVID[4], WILLIAM OSCAR[3], REUBEN[2], RICHARD S[1]), was born June 26, 1948 in Wichita, Sedgwick County, KS. She married WAYNE ARTHUR AUSTIN September 16, 1966 in Eureka, Greenwood County, KS.

Marriage notes for EDITH MOORE and WAYNE AUSTIN:
Copy of marriage license.

Children of EDITH MOORE and WAYNE AUSTIN are:

- 226. i. HEATH WAYNE[7] AUSTIN, b. April 23, 1967, Wichita, Sedgwick County, KS.
- ii. MICHAEL DANIEL AUSTIN, b. April 01, 1969, Wichita, Sedgwick County, KS; m. TRACIE DEANN BALL, March 12, 1994, Augusta, Butler County, KS.

Marriage notes for MICHAEL AUSTIN and TRACIE BALL:
Copy of marriage license.

144. ALAN DEE[6] **MOORE** (ALVA DANIEL[5], REUBEN DAVID[4], WILLIAM OSCAR[3], REUBEN[2], RICHARD S[1]) was born 1950 in Wichita, Sedgwick County, KS. He married KATHLEEN KAY GEORGE September 13, 1973 in Eureka, Greenwood County, KS.

Marriage notes for ALAN MOORE and KATHLEEN GEORGE:
Copy of marriage license.

Children of ALAN MOORE and KATHLEEN GEORGE are:
- i. AMANDA ELAINE[7] MOORE.
- ii. ALAMA DEANN MOORE.

145. AVA LYNNE[6] **MOORE** (ALVA DANIEL[5], REUBEN DAVID[4], WILLIAM OSCAR[3], REUBEN[2], RICHARD S[1]) was born October 23, 1954 in Wichita, Sedgwick County, KS. She married VICTOR LEROY VOGTS January 04, 1975 in El Dorado, Butler County, KS.

Marriage notes for AVA MOORE and VICTOR VOGTS:
Copy of marriage license.

Children of AVA MOORE and VICTOR VOGTS are:
- i. VALECIA LYNNE[7] VOGTS.

    Notes for VALECIA LYNNE VOGTS:
    Copy of graduation announcement and program.

- ii. WESLEY VOGTS.

- iii. NATHAN DANIEL VOGTS.

146. ROSE ANNETTE[6] **MOORE** (ALVA DANIEL[5], REUBEN DAVID[4], WILLIAM OSCAR[3], REUBEN[2], RICHARD S[1]) was born September 24, 1960 in Wichita, Sedgwick County, KS. She married MARTIN GREG BRENTON October 28, 1978 in El Dorado, Butler County, KS, son of GEORGE BRENTON and ROSALIE STOREY.

Marriage notes for ROSE MOORE and MARTIN BRENTON:
Copy of marriage license.

Children of ROSE MOORE and MARTIN BRENTON are:
- i. TYSON GEORGE[7] BRENTON, b. August 29, 1981, El Dorado, Butler County, KS.
- ii. SHELLY RENAE BRENTON, b. June 09, 1984, El Dorado, Butler County, KS.

147. LAVONNE ELAINE[6] BALZER (VEDA MAE[5] MOORE, REUBEN DAVID[4], WILLIAM OSCAR[3], REUBEN[2], RICHARD S[1]) was born June 20, 1952 in Newton, Harvey County, KS. She married CHARLES ROLAND BAKER August 12, 1972 in Potwin, Butler County, KS.

More about LAVONNE ELAINE BALZER:
Occupation: Teacher.

More about CHARLES ROLAND BAKER:
Occupation: School custodian.

Children of LAVONNE BALZER and CHARLES BAKER are:
- i. CARLA JEAN[7] BAKER, b. August 08, 1976, Newton, Harvey County, KS.
- ii. CHANDA MAE BAKER, b. May 26, 1980, Newton, Harvey County, KS.
- iii. JARRET ROLAND BAKER, b. May 26, 1980, Newton, Harvey County, KS.

148. JO ANN[6] BALZER (VEDA MAE[5] MOORE, REUBEN DAVID[4], WILLIAM OSCAR[3], REUBEN[2], RICHARD S[1]) was born February 17, 1956 in Newton, Harvey County, KS. She married DAVID CECIL DENNY October 20, 1980 in Potwin, Butler County, KS.

More about JO ANN BALZER:
Occupation: Expedites for Beech Aircraft.

More about DAVID CECIL DENNY:
Occupation: Buyer for Beech Aircraft.

Child of JO BALZER and DAVID DENNY is:
- i. KATRINA ANN[7] DENNY, b. April 17, 1985, Newton, Harvey County, KS.

149. MILTON LEE[6] BALZER (VEDA MAE[5] MOORE, REUBEN DAVID[4], WILLIAM OSCAR[3], REUBEN[2], RICHARD S[1]) was born February 27, 1964 in Newton, Harvey County, KS. He married JENNIFER LYNN CARR August 03, 1991 in Arkansas City, Cowley County, KS.

More about MILTON LEE BALZER:
Occupation: Finance.

Children of MILTON BALZER and JENNIFER CARR are:
- i. ABBEY MARIE[7] BALZER, b. March 23, 1992, Wichita, Sedgwick County, KS.
- ii. THOMAS LEE BALZER, b. July 21, 1994, Wichita, Sedgwick County, KS.

150. MOREY HOWARD[6] BALZER (VEDA MAE[5] MOORE, REUBEN DAVID[4], WILLIAM OSCAR[3], REUBEN[2], RICHARD S[1]) was born February 27, 1964 in Newton, Harvey County, KS. He married LORI ANN BEAN January 07, 1989 in Newton, Harvey County, KS.

Children of MOREY BALZER and LORI BEAN are:
- i. JORDAN[7] BALZER.
- ii. DERCK BALZER.
- iii. DANIELLE MARIE BALZER, b. January 12, 1995.
- iv. BETHAMY BALZER,

151. LARRY JO[6] MOORE (ELWOOD ORIN[5], ORIN EDGAR[4], WILLIAM OSCAR[3], REUBEN[2], RICHARD S[1]) was born December 13, 1940 in Wichita, Sedgwick County, KS. He married (1) EVELYN SUE GRONAU, daughter of LEO GRONAU. He married (2) LINDA LEE DALTON April 11, 1968.

Notes for LARRY JO MOORE:
Copy of military discharge papers and newspaper articles.

Children of LARRY MOORE and EVELYN GRONAU are:
- i. RANDY RAY[7] MOORE, b. May 23, 1959, Newton, Harvey County, KS; d. May 23, 1959, Newton, Harvey County, KS.

    Notes for RANDY RAY MOORE:
    Copy of funeral home record.

    More about RANDY RAY MOORE:
    Buried Location: May 23, 1956, Whitewater Cemetery, Butler County, KS.
    Cause of Death: Stillborn.

- ii. JEFFREY DEAN MOORE, b. September 01, 1960, Newton, Harvey County, KS.

Children of LARRY MOORE and LINDA DALTON are:
227. iii. ANGELA DAWN[7] MOORE, b. October 17, 1970, Moab, UT.
      iv. SHAWN DEAN MOORE, b. August 28, 1974, Moab, UT.

152. HELEN[6] CROSSFIELD (LEWIS IRA[5], MABEL BLANCHE[4] TAYLOR, MELISSA REBECCA[3] MOORE, REUBEN[2,] RICHARD S[1]). She married GORDON T WEBB.

Children of HELEN CROSSFIELD and GORDON WEBB are:
      i. BARBARA DAWN[7] WEBB, m. ??? GUMPKE.
      ii. MARIE ALAINE WEBB, b. July 12, 1972, Eurenka, Greenwood County, KS.

153. ANN ELIZABETH[6] CROSSFIELD (LELAND FRANCIS[5], MABEL BLANCHE[4] TAYLOR, MELISSA REBECCA[3] MOORE, REUBEN[2], RICHARD S[1]). She married ROBERT OEHLERT.

Children of ANN CROSSFIELD and ROBERT OEHLERT are:
      i. AARON LEE[7] OEHLERT.
      ii. JORDON GLENN OEHLERT.

154. VICKI[6] AMERINE (ELOISE[5] SHARITS, GLADYS HAZEL[4] TAYLOR, MELISSA REBECCA[3] MOORE, REUBEN[2], RICHARD S[1]) She married ??? WELLS.

Children of VICKI AMERINE and ??? WELLS are:
      i. SCOTTIE[7] WELLS.
      ii. TERRI WELLS.
      iii. SHARON WELLS, m. JOHN ALBERT LEA.

155. WAYNE IRVIN[6] BARTLETT (HELEN LOUISE[5] ELLER, STELLA ADALINE[4] WILEY, ETTA ELLEN[3] MOORE, REUBEN[2], RICHARD S[1]) was born September 04, 1931 in Dewey Washington County, OK. He married ROSE MARIE BOND July 08, 1951 in Bartlesville, Washington County, OK, daughter of CHARLES BOND.

Notes for WAYNE IRVIN BARTLETT:
Copy of military separation papers.

More about WAYNE IRVIN BARTLETT:
Fact 1: U.S. Army, #RA 18 343 098 from July 20, 1948 - July 20, 1952.
Occupation: Enforcement officer.

More about ROSE MARIE BOND:
Occupation: Nurse.

Marriage notes for WAYNE BARTLETT and ROSE BOND:
Copy of marriage license.

Children of WAYNE BARTLETT and ROSE BOND are:
228. i. ALICE FAY[7] BARTLETT, b. January 12, 1953, Bartlesville, Nowata County, OK.
229. ii. JOHNNY WAYNE BARTLETT, b. July 09, 1957, Pawhuska, Osage County, OK.
230. iii. CHARLES CLIFFORD BARTLETT. b. November 06, 1958, Pawhuska, Osage County, OK.

156. STELLA MAE[6] BARTLETT (HELEN LOUISE[5] ELLER, STELLA ADALINE[4] WILEY, ETTA ELLEN[3] MOORE, REUBEN[2], RICHARD S[1]) was born February 28, 1934 in Dewey Washington County, OK. She married (1) CALVIN HOOVER PFIEFFF May 22, 1953 in Leipheim, Augsburg, Germany. She married (2) ELMER J PATTERSON November 19, 1978 in Dewey, Dewey County, OK.

Notes for CALVIN HOOVER PFIEFFF:
Copy of military interment paper and veteran identification data sheet

More about CALVIN HOOVER PFIEFFF
Buried Location: February 19, 1963, Fort Gibson Military Cemetery, OK.
Fact 1: WWII, U.S. Army #RA 17192061, 1943-1963.

Marriage notes for STELLA BARTLETT and CALVIN PFIEFFF:
Copy of newspaper announcement of engagement and marriage. Also the wedding invitation.

Marriage notes for STELLA BARTLETT and ELMER PATTERSON:
Copy of marriage license.

Children of STELLA BARTLETT and CALVIN PFIEFFF are:
231. i. EMMA JEAN[7] PFIEFF, b. January 09, 1956, Fort Polk, Vernon County, LA.
232. ii. CYNTHIA LOUISE PFIEFF, b, February 16, 1957, Fort Hood, Coryell County, TX.
      iii. GLEN STEPHEN PFIEFF, b. June 18, 1959, Leipheim, Augsburg, Germany, m. JOAN ???.

157. NORMA JEAN[6] BARTLETT (HELEN LOUISE[5] ELLER, STELLA ADALINE[4] WILEY, ETTA ELLEN[3] MOORE, REUBEN[2], RICH-

ARD S[1]) was born August 23, 1938 in Dewey, Washington County, OK She married (1) J D COTTRELL March 23, 1955 in Pauls Valley, Garvin County, OK. She married (2) RILEY OLIVER July 17, 1956. She married (3) JERRY LEHMAN December 19, 1959 in Pauls Valley, Garvin County, OK.

Child of NORMA BARTLETT and J COTTRELL is:
233.   i.   DIXIE LOUISE[7] COTTRELL, b. May 16, 1955, Pawhuska, Osage County, OK.

Child of NORMA BARTLETT and RILEY OLIVER is:
       ii.   JOHNNIE EUGENE[7] OLIVER, b. July 05, 1957, Memphis, Shelby County, TN.

Children of NORMA BARTLETT and JERRY LEHMAN are:
234.   iii.   BRENDA[7] LEHMAN, b. June 18, 1960, Pauls Valley, Garvin County, OK.
235.   iv.   JERI ANN LEHMAN, b. April 21, 1961, Pauls Valley, Garvin County, OK.
236.   v.   LUCINA RUTH LEHMAN, b, August 13, 1962, Pauls Valley, Garvin County, OK.

158. NITA JO[6] ELLER (GEORGE EVERETT[5], STELLA ADALINE[4] WILEY, ETTA ELLEN[3] MOORE, REUBEN[2], RICHARD S[1]) was born November 21, 1947 in McAllen, Hildago County, TX. She married RONALD A RUSHTON June 07, 1969 in Rock Springs, Sweetwater County, WY.

Notes for NITA JO ELLER:
Called Jody.

More about RONALD A RUSHTON: Occupation: Vice president Yellowstone Pipe Line Co.

Children of NITA ELLER and RONALD RUSHTON are:
       i.   CRAIG ALL[7] RUSHTON, b. February 07, 1970, Bountiful, Davis County, UT.

           More about CRAIG ALL RUSHTON:
           Occupation: Towers operator.

237.   ii.   MICHAEL BRETT RUSHTON, b. November 14, 1972, Madison, Dane County, WI.
238.   iii.   TRACY NOELLE RUSHTON, b. December 11, 1974, Billings, Yellowstone County, MT.

159. BARBARA ELOUISE[6] ELLER (JAMES WILKERSON[5], STELLA ADALINE[4] WILEY, ETTA ELLEN[3] MOORE, REUBEN[2], RICHARD S[1]) was born September 24, 1941 in Dewey, Washington County, OK. She married LOREN JONES June 15, 1958 in Mt View, Kiowa County, OK.

More about BARBARA ELOUISE ELLER:
Occupation: Tulsa World Carrier.

More about LOREN JONES:
Occupation: Trucker.

Marriage notes for BARBARA ELLER and LOREN JONES:
Copy of marriage license.

Children of BARBARA ELLER and LOREN JONES are:
239.   i.   BECKY SUE[7] JONES, b. August 14, 1959, Bartlesville, Washington County, OK.
       ii.   LONNIE LEE JONES, b. April 12, 1960, Bartlesville, Washington County, OK
       iii.   RONNIE JONES, b. November 21, 1963, Bartlesville, Washington County, OK; d. April 05, 1981, Bartlesville, Washington County, OK.

           More about RONNIE JONES:
           Buried Location: April 08, 1981, Dewey Cemetery, Dewey, OK.

240.   iv.   CLIFFORD JONES, b. September 28, 1967, Bartlesville, Washington County, OK.

160. SONYA LOU[6] ELLER (JAMES WILKERSON[5], STELLA ADALINE[4] WILEY, ETTA ELLEN[3] MOORE, REUBEN[2], RICHARD S[1]) was born May 26, 1943 in Bartlesville, Washington County, OK. She married (1) HARRY SMITH. She married (2) BILL ALLISON. December 22, 1962 in Dewey, Washington County, OK.

Marriage notes for SONYA ELLER and BILL ALLISON:
Copy of marriage license.

Children of SONYA ELLER and BILL ALLISON are:
  i.   KRISTIN KAY[7] ALLISON, b. July 31, 1961, Tracy, San Joaquin, CA.
  ii.   JILL ANNETTE ALLISON, b. October 13, 1968, Tracy, San Joaquin, CA.

161. ALICE MARIE[6] ELLER (JAMES WILKERSON[5], STELLA ADALINE[4] WILEY, ETTA ELLEN[3] MOORE, REUBEN[2], RICHARD S[1]) was born July 25, 1953 in Bartlesville, Washington County, OK. She married (1) WILLIAM E JONES December 28, 1970 in Dewey, Washington

County, OK. She married (2) WILLIAM JAMES PHILLIPS April 02, 1979 in Edwardsville, Madison County, IL. She married (3) CLAIRE, ENABINETT August 07, 1996.

Notes for WILLIAM E JONES:
Called Bill.

Marriage notes for ALICE ELLER and WILLIAM JONES:
Copy of marriage license.

More about WILLIAM JAMES PHILLIPS:
Fact 1: U.S. Army 1978-80.

Child of ALICE ELLER and WILLIAM JONES is:
241.   i.   SANDRA LYNN[7] JONES, b. December 04, 1972, Fort Carson, El Paso County, CO.

Children of ALICE ELLER and WILLIAM PHILLIPS are:
    ii.   VIRGINIA ROSE[7] PHILLIPS, b. March 06, 1981, Bartlesville, Washington County, OK.
    iii.   RANDIE RENEE PHILLIPS, b. January 25, 1989, Bartlesville, Washington County, OK.

162. LARRY ERVIN[6] CASE (WILLA MAE[5] ELLER, STELLA ADALINE[4] WILEY, ETTA ELLEN[3] MOORE, REUBEN[2], RICHARD S[1]) was born December 08, 1941 in Dewey Washington County, OK. He married DURENA DALE ELKINS October 05, 1968 in Ardmore, Carter County, OK.

Notes for LARRY ERVIN CASE:
Copy of military discharge paper.

More about LARRY ERVIN CASE:
Fact 1: Army FR 448 40 7677 AF 1863 9824.
Occupation: Mechanic, rancher.

More about DURENA DALE ELKINS:
Ethnicity/Relig: Christian Church.
Occupation: Nurse.

Marriage notes for LARRY CASE and DURENA ELKINS:
Copy of marriage license.

Children of LARRY CASE and DURENA ELKINS are:
    i.   BRETT MICHAEL[7] CASE, b. July 06, 1969, Tinker AFB, Oklahoma County, OK.

        Notes for BRETT MICHAEL CASE:
        Copy of certificate of baptism.

        More about BRETT MICHAEL CASE:
        Ethnicity/Relig: Christian Church.
        Occupation: Welder, mechanic, painter.

    ii.   DESIREE DALE CASE, b. February 16, 1971, Marietta, Cobb County, GA; m. MASON SCOTT THOMAS II, July 06, 1996, Oklahoma City, Oklahoma County, OK.

        More about DESIREE'DALE CASE:
        Ethnicity/Relig: Christian Church.
        Occupation: Store office manager.

        More about MASON SCOTT THOMAS II:
        Occupation: Engineer.

        Marriage notes for DESIREE CASE and MASON THOMAS:
        Copy of marriage license.

    iii.   SCOTT ALLEN CASE, b. February 02, 1975, Bartlesville, Washington County, OK.

        More about SCOTT ALLEN CASE:
        Ethnicity/Relig: Christian Church.
        Occupation: Rancher.

163. GERALD ALLEN[6] CASE (WILLA MAE[5] ELLER, STELLA ADALINE[4] WILEY, ETTA ELLEN[3] MOORE, REUBEN[2], RICHARD S[1]) was born August 26, 1948 in Bartlesville, Washington County, OK. He married JANET LEE WARD June 16, 1973 in Bartlesville, Washington County, OK.

More about GERALD ALLEN CASE:
Ethnicity/Relig: Christian Church.
Occupation: Painter-rancher

More about JANET LEE WARD:
Ethnicity/Relig: Church of God
Occupation: Office manager.

Marriage notes for GERALD CASE and JANET WARD: Copy of marriage license.

Child of GERALD CASE and JANET WARD is:
    i. CALEB LEVI[7] CASE, b. February 15, 1981, Bartlesville, Washington County, OK.

164. MICHAEL WAYNE[6] BROCKHOUSE (ELIZABETH IRENE[5] ELLER, STELLA ADALINE[4] WILEY, ETTA ELLEN[3] MOORE, REUBEN[2], RICHARD S[1]) was born November 12, 1951 in Jacksonville, Duval County, FL. He married DARCY ANN O'BRIEN May 05, 1978 in Kansas City, Jackson County, MO, daughter of RICHARD O'BRIEN and EDITH PADLEY.

Notes for MICHAEL WAYNE BROCKHOUSE:
Copy of birth certificate.

Children of MICHAEL BROCKHOUSE and DARCY O'BRIEN are:
    i. MICHELLE JENETTE[7] BROCKHOUSE, b. December 30, 1978, Kansas City, Jackson County, MO.
    ii. MICHAEL-LEE O'BRIEN BROCKHOUSE, b. July 06, 1982, Overland Park, Johnson County, KS.
    iii. LUKE WAYNE RICHARD BROCKHOUSE, b. January 26, 1998, Salina, Saline County, KS.

165. MADELINE EILEEN[6] BROCKHOUSE (ELIZABETH IRENE[5] ELLER, STELLA ADALINE[4] WILEY, ETTA ELLEN[3] MOORE, REUBEN[2], RICHARD S[1]) was born July 30, 1953 in Kansas City, Jackson County, MO. She married (1) WILLIAM WALLACE ASHURST August 07, 1970 in Kansas City, Jackson County, MO. She married (2) JEFFERY EARL GARMAN July 07, 1995 in Kansas City, Jackson County, MO, son of JAMES GARMAN and JOANNE WALL.

Notes for MADELINE EILEEN BROCKHOUSE:
Copy of birth certificate.

Children of MADELINE BROCKHOUSE and WILLIAM ASHURST are:
242.   i. ROBERT CRAIG[7] ASHURST, b. January 27, 1971, Independence, Jackson County, MO.
    ii. WILLIAM BRANDY ASHURST, b. January 27, 1971, Independence, Jackson County, MO; m. STAHR DENYSE BERTRAND, July 13, 1996, Kansas City, Jackson County, MO.

Notes for WILLIAM BRANDY ASHURST:

Copy of birth certificate.

More about WILLIAM BRANDY ASHURST:
Occupation: Construction.

More about STAHR DENYSE BERTRAND:
Occupation: Insurance.

243.   iii. CHERRY SHERIE ASHURST, b. February 16, 1977, Independence, Jackson County, MO.

166. DARLENE SUE[6] BUTTS (BARBARA LEDORA[5] ELLER, STELLA ADALINE[4] WILEY, ETTA ELLEN[3] MOORE, REUBEN[2], RICHARD S[1]) was born December 04, 1954 in Champaign, Champaign County, IL. She married MELVIN JOHN LYNN July 28, 1973 in Champaign, Champaign County, IL.

More about DARLENE SUE BUTTS:
Ethnicity/Relig: Christian Church.
Occupation: Secretary/ housewife.

More about MELVIN JOHN LYNN:
Ethnicity/Relig: Christian Church.
Occupation: Dry wall-video works.

Children of DARLENE, BUTTS and MELVIN LYNN are:
    i. KIMBERLY DIANE[7] LYNN, b. November 13, 1975, Denver, Arapahoe County, CO; m. JASON EDWARD HARDEN, August 23, 1967, Mahomet, Champaign County, IL.

    Notes for KIMBERLY DIANE LYNN: Psychology Degree 1998 from Urbana University of Illinois.

    More about KIMBERLY DIANE LYNN:
    Ethnicity/Relig: Christian Church.
    Occupation: Clerk.

More about JASON EDWARD HARDEN:
Occupation: Dry wall.

ii. BENJAMIN JOHN LYNN, b. April 29, 1977, Urbana, Champaign County, IL.

More about BENJAMIN JOHN LYNN:
Ethnicity/Relig: Christian Church
Fact 1: Marine 1996.
Occupation: Computers.

iii. ALEXIS ANN LYNN, b. December 09, 1980, Denver, Arapahoe County, CO.

More about ALEXIS ANN LYNN:
Ethnicity/Relig: Christian Church.

167. DIANE SUE[6] BUTTS (BARBARA LEDORA[5] ELLER, STELLA ADALINE[4] WILEY, ETTA ELLEN[3] MOORE, REUBEN[2], RICHARD S[1]) was born November 01, 1956 in Champaign, Champaign County, IL. She married JOHN ROBERT HEMRICH November 22, 1974 in Champaign, Champaign County, IL, son of JOHN HEMRICH and BETTY BENNETT.

More about DIANE SUE BUTTS:
Occupation: Secretary/ housewife.

Notes for JOHN ROBERT HEMRICH:
Copy of military discharge.

More about JOHN ROBERT HEMRICH:
Fact 1: Army 1976-1979
Occupation: Trucker-mechanic.

Children of DIANE BUTTS and JOHN HEMRICH are:
  i. CHRISTINA DIANE[7] HEMRICH, b. January 27, 1980, Urbana, Champaign County, IL.
  ii. CRYSTAL MICHELLE HEMRICH, b. April 11, 1985, Urbana, Champaign County, IL.

168. DEBRA SUE[6] BUTTS (BARBARA LEDORA[5] ELLER, STELLA ADALINE[4] WILEY, ETTA ELLEN[3] MOORE, REUBEN[2], RICHARD S[1]) was born November 27, 1958 in Champaign, Champaign County, IL. She married JOHN FOSTER MILLER II October 05, 1976 in Gulf Port, Harrison County, MS.

More about DEBRA SUE BUTTS:
Ethnicity/Relig: Christian Church.
Occupation: Day Care.

More about JOHN FOSTER MILLER II:
Ethnicity/Relig: Christian Church.
Fact 1: Seebees 1973-77.
Occupation: Warehouse Foreman.

Children of DEBRA BUTTS and JOHN MILLER are:
  i. CHARLES LAWRENCE[7] MILLER, b. September 04, 1979, Champaign, Champaign County, IL.
  ii. KATHERINE DIANE MILLER, b. October 17, 1981, Champaign, Champaign County, IL.
  iii. ASHLEY NICOLE MILLER, b. July 01, 1985, Champaign, Champaign County, IL.
  iv. JOHN ANDREW MILLER, b. March 04, 1989, Champaign, Champaign County, IL.
  v. HANNAH ELIZABETH MILLER, b. September 13, 1990, Champaign, Champaign County, IL.

169. RONALD EUGENE[6] BUTTS (BARBARA LEDORA[5] ELLER, STELLA ADALINE[4] WILEY, ETTA ELLEN[3] MOORE, REUBEN[2], RICHARD S[1]) was born July 11, 1960 in Champaign, Champaign County, IL. He married LEANNE RENAE MACHE January 07, 1984 in St Charles, Kane County, IL.

More about RONALD EUGENE BUTTS:

Ethnicity/Relig: Christian Church.
Occupation: Instructor.

More about LEANNE RENAE MACHE:
Occupation: processor mortgage corp.

Children of RONALD BUTTS and LEANNE MACHE are:
  i. CASI RENAE[7] BUTTS, b. February 01, 1988, Denver, Arapahoe County, CO.
  ii. COURTNEY ANNE BUTTS, b. July 27, 1990, Denver, Arapahoe County, CO.

170. FRED JOHN[6] MCCONEGHY (ZORA DOUTHARD[5] DEXTER, GRACE MAUDE[4] HALL, FRANCIS LEATON[3], SENY[2] MOORE, RICHARD S[1]) was born June 10, 1927 in Elbing, Butler County, KS. He married BETTY LOU OWENS April 18, 1943 in Macon, Bibb County, GA.

Children of FRED MCCONEGHY and BETTY OWENS are:
      i. CATHY LOU[7] MCCONEGHY.
      ii. Kim DEXTER MCCONEGHY.
      iii. RANDY MCCONEGHY.
      iv. BECKY MCCONEGHY.
      v. MICAL MCCONEGHY, stepchild.
      vi. SHARON HOP MCCONEGHY, stepchild.

171. MARILYN SUE[6] BROYLES (VIOLA G[5] DEXTER, GRACE MAUDE[4] HALL, FRANCIS LEATON[3], SENY[2] MOORE, RICHARD S[1]) was born August 06, 1941. She married CHARLES ARTHUR COATS August 24, 1962 in Potwin, Butler County, KS, son of ROY COATS and SARAH BALDWIN.

Notes for MARILYN SUE BROYLES:
Marilyn's real parents names are: Kenneth F Broyles and Betty Lou O'Keefe

Marriage notes for MARILYN BROYLES and CHARLES COATS:
Copy of marriage license.

Child of MARILYN BROYLES and CHARLES COATS is:
244.   i. MICHAEL K[7] COATS, b. September 17, 1963.

172. RODONNA SUE[6] BRENNER (VERL W[5], ALICE ELIZA[4] HALL, FRANCIS LEATON[3], SENY[2] MOORE, RICHARD S[1]) was born August 21, 1945. She married ROBERT ELDENBURG, June 23, 1963 in Potwin, Butler County, KS.

Notes for RODONNA SUE BRENNER:
Was called Sue.

Marriage notes for RODONNA BRENNER and ROBERT ELDENBURG:
Copy of marriage license.

Children of RODONNA BRENNER and ROBERT ELDENBURG are:
245.   i. ROBIN[7] ELDENBURG.
      ii. MIKE ELDENBURG.

173. IVA JO[6] BRENNER (VERL W[5], ALICE ELIZA[4] HALL, FRANCIS LEATON[3], SENY[2] MOORE, RICHARD S[1]) was born July 08, 1946. She married (1) DANNY WHITESIDE. She married (2) JACK OBERST February 08, 1964 in Benton, Butler County, KS.

Notes for IVA JO BRENNER:
Was called Jo.

Child of IVA BRENNER and DANNY WHITESIDE is:
      i. BANDIE[7] WHITESIDE, b. November 06, 1975.

Children of IVA BRENNER and JACK OBERST are:
      ii. SCOTT S[7] OBERST, b. July 06, 1964.
      iii. CHRIS OBERST, b. January 05, 1971.

174. JOAN ANN[6] HALL (CECIL LORNE[5], IRA EMMUTT[4], FRANCIS LEATON[3], SENY[2] MOORE, RICHARD S[1]) was born August 11, 1946 in California. She married JOHN PETERS.

Child of JOAN HALL and JOHN PETERS is:
      i. LUCELLE[7] PETERS.

175. MARY ESTHER[6] KENNEDY (DORIS MAXINE[5] HALL, GUY CHRISTIAN[4], FRANCIS LEATON[3], SENY[2] MOORE, RICHARD S[1]) was born May 13, 1942 in Newton, Harvey County, KS. She married (1) THOMAS GRANT ANDERSON April 26, 1958 in Nogales, Sonora State, Mexico. She married (2) THOMAS HENRY HATCH March 10, 1962 in Wichita, Sedgwick County, KS.

More about THOMAS HENRY HATCH:
Buried Location: April 14, 1993, West Plains, Howell County, MO.
Cause of Death: Cancer.
SSAN: 507-12-5570.

Children of MARY KENNEDY and THOMAS ANDERSON are:
246.   i. THOMAS GRANT[7] ANDERSON JR, b. April 13, 1959, Wichita, Sedgwick County, KS.
      ii. CHARLETTE MAXINE ANDERSON, b. September 07, 1960, Wichita, Sedgwick County, KS; d. January 03, 1961, Wichita, Sedgwick County, KS.

More about CHARLETTE MAXINE ANDERSON:
Buried Location: January 07, 1961, Arkansas City, Cowley County, KS.

    iii.   TONY GRANT ANDERSON, b. December 27, 1962, Wichita, Sedgwick County, KS.

Children of MARY KENNEDY and THOMAS HATCH are:
- iv. NAOMI LUELLA[7] HATCH, b. January 25, 1963, Newton, Harvey County, KS; m. JAMES D COLEMAN, February 17, 1984, U.S. Army Post, Denmark.
- v. ALLEN SCOTT HATCH, b. August 30, 1968, West Plains, Howell County, MO; m. KIMBERLY FRYE, July 18, 1992, Minot, Ward County, ND.

176. MARCELLA JEAN[6] KENNEDY (DORIS MAXINE[5] HALL, GUY CHRISTIAN[4], FRANCIS LEATON[3], SENY[2] MOORE, RICHARD S[1]) was born March 09, 1946 in Newton, Harvey County, KS, and died July 09, 1993 in Iola, Allen County, KS. She married (1) RONALD GENE SEEDS December 10, 1961 in Tajuina, Old Mexico. She married (2) BUSTER E ROGERS August 29, 1975 in Long Beach, Los Angeles County, CA. She married (3) CHARLES JOHN COLE April 21, 1978 in Emporia, Lyon County, KS.

Notes for MARCELLA JEAN KENNEDY:
Copy of birth certificate, death certificate and newspaper obituary.

More about MARCELLA JEAN KENNEDY:
Buried Location: July 12, 1993, Shawnee Mission Cemetery, Shawnee, KS.
Cause of Death: Peritonitis, perforated peptic ulcer.
Medical Information: Chronic steroid usage for polymyositis.
SSAN: 567-62-4564.

Marriage notes for MARCELLA KENNEDY and CHARLES COLE:
Copy of marriage license.

Child Of MARCELLA KENNEDY and RONALD SEEDS is.
- i. RONALD[7] SEEDS JR, b. August 13, 1968, adopted child.

177. CHARLENE WILMA[6] KENNEDY (DORIS MAXINE[5] HALL, GUY CHRISTIAN[4], FRANCIS LEATON[3], SENY[2] MOORE, RICHARD S[1]) was born August 30, 1947 in Eureka, Greenwood County, KS, She married (1) WILLIAM NEIL FOYLE November 26, 1964. She married (2) ROGER JERMO BRANDEL July 07, 1970. She married (3) RAYMOND GOLIGHTLY BRAHIER January 17, 1975 in Long Beach, Los Angeles County, CA.

Child of CHARLENE KENNEDY and WILLIAM FOYLE is:
247.   i.   CHARLOTTE JEAN[7] FOYLE, b. September 01, 1966.

Child of CHARLENE KENNEDY and ROGER BRANDEL is:
- ii. VIVIAN MAXINE[7] BRANDEL, b. July 03, 1970; m. MARK KUHNS, October 25, 1989.

Children of CHARLENE KENNEDY and RAYMOND BRAHIER are:
- iii. RAYMOND EUGENE[7] BRAHIER, b. February 1970; stepchild.
- iv. RICHARD LAWRENCE BRAHIER, b. March 25, 1971; stepchild.
- v. DANIEL JOSEPH BRAHIER, b. February 25, 1973; stepchild.
- vi. RAYMOND GOLIGHTLY BRAHIER JR. b. October 11, 1975, Long Beach, Los Angeles County, CA.

178. DIANA KAY[6] HALL (DUANE DELOISE[5], GUY CHRISTIAN[4], FRANCIS LEATON[3], SENY[2] MOORE, RICHARD S[1]) was born September 29, 1946 in Shawnee, Pottawatomie County, OK. She married DENNIS VINCE ALVAREZ January 27, 1968 in Wichita, Sedgwick County, KS, son of VINCE ALVAREZ.

Marriage notes for DIANA HALL and DENNIS ALVAREZ:
Copy of marriage license.

Children of DIANA HALL. and DENNIS ALVAREZ are:
- i. SCOTT ALLEN[7] ALVAREZ, b. October 21, 1969, Wichita, Sedgwick County, KS; d. October 21, 1969, Wichita, Sedgwick County, KS.

    More about SCOTT ALLEN ALVAREZ:
    Cause of Death: Stillborn.

- ii. KAYLENE LYNN ALVAREZ, b. February 26, 1971, Wichita, Sedgwick County, KS.
- iii. GUY ELDON ALVAREZ, b. October 02, 1973, Shawnee, Pottawatomie County, OK; m. AMY COOK, January 10, 1998, Tulsa, Tulsa County, OK.

    More about AMY COOK:

    Occupation: Teacher.

Marriage notes for GUY ALVAREZ and AMY COOK:
Copy of newspaper article.

179. MARTHA MAY[6] HALL (DUANE DELOISE[5], GUY CHRISTIAN[4], FRANCIS LEATON[3], SENY[2] MOORE, RICHARD S[1]) was born April 29, 1947. She married JAMES C WATHEN April 03, 1971 in Arnesten, AL.

More about MARTHA MAY HALL:
Fact 1: August 08, 1955, Adopted by Duane and Mary.

Children of MARTHA HALL and JAMES WATHEN are:
- 248. i. SHAWN CEHRI[7] WATHEN, b. February 02, 1972, California.
- 249. ii. VERNON JAMES WATHEN, b. May 15, 1974, California.

180. NAOMI LEE[6] HALL (CLAYTON OAKLEY[5], GUY CHRISTIAN[4], FRANCIS LEATON[3], SENY[2] MOORE, RICHARD S[1]) was born June 10, 1952 in Newton, Harvey County, KS. She married STEPHEN CRAIG ANDERSON July 29, 1972 in Wichita, Sedgwick County, KS.

Marriage notes for NAOMI HALL and STEPHEN ANDERSON:
Copy of marriage license.

Children of NAOMI HALL and STEPHEN ANDERSON are:
- i. JOSHUA JUSTIN[7] ANDERSON, b. September 20, 1977, Wichita, Sedgwick County, KS.
- ii. LINDSEY RENEE ANDERSON, b. January 11, 1980, Wichita, Sedgwick County, KS.

181. CATHERINE ANN[6] HALL (CLAYTON OAKLEY[5], GUY CHRISTIAN[4], FRANCIS LEATON[3], SENY[2] MOORE, RICHARD S[1]) was born July 15, 1954 in Newton, Harvey County, KS. She married SKOL RATANAMON June 10, 1978 in Wichita, Sedgwick County, KS.

Children of CATHERINE HALL and SKOL RATANAMON are:
- i. KIMBERLY BETH[7] RATANAMON, b. June 21, 1982, Wichita, Sedgwick County, KS.
- ii. CRAIG AUSTIN RATANAMON, b. March 17, 1986, Wichita, Sedgwick County, KS.

182. VERNON LEROY[6] COSENTINO (WANDA MARLENE[5] HALL, GUY CHRISTIAN[4], FRANCIS LEATON[3], SENY[2] MOORE, RICHARD S[1]) was born August 13, 1950 in Newton, Harvey County, KS. He married CAROLYN LEE NEWTON July 06, 1973 in Neapolis, Lucas County, OH, daughter of WARREN NEWTON and ILA CALKINS.

Marriage notes for VERNON COSENTINO and CAROLYN NEWTON:
Have an invitation card.

Child of VERNON COSENTINO and CAROLYN NEWTON is:
- i. DONALD LEE NEWTON[7] COSENTINO, b. January 29, 1963, Toledo, Lucas County, OH; adopted child.

    More about DONALD LEE NEWTON COSENTINO:
    Fact 1: February 1975, adopted by Vernon Cosentino.

183. GUY VINCENT[6] COSENTINO (WANDA MARLENE[5] HALL, GUY CHRISTIAN[4], FRANCIS LEATON[3], SENY[2] MOORE, RICHARD S[1]) was born June 29, 1951 in Newton, Harvey County, KS. He married SHARON LEE SHRIGLEY June 09, 1973 in State College, Centre County, PA, daughter of ROBERT SHRIGLEY and CHARLOTTE ???.

Marriage notes for GUY COSENTINO and SHARON SHRIGLEY:
Have an invitation card.

Children of GUY COSENTINO and SHARON SHRIGLEY are:
- i. AMY LORRAINE[7] COSENTINO, b. September 23, 1981, State College, Centre County, PA.
- ii. JULIE ALEXIS COSENTINO, b. March 28, 1983, State College, Centre County, PA.
- iii. MARLLENA RENEE COSENTINO, b. January 13, 1986, Dayton, Montgomery County, OH.

184. JAMES HALL[6] COSENTINO (WANDA MARLENE[5] HALL, GUY CHRISTIAN[4], FRANCIS LEATON[3], SENY[2] MOORE, RICHARD S[1]) was born June 07, 1955 in Tucson, Pina County, AZ. He married CORDELIA LYNN BOWLING May 28, 1976 in Phoenix, Maricopa County, AZ, daughter of WILLIAM BOWLING and FRANCIS ???.

Marriage notes for JAMES COSENTINO and CORDELIA BOWLING:
Have an announcement card.

Children of JAMES COSENTINO and CORDELIA BOWLING are:
- i. JAMES HALL[7] COSENTINO II, b. April 30, 1979, Phoenix, Maricopa County, AZ.
- ii. ANGELA DOMENICA LYNN COSENTINO, b. March 17, 1983, Valle Jo, Marine County, CA.
- iii. CHRISTINA COSENTINO, b. 1991.
- iv. VICTORIA ALEXANDRA COSENTINO, b. 1993.

185. SONDRA SUE[6] HOPKINS (AUDREY FAYE[5] HALL, GUY CHRISTIAN[4], FRANCIS LEATON[3], SENY[2] MOORE, RICHARD S[1]) was born April 20, 1952 in Newton, Harvey County, KS. She married (1) WARREN LEE UNRUH March 24, 1973 in Newton, Harvey County, KS. She met (2) EARL CHRISTOPHER MAY 1978.

Marriage notes for SONDRA HOPKINS and WARREN UNRUH:
Copy of marriage license.

Child of SONDRA HOPKINS and WARREN UNRUH is:
    i. SHAWN CHRISTIAN[7] UNRUH, b. August 25, 1975, Newton, Harvey County, KS; m. DOLLI ANN WINSKY, January 07, 1995, Newton, Harvey County, KS.

    Marriage notes for SHAWN UNRUH and DOLLI WINSKY:
    Copy of marriage license.

Children of SONDRA HOPKINS and EARL MAY are:
250.   ii. APRIL MICHELLE[7] MAY, b. July 31, 1979, Wichita, Sedgwick County, KS.
    iii. DANIEL EARL MAY, b. February 27, 1984, Newton, Harvey County, KS.

186. PAMELA KAY[6] HOPKINS (AUDREY FAYE[5] HALL, GUY CHRISTIAN[4], FRANCIS LEATON[3], SENY[2] MOORE, RICHARD S[1]) was born January 18, 1954 in Newton, Harvey County, KS. She married DENNIS LYNN JESSEPH August 16, 1975 in Newton, Harvey County, KS.

Marriage notes for PAMELA HOPKINS and DENNIS JESSEPH:
Copy of marriage license.

Children of PAMELA HOPKINS and DENNIS JESSEPH are:
251.   i. CHASTITY DAWN HOPKINS[7] JESSEPH, b. July 06, 1974, Newton, Harvey County, KS.
    ii. KELLY TANNER JESSEPH, b. May 30, 1977, Ellsworth, Ellsworth County, KS.

    Notes for KELLY TANNER JESSEPH:
    Copy of birth certificate.

187. BRUCE LYNN[6] HOPKINS (AUDREY FAYE[5] HALL, GUY CHRISTIAN[4], FRANCIS LEATON[3], SENY[2] MOORE, RICHARD S[1]) was born May 04, 1955 in Newton, Harvey County, KS. He married KAREN L MOORE May 26, 1981 in Newton, Harvey County, KS, daughter of GEROME MOORE and BEVERLY HUGHES.

Notes for BRUCE LYNN HOPKINS:
Copy of birth certificate.

Marriage notes for BRUCE HOPKINS and KAREN MOORE:
Copy of marriage license.

Child of BRUCE HOPKINS and KAREN MOORE is:
    i. MARIAH MARIE[7] HOPKINS, b. September 21, 1989, Newton, Harvey County, KS.

188. BRENDA JO[6] HOPKINS (AUDREY FAYE[5] HALL, GUY CHRISTIAN[4], FRANCIS LEATON[3], SENY[2] MOORE, RICHARD S[1]) was born September 26, 1957 in Newton, Harvey County, KS. She met (1) JACK EUGENE DOTY 1976, son of GERALD E DOTY. She married (2) JERRY WAYNE SHAY June 07, 1983 in Oklahoma City, Oklahoma County, OK. She married (3) TERRY KEEN February 09, 1988 in New Castle, McClain County, OK.

More about JACK EUGENE DOTY:
Occupation: Santa Fe Railroad.

Marriage notes for BRENDA HOPKINS and TERRY KEEN:
Copy of marriage license.

Child of BRENDA HOPKINS and JACK DOTY is:
    i. LAURA LEE DOTY[7] WALKER, b. September 06, 1975, Eugene, Lane County, OR; m. JOE FOELKE, October 15, 1994, Lebanon, Linn County, OR.

    Notes for LAURA LEE DOTY WALKER:
    Laura was adopted by a family named Walkers. Curtis Lee and Dorothy Ellen.

189. VEDA LOU[6] HOPKINS (AUDREY FAYE[5] HALL, GUY CHRISTIAN[4], FRANCIS LEATON[3], SENY[2] MOORE, RICHARD S[1]) was born January 08, 1959 in Hutchinson, Reno County, KS. She married (1) MICHAEL D HERMAN March 05, 1977 in Wichita, Sedgwick County, KS, son of BOYD HERMANN and GERALDINE ???. She met (2) PHILLIP HAYES 1980. She married (3) LARRY D CRAWFORD November 02, 1985 in El Dorado, Butler County, KS. She married (4) ANDREW LAWRENCE VEAL April 01, 1989 in Wichita, Sedgwick County, KS, son of GENE VEAL and DELORSE HARRISON.

Marriage notes for VEDA HOPKINS and MICHAEL HERMAN:
Copy of marriage license.

More about PHILLIP HAYES: Occupation: Part owner of Hayes Company Inc.

Marriage notes for VEDA HOPKINS and LARRY CRAWFORD:
Copy of marriage license.

Marriage notes for VEDA HOPKINS and ANDREW VEAL:
Copy of marriage license; married, divorced and then remarried.

Child of VEDA HOPKINS and PHILLIP HAYES is:
    i. AMANDA CHRISTINE[7] HOPKINS, b. August 22, 1981, Wichita, Sedgwick County, KS.

190. CYNTHIA LOU[6] MCGINN (NANCY ANN[5] HALL, GUY CHRISTIAN[4], FRANCIS LEATON[3], SENY[2] MOORE, RICHARD S[1]) was born May 28, 1953 in Newton, Harvey County, KS. She married (1) KENNETH EUGENE BEASLEY June 18, 1971. She married (2) MONTE BITTING April 28, 1976. She married (3) SCOTT CARL LEWIS September 29, 1990 in El Dorado, Butler County, KS.

Marriage notes for CYNTHIA MCGINN and SCOTT LEWIS:
Copy of marriage license.

Child of CYNTHIA MCGINN and KENNETH BEASLEY is:
    i. KRISTINE RENEE[7] BEASLEY, b. April 10, 1973, Newton, Harvey County, KS.

Child of CYNTHIA MCGINN and MONTE BITTING is:
    ii. MISTY DAWN[7] BITTING, b. November 29, 1977, Wichita, Sedgwick County, KS.

191. KIMBERLY SUE[6] DEHAVEN (CLARA MAY[5] HALL, GUY CHRISTIAN[4], FRANCIS LEATON[3], SENY[2] MOORE, RICHARD S[1]) was born August 08, 1956 in Newton, Harvey County, KS. She married DOUGLAS L HAGUE December 22, 1979 in Sedgwick, Harvey County, KS.

Marriage notes for KIMBERLY DEHAVEN and DOUGLAS HAGUE:
Copy of marriage license.

Children of KIMBERLY DEHAVEN and DOUGLAS HAGUE are:
    i. MORGAN ASHLEY[7] HAGUE, b. August 29, 1983, Newton, Harvey County, KS.
    ii. MATTHEW D HAGUE, b. April 05, 1985, Newton, Harvey County, KS.
    iii. MOLLY A HAGUE, b. December 20, 1989, Newton, Harvey County, KS.

192. JEFFREY LYNN[6] DEHAVEN (CLARA MAY[5] HALL, GUY CHRISTIAN[4], FRANCIS LEATON[3], SENY[2] MOORE, RICHARD S[1]) was born April 25, 1959 in Newton, Harvey County, KS. He married BRENDA KAY BISHOP April 12, 1980 in Sedgwick, Harvey County, KS.

Marriage notes for JEFFREY DEHAVEN and BRENDA BISHOP:
Copy of marriage license.

Children of JEFFREY DEHAVEN and BRENDA BISHOP are:
    i. TIFFANY M[7] DEHAVEN, b. August 11, 1982, Newton, Harvey County, KS.
    ii. ZACHERY D DEHAVEN, b. January 03, 1986, Newton, Harvey County, KS.

193. RHONDA LEIGH[6] BAIR (JANICE DE LOIS[5] HALL, GUY CHRISTIAN[4], FRANCIS LEATON[3], SENY[2] MOORE, RICHARD S[1]) was born November 24, 1961 in Forbes AFB, Shawnee County, KS. She married (1) IRVING JAMES HUMMEL September 15, 1979 in Venice, Sarasota County, FL, son of IRVING HUMMEL and GRACE NELSON. She married (2) RICHARD LEE JOHNSTON October 22, 1988 in Schertz, Guadalupe County, TX.

Notes for RHONDA LEIGH BAIR:
At the time of her divorce from Irving, Rhonda took back the Bair name.

More about IRVING JAMES HUMMEL II:
Cause of death: Pedestrian - hit by car

Children of RHONDA BAIR and RICHARD JOHNSTON are:
    i. CHRISTINE NICOLE[7] JOHNSTON, b. July 24, 1991, Live Oak, Bexar County, TX.
    ii. MICHELLE ANNETTE JOHNSTON, b. September 02, 1995, San Antonio, Bexar County, TX.

194. TERESA RENEA[6] BAIR (JANICE DE LOIS[5] HALL, GUY CHRISTIAN[4], FRANCIS LEATON[3], SENY[2] MOORE, RICHARD S[1]) was born September 24, 1962 in Port Lyautey NAS, Morocco. She married RONALD PHILLIP WOODS November 24, 1990 in Venice, Sarasota County, FL.

Notes for TERESA RENEA BAIR:
Teresa was born in a Navy hospital at Port Lyautey NAS, Morocco. She received a certificate of birth from the Navy Hospital. Because it was on foreign soil, she could not have a birth certificate. To the laws of the USA, these are different. Her mother and father had to apply to the U.S. Government for a certificate of citizenship and verify that she was our child in federal court. A lot of paperwork and six months waiting to get it through the federal court system. Without this certificate, there was no way for her to prove that she was an American citizen.

More about TERESA RENEA BAIR:
Fact 1: Certificate of citizenship # AA-242458.

Child of TERESA BAIR and RONALD WOODS is:
    i. TYLER CHRISTIAN LORNE[7] WOODS, b. June 07, 1995, Bradenton, Manatee County, FL.

195. JOYCE ANN[6] DUNCAN (MARGARET ELNORA[5] PENNER, ENUICE MARJORIE[4] JACOBS, FLORENCE ANN[3] HALL, SENY[2] MOORE, RICHARD S[1]) was born July 28, 1944 in California. She married ROBERT MELTON.

Children of JOYCE DUNCAN and ROBERT MELTON are:
  i. JASON WALTER[7] MELTON, b. May 03, 1970, California.
  ii. DARREN ROBERT MELTON, b. December 01, 1972, California.

196. FAITH EILEEN[6] DUNCAN (MARGARET ELNORA[5] PENNER, ENUICE MARJORIE[4] JACOBS, FLORENCE ANN[3] HALL, SENY[2] MOORE, RICHARD S[1]) was born January 14, 1948 in California. She married CRAIG BAKER.

Children of FAITH DUNCAN and CRAIG BAKER are:
  i. ANGELA MARGARET[7] BAKER, b. August 03, 1967, Palmdale, Los Angeles County, CA.
  ii. HEATHER RENEE BAKER, b. September 23, 1970, Palmdale, Los Angeles County, CA.

197. DAVID ROBERT[6] DUNCAN (MARGARET ELNORA[5] PENNER, ENUICE MARJORIE[4] JACOBS, FLORENCE ANN[3] HALL, SENY[2] MOORE, RICHARD S[1]) was born February 05, 1951 in California. He married (1) JAN ???. He married (2) CHRIS ???.

Children of DAVID DUNCAN and JAN ??? are:
  i. CHRISTINE[7] DUNCAN.
  ii. BRYON DUNCAN.

198. ROBERT STEVEN[6] MORSE (NORMA FRANCES[5] PENNER, ENUICE MARJORIE[4] JACOBS, FLORENCE ANN[3] HALL, SENY[2] MOORE, RICHARD S[1]) was born September 28, 1947 in Wichita, Sedgwick County, KS. He married RITA SUE CANNON October 23, 1971 in Howard, Elk County, KS.

Marriage notes for ROBERT MORSE and RITA CANNON:
Copy of marriage license.

Children of ROBERT MORSE and RITA CANNON are:
  i. PHYLLIS ANN[7] MORSE, b. May 01, 1974, Independence, Montgomery County, KS.
  ii. VANCE STEVEN MORSE, b. January 27, 1976, El Dorado, Butler County, KS.

199. TERESA ANNE[6] MORSE (NORMA FRANCES[5] PENNER, ENUICE MARJORIE[4] JACOBS, FLORENCE ANN[3] HALL, SENY[2] MOORE, RICHARD S[1]) was born January 19, 1950 in Independence, Montgomery County, KS. She married RALPH VESTEL FOWLER JR November 27, 1970 in Longton, Elk County, KS.

Marriage notes for TERESA MORSE and RALPH FOWLER:
Copy of marriage license.

Children of TERESA MORSE and RALPH FOWLER are:
  i. KEVIN LEE[7] FOWLER, b. November 30, 1974, Iowa.
  ii. BRIAN CARL FOWLER, b. April 28, 1977, Chicago Heights, Cook County, IL.

200. CONNIE ARLENE[6] MORSE (NORMA FRANCES[5] PENNER, ENUICE MARJORIE[4] JACOBS, FLORENCE ANN[3] HALL, SENY[2] MOORE, RICHARD S[1]) was born July 13, 1952 in Eureka, Greenwood County, KS. She married (1) DEWEY ALLEN EASUM June 05, 1971 in Longton, Elk County, KS. She married (2) VICTOR LEE ALBERT February 14, 1975.

Children of CONNIE MORSE and VICTOR ALBERT are:
  i. CHRISTINE MARIE[7] ALBERT, b. June 16, 1975, Wichita, Sedgwick County, KS.
  ii. JENNIFER DAWN ALBERT, b. September 28, 1977, Independence, Montgomery County, KS.

201. REX ELDON[6] MORSE (NORMA FRANCES[5] PENNER, ENUICE MARJORIE[4] JACOBS, FLORENCE ANN[3] HALL, SENY[2] MOORE, RICHARD S[1]) was born December 09, 1956 in Eureka, Greenwood County, KS. He married TREVA SUE AEMISEGGER November 26, 1976 in Independence, Montgomery County, KS.

Marriage notes for REX MORSE and TREVA AEMISEGGER:
Copy of marriage license.

Children of REX MORSE and TREVA AEMISEGGER are:
  i. CORRIN MOONYEON[7] MORSE, b. November 30, 1978, Independence, Montgomery County, KS.
  ii. NICKOLAS LEROY MORSE, b. May 27, 1982, Independence, Montgomery County, KS.

202. JOY SUE[6] JACOBS (CHARLES FORREST[5], HOMER[4], FLORENCE ANN[3] HALL, SENY[2] MOORE, RICHARD S[1]) was born September 22, 1945 in El Dorado, Butler County, KS. She married WILLIAM RUSSELL DUGAN September 09, 1972 in Warrensburg, Johnson County, MO.

Child of JOY JACOBS and WILLIAM DUGAN is:
  i. EDWARD W[7] DUGAN, b. September 09, 1977, Little Rock, Pulaski County, AR.

203. JOHN ERIC[6] JACOBS (CHARLES FORREST[5], HOMER[4], FLORENCE ANN[3] HALL, SENY[2] MOORE, RICHARD S[1]) was born November 27, 1947 in Manhattan, Pottawatomie County, KS. He married DEBRA ANN MUNFORD July 07, 1969, daughter of WILLIAM MUNFORD and MARGARET DAVIDSON.

Children of JOHN JACOBS and DEBRA MUNFORD are:
    i. JULIA ANN[7] JACOBS, b. March 26, 1971.
    ii. ELIZABETH ELLEN JACOBS, b. March 09, 1977.
    iii. ERICA LYNN JACOBS, b. September 06, 1979.

204. JANICE ALLENE[6] JACOBS (CHARLES FORREST[5], HOMER[4,] FLORENCE ANN[3] HALL, SENY[2] MOORE, RICHARD S[1]) was born November 13, 1949) in El Dorado, Butler County, KS. She married KENNETH D JORNS November 12, 1983 in Towanda, Butler County, KS. son of B JORNS and MARIA TROELLER.

Child of JANICE JACOBS and KENNETH JORNS is:
    i. BURKE JACOBS[7] JORNS, b. March 15, 1988.

205. GARY FORREST[6] JACOBS (CHARLES FORREST[5], HOMER[4], FLORENCE ANN[3] HALL, SENY[2] MOORE, RICHARD S[1]) was born December 05, 1954 in Wichita, Sedgwick County, KS. He married JOAN KAY RACICKY November 04, 1983 in El Dorado, Butler County, KS.

Marriage notes for GARY JACOBS and JOAN RACICKY:
Copy of marriage license.

Children of GARY JACOBS and JOAN RACICKY are:
    i. HANNAH MARIE[7] JACOBS, b. May 27, 1986, Wichita, Sedgwick County, KS.
    ii. CHRISTIAN FORREST JACOBS, b. August 25, 1989, Garden City, Finney County, KS.
    iii. JONATHON WADE JACOBS, b. March 29, 1991, Garden City, Finney County, KS.

206. JIM C[6] LONG (JOAN[5] JACOBS, HOMER[4,] FLORENCE ANN[3] HALL, SENY[2] MOORE, RICHARD S[1]) was born July 11, 1957 in Liberal, Seward County, KS. He married LORI PERKINS April 27, 1984 in Grapevine, Tarrant County, TX.

Children of JIM LONG and LORI PERKINS are:
    i. RACHELL ANN[7] LONG, b. Grapevine, Tarrant County, TX.
    ii. SARA NELL LONG, b. September 27, 1985, Grapevine, Tarrant County, TX.

207. ANNE E[6] LONG (JOAN[5] JACOBS, HOMER[4,] FLORENCE ANN[3] HALL, SENY[2] MOORE, RICHARD S[1]) was born August 21, 1958 in Hutchinson, Reno County, KS. She married JOHN K FARLEY April 17, 1983 in Hutchinson, Reno County, KS.

Children of ANNE LONG and JOHN FARLEY are:
    i. TESSA JANE[7] FARLEY, b. March 06, 1984, Hutchinson, Reno County, KS.
    ii. SETH KELLY FARLEY, b. March 17, 1986, Hutchinson, Reno County, KS.

208. SCOTT JACOBS[6] LONG (JOAN[5] JACOBS, HOMER[4,] FLORENCE ANN[3] HALL, SENY[2] MOORE, RICHARD S[1]) was born October 08, 1962 in Hutchinson, Reno County, KS. He married TENLEY WIARD April 06, 1987 in Hutchinson, Reno County, KS.

Child of SCOTT LONG and TENLEY WIARD is:
    i. KYLE JACOBS[7] LONG, b. May 08, 1989, Hutchinson, Reno County, KS.

209. ANGELA RAE[6] JACOBS (CHARLES RAY[5], LESTON LYLE[4], FLORENCE ANN[3] HALL, SENY[2] MOORE, RICHARD S[1]) was born October 22, 1964 in Wichita, Sedgwick County, KS. She married RONALD DAVID KROPP July 18, 1988 in Naperville, DuPage County, IL.

Children of ANGELA JACOBS and RONALD KROPP are:
    i. TREVOR CHARLES[7] KROPP.
    ii. ERIKA RUTH KROPP, b. June 05, 1992.
    iii. KAITLYN ANN KROPP, b. January 09, 1993.
    iv. TYLER DAVID KROPP, b. December 18, 1996.

210. MICHAEL ERNEST[6] SEARS (GERALD ORLANDO[5], PHYLLIS USEBA MAE[4] COPELAND, ADA FRANCIS[3] ATKINSON, SUSAN N[2] MOORE, RICHARD S[1]) was born March 28, 1946 in Vinita, Craig County, OK. He married (1) CHERYL ANN KITCHELL September 03, 1965 in Bartlesville, Washington County, OK. He married (2) CLAUDIA OPENSHAW March 28, 1982 in Carson City, Carson City County, NV.

Marriage notes for MICHAEL SEARS and CHERYL KITCHELL:
Copy of marriage license.

Children of MICHAEL SEARS and CHERYL KITCHELL are:
252. i. KIABERLI MARIE[7] SEARS, b. May 24, 1967, Tahlequah, Cherokee County, OK.
253. ii. STACY BROCK SEARS, b. July 03, 1969, Bartlesville, Washington County, OK.
254. iii. TRACY LANCE SEARS, b. July 03, 1969, Bartlesville, Washington County, OK.

Children of MICHAEL SEARS and CLAUDIA OPENSHAW are:
    iv. DANIELLE ELIZABETH[7] SEARS, b. March 07, 1983, Modesto, Stanislaus, CA.
    v. CHRISTINA MICHELLE SEARS, b. January 07, 1985, Thousand Oaks, Ventura County, CA.

211. JANET SUE[6] SEARS (GERALD ORLANDO[5], PHYLLIS USEBA MAE[4] COPELAND, ADA FRANCIS[3] ATKINSON, SUSAN N[2] MOORE, RICHARD S[1]) was born December 24, 1955 in Bartlesville, Washington County, OK. She married MARSHALL RICHARD NEWMAN March 16, 1985 in Hobbs, Lea County, NM.

Children of JANET SEARS and MARSHALL NEWMAN are:
    i.   AMANDA RENE[7] NEWMAN, b. July 21, 1986, Hobbs, Lea County, NM.
    ii.   CANDICE JILL STANFIELD NEWMAN, b. August 19, 1981, Hobbs, Lea County, NM.

212. DEBBIE[6] HAWKINS (JAN[5] SMITHHISLER, LEONA BELLE[4] COPELAND, ADA FRANCIS[3] ATKINSON, SUSAN N[2] MOORE, RICHARD S[1]). She married ??? WERNER.

Child of DEBBIE HAWKINS and ??? WERNER is:
    i.   JUDY[7] WERNER.

Generation No. 7

213. DIANA LEEANN[7] DENNETT (MIRIAM ANN[6] MOORE, WILLIAM REUBEN[5], REUBEN DAVID[4], WILLIAM OSCAR[3], REUBEN[2], RICHARD S[1]) was born November 23, 1957 in Wichita, Sedgwick County, KS. She married EUGENE THOMAS CORL July 13, 1985, son of EUGENE CORL and JEAN LEBLANC.

More about DIANA LEEANN DENNETT:
Occupation: Accountant.

More about EUGENE THOMAS CORL:
Fact 1: U.S. Navy.
Occupation: Computer tech.

Children of DIANA DENNETT and EUGENE CORL are:
- i. DANIELLE DAWN[8] CORL, b. June 19, 1986, Denver, Arapahoe County, KS.
- ii. HEATHER LYNN CORL, b. July 15, 1988, Denver, Arapahoe County, KS.
- iii. DERIK EUGENE CORL, b. September 28, 1993, Denver, Arapahoe County, KS.

214. RICHARD NHEIL ALLISON[7] WULZ (WILLIA PAULINE[6] MOORE, WILLIAM REUBEN[5], REUBEN DAVID[4], WILLIAM OSCAR[3], REUBEN[2], RICHARD S[1]) was born January 19, 1955 in McConnell AFB, Sedgwick County, KS. He married (1) CLAUDIA MARIA SCHWEHR August 28, 1978 in Twrstringen, GE, daughter of FRANZ SCHWEHR and MARIA BAVENDIEK. He married (2) PATRICIA LYNNE SANNER December 29, 1984 in Derby, Sedgwick County, KS, daughter of JAMES SANNER and WANDA BECKER.

Notes for RICHARD NHEIL ALLISON WULZ:
Was adopted by James Wulz on October 11, 1964.

More about RICHARD NHEIL ALLISON WULZ:
Fact 1: Army

Marriage notes for RICHARD WULZ and PATRICIA SANNER:
Copy of computer printout of marriage application and license.

Child of RICHARD WULZ and CLAUDIA SCHWEHR is:
- i. RENEE MARIA[8] ALLISON, b. December 09, 1978, Holzwickde, GE.

Child of RICHARD WULZ and PATRICIA SANNER is:
- ii. JAMES PATRICK NHEIL[8] WULZ, b. October 06, 1984, Wichita, Sedgwick County, KS.

215. RONALD RAY ALLISON[7] WULZ (WILLIA PAULINE[6] MOORE, WILLIAM REUBEN[5], REUBEN DAVID[4], WILLIAM OSCAR[3], REUBEN[2], RICHARD S[1]) was born May 18, 1957 in Winfield, Cowley County, KS. He met (1) LINDA BENOIT. He married (2) DEBORAH ANN FUDGER BRINDLE August 05, 1978 in Jacksonville, Nassau County, FL, daughter of JAMES FUDGER and KATHLEEN GROSHA. He married (3) SHAWN SUZANNE SNYDER November 29, 1986 in Wichita, Sedgwick County, KS, daughter of ROBERT SNYDER and EDITH MARTIN. He married (4) VICKI MCQUEEN December 31, 1991.

Notes for RONALD RAY ALLISON WULZ:
Was adopted by James Wulz on October 11, 1964.

Marriage notes for RONALD WULZ and SHAWN SNYDER:
Copy of computer printout of marriage application and marriage license.

Child of RONALD WULZ and LINDA BENOIT is:
- i. COLLEEN[8] BENOIT, b. February 15, 1985, Long Beach, Los Angeles, CA.

Child of RONALD WULZ and DEBORAH BRINDLE is:
- ii. STEPHANIE RENEE[8] ALLISON, b. April 12, 1980, Jacksonville, Nassau County, FL.

Child of RONALD WULZ and SHAWN SNYDER is:
- iii. MEGAN LEIGH[8] ALLISON, b. February 18, 1989, Long Beach, Los Angeles County, CA.

216. TAMMY RAE[7] MOORE (JAMES REUBEN[6], WILLIAM REUBEN[5], REUBEN DAVID[4], WILLIAM OSCAR[3], REUBEN[2], RICHARD S[1]) was born August 21, 1965 in Wichita, Sedgwick County, KS. She married GEORGE ARTHUR CRAIG March 30, 1991, son of GEORGE CRAIG and MARY LUC.

Children of TAMMY MOORE and GEORGE CRAIG are:
- i. CODY JAMES[8] CRAIG, b. November 11, 1991, Columbus, Polk County, NC.
- ii. DYLAN REESE CRAIG, b. September 04, 1994, Columbus, Polk County, NC.
- iii. WYATT WILLAM CRAIG, b. June 10, 1996, Columbus, Polk County, NC.

217. WESLEY WAYNE[7] MOORE (JAMES REUBEN[6], WILLIAM REUBEN[5], REUBEN DAVID[4], WILLIAM OSCAR[3], REUBEN[2], RICHARD S[1]) was born May 04, 1968 in Wichita, Sedgwick County, KS. He married RICHELLE LYNN ANTEL November 30, 1991 in Mulvane, Sumner County, KS, daughter of RICK ANTEL and KAYE WILSON.

Children of WESLEY MOORE and RICHELLE ANTEL are:
    i. JOSHUA SHANE[8] MOORE, b. October 13, 1991.
    ii. JORDAN JAYNE MOORE, b. January 21, 1993.

218. CINDY D[7] RAY (VELMA RUTH[6] TALLMAN, VIOLET MARIE[5] MOORE, REUBEN DAVID[4], WILLIAM OSCAR[3], REUBEN[2], RICHARD S[1]) was born August 28, 1954 in Wichita, Sedgwick County, KS. She married ??? HERRMAN.

Children of CINDY RAY and ??? HERRMAN are:
    i. SHAWN[8] HERRMAN, b. October 20, 1976.
    ii. KAYCI HERRMAN, b. January 18, 1978.
    iii. JORDAN HERRMAN, b. November 05, 1986.
    iv. JOSHUA HERRMAN, b. November 05, 1986.

219. CINDY D[7] CAIN (VELMA RUTH[6] TALLMAN, VIOLET MARIE[5] MOORE, REUBEN DAVID[4], WILLIAM OSCAR[3], REUBEN[2], RICHARD S[1]) was born August 28, 1954 in Wichita, Sedwick County, KS. She married ??? HERMAN.

Children of CINDY CAIN and ??? HERMAN are:
    i. SHAWN[8] HERMAN, b. October 20, 1976.
    ii. KAYCI HERMAN, b. January 18, 1978.
    iii. JORDAN HERMAN, b. November 05, 1986,
    iv. JOSHUA HERMAN, b. November 05, 1986.

220. DANNY J[7] CAIN (VELMA RUTH[6] TALLMAN, VIOLET MARIE[5] MOORE, REUBEN DAVID[4], WILLIAM OSCAR[3], REUBEN[2], RICHARD S[1]) was born December 23, 1958 in El Dorado, Butler County, KS. He married TERRY L ???.

Children of DANNY CAIN and TERRY ??? are:
    i. MICHAEL[8] CAIN, b. June 21, 1988.
    ii. SHELDON CAIN, b. July 23, 1990.

221. CHARLES RICHARD[7] EDRIS (THELMA ELIZABETH[6] TALLMAN, VIOLET MARIE[5] MOORE, REUBEN DAVID[4], WILLIAM OSCAR[3], REUBEN[2], RICHARD S[1]) was born May 30, 1955 in Newton, Harvey County, KS. He married SANDY LEE JONES March 05, 1977 in Newton, Harvey County, KS, daughter of SAMUEL LEE and APRIL BLOOMER.

More about CHARLES RICHARD EDRIS:
Occupation: Flour miller.

Children of CHARLES EDRIS and SANDY JONES are:
    i. TAWNYA CHRISTINE[8] EDRIS, b. September 10, 1978, Newton, Harvey County, KS.
    ii. TRAVIS CHARLES EDRIS, b. September 03, 1980, Newton, Harvey County, KS.
    iii. TIFFANY CRYSTAL EDRIS, b. November 22, 1981, Newton, Harvey County, KS.

222. DENNIS LEE[7] EDRIS (THELMA ELIZABETH[6] TALLMAN, VIOLET MARIE[5] MOORE, REUBEN DAVID[4], WILLIAM OSCAR[3], REUBEN[2], RICHARD S[1]) was born December 25, 1958 in Newton, Harvey County, KS. He married DEBORAH SUE HOPKINS April 20, 1985 in Elmira, Lane County, OR, daughter of EVERETT HOPKINS and RUTH JOHNSON.

More about DENNIS LEE EDRIS:
Occupation: Manufacturing supervisor.

More about DEBORAH SUE HOPKINS:
Occupation: Restitution Clerk.

Children of DENNIS EDRIS and DEBORAH HOPKINS are:
    i. JOSHUA NATHANIEL[8] EDRIS, b. March 06, 1974, Tucson, Pima County, AR; m. HEIDI JEAN DURHAM, August 20, 1993, Eugene, Lane County, OR.
    ii. JACOB LOGAN EDRIS, b. November 14, 1986, Eugene, Lane County, OR.

223. BRUCE LEON[7] EDRIS(THELMA ELIZABETH[6] TALLMAN, VIOLET MARIE[5] MOORE, REUBEN DAVID[4], WILLIAM OSCAR[3], REUBEN[2], RICHARD S[1]) was born March 01, 1960 in Newton, Harvey County, KS.

Child of BRUCE LEON EDRIS is:
    i. KRISTAIN DALE[8] EDRIS, b. March 03, 1992, Newton, Harvey County, KS.

224. SUE CHARLENE[7] EDRIS (THELMA ELIZABETH[6] TALLMAN, VIOLET MARIE[5] MOORE, REUBEN DAVID[4], WILLIAM OSCAR[3], REUBEN[2], RICHARD S[1]) was born July 12, 1962 in Newton, Harvey County, KS. She married RAYMOND LEE ARCHER May 30, 1981 in Whitewater, Butler County, KS, son of JERALD ARCHER and CHARLOTTE JONES.

More about SUE CHARLENE EDRIS:
Occupation: Banker.

More about RAYMOND LEE ARCHER:
Occupation: Auto body repairman.

Children of SUE EDRIS and RAYMOND ARCHER are:
      i. AARON JAMES[8] ARCHER, b. November 01, 1984, Newton, Harvey County, KS.
      ii. AMANDA RAE ARCHER, b. October 04, 1986, Newton, Harvey County, KS.

225. TINA MARIE[7] EDRIS (THELMA ELIZABETH[6] TALLMAN, VIOLET MARIE[5] MOORE, REUBEN DAVID[4], WILLIAM OSCAR[3], REUBEN[2], RICHARD S[1]) was born November 17, 1965 in Newton, Harvey County, KS. She married (1) ??? MACY. She married (2) AMOS LELAND HASTINGS III July 23, 1994 in Whitewater, Butler County, KS, son of AMOS HASTINGS and KAY CUTLER.

More about TINA MARIE EDRIS:
Occupation: Dental assistant.

More About AMOS LELAND HASTINGS III:
Occupation: Sales rep.

Children of TINA EDRIS and ??? MACY are:
      i. HEATHER KAY[8] MACY, b. December 20, 1985, Newton, Harvey County, KS.
      ii. TATUM LYN MACY, b. November 19, 1987, Newton, Harvey County, KS.

226. HEATH WAYNE[7] AUSTIN (EDITH VALETTA[6] MOORE, ALVA DANIEL[5], REUBEN DAVID[4], WILLIAM OSCAR[3], REUBEN[2], RICHARD S[1]) was born April 23, 1967 in Wichita, Sedgwick County, KS. He married MICHAL MAUREEN COATES April 04, 1987 in El Dorado, Butler County, KS.

Marriage notes for HEATH AUSTIN and MICHAL COATES:
Copy of marriage license.

Children of HEATH AUSTIN and MICHAL COATES are:
      i. AUDIE[1] AUSTIN.
      ii. CODY AUSTIN.

227. ANGELA DAWN[7] MOORE (LARRY JO[6], ELWOOD ORIN[5], ORIN EGAR[4], WILLIAM OSCAR[3], REUBEN[2], RICHARD S[1]) was born October 17, 1970 in Moab, UT. She married GEORGE AMASA LARSEN January 07, 1991 in Moab, UT.

Children of ANGELA MOORE and GEORGE LARSEN are:
      i. SHAYLA MICHALLE[8] LARSEN, b. August 08, 1988, Moab, UT.
      ii. JESSICA DARLENE LARSEN, b. December 10, 1989, Moab, UT.
      iii. RAYMON AMASA LARSEN, b. January 30, 1993, Moab, UT.

228. ALICE FAY[7] BARTLETT (WAYNE IRVIN[6], HELEN LOUISE[5] ELLER, STELLA ADALINE[4] WILEY, ETTA ELLEN[3] MOORE, REUBEN[2], RICHARD S[1]) was born January 12, 1953 in Bartlesville, Nowata County, OK. She married JOHN EUGENE. ORCUTT April 20, 1973 in Fountain, El Paso County, CO.

Notes for JOHN EUGENE ORCUTT: Copy of military separation papers.

More about JOHN EUGENE ORCUTT:
Fact 1: Navy 1966-1970 Electrician mate 3rd class petty officer.

Children of ALICE BARTLETT and JOHN ORCUTT are:
255.   i. TRAVIS EUGENE[8] ORCUTT, b. July 23, 1974, Colorado Springs, El Paso County, CO.
256.   ii. AMANDA MICHELLE ORCUTT, b. May 22, 1977, Colorado Springs, El Paso County, CO.

229. JOHNNY WAYNE[7] BARTLETT (WAYNE IRVIN[6], HELEN LOUISE[5] ELLER, STELLA ADALINE[4] WILEY, ETTA ELLEN[3] MOORE, REUBEN[2], RICHARD S[1]) was born July 09, 1957 in Pawhuska, Osage County, OK. He married (1) SUSAN ??? December 1978 in Fountain, El Paso County, CO. He married (2) DARLENE ??? July 15, 1989.

Child of JOHNNY BARTLETT and SUSAN ??? is:
      i. ALISSA CHRISTINA[8] BARTLETT, b. December 07, 1979, Colorado Springs, El Paso County, CO.

230. CHARLES CLIFFORD[7] BARTLETT (WAYNE IRVIN[6], HELEN LOUISE[5], STELLA ADALINE[4] WILEY, ETTA ELLEN[3] MOORE, REUBEN[2], RICHARD S[1]) was born November 06, 1958 in Pawhuska, Osage County, OK. He married JUDY TAYLOR September 25, 1982 in Fountain, El Paso County, CO.

Children of CHARLES BARTLETT and JUDY TAYLOR are:
      i. HEATHER[8] BARTLETT. b. June 15, 1980, Colorado Springs, El Paso County, CO.
      ii. JACOB BRIAN BARTLETT, b. October 31, 1986, Colorado Springs, El Paso County, CO.

231. EMMA JEAN[7] PFIEFF (STELLA MAE[6] BARTLETT, HELEN LOUISE[5] ELLER, STELLA ADALINE[4] WILEY, ETTA ELLEN[3] MOORE, REUBEN[2], RICHARD S[1]) was born January 09, 1956 in Ft Polk, Vernon County, LA. She married (1) MIKE NICHOLSON October 01, 1973 in Pauls Valley, Garvin County, OK. She married (2) SAM REECE November 28, 1978 in Pauls Valley, Garvin County, OK.

More about SAM REECE: Occupation: Trucker.

Child of EMMA PFIEFF and MIKE NICHOLSON is:
  i. ROBERT ALLEN[8] NICHOLSON, b. October 31, 1974, Pauls Valley, Garvin County, OK.

More about ROBERT ALLEN NICHOLSON:
Fact 1: Army.

Children of EMMA PFIEFF and SAM REECE are:
  ii. NATHAN EDWARD[8] REECE, b. November 01, 1979, Pauls Valley, Garvin County, OK.
  iii. JONATHAN ADRIAN REECE, b. November 02, 1980, Pauls Valley, Garvin County, OK.
  iv. THOMAS RAY REECE, b. October 24, 1982, Pauls Valley, Garvin County, OK.
  v. ALISHA DAWN REECE, b. September 21, 1985, Pauls Valley, Garvin County, OK
  vi. CHRISTINA ELIZABETH REECE, b. November 05, 1992, Pauls Valley, Garvin County, OK.

Notes for CHRISTINA ELIZABETH REECE:
Called Chrissy.

232. CYNTHIA LOUISE[7] PFIEFF (STELLA MAE[6] BARTLETT, HELEN LOUISE[5] ELLER, STELLA ADALINE[4] WILEY, ETTA ELLEN[3] MOORE, REUBEN[2], RICHARD S[1]) was born February 16, 1957 in Ft Hood, Coryell County, TX. She married (1) BILL SHERRELL February 13, 1976 in Pauls Valley, Garvin County, OK. She married (2) PAGET LOPER July 22, 1994 in Pauls Valley, Garvin County, OK.

Notes for CYNTHIA LOUISE PFIEFF: Called Cindy.

More about PAGET LOPER: Occupation: Trucker.

Child of CYNTHIA PFIEFF and BILL SHERRELL is:
  i. BILLY DON[8] SHERRELL, b. August 25, 1978, Pauls Valley, Garvin County, OK.

Child of CYNTHIA PFIEFF and PAGET LOPER is:
  ii. PATRICIA LEE[8] LOPER, b. August 09, 1995, Pauls Valley, Garvin County, OK.

233. DIXIE LOUISE[7] COTTRELL (NORMA JEAN[6] BARTLETT, HELEN LOUISE[5] ELLER, STELLA ADALINE[4] WILEY, ETTA ELLEN[3] MOORE, REUBEN[2], RICHARD S[1]) was born May 16, 1955 in Pawhuska, Osage County, OK. She married J D BLEVINS June 08, 1973 in Pauls Valley, Garvin County, OK.

Marriage notes for DIXIE, COTTRELL and J BLEVINS:
Copy of marriage license.

Children of DIXIE COTTRELL and J BLEVINS are:
257. i. MELINDA DAWN[8] BLEVINS, b. January 27, 1975, Pauls Valley, Garvin County, OK.
  ii. JAMES DAVID) BLEVINS, b. July 15, 1980. Pauls Valley, Garvin County, OK.

234. BRENDA[7] LEHMAN (NORMA JEAN[6] BARTLETT, HELEN LOUISE[5] ELLER, STELLA ADALINE[4] WILEY, ETTA ELLEN[3] MOORE, REUBEN[2], RICHARD S[1]) was born June 18, 1960 in Pauls Valley, Garvin County, OK. She married (2) JIMMY SHERRELL June 18, 1984 in Pauls Valley, Garvin County, OK.

Child of BRENDA LEHMAN is:
  i. ANGEL MARIE[8] LEHMAN, b. December 04, 1978, Pauls Valley, Garvin County, OK; m. BILLY FETGATTE , March 27, 1998.

Children of BRENDA LEHMAN and JIMMY SHERRELL are:
  ii. JERI SUE[8] SHERRELL, b. August 06, 1985, Pauls Valley, Garvin County, OK.
  iii. GARY DON SHERRELL, b. January 05, 1988, Pauls Valley, Garvin County. OK

235. JERI ANN[7] LEHMAN (NORMA JEAN[6] BARTLETT, HELEN LOUISE[5] ELLER, STELLA ADALINE[4] WILEY, ETTA ELLEN[3] MOORE, REUBEN[2], RICHARD S[1]) was born April 21, 1961 in Pauls Valley, Garvin County, OK. She met (1) BILLY SHERRELL. She married (2) LARRY SHERRELL January 1979 in Pauls Valley, Garvin County, OK She married (3) JOHN TOWLER JR June 18, 1984.

Children of JERI LEHMAN and LARRY SHERRELL are:
  i. JERRY RAY[8] SHERRELL, b. February 14, 1980, Pauls Valley, Garvin County, OK.
  ii. REBECCA ANN SHERRELL, b. August 11, 1981, Pauls Valley, Garvin County, OK.

Children of JERI LEHMAN and JOHN TOWLER are:
  iii. CAROL JEAN[8] TOWLER, b. July 08, 1984, Pauls Valley, Garvin County, OK.
  iv. SAVANNA TOWLER, b. October 30, 1989, Pauls Valley, Garvin County, OK.

236. LUCINA RUTH[7] LEHMAN (NORMA JEAN[6] BARTLETT, HELEN LOUISE[5] ELLER, STELLA ADALINE[4] WILEY, ETTA ELLEN[3] MOORE, REUBEN[2], RICHARD S[1]) was born August 13, 1962 in Pauls Valley, Garvin County, OK. She married (1) DANNY WILLIAMS June 02, 1978 in Pauls Valley, Garvin County, OK. She married (2) MIKE L HOCKERSMITH July 01, 1985.

Notes for LUCINA RUTH LEHMAN:
Called Lucy.

More about MIKE L HOCKERSMITH:
Occupation: Manager fast foods.

Children of LUCINA LEHMAN and DANNY WILLIAMS are:
    i. KRISTA GAIL[8] WILLIAMS, b. January 30, 1979, Pauls Valley, Garvin County, OK.
    ii. JONATHAN PAUL WILLIAMS, b. February 21, 1980, Pauls Valley, Garvin County, OK.
    iii. KENNETH WAYNE WILLIAMS, b. December 14, 1982, Pauls Valley, Garvin County, OK.

Children of LUCINA LEHMAN and MIKE HOCKERSMITH are:
    iv. DAVID[8] HOCKERSMITH.
    v. BRANDON M HOCKERSMITH, b. September 05, 1989, Pauls Valley, Garvin County, OK.
    vi. STEPHEN NICHOLAS HOCKERSMTH, b. November 17, 1997, Pauls Valley, Garvin County, OK.
    vii. STEPHANIE NICHOLE HOCKERSMITH b. November 17, 1997, Pauls Valley, Garvin County, OK.

237. MICHAEL BRETT[7] RUSHTON (NITA JO[6] ELLER, GEORGE EVERETT[5], STELLA ADALINE[4] WILEY, ETTA ELLEN[3] MOORE, REUBEN[2], RICHARD S[1]) was born November 14, 1972 in Madison, Dane County, WI. He married JANELLE LYNN COTTRELL July 23, 1994 in Houston, Harris County, TX.

Marriage notes for MICHAEL RUSHTON and JANELLE COTTRELL:
Copy of marriage license.

Children of MICHAEL RUSHTON and JANELLE COTTRELL are:
    i. HUNTER AUSTIN[8] RUSHTON, b. September 28, 1994, Augusta, Richmond County, GA.
    ii. TYLER MICHAEL RUSHTON, b. April 14, 1996, Augusta, Richmond County, GA.

238. TRACY NOELLE[7] RUSHTON (NITA JO[6] ELLER, GEORGE EVERETT[5], STELLA ADALINE[4] WILEY, ETTA ELLEN[3] MOORE, REUBEN[2], RICHARD S[1]) was born December 11, 1974 in Billings, Yellowstone County, MT. She married LOREN CULLEY STATON March 23, 1996 in Houston, Harris County, TX, son of DAVID STATON and SHARON ???.

Marriage notes for TRACY RUSHTON and LOREN STATON:
Copy of marriage license.

Child of TRACY RUSHTON and LOREN STATON is:
    i. HALEY LOREN[8] STATON, b. November 19, 1997, Houston, Harris County, TX.

239. BECKY SUE[7] JONES (BARBARA ELOUISE[6] ELLER, JAMES WILKERSON[5], STELLA ADALINE[4] WILEY, ETTA ELLEN[3] MOORE, REUBEN[2], RICHARD S[1]) was born August 14, 1959 in Bartlesville, Washington County, OK. She married (2) KENT BARNES June 09, 1984 in Bartlesville, Washington County, OK.

Child of BECKY SUE JONES is:
    i. MICHAEL[8] JONES, b. May 09, 1980, Bartlesville, Nowata County, OK.

Child of BECKY JONES and KENT BARNES is:
    ii. SHANNON RENEE[8] BARNES, b. February 03, 1987, Bartlesville, Washington County, OK.

240. CLIFFORD[7] JONES (BARBARA ELOUISE[6] ELLER, JAMES WILKERSON[5], STELLA ADALINE[4] WILEY, ETTA ELLEN[3] MOORE, REUBEN[2], RICHARD S[1]) was born September 28, 1967 in Bartlesville, Washington County, OK. He married (2) KAREN GRIGGS January 03, 1986 in Bartlesville, Washington County, OK.

Children of CLIFFORD JONES and KAREN GRIGGS are:
    i. KARA DAWN[8] JONES, b. October 16, 1987, Bartlesville, Washington County, OK.
    ii. CLIFFA JONES.

241. SANDRA LYNN[7] JONES (ALICE MARIE[6] ELLER, JAMES WILKERSON[5], STELLA ADALINE[4] WILEY, ETTA ELLEN[3] MOORE, REUBEN[2], RICHARD S[1]) was born December 04, 1972 in Ft Carson, El Paso County, CO. She married MIKE SCHOPANSKY February 13, 1991 in Bartlesville, Washington County, OK.

Children of SANDRA JONES and MIKE SCHOPANSKY are:
    i. WILLIAM CODY[8] SCHOPANSKY, b. October 15, 1991, Bartlesville, Washington County, OK.
    ii. JAMES ALLEN SCHOPANSKY, b. October 04, 1993, Bartlesville, Washington County, OK.

242. ROBERT CRAIG[7] ASHURST (MADELINE EILEEN[6] BROCKHOUSE, ELIZABETH IRENE[5] ELLER, STELLA ADALINE[4] WILEY, ETTA ELLEN[3] MOORE, REUBEN[2], RICHARD S[1]) was born January 27, 1971 in Independence, Jackson County, MO. He met RHONDA LYNNE BALDWIN, daughter of JOSEPH BALDWIN and DEBORAH TIPPETT.

Notes for ROBERT CRAIG ASHURST:
Copy of birth certificate.

More about ROBERT CRAIG ASHURST:
Occupation: Printer.

Children of ROBERT ASHURST and RHONDA BALDWIN are:
    i. CHELSEY LYNNE[8] ASHURST, b. April 21, 1992, Kansas City, Jackson County, MO.
    ii. JOSEPH TIMOTHY ASHURST, b. December 18, 1993, Kansas City, Jackson County. MO.

243. CHERRY SHERIE[7] ASHURST (MADELINE EILEEN[6] BROCKHOUSE, ELIZABETH IRENE[5] ELLER, STELLA ADALINE[4] WILEY, ETTA ELLEN[3] MOORE, REUBEN[2], RICHARD S[1]) was born February 16, 1977 in Independence, Jackson County, MO. She married JAMES EDWARD ALEXANDER WILLIAMS November 30, 1992 in Lee Summit, Jackson County, MO.

Notes for JAMES EDWARD ALEXANDER WILLAMS:
Called Alex.

Child of CHERRY ASHURST and JAMES WILLAMS:
    i. HALEY NICOLE MARIE[8] WILLAMS, b. March 14, 1993, Kansas City, Jackson County, MO.

244. MICHAEL K[7] COATS (MARILYN SUE[6] BROYLES, VIOLA G[5] DEXTER, GRACE MAUDE[4] HALL, FRANCIS LEATON[3] SENY[2] MOORE, RICHARD S[1]) was born September 17, 1963. He married GINGER G SMITH KITTEMASA July 12, 1984 in Whitewater, Butler County, KS.

Children of MICHAEL COATS and GINGER KITTEMASA are:
258.   i. PAMELA A[8] COATS, b. April 08, 1970; adopted child.
    ii. JACOB M COATS, b. March 07, 1986.
    iii. JACKLYN N COATS, b. December 11, 1988.

245. ROBIN[7] ELDENBURG (RODONNA SUE[6] BRENNER, VERL W[5], ALICE ELIZA[4] HALL, FRANCIS LEATON[3], SENY[2] MOORE, RICHARD S[1]). She married JOHN SMITH.

Child of ROBIN ELDENBURG and JOHN SMITH is:
    i. AMBER[8] SMITH.

246. THOMAS GRANT[7] ANDERSON JR (MARY ESTHER[6] KENNEDY, DORIS MAXINE[5] HALL, GUY CHRISTIAN[4], FRANCIS LEATON[3], SENY[2] MOORE, RICHARD S[1]) was born April 13, 1959 in Wichita, Sedgwick County, KS. He married (1) DONNA SELLERS April 18, 1970 in West Plans, Howell County, MO. He married (2) ELIZABETH MAXINE COLE March 30, 1985.

Children of THOMAS ANDERSON and DONNA SELLERS are:
    i. CHRISTINA MARIA[8] ANDERSON, b. June 25, 1977, Wichita, Sedgwick County, KS.
    ii. CHARLES ANDERSON, b. October 16, 1978, Wichita, Sedgwick County, KS.
    iii. MICHELLE LYNN ANDERSON, b. March 03, 1982, West Plains, Howell County, MO.

Child of THOMAS ANDERSON and ELIZABETH COLE is:
    iv. LYLE LYNN[8] ANDERSON, b. February 23, 1986, Phoenix, Maricopa County, AZ.

247. CHARLOTTE JEAN[7] FOYLE (CHARLENE WILMA[6] KENNEDY, DORIS MAXINE[5] HALL, GUY CHRISTIAN[4], FRANCIS LEATON[3], SENY[2] MOORE, RICHARD S[1]) was born September 01, 1966. She married STEVE REEVES May 26, 1984.

Children of CHARLOTTE FOYLE and STEVE REEVES are:
    i. DUSTIN DWIGHT[8] REEVES, b. November 28, 1985, Fort Worth, Parker County, TX
    ii. MATTHEW LEVI REEVES, b. April 23, 1987, Fort Worth, Parker County, TX.

248. SHAWN CEHRI[7] WATHEN (MARTHA MAY[6] HALL, DUANE DELOISE[5], GUY CHRISTIAN[4], FRANCIS LEATON[3], SENY[2] MOORE, RICHARD S[1]) was born February 02, 1972 in California. She married CHARLES HARRIS 1990.

Children of SHAWN WATHEN and CHARLES HARRIS are:
    i. BRENNA SAMORA[8] HARRIS, b. August 09, 1989, California.
    ii. JAMES DUANE HARRIS, b. October 02, 1992, California.

249. VERNON JAMES[7] WATHEN (MARTHA MAY[6] HALL, DUANE DELOISE[5], GUY CHRISTIAN[4], FRANCIS LEATON[3], SENY[2] MOORE, RICHARD S[1]) was born May 15, 1974 in California. He married CHRISTY ???.

Child of VERNON WATHEN and CHRISTY ??? is:
    i. SLOAN COURTNEY[8] WATHEN, b. January 25, 1994, California.

250. APRIL MICHELLE[7] MAY (SONDRA SUE[6] HOPKINS, AUDREY FAYE[5] HALL, GUY CHRISTIAN[4], FRANCIS LEATON[3], SENY[2] MOORE, RICHARD S[1]) was born July 31, 1979 in Wichita, Sedgwick County, KS. She met MICHAEL DAINES 1997,

Child of APRIL MAY and MICHAEL DAINES is:
    i. WILLIAM MICHAEL^8 DAINES, b. December 27, 1997, Newton, Harvey County, KS.

Notes for WILLIAM MICHAEL, DANES:
Copy of birth certificate.

251. CHASTITY DAWN HOPKINS^7 JESSEPH (PAMELA KAY^6 HOPKINS, AUDREY FAYE^5 HALL, GUY CHRISTIAN^4, FRANCIS LEATON^3, SENY^2 MOORE, RICHARD S^1) was born July 06, 1974 in Newton, Harvey County, KS. She married LEE CHARLES BRISCOE December 14, 1996 in Little River, Rice County, KS, son of HENRY BRISCOE and ARAH ALTON.

Notes for CHASTITY DAWN HOPKINS JESSEPH:
Copy of birth certificate.

Marriage notes for CHASTITY JESSEPH and LEE BRISCOE:
Have an announcement card, Copy of marriage license.

Child of CHASTITY JESSEPH and LEE BRISCOE is:
    i. ABIGAIL DENISE^8 BRISCOE, b. January 13, 1998, McPherson, McPherson County, KS.

Notes for ABIGAIL DENISE BRISCOE:
Copy of birth certificate.

252. KIABERLI MARIE^7 SEARS (MICHAEL ERNEST^6, GERALD ORLANDO^5, PHYLLIS USEBA MAE^4 COPELAND, ADA FRANCIS^3 ATKINSON, SUSAN N MOORE, RICHARD S^1) was born May 24, 1967 in Tahlequah, Cherokee County, OK. She married TERRANCE LEON HYCHE April 02, 1988 in Bartlesville, Washington County, OK.

Marriage notes for KIABERLI SEARS and TERRANCE HYCHE:
Copy of marriage license.

Child of KIABERLI SEARS and TERRANCE HYCHE is:
    i. BREANNE MICHELLE^8 HYCHE, b. August 07, 1988, Bartlesville, Washington County, OK.

253. STACY BROCK^7 SEARS (MICHAEL ERNEST^6, GERALD ORLANDO^5, PHYLLIS USEBA MAE^4 COPELAND, ADA FRANCIS^3 ATKINSON, SUSAN N^2 MOORE, RICHARD S^1) was born July 03, 1969 in Bartlesville, Washington County, OK.

Child of STACY BROCK SEARS is:
    i. JUSTIN BROCK^8 SEARS, b. April 05, 1997, Waco, McLennon County, TX.

254. TRACY LANCE^7 SEARS (MICHAEL ERNEST^6, GERALD ORLANDO^5, PHYLLIS USEBA MAE^4 COPELAND, ADA FRANCIS^3 ATKINSON, SUSAN N^2 MOORE, RICHARD S^1) was born July 03, 1969 in Bartlesville, Washington County, OK. He married DAWN MARIE LIMPERT April 28, 1990 in Bartlesville, Washington County, OK, daughter of LEO LIMPERT and LUCILLE LUCK.

Marriage notes for TRACY SEARS and DAWN LIMPERT:
Copy of marriage license.

Children of TRACY SEARS and DAWN LIMPERT are:
    i. CAMERON JACOB^8 SEARS, b. July 31, 1991, St Louis, St Louis County, MO.
    ii. ALEC TANNER SEARS, b. July 13, 1993, St Louis, St Louis County, MO.

Generation No. 8

255. TRAVIS EUGENE[8] ORCUTT (ALICE FAY[7] BARTLETT, WAYNE IRVIN[6], HELEN LOUISE[5] ELLER, STELLA ADALINE[4] WILEY, ETTA ELLEN[3] MOORE, REUBEN[2], RICHARD S[1]) was born July 23, 1974 in Colorado Springs, El Paso County, CO. He married CARMEN BARTELS April 19, 1997 in Fountain, El Paso County, CO.

Child of TRAVIS ORCUTT and CARMEN BARTELS is:
    i.   CARLY SAVANNAH[2] ORCUTT b. July 25, 1996, Fountain, El Paso County, CO.

256. AMANDA MICHELLE[8] ORCUTT (ALICE FAY[7] BARTLETT, WAYNE IRVIN[6], HELEN LOUISE[5] ELLER, STELLA ADALINE[4] WILEY, ETTA ELLEN[3] MOORE, REUBEN[2], RICHARD S[1]) was born May 22, 1977 in Colorado Springs, El Paso County, CO.

Child of AMANDA MICHELLE ORCUTT is:
    i.   ALEXANDER CHANCE[9] ORCUTT, b. January 23, 1996, Fountain, El Paso County, CO.

257. MELINDA DAWN[8] BLEVINS (DIXIE LOUISE[7] COTTRELL, NORMA JEAN[6] BARTLETT, HELEN LOUISE[5] ELLER, STELLA ADALINE[4] WILEY, ETTA ELLEN[3] MOORE, REUBEN[2], RICHARD S[1]) was born January 27, 1975 in Pauls Valley, Garvin County, OK. She married GLEN REISER February 20, 1993 in Pauls Valley, Garvin County, OK.

Marriage notes for MELINDA BLEVINS and GLEN REISER:
Copy of marriage license.

Children of MELINDA BLEVINS and GLEN REISER are:
    i.   TIFFANY RENEE[9] REISER, b. June 06, 1993, Pauls Valley, Garvin County, OK.
    ii.   BRITTANY NICOLE REISER, b. November 28, 1994, Pauls Valley, Garvin County, OK.

258. PAMELA A[8] COATS (MICHAEL K[7], MARILYN SUE[6] BROYLES, VIOLA G[5] DEXTER, GRACE MAUDE[4] HALL, FRANCIS LEATON[3], SENY[2] MOORE, RICHARD S[1]) was born April 08, 1970. She married ROGER B MCQUISTON October 20, 1996.

Child of PAMELA COATS and ROGER MCQUISTON is:
    i.   BRIAN M[9] MCQUISTON, b. February 11, 1998.

Family Group Sheet

Husband's Full Name: Archibald Owens   **Chart No.**

	Day Month Year	City, Town or Place	County or Province, etc.	State or Country	Add. Info. on Husband
Birth	1786			NC	
Chr'nd					
Marr.	22-12-1810		Wilkes	NC	
Death	1-11-1869	Plano	Kendall	Ill.	
Burial		Griswold Cem.			

Places of Residence:
Occupation: Church Affiliation: Military Rec:

His Father: **Mother's Maiden Name:** Moore

Wife's Full Maiden Name: Nancy Judd

	Day Month Year	City, Town or Place	County or Province, etc.	State or Country	Add. Info. on Wife
Birth	1783			NC	
Chr'nd					
Death	11-5-1870	Plano	Kendall Co.	Ill.	
Burial		Griswold Cem.			

Places of Residence:
Occupation: Church Affiliation: Military Rec:

Her Father: Nathaniel Judd   **Mother's Maiden Name:** Elizabeth Owens

Sex	Children's Names in Full		Day Month Year	City, Town or Place	County or Province, etc.	State or Country	Add. Info on Children
F	1 Susannah Owens	Birth	21-10-1811			NC	
		Marr.	17-10-1831	Kingston	Roane Co.	Tn.	
	Full Name of Spouse	Death	23-12-1885	Plano	Kendall Co.	Ill.	
	Abram Darnell	Burial		Griswold Cem.			
F	2 Rebecca Owens	Birth	1813 ca.			NC	
		Marr.					
	Full Name of Spouse	Death					
	Richard S. Moore	Burial					
F	3 Charlotte Owens	Birth	1817			NC	
		Marr.	1-12-1833	Hennepin	Putnam Co.	Ill.	
	Full Name of Spouse	Death	20-12-1891	Lawrence	Pottowatomie	Ks.	
	James Darnell	Burial					
M	4 Reuben Owens	Birth	27-4-1820		Wilkes	NC	
		Marr.	20-12-1844	Long Grove	Kendall	Ill.	
	Full Name of Spouse	Death	9-10-1899	Little Rock	Kendall	Ill.	
	Lucinda Ryon	Burial		Griswold Cem.			

Susannah Owens   Reuben Owens

Family Group Sheet

Husband's Full Name: Richard S. Moore — Chart No.

	Day Month Year	City, Town or Place	County or Province, etc.	State or Country	Add. Info on Husband
Birth	1811			Va.	
Chr'nd					
Marr.	1833				
Death					
Burial					

Places of Residence:
Occupation: Farmer-Stonemaker   Church Affiliation: Military Rec:

His Father: Mother's Maiden Name:

Wife's Full Maiden Name: Rebecca Owen(s)

	Day Month Year	City, Town or Place	County or Province, etc.	State or Country	Add. Info on Wife
Birth	1814			NC	
Chr'nd					
Death					
Burial					

Places of Residence:
Occupation: Church Affiliation: Military Rec:

Her Father: Archibald Owen(s)   Mother's Maiden Name: Nancy Judd

Sex	Children's Names in Full		Day Month Year	City, Town or Place	County or Province, etc.	State or Country	Add. Info on Children
M	1 William H. Moore	Birth	1833 ca			Ill.	
	Full Name of Spouse	Marr.					
		Death					
		Burial					
M	2 Reuben Moore	Birth	29-11-1834		Kendall Co.	Ill.	
	Full Name of Spouse	Marr.	23-8-1851	Penn Field	Kendall Co.	Ill.	
	Melvina Paul	Death	8-3-1884	Elgin	Chautauqua Co.	Kans.	
		Burial	3-1884	Oak Grove	Chauaqua Co.	Kans.	
F	3 Sena Moore	Birth	17-8-1836	Aurora	Kendall Co.	Ill.	
	Full Name of Spouse	Marr.	7-5-1857		Kendall Co.	Ill.	
	Edmund Hall	Death	15-11-1908	Inglewood	Los Angeles	Calif.	
		Burial	11-1908	Shaffer Cem.	Potwin,	Kans.	
F	4 Matilda Jane Moore	Birth	11-3-1837	Plano	Kendall Co.	Ill.	
	Full Name of Spouse	Marr.	23-10-1856		Kendall Co.	Ill.	
	Harvey I. Greenfield	Death	24-4-1926	Jefferson	Greene Co.	Ia.	cert/obit
		Burial	26-4-1926	Pleasant Hill Cem.		Ia.	no marker
MM	5 Thomas S. Moore	Birth	1840 ca.			Ill.	
	Full Name of Spouse	Marr.	8-1-1863		Kendall Co.	Ill.	
	Adeline Isabell	Death	1939				
		Burial					
M	6 James C. Moore	Birth	4-3-1844		Kendall Co.	Ill.	
	Full Name of Spouse	Marr.	31-12-1868		Madison Co.	Ia.	
	Martha M. Shearer	Death	18-12-1915	Lincoln Twp.	Madison Co.	Ia.	
		Burial		Peru Cem.			
M	7 Calvin W. Moore	Birth	2-1845 ca.			Ill.	
	Full Name of Spouse	Marr.	1873				
	Carinda	Death					
		Burial					
F	8 Martha Moore	Birth	1846 ca			Ill.	
	Full Name of Spouse	Marr.					
	Thomas Bascom	Death					
		Burial					

Compiler:
Address:
City, State, Zip:
Date:

Notes:

Family Group Sheet

page 2

Husband's Full Name Richard S. Moore   Chart No.

	Day	Month	Year	City, Town or Place	County or Province, etc.	State or Country	Add. Info on Husband
Birth			1811			Va.	
Chr'nd							
Marr			1833				
Death							
Burial							

Places of Residence:

Occupation: Farmer-Stonemaker   Church Affiliation: Military Rec:

His Father: Mother's Maiden Name:

Wife's Full Maiden Name Rebecca Owen(s)

	Day	Month	Year	City, Town or Place	County or Province, etc.	State or Country	Add. Info on Wife
Birth			1814			NC	
Chr'nd							
Death							
Burial							

Places of Residence:

Occupation: Church Affiliation: Military Rec:

Her Father: Archibald Owen(s)   Mother's Maiden Name: Nancy Judd

Sex	Children's Names in Full		Day	Month	Year	City, Town or Place	County or Province, etc.	State or Country	Add. Info on Children
F	9 Charlotte M. Moore	Birth			1849			Ill.	1876 Madison Co. Iowa
	Full Name of Spouse: Geo. C. Gaylord / Thomas Garrity	Marr.	26	12	1867	Kendall Co.		Ill.	
		Death							
		Burial							
F	10 Phoebe C. Moore	Birth			1850 ca.			Ill.	
	Full Name of Spouse: James H. Colley	Marr.	12	10	1969	ElDorado	Butler Co.	Kans.	
		Death							
		Burial							
M	11 Marion M. Moore	Birth			1854			Ill.	
	Full Name of Spouse	Marr.							
		Death							
		Burial							
F	12 Susan Nancy Moore	Birth	3	10	1855		Putnam Co.	Ill.	
	Full Name of Spouse: Samuel R. Atkinson	Marr.							
		Death	31	8	1939	Independence	Mong.-Co.	Kans.	
		Burial		8	1939	Mt. Hope Cem.	Mong. Co.	Kans.	
M	13 George Moore	Birth							
	Full Name of Spouse	Marr.							
		Death							
		Burial							
	6	Birth							
	Full Name of Spouse	Marr.							
		Death							
		Burial							
	7	Birth							
	Full Name of Spouse	Marr.							
		Death							
		Burial							
	8	Birth							
	Full Name of Spouse	Marr.							
		Death							
		Burial							

Compiler: Notes:
Address:
City, State, Zip:
Date:

Family Group Sheet

Husband's Full Name: William H. Moore **Chart No.**

	Day	Month	Year	City, Town or Place	County or Province, etc.	State or Country	Add. Info. on Husband
Birth			1833			Ill.	
Chr'nd							
Marr.							
Death							
Burial							

Places of Residence:
Occupation: Church Affiliation: Military Rec.:

His Father: Richard S. Moore   **Mother's Maiden Name:** Rebecca Owen(s)

Wife's Full Maiden Name:

	Day	Month	Year	City, Town or Place	County or Province, etc.	State or Country	Add. Info. on Wife
Birth							
Chr'nd							
Death							
Burial							

Places of Residence:
Occupation: Church Affiliation: Military Rec.:

Her Father: **Mother's Maiden Name:**

Sex	Children's Names in Full		Day	Month	Year	City, Town or Place	County or Province, etc.	State or Country	Add. Info on Children
1	Clarence	Birth							
		Marr.							
	Full Name of Spouse	Death							
		Burial							
2	Josephine	Birth							
		Marr.							
	Full Name of Spouse	Death							
		Burial							
3		Birth							
		Marr.							
	Full Name of Spouse	Death							
		Burial							

September 25, 1997

AUDREY F HOPKINS
RR 3 BOX 190B
INDEPENDENCE KS 69301-9304

RE: WILLIAM MOORE

Dear Ms. Hopkins:

The Office of Vital Statistics began filing birth certificates on July 1, 1911. The record you requested is for an event which occurred before that date, therefore we are unable to process your request.

Since we are unable to process your request, a $10.00 refund will be processed and mailed to you in approximately three to four weeks.

If we can be of further assistance, please feel free to contact Holly Borsdorf at (785) 296-0859.

Sincerely,

Donna Calabrese

Donna Calabrese, Supervisor
Customer Service
Office of Vital Statistics

Family Group Sheet

Husband's Full Name: Reuben Moore   **Chart No.**

	Day Month Year	City, Town or Place	County or Province, etc.	State or Country	Add. Info on Husband
Birth	29-11-1834		Kendall Co.	Ill.	m. by Justice of Peace
Chr'nd					Joseph Laymar
Marr.	23-8-1851	Pennfield	Kendall Co.	Ill.	
Death	8-3-1884	Elgin	Chatauqua Co.	Kansas	
Burial	3-1884	Oak Grove cem. Elgin Chautauqua Co.		Kansas	

Places of Residence: Elgin, Kansas
Occupation: Farmer   **Church Affiliation:**   **Military Rec:**
Other wives: Elizabeth A. Pitts married June 26, 1883 in Sedan, Kansas
His Father: Richard S. Moore   **Mother's Maiden Name:** Rebecca Owen

Wife's Full Maiden Name: Melvina Barbara Paul

	Day Month Year	City, Town or Place	County or Province, etc.	State or Country	Add. Info on Wife
Birth	7-12-1833		Kendall Co.	Ill.	
Chr'nd					
Death	12-1-1883				
Burial	1-1883	Oak Grove Cem. Elgin	Chatauqua Co.	Kansas	

Places of Residence: Elgin, Kansas
Occupation: Housewife   **Church Affiliation:**   **Military Rec:**
Her Father: **Mother's Maiden Name:**

Sex	Children's Names in Full		Day Month Year	City, Town or Place	County or Province, etc.	State or Country	Add. Info on Children
M	1. William Oscar Moore	Birth	31-5-1852		Kendall Co.	Ill.	Killed by a street car
		Marr.					
	Spouse: Louise M. Adams	Death	17-9-1921	Whitewater	Butler Co.	Kans.	
		Burial	19-9-1921	Potwin	Butler Co.	Kans.	
M	2. Richard Edgar Moore	Birth	3-7-1854		Chatauqua Co.	Kans.	
		Marr.	1-1-1882	Cariboo	Butler Co.	Kans.	
	Spouse: Eunice E. Adams	Death	21-1-1934				
		Burial	1-1934				
M	3. John Edward Moore	Birth	1-8-1857		Chatauqua Co.	Kans.	12 yrs. 1 mo. 12 days
		Marr.					
		Death	22-9-1869	Potwin	Butler Co.	Kans.	
		Burial	9-1869	Shaffer cem. Potwin Butler Co.			
M	4. James Monroe Moore	Birth	26-10-1859	near Lawrence	Douglas Co.	Ks.	
		Marr.	17-8-1884	Elgin	Chatauqua Co.	Kans.	
	Spouse: Julia Bell Smith	Death	20-7-1954	Elgin	Chatauqua Co.	Kans.	
		Burial	7-1954	Oak Grove cem. Elgin, Kans.			
F	5. Melissa Rebecca M.	Birth	19-12-1862		Douglas Co.	Kans.	
		Marr.	4-7-1881	Elgin	Chatauqua Co.	Kans.	
	Spouse: John Taylor	Death	30-5-1923	Berryville	Carroll Co.	Ark.	
		Burial	5-1923	Altoona	Wilson Co.	Kansas	
F	6. Sarah Louise Moore	Birth	26-7-1866		Chautauqua Co.	Kansas	
		Marr.	6-2-1885				
	Spouse: William L. Smith	Death	15-2-1889	Elgin	Chautauqua Co.	Kansas	
		Burial	2-1889	Oak Grove Cem. Elgin, Kans.			
F	7. Etta Ellen Moore	Birth	27-10-1874		Butler Co.	Kans.	
		Marr.	14-3-1893	Altoona	Wilson Co.	Kans.	
	Spouse: George Alan Wiley	Death	3-10-1945	Dewey	Washington Co.	Okla.	
		Burial	10-1945	Altoona	Wilson Co.	Kans.	

Reuben Moore - uniform in Civil War, 1884.

Reuben Moore and Melvina Barbara Paul

Deed to this place

INDEX DEEDS.

Time of Reception.	NAME OF GRANTOR.	NAME OF GRANTEE.	Nature of Instrum
No. 1358	Receiver's Office at Augusta Kan Nov 15th 1871. Received from Samuel K. Hall of Butler County Kansas the sum of Two Hundred dollars and —— cents being in full for the South East quarter of Section No. 19 in Township No. 28 South of Range 4 East containing 160 acres and — Hundredths at $1.25 per acre		
$200	W. A. Shannon Receiver		
State of Kansas Butler County } SS	This Instrument was filed for Record on the 11th day of March A.D. 1874 at 4½ O'clock P.M. and duly recorded		
Final Receiver's Receipt No. 297	Homestead. Receiver's Office Wichita Kansas March 4, 1874. Application No. 2163		
	Received of Reuben Moore the sum of four dollars — cents being the second half of compensation of Register and Receiver and balance of payment required by law for the entry of South ½ of North East ¼ and North ½ of South East ¼ Section 19 in Township 28 S of Range 3 E containing 160 acres under the acts of Congress approved May 20 1862 and March 21 1864 entitled "An Act to secure Homesteads to actual settlers on the public domain."		
$4	J. C. Redfield Receiver		
State of Kansas Butler County } SS	This instrument was filed for record on the 14th day of March A.D. 1874 at 4½ O'clock P.M. and duly recorded		

He paid 0.83 cents a Acre
240 Acres.

WARRANTY DEED. Walnut Valley Times Print.

This Deed, Made this twenty-sixth day of April in the year of our Lord One Thousand Eight Hundred and Seventy-seven between Melvina B. Moore and Reuben Moore of Murdock Twp, County of Butler, and State of Kansas of the first part, and William A. Moore of Murdock Twp, County of Butler and State of Kansas, of the second part: WITNESSETH, that the said party of the first part, for and in consideration of the sum of Eight Hundred Dollars, to them in hand paid by the said party of the second part, the receipt whereof is hereby acknowledged, do by these presents Grant, Bargain, Sell, Remise, Release, Alien Convey and Confirm unto the said party of the second part, and to his heirs and assigns forever, all of the following described tract, piece, and parcel of land, lying and situate in the County of Butler, and State of Kansas, to-wit:

The South half of the South West quarter of Section One Twelve, in Township No. Twenty-eight (28) South of Range No. Three (3) East of the Sixth Prin. Mer. Containing Eighty acres, more or less by Government Survey

Together with all and singular, the hereditaments and appurtenances thereunto belonging, or in anywise appertaining: To Have and to Hold the same unto the said party of the second part, his heirs and assigns, forever. And the said Melvina B. Moore and Reuben Moore for themselves and their heirs, do hereby covenant and agree to and with the said party of the second part, his heirs and assigns, that they will Warrant and forever Defend the same lands and appurtenances, and every part and parcel thereof unto the said party of the second part, his heirs and assigns, against the said party of the first part, and their heirs, and against all and every person or persons whomsoever, lawfully claiming or to claim the same.

IN TESTIMONY WHEREOF, the said party of the first part have hereunto set their hands, the day and year first above written.

Executed and Delivered in the Presence of
John ... Snee
Mary C. ...

Melvina B. Moore (SEAL)
Reuben Moore (SEAL)

STATE OF KANSAS, County of Butler, SS.

Be it Remembered, That on this 26th day of April A. D. 1877 before me, the undersigned, a Justice of the Peace in and for the County and State aforesaid came Melvina B. Moore and Reuben Moore who are personally known to me to be the same persons who executed the foregoing instrument of writing and duly acknowledged the execution of the same.

In Testimony Whereof, I have hereunto set my hand and affixed my official seal, the day and year last above written.

M. C. ..., J.P.

STATE OF ILLINOIS, KENDALL COUNTY, ss.

Certificate of Record of Marriage.

I, William Hall Clerk of the County Court of said County, hereby certify that Mr. Reuben Moore was married to Miss Melvina B. Pau... in said County on the twenty third day of August A. D. 1851 by Josiah Lehman a Justice of the Peace duly authorized to solemnize marriages by the Statute of the State of Illinois, as appears by his return and certificate of marriage attached to the license granted therefor by the Clerk of this Court, and now on file in my office.

In Witness Whereof, I have hereunto subscribed my name and attached the seal of said County Court, at my Office in Yorkville, this 24th day of July A. D. 1895

Wm Hall
Clerk of the County Court

In Memoriam

Grandma Moore who saw a vast change wrought thru her nearly a century of living in this old world, just grew tired of trying to live so the beats of her weary-worn heart grew fainter thru the weeks of her convalescence, until they ceased altogether Thursday morning of last week.

She had lived her life to the fullest and richest; she had accomplished her mission on earth and was ready for a new Home and a new life. For over 96 years she walked upon the earth, courageously and faithfully, never faltering in her trust of a Heavenly Father to watch over her and to care for her. She possessed a volume of sparkling wit—she was ever ready with an answer that stumped you. She was loved and loving; she was sincere and steadfast always; she was a devoted mother thru all those years.

She was tiny in stature but she had a mighty spirit. She believed in decency—the old-fashioned kind she knew and grew up with; she believed in doing for those in need; she loved her church and its work; and she loved her home and all of its sorrows and joys. But as the years rolled by, Lovisa Moore saw the buggy days pass away into the coming of cars and airplanes; she saw radio and television both brought into reality; she saw the changing fashions of men and women, and the changing morals of a war-torn world. In fact she lived thru the Civil War, the Spanish-American War, two World Wars and the Korean conflict, but thru it all she ever remained loyal and held steadfast to the love of a dying Saviour's promise of eternal life. Above her lavendar clad body

Mother's great great grandfather came from Scotland and was shipwrecked five miles off shore. He had his money belt strapped around his waist. He swam ashore and there he found a woman washing clothes. He gave her five dollars for some clothes.

Her people (don"t know which one) homesteaded the land where Chicago now stands. They were quite wealthy, one night a burglar placed a ladder to an upstairs window but when he reached his hand inside the window, one of the women cut his finger off with a sword.

Her great grandfather, Reuben Moore helped the negro slaves to escape on their way north by helping them to hide and feeding them.

(found in family Bible by Eva Moore)

Family Group Sheet

Husband's Full Name: William Oscar Moore — Chart No.

	Day Month Year	City, Town or Place	County or Province, etc.	State or Country	Add. Info on Husband
Birth	31-5-1852		Kendall Co.	Ill.	killed by a street car
Chr'nd					
Marr	16-4-1876	Towanda	Butler Co.	Kans.	
Death	17-9-1921	Whitewater	Butler Co.	Kans.	
Burial	9-1921	Shaffer cem.	Butler Co.	Kans.	

Places of Residence:
Occupation: Farmer Church Affiliation: Christian Military Rec:

His Father: Reuben Moore Mother's Maiden Name: Melvina Barbara Paul

Wife's Full Maiden Name: Louisa M. Adams

	Day Month Year	City, Town or Place	County or Province, etc.	State or Country	Add. Info on Wife
Birth	28-9-1856		Grundy Co.	Ill.	
Chr'nd					
Death	26-2-1953	ElDorado	Butler Co.	Kans.	
Burial	2-1953	Shaffer cem. Potwin	Butler Co.	Kans.	

Places of Residence:
Occupation: Housewife Church Affiliation: Christian Military Rec:

Her Father: David Adams Mother's Maiden Name: J. Sarah Ky.

Sex	Children's Names in Full		Day Month Year	City, Town or Place	County or Province, etc.	State or Country	Add. Info on Children
M	1. E. William Moore	Birth	1877				17 yrs. old
		Marr.					
	Full Name of Spouse	Death	1894				
		Burial		Shaffer cem.	Butler Co.	Kans.	
F	2. Effie Sarah Moore	Birth	27-6-1879				
		Marr.					
	Full Name of Spouse	Death	8-1977	Boise	Ada Co.	Idaho	
	#1 Corter #2 Pickrell	Burial	8-1977	Enid	Garfield Co.	Okla.	
M	3. Leon Arthur Moore	Birth	11-10-1883	Potwin	Butler Co.	Kans.	
		Marr.					
	Full Name of Spouse "Millie" Nellie Metz	Death	18-10-1969	Wichita	Sedgwick Co.	Kans.	
		Burial	10-1969		South Haven	Kans.	
M	4. Reuben David Moore	Birth	12-11-1886	Murdock Township	Butler Co.	Ks.	
		Marr.	12-2-1908	Potwin	Butler Co.	Kans.	
	Full Name of Spouse	Death	14-4-1963	ElDorado	Butler Co.	Kans.	
	Edith L Taylor	Burial	4-1963	Towando cem.	Butler Co.	Kansas	
M	5. Orin Edgar Moore	Birth	29-11-1888	Potwin	Butler Co.	Kans.	
		Marr.	3-3-1913	Potwin	Butler Co.	Kans.	
	Full Name of Spouse	Death	9-8-1982	Newton	Harvey	Kans.	
	Susan May Keys	Burial	8-1982	Whitewater cem.	Butler co.	Ks.	
M	6. Elmer Moore	Birth	1891	Potwin	Butler Co.	Kans.	Dipthera
		Marr.					
	Full Name of Spouse	Death	1967	Potwin	Butler Co.	Kans.	
		Burial	1967	Shaffer cem. Potwin	Butler Co.		
F	7. Ruth Moore	Birth	1893	Potwin	Butler Co.	Kans.	3 yrs. old when died Dipthera
		Marr.					
	Full Name of Spouse	Death	1908	Potwin	Butler Co.	Kans.	
		Burial	1908	Shaffer cem. Potwin	Butler Co.	Ks.	
M	8. Raymond I. Moore	Birth	3-4-1896	Potwin	Butler Co.	Kans.	
		Marr.	10-1-1917	Potwin	Butler Co.	Kans.	
	Full Name of Spouse	Death	18-12-1979	Newton	Harvey Co.	Kans.	
	Vida M. Maxwell	Burial	12-1979	Pleasant View cem.		Kans.	

Guardians Deed

This Indenture Made this 7" day of October AD 1887 between W.O. Moore guardian of Ettie E Moore minor heir of Reuben Moore of Chautauqua County and State of Kansas deceased of the first part and W. D. Stallard of Chautauqua County and State of Kansas of the second part Witnesseth That said party of the first part by virtue of an order of sale issued out of the Probate Court of Chautauqua County in the State of Kansas and dated the 19" day of September AD 1887 has sold to W.D. Stallard the Real property hereinafter described in conformity with said order and sale thereof confirmed as required by law and in conformity with the provisions of the acts of the legislature of the State of Kansas entitled "An Act concerning Guardians and Wards." approved February 29 1868 and "An Act regulating Executors and Administrators and the Settlement of the estates of deceased Persons" approved February 28 1868 and in consideration of the sum of ($200) Two Hundred Dollars (the same being more than three fourths of the appraised value of said real property.) the receipt of which is hereby acknowledged does by these presents Grant Bargain Sell And Convey unto the said party of the second part his heirs and assigns forever all the right title and interest of said minor in and to all the following described real estate situated in the County of Chautauqua and State of Kansas to wit

The South half (½) of the South West quarter (¼) and the South West quarter (¼) of the South East quarter (¼) all in Section No Five (5) Township No Thirty Five (35) South of Range No Eleven (11) East of 6" P.M. Chautauqua County Kansas

To Have and to Hold the above granted premises together with the appurtenances and every part thereof unto the said party of the second part his heirs and assigns forever And the said party of the first part do hereby covenant with the said party of the second part his heirs and assigns that he has in all things observed the requirements of law and of all orders in and concerning said sale

In Witness Whereof the said party of the first part has hereunto set his hand and seal the day and year first above written.

Signed sealed and acknowledged in presence of H. Kilmer
W.R. Hillman,

W.O. Moore Guardian (Seal)

State of Kansas Chautauqua Co ss.

Be it Remembered That on this 7th day of October A.D. 1887 before me the undersigned a Probate Judge in and for said County and State came W.O. Moore Guardian of the person and estate of Ettie E. Moore minor heir of Reuben Moore deceased who is personally known to me to be the same person who executed the within instrument of writing and such person duly acknowledged

William Oscar Moore was born in Kendall Co. Ill. May 31, 18..
Departed this life Sept. 17, 192..
Aged 69 yrs. 3 mo. and 17 d..
He with his parents moved to Douglass Co., Kans. in the fall of '58. In the fall of '68 he moved to Butler county, Kansas where he grew to manhood and was united in marriage to Louisa M. Adams of Towanda Kansas on April 16, 1876. To this union were born 10 children. Two sons and three daughters having preceeded him to the Great Beyond. Those left to mourn his departure are his wife Louisa M. Moore of Whitewater Kans., 4 sons, Arthur and Ruby, of Potwin Kansas, Orin of Whitewater and Ray of Maize, one daughter Effie Courter of Enid Okla., one grand daughter Hazel Newcom who has made her home with her grandparents from infancy and 16 other grand children. Also 2 brothers and 2 sisters, Edgar of Herring, Okla., Monroe of Elgin Okla., Etta Wiley of Dewey Okla., all of whom are present and Melissa Taylor of Holly Colo.

He united with the Christian church at Golden Gate in the spring of 1878 and from then to the time of his death has lived true christian life.

The funeral service was held from the Christian church here Tuesday afternoon at 2 o'clock conducted by Rev. Higdon and Rev. Guinty of Whitewater. It was one of the largest, if not the largest funeral ever held from the Christion church in Potwin. Mr. Moore was well known and respected by scores of friends and neighbors in this vicinity and Whitewater.

W. O. MOORE KILLED IN AUTO ACCIDENT AT WICHITA

Onr city and community were shocked and saddened by the news that came over the wires Saturday evening that W. O. Moore was seriously injured and died in a Wichita hospital. The accident happened at 3:30 p. m. at the Thirteenth street crossing, the automobile he was in was struck by an interurban car and totally demolished. His son, Ray, who was driving, escaped without injury.

The body of Mr. Moore was brought up from Wichita on the Rock Island No. 12 Monday morning.

Mr. Moore was well known and very highly esteemed, an old Butler County settler, always took part in public affairs in and around Whitewater. The 80 that he owned in Murdock township he bought in the year 1876, all this section of Butler County clear to Marion County line was then known as Towanda township. Mr. Moore came to this county with his parents from Iowa and was about 60 years old. His son, Ray, who was with him in the accident is 25.

His wife and five children are left to mourn ... Effie Courter, Lahoma, Oklahoma; Arthur Moore, South Haven; Reuben and Oren, Whitewater; and Ray, Benton.

The Furley State Bank suffered from a yegg gang early Sunday morning, the robbers carrying off about $350 worth of bonds and securities which were in the safety deposit boxes. A severe battering of the safe failed to gain entrance for the yeggs and the several thousand dollars waited for an expert safe opener to bring it out for the business of the bank. The job looks like the same kind that was pulled off at Andover last Thursday night.

broken. The Senior girls seemed have a typical look that took ... Freshman boys eye for everyone ... a gasp of astonishment when the Sen... girls started home with a Freshm... boy dangling on their arm. Many ... the Junior girls thot they had infatu... the Freshman boys but the Senior gi... looks were too facinating.

The next morning the faculty se... to have a sad look and when they w... asked what was the matter they p... dicted that they were afraid that ... Senior girls would be a victim of ... "matermonial dispepsy" and wo... pass away from H. S. before May 2...

OBITUARY.

William Oscar Moore was born Kendall County, Illinois, May 31, 18... Departed this life September 17th, 19... aged 69 years, 3 months and 17 days.

He, with his parents, moved to Douglass County, Kansas, in the fall of '5... In the spring of '68, they moved ... Butler County, Kansas, here he grew ... manhood and was united in marriage ... Lovisa Adams of Towenda, Kansas, o... April ..., 1876. To this union were bor... ... preceeded to the Grea... Beyond. The living are: four sons Arthur and Ruby, of Potwin, Kansas Orin of Whitewater and Ray of Maize Kansas; one daughter, Effie Courter of Enid, Oklahoma, and granddaughter Hazel Newcom who ... made her home with her grandparents from infancy also sixteen other grandchildren.

He also leaves two brothers, Edgar Moore of Herring, Oklahoma, and Monroe Moore of Elgin, Kansas; two sisters, Mrs. Etta Wiley of Dewey, Oklahoma, all of whom were present, and Mrs. Melissa Taylor of Holly, Colorado.

He united with the Christian Church at Golden Gate in the spring of 1878, and from then to the time of his death, has lived a True Christian life.

Family Group Sheet

page 2

Husband's Full Name: William Oscar Moore   Chart No. ___

	Day Month Year	City, Town or Place	County or Province, etc.	State or Country	Add. Info on Husband
Birth	31-5-1852		Kendall Co.	Ill.	killed by a street car
Chr'nd					
Marr	16-4-1876	Towanda	Butler Co.	Kans.	
Death	17-9-1921	Whitewater	Butler Co.	Kans.	
Burial	9-1921	Shaffer cem.	Butler Co.	Kans.	

Places of Residence:
Occupation: Farmer   Church Affiliation: Christian   Military Rec:

His Father: Reuben Moore   Mother's Maiden Name: Melvina Barbara Paul

Wife's Full Maiden Name: Louisa M. Adams

	Day Month Year	City, Town or Place	County or Province, etc.	State or Country	Add. Info. on Wife
Birth	28-9-1856		Grundy Co.	Ill.	
Chr'nd					
Death	26-2-1953	ElDorado	Butler Co.	Kans.	
Burial	2-1953	Shaffer cem. Potwin	Butler Co.	Kans.	

Places of Residence:
Occupation: Housewife   Church Affiliation: Christian   Military Rec:

Her Father: David Adams   Mother's Maiden Name: J. Sarah (Ky.)

Sex	Children's Names		Day Month Year	City, Town or Place	County or Province, etc.	State or Country	Add. Info on Children
9	Infant	Birth	1899	Potwin	Butler Co.	Kans.	
		Marr.					
	Full Name of Spouse	Death	1899				
		Burial		Shaffer cem. Potwin Butler Co.			
10	Olive Moore	Birth	1881				
		Marr.					died in child birth
	Full Name of Spouse	Death	22-3-1902				
	Boyd Newcomb	Burial					

William Oscar Moore

W. Oscar Moore, a prominent farmer and stockman of Murdock township, is a member of one of Butler county's old pioneer families. He was born in Kendall county, Illinois, in May, 1852. His parents were Reuben and Minerva (Paul) Moore, both natives of Illinois. In the early days the family went from Illinois to Iowa and from there to Texas, and thence to Missouri. In 1857 they settled in Douglass county in the Territory of Kansas. This was four years before Kansas was admitted to the Union. After remaining in Douglass county for ten years, the family removed to Butler county in 1867, settling in Murdock county, being among the very first settlers of that section, and here the father engaged in farming and stock raising and spent the remainder of his life. To Reuben and Minerva (Paul) Moore were born the following children: Edgar, Lawton, Okla.; J. Monroe, Elgin, Kans.; W. Oscar, the subject of this sketch; Mrs. Melissa Taylor, Toronto, Kans., and Mrs. Etta Wiley, Altoona, Kans.

842 HISTORY OF BUTLER COUNTY

W. Oscar Moore grew to manhood on his father's farm in Murdock township and started in life for himself by purchasing eighty acres of land from his father in 1876. He immediately began work on his new place, breaking out a little prairie during the summer of the first year and then he was compelled to sell his team in order to get money to build a little house and live during the winter. The next year he had a good crop of wheat, although he had but seven acres. This gave him a start and since that time he has met with unvarying success and is one of the substantial men of Murdock township.

Mr. Moore was married in April, 1872, to Miss Louisa Adams, a daughter of David and Sarah Adams. The Adams family consisted of the parents and three children, as follows: Mrs. Lavina Turner, of Wichita; Elmer, Duncan, Okla., and the wife of W. Oscar Moore, the subject of this sketch. To Mr. and Mrs. Moore have been born five children, as follows: Mrs. Effie Courter, Tahoma, Okla.; Arthur, South Haven, Kans.; Reuben, Whitewater, Kans.; Orin, Whitewater, Kans., and Ray, Benton, Kans. Hazel Newcomb, a granddaughter of Mr. and Mrs. Moore, makes her home with them and is attending school. The members of the Moore family are well known and highly respected and number among the leading citizens of the locality where they reside.

Family Group Sheet

Husband's Full Name Boyd Newcomb — **Chart No.**

	Day	Month	Year	City, Town or Place	County or Province, etc.	State or Country	Add. Info on Husband
Birth							
Chr'nd							
Marr							
Death							
Burial							

Places of Residence

Occupation — Church Affiliation — Military Rec

His Father — Mother's Maiden Name

Wife's Full Maiden Name Olive Moore

	Day	Month	Year	City, Town or Place	County or Province, etc.	State or Country	Add. Info on Wife
Birth			1881				died of child birth
Chr'nd							
Death	22	3	1902				
Burial							

Places of Residence

Occupation — Church Affiliation — Military Rec

Her Father: William Oscar Moore — Mother's Maiden Name: M. Louisa Moore

Sex	Children's Names		Day	Month	Year	City, Town or Place	County or Province, etc.	State or Country	Add. Info on Children
F	1 Hazel Newcomb	Birth	22	3	1902				
	Full Name of Spouse: Witt	Marr.							
		Death							
		Burial							

In Loving Remembrance of
Mrs. Boyd Newcom,
Died March 22, 1902.
Age 21 yrs. 6 mos. 6 days.

Gone but not forgotten

'Tis hard to break the tender cord
When love has bound the heart;
'Tis hard, so hard, to speak the words
"We must forever part."
Dearest loved one, we must lay thee
In the peaceful grave's embrace,
But thy memory will be cherished
Till we see thy heavenly face.

Olive Moore Newcomb

Hazel and Boyd Newcomb

Family Group Sheet

Husband's Full Name Earl Chester Witt **Chart No.**

	Day	Month	Year	City, Town or Place	County or Province, etc.	State or Country	Add. Info on Husband
Birth							
Chr'nd							
Marr							
Death							
Burial							

Places of Residence

Occupation **Church Affiliation** **Military Rec**

His Father **Mother's Maiden Name** Olive

Wife's Full Maiden Name Hazel Newcomb

	Day	Month	Year	City, Town or Place	County or Province, etc.	State or Country	Add. Info. on Wife
Birth	22	3	1902				
Chr'nd							
Death							
Burial							

Places of Residence

Occupation **Church Affiliation** **Military Rec**

Her Father Boyd Newcomb **Mother's Maiden Name** Olive Moore

Sex	Children's Names in Full	Day	Month	Year	City, Town or Place	County or Province, etc.	State or Country	Add. Info on Children

Husband's Full Name

Address

City, State, Zip

Date

Family Group Sheet
Clarence Courter

Husband's Full Name — Chart No.

	Day Month Year	City, Town or Place	County or Province, etc.	State or Country	Add. Info. on Husband
Birth	5-12-1960	LaHoma Enid	Garfield Co.	Okla.	
Chr'nd					
Marr	1923	Enid	Garfield Co.	Okla.	
Death	4 - 1981	Santa Rosa	Sonoma	Calif.	
Burial	1981				

Places of Residence: Riverside-Healdsburg-Santa Rosa-California
Occupation: Lumberman

His Father: Robert Courter
Mother's Maiden Name: Effie Sarah Moore

Wife's Full Maiden Name Edna G. Smart

	Day Month Year	City, Town or Place	County or Province, etc.	State or Country	Add. Info. on Wife
Birth	1900	Anthony	Harper Co.	Kansas	
Chr'nd					
Death	1958	Fresno	Fresno Co.	Calif.	
Burial					

Places of Residence: Riverside, California
Occupation: Teacher

Her Father:
Mother's Maiden Name:

Sex	Children's Names in Full		Day Month Year	City, Town or Place	County or Province, etc	State or Country	Add. Info. on Children
M	1 Max Courter	Birth	1924	Enid	Garfield Co.	Okla.	
		Marr.	1949				
	Spouse: Dorothy Mehling	Death					
		Burial					
F	2 Doris Tea Courter	Birth	1927	Enid	Garfield Co.	Okla.	
		Marr.	1950				
	Spouse: Bruce Wilson	Death					
		Burial					
	3	Birth					
		Marr.					
		Death					
		Burial					

Effie S. Moore and Robert Courter

Freda - Cecil
Courters
Clarence - Kenneth

Family Group Sheet

Husband's Full Name: Max Courter
Chart No.

Husband's Data	Day Month Year	City, Town or Place	County or Province, etc.	State or Country	Add. Info on Husband
Birth	1924	Enid	Garfield Co.	Okla.	
Chr'nd					
Marr	1949	Fresno	Fresno Co.	Calif.	
Death					
Burial					

Places of Residence: Riverside-Healdsburg-Santa Rosa, California
Occupation: Lumberman **Church Affiliation:** **Military Rec:** US Army 1942-1945
His Father: Clarence Courter **Mother's Maiden Name:** Edna Smart

Wife's Full Maiden Name: Dorothy Mehling

Wife's Data	Day Month Year	City, Town or Place	County or Province, etc.	State or Country	Add. Info on Wife
Birth	1924	Fresno	Fresno, Co.	Calif.	
Chr'nd					
Death					
Burial					

Places of Residence: Fresno-Santa Rosa, California
Occupation: Teacher **Church Affiliation:** **Military Rec:**
Her Father: Conrad Mehling **Mother's Maiden Name:** Margaret Seiler

Sex	Children's Names in Full	Children's Data	Day Month Year	City, Town or Place	County or Province, etc.	State or Country	Add. Info on Child
M	1. Ross Courter / Spouse: Renee Ebejer	Birth	1960	Santa Rosa	Sonoma Co.	Calif.	
F	2. Susan Courter / Spouse: John Wertz	Birth	1952	Healdsburg	Sonoma Co.	Calif.	
F	3. Denise Courter / Spouse: Dennis Scott	Birth	1950	Healdsburg	Sonoma Co.	Calif.	

Family Group Sheet

Husband's Full Name: Robert Courter   **Chart No.**

	Day Month Year	City, Town or Place	County or Province, etc.	State or Country	Add. Info. on Husband
Birth	9- 1-1872	Saranac	Ionia Co.	Michigan	
Chr'nd					
Marr.	30- 5-1897	Murdock		Kansas	
Death	30- 8-1935	Enid	Garfield Co.	Okla.	
Burial	8-1935	Enid	Garfield Co.	Okla.	

Places of Residence:
Occupation: Farmer   Church Affiliation: Military Rec:

His Father: John A. Courter   **Mother's Maiden Name:** Maggie McCloud

Wife's Full Maiden Name: Effie Sarah Moore   S.S. 318-82--1860

	Day Month Year	City, Town or Place	County or Province, etc.	State or Country	Add. Info. on Wife
Birth	27-6-1878	Whitewater	Butler Co.	Kansas	
Chr'nd					
Death	7- 8-1977	Boise	Ada Co.	Idaho	83702
Burial	8-1977	Enid	Garfield Co.	Oklahoma	

Places of Residence:
Occupation: Housewife   Church Affiliation: Military Rec:
Other husbands: George Pickell

Her Father: William Oscar Moore   **Mother's Maiden Name:** M. Louvisa Adams

Sex	Children's Names in Full		Day Month Year	City, Town or Place	County or Province, etc.	State or Country	Add. Info. on Children
M	1 556-10-6533 Cecil Courter	Birth	27- 7-1898	LaHoma	Garfield Co.	Okla.	
	Full Name of Spouse: Ruth Linden	Marr.					
		Death	27- 8-1990				
		Burial					
M	2 358-10-6428 Clarence Courter	Birth	5-12-1900	LaHoma	Garfield Co.	Okla.	Healdsberg 95448 Calif.
	Full Name of Spouse:	Marr.					
		Death	4- 1981				
		Burial					
F	3 Freda Courter	Birth	26- 6-1904	LaHoma	Garfield Co.	Okla.	
	Full Name of Spouse: Forrest F. Zirkle	Marr.	2 -10-1927	LaHoma	Garfield Co.	Okla.	
		Death					
		Burial					
M	4 353-07-1520 Kenneth Courter	Birth	25-12-1905	LaHoma	Garfield Co.	Okla.	Roseburg, Ca 97470
	Full Name of Spouse:	Marr.					
		Death	12- 1981				
		Burial					
	5	Birth					

Family Group Sheet

Husband's Full Name: Cecil Courter — Chart No.

	Day Month Year	City, Town or Place	County or Province, etc.	State or Country	Add. Info on Husband
Birth	27-7-1898	LaHoma	Garfield Co.	Okla.	
Chr'nd					
Marr					
Death	27-8-1990				
Burial	1990				

Places of Residence:
Occupation: — Church Affiliation: — Military Rec:

His Father: Robert Courter   **Mother's Maiden Name:** Effie Sarah Moore

Wife's Full Maiden Name: Ruth Linden

	Day Month Year	City, Town or Place	County or Province, etc.	State or Country	Add. Info on Wife
Birth					
Chr'nd					
Death					
Burial					

Places of Residence:
Occupation: — Church Affiliation: — Military Rec:

Her Father: — **Mother's Maiden Name:**

Sex	Children's Names in Full		Day Month Year	City, Town or Place	County or Province, etc.	State or Country	Add. Info on Children
1		Birth					
		Marr.					
	Full Name of Spouse	Death					
		Burial					
2		Birth					
		Marr.					
	Full Name of Spouse	Death					
		Burial					
3		Birth					
		Marr.					
	Full Name of Spouse	Death					
		Burial					
4		Birth					
		Marr.					

State of Kansas, Butler County. OFFICE OF PROBATE JUDGE OF SAID COUNTY.

BE IT REMEMBERED, That on the 29th day of May A.D. 1897, there was issued from the office of said Probate Judge, a Marriage License, of which the following is a true copy:

MARRIAGE LICENSE.

El Dorado, Butler County. State of Kansas, May 29th A.D. 1897

To any Person Authorized by Law to Perform the Marriage Ceremony—Greeting:

You are hereby authorized to join in Marriage Robert H. Courter of Butler County Kans aged 26 and Effie Moor of Butler County Kans aged 19 and of this License you will make due return to my office within thirty days. (SEAL) J.M. Caudell Probate Judge

And which said Marriage License was afterwards, to wit: on the 13th day of June A.D. 1897, returned to said Probate Judge, with the following Certificate endorsed thereon, to wit:

State of Kansas, Butler County, ss.

I, Clergyman Christian Church do hereby certify, that in accordance with the authorization of the within License, I did, on the 30th day of May A.D. 1897, at Bride's Home in said County, join and unite in Marriage the within named Robert H. Courter and Effie Moon

WITNESS MY HAND and seal the day and year above written.

Attest: J. Mooney
Probate Judge   Clergyman

---

interest *** Aunt Effie was finding herself feeling a bit low Sunday—and was as low as one could get—on the floor, the telephone rang and her daughter's voice came over the wires from Pendleton, Oregon. After talking to her daughter Aunt Effie says she felt so much better because just talking oft times with loved ones when blue or lonely, it helps to raise those depressing clouds and the sun of love and tenderness comes shining thru.
F.M.P

Family Group Sheet

Husband's Full Name Kenneth Courter (SS553-07=1520)   Chart No.

	Day Month Year	City, Town or Place	County or Province, etc.	State or Country	Add. Info on Husband
Birth	25-12-1905	LaHoma	Garfield Co.	Okla.	
Chr'nd					
Marr					
Death	1981				
Burial					

Places of Residence
Occupation   Church Affiliation   Military Rec
Other wives, if any, No. (1)(2) etc. Make separate sheet for each marr.
His Father   ,   Mother's Maiden Name

Wife's Full Maiden Name

	Day Month Year	City, Town or Place	County or Province, etc.	State or Country	Add. Info. on Wife
Birth					
Chr'nd					
Death					
Burial					

Places of Residence
Occupation   Church Affiliation   Military Rec
Other husbands, if any, No. (1)(2) etc. Make separate sheet for each marr.
Her Father   Mother's Maiden Name

Sex	Children's Names in Full		Day Month Year	City, Town or Place	County or Province, etc.	State or Country	Add. Info on Children
	1	Birth					
		Marr.					
	Full Name of Spouse	Death					
		Burial					
	2 Full Name						
	3 Full Name						
	4 Full Name						
	5 Full Name						
	6 Full Name						
	7 Full Name						
	8	Birth					
		Marr.					
	Full Name of Spouse	Death					
		Burial					

Compiler   Notes
Address
City, State, Zip
Date

Family Group Sheet

Husband's Full Name: Forrest Zirkle — **Chart No.**

	Day Month Year	City, Town or Place	County or Province, etc.	State or Country	Add. Info on Husband
Birth	27-10-1905	LaHoma	Garfield Co.	Okla.	
Chr'nd					
Marr	2-10-1927	LaHoma	Garfield Co.	Okla.	
Death					
Burial					

Places of Residence

Occupation: Lumber-Bowling   Church Affiliation   Military Rec

His Father: Bert Zirkle   **Mother's Maiden Name:** Malinda Mae Kitchen

Wife's Full Maiden Name: Freda Courter

	Day Month Year	City, Town or Place	County or Province, etc.	State or Country	Add. Info on Wife
Birth	26-6-1904	LaHoma	Garfield Co.	Okla.	
Chr'nd					
Death					
Burial					

Places of Residence

Occupation: Bookkeeper   Church Affiliation   Military Rec

Her Father: Robert Courter   **Mother's Maiden Name:** Effie Sarah Moore

Sex	Children's Names in Full		Day Month Year	City, Town or Place	County or Province, etc.	State or Country	Add. Info on Children
F	1. Joyce Ellen Zirkle	Birth	11-12-1929	Enid	Garfield Co.	Okla.	
		Marr.	1-2-1953	LaHoma	Garfield Co.	Okla.	
	Full Name of Spouse: Edward V. Whyde	Death					
		Burial					
F	2. Suzanne Zirkle	Birth	24-7-1932	Enid	Garfield Co.	Okla.	4 yrs. old
		Marr.					
	Full Name of Spouse	Death	4-1936	Enid	Garfield Co.	Okla.	
		Burial	4-1936	Enid	Garfield Co.	Okla.	
M	3. Jay Robert Zirkle	Birth	2-5-1936	Enid	Garfield Co.	Okla.	
		Marr.	1-3-1958	Pendleton	Umatilla Co.	Oregon	
	Full Name of Spouse: Kellie Jay Overholt	Death					
		Burial					

Freda Courter Zirkle

Family Group Sheet

Husband's Full Name: Edward V. Whyde

Chart No. —

	Day Month Year	City, Town or Place	County or Province, etc.	State or Country	Add. Info on Husband
Birth	22-1-1926	Chicago	Cook Co.	Ill.	
Chr'nd					
Marr	1-2-1953	Pendleton	Umatilla Co.	Oregon	
Death					
Burial					

Places of Residence:
Occupation: Retired   Church Affiliation: Military Rec:

His Father: John Woycheese   **Mother's Maiden Name:** Adele

Wife's Full Maiden Name: Joyce Ellen Zirkle

	Day Month Year	City, Town or Place	County or Province, etc.	State or Country	Add. Info on Wife
Birth	11-12-1929	Enid	Garfield Co.	Oklahoma	
Chr'nd					
Death					
Burial					

Places of Residence:
Occupation: Retired   Church Affiliation: Military Rec:

Her Father: Forrest F. Zirkle   **Mother's Maiden Name:** Freda Courter

Sex	Children's Names		Day Month Year	City, Town or Place	County or Province, etc.	State or Country	Add. Info on Children
M	1. Gregory Whyde	Birth	23-1-1954	Salt Lake City	Salt Lake	Utah	
		Marr.	27-9-1986	Boise	Ada Co.	Idaho	
	Full Name of Spouse	Death					
	Cathie Whyde	Burial					
M	2. Michael Whyde	Birth	6-4-1957	Syracuse	Onadago Co.	New York	
		Marr.	2-9-1985				
	Full Name of Spouse: Terry Eller	Death					
		Burial					
	3.	Birth					
		Marr.					
	Full Name of Spouse	Death					
		Burial					
	4.	Birth					
		Marr.					
	Full Name of Spouse	Death					
		Burial					
	5.	Birth					
		Marr.					
	Full Name of Spouse	Death					
		Burial					
	6.	Birth					
		Marr.					
	Full Name of Spouse	Death					
		Burial					
	7.	Birth					
		Marr.					
	Full Name of Spouse	Death					
		Burial					
	8.	Birth					
		Marr.					
	Full Name of Spouse	Death					
		Burial					

Compiler:
Address: 711 North 19th St.
City, State, Zip: Boise, Idaho 83702
Date:

Notes:

Family Group Sheet

Husband's Full Name: Gregory Whyde — **Chart No.**

	Day Month Year	City, Town or Place	County or Province, etc.	State or Country	Add Info on Husband
Birth	23-1-1954	Salt Lake City	Salt Lake Co.	Utah	
Chr'nd					
Marr	27-9-1986	Boise	Ada Co.	Idaho	
Death					
Burial					

Places of Residence:
Occupation: Ast. Analyist Computer-related
Church Affiliation:
Military Rec:

His Father: Edward V. Whyde   **Mother's Maiden Name:** Joyce Ellen Zirkle

Wife's Full Maiden Name: Marie Woods

	Day Month Year	City, Town or Place	County or Province, etc.	State or Country	Add Info on Wife
Birth	31-1-1954	Jerome	Jerome Co.	Idaho	
Chr'nd					
Death					
Burial					

Places of Residence:
Occupation: Lawyer
Church Affiliation:
Military Rec:

Her Father: Robert Woods   **Mother's Maiden Name:** Eileen Billcrad

Sex	Children's Names in Full		Day Month Year	City, Town or Place	County or Province, etc.	State or Country	Add Info on Children
F	1 Gracelynn Whyde	Birth	24-10-1987	Boise	Ada Co.	Idaho	
	Full Name of Spouse	Marr					
		Death					
		Burial					
	2	Birth					

Family Group Sheet

Husband's Full Name: Michael Whyde — **Chart No.**

	Day Month Year	City, Town or Place	County or Province, etc.	State or Country	Add Info on Husband
Birth	6-4-1957	Syracuse	Onondago Co.	New York	
Chr'nd					
Marr	2-9-1985	Boise	Ada Co.	Idaho	
Death					
Burial					

Places of Residence:
Occupation: C P A
Church Affiliation:
Military Rec:

His Father: Edward V. Whyde   **Mother's Maiden Name:** Joyce Ellen Zirkle

Wife's Full Maiden Name: Terry Eller

	Day Month Year	City, Town or Place	County or Province, etc.	State or Country	Add Info on Wife
Birth	13-12-1956	Fort Atkinson	Jefferson Co.	Wisconsin	
Chr'nd					
Death					
Burial					

Places of Residence:
Occupation: Lawyer
Church Affiliation:
Military Rec:

Her Father: Benjamine Eller   **Mother's Maiden Name:** Cora Chamber

Sex	Children's Names in Full		Day Month Year	City, Town or Place	County or Province, etc.	State or Country	Add Info on Children
	1	Birth					
	Full Name of Spouse	Marr					
		Death					
		Burial					
	2	Birth					

Family Group Sheet

Husband's Full Name: Leon Arthur Moore s.s. 510-30-6??   **Chart No.**

	Day Month Year	City, Town or Place	County or Province, etc.	State or Country	Add. Info on Husband
Birth	17-4-1884	Benton	Butler Co.	Kans.	
Chr'd					
Marr.	1904	Potwin	Butler Co.	Kans.	
Death	18-10-1969	Wichita	Sedgewick Co.	Kans.	
Burial	10-1969	Rose Hill Cem.	South Haven	Kans.	

Places of Residence:
Occupation: Farmer   **Church Affiliation:**   **Military Rec:**
Other wives: #2 Martha Loomis died 1954 Wichita, Kans.
His Father: William Oscar Moore   **Mother's Maiden Name:** Lovisa Adams

Wife's Full Maiden Name: Nellie Mae Metz

	Day Month Year	City, Town or Place	County or Province, etc.	State or Country	Add. Info. on Wife
Birth	1887			Kans.	
Chr'd					
Death	7-1944	Wichita	Sedgewick Co.	Kans.	
Burial	7-1944	Rose Hill Cem.	South Haven	Kans.	

Places of Residence:
Occupation: Housewife   **Church Affiliation:**   **Military Rec:**
Her Father: **Mother's Maiden Name:**

Sex	Children's Names in Full		Day Month Year	City, Town or Place	County or Province, etc.	State or Country	Add. Info on Children
M	1 Floyd V. Moore	Birth	29-4-1906	Potwin	Butler	Kans.	
		Marr.	6-6-1935	Wichita	Sedgwick Co.	Kans.	
	Full Name of Spouse: Frances E. Whitney	Death	5-6-1995	Wichita	Sedgewick Co.	Kans.	
		Burial	8-6-1995	Jamesburg Park cem.		Kans.	
F	2 Zelma Elva Moore	Birth	8-11-1908	Syracuse	Hamilton Co.	Kans.	
		Marr.					
	Full Name of Spouse: William Henry Myers	Death	22-2-1998	Clearwater	Sedgwick Co.	Kans	
		Burial	24-2-1998				
M	3 Richard Donald M.	Birth	1-9-1913	Potwin	Butler Co.	Kans.	
		Marr.	28-8-1938	Douglas	Butler Co.	Kans.	
	Full Name of Spouse: Erma Lucille Kibbe	Death					
		Burial					
M	4 Raymond Moore	Birth	13-7-1915	S. Haven	Sumner Co.	Kans.	died of Whooping cough
		Marr.					
	Full Name of Spouse	Death	16-8-1916	S. Haven	Sumner Co.	Kans.	
		Burial	8-1916	S. Haven	Sumner Co.	Kans.	
F	5 Arlene Moore	Birth	1923				
		Marr.					
	Full Name of Spouse	Death	10-9-1933	Wichita	Sedgewick Co.	Kans.	killed when 10 yrs. old
		Burial	9-1933	S. Haven	Sumner Co.	Kans.	

Notes: Wife # 3 Edna Oneita Lanferman Kenny born March 15, 1893 Dexter Cowly Co. Ks death May 27, 1991 Wichita Sedgewick Co. Kansas

Arthur and Nellie

Names and Addresses of Surviving Relatives

Husband or Wife Living Yes Name Edna
Parents
Daughters Zelma Myers; Wichita

Sons Floyd Moore
      Richard Moore
2-deceased Raymond, Arlene

Sisters Effie Pickrell; Boise, Idaho

Brothers Ray Moore; Newton, Kansas
          Oran Moore; Whitewater, Kansas

Place of Funeral Culbertson Mortuary Chapel
Day Thursday Time 1:00 P.M. Date 10-16-19 69
Minister Rev. John E. Greenlee
          West Side Christian Church
Place of Burial or Removal Rose Hill Cemetary
South Haven, Kansas Date 19
Songs "Meet Me There"
       "How Great Thou Art"
Singers Bud Hansen
Accompanist Ada Whitcomb
Bearers 1. Wiley Clute   4. Earl Parker
         2. Bob Myers   5. Harold Wilhelm
         3. Don Moore   6. Howard Moore

Full Name Leon Arthur Moore
Residence 1229 S. Wichita
Place of Death Wichita Sedgwick St. Joseph Hos.
               City   County   Street or Hospital
Date of Birth 10-11-1883 Age 86 Yrs. Mo. Days
Birthplace Butler County, Kansas
Sex Male Color White Single Married Widowed Divorced
Military Record None
Occupation Retired Farmer
Work For
Social Security No. 510-30-6531-A
Name of Father Oscar Moore
Maiden Name of Mother Lavisa Adams
Deceased Came From Maize, as a farmer in 1929

Church Affiliation West Side Christian Church
Fraternal Orders None

Informant Floyd Moore
Date of Death October 14 1969 Hour 12:35 P.M.
Cause of Death (illegible)
Physician Dr. D. Trees
Additional Information

234 Year 13 Month

Names and addresses of surviving relatives:

wife Arthur Leon 61
Mrs. Hettie Metz - 709 S. Seneca
daughters Mrs. W. H. Myers - at home
          daughter Arlene Moore preceded her in death

sons Floyd - 1108 S. Martinson
      Richard - 228 S. Athenian
son Raymond preceded her in death

sisters Mrs. Oden Harris - Medicine Lodge, Ks.

Brothers Avery Metz - 150 S. Seneca
          Charlie Metz - Garden City, Ks.
          5 Grand-

Interment at Noon at 9 a.m.

This Information for Death Certificate and Newspapers

Full Name Nellie Mae Moore
Place of death Wesley
               County, Township, City, street or hospital
Residence 215 N. Vine How long at place of death 1 week
Military Record

Sex F Color W Single—Married, Widowed, Divorced
Occupation Housewife
           Filling Station for Gas & Gasoline & Oil
Date Last Worked at Same Total Years Spent at Same
Date of Birth Aug 7 1887 Age 56 years 7 months 1 days
Birthplace Near Benton (Butler Co.) Kansas
                          City   State
Name of Father Geo. Metz
Birthplace of Father Missouri
Maiden Name of Mother Hettie Main
Birthplace of Mother Oilmont Michigan
Deceased came from Whitewater & Potwin
                    community to Maize about
                    1927 to Wichita 1929
Was a member of what church W.S. Christian
What Fraternal Orders? Supt. of Beginners Dept.
                        Very good Sunday worker

Informant
Address

Medical Certificate
Date of Death 3-8-1944 Hour 10:00 P.M.
Cause of death
Physician Tihen
Address   Phone
Place of burial or removal S. Haven Date

Arthur

Family Group Sheet

Husband's Full Name: Floyd Virgil Moore SS 510-30-6584 Chart No.

	Day Month Year	City, Town or Place	County or Province, etc.	State or Country	Add. Info on Husband
Birth	29- 4-1906	Potwin	Butler Co.	Kans.	
Chr'nd	1915				
Marr	6- -6-1935	Wichita	Sedgewick Co.	Kans.	
Death	5- -6-1995	Wichita	Sedgwick Co.	Kans.	
Burial	8- -6-1995	Jamesburg Park	Sedgwick Co.	Kans.	

Places of Residence: Rural Butler Co. -Maize- Whitewater-Wichita
Occupation: Teacher Administrator **Church Affiliation:** Christian **Military Rec:**

His Father: Leon Arthur Moore **Mother's Maiden Name:** Nellie May Metz

Wife's Full Maiden Name: Frances Ethlyn Whitney

	Day Month Year	City, Town or Place	County or Province, etc.	State or Country	Add. Info on Wife
Birth	20- 5-1913	Belle Plains	Sumner Co.	Kans.	
Chr'nd	1930				
Death					
Burial					

Places of Residence: Rural Sumner Co. -Whitewater-Maize-Wichita, Kansas
Occupation: Housewife **Church Affiliation:** Christian **Military Rec:**

Her Father: Herbert W. Whitney **Mother's Maiden Name:** Lula Thomas

Sex	Children's Names in Full		Day Month Year	City, Town or Place	County or Province, etc.	State or Country	Add. Info on Children
M	1 Alan Arthur Moore	Birth	5- 8-1939	Wichita	Sedgwick Co.	Ks.	
		Marr	28-8-1963				
	Full Name of Spouse	Death	1- -2-1996	Minneapolis	Hennepin Co.	Minn.	
	Della Jean Turpin	Burial	4- 2-1996	Park Rapids	Hubbard Co.	Minn.	
M	2 Wayne Virgil Moore	Birth	3- 5-1942	Wichita	Sedgwick Co.	Kans.	
		Marr	10-8-1963	Wichita	Sedgwick Co.	Kans.	
	Full Name of Spouse Edminster	Death					
	Peggy Charline	Burial					

Arthur and Floyd Moore
Nellie Metz Moore

Frances Whitney Moore

Floyd Moore

Floyd Moore and Frances Whitney

Hillside Funeral Home West
2929 WEST 13th STREET
Wichita, Kansas
943-2929

A division of Quiring Monument Company

CASE # W303 95 DIRECTOR K/Dale

NAMES AND ADDRESSES OF THOSE SURVIVING
- WIFE — FRANCES — HOME
- SONS — ALAN — MINNEAPOLIS, MINN
- DR. WAYNE — KANSAS CITY, KS
- BROTHERS — RICHARD — WICHITA
- SISTER — ZELMA MYERS — WICHITA
- 5 GRANDCHILDREN
- 2 GREAT GRANDCHILDREN

NAME: Floyd V. Moore
ADDRESS: 1721 Westridge CITY: Wichita ZIP: 67203 PHONE: 943-0892
AGE: 89 BORN WHEN? 4-29-06 WHERE? Butler Co., Kansas
OCCUPATION: Retired School Teacher & Administrator
WHEN LAST WORKED: 1971 S.S. 510-30-6584
PLACE OF DEATH: Lakewood Heights
DAY AND DATE OF DEATH: Monday TIME: 5-95 HOUR: 3:30 AM
PHYSICIAN SIGNING D.C.: Kevin Bryant
NAME OF FATHER: L. Arthur Moore
NAME OF MOTHER: Nellie Metz
ANCESTRY / EDUCATION: German/English 18
IF MARRIED, TO WHOM? (MAIDEN NAME): Frances Whitney 6-6-35 Wichita
IS SPOUSE LIVING? Yes IF NOT, DATE OF DEATH: ___
CHURCH MEMBERSHIP: Westside Christian Church

MEMORIALS TO: West Side Christian Church 1819 W. Douglas 67213
FUNERAL SERVICES: West Side Christian Church 2635269
DATE, DAY OF SERVICES: Thurs 6-8-95 TIME: 2 PM
OFFICIATING: Dr. David McCord
CHURCH: West Side Christian Church
INTERMENT: Resthaven Park No. Tyler
ORGANIST: Anna Mae Berwick SOLOIST: Charles Stinson 755-1027
SONGS: How Great Thou Art, Shall We Gather At The River

VETERAN? NO FLAG: NO BENEFITS: NO MARKER: NO
YES/NO: open before for everyone in back of church — open after just for family

MARRIAGE LICENSE RECORD

State of Kansas, Sedgwick County, ss:
June 3rd, 1935
...herewith files application and affidavit for Marriage License to be issued to Floyd V. Moore and Frances Evelyn Whitney...

Office of the Probate Judge of Said County
BE IT REMEMBERED, That on the 3rd day of June, A.D. 1935...

MARRIAGE LICENSE
State of Kansas, County of Sedgwick
Wichita, Kansas, June 3rd, 1935

YOU ARE HEREBY AUTHORIZED TO JOIN IN MARRIAGE
Floyd V. Moore of Wichita, Kansas, aged 29
Frances Evelyn Whitney, Wichita, Kansas, aged 22

TO WHOM IT MAY CONCERN:
I hereby certify that I performed the ceremony joining in marriage the above-named couple on the 6th day of June, 1935, at Wichita.
Signed: Frank L Walker
Title: Christian Minister
Address: 2413 E. Douglas

Floyd Moore was Mr. Discipline in his schools

By Tim Potter
The Wichita Eagle

OBITUARY

As a principal, Floyd V. Moore emphasized discipline.

"If he said something, we all did it," said Zola Dean, a retired English teacher who admired Mr. Moore's leadership when he was principal of Hadley Junior High School.

During a career spanning 43 years, Mr. Moore also served as superintendent in Maize and Whitewater and as principal of Longfellow, Stanley, and Washington elementary schools and Allison Junior High.

Mr. Moore died Monday after a recent illness. He was 89.

Although he was a firm disciplinarian, he also was forgiving. One day he would deal with a misbehaving child. The next day, he could be seen walking down the hallway with his arm around the former troublemaker, said Frances Moore, his wife of almost 60 years. "He always saw the good in everyone," she said. "He never gave up on a child."

As a young man, Mr. Moore learned discipline himself as fullback on the football team and as center on the basketball team at Friends University. Later, he taught discipline as a teacher and coach at Maize, where he became superintendent before moving on to Whitewater and then to Wichita.

At Maize, Mr. Moore started softball, basketball and track teams for girls. At the time — the late 1930s — organized competition for girls was a revolutionary concept, said Mr. Moore's son Alan.

Mr. Moore started teaching at age 17, right out of high school, which was allowed in Kansas in the 1920s. His first teaching job was in a one-room school house in Butler County, where, as his family tells it, rowdy children had scared off two previous teachers. But when strapping Mr. Moore, who eventually reached 6 feet 3 inches tall, entered the troubled school, the students quickly started behaving. His size helped him get respect, his son said.

While Mr. Moore took on increasingly challenging jobs in school administration he always seemed to be able to handle the stress.

"I never saw him get irritated at another person," said Alan Moore.

His father had a talent for resolving conflicts, and that's why he was often asked to referee at athletic events.

To relieve the stress of administration, Mr. Moore raised a five-acre garden and orchard bursting with peaches, plums, cherries and a bed of asparagus. He also raised pigs, sheep and turkeys — at one time about 600 of the birds.

The first principal of Hadley Junior High, Mr. Moore watched the enrollment grow from 400 students to 1,500 when he retired in 1971.

After retirement, Mr. Moore continued to be active as a deacon and elder at West Side Christian Church.

And he continued to grow his garden. As his stamina decreased, he used a chair for support while he pulled weeds between the rows. After his eyesight began to fail, he had to depend on others to pull weeds that grew close to his plants.

But Mr. Moore continued to nurture his garden as long as he could, his son said.

A hard worker, Mr. Moore also was self-reliant, said his granddaughter, Marisa Moore. About two years ago, she said, he told her, "I don't want to ever have to depend on anyone."

A service for Mr. Moore will be at 2 p.m. today at West Side Christian Church. Other survivors include a son, Wayne of Kansas City, Kan.; a brother, Richard, and a sister, Zelma Myers, both of Wichita; five grandchildren and two great-grandchildren. A memorial has been established with West Side Christian Church.

Family Group Sheet

Husband's Full Name: Alan Moore — **Chart No.**

Husband's Data	Day Month Year	City, Town or Place	County or Province, etc.	State or Country	Add. Info. on Husband
Birth	5- 8-1939	Wichita	Sedgwick Co.	Kansas	
Chr'nd					
Marr	28-8-1963				
Death	1- 2-1996	Minneapolis	Hennepin Co.	Minnesota	
Burial	4- 2-1996	Park Rapids	Hubbard Co.	Minnesota	

Places of Residence:
Occupation: Church Affiliation: Military Rec:

His Father: Floyd Virgil Moore   **Mother's Maiden Name:** Frances Whitney

Wife's Full Maiden Name: Della Jean Turpin

Wife's Data	Day Month Year	City, Town or Place	County or Province, etc.	State or Country	Add. Info. on Wife
Birth					
Chr'nd					
Death					
Burial					

Places of Residence:
Occupation: Church Affiliation: Military Rec:

Her Father: **Mother's Maiden Name:**

Sex	Children's Names in Full	Children's Data	Day Month Year	City, Town or Place	County or Province, etc.	State or Country	Add. Info. on Children
M	1 Cade Moore	Birth					
	Full Name of Spouse	Marr.					
		Death					
		Burial					
F	2 Marissa Moore	Birth					
	Full Name of Spouse	Marr.					
		Death					
		Burial					
F	3 Ginger Moore	Birth					
	Full Name of Spouse	Marr.					
		Death					
		Burial					
M	4 Andrew Moore	Birth					
	Full Name of Spouse	Marr.					
		Death					
		Burial					
F	5 Lauren Moore	Birth					
	Full Name of Spouse	Marr.					
		Death					
		Burial					
	6	Birth					
	Full Name of Spouse	Marr.					
		Death					
		Burial					
	7	Birth					
	Full Name of Spouse	Marr.					
		Death					
		Burial					
	8	Birth					
	Full Name of Spouse	Marr.					
		Death					
		Burial					

Compiler: Notes:
Address:
City, State, Zip:
Date:

Family Group Sheet

Husband's Full Name: Wayne V. Moore — **Chart No.**

	Day Month Year	City, Town or Place	County or Province, etc.	State or Country	Add. Info on Husband
Birth	3-5-1942	Wichita	Sedgwick Co.	Kans.	
Chr'nd					
Marr	10-8-1963	Wichita	Sedgwick Co.	Kans.	
Death					
Burial					

Places of Residence:
Occupation: Physician **Church Affiliation:** Christian **Military Rec:** 1972-74 Navy Lt. Col.

His Father: Floyd Virgil Moore **Mother's Maiden Name:** Frances Whitney

Wife's Full Maiden Name: Peggy Edminster

	Day Month Year	City, Town or Place	County or Province, etc.	State or Country	Add. Info on Wife
Birth	17-10-1940	Wichita	Sedgwick Co.	Kans.	
Chr'nd					
Death					
Burial					

Places of Residence: Wichita-Minnesota-Maryland-Kansas City, Kansas
Occupation: Minister **Church Affiliation:** Christian **Military Rec:**

Her Father: Leichester (Corky) Edminster **Mother's Maiden Name:** Winfred Clark

Sex	Children's Names in Full		Day Month Year	City, Town or Place	County or Province, etc.	State or Country	Add. Info on Children
F	1 Kirsten Lee Moore	Birth	14-5-1967	Minneapolis	Hennepin Co.	Minn.	
		Marr.	1989			Kansas	
	Full Name of Spouse: Pat Shartzer /tod/ /Wellmer/	Death					
		Burial					
F	2 Kari Cozette Moore	Birth	23-12-1969	Minn.	Hennepin Co.	Minnesota	
		Marr.	19-6-1994	Kansas City	Wyandotte Co.	Ks.	
	Full Name of Spouse: Brett Richard Larson	Death					
		Burial					

APPLICATION AND AFFIDAVIT FOR MARRIAGE LICENSE No. 88710

STATE OF KANSAS, COUNTY OF SEDGWICK, ss: IN THE PROBATE COURT IN AND FOR SAID COUNTY AND STATE

Wayne V. Moore of Wichita, State of Kans. hereby makes application to marry Peggy C. Edminster of Wichita, State of Kans. and further applies for a marriage license addressed to any person authorized by law to unite said parties in marriage; being duly sworn deposes:

That said Wayne V. Moore is 21 years of age and that he has no living wife and that the said Peggy C. Edminster 22 years of age and that she has no living husband.

That said contracting parties are not related to each other in any of the degrees prohibited by law, to-wit: Parent and child, grandparent and grandchild in any degree, brother and sister of the whole or the half blood, uncle or niece, aunt or nephew, nor first cousins, and neither has been divorced within the past six months.

That neither of said parties is or has ever been feeble minded or insane; or if either is or has ever been afflicted, then that the woman is more than forty-five years of age.

(1) Have you or has the person you are expecting to marry ever been adjudicated insane or afflicted with feeble-mindedness? No
(2) If your answer to question (1) is yes, have all the persons adjudicated been discharged as restored?

That neither of said parties was born subsequent to the insanity of either of his or her parents, or if so that the woman about to be married is more than forty-five years of age.

Further affiant saith not.

Subscribed and sworn to before me this 5 day of August, 1963. Wayne V. Moore

Vanna Hunter, Notary Public

Commission expires 8-11-65 (SEAL) Probate Judge

Marriage License issued 8-8-63 No. 88710 Health Certificate filed 8-8-63 No.

State of Kansas, Central Division of Vital Statistics **MARRIAGE LICENSE** No. 88710 Aug 8, 1963

P. J. No.

IN THE PROBATE COURT OF SEDGWICK COUNTY

TO ANY PERSON IN THE STATE OF KANSAS AUTHORIZED BY LAW TO PERFORM THE MARRIAGE CEREMONY, GREETING: YOU ARE HEREBY AUTHORIZED TO JOIN IN MARRIAGE

Wayne V. Moore of Wichita, Kansas, Age 21
Peggy C. Edminster of Wichita, Kansas, Age 22

with the consent of _____ and this license duly endorsed, you will make return to my office at Wichita, Kansas, within ten days after performing the ceremony.

(SEAL) Clark V. Owens, Probate Judge

ENDORSEMENT
TO WHOM IT MAY CONCERN:
I certify that I performed the ceremony joining in marriage the above named couple, on the 10th day of August, 1963, at Wichita, Kansas.

Signed W. A. Young and George K. Didier

103

E. Military Service Record

Name of Veteran ___Moore_____ ___Wayne_____ ___Virgil_____
                        last   first   middle

State from Which Served _____

War in Which, or Dates between Which, He Served _____

If Service Was Civil War:

    Union _____ Confederate _____

Unit in Which He Served:

    Name or Number of Regiment _____

    Company _____

    Name of Ship _____

Branch in Which He Served: 1973—1974

    Infantry_____ Cavalry_____ Artillery_____ Navy_____ Other_____

Kind of Service: Volunteers _____ Regulars _____

Pension File Number _____

Bounty Land File Number (for Service before 1856 Only) _____

Military Record Number _____

Date of Birth ___May 3, 19_____

Place of Birth ___Wichita_____ ___Sedgwick_____ ___Kansas_____
                        city   county   state

Name of Widow or Other Claimant _____

Date of Death _____

Place of Death _____
                        city   county   state

Places Lived after Service _____

_____

_____

If Veteran Lived in a Home for Soldiers:

    Location _____
                        city   state

Family Group Sheet

Husband's Full Name: Todd Weltmer — **Chart No.**

	Day Month Year	City, Town or Place	County or Province, etc.	State or Country	Add. Info on Husband
Birth					
Chr'nd					
Marr	21- 2-1998	Las Vegas	Clark Co.	Nevada	
Death					
Burial					

Places of Residence:
Occupation: Church Affiliation: Military Rec.:
His Father: Mother's Maiden Name:

Wife's Full Maiden Name: Kirsten Lee Moore

	Day Month Year	City, Town or Place	County or Province, etc.	State or Country	Add. Info on Wife
Birth	14- 5-1967	Minneapolis	Hennepin Co.	Minnesota	
Chr'nd					
Death					
Burial					

Places of Residence:
Occupation: Church Affiliation: Military Rec.:
Her Father: Wayne V. Moore   Mother's Maiden Name: Peggy Edminster

Sex	Children's Names in Full		Day Month Year	City, Town or Place	County or Province, etc.	State or Country	Add. Info on Children
1		Birth					
		Marr					

Family Group Sheet

Husband's Full Name: Brett Richard Larson — **Chart No.**

	Day Month Year	City, Town or Place	County or Province, etc.	State or Country	Add. Info on Husband
Birth					
Chr'nd					
Marr	19-6-1994	Overland Park,	Johnson Co.	Kans.	
Death					
Burial					

Places of Residence:
Occupation: Church Affiliation: Military Rec.:
His Father: Mother's Maiden Name:

Wife's Full Maiden Name: Kari Cozette Moore

	Day Month Year	City, Town or Place	County or Province, etc.	State or Country	Add. Info on Wife
Birth	23-12-1969	Minneapolis	Hennepin Co.	Minnesota	
Chr'nd					
Death					
Burial					

Places of Residence:
Occupation: Church Affiliation: Military Rec.:
Her Father: Wayne V. Moore   Mother's Maiden Name: Peggy Edminster

Sex	Children's Names in Full		Day Month Year	City, Town or Place	County or Province, etc.	State or Country	Add. Info on Children
1		Birth					
		Marr.					
	Full Name of Spouse	Death					
		Burial					
2		Birth					
		Marr.					
	Full Name of Spouse	Death					
		Burial					

Family Group Sheet

Husband's Full Name: William Henry Myers SS 441-05-8559 Chart No.

	Day Month Year	City, Town or Place	County or Province, etc.	State or Country	Add. Info. on Husband
Birth	4-4-1907	Blackwell	Kay Co.	Okla.	
Chr'nd					
Marr.					
Death	2-11-1991	Wichita	Sedgwick Co.	Kans.	
Burial	6-11-1991				

Places of Residence:
Occupation: Boeing   Church Affiliation: Christian   Military Rec:

His Father: Mother's Maiden Name:

Wife's Full Maiden Name: Zelma Elva Moore

	Day Month Year	City, Town or Place	County or Province, etc.	State or Country	Add. Info. on Wife
Birth	7-11-1908	Syracuse	Hamilton Co.	Kans.	
Chr'nd					
Death	22-2-1998	Clearwater	Sedgwick Co.	Kans.	
Burial	24-2-1998				

Places of Residence: Rural Butler Co. Houston, Texas Rifle Co. Ada, Okla.
Occupation: Teacher   Church Affiliation: Christian   Military Rec:

Her Father: Leon Arthur Moore   Mother's Maiden Name: Nellie May Metz

Sex	Children's Names in Full		Day Month Year	City, Town or Place	County or Province, etc.	State or Country	Add. Info. on Children
M	1 William Harold M.	Birth	13-11-1938	Ada	Pontotoc Co.	Okla.	
	Full Name of Spouse	Marr.					
		Death					
		Burial					
F	2 Carolyn June Myers	Birth	31-10-1942	Houston	Harris Co.	Texas	
		Marr.	6-7-1962	Wichita	Sedgwick Co.	Kans.	
	Full Name of Spouse	Death					
	Robert Gordon Wainscott	Burial					
M	3 Robert Glen Myers	Birth	1-9-1944	Wichita	Sedgwick Co.	Kans.	
		Marr.					

Myers, Zelma Elva, 89, retired Wichita public school teacher, died Sunday, Feb. 22, 1998. Service 3 p.m. today, Resthaven Mortuary.

Survivors: sons, William of Amarillo, Texas, Robert of Wichita; daughter, Carolyn Wainscott of Spring, Texas; brother, Richard Moore of Wichita; three grandchildren; one great-grandchild.

William Myers and Zelma Moore

Zelma Moore

106

Family Group Sheet

Husband's Full Name William Harold Myers — **Chart No.**

Husband's Data	Day Month Year	City, Town or Place	County or Province, etc.	State or Country	Add. Info on Husband
Birth	13-11-1938	Ada	Pontotoc Co.	Okla.	
Chr'nd					
Marr					
Death					
Burial					

Places of Residence

Occupation — **Church Affiliation** — **Military Rec**

His Father William Henry Myers — **Mother's Maiden Name** Zelma Elva Moore

Family Group Sheet

Husband's Full Name Gordon Robert Wainscott — **Chart No.**

Husband's Data	Day Month Year	City, Town or Place	County or Province, etc.	State or Country	Add. Info on Husband
Birth	7-11-1941	Wichita	Sedgwick Co.	Kansas	
Chr'nd					
Marr	6-6-1962	Wichita	Sedgwick Co.	Kansas	
Death					
Burial					

Places of Residence Wichita, Ks.-Dallas and Houston, Texas- Slidell, La.

Occupation Geo-Physicist — **Church Affiliation** Christian — **Military Rec**

His Father Gordon A. Wainscott — **Mother's Maiden Name** Maxine Moutray

Wife's Full Maiden Name Carolyn June Myers

Wife's Data	Day Month Year	City, Town or Place	County or Province, etc.	State or Country	Add. Info on Wife
Birth	31-10-1942	Houston	Harris Co.	Texas	
Chr'nd					
Death					
Burial					

Places of Residence

Occupation Housewife — **Church Affiliation** Christian — **Military Rec**

Her Father William Henry Myers — **Mother's Maiden Name** Zelma Elva Moore

Sex	Children's Names in Full	Children's Data	Day Month Year	City, Town or Place	County or Province, etc.	State or Country	Add. Info on Children
F	1 Jodi Lynn Wainscott	Birth	30-3-1963	Wichita	Sedgwick Co.	Kans.	
	Full Name of Spouse: David Buchanan	Marr	22-10-1988	Spring	Harris Co.	Tx.	
		Death					
		Burial					
M	2 Steve Lee Wainscott	Birth	23-9-1967	Wichita	Sedgwick Co.	Kans.	
	Full Name of Spouse	Marr					
		Death					
		Burial					
M	3 David Shawn Wainscott	Birth	2-12-1971	Garland	Dallas Co.	Texas	
	Full Name of Spouse	Marr					
		Death					
		Burial					
	8	Birth					
	Full Name of Spouse	Marr					
		Death					
		Burial					

Compiler Carolyn Wainscott
Address 6607 Sunner Isle Court
City, State, Zip Spring, Texas 77379
Date

Jodi Lynn Wainscott

108

Family Group Sheet

Husband's Full Name: David Buchanan
Chart No.

	Day Month Year	City, Town or Place	County or Province, etc.	State or Country	Add Info on Husband
Birth					
Chr'nd					
Marr	22-10-1988	Spring	Harris Co.	Texas	
Death					
Burial					

Places of Residence:
Occupation: Church Affiliation: Military Rec:

His Father: Mother's Maiden Name:

Wife's Full Maiden Name: Jodi Lynn Wainscott

	Day Month Year	City, Town or Place	County or Province, etc.	State or Country	Add Info on Wife
Birth	30-3-1963	Wichita	Sedgwick Co.	Kans.	
Chr'nd					
Death					
Burial					

Places of Residence:
Occupation: Church Affiliation: Military Rec:

Her Father: Gordon Robert Wainscott Mother's Maiden Name: Carolyn June Myers

Sex	Children's Names in Full		Day Month Year	City, Town or Place	County or Province, etc.	State or Country	Add Info on Children
F	1. Buchanan, Lea Grace	Birth / Marr / Death / Burial					

Lea Grace Buchanan, 4 mo. old

109

Family Group Sheet

Husband's Full Name Robert Glenn Myers SS-509-44-2680 **Chart No.**

	Day Month Year	City, Town or Place	County or Province, etc.	State or Country	Add. Info. on Husband
Birth	1-9-1944	Wichita	Sedgwick Co.	Kansas	
Chr'nd					
Marr					
Death					
Burial					

Places of Residence

Occupation   Church Affiliation   Military Rec

His Father **William Henry Myers**   Mother's Maiden Name **Zelma Elva Moore**

THE UNITED STATES OF AMERICA
DEPARTMENT OF COMMERCE
BUREAU OF THE CENSUS

Notification of Birth Registration

This certifies that the following Record of Birth is registered and preserved in the office of the State Registrar of Vital Statistics at **Topeka, Kansas**

Name *Robert Glenn Myers* Sex *Male* No. 287-68689
Date of Birth 9-1-44 Place of Birth WICHITA
Name of Father *William Henry Myers*
Maiden Name of Mother *Zelma Elva Moore*

Minnie Fleming
Special Agent, Bureau of the Census

J.C. Capt, Director of the Census.

509-44-2680
[SOCIAL SECURITY ACCOUNT NUMBER]

Robert Glenn Myers
1649 West Ridge Dr.
Wichita 12, Kans.

SIGNATURE
FOR SOCIAL SECURITY PURPOSES • NOT FOR IDENTIFICATION

Honorable Discharge

from the Armed Forces of the United States of America

This is to certify that ROBERT GLEN MYERS   599 91 33 SN   USNR
was Honorably Discharged from the

United States Navy

on the 10TH day of JULY 1968 This certificate is awarded as a testimonial of Honest and Faithful Service

D. E. Oglevee, Captain, USNR
Commanding Officer
Naval Reserve Manpower Center

---

4 Full Name	
5 Full Name	
6 Full Name	
7 Full Name	
8 Full Name	

Comp'er
Address
City, State, Zip
Date

237

E. Military Service Record

Name of Veteran __Myers_____ __Robert_____ __Glenn___
                        last   first   middle

State from Which Served __Kansas_____

War in Which, or Dates between Which, He Served _____

If Service Was Civil War:

    Union _____ Confederate _____

Unit in Which He Served:

    Name or Number of Regiment _____

    Company _____

    Name of Ship __U. S. S. Frank Knox DD 742__

Branch in Which He Served:

    Infantry _____ Cavalry _____ Artillery _____ Navy __X__ Other _____

Kind of Service: Volunteers _____ Regulars __X__

Pension File Number __509-91-33__

Bounty Land File Number (for Service before 1856 Only) _____

Military Record Number _____

Date of Birth _____

Place of Birth _____
            city   county   state

Name of Widow or Other Claimant _____

Date of Death _____

Place of Death _____
            city   county   state

Places Lived after Service __Wichita, Kansas__

_____

_____

If Veteran Lived in a Home for Soldiers:

    Location _____
             city   state

Family Group Sheet

Husband's Full Name: Richard (Dick) Donald Moore — Chart No.

	Day	Month	Year	City, Town or Place	County or Province, etc.	State or Country	Add. Info on Husband
Birth	1	9	1913	Whitewater	Butler Co.	Kansas	
Chr'nd							
Marr	27	8	1938	Douglas	Butler Co.	Kansas	
Death							
Burial							

Places of Residence:
Occupation: Boeing Flight Line **Church Affiliation:** **Military Rec:**

His Father: Leon Arthur Moore **Mother's Maiden Name:** Nellie Mae Metz

Wife's Full Maiden Name: Erma Lucile Kibbe

	Day	Month	Year	City, Town or Place	County or Province, etc.	State or Country	Add. Info on Wife
Birth	8	10	1913	Lincoln	Lancaster Co.	Nebraska	
Chr'nd							
Death	23	7	1997	Wichita	Sedgwick Co.	Kansas	
Burial		7	1997	Resthaven cem. Wichita	Sedgwick Co.	Kansas	

Places of Residence:
Occupation: Southwestern Bell **Church Affiliation:** **Military Rec:**

Her Father: Walter E. Kibbe **Mother's Maiden Name:** Hallie Edith Wilson

Sex	Children's Names in Full		Day	Month	Year	City, Town or Place	County or Province, etc.	State or Country	Add. Info on Children
M	1. Donald Jay Moore	Birth	7	4	1942	Wichita	Sedgwick Co.	Kans.	
		Marr	21	12	1974	Wichita	Sedgwick Co.	Kans.	
	Full Name of Spouse: Suzanne Elizabeth Schabell	Death							
		Burial							
F	2. Judith Diane Moore	Birth	9	5	1944	Wichita	Sedgwick Co.	Kans.	
		Marr							
	Full Name of Spouse: Lloyd Eugene Krase	Death							
		Burial							
F	3. Karen Sue Moore	Birth	24	8	1950	Wichita	Sedgwick Co.	Kans.	
		Marr	18	5	1991	Wichita	Sedgwick Co.	Kans.	
	Full Name of Spouse: Paul Richard Holliday	Death							
		Burial							

Richard and Erma Moore
August 28, 1964

Richard Moore

Saturday, August 27, 1938 . . . . . .

ERMA LUCILLE KIBBE

and

RICHARD DONALD MOORE

exchanged wedding vows on Saturday evening in Douglass, Ks. Witnesses were Burr and Helen Kibbe. Officiating at the ceremony was Reverend Charles Neff. (The reverend mistakenly dated their marriage certificate for the 28th of August.)

That was 50 years ago . . . . . .

50 years ago...

The year was 1938, President Roosevelt signed the Wage and Hour Act, raising minimum wage for workers engaged in interstate commerce from 25¢ to 40¢ an hour. It was the year Dupont marketed the first nylon product - a toothbrush.

"Invasion From Mars," a radio play produced by Orson Welles pervaded the air waves causing panic when listeners believed an attack from Mars was an actual news broadcast.

In Wichita, Ks. Saturday, August 27, 1938 the Air Capital Market at 204 N. Main featured:
- Bacon (sliced) 1 lb. 19¢
- Oranges . . . . 1¢ ea.
- Folgers Coffee 1 lb. can . . . . 23¢

Playing at the Miller Theater was Irving Berlin's "Alexander's Ragtime Band" . . . . admission was 25¢. The Wichita Eagle sold for 3¢ a copy and reported temperatures for that day to be in the upper 90's.

Dear Family and Friends,

We would like to invite you to help us celebrate our parents' Golden Wedding Anniversary in Minnesota on August 27th by sending them a greeting or a note. Their address is:

Richard and Erma Moore
Box 144
R.R. 4 Stony Lake
Park Rapids, Mn. 56470

We are planning to be with them on that date to enjoy the moment and acknowledge this milestone.

Thanks for being a part of their lives,

Don, Judy, Karen & families

Richard Moore and Erma Kibbe

Family Group Sheet

Husband's Full Name Lloyd Eugene Krase — Chart No.

Husband's Data	Day Month Year	City, Town or Place	County or Province, etc.	State or Country	Add. Info. on Husband
Birth	24-5-1943	Kingman	Kingman	Kansas	
Chr'nd					
Marr	28-8-1964	Wichita	Sedgwick Co.	Kansas	
Death					
Burial					Viet Nam vet

Places of Residence: Murdock, Wichita, Topeka, Ft. Leavenworth, Ks. Carlisle, Pa.
Occupation: Ret. Nat. Guard Tech Church Affiliation: Topeka Bible Church Military Rec: Ks. National Guard
Other wives: Current: Deputy Dir. Emergency Management Kansas (Brig. Gen)
His Father: Lloyd Cicero Krase Mother's Maiden Name: Elizabeth Mary Hart

Wife's Full Maiden Name Judith Diane Moore

Wife's Data	Day Month Year	City, Town or Place	County or Province, etc.	State or Country	Add. Info. on Wife
Birth	9-5-1944	Wichita	Sedgwick Co.	Kansas	
Chr'nd					
Death					
Burial					

Places of Residence: Wichita, Goddard, Topeka, Ft. Leavenworth, (Ks) Carlisle, Pa.
Occupation: Homemaker Church Affiliation: Bible Church-Topeka Military Rec: Viet Nam vet.
Other husbands: (Sec'y-State House Jan. thru April-9 yrs. currently)
Her Father: Richard Donald Moore Mother's Maiden Name: Erma Lucile Kibbe

Sex	Children's Names in Full		Day Month Year	City, Town or Place	County or Province, etc.	State or Country	Add. Info. on Children
F	1 Shelly Anne Krase	Birth	6-1-1968	Wichita	Sedgwick Co.	Kans.	
		Marr	27-5-1990	Topeka	Shawnee Co.	Kans.	
	Full Name of Spouse: Kenneth James Savoy	Death					
		Burial					
F	2 Jill Diane Krase	Birth	20-2-1972	Wichita	Sedgwick Co.	Ks.	
		Marr	27-6-1992	Wichita	Sedgwick Co.	Ks.	
	Full Name of Spouse: Scott Edward Spradlin	Death					
		Burial					

Judith Diane Moore and Lloyd Eugene Krase wedding, August 28, 1964

Certificate

STATE OF KANSAS } SS:
SEDGWICK COUNTY }

I, CLARK V. OWENS, Probate Judge of Sedgwick County, Kansas, do hereby certify that, according to our records Lloyd Eugene Krase Murdock, Kans. aged 21 years, and Judith Diane Moore Wichita, Ks. aged 20 years, were married by Rev. N. Gene Carlson on the 28 day of August, 1964, as the same appear in Volume HHHH at Page 448.

WITNESS my seal and signature this 6 day of May, 1966.

By _____ Deputy Clerk   _____ Probate Judge, Sedgwick County, Kansas

LLOYD EUGENE KRASE - BIRTH CERT.

JUDITH DIANE MOORE - BIRTH CERT.

Mr. and Mrs. Lloyd E. Krase
invite you to share in the joy
of seeing their daughter

Jill Diane

united with

Scott Edward Spradlin

Saturday, the twenty-seventh of June
nineteen hundred and ninety-two
at six-thirty in the evening
Westlink Christian Church
Wichita, Kansas

Mr. and Mrs. Lloyd E Krase
request the honor of your presence
at the marriage of their daughter

Shelley Anne

to

Mr. Kenneth James Savoy

on Sunday, the twenty-seventh of May
Nineteen hundred and ninety
at five o'clock in the afternoon
Historic Ward-Meade Park
Topeka, Kansas

Reception following
Ceremony

EDUCATION DATA as of 1997

Lloyd Eugene Krase
Cheney Rural High School, Cheney, KS
Bachelors of Business Administration (Accounting/Economics),
Wichita State University, Wichita, KS
Masters of Science (Public Administration)
Shippensburg University, Shippensburg, PA

Judith Diane (Moore) Krase
Goddard High School, Goddard, KS
One year, Emporia State University,
Emporia, KS

Shelley Anne (Krase) Savoy
Leavenworth High School, Leavenworth, KS
Bachelors of Business Administration (Economics)
Wichita State University, Wichita, KS
Bachelors of Science (French)
Wichita State University, Wichita, KS
Masters of Science (Economics)
Wichita State University, Wichita, KS

Kenneth James Savoy
Leavenworth High School, Leavenworth, KS
Bachelors of Science (Electrical Engineering)
Wichita State University, Wichita, KS
Masters of Science (Electrical Engineering)
Wichita State University, Wichita, KS
Currently pursuing Masters of Business Administration,
University of Missouri-St Louis

Jill Diane (Krase) Spradlin
Shawnee Heights High School, Topeka, KS
Bachelors of Science (Psychology)
Kansas State University, Manhattan, KS
Currently pursuing Masters/Doctorate (Psychology)
George Fox University, Newburg, OR

Scott Edward Spradlin
Northwest High School, Wichita, KS
Bachelors of Art (Bible and Family)
Manhattan Christian College, Manhattan, KS
Masters of Science (Counseling)
Covenant Theological Seminary, St. Louis, MO

Family Group Sheet

Husband's Full Name Scott Edward Spradlin — **Chart No.**

Husband's Data	Day Month Year	City, Town or Place	County or Province, etc.	State or Country	Add. Info. on Husband
Birth					
Chr'nd					
Marr	27-6-1992	Wichita	Sedgwick Co.	Kansas	
Death					
Burial					

Places of Residence:
Occupation: Church Affiliation: Military Rec:
Other wives (if any)
His Father: Mother's Maiden Name:

Wife's Full Maiden Name Jill Diane Krase

Wife's Data	Day Month Year	City, Town or Place	County or Province, etc.	State or Country	Add. Info. on Wife
Birth	20-2-1972	Wichita	Sedgwick Co.	Kansas	
Chr'nd					
Death					
Burial					

Places of Residence:
Occupation: Church Affiliation: Military Rec:
Other husbands (if any)
Her Father: Lloyd E. Krase   Mother's Maiden Name: Judith Diane Moore

---

Family Group Sheet

Husband's Full Name Kenneth James Savory — **Chart No.**

Husband's Data	Day Month Year	City, Town or Place	County or Province, etc.	State or Country	Add. Info. on Husband
Birth				Kansas	
Chr'nd					
Marr	27-5-1990	Topeka	Shawnee Co.	Kansas	
Death					
Burial					

Places of Residence:
Occupation: Church Affiliation: Military Rec:
Other wives (if any)
His Father: Mother's Maiden Name:

Wife's Full Maiden Name Shelly Anne Krase

Wife's Data	Day Month Year	City, Town or Place	County or Province, etc.	State or Country	Add. Info. on Wife
Birth	6-1-1968	Wichita	Sedgwick Co.	Kansas	
Chr'nd					
Death					
Burial					

Places of Residence: Ireland, St. Louis, Pa., Manhattan and Topeka, Kansas
Occupation: Psychology Grad. student   Church Affiliation: Christian   Military Rec:
Other husbands (if any)
Her Father: Lloyd Krase   Mother's Maiden Name: Judith Moore

Sex	Children's Names in Full	Children's Data	Day Month Year	City, Town or Place	County or Province, etc.	State or Country	Add. Info. on Children
	1	Birth					
		Marr.					
	Full Name of Spouse	Death					
		Burial					
	2	Birth					
		Marr.					
	Full Name of Spouse	Death					
		Burial					

City, State, Zip:
Date:

Family Group Sheet

Husband's Full Name: Paul Richard Holliday — **Chart No.**

	Day Month Year	City, Town or Place	County or Province, etc.	State or Country	Add. Info on Husband
Birth	4- 4-1947	Norton	Norton Co.	Kansas	
Chr'nd					
Marr	18- 5-1991	Wichita	Sedgwick Co.	Kansas	
Death					
Burial					

Places of Residence: Johnson, Ks. Wesleyan
Occupation: Farmer — **Church Affiliation:** — **Military Rec:**

His Father: Myron Murphey Holliday — **Mother's Maiden Name:** Marjorie Marie Inem

Wife's Full Maiden Name: Karen Sue Moore

	Day Month Year	City, Town or Place	County or Province, etc.	State or Country	Add. Info. on Wife
Birth	24- 8-1950	Wichita	Sedgwick Co.	Kansas	
Chr'nd					
Death					
Burial					

Places of Residence: Johnson, Kansas
Occupation: Graphic design-Drafting — **Church Affiliation:** — **Military Rec:**

Her Father: Richard Donald Moore — **Mother's Maiden Name:** Erma Lucile Kibble

Sex	Children's Names in Full	Children's Data	Day Month Year	City, Town or Place	County or Province, etc.	State or Country	Add. Info on Children
M	Heath Ray Holliday	Birth	17-9-1977	Ulysses	Grant Co.	Kansas	step-son
		Marr.					
	Full Name of Spouse	Death					
		Burial					
M 2	Adam Blair Holliday	Birth	28- 3-1980	Ulysses	Grant Co.	Kansas	step-son
		Marr.					
	Full Name of Spouse	Death					
		Burial					
F 3	Emie Lea Holliday	Birth	25-10-1983	Ulysses	Grant, Co.	Kansas	step-daught
		Marr.					
	Full Name of Spouse	Death					
		Burial					
M 4	Seth Myron Holliday	Birth	1- 8-1993	Garden City	Finney Co.	Kans.	
		Marr.					

Paul Holliday and Karen Moore
May 18, 1991

Adam Blair Holliday
Senior, March 28, 1980

Ernie Lea Holliday
8th Grade, Stanton Middle School
Oct. 25, 1983

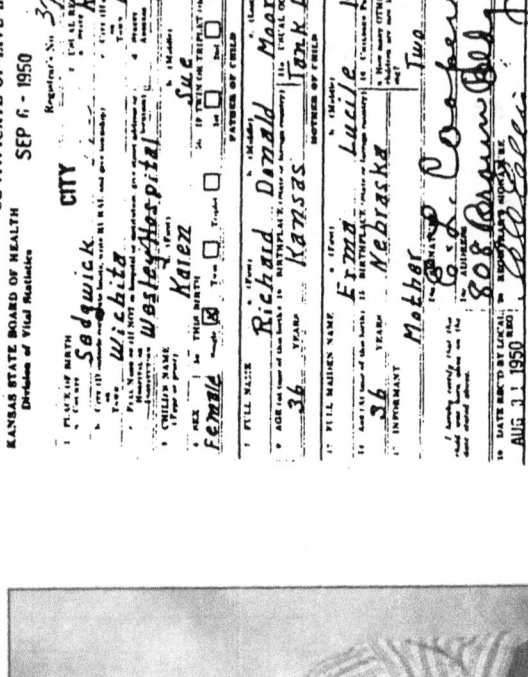

Seth Myron Holliday
pre-school (2nd yr.)
August 1, 1993

Heath Ray Holliday
Soph. at KU
Sept. 17, 1977

Heath, Adam, Ernie are Paul's children by first wife, Jonnie Wartman

Family Group Sheet

SON Full Name: Raymond Moore — Chart No.

	Day Month Year	City, Town or Place	County or Province, etc.	State or Country	Add. Info. on Husband
Birth	13-07-1915	South Haven	Sumner, Co.	Kansas	
Chr'nd					
Marr					
Death	16-08-1916	South Haven	Sumner, Co.	Kansas	
Burial	08-1916	South Haven Cem.	Sumner, Co.	Kansas	

Places of Residence:
Occupation: Church Affiliation: Military Rec.:

His Father: Leon Arthur Moore   Mother's Maiden Name: Nellie Mae Metz

DAUGHTER Full Maiden Name: Arlene Moore

	Day Month Year	City, Town or Place	County or Province, etc.	State or Country	Add. Info. on Wife
Birth	1923	Potwin	Buther, Co.	Kansas	
Chr'nd					
Death	1933 ?	Wichita	Sedgwick, Co.	Kansas	
Burial	1933	South Haven Cem.	Sumner, Co.	Kansas	

Places of Residence:
Occupation: Church Affiliation: Military Rec.:

Her Father: Leon Arthur Moore   Mother's Maiden Name: Nellie Mae Metz

1   Full Name of Spouse:
- Birth: RAYMOND TOOK CHICKEN POX FROM HIS BROTHER FLOYD AND IT TURNED INTO PNEUMONIA AND HE DIED AT
- Marr:
- Death: 1 YEAR OLD.
- Burial:

2
- Birth: ARLENE WAS RIDING IN A TRAILER HER PARENTS
- Marr: WAS PULLING ON 13th STREET IN WICHITA, KANSAS THE TRAILER UNHOOKED, AND ANOTHER VEHICLE HIT THE TRAILER AND KILLED HER. SHE WAS 10 YEARS OLD.

Arlene Moore

Hazel Newcomb and Raymond Moore

ARLINE R MOORE DEC 4 1925 — SEPT 10 1934

Family Group Sheet

Husband's Full Name: Reuben David Moore SS-511-32-7161   Chart No.

	Day Month Year	City, Town or Place	County or Province, etc.	State or Country	Add. Info on Husband
Birth	21-11-1886	Murdock Township	Butler Co.	Kansas	
Chr'nd	11-1902	Potwin	Butler Co.	Kansas	
Marr	12- 2-1908	Potwin	Butler Co.	Kansas	
Death	14- 4-1963	ElDorado	Butler Co.	Kansas	
Burial	17- 4-1963	Towanda Ks.	Butler Co.	Kansas	

Places of Residence:

Occupation: Farmer   **Church Affiliation:** Christian   **Military Rec.:**

His Father: William Oscar Moore   **Mother's Maiden Name:** Louisa Mae Adams

Wife's Full Maiden Name: Edith Leona Taylor

	Day Month Year	City, Town or Place	County or Province, etc.	State or Country	Add. Info on Wife
Birth	16- 9-1889	Danville	Vermillion Co.	Illinois	
Chr'nd	8-1903				
Death	24- 1-1975	ElDorado	Butler Co.	Kansas	
Burial	28- 1-1975	Towanda	Butler Co.	Kansas	

Places of Residence:

Occupation: Housewife   **Church Affiliation:** Christian   **Military Rec.:**

Her Father: William H. Taylor   **Mother's Maiden Name:** Sarah Katherine Liggett

Sex	Children's Names in Full		Day Month Year	City, Town or Place	County or Province, etc.	State or Country	Add. Info on Children
M	1. William Reuben Moore	Birth	1- 8-1909	Potwin	Butler Co.	Kans.	
		Marr.	27- 6-1932	Wichita	Sedgwick Co.	Kans.	
	Full Name of Spouse	Death		Wichita	Sedgwick Co.	Kans.	
	Wanda Pickens	Burial		Peck	Summer, CO	Kans.	
F	2. Violet Marie Moore	Birth	15- 7-1911	Potwin	Butler Co.	Kans.	
		Marr.	31- 7-1932	Potwin	Butler Co.	Kans.	
	Full Name of Spouse	Death	9- 7-1996		Butler Co.	Kans.	
	Charles Tallman	Burial	13- 7-1996	Towanda	Butler Co.	Kans.	
M	3. Glenn Leon Moore	Birth	2- 3-1913	Potwin	Butler Co.	Kans.	
		Marr.	17-10-1943	Sacramento	Sacramento Co.	Calif.	
	Full Name of Spouse	Death					
	Emily Weisker	Burial					
M	4. Lloyd Merle Moore	Birth	18- 6-1915	Potwin	Butler Co.	Kans.	
		Marr.	10- 9-1934	ElDorado	Butler Co.	Kans.	
	Full Name of Spouse	Death					
	Naomi Ullum	Burial					
F	5. Ruth Beula Moore	Birth	4-11-1917	Potwin	Butler Co.	Kans.	
		Marr.	21-12-1940	Potwin	Butler Co.	Kans.	
	Full Name of Spouse	Death					
	John Harold Turner	Burial					
F	6. Opal Miriam Moore	Birth	22- 8-1922	Potwin	Butler Co.	Kans.	
		Marr.	20- 9-1942	ElDorado	Butler Co.	Kans.	
	Full Name of Spouse	Death					
	Merle Harlan	Burial					
M	7. Alva Daniel Moore	Birth	28-11-1927	Potwin	Butler Co.	Kans.	
		Marr.	30-11-1946	Benton	Butler Co.	Kans.	Divorce
	Full Name of Spouse	Death					
	Lois Valette Bachelder	Burial					
F	8. Veda Mae Moore	Birth	22- 7-1930	Potwin	Butler Co.	Kans.	
		Marr.	29-12-1950	Potwin	Butler Co.	Kans.	
	Full Name of Spouse	Death					
	Howard Blazier	Burial					

Compiler:
Address:
City, State, Zip:
Date:

Notes:

Edith Taylor and Reuben D. Moore

STATE OF KANSAS,
BUTLER COUNTY. Office of PROBATE JUDGE OF SAID COUNTY.

Be it Remembered, That on the 10 day of Feb. A.D. 1908, there was issued from the office of said Probate Judge, a Marriage License, of which the following is a true copy:

MARRIAGE LICENSE.

El Dorado, Butler County, State of Kansas, Feb. 10 A.D. 1908.

ANY PERSON AUTHORIZED BY LAW TO PERFORM THE MARRIAGE CEREMONY—GREETING:

YOU ARE HEREBY AUTHORIZED to join in Marriage Ruben D. Moore Butler Co., Kansas aged 21 and Edith Leona Taylor Butler Co., Kansas aged 18 and of this License you will make due return to my office within thirty days. [SEAL] James T. Nye Probate Judge.

And which said Marriage License was afterwards, to-wit: on the 14 day of Feb. A.D. 1908, returned to said Probate Judge, with the following Certificate endorsed thereon, to-wit:

STATE OF KANSAS,
BUTLER COUNTY. ss.

I, Homer E. Moore, do hereby certify, that in accordance with the authorization of the within License, I did, on the 12th day of Feb. 1908, at Residence of Brides Parents in said County, join and unite in Marriage the within named Ruben D. Moore and Edith Leona Taylor.

WITNESS my hand and seal, the day and year above written.

Attest: James T. Nye, Probate Judge.

Homer E. Moore
Minister of the Gospel

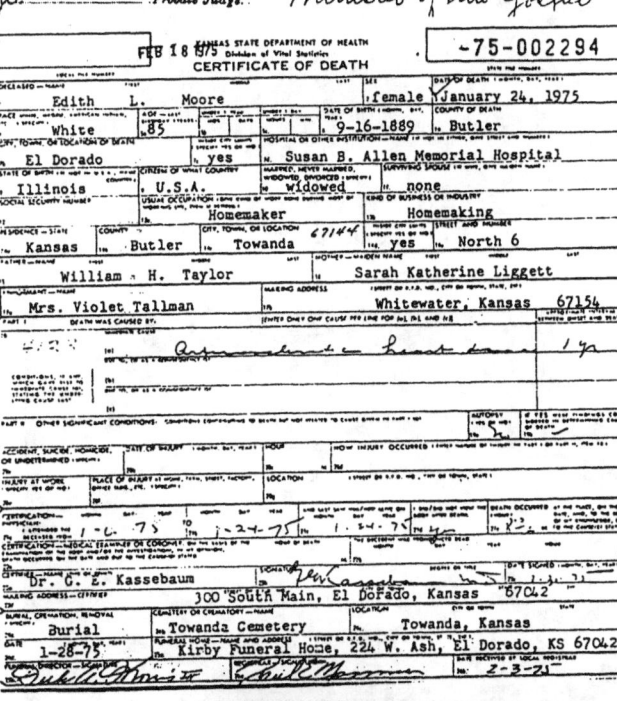

[Certificate of Death — Reuben David Moore, Butler County, Kansas; died April 14, 1963; born 11-21-1886; father William Oscar Moore; mother Lovisa M. Adams; burial Towanda, 4-17-63, Kirby Funeral Home, El Dorado, Ks.]

[Certificate of Death — Edith L. Moore, died January 24, 1975; born 9-16-1889 Butler; El Dorado, Susan B. Allen Memorial Hospital; widowed; Homemaker; Kansas, Butler, Towanda 67144; father William H. Taylor; mother Sarah Katherine Liggett; Mrs. Violet Tallman, Whitewater, Kansas 67154; burial Towanda Cemetery, Towanda, Kansas; Kirby Funeral Home, 224 W. Ash, El Dorado, KS 67042.]

STATE OF ILLINOIS } SS.
Vermilion County

Danville, Illinois, Sept. 23 1997

Upon examination of the records I do not find a record of birth for Edith Leona Taylor in the year 1858-1915.

Upon receipt of $7.00, I will mail you a certificate. Please return this card with your remittance. Additional copies $4.00 each.

No. —

Lynn Foster
County Clerk ML

October 2, 1997

AUDREY F HOPKINS
RR 3 BOX 190B
INDEPENDENCE KS 67301-9304

RE: REUBEN MOORE
    NOVEMBER 21, 1886
    BUTLER COUNTY

Dear Ms. Hopkins:

Our office began filing birth certificates on July 1, 1911. In 1940, we began filing delayed birth certificates for persons born prior to July 1911, who had no birth certificate on file. The oldest of these records dates back to approximately 1875.

Based on the information provided, we conducted a search of our delayed birth records but were unable to locate a record. In compliance with state regulations, we retained a $10.00 fee for the search provided.

If we can be of further assistance, please contact Holly Borsdorf at (785) 296-0859.

Sincerely,

Donna Calabrese
Donna Calabrese, Supervisor
Customer Service
Office of Vital Statistics

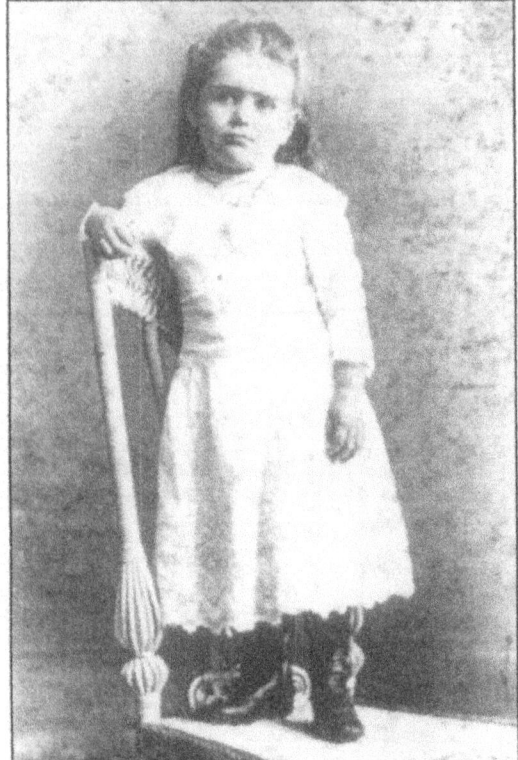
Edith Taylor

Glenn, Alva, Opal, Violet, Lloyd and Veda Moore

Reuben D. Moore, Towanda, Is Dead

Reuben David Moore, of Towanda, died Sunday in Allen Memorial hospital. He was 76.

Funeral services will be held Wednesday at 2 p.m. from the Kirby Funeral Home with the Rev. Z. M. Bressler, pastor of the Towanda Congregational Christian Church officiating.

Burial will be in the Towanda cemetery.

Mr. Moore had been a resident of Butler county all of his life except for two years during which time he lived in Colorado.

He had been a resident of Towanda since 1951.

He was a member of the Towanda Congregational Church.

Mr. Moore was born Nov. 12, 1886 in Murdock Township, Butler County, and was married to Edith Taylor on Feb. 12, 1908, in Murdock Township.

Survivors include his wife, of the home; four daughters, Mrs. Violet M. Tallman of Whitewater, Mrs. Ruth B. Turner of Potwin, Mrs. Opal M. Harlan, Madison, Kans., Mrs. Veda Balzer of Benton; four sons, William R. of Mulvane, Glenn L. of Sacramento, Calif., Lloyd M. of Augusta, Alva D., of Eureka; a sister, Mrs. Effie Pickrell, of Covina, Calif.; three brothers, Arthur, of Wichita, Oren E. of Whitewater, Ray, Valley Center; 27 grandchildren and 20 great-grandchildren.

Edith L. Moore Services Held Last Tuesday

Mrs. Edith L. Moore, 85, of Towanda, died Friday, January 24, at Susan B. Allen Memorial Hospital, El Dorado.

Mrs. Moore was born September 16, 1889 in Danville, Illinois. She married Reuben D. Moore on February 12, 1907, in Murdock Township in Butler county. He died April 14, 1963.

She came to Kansas at the age of four. She was a member of the Towanda United Methodist Church of Christ.

Services were held Tuesday afternoon, January 28, at the Kirby Funeral Home Chapel, El Dorado, with the Rev. George Wattenbarger officiating. Vocalist Glen Lehman, Jr., sang "When They Ring the Golden Bell" and "No Night There." Organist was Mrs. H. W. Bullerdiek.

Casketbearers were Howard Moore, Gary Moore, Alva Moore, James Moore, Roger Tallman and Mervin Harlan.

Survivors include four daughters, Mrs. Violet Tallman of Whitewater, Mrs. Ruth Turner and Mrs. Vida Balzer, both of Potwin, and Mrs. Opal Harlan of Madison; four sons, William of Mulvane, Glen of Sacramento, California, Lloyd of Augusta, and Alva of Cassoday; one brother, Kenneth Taylor of Whitewater; and 28 grandchildren, 37 great-grandchildren. She was preceded in death by her husband, four brothers, one grandchild and one great-grandchild.

Interment was in the Towanda Cemetery.

Alva Moore, Ruth Turner, Willa Case, Elwood Moore.
Glenn Moore, Opal Halon, Lloyd Moore.

George Pickel, Orin Moore, Reuben Moore, Ray Moore.
Susie Moore, Edith Moore, Vida Moore, Aunt Effie, Dad's sister.

Effie, Eva, Stella, Orin, Reuben, Ray Moore, Oscar and Mary Smith, June 10, 1956.

Back: Lloyd, Ruth, Alva, Glenn, Violet, Bill. Front: Opal, Reuben, Edith, Vida Moore, 1946.

Sue Moore, Edith, Vida, Stella Eller and Lavine Porterfield, Marie W., Gladys Stewart, Maxine, Cora, Stella Schisler. June 10, 1956.

Family Group Sheet

Husband's Full Name William Reuben Moore SS-512-10-0678 Chart No.

Husband's Data	Day Month Year	City, Town or Place	County or Province, etc.	State or Country	Add. Info. on Husband
Birth	8-1-1909	Potwin	Butler Co.	Kans.	
Chr'nd					
Marr.	25-6-1932	Wichita Presbyterian church	Sedgwick Co.	Kans.	
Death	5-4-1987	Wichita	Sedgwick Co.	Kans.	
Burial	4-1987	Council Hill cem.	Peck	Kans.	

Places of Residence 310 N. Second Mulvane, Ks.
Occupation Aircraft Technician Church Affiliation Methodist Military Rec

His Father Reuben David Moore Mother's Maiden Name Edith Leona Taylor

Wife's Full Maiden Name Wanda Lucinda Pickens

Wife's Data	Day Month Year	City, Town or Place	County or Province, etc.	State or Country	Add. Info. on Wife
Birth	16-12-1910	Ashland		Kansas	
Chr'nd					
Death					
Burial					

Places of Residence 310 N. Second Mulvane, Ks. Villa Maria Nursing Home-Mulvane, Ks.
Occupation Silk Screen Maker Church Affiliation Methodist Military Rec

Her Father Homer Orsen Pickens Mother's Maiden Name Maude Hazel Anderson

Sex	Children's Names in Full		Day Month Year	City, Town or Place	County or Province, etc.	State or Country	Add. Info. on Children
F	1 Mirran Ann Moore	Birth	5-3-1933	Wesley hospital Wichita		Kans.	divorced
		Marr.	11-2-1952	Mulvane United Meth.		Kans.	23 Sept. 1983
	Full Name of Spouse Robert Lee Dennett	Death					
		Burial					
F	2 Willia Pauline M.	Birth	4-5-1935		Butler Co.	Ks.	
		Marr.	14-10-1961	Wichita	Sedgwick Co.	Ks.	
	Full Name of Spouse James Elwyn Wulz	Death					
		Burial					
M	3 Howard Ray Moore	Birth	27-11-1936	Wichita	Sedgwick Co	Ks	
		Marr.	26-2-1960	Wichita	Sedgwick Co	Ks	
	Full Name of Spouse Margaret Ann Hornecker	Death					
		Burial					
M	4 James Reuben Moore	Birth	20-6-1942	Wesley hospital Wichita	Sedg. Co.	Ks.	
		Marr.	7-7-1963				
	Full Name of Spouse Judy Arlene Hayes	Death					
		Burial					
	5	Birth					
		Marr.					

1982

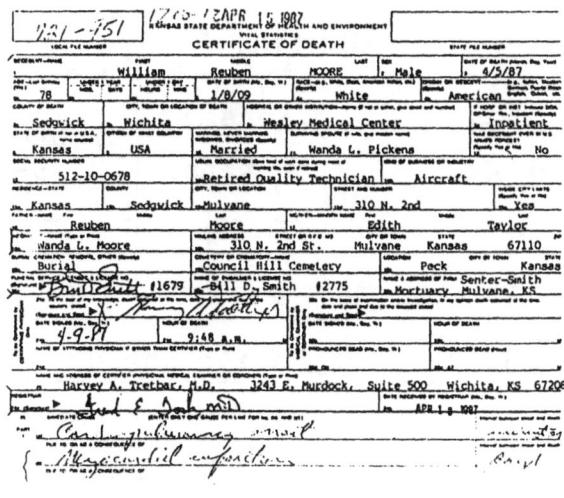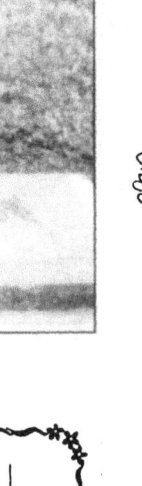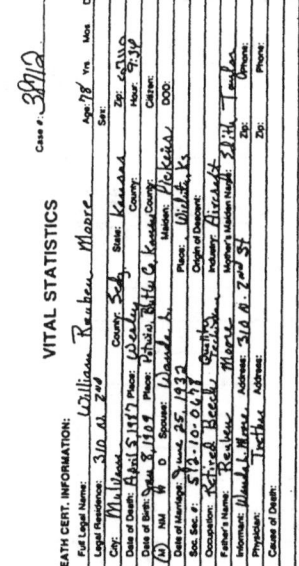

Family Group Sheet

Husband's Full Name: Robert Lee Dennett
Chart No.:

	Day Month Year	City, Town or Place	County or Province, etc.	State or Country	Add. Info on Husband
Birth	8-1-1932	Shady Rest	Butler Co.	Kansas	Divorced 23-9-198
Chr'nd					
Marr	11-2-1952	Methodist Mulvane	Sedgwick Co.	Kans.	
Death					
Burial					

Places of Residence: Augusta, Kansas
Occupation: Unlcan **Church Affiliation:** **Military Rec:**

His Father: Leo Glen Dennett **Mother's Maiden Name:** Eleanor Margaurite Sharon

Wife's Full Maiden Name: Miriam Ann Moore

	Day Month Year	City, Town or Place	County or Province, etc.	State or Country	Add. Info on Wife
Birth	4-5-1933	Wesley Wichita	Sedgwick Co.	Kansas	
Chr'nd					
Death					
Burial					

Places of Residence: 10310 SW 110th, Augusta, Kansas
Occupation: Seamstress **Church Affiliation:** **Military Rec:**

Her Father: William R. Moore **Mother's Maiden Name:** Wanda Lucinda Pickins

Sex	Children's Names in Full		Day Month Year	City, Town or Place	County or Province, etc.	State or Country	Add. Info on Children
M	1. Carl Leland Dennett	Birth	21-1-1956	Wichita	Sedgwick Co.	Kans.	
		Marr.					
	Full Name of Spouse	Death					
		Burial					
F	2. Diana LeeAnn D.	Birth	23-11-1957	Wichita	Sedgwick Co.	Kans.	
		Marr.	1985				
	Full Name of Spouse: Eugene Thomas Corl	Death					
		Burial					

Family Group Sheet

Husband's Full Name: Carl LeLand Dennett

Chart No.

	Day Month Year	City, Town or Place	County or Province, etc.	State or Country	Add. Info on Husband
Birth	21-1-1956	Wichita	Sedgwick Co.	Kansas	
Chr'nd					
Marr.					
Death					
Burial					

Places of Residence:

Occupation: Electronic Technician **Church Affiliation:** **Military Rec:** U.S. Navy

His Father: Robert L. Dennett   **Mother's Maiden Name:** Miriam Ann Moore

Wife's Full Maiden Name:

	Day Month Year	City, Town or Place	County or Province, etc.	State or Country	Add. Info on Wife
Birth					
Chr'nd					
Death					
Burial					

Places of Residence:

Occupation: **Church Affiliation:** **Military Rec:**

Her Father: **Mother's Maiden Name:**

Sex	Children's Names in Full	Children's Data	Day Month Year	City, Town or Place	County or Province, etc.	State or Country	Add. Info on Child
	1	Birth					
		Marr.					
	Full Name of Spouse	Death					
		Burial					
	2	Birth					
		Marr.					
	Full Name of Spouse	Death					
		Burial					
	3	Birth					
		Marr.					
	Full Name of Spouse	Death					
		Burial					
	4	Birth					
		Marr.					
	Full Name of Spouse	Death					
		Burial					
	5	Birth					
		Marr.					
	Full Name of Spouse	Death					
		Burial					
	6	Birth					
		Marr.					
	Full Name of Spouse	Death					
		Burial					
	7	Birth					
		Marr.					
	Full Name of Spouse	Death					
		Burial					
	8	Birth					
		Marr.					
	Full Name of Spouse	Death					
		Burial					

Compiler:
Address:
City, State, Zip:
Date:

Notes:

Family Group Sheet

Husband's Full Name: Eugene Thomas Corl

Chart No.

	Day Month Year	City, Town or Place	County or Province, etc.	State or Country	Add. Info on Husband
Birth	25- 7-1957	Syracuse	Onondago Co.	New York	
Chr'nd					
Marr	13- 7-1985				
Death					
Burial					

Places of Residence:

Occupation: Computer Systems Tech   **Church Affiliation:**   **Military Rec:** Navy

His Father: Eugene Thomas Corl II   **Mother's Maiden Name:** Jean Louise LeBlanc

Wife's Full Maiden Name: Diana Leeann Dennett

	Day Month Year	City, Town or Place	County or Province, etc.	State or Country	Add. Info on Wife
Birth	23-11-1957	Wichita	Sedgwick Co.	Kansas	
Chr'nd					
Death					
Burial					

Places of Residence: 820 Elm Forrest Drive   Claremont, Florida

Occupation: Accountant   **Church Affiliation:** Methodist   **Military Rec:**

Her Father: Robert L. Dennett   **Mother's Maiden Name:** Miriam Ann Moore

Sex	Children's Names in Full		Day Month Year	City, Town or Place	County or Province etc.	State or Country	Add. Info on Children
F	1 Danielle Dawn Corl	Birth	19- 6-1986	Denver	Denver Co.	Colo.	
	Full Name of Spouse	Marr.					
		Death					
		Burial					
F	2 Heather Lynn Corl	Birth	15- 7-1988	Denver	Denver Co.	Colo.	
	Full Name of Spouse	Marr.					
		Death					
		Burial					
M	3 Derik Eugene Corl	Birth	28- 9-1993	Denver	Denver Co.	Colo.	
	Full Name of Spouse	Marr.					
		Death					
		Burial					

Diana LeeAnn Dennett, Thomas Eugene Corl, Danielle Dawn, Heather Lynn and Derik Eugene Corl

Family Group Sheet

Husband's Full Name: James Elvyn Wulz **Chart No.**

	Day Month Year	City, Town or Place	County or Province, etc	State or Country	Add. Info. on Husband
Birth	15-7-1932	Kremlin	Garfield Co.	Okla.	
Chr'nd					
Marr	14-10-1961	Wichita	Sedgwick Co.	Kansas	
Death					
Burial					

Places of Residence: P.O. Box 624 Shell Knob, Mo. 65747
Occupation: Program Manager Boeing **Church Affiliation:** Methodist **Military Rec:** U.S. Army
His Father: Gilbert Charles Wulz **Mother's Maiden Name:** Gretchen Irene Hamil

Wife's Full Maiden Name: Willa Pauline Moore

	Day Month Year	City, Town or Place	County or Province, etc	State or Country	Add. Info. on Wife
Birth	5-4-1935		Butler Co.	Kansas	
Chr'nd					
Death					
Burial					

Places of Residence: P.O. Box 624 Shell Knob, Mo. 65747
Occupation: Human Res. Dir. Commerce Bank Methodist **Military Rec:**
Other husbands: 1st. Richard Nheil Allison 17-?-1954 Divorced in 1957
Her Father: William R. Moore **Mother's Maiden Name:** Wanda Lucinda Pickell

Sex	Children's Names in Full		Day Month Year	City, Town or Place	County or Province, etc	State or Country	Add. Info. on Children
M	1 Richard Nheil Wulz	Birth	19-1-1955	McConnell AFB Wichita		Kans.	Divorced
	#1 Claudia Marie Schwehm	Marr.	28-8-1978	Twistringen		Germany	23-8-1982
	#2 Patricia Sanner	Death					
		Burial					
M	2 Ronald Ray Wulz	Birth	18-5-1957	Winfield	Cowley Co	Kans.	
		Marr.	31-12-1991				
	Vicki McQueen	Death					
		Burial					
F	3 Susan Rene Wulz	Birth	3-2-1965				
		Marr.					
		Death	5-2-1965				
		Burial	2-1965	Council Hill cem. Peck Sumner Co. Ks.			

Compiler: Willa Wulz
Notes: Richard and Ronald were adopted by James Wulz on 11 October 1964 their Biological father was Richard Nheil Allison, born 19-12-1933 deceased 15-1-1995

Gravestone: SUSAN RENE WULZ FEB. 3, FEB. 5, 1965

129

E. Military Service Record

Name of Veteran: Wulz (last) James (first) Elvyn (middle)

State from Which Served: Oklahoma

War in Which, or Dates between Which, He Served: January 1953 === January 1955 KOREAN

If Service Was Civil War:

Union _____ Confederate _____

Unit in Which He Served:

Name or Number of Regiment: 123rd ARMORED ORDNANCE BATTALION

Company: Headquarters Detachment

Name of Ship: _____

Branch in Which He Served: Basic Training — After Basic Traing Armore

Infantry __X__ Cavalry ____ Artillery ____ Navy ____ Other __X__

Kind of Service: Volunteers _____ Regulars __X__

Pension File Number: N/A

Bounty Land File Number (for Service before 1856 Only): N/A

Military Record Number: US 54050841

Date of Birth: 15 July, 1932

Place of Birth: Kremlin (city) Garfield; Co. (county) Oklahoma (state)

Name of Widow or Other Claimant: _____

Date of Death: _____

Place of Death: _____ (city) _____ (county) _____ (state)

Places Lived after Service: Stillwater, OK.==Wichita, Ks.== Derby, Ks.== Shell Knob, Missouri

If Veteran Lived in a Home for Soldiers:

Location: _____ (city) _____ (state)

Family Group Sheet

Husband's Full Name Richard NHeil Wulz — **Chart No.**

Husband's Data	Day Month Year	City, Town or Place	County or Province, etc.	State or Country	Add. Info. on Husband
Birth	19-1-1955	McConnell AFB Wichita	Sedgwick Co.	Kansas	Divorced 23-8-1982
Chr'nd	29-1-1955				
Marr	28-8-1978	Tnistringen		Germany	
Death					
Burial					

Places of Residence Florida
Occupation Salesperson **Church Affiliation** Methodist **Military Rec.** U.S. Army
His Father James E. Wulz **Mother's Maiden Name** Willa P. Moore

Wife's Full Maiden Name Claudia Marie Schwehr

Wife's Data	Day Month Year	City, Town or Place	County or Province, etc.	State or Country	Add. Info. on Wife
Birth	21-12-1957	Twistringen		Germany	
Chr'nd					
Death					
Burial					

Places of Residence Twistringen Germany
Occupation Radiation Therapist **Church Affiliation** Catholic **Military Rec.**
Her Father Franz Joseph Schwehr **Mother's Maiden Name** Marie Magdalena Bavendiek

Sex	Children's Names in Full	Children's Data	Day Month Year	City, Town or Place	County or Province, etc.	State or Country	Add. Info. on Children
F	Renee Maria Wulz	Birth	9-12-1979	Holzwickde		Germany	
		Marr.					

Family Group Sheet

Husband's Full Name Richard NHeil Wulz — **Chart No.**

Husband's Data	Day Month Year	City, Town or Place	County or Province, etc.	State or Country	Add. Info. on Husband
Birth	19-01-1955	McConnell AFB Wichita, Sedgwick, Co.		Kansas	Divorced 17-08-198
Chr'nd					
Marr	29-12-1984	Derby	Sedgwick, Co.	Kansas	
Death					
Burial					

Places of Residence Florida
Occupation Sale Person **Church Affiliation** Methedist **Military Rec.** US Army
His Father James E. Wulz **Mother's Maiden Name** Willa P. Moore

Wife's Full Maiden Name Patrick Lynne Sanner

Wife's Data	Day Month Year	City, Town or Place	County or Province, etc.	State or Country	Add. Info. on Wife
Birth	12-10-1954	Wellington	Sumner, Co.	Kansas	
Chr'nd					
Death					
Burial					

Places of Residence 2122 South Market === Wichita, Kansas
Occupation Hair Dresser **Church Affiliation** Evangelical **Military Rec.**
Her Father James Carroll Sanner **Mother's Maiden Name** Wanda Lee Beck

Sex	Children's Names in Full	Children's Data	Day Month Year	City, Town or Place	County or Province, etc.	State or Country	Add. Info. on Children
MM	1 James Patrick NHeil Wulz	Birth	06-10-1984	Wichita	Sedgwick, Co.	Kansas	
	Full Name of Spouse	Marr.					
		Death					
		Burial					
	2	Birth					
		Marr.					
	Full Name of Spouse	Death					
		Burial					

Family Group Sheet

Husband's Full Name _____   **Chart No.** _____

	Day Month Year	City, Town or Place	County or Province, etc.	State or Country	Add. Info. on Husband
Birth					
Chr'nd					
Marr					
Death					
Burial					

Places of Residence

Occupation _____ Church Affiliation _____ Military Rec. _____

His Father _____ Mother's Maiden Name _____

Wife's Full Maiden Name Renee Maria Wulz

	Day Month Year	City, Town or Place	County or Province, etc.	State or Country	Add. Info. on Wife
Birth	09-12-1979	Holzwickde		Germany	
Chr'nd					
Death					
Burial					

Places of Residence

Occupation _____ Church Affiliation _____ Military Rec. _____

Her Father Richard NHeil Wulz   Mother's Maiden Name Claudia Marie Schwehr

Sex	Children's Names in Full		Day Month Year	City, Town or Place	County or Province, etc.	State or Country	Add. Info. on Child
F	1 Sophie Wulz	Birth	-01-1988	Twistringen		Germany	
		Marr.					
	Full Name of Spouse	Death					
		Burial					
	2	Birth					
		Marr.					
	Full Name of Spouse	Death					
		Burial					
	3	Birth					
		Marr.					
	Full Name of Spouse	Death					
		Burial					
	4	Birth					

```
PF1-MENU,2-BWDS,3-FWD,4-APP XREF,5-APP,6-LIC XREF,7-CLERGY,8-CLERGY XREF,9-RCPT
06 APPLICATION/LICENSE NUMBER: 85ML 00065  CLERGY:           10/31/97 F10 XK36
APPLICATION DATE: 03-23-84          APPLICANT: GROOM
GROOMS    NAME:         ▓▓▓▓▓▓▓
RESIDENCE-CITY:
STATE: KANSAS
BRIDES    NAME:         ▓▓▓▓ LYNNE ▓              ▓▓▓▓▓ 04-19-55▓
RESIDENCE CITY:
STATE: KANSAS                                      ▓▓▓▓▓▓ 10-12-▓
                         (CONSENTING PARENTS)
LICENSE NUMBER:
DATE ISSUED:            B:
DATE EXPIRED:           COURT OFFICIAL: TANNER, SUSAN
MARRIAGE DATE:          ▓▓▓▓▓▓▓▓▓▓▓▓▓▓▓    ▓▓▓▓▓▓▓▓▓▓▓
LOCATION:               ▓▓▓▓▓▓▓▓▓▓▓       DISTRICT COURT JUDGE
COUNTY:                                    COURTHOUSE
COUNTY REG: NOT REGISTERED
WITNESSES:              ▓▓▓▓▓▓▓▓▓▓         ▓BARA A. CLASS▓
DATE RECEIVED:          DATE RECORDED: 01-08-85    PRINT COPIES:
```

Comp'er		
Address		
City, State, Zip		Notes:
Date		

Family Group Sheet

Husband's Full Name Ronald Ray Wulz **Chart No.**

Husband's Data	Day	Month	Year	City, Town or Place	County or Province, etc.	State or Country	Add. Info. on Husband
Birth	18	05	1957	Winfield,	Cowley County	Kansas KS	
Chr'nd		06	1957	Mulvane,	Sedgwick County	Kansas	
Marr	05	08	1978	Jacksonville,	Duval County	Florida	Div. 1983
Death							
Burial							

Places of Residence

Occupation **Church Affiliation** **Military Rec.**

Other wives if any: Linda Benoit, Domestic Partner

His Father James Wulz **Mother's Maiden Name** Willa Moore

Wife's Full Maiden Name Deborah Ann Brindle

Wife's Data	Day	Month	Year	City, Town or Place	County or Province, etc.	State or Country	Add. Info. on Wife
Birth	13	10	1949	Amsterdam	Montgomery County	New York	
Chr'nd							
Death							
Burial							

Places of Residence Omaha, Nebraska

Occupation Nurse **Church Affiliation** **Military Rec.**

Her Father James D. Fudges **Mother's Maiden Name** Katherine May Grosha

Sex	Children's Names in Full (arranged in order of birth)	Children's Data	Day	Month	Year	City, Town or Place, County or Province, etc. State or Country	Add. Info. on Children
F	1. Stephanie Renee Wulz	Birth	12	04	1980	Jacksonville, Duval Co. Florida	1st wife
	Full Name of Spouse	Marr.					
		Death					
		Burial					
F	2. Colleen Benoit Wulz	Birth	15	02	1985	Long Beach, Los Angeles Co. CA	2nd wife
	Full Name of Spouse	Marr.					
		Death					
		Burial					
	3.	Birth					
		Marr.					
	Full Name of Spouse	Death					
		Burial					
	4.	Birth					
		Marr.					
	Full Name of Spouse	Death					
		Burial					
	5.	Birth					
		Marr.					
	Full Name of Spouse	Death					
		Burial					
	6.	Birth					
		Marr.					
	Full Name of Spouse	Death					
		Burial					
	7.	Birth					
		Marr.					
	Full Name of Spouse	Death					
		Burial					
	8.	Birth					
		Marr.					
	Full Name of Spouse	Death					
		Burial					

Compiler:
Address:
City, State, Zip:
Date:

Notes:

Family Group Sheet

Husband's Full Name Ronald Ray Wulz — **Chart No.**

Husband's Data	Day Month Year	City, Town or Place	County or Province, etc	State or Country	Add. Info. on Husband
Birth	18-5-1957	Winfield	Cowley Co.	Kansas	Divorced
Chr'nd	6-1957	Mulvane	Sedgwick Co.	Kans.	1983
Marr	29-11-1986	Wichita	Sedgwick Co.	Kans.	# 1 wife
Death					
Burial					

Places of Residence:
Occupation: Church Affiliation: Military Rec:

His Father: Mother's Maiden Name:

#3 **Wife's Full Maiden Name** Shawn Suzanne Snyder

Wife's Data	Day Month Year	City, Town or Place	County or Province, etc.	State or Country	Add. Info. on Wife
Birth	24-7-1959	Ft. Bragg		North Carolina	
Chr'nd					
Death					
Burial					

Places of Residence:
Occupation: Acct Manager   Church Affiliation: Protestant   Military Rec:

Her Father: Robert Lee Snyder   Mother's Maiden Name: Edith Jane Martin

Sex	Children's Names in Full	Children's Data	Day Month Year	City, Town or Place	County or Province, etc.	State or Country	Add. Info. on Children
F	1 Megan Leigh Wulz (Henning)	Birth	18-2-1989	Long Beach	Los Angeles Co.	Ca.	
	Full Name of Spouse	Marr.					
		Death					
		Burial					
	2	Birth					
		Marr.					
	Full Name of Spouse	Death					
		Burial					
	3	Birth					
		Marr.					
	Full Name of Spouse	Death					
		Burial					
	4	Birth					
		Marr.					
	Full Name of Spouse	Death					
		Burial					
	5	Birth					
		Marr.					
	Full Name of Spouse	Death					

```
PF1-MENU,2-BWDS,3-FWD,4-APP XREF,5-APP,6-LIC XREF,7-CLERGY,8-CLERGY XREF,9-RCPT
06 APPLICATION/LICENSE NUMBER: 86ML 04230  CLERGY:           10/31/97 F10 XK26
APPLICATION DATE: 11-21-86          APPLICANT: BRIDE
GROOMS  NAME:    ███████ RONALD RAY
RESIDENCE-CITY:  ████████
STATE: CALIFORNIA                                   DATE/BIRTH: 05-18-57
BRIDES  NAME:           SHAWN SUZANNE
RESIDENCE-CITY:  ████████
STATE: CALIFORNIA                                   DATE/BIRTH: 07-24-59
                         (CONSENTING PARENTS)
LICENSE NUMBER: ██████████
DATE ISSUED:      11-25-86   B:
DATE EXPIRED:                COURT OFFICIAL: TANNER, SUSAN
MARRIAGE DATE: ████████      PERFORMED ██████████████
LOCATION: ████████                        ████ CLERGY
COUNTY: ████████                          ADDR: WICHITA, KS.
COUNTY REG: RENO
WITNESSES: ████████████                   ████████████
DATE RECEIVED ████████       DATE RECORDED: 12-02-86     PRINT COPIES:
```

Family Group Sheet

Husband's Full Name Ronald Ray Wulz — **Chart No.**

Husband's Data	Day Month Year	City, Town or Place	County or Province, etc.	State or Country	Add. Info. on Husband
Birth	18-05-1957	Fort Collins	Larimer, Co.	Colorado	
Chr'nd					
Marr	-02-1998	Fort Collins	Larimer, Co.	Colorado	
Death					
Burial					

Places of Residence
Occupation — Church Affiliation — Military Rec.

His Father James E. Wulz — **Mother's Maiden Name** Willa P. Moore

Wife's Full Maiden Name Ruth Arenas

Wife's Data	Day Month Year	City, Town or Place	County or Province, etc.	State or Country	Add. Info. on Wife
Birth	1957	Fort Collins	Larimer, Co.	Colorado	
Chr'nd					
Death					
Burial					

Places of Residence
Occupation — Church Affiliation — Military Rec.

Her Father — **Mother's Maiden Name**

Sex	Children's Names in Full	Children's Data	Day Month Year	City, Town or Place	County or Province, etc.	State or Country	Add. Info on Child
M	1. James Wyett Wulz	Birth	30-05-1998	Fort Collins	Larimer, Co.	Colorado	
	Full Name of Spouse	Marr. / Death / Burial					
	2.						
	3.						
	4.						
	5.						
	6.						
	7.						
	8.						

Compiler:
Address:
City, State, Zip:
Date:
Notes:

Family Group Sheet

Husband's Full Name: Howard Ray Moore — Chart No.

	Day Month Year	City, Town or Place	County or Province, etc.	State or Country	Add. Info. on Husband
Birth	27-11-1936	Wesley Hospital Wichita	Sedgwick Co.	Kans.	
Chr'nd					
Marr	26-2-1960	Wichita	Sedgwick Co.	Kans.	
Death					
Burial					

Places of Residence: 1500 Wheatridge Drive Wichita, Kansas
Occupation: Asst. Principal **Church Affiliation:** Methodist **Military Rec:** US Army

His Father: William R. Moore **Mother's Maiden Name:** Wanda Lucinda Pickens

Wife's Full Maiden Name: Margaret Ann Hornecker

	Day Month Year	City, Town or Place	County or Province, etc.	State or Country	Add. Info. on Wife
Birth	3-12-1938	St. Frances hospital Wichita	Sedgwick Co.	Kans.	
Chr'nd					
Death					
Burial					

Places of Residence: 1500 Wheatridge Drive Wichita, Kansas
Occupation: Nurse

Her Father: Charles Hornecker **Mother's Maiden Name:** LaVerne Dixon

Sex	Children's Names in Full		Day Month Year	City, Town or Place	County or Province, etc.	State or Country	Add. Info. on Children
M	1 Troy Douglas Moore	Birth	28-12-1960	St. Frances Wichita		Kansas	
		Marr.	30-12-1995	San Diego	San Diego Co.	Calif.	
	Full Name of Spouse: Jacqueline Guajardo	Death					
		Burial					
M	2 Michael Alan Moore	Birth	3-12-1965	Wichita	Sedgwick Co.	Kans.	
		Marr.	14-8-1993				
	Full Name of Spouse: Jean Covert Joni	Death					
		Burial					
F	3 Sheryl Ann Moore	Birth	3-2-1975	Wesley hospital Wichita		Ks.	
		Marr.					
	Full Name of Spouse	Death					
		Burial					

Howard and Margaret Moore, 1997

E. Military Service Record

Name of Veteran Moore   Howard   Ray

State from Which Served Kansas
War in Which, or Dates between Which, He Served:
    5 April 1960 - 26 December 1991

Unit in Which He Served:

   Name or Number of Regiment:
        HQs 89th Regional Support Command, Wichita, Ks
        HQs 102nd USARCOM St Louis, Mo
        HQs 3rd Region ROTC Ft Riley, Ks

Branch in Which He Served:

   Infantry Yes
   Other   Adjutant General
   Other   Inspector General

Kind of Service:

   Volunteers Yes

Military Record Number   510-30-9956

Date of Birth   27 November 1936

Place of Birth Wichita   Segwick   Kansas
                City   County   State

Name of Widow or Other Claimant Margaret

Places Lived after Service Wichita, Ks

Enlisted Service:
  Kansas Army National Guard Wichita, Ks   E1 - E2
       5 April '60 - 1 February '61

  325th Tans Company Salina, Ks   E2 - E3
       Dec '61 - Aug '63

  HQs 1st Battalion 89th Divison Training (CST) Holton, Ks   E3 - E4
       Aug '63 - Jul '65

  HQs 89th Division Training Wichita, Ks   E4 - E5

Commissioned Service:

  Transportation Company   1st Lt (2 SED GC) Direct Appointment

       Sept '66 - Aug '68

HQs 89th Division Training Wichita, Ks
    1st Lt to Captain (19 Dec 69)
        Aug '68 - Nov '73

Commander, 430th Personnel Services Company, Type C
    Promoted to Major (15 June '74)
        1 Nov '73 - 15 Feb '76

USAR Control Group, REINF St Louis, Mo

HQs 89th United States Army Reserve Command Wichita, Ks
        Inspector General
        21 Aug '76 - 1 Nov '78

Assistant Deputy Chief of Staff Resource Management
    Promoted to Lt Colonel (15 Aug '80)

Active Guard Reserve Program Wichita, Ks (Active Duty) May '84
    Promoted to Colonel (15 Nov '85)

Inspector General 102 nd USARCDM St Louis, Mo
        9 April '87 - 9 May '90

United States Army Reserve Advisor to The Commanding General
Third Region Headquarters (ROTC) Cadet Command, Ft Riley, Ks
        10 May '90 - 26 Dec '91
        Retired, Colonel, AUS

Army Schools attended Adjutant General Officer Basic & Advanced Course Ft Benjamin Harrison, In., Command and General Staff College Ft Leavenworth, Ks, National Security Seminar, Washington, D.C., Inspector General Course Ft Belvoir, Va.

Graduated Friends University, Ba Degree 1960; Wichita State
   University, Wichita, Ks
Master of Education Degree 1971: Wichita State University, Wichita,
   Ks
Specialist Education Degree 1976; Oklahoma State University 1989
   Doctor of Education, Stillwater, Ok.

Family Group Sheet

Husband's Full Name: Troy Douglas Moore — **Chart No.**

	Day Month Year	City, Town or Place	County or Province, etc.	State or Country	Add. Info. on Husband
Birth	28-12-1960	St. Frances Hospital Wichita	Sedgwick Co.	Kans.	
Chrnd					
Marr	30-12-1995	San Diego	San Diego Co.	Calif.	
Death					
Burial					

Places of Residence:
Occupation: Adv. Exec. **Church Affiliation:** Methodist **Military Rec:** US Army

His Father: HOWARD RAY MOORE **Mother's Maiden Name:** MARGARET HORNECKER

Wife's Full Maiden Name: Jacqueline Nicole Guajardo

	Day Month Year	City, Town or Place	County or Province, etc.	State or Country	Add. Info. on Wife
Birth	30-7-1964	San Diego	San Diego Co.	Calif.	
Chrnd					
Death					
Burial					

Places of Residence:
Occupation: Graduate Student **Church Affiliation:** Catholic **Military Rec:**

Her Father: Robert Guajardo **Mother's Maiden Name:** Ella Mae Fernandy

Sex	Children's Names in Full		Day Month Year	City, Town or Place	County or Province, etc.	State or Country	Add. Info. on Children
	1	Birth					
		Marr.					
	Full Name of Spouse	Death					
		Burial					
	2	Birth					
		Marr.					

Family Group Sheet

Husband's Full Name: Michael Alan Moore — **Chart No.**

	Day Month Year	City, Town or Place	County or Province, etc.	State or Country	Add. Info. on Husband
Birth	3-12-1965	Wichita	Sedgwick Co.	Kansas	
Chrnd					
Marr	14-8-1993	East Liver Pool		Ohio	
Death					
Burial					

Places of Residence:
Occupation: Systems Analyst **Church Affiliation:** Methodist **Military Rec:** US Army

His Father: Howard Ray Moore **Mother's Maiden Name:** Margaret Ann Hornecker

Wife's Full Maiden Name: Joni Mae Covert

	Day Month Year	City, Town or Place	County or Province, etc.	State or Country	Add. Info. on Wife
Birth	31-8-1966	East Liver Pool		Ohio	
Chrnd					
Death					
Burial					

Places of Residence:
Occupation: US Army **Church Affiliation:** Catholic **Military Rec:** Lt.Meb Intel. Spec.

Her Father: Carol Covert **Mother's Maiden Name:** Anna Mae King

Sex	Children's Names in Full		Day Month Year	City, Town or Place	County or Province, etc.	State or Country	Add. Info. on Children
	1	Birth					
		Marr.					
	Full Name of Spouse	Death					
		Burial					

Family Group Sheet

Husband's Full Name: James Reuben Moore   **Chart No.**

	Day Month Year	City, Town or Place	County or Province, etc.	State or Country	Add. Info. on Husband
Birth	20-6-1942	Wesley hospital Wichita	Sedgwick Co.	Kansas	
Chr'nd					
Marr	7-7-1963	Mulvane Baptist Church	Sedgwick Co.	Kansas	
Death					
Burial					

Places of Residence: 418 N. Second Mulvane, Kansas
Occupation: Vulcan   **Church Affiliation:** Step-to-Life   **Military Rec.**
His Father: William R. Moore   **Mother's Maiden Name:** Wanda L. Pickens

Wife's Full Maiden Name: Judy Arlene Hayes

	Day Month Year	City, Town or Place	County or Province, etc.	State or Country	Add. Info. on Wife
Birth	8-5-1945	Susan B. Allen Hosp. ElDorado	Butler Co.	Kansas	
Chr'nd	1963	baptized in 1st Baptist Church Mulvane	Sedgwick Co.	Ks.	
Death					
Burial					

Places of Residence: 418 N. Second Mulvane, Kansas
Occupation: Clerk   **Church Affiliation:** 1st. Baptist   **Military Rec.**
Her Father: Ralph Lee Hayes   **Mother's Maiden Name:** Helen Marie Shipley Sk.

Sex	Children's Names in Full		Day Month Year	City, Town or Place	County or Province, etc.	State or Country	Add. Info. on Children
F	Tammy Rae Moore	Birth	21-8-1965	St. Joseph hosp. Wichita		Kans.	
		Marr.	30-3-1991				
	Full Name of Spouse	Death					
	George Arthur Craig	Burial					
M	2 Wesley Wayne Moore	Birth	4-5-1968	Wesley hosp. Wichita Sedg.		Kans.	
		Marr.	30-11-1991				
	Full Name of Spouse	Death					
	Richelle (Shel) Lynn Antle	Burial					
	3	Birth					
		Marr.					
	Full Name of Spouse	Death					
		Burial					
	4	Birth					

Jim and Judy Moore

Notes:

Address:
City, State, Zip:
Date:

Family Group Sheet

Husband's Full Name: George Arthur Craig — Chart No.

	Day Month Year	City, Town or Place	County or Province, etc.	State or Country	Add. Info on Husband
Birth	5-9-1964	Kershaw	Lancaster Co.	South Carolina	
Chr'nd					
Marr	30-3-1991	Antioch Bap. Church Lancaster	Lan. Co.	S. Carolina	
Death					
Burial					

Places of Residence:
Occupation: Coach & Teacher   **Church Affiliation:** Baptist   **Military Rec:**

His Father: George Arthur Craig, Sr.   **Mother's Maiden Name:** Mary Elizabeth

Wife's Full Maiden Name: Tammy Rae Moore

	Day Month Year	City, Town or Place	County or Province, etc.	State or Country	Add. Info. on Wife
Birth	21-8-1965	St. Joseph hosp. Wichita	Sedgwick Co.	Kansas	
Chr'nd					
Death					
Burial					

Places of Residence:
Occupation: Teacher   **Church Affiliation:** Baptist   **Military Rec:**

Her Father: James R. Moore   **Mother's Maiden Name:** Judy Arlene Hayes

Sex	Children's Names in Full		Day Month Year	City, Town or Place	County or Province, etc.	State or Country	Add. Info on Children
M	1. Cody James Craig	Birth	29-11-1991	Columbia	Richland Co.	S. Carolina	
	Full Name of Spouse	Marr.					
		Death					
		Burial					
M	2. Dylan Rase Craig	Birth	4-9-1994	Columbia	Richland Co.	S. Carolina	
	Full Name of Spouse	Marr.					
		Death					
		Burial					
M	3. Wyatt William Craig	Birth	10-05-1996	Columbia	Richand, Co.	S. Caroline	
	Full Name of Spouse	Marr.					
		Death					
		Burial					

Family Group Sheet

Husband's Full Name: Wesley Wayne Moore — **Chart No.**

	Day Month Year	City, Town or Place	County or Province, etc.	State or Country	Add. Info. on Husband
Birth	04-05-1968	Wesley Hospital Wichita	Sedgwick, Co.	Kansas	
Chr'nd					
Marr	30-11-1991	1st. Baptist Church Mulvane	Sedgwick, Co.	Kansas	
Death					
Burial					

Places of Residence: 9206 Manchester Kansas City, Missouri
Occupation: Mason **Church Affiliation:** **Military Rec.:** US Army

His Father: James R. Moore **Mother's Maiden Name:** Judy Arlene Hayes

Wife's Full Maiden Name: Richelle "Shel" Lynn Antle

	Day Month Year	City, Town or Place	County or Province, etc.	State or Country	Add. Info. on Wife
Birth					
Chr'nd					
Death					
Burial					

Places of Residence:
Occupation: Ind. Hygienist **Church Affiliation:** **Military Rec.:**

Her Father: Rick Antle **Mother's Maiden Name:** Kaye Wilson

Sex	Children's Names in Full		Day Month Year	City, Town or Place	County or Province, etc.	State or Country	Add. Info. on Child
M	1. Jordan Wayne Moore	Birth	21-01-1993	Kansas City	Jackson, Co.	Missouri	
	Full Name of Spouse	Marr.					
		Death					
		Burial					
M	2. Joshua Shane Moore	Birth	13-10-1995	Kansas City	Jackson, Co.	Missouri	
	Full Name of Spouse	Marr.					
		Death					
		Burial					

Compiler:
Address:
City, State, Zip:
Date:

Violet Marie Moore

MARRIAGE LICENSE

Charles Wesley Tallman and Violet Marie Moore Affidavit showing that said Parties are legally entitled to License to marry is ordered filed and numbered E13022

Office of the Probate Court of Said County

BE IT REMEMBERED, That on the 30th day of July, A.D. 1932, there was issued from the office of said Probate Judge a Marriage License, of which the following is a true copy:

State of Kansas, County of Sedgwick
Wichita, Kansas, July 30, 1932

To any person authorized by law to perform the Marriage Ceremony, Greeting:

YOU ARE HEREBY AUTHORIZED TO JOIN IN MARRIAGE Charles Wesley Tallman of Benton, Kansas, aged 25 (Groom) Violet Marie Moore of Potwin, Kansas, aged 21 (Bride)

with the consent of _____ (Name of Parent or Guardian Consenting)

and of this license, duly endorsed, you will make due return to my office at Wichita, Kansas, within ten days after performing the ceremony.

(SEAL)   J. D. Dickerson, Probate Judge.

ENDORSEMENT

TO WHOM IT MAY CONCERN:
I hereby certify that I performed the ceremony joining in marriage the above-named couple on the 31st day of July, 1932, at Potwin, Kansas

Signed: J. H. Higdon
Title: Minister
Address: Potwin, Kansas

Glenn, Alva, Opal, Violet, Lloyd and Veda

CARLSON FUNERAL HOME INFORMATION SHEET

Florist OK, Times OK, Eagle OK, KSRX ___, Other OK Eureka & Newton

Deceased Name: Violet Marie Tallman
Address: Rt. 1, Box 114 Eureka 67045, Phone #: 853-2267
Informant's Name: Roger Tallman
Address: Box 196 Whitewater 67154, Phone #: 799-2351
Age: 84-11-24, Born: July 15, 1911, Where: Benton, Kansas
Occupation: Homemaker

Date Last Worked: _____, SS#: 509-58-0281
Date of Death: July 9, 1996 (Tuesday), Time: 3:30 P.M.
Place of Death: Susan B. Allen Memorial Hospital, DOA (Auto Accident)
How Long Lived Here: Butler Co. all of life
Lived Where Previously: Whitewater than to Reece, Ks.

Signing Doctor: Dr. Robert Proctor   Dr. Varner
Address: 119 Jones El Dorado, Kansas 67042
Name of Father: Rueben Moore
Name of Mother (Maiden): Edith Taylor
Spouses Name (Maiden): Charles Tallman
Date of Marriage: July 31, 1932, Place: Potwin, Kansas
Is Spouse Living: yes, D.o.D. _____, D.o.B. June 16, 1907
Member of What Church: Potwin Christian Church
Member of What Organizations: none

Military: no   Education: 12

Survivors:
Husband—Charles   Reece, Kansas
Son—Roger Tallman   Whitewater, Kansas
Daughters—Velma Cain   Potwin, Kansas 752-3367
→305 North Sturgis
Thelma Edris   Whitewater, Ks. 799-2612
Brothers—Glenn Moore   Sacramento, California
Lloyd Moore   Independence, Kansas
Alva Moore   Independence, Kansas
Sisters—Opal Harlan   Emporia, Kansas
Ruth Turner   Paducah, Kentucy
Veda Balzer   Potwin, Kansas
13 Grandchildren   26 Great Grandchildren
4 Great Great Grandchildren
*Preceded in death by parents, son-(Glenn Tallman)
Memorials: 1 brother, 1 Grandson
Potwin Christian Church

SERVICE INFORMATION

Place: Potwin Christian Church, Time: 2:00 P.M.
Day and Date of Service: Saturday, July 13, 1996
Officiant: Reverend Rick McNary
Church: _____
Cemetery: Towanda Cemetery
Special Service: _____
Organist: Cynthia Lemke   Vocalist: LaVonne Baker

Songs: "His Eye On The Sparrow" "In The Garden"

Casket Bearers: Honorary Casket Bearers:
Cotton Thorpe
Jim Elting
Bill Williams
Dean Lawrence
Jim Jackson
Steve Mock

Family Group Sheet

Husband's Full Name: Charles W. Tallman — Chart No.

	Day Month Year	City, Town or Place	County or Province, etc.	State or Country	Add. Info. on Husband
Birth	16-6-1907	Wichita	Sedgwick Co.	Kansas	
Chr'nd					
Marr	31-7-1932	Potwin	Butler Co.	Kansas	
Death					
Burial					

Places of Residence:
Occupation: Farmer-Mechanic **Church Affiliation:** Christian **Military Rec:**

His Father: Charles Tallman **Mother's Maiden Name:** Elizabeth Skinner

Wife's Full Maiden Name: Violet Marie Moore SS 509-58-0281

	Day Month Year	City, Town or Place	County or Province, etc.	State or Country	Add. Info. on Wife
Birth	15-7-1911	Benton	Butler Co.	Kansas	
Chr'nd					
Death	9-7-1996	US 54	Butler Co.	Kansas	
Burial	13-7-1996	Towanda cem.	Butler Co.	Kansas	

Places of Residence:
Occupation: Housewife **Church Affiliation:** Christian **Military Rec:**

Her Father: Ruben David Moore **Mother's Maiden Name:** Edith Taylor

Sex	Children's Names in Full		Day Month Year	City, Town or Place	County or Province, etc.	State or Country	Add. Info. on Children
F	1. Velma R. Tallman	Birth	11-6-1933	Benton	Butler Co.	Kansas	
		Marr.	30-11-1956	Newton	Harvey Co.	Kansas	
	Spouse: Harry Cain	Death					
		Burial					
F	2. Thelma E. Tallman	Birth	28-9-1934	Benton	Butler Co.	Kansas	
		Marr.	18-1-1955	Newton	Butler Co.	Kansas	
	Spouse: Richard Dale Edris	Death					
		Burial					
M	3. Roger D. Tallman	Birth	10-6-1938	Benton	Butler Co.	Kansas	
		Marr.	26-2-1965	Turley	Sedgwick Co.	Kansas	
	Spouse: Nancy Lou Edwards	Death					
		Burial					
M	4. Glenn E. Tallman	Birth	4-11-1940	Benton	Butler Co.	Kansas	Divorced
		Marr.					
	Spouse: Sherry Taylor	Death	1-12-1995	ElDorado	Butler Co.	Kansas	
		Burial	5-12-1995	Fairview cem. ElDorado		Kansas	

144

Family Group Sheet

Husband's Full Name: Harry Russell Cain — **Chart No.**

	Day Month Year	City, Town or Place	County or Province, etc.	State or Country	Add. Info. on Husband
Birth	26- 5-1932				
Chr'nd					
Marr	30-11-1956	Newton	Harvey Co.	Kansas	
Death					
Burial					

Places of Residence:
Occupation: Farmer **Church Affiliation:** Christian **Military Rec.**
His Father: **Mother's Maiden Name:**

Wife's Full Maiden Name: Velma Ruth Tallman SS 509-30-0024

	Day Month Year	City, Town or Place	County or Province, etc.	State or Country	Add. Info. on Wife
Birth	11- 6-1933	Benton	Butler Co.	Kansas	
Chr'nd					
Death	18- 5-1998	Wichita	Sedgwick Co.	Kansas	
Burial	20- 5-1998	McGill cem. Potwin	Butler Co.	Kansas	

Places of Residence: Potwin, Kansas
Occupation: Housewife **Church Affiliation:** Christian **Military Rec.**
Her Father: Charles Tallman **Mother's Maiden Name:** Violet Marie Moore

Sex	Children's Names in Full		Day Month Year	City, Town or Place	County or Province, etc.	State or Country	Add. Info. on Children
F	1 Cindy D. Ray Spouse: Herman	Birth Marr. Death Burial	28- 8-1954	Wichita	Sedgwick Co.	Kans.	
M	2 Harry Cain Spouse:	Birth Marr. Death Burial	13- 9-1957 3- 1-1991 -/- 1991	Newton McGill Cem. Potwin Butler Co. KS	Harry Co.	Kansas	
M	3 Danny J. Cain Spouse: Terry L.	Birth Marr. Death Burial	23-12-1958	ElDorado	Butler Co.	Kansas	
M	4 Jerry D. Cain Spouse:	Birth Marr. Death Burial	18- 5-1961	ElDorado	Butler Co.	Kansas	
F	5 Bonnie L. Cain Spouse: Stephans C. Lavan	Birth Marr. Death Burial	26- 2-1963 10-11-1984	ElDorado Benton	Butler Co. Butler Co.	Kansas Kansas	

Address: 312 North Sturges
City, State, Zip: Potwin, Kansas 67123
Date: 316-752-3367

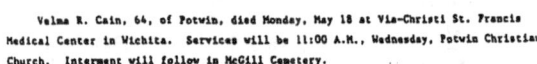

Velma R. Cain, 64, of Potwin, died Monday, May 18 at Via-Christi St. Francis Medical Center in Wichita. Services will be 11:00 A.M., Wednesday, Potwin Christian Church. Interment will follow in McGill Cemetery.

She was born June 11, 1933 at Benton, the daughter of Charles and Violet Marie Moore Tallman. She was a homemaker and had also worked for Walmart for 5 years. She was a member of the Potwin Christian Church.

On November 30, 1956, she married Harry R. Cain at Newton.

Those who survive are her husband—Harry Cain, of the home. Two sons—Danny J Cain, Potwin; Jerry D. Cain, El Dorado. Two daughters—Cindy D. Herrman, Potwin; Bonnie L. Stephens, Benton; Her father—Charles Tallman, Whitewater; One brother— Roger Tallman and one sister—Thelma Edris, both of Whitewater. Eight grandchildren and three great-grandchildren also survive.

She was preceded in death by her mother; one brother and one son.

Memorials in her memory for the Potwin Christian Church may be left at Carlson Funeral Home who are in charge of the services.

Glenn, Veda, Alva, Opal, Lloyd and Violet Moore

Lloyd, Alva, Glenn, William, Violet, Opal, Ruth and Velda, 1986.

Family Group Sheet

Husband's Full Name Herrman — **Chart No.**

	Day Month Year	City, Town or Place	County or Province, etc.	State or Country	Add. Info on Husband
Birth					
Chr'nd					
Marr					
Death					
Burial					

Places of Residence:
Occupation: Church Affiliation: Military Rec:
Other wives, if any...
His Father: Mother's Maiden Name:

Wife's Full Maiden Name Cindy D. Ray

	Day Month Year	City, Town or Place	County or Province, etc.	State or Country	Add. Info. on Wife
Birth	28-8-1954	Wichita	Sedgwick, Co.	Kansas	
Chr'nd					
Death					
Burial					

Places of Residence:
Occupation: Church Affiliation: Military Rec:
Her Father: Harry R. Cain Mother's Maiden Name: Velma Ruth Tallman

Sex	Children's Names		Day Month Year	City, Town or Place	County or Province, etc.	State or Country	Add. Info on Children
M	1 Shawn	Birth	20-10-1976				
	Full Name of Spouse	Marr. / Death / Burial					
F	2 Kayci	Birth	18-1-1978				
	Full Name of Spouse	Marr. / Death / Burial					
M	3 Jordan	Birth	5-11-1986				
	Full Name of Spouse	Marr. / Death / Burial					
M	4 Joshua	Birth	5-11-1986				
	Full Name of Spouse	Marr. / Death / Burial					
	5	Birth					

Family Group Sheet

Husband's Full Name Harry Cain — **Chart No.**

	Day Month Year	City, Town or Place	County or Province, etc.	State or Country	Add. Info on Husband
Birth	13-9-1957	Newton	Harry Co.	Kansas	killed in car accident
Chr'nd					
Marr					
Death	3-1-1991				
Burial	1-1991	McGill Cem. Potwin	Butler Co	Kansas	

Places of Residence:
Occupation: Church Affiliation: Military Rec:
His Father: Harry Russell Cain Mother's Maiden Name: Velma Ruth Tallman
Compiler: Notes:
Address:
City, State, Zip:
Date:

Family Group Sheet

Husband's Full Name: Danny J. Cain   **Chart No.** —

	Day Month Year	City, Town or Place	County or Province, etc.	State or Country	Add. Info. on Husband
Birth	23-12-1958	ElDorado	Butler Co.	Kansas	
Chr'nd					
Marr					
Death					
Burial					

Places of Residence:
Occupation: Church Affiliation: Military Rec:

His Father: Harry R. Cain   **Mother's Maiden Name:** Velma Ruth Tallman

Wife's Full Maiden Name: Terry L.

	Day Month Year	City, Town or Place	County or Province, etc.	State or Country	Add. Info. on Wife
Birth	22- 7-1962				
Chr'nd					
Death					
Burial					

Places of Residence:
Occupation: Church Affiliation: Military Rec:

Her Father: **Mother's Maiden Name:**

Sex	Children's Names in Full		Day Month Year	City, Town or Place	County or Province, etc.	State or Country	Add. Info. on Children
M	1 Michael	Birth	21- 6-1988				
	Full Name of Spouse	Marr.					
		Death					
		Burial					
M	2 Sheldon	Birth	23- 7-1990				
	Full Name of Spouse	Marr.					
		Death					
		Burial					
	3	Birth					
		Marr.					
	Full Name of Spouse	Death					
		Burial					
	4	Birth					
		Marr.					
	Full Name of Spouse	Death					
		Burial					
	5	Birth					

Family Group Sheet

Husband's Full Name: Jerry D. Cain   **Chart No.** —

	Day Month Year	City, Town or Place	County or Province, etc.	State or Country	Add. Info. on Husband
Birth	18- 5-1961	ElDorado	Butler Co.	Kansas	
Chr'nd					
Marr					
Death					
Burial					

Places of Residence:
Occupation: Church Affiliation: Military Rec:

His Father: Harry Russell Cain   **Mother's Maiden Name:** Velma Ruth Tallman

Compiler: Notes:
Address:
City, State, Zip:
Date:

Family Group Sheet

Husband's Full Name: Craig Lavan Stephens   **Chart No.**

	Day Month Year	City, Town or Place	County or Province, etc.	State or Country	Add. Info on Husband
Birth	3-28-1963	Wichita	Sedgwick Co.	Kansas	
Chr'nd					
Marr	11-10-1984	Benton Christian Church	Butler Co.	Kansas	
Death					
Burial					

Places of Residence: 668 NW Tawakoni Rd. Benton, Kansas 67017
Occupation: Maintenance   **Church Affiliation:**   **Military Rec:**

His Father: Dexter Lavan Stephens   **Mother's Maiden Name:** Juanita Joyce Boyd

Wife's Full Maiden Name: Bonnie Lou Cain

	Day Month Year	City, Town or Place	County or Province, etc.	State or Country	Add. Info on Wife
Birth	2-26-1963	Susan B. Allen ElDorado	Butler Co.	Kansas	
Chr'nd					
Death					
Burial					

Places of Residence: 668 NW Tawakoni Rd. Benton, Kansas 67017
Occupation: Management   **Church Affiliation:** Potwin Christian   **Military Rec:**

Her Father: Harry Russell Cain   **Mother's Maiden Name:** Velma Ruth Tallman

---

Susan B Allen Memorial Hospital, ElDorado, Kansas
BIRTH CERTIFICATE

This Certifies that Bonnie Lou Cain was born to Mr. & Mrs. Harry Russell Cain in this hospital at 2:36 a.m. on Tuesday the 26th day of February 1963.

IN WITNESS WHEREOF the said Hospital has caused this Certificate to be signed by its duly authorized officer, and its Official Seal to be hereunto affixed.

License No. 111849

STATE OF KANSAS
THE KANSAS STATE DEPARTMENT OF HEALTH AND ENVIRONMENT
Bureau of Vital Statistics

Marriage License

In the District Court of Sedgwick County, November 2, 1984

To Any Person in the State of Kansas Authorized by Law to Perform the Marriage Ceremony, Greetings:

YOU ARE HEREBY AUTHORIZED TO JOIN IN MARRIAGE

Craig Lavan Stephens of Wichita, Kansas   Age 21
Bonnie Lou Cain of Benton, Kansas   Age 21

...and with this license duly endorsed, you will make return to my office at Wichita, Kansas, within ten days after performing the ceremony.

Chief Deputy Clerk

ENDORSEMENT

TO WHOM IT MAY CONCERN:
I hereby certify that I, the undersigned, performed the ceremony joining in marriage the above named couple on the Tenth day of November 1984 at Benton, Kansas, in Butler County. My credentials are recorded in the D.C.'s office of Butler Co., Ks.

Title: Minister, Benton Christian Church
Address: P.O. Box 246, Benton, KS 67017

Bonnie Lou Cain and Craig L. Stephens
December 1994

149

Family Group Sheet

Husband's Full Name: Richard Dale Edris

Chart No.:

	Day Month Year	City, Town or Place	County or Province, etc.	State or Country	Add. Info on Husband
Birth	12- 2-1934	Newton	Harvey Co.	Kansas	
Chr'nd					
Marr	18- 1-1954	Newton	Harvey Co.	Kansas	
Death	30- 5-1998	Wichita	Sedgwick Co.	Kansas	
Burial	3- 6-1998	Whitewater cem.	Whitewater Butler Co.	Kansas	

Places of Residence: Whitewater, Kansas
Occupation: Cargil Mill **Church Affiliation:** Federated Church **Military Rec:**

His Father: Charles J. Edris **Mother's Maiden Name:** Emma E. Brockway

Wife's Full Maiden Name: Thelma Elizabeth Tallman

	Day Month Year	City, Town or Place	County or Province, etc.	State or Country	Add. Info on Wife
Birth	28- 9-1934	Benton	Butler Co.	Kansas	
Chr'nd					
Death					
Burial					

Places of Residence: Whitewater, Kansas
Occupation: Food Server **Church Affiliation:** Federated Church **Military Rec:**

Her Father: Charles Tallman **Mother's Maiden Name:** Violet Marie Moore

Sex	Children's Names in Full		Day Month Year	City, Town or Place	County or Province, etc.	State or Country	Add. Info on Children
M	1 Charles Richard E.	Birth	30- 5-1955	Newton	Harvey Co.	Kansas	divorced 10-1987
	Full Name of Spouse: Sandy Lee Jones	Marr.	5- 3-1977	Newton	Harvey Co.	Kansas	
		Death					
		Burial					
M	2 Harry L. Edris	Birth	23-10-1956	Newton	Harvey Co	Kansas	
	Full Name of Spouse: Kim Leigh Hatfield	Marr.	4-2-1987				
		Death					
		Burial					
M	3 Dennis L. Edris	Birth	25-12-1958	Newton	Harvey Co.	Kansas	
	Full Name of Spouse: Deborah Sue Hopkins	Marr.	20- 4-1985	Elmiro	Lane Co.	Oregon	
		Death					
		Burial					
M	4 Bruce L Edris	Birth	1- 3-1960	Newton	Harvey Co.	Kansas	
	Full Name of Spouse:	Marr.					
		Death					
		Burial					
F	5 Sue Charlene Edris	Birth	12- 7-1962	Newton	Harvey Co.	Kansas	
	Full Name of Spouse: Raymond Lee Archer	Marr.	30- 5-1981	Whitewater	Butler Co.	Kansas	
		Death					
		Burial					
F	6 Tina Marie Edris	Birth	17-11-1965	Newton	Harvey Co.	Kansas	
	Full Name of Spouse: Amos Leland Hasting 1l	Marr.	23- 7-1994	Whitewater	Butler Co.	Kansas	
		Death					
		Burial					

Compiler:
Address:
City, State, Zip:
Date:

Family Group Sheet 1

Husband's Full Name: Harry L. Edris — Chart No.

	Day Month Year	City, Town or Place	County or Province, etc.	State or Country	Add. Info on Husband
Birth	25-10-1956	Newton	Harvey Co.	Kansas	
Chr'nd					
Marr	4-2-1984			Kansas	
Death					
Burial					

His Father: Richard Dale Edris **Mother's Maiden Name:** Thelma Elizabeth Tallman

Wife's Full Maiden Name: Kim Leigh Hatfield

	Day Month Year	City, Town or Place	County or Province, etc.	State or Country	Add. Info. on Wife
Birth	4-2-1957				
Chr'nd					
Death					
Burial					

Her Father: **Mother's Maiden Name:**

Children

Sex	Name	Event	Day Month Year	City, Town or Place	County or Province, etc.	State or Country
M	1. Daniel R. Edris	Birth	3-12-1978	Newton	Harvey Co.	Kansas
	Spouse: Janell M. Haliburton	Marr.	23-3-1998			
		Death				
		Burial				
M	2. Brianane Edris	Birth	20-10-1979	Newton	Harvey Co.	Kansas
		Marr.				
		Death				
		Burial				
F	3. Brandie Edris	Birth	31-5-1981	Newton	Harvey Co.	Kansas
		Marr.				

Family Group Sheet 2

Husband's Full Name: Daniel R. Edris — Chart No.

	Day Month Year	City, Town or Place	County or Province, etc.	State or Country	Add. Info on Husband
Birth	3-12-1978	Newton	Harvey Co.	Kansas	
Chr'nd					
Marr	22-3-1998				
Death					
Burial					

His Father: Harry L. Edris **Mother's Maiden Name:** Kim Leigh Hatfield

Wife's Full Maiden Name: Janell M. Haliburton

	Day Month Year	City, Town or Place	County or Province, etc.	State or Country	Add. Info. on Wife
Birth	6-1-1980				
Chr'nd					
Death					
Burial					

Her Father: **Mother's Maiden Name:**

Children

Sex	Name	Event	Day Month Year	City, Town or Place	County or Province, etc.	State or Country
F	1. Vineisa M. Edris	Birth	25-6-1997	Newton	Harvey Co.	Kansas
		Marr.				
		Death				

Family Group Sheet

Husband's Full Name: Charles Richard Edris — Chart No.

	Day Month Year	City, Town or Place	County or Province, etc.	State or Country	Add. Info. on Husband
Birth	30-5-1955	Newton	Harvey Co.	Kansas	
Chr'nd					Divorced
Marr	5-3-1977	Newton	Harvey Co.	Kansas	10/87
Death					
Burial					

Places of Residence: Whitewater-Newton Kansas
Occupation: Flour Miller   Church Affiliation: Military Rec:

His Father: Richard D. Edris   **Mother's Maiden Name:** Thelma E. Tallman

Wife's Full Maiden Name: Sandy Lee Jones

	Day Month Year	City, Town or Place	County or Province, etc.	State or Country	Add. Info. on Wife
Birth	25-2-1959	Marion	Marion Co.	Kansas	
Chr'nd					
Death					
Burial					

Her Father: Samuel Lee Jones   **Mother's Maiden Name:** April Ann Bloomer

Sex	Children's Names in Full		Day Month Year	City, Town or Place	County or Province, etc.	State or Country
F	1. Tawnya Christine E.	Birth	10-9-1978	Newton	Harvey Co.	Kansas
M	2. Travis Charles E.	Birth	3-9-1980	Newton	Harvey Co.	Kansas
F	3. Tiffany Crystal E.	Birth	22-11-1981	Newton	Harvey Co.	Kansas

MARRIAGE LICENSE

J. No. _____

IN THE PROBATE COURT OF HARVEY COUNTY, January 18, 1955.

To Any Person in the State of Kansas Authorized by Law to Perform the Marriage Ceremony, Greeting:

YOU ARE HEREBY AUTHORIZED To Join in Marriage

Richard Dale Edris (Groom) of Whitewater, Ks. Age 20

Thelma Elizabeth Tallman (Bride) of Whitewater, Ks. Age 20

with the consent of Mrs. Chas. Edris, mother (Name of Parent or Guardian Consenting) and of this license, duly endorsed, you will make return to my office at Newton, Kansas, within ten days after performing the ceremony.

(SEAL)   Sam H. Sturm, Probate Judge.

ENDORSEMENT

To Whom It May Concern:

I HEREBY CERTIFY That I performed the ceremony joining in marriage the above named couple on the 18th day of January, 1955, at Peturia, Kansas.

Signed: Clinton M. Thomas
Title: Minister of Christian Church
Address: Peturia, Kansas

Compiler: Charles Edris
Address: 111 S. Elm
City, State, Zip: Whitewater, KS 67154
Date: 6-7-95

Family Group Sheet

Husband's Full Name: Dennis Lee Edris — Chart No.

	Day Month Year	City, Town or Place	County or Province, etc.	State or Country	Add. Info. on Husband
Birth	25-12-1958	Newton	Harvey Co.	Kansas	
Chr'nd					
Marr	20-4-1985	Elmira	Lane Co.	Oregon	
Death					
Burial					

Places of Residence: Whitewater, Ks.   Elmira, Oregon
Occupation: Manufacturing Supervisor   **Church Affiliation:**   **Military Rec:**

His Father: Richard Dale Edris   **Mother's Maiden Name:** Thelma Tallman

Wife's Full Maiden Name: Deborah Sue Hopkins

	Day Month Year	City, Town or Place	County or Province, etc.	State or Country	Add. Info. on Wife
Birth	3-4-1951	Kansas City,	Butler Co.	Missouri	
Chr'nd					
Death					
Burial					

Places of Residence: LaCygne, Ks.   Tucson, Ariz.   Elmira, Oregon
Occupation: Restitution Clerk   **Church Affiliation:**   **Military Rec:**

Her Father: Everett Harrison Hopkins   **Mother's Maiden Name:** Ruth Maxine Johnson

Sex	Children's Names in Full		Day Month Year	City, Town or Place	County or Province, etc.	State or Country	Add. Info. on Children
M	1. Joshua Nathaniel E	Birth	6-3-1974	Tucson	Pima	Arizona	
	Full Name of Spouse: Heidi Jean Durham	Marr.	20-8-1993	Eugene	Lane	Oregon	
		Death					
		Burial					
M	2. Jacob Logan Edris	Birth	14-11-1986	Eugene	Lane	Oregon	
	Full Name of Spouse:	Marr.					
		Death					
		Burial					

Richard Dale Edris — The Newton Kansan, Monday, June 1, 1998

WHITEWATER — Richard Dale Edris, 64, died Saturday (May 30, 1998) in Wichita.

He was born Feb. 12, 1934, in Newton to Charles Edris and Emma (Brockway) Edris. He married Jeep Tallman on Jan 18, 1954, in Potwin. She survives of the home.

He was a member of The Federated Church in Whitewater.

He graduated from Whitewater High School and was a lifetime Whitewater resident.

Other survivors include: four sons, Charles Edris and Harry Edris, both of Whitewater, Dennis Edris of Elmira, Ore., and Bruce Edris of Newton; two daughters, Sue Archer of Whitewater and Tina Hastings of Hutchinson; 13 grandchildren; and three great-grandchildren. He was preceded in death by his parents, three bothers, and one sister.

Funeral services will be at 11 a.m. Wednesday at The Federated Church in Whitewater with Pastor Scott Martin officiating. Friends may call from 9 a.m. to 8:30 p.m. Tuesday at Bob Lamb Funeral Home in Whitewater. Family will greet friends from 7 to 8:30 p.m. Tuesday at the funeral home.

Memorials have been established with the Whitewater Cemetery in care of the funeral home.

Family Group Sheet

Husband's Full Name: Bruce Leon Edris — Chart No.

	Day Month Year	City, Town or Place	County or Province, etc.	State or Country	Add. Info on Husband
Birth	1-3-1960	Newton	Harvey	Kansas	
Chr'nd					
Marr					
Death					
Burial					

Places of Residence: Whitewater, Ks. Newton, Ks.
Occupation: **Church Affiliation:**   **Military Rec:**

His Father: Richard Dale Edris   **Mother's Maiden Name:** Thelma Tallman

Wife's Full Maiden Name:

	Day Month Year	City, Town or Place	County or Province, etc.	State or Country	Add. Info on Wife
Birth					
Chr'nd					
Death					
Burial					

Places of Residence:
Occupation: **Church Affiliation:**   **Military Rec:**

Her Father: **Mother's Maiden Name:**

Sex	Children's Names in Full		Day Month Year	City, Town or Place	County or Province, etc.	State or Country	Add. Info on Children
M	1 Kristain Dale	Birth	3-3-1992	Newton	Harvey	Kansas	
		Marr					

Family Group Sheet

Husband's Full Name: Raymond Lee Archer — Chart No.

	Day Month Year	City, Town or Place	County or Province, etc.	State or Country	Add. Info on Husband
Birth	11-9-1959	Winfield	Cowley Co.	Kansas	
Chr'nd					
Marr	30-5-1981	Whitewater	Butler Co.	Kansas	
Death					
Burial					

Places of Residence: ElDorado, Ks.   Whitewater, Ks.
Occupation: Body man (cars)   **Church Affiliation:** Reorganized church of Latter Day Saints   **Military Rec:**

His Father: Jerald Dean Archer   **Mother's Maiden Name:** Charlotte Jones

Wife's Full Maiden Name: Sue Edris

	Day Month Year	City, Town or Place	County or Province, etc.	State or Country	Add. Info on Wife
Birth	12-7-1962	Artell hospital Newton	Harvey Co.	Kansas	
Chr'nd					
Death					
Burial					

Places of Residence: Whitewater, Kansas
Occupation: **Church Affiliation:**   **Military Rec:**

Her Father: Richard Dale Edris   **Mother's Maiden Name:** Thelma (Jeep) Tallman

Sex	Children's Names in Full		Day Month Year	City, Town or Place	County or Province, etc.	State or Country	Add. Info on Children
M	1 Aaron James Archer	Birth	1-11-1984	Newton	Harvey Co.	Kans.	
	Full Name of Spouse	Marr					
		Death					
		Burial					
F	2 Amanda Rae Archer	Birth	4-10-1986	Newton	Harvey Co.	Kans.	
	Full Name of Spouse	Marr					
		Death					
		Burial					

Family Group Sheet

Husband's Full Name: Amos Leland Hastings lll **Chart No.**

Husband's Data	Day Month Year	City, Town or Place	County or Province, etc.	State or Country	Add. Info on Husband
Birth	31-12-1967	Bitgerge		Germany	
Chr'nd					
Marr	23- 7-1994	Whitewater	Butler	Kansas	
Death					
Burial					

Places of Residence: Hutchinson, Kansas
Occupation: Sales Rep. **Church Affiliation:** **Military Rec:**

His Father: Amos Leland Hastings, Jr. **Mother's Maiden Name:** Kay Cutler

Wife's Full Maiden Name: Tina Marie Edris

Wife's Data	Day Month Year	City, Town or Place	County or Province, etc.	State or Country	Add. Info on Wife
Birth	17-11-1965	Newton	Harvey Co.	Kansas	
Chr'nd					
Death					
Burial					

Places of Residence: Hutchinson, Ks. Whitewater, Ks.
Occupation: Dental Asst. **Church Affiliation:** **Military Rec:**

Her Father: Richard Dale Edris **Mother's Maiden Name:** Thelma E. Tallman

Sex	Children's Names in Full	Children's Data	Day Month Year	City, Town or Place	County or Province, etc.	State or Country	Add. Info on Children
F	1. Heather Kay Macy	Birth	20-12-1985	Newton	Harvey Co.	Kans.	
		Marr.					
	Full Name of Spouse	Death					
		Burial					
F	2. Tatum Lyn Macy	Birth	19-11-1987	Newton	Harvey Co.	Kans.	
		Marr.					
	Full Name of Spouse	Death					
		Burial					

Family Group Sheet

Husband's Full Name: Roger Dennie Tallman
Chart No.:

Husband's Data	Day Month Year	City, Town or Place	County or Province, etc.	State or Country	Add. Info. on Husband
Birth	10- 6-1938	Benton	Butler Co.	Kansas	
Chr'nd					
Marr	26- 2-1965	Furley	Sedgwick Co.	Kansas	
Death					
Burial					

Places of Residence: Potwin, Whitewater, Newton, Kansas
Occupation: Mechanic **Church Affiliation:** United Methodist **Military Rec:** US Army
His Father: Charles Tallman **Mother's Maiden Name:** Violet Moore

Wife's Full Maiden Name: Nancy Lou Edwards

Wife's Data	Day Month Year	City, Town or Place	County or Province, etc.	State or Country	Add. Info. on Wife
Birth	4-11-1935	Newton	Harvey Co.	Kansas	
Chr'nd					
Death					
Burial					

Places of Residence: Whitewater, Newton, Kansas
Occupation: Reg. Nurse **Church Affiliation:** United Methodist **Military Rec.:**
Her Father: Orlan Edwards **Mother's Maiden Name:** Blanche Root

Sex	Children's Names in Full	Children's Data	Day Month Year	City, Town or Place	County or Province, etc.	State or Country	Add. Info. on Children
M	1. Charles West T.	Birth	5- 7-1966	Newton	Harvey Co.	Kansas	
		Marr.	4-10-1985	Newton	Harvey Co.	Kansas	
	Full Name of Spouse	Death					
		Burial					

Roger and Nancy Tallman

Roger Tallman

156

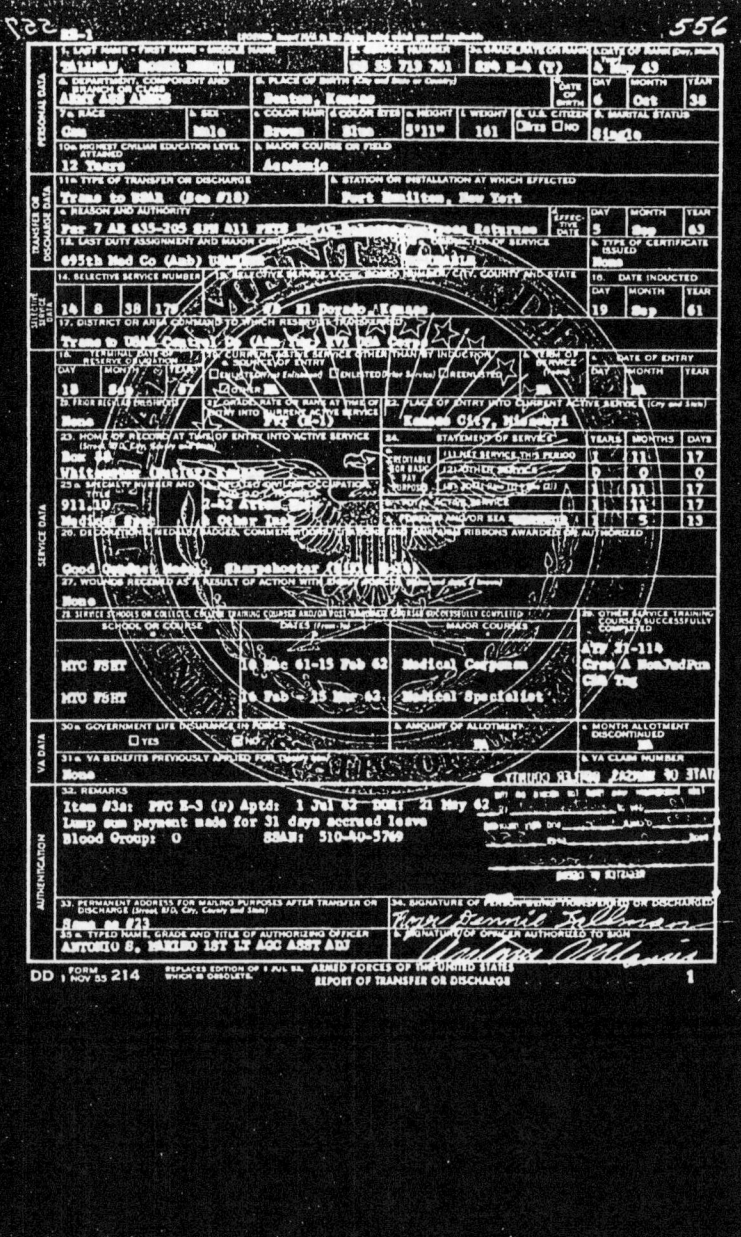

Family Group Sheet

Husband's Full Name: Charles West Tallman — Chart No.

	Day Month Year	City, Town or Place	County or Province, etc.	State or Country	Add. Info. on Husband
Birth	7-5-1966	Newton	Harvey Co.	Kansas	
Chr'nd					
Marr	5-10-1985	Newton	Harvey Co.	Kansas	
Death					
Burial					

Places of Residence: Newton, Whitewater Kansas
Occupation: Truck Driver   **Church Affiliation:** United Methodist   **Military Rec:**
His Father: Roger Tallman   **Mother's Maiden Name:** Nancy Edwards

Wife's Full Maiden Name: Marci Lynn McCurdy

	Day Month Year	City, Town or Place	County or Province, etc.	State or Country	Add. Info. on Wife
Birth	21-6-1967	Newton	Harvey Co.	Kansas	
Chr'nd					
Death					
Burial					

Places of Residence: Whitewater, Kansas
Occupation: Admissions Registry/WMC   **Church Affiliation:** United Methodist   **Military Rec:**
Her Father: Carl McCurdy   **Mother's Maiden Name:** Catherine Higgins

Sex	Children's Names in Full		Day Month Year	City, Town or Place	County or Province, etc.	State or Country	Add. Info. on Children
M	Ryan Charles T.	Birth	4-8-1986	Newton	Harvey Co.	Kans.	
		Marr.					
	Full Name of Spouse	Death					
		Burial					
F	Elizabeth Blanche	Birth	11-3-1991	Wichita	Sedgwick Co.	Kans.	
		Marr.					
	Full Name of Spouse	Death					
		Burial					

Parents: Cathy and Carl McCurdy / Nancy and Roger Tallman
Grandparents: Margaret Wright / Clara and Gene Smith / Violet and Charles Tallman / Blanche and Orlan Edwards

Ministers: Rev. Leon Jennings / Rev. Bob Gleason
Maid of Honor: Mary Tilley
Bridesmaids: Kelli McCurdy / Kristi McCurdy
Best Man: Mike Willis
Groomsmen: Rob McCoy / Ryan Spoerke
Flower Girl: Amanda Reese
Ring Bearer: James Elfers
Candlelighters and Ushers: Wesley Tallman / Tony McCurdy
Soloist: Nancy Tallman
Organist: Rev. Bill Ruster
Pianist: Debra Ewing
Guest Book Attendant: Shane McCurdy
Gift Attendants and Servers: Diane Brooks / Bekki Thies / Sheryl Holmes / Carmen Wrubl / Brenda Wogul / Sandy Moulds

Marci Lynn McCurdy
and
Charles West Tallman
2 P.M., Saturday, October 5, 1985
The First Church of the Nazarene
Newton, Kansas

Organ Prelude
Solo — "Sunrise, Sunset" — Nancy Tallman
Processional
Words of Blessing — Rev. Bob Gleason
Vows — Rev. Leon Jennings
Prayer — Rev. Bob Gleason
Solo — "O Perfect Love" — Nancy Tallman
Ring Ceremony
Solo — "What a Difference You've Made in My Life"
Ring Ceremony
Pronouncement and Blessing
Recessional

Reception following
Family Hall
The First Church of the Nazarene

Marriage License
STATE OF KANSAS
THE KANSAS STATE DEPARTMENT OF HEALTH AND ENVIRONMENT
License No. 119957
D.C. No. — HARVEY County
In the District Court of...
To Any Person in the State of Kansas Authorized by Law to Perform the Marriage Ceremony, Greetings:
YOU ARE HEREBY AUTHORIZED TO JOIN IN MARRIAGE
CHARLES WEST TALLMAN of NEWTON, KANSAS Age 19
MARCI LYNN MCCURDY of NEWTON, KANSAS Age 18
SEPTEMBER 30, 1985

Husband's Full Name: Glenn Edward Tallman
Chart No.:

	Day Month Year	City, Town or Place	County or Province, etc.	State or Country	Add. Info on Husband
Birth	4-11-1940	Potwin	Butler Co.	Kansas	
Chr'nd					Divorced
Marr	1967				
Death	1-12-1995	ElDorado	Butler Co.	Kansas	
Burial	5-12-1995	Fairview cem. ElDor.	Butler Co.	Kansas	

Places of Residence:
Occupation: Cowboy
Church Affiliation:
Military Rec: US Army-Viet Nam

His Father: Charles Tallman
Mother's Maiden Name: Violet Marie Moore

Wife's Full Maiden Name: Sharnon Taylor

	Day Month Year	City, Town or Place	County or Province, etc.	State or Country	Add. Info on Wife
Birth	13- 6-1945				
Chr'nd					
Death	17-11-1984				
Burial	19-11-1984				

Places of Residence:
Occupation:
Church Affiliation:
Military Rec:

Her Father: Norman Taylor
Mother's Maiden Name: Dorothy Carnahon

Sex	Children's Names in Full		Day Month Year	City, Town or Place	County or Province, etc.	State or Country	Add. Info on Children
M	1 Wesley Edward T.	Birth	9- 3-1970				
		Marr.	9-1993				
	Full Name of Spouse: Leslie Pinkerton	Death					
		Burial					
	2	Birth					
		Marr.					
	Full Name of Spouse	Death					
		Burial					
	3	Birth					
		Marr.					

Much Ado About Everything
Remembering a true cowboy

December 11, 1995

Glenn Tallman died the other day. He was only 55 years old. I had not had the pleasure of knowing Glenn. I am sorry I had not had that pleasure.

And I know it would have been a pleasure, too. You see, he was a cowboy.

The Times columnists Jim Hoy and Tom Isern know a lot more about "cowboying" than I. Jim's dad, Ken Hoy, and his late uncle, Marshall Hoy, even from that time, and until his death, Glenn was, to all intents and purposes, totally disabled.

But, even though a full schedule of work was impossible, Glenn continued to train horses. He was the best horse trainer around, his son, Wes, asserted stoutly. And other people confirmed that assessment, too.

Wes himself trains horses now. "I do pretty well," he says, "but I can't hole a candle to my dad."

In more recent times, Wes has worked out of the carpenters' union in Wichita. Do you think of yourself as a carpenter? I asked. Oh, my, no, Wes replied, but I can make more money as a carpenter, than I can at anything else I've done.

"I hate to say I'm a cowboy, or a horse trainer; somebody might question it," Wesley says, his voice tinged with some regret, "but that's what I enjoy most. And, if I could make as much money as a cowboy, or a horse trainer, as I can as a carpenter, I'd work with horses, gladly."

Wesley thinks he and his dad made a pretty good team.

But his dad and Chico made a good team, too—a great team. But who in the world was Chico?

Chico was a big brown Southern-Star-bred horse. He was 16-plus hands high, and weighed about 1,500 pounds. Chico "knew the drill," so to speak. When Glenn Tallman was roping calves, Chico would slow down the calf; if Glenn missed the calf with his lariat. Then, when Glenn had had a chance to form another loop, for a second throw, Chico would back away, so Glenn would have a clear shot at the calf. Wes used to smile at how smart Chico was.

"Were you working with horses because you enjoyed it, or so of thought these last few weeks, you could be with your dad, I asked Wes.

Wes' answer was illuminating. "Always thought I was working with horses for myself. In retrospect, I think I was doing it for my dad."

Will you go back to working with horses, or not?

"I just don't know, was Wes' response, but I've given it a lot of thought these last few weeks, and especially, these last few days.

"I'm going to miss my dad's advice and, as you might expect, I need it right now, more than I've ever needed it in all of my life.

knowing Glenn. I am sorry I had not had that pleasure.

A lovely young Asian woman—a former student of mine—lives with her husband in Singapore. She has visited me, from time to time, in Kansas. On one of those visits, I asked her where she would like to go, or what she would like to see, or do.

She told me she had always wanted to ride horseback. Could I arrange for her to ride horseback, while she was in Kansas? I telephoned a friend of mine who operates a riding academy in Wichita. Yen and I were invited to visit the riding academy, and Yen, most certainly, was allowed to ride a horse.

The only trouble was, Yen was terrified, and, as long as she was aboard that gentle animal, she hung on for dear life.

I was surprised, because Yen had ridden elephants and camels, without fear, but a horse—well, horses, Yen told me, were "different."

Glenn Tallman, however, was, in the words of his son, Wesley, "a horse nut." Throughout his early years, Glenn had wanted to be a jockey, and was small and slight enough to fill the bill, but, at age 14, he began to grow and grow—and grow, so that was that.

Glenn rode in rodeos for some ten years, but his principal forte was saddle bronc riding.

Glenn felt a special affinity for Marshall Hoy, and the Hoy he knew best. Marshall kept cattle, and used to allow Glenn to rope cattle for him, just for fun, and Glenn regarded Marshall as his friend.

Glenn married Sharon Taylor from Whitewater, and Wesley was the couple's only child. Sharon died when Wesley was only 14 years old and, after his mother's death, Wesley continued to live with his father. Wesley felt he and his father were particularly close—in part, because their interests were the same and, in part, too, because father and son lived together, after Sharon's death.

When Glenn was about 40 years of age, he discovered he had emphysema. At that time, he was working for the Southern Star Land and Cattle Company, but he continued to work for that outfit, as long as his health permitted. By 1982 or 1983, however, Glenn's emphysema made regular and sustained work impossible, and, so,

more. They have all been cowboys.

It may not count, but I am a cowboy by marriage. That is to say, an uncle of mine was an honest-to-goodness cowboy.

I am speaking of Creighton Hotchkiss—Uncle Creight who married my father's youngest sister, and began a whole slew of first cousins.

At that time, Uncle Creight was the only cowboy I had ever known, but I had been weaned on Zane Gray and Clarence E. Mulford and other writers of that period, who had romanticized the life of the cowboy, and here I found I had one of my very own, right in the bosom of my family!

What a lucky guy I thought I was—and what a lucky guy I actually was, too, for Uncle Creight exemplified all of those sterling traits of character, possessed by the fictionalized cowboy.

Yes, in no small part because of Uncle Creight, I have always been congenially disposed toward cowboys, interested in cowboys and pleased to have a chance to rub elbows with anyone who shared my passion for this disappearing breed.

So you can see why I was sorry never to have known Glenn Tallman.

I never was, nor could I have been, a cowboy. I don't have what it takes, but I admire those who do.

I am apprehensive of creatures that can kick me through barn doors, or over the roof of the barn. And I am not alone in this.

The late Milton Eisenhower, President Eisenhower's brother, had this to say: "My grandfather drove a horse and buggy, but was afraid of automobiles.

Family Group Sheet

Husband's Full Name: Wesley Edward Tallman Chart No.

	Day Month Year	City, Town or Place	County or Province, etc.	State or Country	Add. Info on Husband
Birth	9-3-1970	Newton	Harvey Co.	Kansas	
Chr'nd					
Marr	25-9-1993	ElDorado	Butler Co.	Kansas	
Death					
Burial					

Places of Residence:
Occupation: Welder   Church Affiliation: Military Rec:

His Father: Glenn E. Tallman   Mother's Maiden Name: Sharnon Taylor

Wife's Full Maiden Name: Leslie Pinkerton

	Day Month Year	City, Town or Place	County or Province, etc.	State or Country	Add. Info on Wife
Birth	7-12-1973	ElDorado	Butler Co.	Kansas	
Chr'nd					
Death					
Burial					

Places of Residence:
Occupation: Cake Decorator   Church Affiliation: Military Rec:

Her Father: Billie Pinkerton   Mother's Maiden Name: Lois Harris

Sex	Children's Names in Full		Day Month Year	City, Town or Place	County or Province, etc.	State or Country	Add. Info on Children
M 1	Clayton Tallman	Birth	1-2-1994	Wichita	Sedgwick Co.	Kans.	
	Full Name of Spouse	Marr.					
		Death					
		Burial					
F 2	Laura Ann Tallman	Birth	9-10-1995	Wichita	Sedgwick Co.	Kans.	
	Full Name of Spouse	Marr.					
		Death					

TALLMAN — BELOVED FATHER GLENN E. TALLMAN NOV. 4, 1940 – DEC. 1, 1995 "One of the Best"

GLENN EDWARD TALLMAN SP4 US ARMY VIETNAM NOV 4 1940 DEC 1 1995

Family Group Sheet

Husband's Full Name: Glenn Leon Moore — Chart No.

	Day Month Year	City, Town or Place	County or Province, etc.	State or Country	Add. Info on Husband
Birth	2-3-1913	Benton	Butler Co.	Kansas	
Chr'nd					
Marr	17-10-1943	Sacramento	Sacramento Co.	California	
Death					
Burial					

Places of Residence: Butler Co., Kansas   Sacramento, Calif.
Occupation: Retired   **Church Affiliation:** First Baptist   **Military Rec:** Air Force
His Father: Reuben David Moore   **Mother's Maiden Name:** Edith Taylor

Wife's Full Maiden Name: Emily Frances Weisker

	Day Month Year	City, Town or Place	County or Province, etc.	State or Country	Add. Info on Wife
Birth	23-8-1919	Sacramento	Sacramento Co.	California	
Chr'nd					
Death					
Burial					

Places of Residence: Sacramento, California
Occupation: Retired   **Church Affiliation:** Baptist   **Military Rec:**
Her Father: William Weisker   **Mother's Maiden Name:** Georgia Bunch

Sex	Children's Names in Full		Day Month Year	City, Town or Place	County or Province, etc.	State or Country	Add. Info on Children
M	1 Arthur Leon Moore	Birth	25-4-1947	Sacramento	Sacramento	Calif.	
		Marr.	7-7-1984	San Francis	San Francis	Calif.	
	Full Name of Spouse: Meg Ann Delahanty	Death					
		Burial					
M	2 William David M.	Birth	6-4-1950	Sacramento	Sacramento	Calif.	
		Marr.		Sacramento	Sacramento	Calif.	
	Full Name of Spouse: Mary Teresa Goebel	Death					
		Burial					
F	3 Nancy Ann Moore	Birth	24-3-1954	Sacramento	Sacramento	Calif.	
		Marr.	30-8-1981	Sacramento	Sacramento	Calif.	
	Full Name of Spouse: Raymond Hoagland	Death					
		Burial					

E. Military Service Record

Name of Veteran Moore, Glenn Leon
 last / first / middle

State from Which Served Kansas

War in Which, or Dates between Which, He Served Dec.-1939 – Jan. 1946

If Service Was Civil War:

Union _____ Confederate _____

Unit in Which He Served:

Name or Number of Regiment _____

Company _____

Name of Ship _____

Branch in Which He Served:

Infantry ____ Cavalry ____ Artillery ____ Navy ____ Other AIR CORPS

Kind of Service: Volunteers X   Regulars ____

Pension File Number _____

Bounty Land File Number (for Service before 1856 Only) _____

Military Record Number _____

Date of Birth March 2, 1913

Place of Birth _____ Butler County _____ Kansas
 city / county / state

Name of Widow or Other Claimant _____

Date of Death _____

Place of Death _____
 city / county

Places Lived after Service California

If Veteran Lived in a Home for Soldiers:

Location _____
 city / state

Family Group Sheet

Husband's Full Name: Arthur Leon Moore — **Chart No.**

	Day Month Year	City, Town or Place	County or Province, etc.	State or Country	Add. Info. on Husband
Birth	25-4-1947	Sacramento	Sacramento Co.	Calif.	
Chr'nd					
Marr	7-7-1984	San Francisco	San Francisco Co.	Calif.	
Death					
Burial					

Places of Residence: Milwaukie-Oregon
Occupation: Federal Clerk-Musician **Church Affiliation:** Catholic **Military Rec:** Army

His Father: Glenn Leon Moore **Mother's Maiden Name:** Emily Francis Weisker

Wife's Full Maiden Name: Meg Anne Delahanty

	Day Month Year	City, Town or Place	County or Province, etc.	State or Country	Add. Info. on Wife
Birth	9-2-1955	Iowa City	Johnson Co.	Iowa	
Chr'nd					
Death					
Burial					

Places of Residence: Milwaukie, Oregon
Occupation: Homemaker **Church Affiliation:** Catholic **Military Rec:**

Her Father: Donald W. Delahanty **Mother's Maiden Name:** Jacoyeline Murphy

Sex	Children's Names in Full	Children's Data	Day Month Year	City, Town or Place	County or Province, etc.	State or Country	Add. Info. on Children
M	1. George Arthur Moore	Birth	29--3-1985	San Francisco	SanFrancisco	Ca.	
	Full Name of Spouse	Marr.					
		Death					
		Burial					
M	2. Samuel W. Moore	Birth	29-12-1987	San Francisco	SanFrancisco	Ca.	
	Full Name of Spouse	Marr.					
		Death					
		Burial					
F	3. Rosemary E. Moore	Birth	9-1-1991	Milwaukie	Clackamas Co.	Ore.	
	Full Name of Spouse	Marr.					
		Death					
		Burial					

Compiler: Meg Moore
Address: 15700 SE Orville Ave.
City, State, Zip: Milwaukie, Oregon 97267
Date:

Family Group Sheet

Husband's Full Name: William David Moore
Chart No.:

	Day Month Year	City, Town or Place	County or Province, etc.	State or Country	Add. Info on Husband
Birth	6- 4-1950	Sacramento	Sacramento Co.	California	
Chr'nd					
Marr					
Death					
Burial					

Places of Residence: Sacramento-Cituel Heights, California
Occupation: Insurance Broker **Church Affiliation:** Catholic **Military Rec.:**

His Father: Glenn C. Moore **Mother's Maiden Name:** Emily Francis Weisker

Wife's Full Maiden Name: Mary Teresa Goebel

	Day Month Year	City, Town or Place	County or Province, etc.	State or Country	Add. Info on Wife
Birth	11-11-1947	Wichita	Sedgwick Co.	Kansas	
Chr'nd					
Death					
Burial					

Places of Residence: Wichita, Kansas Littleton, Colo. Rancho, Colo. California
Occupation: Registered Nurse **Church Affiliation:** Catholic **Military Rec.:**
Other husbands: Thomas Brahter

Her Father: Edwin Goebel **Mother's Maiden Name:** Milbola O'Reily

Sex	Children's Names in Full		Day Month Year	City, Town or Place	County or Province, etc.	State or Country	Add. Info on Children
M	1. Br. Thomas Moore	Birth	21- 3-1969	Rancho	Cordova Co.	Calif.	Adopted
		Marr.					
	Full Name of Spouse	Death					
		Burial					
M	2. Christopher Lee M.	Birth	26- 3-1971	Rancho	Cordova Co.	Calif.	Adopted
		Marr.					
	Full Name of Spouse	Death					
		Burial					
F	3. Karen Anne Moore	Birth	6- 3-1979	Cormuhead		Calif.	
		Marr.					
	Full Name of Spouse	Death					
		Burial					
M	4. Kyle William Moore	Birth	20-8-1980	Cormrehead		Calif.	
		Marr.					
	Full Name of Spouse	Death					
		Burial					
	5.	Birth					
		Marr.					
	Full Name of Spouse	Death					
		Burial					
	6.	Birth					
		Marr.					
	Full Name of Spouse	Death					
		Burial					
	7.	Birth					
		Marr.					
	Full Name of Spouse	Death					
		Burial					
	8.	Birth					
		Marr.					
	Full Name of Spouse	Death					
		Burial					

Compiler: William Moore **Notes:**
Address: 4604 Laureheard Way
City, State, Zip: Sacramento, California 95864
Date:

Family Group Sheet

Husband's Full Name #3 Ray Hoagland — **Chart No.**

	Day Month Year	City, Town or Place	County or Province, etc.	State or Country	Add. Info on Husband
Birth					
Chr'nd					
Marr	30- 8-1984	Sacramento	Sacramento Co.	California	
Death					
Burial					

Places of Residence

Occupation — **Church Affiliation** — **Military Rec.**

His Father — **Mother's Maiden Name**

Wife's Full Maiden Name Nancy Ann Moore

	Day Month Year	City, Town or Place	County or Province, etc.	State or Country	Add. Info. on Wife
Birth	24- 3-1954	Sacramento	Sacramento Co.	California	
Chr'nd					
Death					
Burial					

Places of Residence

Occupation — **Church Affiliation** — **Military Rec.**

Other husbands: #1 Donald P. Jordan 25-3-1972 (divorce) #2 Edward Rainwater

Her Father Glenn Leon Moore — **Mother's Maiden Name** Emily Francis Wersker

Sex	Children's Names in Full		Day Month Year	City, Town or Place	County or Province, etc.	State or Country	Add. Info on Children
F	1 Robin Rainwater	Birth	11- 7-1978				
	Full Name of Spouse	Marr.					
		Death					
		Burial					

Mr. and Mrs. Glenn Moore
have the honour of announcing
the marriage of their daughter
Nancy Ann
to
Mr. Donald P. Jordan
on Saturday, the twenty-fifth of March
one thousand nine hundred seventy-two
Sacramento, California

Reception: for the newlyweds
Saturday, April first, 1972, 2 - 4 p.m.
First Baptist Church
24th and L Streets
Sacramento, California

SACRAMENTO COUNTY
SACRAMENTO, CALIFORNIA

STATE OF CALIFORNIA — MARRIAGE LICENSE — Book 112 Page 207 — COUNTY OF SACRAMENTO

TO ANY JUSTICE OF THE SUPREME COURT, JUSTICE OF THE DISTRICT COURT OF APPEAL, JUDGE OF THE SUPERIOR COURT, JUDGE OF THE JUSTICE COURT, PRIEST OR MINISTER OF THE GOSPEL OF ANY DENOMINATION:

YOU ARE HEREBY AUTHORIZED AND LICENSED TO SOLEMNIZE, WITHIN SAID COUNTY, THE MARRIAGE OF

Glenn Leon Moore, NATIVE OF Kansas, COLOR OR RACE white, AGED 30 YEARS, RESIDING AT Mather Field, CALIFORNIA, AND Emily Frances Weisker, NATIVE OF California, COLOR OR RACE white, AGED 24 YEARS, RESIDING AT Sacramento, CALIFORNIA.

THE DULY VERIFIED WRITTEN CONSENT ... TO THE ISSUANCE OF THIS LICENSE TO THE ABOVE NAMED MINOR HA... BEEN PRESENTED TO AND FILED BY ME.

IN WITNESS WHEREOF, I HAVE HEREUNTO SET MY HAND AND SEAL, THIS 13 DAY OF October 1943.

C. C. LaRue
County Clerk and Ex-Officio Clerk of the Superior Court in and for the County of Sacramento, State of California

(SEAL)
Deputy

CERTIFICATE OF MARRIAGE
STATE OF CALIFORNIA — ORIGINAL — COUNTY OF SACRAMENTO

I HEREBY CERTIFY THAT ON THE 17th DAY OF October 1943 AT Sacramento, IN THE COUNTY OF SACRAMENTO, STATE OF CALIFORNIA, UNDER AUTHORITY OF A LICENSE ISSUED BY THE COUNTY CLERK OF SAID COUNTY, I, THE UNDERSIGNED, AS A Minister of the First Baptist Church, JOINED IN MARRIAGE Glenn Leon Moore AND Emily Frances Weisker, IN THE PRESENCE OF Elmer Wm Noll, RESIDING AT Sacramento, Cal, AND Mrs. Martha Anne Webb, RESIDING AT Sacramento, Cal, CALIFORNIA, WHO WITNESSED THIS CEREMONY.

Rev. Charles A. Carman, D.D.

5506 — CERTIFIED COPY OF VITAL RECORDS — STATE OF CALIFORNIA, COUNTY OF SACRAMENTO — DATED ISSUED MAY 12 1997

SACRAMENTO COUNTY
SACRAMENTO, CALIFORNIA

DO NOT WRITE ON THIS SIDE. ALL BLANKS BELOW ARE FOR USE OF COUNTY RECORDER

STATE OF CALIFORNIA — Department of Public Health — VITAL STATISTICS — Standard Certificate of Marriage — PERSONAL AND STATISTICAL PARTICULARS

County of SACRAMENTO — Local Registered No. 1443

	GROOM	BRIDE
FULL NAME	Glenn Leon Moore	Emily Frances Weisker
RESIDENCE	Mather Field, California	4321 H Street
COLOR OR RACE	white	white
AGE AT LAST BIRTHDAY	30	24
SINGLE, WIDOWED OR DIVORCED	single	single
NUMBER OF MARRIAGE	1st	1st
BIRTHPLACE	Kansas	Sacramento, California
OCCUPATION	U.S. Army	Clerk
NAME OF FATHER	R. D. Moore	William C. Weisker
BIRTHPLACE OF FATHER	Kansas	California
NAME OF MOTHER	Edith L. Taylor	Georgia G. Bunch
BIRTHPLACE OF MOTHER	Illinois	Oregon

MAIDEN NAME OF BRIDE, IF SHE WAS PREVIOUSLY MARRIED

We, the groom and bride named in this Certificate, hereby certify that the information given therein is correct, to the best of our knowledge and belief.

Glenn Leon Moore — Groom
Emily Frances Weisker — Bride

CERTIFICATE OF PERSON PERFORMING CEREMONY

I Hereby Certify that Glenn Leon Moore and Emily Frances Weisker were joined in marriage by me in accordance with the laws of the State of California, at Sacramento, this 17th day of October 1943.

Signature of Witness to the Marriage: Elmer W. Noll
Residence: Sacramento, Calif.

Signature of Person Performing the Ceremony: Rev. Charles A. Carman, D.D.
Official position: Minister-First Baptist Ch.
Residence: 2524 L St. Sacto, Cal

Filed October 19th, 1943

Witnessed in the presence of: 7. B. Kleinsorge

235505 — CERTIFIED COPY OF VITAL RECORDS — STATE OF CALIFORNIA, COUNTY OF SACRAMENTO — DATED ISSUED MAY 12 1997

Family Group Sheet

Husband's Full Name: Lloyd Merle Moore — Chart No.

	Day Month Year	City, Town or Place	County or Province, etc.	State or Country	Add. Info on Husband
Birth	18-6-1915	Whitewater	Butler	Kansas	
Chr'nd	4 1925	baptised - Christian church Potwin Butler Co. Kans.			
Marr	9-10-1934	ElDorado	Butler Co.	Kansas	
Death					
Burial					

Places of Residence: Potwin, Augusta, Independence, Kansas
Occupation: Oil Refinery
Other: #2 Melba Marie Ellis (M) 22-Jan.-1983 Ind. Ks. born 13-Feb.-1921
His Father: Reuben David Moore **Mother's Maiden Name:** Edith Taylor / Cedar Vale

Wife's Full Maiden Name: Naomi Hazel Ullum

	Day Month Year	City, Town or Place	County or Province, etc.	State or Country	Add. Info on Wife
Birth	9-5-1914	Potwin	Butler	Kansas	
Chr'nd					
Death					
Burial					

Places of Residence: Potwin-Whitewater-Augusta, Kansas
Occupation: Housewife
Her Father: Randolph Ullum **Mother's Maiden Name:** Gertrude Staltz

Sex	Children's names in Full		Day Month Year	City, Town or Place	County or Province, etc.	State or Country	Add. Info on Child
M	1 Gary Lloyd Moore	Birth	6-12-1935	Potwin	Butler Co.	Kansas	
		Marr.	26-8-1954	Augusta	Butler Co.	Kansas	
	Full Name of Spouse	Death	18-1-1993	Augusta	Butler Co.	Kansas	
	Beverly Tyler	Burial	21-1-1993	Augusta	Butler Co.	Kansas	
M	2 Tony Brent Moore	Birth	4-4-1942	Augusta	Butler Co.	Kansas	
		Marr.	8-1-1963	Augusta	Butler Co.	Kansas	
	Full Name of Spouse	Death					
	Karen Jean Lackey	Burial					
	3	Birth					
		Marr.					
	Full Name of Spouse	Death					

Lloyd and Naomi Ullum Moore, 1977

No. F 1876
P. J. No. 5576

STATE OF KANSAS CENTRAL, DIVISION OF VITAL STATISTICS

MARRIAGE LICENSE

IN THE PROBATE COURT OF BUTLER COUNTY.   El Dorado, Kansas, Sept 10, 1934.

To any Person Authorized by Law to Perform the Marriage Ceremony, Greeting:

YOU ARE HEREBY AUTHORIZED TO JOIN IN MARRIAGE

Lloyd M. Moore of Potwin, of Butler County, Kansas, Age 21.
Naomi Ullum of Potwin, of Butler County, Kansas, Age 19.

with the consent of _____ (Name of parent or guardian consenting.)

and of this license, duly indorsed, you will make return to my office at El Dorado, Kansas, within ten days after performing the ceremony.

[SEAL]   W N Calkins, Probate Judge.

INDORSEMENT

TO WHOM IT MAY CONCERN:

I hereby certify that I performed the ceremony joining in marriage the above-named couple, on the 10th day of September, 1934, at Eldorado, Kansas.

SIGNED: W N Calkins
TITLE: Probate Judge
ADDRESS: El Dorado, Kans.

p. 497

Compiler: Lloyd Merle Moore
Address:
City, State, Zip: Independence, Kansas 67301
Date:

Lloyd Moore and Melba McDowell

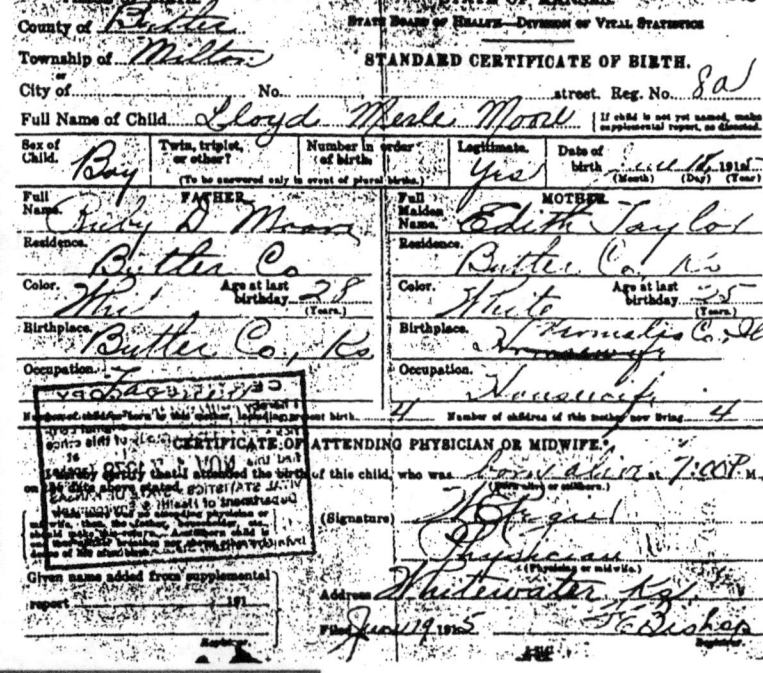

Lloyd Moore

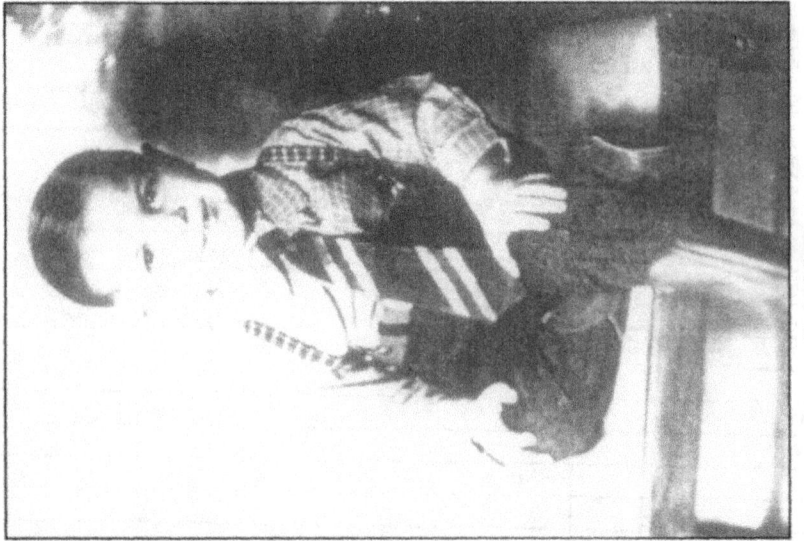

Gary Moore

Family Group Sheet

Husband's Full Name: Gary Lloyd Moore   SS-515-28-4749   Chart No.

Husband's Date	Day Month Year	City, Town or Place	County or Province, etc.	State or Country	Add. Info on Husb.
Birth	6-12-1935	Potwin	Butler Co.	Kansas	
Chr'nd					
Marr	26-8-1934	Augusta	Butler Co.	Kansas	
Death	18-1-1993	Augusta	Butler Co.	Kansas	
Burial	21-1-1993	Augusta	Butler Co.	Kansas	

Places of Residence: Augusta, Kansas
Occupation: Meat Cutter **Church Affiliation:** First Christian **Military Rec:**

His Father: Lloyd M. Moore   **Mother's Maiden Name:** Naomi H. Ullum

Wife's Full Maiden Name: Beverly Tyler

Wife's Date	Day Month Year	City, Town or Place	County or Province, etc.	State or Country	Add. Info on Wife
Birth	16-5-1937	Salina	Salina Co.	Kansas	
Chr'nd					
Death					
Burial					

Places of Residence:
Occupation: **Church Affiliation:** **Military Rec:**

Her Father: Ira C. Tyler   **Mother's Maiden Name:** Margaret Blick

Sex	Children's Names in Full	Children's Data	Day Month Year	City, Town or Place	County or Province, etc.	State or Country	Add. Info on Child
F	1 Valerie Jean Moore	Birth	6-9-1955	Augusta	Butler Co.	Kans.	
	Full Name of Spouse: Mark Smith	Marr.	7-9-1973	Augusta	Butler Co.	Kans.	
		Death					
		Burial					
F	2 Angela Denise Moore	Birth	14-2-1958	Hutchinson	Reno Co.	Kans.	
	Full Name of Spouse	Marr.					
		Death					
		Burial					
F	3 Brenda Sue Moore	Birth	27-12-1960	Augusta	Butler Co.	Kans.	
	Full Name of Spouse: #1 Cory Duke #2 Bill Lantz	Marr.					
		Death					
		Burial					
M	4 Gary Lloyd Moore, Jr	Birth	22-12-1962	Augusta	Butler Co.	Kans.	
	Full Name of Spouse	Marr.					
		Death					
		Burial					
M	5 Stephan Scott Moore	Birth	20-1-1964	Augusta	Butler Co.	Kans.	
	Full Name of Spouse	Marr.					
		Death					
		Burial					
M	6 Michael Moore	Birth	24-8-1959	Augusta	Butler Co.	Kan.	
	Full Name of Spouse	Marr.					
		Death	23-2-1960	Augusta	Butler Co.	Kan.	
		Burial	2-1960	Augusta	Butler Co.	Kan.	

Gary L. Moore and Beverly Tyler Family
Back row: Lloyd Moore - Father of Gary L. Moore, Jermy Linn, Mark Smith, Gary Moore Jr.
Third row: Bill Lantz, Briana Duke, Erins Smith Valerie Smith, Matthew, Julia, Brett Moore.
Second row: Stephan Moore, Brenda, Amenda Smith, Beverly Moore, Angela, Brenda, Gary J., Stephan, Angela, Cory Duke, Cobby Moore.
Front row: Carla Moore, Nathan, Blaine Moore, Elizabeth Moore, Brendon Moore.

Gary Moore

Family Group Sheet

Husband's Full Name: Mark Lindsey Smith — **Chart No.**

	Day Month Year	City, Town or Place	County or Province, etc.	State or Country	Add Info on Husb
Birth					
Chr'nd					
Marr	7-9-1973	Augusta	Butler Co.	Kans.	
Death					
Burial					

Places of Residence

Occupation — Church Affiliation — Military Rec

His Father: Robert E. Smith — **Mother's Maiden Name:**

Wife's Full Maiden Name: Valerie Jean Moore

	Day Month Year	City, Town or Place	County or Province, etc.	State or Country	Add Info on Wife
Birth	6-9-1955	Augusta	Butler Co.	Kansas	
Chr'nd					
Death					
Burial					

Places of Residence

Occupation — Church Affiliation — Military Rec.

Her Father: Gary Lloyd Moore — **Mother's Maiden Name:** Beverly Tyler

Baby's here! And are we glad — We're the proudest, happiest Mother and Dad!

NAME Valerie Jean
DATE OF ARRIVAL 9/6/55 WEIGHT 6 lbs
PARENTS Beverly & Gary Moore

Valerie Moore, 1986

171

Family Group Sheet

Husband's Full Name — **Chart No.**

	Day Month Year	City, Town or Place	County or Province, etc.	State or Country	Add. Info on Husband
Birth					
Chr'nd					
Marr					
Death					
Burial					

Places of Residence:
Occupation: Church Affiliation: Military Rec:
Other wives, if any...
His Father: Mother's Maiden Name:

Wife's Full Maiden Name — Angela Denise Moore

	Day Month Year	City, Town or Place	County or Province, etc.	State or Country	Add. Info. on Wife
Birth	14-2-1958	Augusta	Butler Co.	Kansas	
Chr'nd					
Death					
Burial					

Places of Residence:
Occupation: Church Affiliation: Military Rec:
Other husbands...
Her Father: Gary Lloyd Moore   Mother's Maiden Name: Beverly Tyler

Sex	Children's Names in Full		Day Month Year	City, Town or Place	County or Province, etc	State or Country	Add. Info on Children
	1	Birth					
		Marr.					
	Full Name of Spouse	Death					
		Burial					
	2	Birth					
		Marr.					
	Full Name of Spouse	Death					
		Burial					
	3	Birth					
		Marr.					
	Full Name of Spouse	Death					
		Burial					
	4	Birth					
		Marr.					
	Full Name of Spouse	Death					
		Burial					
	5	Birth					
		Marr.					
	Full Name of Spouse	Death					
		Burial					
	6	Birth					

Family Group Sheet

Husband's Full Name — Michael Brent Moore — **Chart No.**

	Day Month Year	City, Town or Place	County or Province, etc.	State or Country	Add. Info on Husb
Birth	24-8-1959	Augusta	Butler Co.	Kansas	
Chr'nd					
Marr					
Death	23-2-1960	Augusta	Butler Co.	Kansas	
Burial	2-1960	Augusta	Butler Co.	Kansas	

Places of Residence:
Occupation: Church Affiliation: Military Rec:
Other wives...
His Father: Gary Moore   Mother's Maiden Name: Beverly Tyler

Family Group Sheet

Husband's Full Name Cory Duke — Chart No.

Husband's Date	Day	Month	Year	City, Town or Place	County or Province, etc.	State or Country	Add. Info. on Husband
Birth							
Chr'nd							
Marr							
Death							
Burial							

Places of Residence

Occupation — Church Affiliation — Military Rec

Other wives if any No (1) (2) etc. Make separate sheet for each marr.

His Father — Mother's Maiden Name

Wife's Full Maiden Name Brenda Sue Moore

Wife's Date	Day	Month	Year	City, Town or Place	County or Province, etc.	State or Country	Add. Info. on Wife
Birth	27	12	1960	Augusta	Butler Co.	Kansas	
Chr'nd							
Death							
Burial							

Places of Residence

Occupation — Church Affiliation — Military Rec

Other husbands: #2 William Lantz

Her Father: Gary Lloyd Moore — Mother's Maiden Name: Beverly Tyler

Sex	Children's Names in Full	Children's Data	Day	Month	Year	City, Town or Place	County or Province, etc.	State or Country	Add. Info. on Children
1		Birth							
		Marr.							

Family Group Sheet

Husband's Full Name Gary Lloyd Moore, Jr. — Chart No.

Husband's Date	Day	Month	Year	City, Town or Place	County or Province, etc.	State or Country	Add. Info. on Husband
Birth	22	12	1962	Augusta	Butler Co.	Kansas	
Chr'nd							
Marr	11	12	1982	Augusta	Butler Co.	Kansas	
Death							
Burial							

Places of Residence

Occupation — Church Affiliation — Military Rec

His Father: Gary Lloyd Moore — Mother's Maiden Name: Beverly Tyler

Wife's Full Maiden Name Cathryn Kay Valle

Wife's Date	Day	Month	Year	City, Town or Place	County or Province		
Birth							
Chr'nd							
Death							
Burial							

Places of Residence

Occupation — Church Affiliation

Her Father — Mother's Maiden N

Sex	Children's Names in Full	Children's Data	Day	Month	Year	City, Town or P
1		Birth				
		Marr.				
	Full Name of Spouse	Death				
		Burial				
2		Birth				
		Marr.				

City, State, Zip

Date

License No. 43656

D. C. No. 82397

STATE OF KANSAS
THE KANSAS STATE DEPARTMENT OF HEALTH AND ENVIRONMENT
Bureau of Vital Statistics
MARRIAGE LICENSE

IN THE DISTRICT COURT OF BUTLER COUNTY. _____ December 7 _____ 19 82

To Any Person in the State of Kansas Authorized by Law to Perform the Marriage Ceremony, Greetings:
YOU ARE HEREBY AUTHORIZED TO JOIN IN MARRIAGE

Gary Lloyd Moore, Jr. of Augusta, Kansas, Age 19
(Name of Groom) (Residence—City & State)

Cathryn Kay Valle of Augusta, Kansas, Age 17
(Name of Bride) (Residence—City & State)

with the consent of Dixie L. Valle, mother of the bride;
(Name of parent or guardian consenting)
and Assoc. Dist. Judge

and with this license duly endorsed, you will make return to my office at El Dorado, Kansas, within ten days after performing the ceremony.

[SEAL]

s/John M. Javorsky, Associate Districts Judge
Name and Title of Court Official

ENDORSEMENT
TO WHOM IT MAY CONCERN

Signature of Witnesses:
Eric A. Williams
Lorene K. Ralph

Date Received by District Court: Dec 15, 19 82
Date Recorded by District Court: Dec 15, 19 82

NOTE—After recording, the judge shall forward the original marriage license to the State Registrar, Topeka, Kansas, not later than the third day of following month.

Filed Dec 15, 19 82

I hereby certify that I, the undersigned, performed the ceremony joining in marriage the above named couple on the 11 day of December, 19 82 at Augusta, Ks, Kansas, in Butler County.
My credentials are recorded in the D.C.'s office of Butler & Rawlins Co. Ks.

Signed: Richard M. Bacon
Title: Sr. Pastor
Address: 1600 State, Augusta

Name and Title of Court Official

Family Group Sheet

Husband's Full Name: Stephen Scott Moore   **Chart No.**

Husband's Data	Day Month Year	City, Town or Place	County or Province, etc.	State or Country	Add. Info. on Husband
Birth	20-01-1964	Augusta	Butler, Co.	Kansas	
Chr'nd					
Marr	19-02-1994	Arkansas City	Cowley, Co.	Kansas	
Death					
Burial					

Places of Residence: 335 East Fourteenth 14th Augusta, Kansas 67010
Occupation: Plumber/Self Employed   **Church Affiliation:** 1st Baptist   **Military Rec.**

His Father: Gary Lloyd Moore   **Mother's Maiden Name:** Beverly (Mick) Tyler

Wife's Full Maiden Name: Carla Jean Clark

Wife's Data	Day Month Year	City, Town or Place	County or Province, etc.	State or Country	Add. Info. on Wife
Birth	01-05-1966	Arkansas City	Cowley, Co.	Kansas	
Chr'nd					
Death					
Burial					

Places of Residence: Same as Stephen Moore
Occupation: Cosmetologist   **Church Affiliation:** 1st Baptist   **Military Rec.**

Her Father: Joseph Bernard Clark   **Mother's Maiden Name:** Nelora Mary Kannebach

Sex	Children's Names in Full	Children's Data	Day Month Year	City, Town or Place	County or Province, etc.	State or Country	Add. Info on Child
F	1 Elizabeth Tyler Moore	Birth	24-01-1995	Wichita	Sedgwick, Co.	Kansas	the
		Marr.					four
	Full Name of Spouse	Death					children
		Burial					were born
M	2 Nathan Glenn Moore	Birth	30-07-1996	Wichita	Sedgwick, Co.	Kansas	at
		Marr.					the
	Full Name of Spouse	Death					Wesley
		Burial					Hospital
F	3 Annie Jean Moore	Birth	01-04-1998	Wichita	Sedgwick, Co.	Kansas	
		Marr.					
	Full Name of Spouse	Death					
		Burial					
M	4 Joshua Scott Moore	Birth	01-04-1998	Wichita	Sedgwick, Co.	Kansas	
		Marr.					
	Full Name of Spouse	Death					
		Burial					
	5	Birth					
		Marr.					
	Full Name of Spouse	Death					

He's awfully cute,

He's a thing of joy,

We mean, of course,

Our brand-new Boy

name Stephen Scott

arrived 10:25 AM
Jan 20, 1964

weight 8lb 6 5/8 ozs.

parents Beverly & Gary

Michael Brent
name

August 24, 1959
arrived

8 lbs 13 ozs
weighed

Mr & Mrs Gary Moore
Parents

Family Group Sheet

Husband's Full Name: Tony Brent Moore — Chart No.

	Day Month Year	City, Town or Place	County or Province, etc.	State or Country	Add Info on Husb
Birth	4-4-1942	Potwin	Butler Co.	Kansas	
Chr'nd					
Marr	8-1-1963	ElDorado	Butler Co.	Kansas	
Death					
Burial					

Places of Residence: Potwin-Augusta, Kansas
Occupation: Oil Refinnery   **Church Affiliation:** First Christian   **Military Rec.**

His Father: Lloyd Moore   **Mother's Maiden Name:** Naomi H. Ullum

Wife's Full Maiden Name: Karen Jean Lackey

	Day Month Year	City, Town or Place	County or Province, etc.	State or Country	Add. Info. on Wife
Birth	8-4-1944	ElDorado	Butler Co.	Kansas	
Chr'nd					
Death					
Burial					

Places of Residence: Augusta
Occupation: Bank Clerk   **Church Affiliation:** Baptist   **Military Rec.**

Her Father: Floyd Eddie Lackey   **Mother's Maiden Name:** Ruby Venus Woolery

Sex	Children's names in Full		Day Month Year	City, Town or Place	County or Province, etc.	State or Country	Add Info on Child
F	1 LaVina Jean Moore	Birth	3-9-1963	Winfield	Cowley Co.	Kansas	
		Marr	12-2-1990	Augusta	Butler Co.	Kansas	
	Full Name of Spouse: Robert Doyle Blake	Death					
		Burial					
M	2 Rick Dean Moore	Birth	26-8-1964	Wichita	Sedgwick Co.	Kansas	
		Marr	24-6-1994	Wichita	Sedgwick Co.	Kansas	
	Full Name of Spouse: Rhonda Rogers	Death					
		Burial					
F	3 Paula Lynn Moore	Birth	29-6-1967	Wichita	Sedgwick Co.	Kansas	
		Marr	6-8-1994	Augusta	Butler Co.	Kansas	
	Full Name of Spouse: #1 Duke Brandt #2 Larry Barg	Death					
		Burial					
	4	Birth					

Tony Moore

No. _____   **THE KANSAS STATE BOARD OF HEALTH**
P.J. No. 14,326   **DIVISION OF VITAL STATISTICS**

MARRIAGE LICENSE

IN THE PROBATE COURT OF BUTLER COUNTY.   January 7th, 19 63

To any Person in the State of Kansas Authorized by Law to Perform the Marriage Ceremony, Greeting:

YOU ARE HEREBY AUTHORIZED TO JOIN IN MARRIAGE

Tony Brent Moore (Groom) of Augusta, Kansas, Age 20

Karen Jean Lackey (Bride) of Augusta, Kansas, Age 18

with the consent of Mrs. Lloyd Moore, mother of groom (Name of parent or guardian consenting)

and of this license, duly endorsed, you will make return to my office at El Dorado, Kansas, within ten days after performing the ceremony.

(SEAL)   Roy S. Darlington, Probate Judge

ENDORSEMENT

TO WHOM IT MAY CONCERN:

I hereby certify that I performed the ceremony joining in marriage the above named couple, on the 3 day of January, 19 63, at El Dorado, Kansas.

Signed: Donald McCracken
Title: Pastor First Baptist Church
Address: Box 104, El Dorado, Kansas

p.335

Tony Moore

Tony, Karen, Rick, Paula, LaVina, Easter 1998

Family Group Sheet

Husband's Full Name Robert Doyle Blake — Chart No.

Husband's Date	Day Month Year	City, Town or Place	County or Province, etc.	State or Country	Add. Info on Husband
Birth					
Chr'nd					
Marr	12-2-1990	Augusta	Butler Co.	Kansas	
Death					
Burial					

Places of Residence
Occupation — Church Affiliation — Military Rec.

His Father — Mother's Maiden Name

Wife's Full Maiden Name LaVina Jean Moore

Wife's Date	Day Month Year	City, Town or Place	County or Province, etc.	State or Country	Add. Info on Wife
Birth	3-9-1963	Winfield	Cowley Co.	Kansas	
Chr'nd					
Death					
Burial					

Places of Residence
Occupation — Church Affiliation — Military Rec.

Her Father Tony B. Moore — Mother's Maiden Name Karen Jean Lackey

Sex	Children's Names in Full	Children's Date	Day Month Year	City, Town or Place	County or Province, etc.	State or Country	Add Info on Child
1		Birth					
		Marr.					
	Full Name of Spouse	Death					
		Burial					
2		Birth					
		Marr.					

Family Group Sheet

Husband's Full Name: Ricky Dean Moore
Chart No.

	Day Month Year	City, Town or Place	County or Province, etc.	State or Country	Add. Info on Husb.
Birth	26-8-1964	Wichita	Sedgwick Co.	Kansas	
Chr'nd					
Marr	24-6-1994	Wichita	Sedgwick Co.	Kansas	
Death					
Burial					

Places of Residence:
Occupation: **Church Affiliation:** **Military Rec.:**

His Father: Tony B. Moore **Mother's Maiden Name:** Karen Jean Lackey

Wife's Full Maiden Name: Rhonda Lee Rogers

	Day Month Year	City, Town or Place	County or Province, etc.	State or Country	Add. Info on Wife
Birth	25-4-1964	Lerington		Nebraska	
Chr'nd					
Death					
Burial					

Places of Residence:
Occupation: **Church Affiliation:** **Military Rec.:**

Her Father: Charles Robert Rogers **Mother's Maiden Name:** Janet Lee Bauer

Sex	Children's Names in Full		Day Month Year	City, Town or Place	County or Province, etc.	State or Country	Add. Info on Child
M	1. Charles Caleb Rogers	Birth	26-12-1986	Wichita	Sedgwick Co.	Kans.	
	Full Name of Spouse	Marr. / Death / Burial					
F	2. Jodi Caitlin Rogers	Birth	20-6-1990	Wichita	Sedgwick Co.	Kans.	
	Full Name of Spouse	Marr. / Death / Burial					
F	3. Carody Bauer Rogers	Birth	10-6-1992	Wichita	Sedgwick Co.	Kans.	
	Full Name of Spouse	Marr. / Death / Burial					
F	4. Carly Jae Rogers	Birth	10--6-1992	Wichita	Sedgwick Co.	Kans.	
	Full Name of Spouse	Marr. / Death / Burial					
M	5. Taylor Thomas Moore	Birth	5-8-1992	Wichita	Sedgwick Co.	Kans.	
	Our new arrival!	Marr.					

Baby's name **Taylor Thomas**
Birthdate **August 5, 1992**
Weight **10 lbs. 3 ozs.**
Height **22 ½ inches**
Happy family **Andee and Rick Moore**

Ricky and Taylor Moore, 1992

Family Group Sheet

Husband's Full Name: Larry Allen Barg — **Chart No.**

	Day Month Year	City, Town or Place	County or Province, etc.	State or Country	Add Info on Husband
Birth	7- 6-1970	ElDorado	Butler Co.	Kansas	
Chr'nd					
Marr					
Death					
Burial					

Places of Residence:
Occupation: — **Church Affiliation:** — **Military Rec:**

His Father: Larry Dee Barg — **Mother's Maiden Name:** Claudetta Wilene Mitchell

Wife's Full Maiden Name: Paula Lynn Moore

	Day Month Year	City, Town or Place	County or Province, etc.	State or Country	Add Info on Wife
Birth	29- 6-1967	Wichita	Sedgwick Co.	Kansas	
Chr'nd	1975				
Death					
Burial					

Places of Residence:
Occupation: — **Church Affiliation:** — **Military Rec:**

Her Father: Tony Brent Moore — **Mother's Maiden Name:** Karen Jean Lackey

Sex	Children's Names		Day Month Year	City, Town or Place	County or Province, etc.	State or Country
M	1. Drew Tyler Brandt	Birth	27- 1-1989	Wichita	Sedgwick Co.	Kans.
	Full Name of Spouse	Marr. / Death / Burial				
	2.	Birth / Marr. / Death / Burial				
	3.	Birth / Marr. / Death / Burial				

Paula Moore

Drew Brandt, 3 1/2 yrs., 9-20-1992

Compiler:
Address:
City, State, Zip:
Date:

Family Group Sheet

Husband's Full Name: John Harold Turner, Sr. SS-511-07-2715

	Day Month Year	City, Town or Place	County or Province, etc.	State or Country	Add. Info on Husband
Birth	2-5-1917	Hale	Carroll Co.	Missouri	killed in car accident
Chr'nd					
Marr	21-12-1940	Potwin	Butler Co.	Kansas	
Death	10-6-1969	Near Marion, Ks.	Marion Co.	Kansas	
Burial	14-6-1969	Towanda cem.	Butler Co.	Kansas	

Places of Residence: Potwin, Kansas
Occupation: Vickers Petroleum Co.   **Church Affiliation:** Christian   **Military Rec:** US Army WW2
His Father: Lee Turner   **Mother's Maiden Name:** Faye Arlene Adams

Wife's Full Maiden Name: Ruth Beula Moore

	Day Month Year	City, Town or Place	County or Province, etc.	State or Country	Add. Info on Wife
Birth	4-11-1917	Potwin	Butler Co.	Kansas	
Chr'nd					
Death					
Burial					

Places of Residence: Paducah, Kentucky
Occupation: Beech Aircraft   **Church Affiliation:** Christian   **Military Rec:**
Her Father: Reuben Moore   **Mother's Maiden Name:** Edith Taylor

Sex	Children's names		Day Month Year	City, Town or Place	County or Province, etc.	State or Country
M	1. John Harold Turner, Jr.	Birth	12-3-1942	Newton	Harvey Co.	Kansas
		Marr.	15-8-1964	Presidio	San Francisco	Ca
	Spouse: Suzanne Keisel	Death	20-5-1968	Thung Duc		Viet Nam
		Burial		Towanda cem.	Butler Co.	Kansas
M	2. David P. Turner	Birth	1-10-1944	Newton	Harvey Co.	Kansas
		Marr.	14-6-1969	Glendale	Los Angeles Co.	Calif.
	Spouse: Nanette Constable	Death				
		Burial				
	3.	Birth				
		Marr.				
	Spouse:	Death				
		Burial				

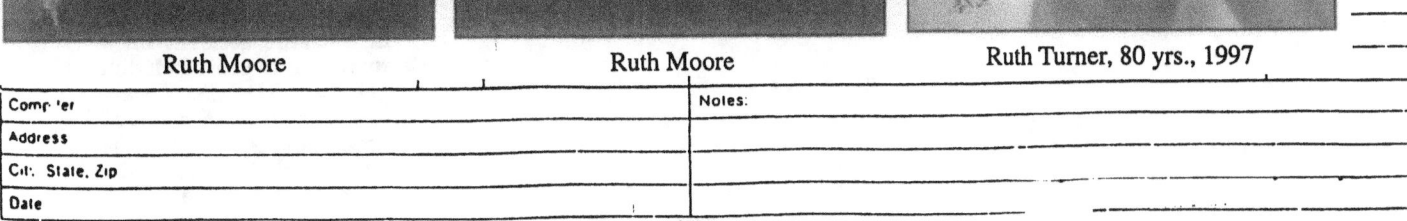

Ruth Moore   Ruth Moore   Ruth Turner, 80 yrs., 1997

RECORD OF FUNERAL

189

Total No. 2463 Yearly No. 81 Date of Entry June 9, 1969

Name of Deceased: John H. Turner, Sr. (What Race) W
☑ Married ☐ Single ☐ Widowed ☐ Divorced ☑ Husband ☐ Wife ☐ Widow of Ruth
Residence: Potwin, Kansas Age of Husband or Wife (if living) _____ Years
Charge to: _____
Address: _____
Order given by: _____ (or Informant)
How secured: _____
Veteran, Name of War: W.W. II
Occupation: Gauger 511-07-2715 (Social Security Number)
Employer and Address: Vickers
Date of Death: June 10, 1969
Date of Birth: May 2, 1917 Age 52
Name of Father: Lee Turner
His Birthplace: _____
Maiden Name of Mother: Faye Arlene Adams
Her Birthplace: _____
Date of Funeral: 9/14/69 Saturday 2:00 P.M.
Services at: Potwin Christian Church
Clergyman: Rev. Larry Cook & Rev. Herbert Keller
Religion of the Deceased: Christian
Birthplace: Hale, Missouri
Resided in the State: Potwin 37
Place of Death: near Marion, Ka.
Cause of Death: _____
Contributory Causes: _____
Certifying Physician: _____ (or Coroner)
His Address: _____
Ship Remains to: _____
Type of Casket: Crest Silver Silver
Manufactured by: National Casket Co.
Cemetery/Crematory: Towanda

Lot No. _____
Grave No. _____
Section No. _____
Block No. _____
Owner _____

Diagram of Lot or Vault

No. H 29223 STATE OF KANSAS, CENTRAL DIVISION OF VITAL STATISTICS
P. J. No. 7623

MARRIAGE LICENSE

IN THE PROBATE COURT OF BUTLER COUNTY, Dec. 14th, 1940
in the State of Kansas
To any Person Authorized by Law to Perform the Marriage Ceremony, Greeting:

YOU ARE HEREBY AUTHORIZED TO JOIN IN MARRIAGE

John Harold Turner (Groom) of Potwin, Kans., Age 23
Beulah Ruth Moore (Bride) of Potwin, Kans., Age 23

with the consent of _____ (Name of parent or guardian consenting)

and of this license, duly endorsed, you will make return to my office at El Dorado, Kansas, within ten days after performing the ceremony.

(SEAL)

W. N. Calkins
Probate Judge

ENDORSEMENT

TO WHOM IT MAY CONCERN:

I hereby certify that I performed the ceremony joining in marriage the above named couple, on the _____ day of December, 1940, at The Potwin Christian Church.

SECTION 5.—Every person who shall perform any marriage ceremony under the provisions of this act, shall, within ten days after such marriage, return the said license to the probate judge who issued the same, with his certificate of such marriage endorsed thereon, etc.

NOTE.—After recording, the probate judge shall forward this original marriage license to the State Registrar, at Topeka, Kansas, not later than the third day of the following month.

Signed Rev. L. R. Hobert
Title Pastor of Christian Church
Address Potwin, Kansas

Potwin Services For John Turner, Accident Victim

POTWIN, Kan. — Services for John H. Turner, 52, employe of Vickers Oil Co. who was killed Monday when two trucks collided on a county road near Marion, Kan., will be at 2 p.m. Saturday at Potwin Christian Church. Burial will be in Towanda, Kan., Cemetery.

Born at Hale, Mo., he came here in 1932.

Survivors include his widow, Ruth; a son, David, Spokane, Wash.; his father, Lee Turner, Van Tassell, Wyo., and a brother, Nelson, Edgerton, Kan.

Kirby Funeral Home has charge.

ies in crash

John H. Turner, 52, of Potwin, was killed Monday in a traffic accident on a rural road in central Marion county. Details were lacking. Funeral arrangements will be announced through the Kirby Funeral home.

FATHER
JOHN H. TURNER SR.
1917 — 1969

Family Group Sheet

Husband's Full Name: John Harold Turner, Jr. — Chart No.

	Day Month Year	City, Town or Place	County or Province, etc.	State or Country	Add Info on Husb
Birth	12- 3-1942	Newton	Harvey Co.	Kansas	
Chr'nd					
Marr	14- 8-1964	Corte Madera	Marin Co.	California	
Death	20- 5-1968	Thung Duc		Viet Nam	
Burial	5-1968	Towanda Cem	Towanda Butler Co.	Kansas	

Places of Residence

Occupation: Church Affiliation: Military Rec. **US Army**

His Father: **John Harold Turner, Sr.**   Mother's Maiden Name: **Ruth B. Moore**

Wife's Full Maiden Name: Suzanne Prince Keisel

	Day Month Year	City, Town or Place	County or Province, etc.	State or Country	Add Info on Wife
Birth	24-11-1942	San Diego	San Diego Co.	California	
Chr'nd					
Death					
Burial					

Places of Residence

Occupation: **Clerical of Bank**   Church Affiliation: Military Rec.

Her Father: **Walter I. Keisel**   Mother's Maiden Name: **Otila Shields**

Sex	Children's names in Full		Day Month Year	City, Town or Place	County or Province, etc.	State or Country	Add Info on Child
F	Suzanne K. Turner	Birth	2- 4-1965	San Diego	San Diego Co.	Calif.	
		Marr	29-5-1988	San Diego	San Diego Co.	Calif.	Divorce
	Full Name of Spouse: Todd Rossiter	Death					
		Burial					

Lt. John H. Turner Jr.

Suzanne Beach (John Jr.'s daughter) and her daughter Stephanie Rossiter, Nov. 1995.

KIRBY FUNERAL HOME
224 West Ash, El Dorado, Kansas

This Information for Death Certificates and Newspapers

- Full Name: S/Sgt. John H. Turner, Jr.
- Residence: Potwin
- Date of Death: May 20, 1968
- Time: —
- Place of Death: Vietnam
- Date and Place of Birth: March 12, 1942 – Newton, Ks.
- Date and Place of Marriage: —
- How Long Ill?: —
- How Long Lived Here?: in Potwin all of life

Graduate of Ponca City Military Academy.

Entered military service in 1961, went to Vietnam in March 1968 on 2nd hitch which was 1962–1966. Killed in action.

- Occupation: —
- Employer: —
- Father's Name: John H. Turner
- Mother's Maiden Name: Ruth _____
- Social Security Number: —
- If Veteran, Specify War and Unit: —
- Entered Service: 1962
- Service No.: RA17629987
- Discharged: —
- Rank or Rating: S/Sgt.
- Cause of Death: —
- Physician: —
- Address: —
- Was a Member of What Church?: Potwin Christian Church
- What Fraternal Orders?: —

Names and Addresses of Surviving Relatives

- Husband or Wife: Ruth (?)
- Father: ___ Turner, Van Tasell, Wyo.
- Mother: —
- Daughters: —
- 1 son: David Turner, Lynnwood, Washington
- (1 son S/Sgt John H. Turner, Jr. predeceased) 5-20-68
- Sisters: —
- 1 Brother: James Turner, Virginia, Kas.
- 1 grandson: Wayne Turner, Los Angeles, Calif.

Services

- Date, Hour, Place: ___
- Minister: Rev. ___
- Place of Burial: Potwin
- Bearers: Fred Weber, Jr., Jack Hagins, Jack Weiser, Jim King, Lawrence ___, Jr., Bud Winter
- Music Singer: Richard ___, Edgar Thiessen, Willard ___, Wm Tom Taylor
- Songs: "My Future Person At All", "How Beautiful ___ ___", "_____"
- Organist: Candy ___
- Organizations Attending in a Body: —

Dist Flag
Cash't to ___
Card #315

510-40-3165

TURNER, JOHN H.
RA17629987
510-40-3165

1. NAME (Last, first, middle initial) AND SERVICE NUMBER

9. RELIGION: Christian
10. MAR. STATUS and NO. DEPN: M 2

2. GRADE	3. DATE OF RANK	4. PPD	5. ADD PAY ELIG	6. DATE OF BIRTH	7. RACE	8. DUTY MOS
SSG E-6	30Sep66	—	—	12Mar42	CAU	00F4B

22. MILITARY OCCUPATIONAL SPECIALTIES

VORN	TYPE	CODE	TITLE	DATE
S	MOS	11B4O	Lt Weapons Inf'man (MW652 5May64)	
P	MOS	11F4B	Inf Opns & Intel Spec	90ct64
	MOS		(19Jul65)	

11. ENLISTED, INDUCTED, REENLISTED, EXTENDED, AND/OR OAD

COMPONENT	EFFECTIVE DATE	LENGTH	EXPIRATION DATE
RA	29Jul64	6yrs	28Jul70

13. ENLISTED OR VOLUNTEERED FOR: OCS VOL AR 350-50

24. APTITUDE TESTS

FORM	SCORE	RETEST SCORE	APTITUDE AREAS	SCORE	RETEST SCORE
VE	116		IN	133	
AR	130		AE	110	
SM	111		EL	113	
PA	124		GM	115	
ACS	126		MM	115	
AI	107		CL	123	
MA	130		GT	123	
ELI	104		RC	113	
GIT	112		CO-A	126	
CI	135		CO-B	128	
ARC	111				

25. OTHER TESTS

TEST	SCORE	GROUP	DATE
MOS-1	141		1Aug62
OCT-2	95	III	1Aug62
ALAT	40		1Aug62
OCT-2	122	II	6Nov63
ARWQBT	169		20Apr66

16. SERVICE DATES

TYPE	DATE
BASD	27Jul62
BPED	27Jul62
BESD	
LAST PCS	Ft Field, Mo
FSA CODE	

PLACE TESTED: Ft Lv Mo
DATE TESTED: 31Jul62

27. MILITARY EDUCATION

TITLE OF COURSE	MOS CODE	SCHOOL	WEEKS	YEAR
ATP				
Drill Sgt Sch	00F4B	Ft Ord Calif	6	67
Basic NCO Acad credit		USATS	12	67

17. PHYSICAL STATUS

CODE: A DATE: 2Jul67
HEIGHT: 6ft 3 1/2 in WEIGHT: 205 lbs GLASSES: No

18. ASSIGNMENT LIMITATIONS: —

19. INVESTIGATIONS AND CLEARANCES: NAC 27Jul64 64 NAC 27Jul64
Validated 62 Ft Ord 10Jan67
SIH compl 15Jun64

28. SPECIALIZED TRAINING

TYPE	WEEKS	COMPLETED
ATP 21-114		28Sep62
CBR tng		11Mar67
Code of Cond		28Sep62
RVN TNG		13Feb68

29. QUALIFICATION IN ARMS

WEAPON	COURSE	QUAL	SCORE	DATE
Rifle M1	TF	NM1	64	7Sep66
Pistol 95	FAM	—	—	17Oct66
3.5 RL	FAM	—	—	18Oct66
MG cal 50	A	264	72	23Aug64
Rifle M14	KD	EX	828	24Oct__
M14	T	55	49	8Jul62

20. BIRTHPLACE AND CITIZENSHIP

	RESIDENCE	COUNTRY
SELF	Newton, Kas	US
SPOUSE	La Jolla, Calif	US
FATHER	Hale, Mo	US
MOTHER	Potwin, Kas	US

Family Group Sheet

Husband's Full Name: Todd Rossiter   **Chart No.**

Husband's Data	Day Month Year	City, Town or Place	County or Province, etc.	State or Country	Add Info on Husband
Birth					
Chr'nd					
Marr	29-5-1988	San Diego	San Diego Co.	California	divorced
Death					
Burial					

Places of Residence:

Occupation: **Church Affiliation:**   **Military Rec.:**

Other wives if any, No. (1st) 2nd etc. Make separate sheet for each marr.

His Father: **Mother's Maiden Name:**

Wife's Full Maiden Name: Suzanne K. Turner

Wife's Data	Day Month Year	City, Town or Place	County or Province, etc.	State or Country	Add. Info on Wife
Birth	2-4-1965	San Diego	Ft. Ord, Monterey	California	
Chr'nd					
Death					
Burial					

Places of Residence: San Diego

Occupation: Financial Analyst   **Church Affiliation:** Episcopalion   **Military Rec.:**

Other husbands if any, No. (1st) 2nd etc.: 2nd. Victor Beach-married in Nov.

Her Father: John Harold Turner, Jr.   **Mother's Maiden Name:** Suzanne Prince Keisel

---

Sex	Children's names in Full	Children's Data	Day Month Year	City, Town or Place	County or Province, etc.	State or Country	Add Info on Child
F	1 Stephanie Rachel Rossiter	Birth	7-12-1991	San Diego	San Diego Co.	Calif.	
	Full Name of Spouse	Marr.					
		Death					
		Burial					
F	2 Rossiter Rebecca Lynn	Birth	7-12-1991	San Diego	San Diego Co.	Calif.	
	Full Name of Spouse	Marr.					
		Death					

HEADQUARTERS DEPARTMENT OF THE ARMY OFFICE OF THE ADJUTANT GENERAL WASHINGTON, D. C. 20315

REPORT OF CASUALTY

REPORT NUMBER AND TYPE	DATE PREPARED
A 6548 FINAL RVN 2318	3 June 1968

1. **SERVICE IDENTIFICATION** (Name, Service Number, Grade or Rate, Component, Branch and Organization)
TURNER, JOHN HAROLD; RA 17 629 987; SSG; RA; ADV TM #1, MACV, VIETNAM

2. **CASUALTY STATUS** ☐ BATTLE ☒ NON-BATTLE
DIED 20 May 1968 in Vietnam from gunshot wound received while in quarters when a loaded shotgun which was hanging on the wall fell to the floor and discharged.
Commenced tour in Vietnam 6 Mar 68

3. **DATE AND PLACE OF BIRTH, RACE, RELIGIOUS PREFERENCE**
12 March 1942   Newton, Kansas   Caucasian   Protestant

4. **DATE AND PLACE OF LAST ENTRY ON ACTIVE DUTY IN CURRENT STATUS AND HOME OF RECORD AT TIME**
29 July 1964 San Francisco, California   Potwin, Kansas

5. **SOCIAL SECURITY NUMBER, PAY GRADE, LENGTH OF SERVICE FOR PAY, BASIC PAY, INCENTIVE PAY**
510-40-3165   E-6   Over 4 years $322.50

6. **DUTY STATUS**
ACTIVE: ON DUTY

7. **INTERESTED PERSONS** (Name, Address, Relationship)
Mrs. Suzanne K. Turner, 4361 Ventura Canyon Avenue, Apt 10, Sherman Oaks, California 91403; Wife 1,3
Notified 23 May 1968
Mr. John H. Turner, 310 Anita, Potwin, Kansas 67123; Father
Mrs. Ruth B. Turner, 389 Leinbach Avenue, Ft. Ord, California 93941; Mother 4

8. **REPORTING COMMAND AND DATE REPORT RECEIVED IN DEPARTMENT**
CG USARV LBN RVN   22 May 1968

9. **REPORT FOR VA TO FOLLOW** ☒ YES ☐ NO

10. **SELECTIVE SERVICE NUMBER, LOCAL BOARD, AND LOCATION** (if minor, enter date and place of first entry in Armed Services)
14 8 42 61   LBf 8 Eldorado, Kansas

11. **PRIOR SERVICE DATA** ☒ YES ☐ NO

12. **REMARKS**
Mr. David P. Turner, 310 Anita, Potwin, Kansas 67123; Brother 2
DA Form 41 dated 7 Feb 68
FOR VA: Certification of Basic Pay UP PL 89-622 None

QUANG NAM (03) 1 CIZ
FOOTNOTES:
1. Adult next of kin.
2. Beneficiary for gratuity pay.
3. Beneficiary for unpaid pay and allowances.
4. ...

BY ORDER OF THE SECRETARY OF THE ARMY:
Adjutant General

DISTRIBUTION: B VI

DD Form 1300

Family Group Sheet

Husband's Full Name Victor Beach   **Chart No.**

	Day Month Year	City, Town or Place	County or Province, etc.	State or Country	Add Info on
Birth					
Chr'nd					
Marr.	11-1997				
Death					
Burial					

Places of Residence
Occupation   **Church Affiliation**   **Military Rec.**

His Father   **Mother's Maiden Name**

Wife's Full Maiden Name Suzanne K. Turner

	Day Month Year	City, Town or Place	County or Province, etc.	State or Country	Add Info on
Birth	2-4-1965	San Diego (Ft. Ord)	San Diego Co.	Calif.	
Chr'nd					
Death					
Burial					

Places of Residence
Occupation Financial Analyst   **Church Affiliation** Episcopalian   **Military Rec.**

Other husbands: #1 Todd Rossiter

Her Father John Harold Turner, Jr.   **Mother's Maiden Name** Suzanne Prince Keisel

Sex	Children's Names in Full		Day Month Year	City, Town or Place	County or Province, etc.	State or Country	Add Info on Ch
	1	Birth					
		Marr.					
	Full Name of Spouse	Death					
		Burial					
	2	Birth					
		Marr.					
	Full Name of Spouse	Death					
		Burial					
	3	Birth					
		Marr.					
	Full Name of Spouse	Death					
		Burial					
	4	Birth					
		Marr.					
	Full Name of Spouse	Death					
		Burial					
	5	Birth					
		Marr.					
	Full Name of Spouse	Death					
		Burial					
	6	Birth					
		Marr.					
	Full Name of Spouse	Death					
		Burial					
	7	Birth					
		Marr.					
	Full Name of Spouse	Death					
		Burial					
	8	Birth					
		Marr.					
	Full Name of Spouse	Death					
		Burial					

Compiler   **Notes**
Address
City, State, Zip
Date

Family Group Sheet

Husband's Full Name David P. Turner **Chart No.**

	Day Month Year	City, Town or Place	County or Province, etc.	State or Country	Add. Info. on Husband
Birth	1-10-1944	Newton	Harvey Co.	Kansas	
Chr'nd					Divorced 1986
Marr	9-6-1969	Glendale	Los Angeles Co.	Calif.	
Death					
Burial					

Places of Residence Paducah, Kentucky
Occupation Owner Turner Pub. Co. **Church Affiliation** **Military Rec** USAF

For additional information see next page.

His Father John Harold Turner, Sr. **Mother's Maiden Name** Ruth B. Moore

Wife's Full Maiden Name Nanette Constable

	Day Month Year	City, Town or Place	County or Province, etc.	State or Country	Add. Info. on Wife
Birth	31-1-1950	Kansas City	Wyandotte Co.	Kansas	
Chr'nd					
Death					
Burial					

Places of Residence
Occupation Owner of Computor Co **Church Affiliation** **Military Rec**

Her Father Erle Constable **Mother's Maiden Name** Eugenia Goff

Sex	Children's Names in Full		Day Month Year	City, Town or Place	County or Province, etc.	State or Country	Add. Info. on Children
M	1 Justin David Turner	Birth	5-6-1974	Longview	Gregg Co.	Texas	
	Full Name of Spouse: Heather	Marr.					
		Death					
		Burial					
M	2 Jeremy John Turner	Birth	26-8-1978	Lubbock	Lubbock Co.	Texas	
	Full Name of Spouse	Marr.					
		Death					
		Burial					
	3	Birth					
	Full Name of Spouse	Marr.					
		Death					
		Burial					

Ruth Turner with grandson, Justin Turner.

Heather (Justin's wife) and children: Blake and Abby.

Jeremy Turner and Gabriela Reyes

DAVID P. TURNER

David (Dave) Turner, son of John H. and Ruth B. Turner, was born in Newton, KS. He graduated from high school in El Dorado, KS and from Whitworth College in Spokane, WA. He served in the United States Air Force as the Base Commander's Aide in Spokane.

Rachelle (Shelly) Lee Murt Turner, daughter of Carl and Cookie Murt was born July 1, 1961 in Paducah, KY. She graduated from Reidland High School.

Dave and Shelly were married in 1991. Dave has two sons, Justin and Jeremy, from a previous marriage. Dave and Shelly have been attending Broadway Methodist Church since 1992.

Dave worked in Public Relations for Whitworth College in Spokane, WA; Simpson College in San Francisco, CA; and Le Turneau College in Longview, TX before starting Turner Publishing Company in 1977.

Shelly has also been very active in the continuing success of Turner Publishing Company. She spends many an hour handling customer service calls and is one of the main icons at the Turner booths set up at military functions across the nation.

Turner Publishing has published more than 700 titles nationwide. The company has 25 employees and is based in Paducah.

Dave Turner with his mom, Ruth.

Jeremy and Justin Turner with Justin's one year old son, Blake, Nov. 11, 1992.

Corporal Justin Turner, USMC

Shelly and Dave Turner

Military Unit Histories A Success Story For Paducah, KY, Publisher

187

Memorial to My Brother and Father

John Harold Turner Jr.

JOHN HAROLD TURNER JR.
March 12, 1942-May 20, 1968
Killed in Viet Nam War

JOHN HAROLD TURNER SR.
May 2, 1917-June 9, 1969
Killed in Auto Accident

Dave Turner's Family History located elsewhere in this book has more information.

John Harold Sr., John Harold Jr., Ruth B. holding David P. Turner

John Sr. and Ruth Turner — 1963

Family Group Sheet

Husband's Full Name Merle Dean Harlan — **Chart No.**

	Day Month Year	City, Town or Place	County or Province, etc.	State or Country	Add. Info on Husband
Birth	29-12-1916	Emporia	Lyons Co.	Kansas	
Chr'nd		Christian Church	Madison	Kansas	
Marr	20- 9-1942	ElDorado	Butler Co.	Kansas	
Death					
Burial					

Places of Residence

Occupation Farmer-Welder   Church Affiliation Christian   Military Rec

His Father Pay S. Harlan   Mother's Maiden Name Mae Lillian Duby

Wife's Full Maiden Name Opal Marian Moore

	Day Month Year	City, Town or Place	County or Province, etc.	State or Country	Add. Info on Wife
Birth	8- 8-1922	Murdock Township	Butler Co.	Kansas	
Chr'nd	10-10-1934	Christian Church Potwin	Butler Co.	Kansas	
Death					
Burial					

Places of Residence

Occupation Secretary-Housewife   Church Affiliation Christian   Military Rec

Her Father Reuben David Moore   Mother's Maiden Name Edith Grace Taylor

Sex	Children's Names in Full		Day Month Year	City, Town or Place	County or Province, etc.	State or Country	Add. Info on Children
F	1 Janice Kay Harlan	Birth	15-11-1943	Wichita	Sedgwick Co.	Kansas	1960
	Full Name of Spouse Steinback	Marr.	1963				
	Ron Sheets/Alan	Death					
		Burial					
M	2 Mervin Jay Harlan	Birth	21-8-1946	Wichita	Sedgwick Co.	Kan.	
		Marr.					
	Full Name of Spouse	Death					
		Burial					
F	3 Harlan Barbara Louise	Birth	24- 7-1953	Emporia	Lyon Co.	Kans.	
		Marr.	1976				
	Full Name of Spouse	Death					
	Duane T. Schroder	Burial					

Opal Moore

Merle and Opal Harlan, 55th Anniversary, 1997.

Merle Harlan and Opal Moore Harlan, Barbara Harlan Schroeder, Mervin Harlan, Janice Harlan Steinback

Family Group Sheet

Husband's Full Name: Ronald Hiram Sheets — **Chart No.**

	Day Month Year	City, Town or Place	County or Province, etc.	State or Country	Add. Info on Husband
Birth					
Chr'nd					
Marr	16-2-1963	Madison Methodist	Greenwood	Kansas	divorced 1979
Death					
Burial					

Places of Residence:
Occupation: Church Affiliation: Military Rec:
Other wives, if any:
His Father: Mother's Maiden Name:

Wife's Full Maiden Name: Janice Kay Harlan

	Day Month Year	City, Town or Place	County or Province, etc.	State or Country	Add. Info on Wife
Birth	15-11-1943	Wichita	Oesteopathic hospital Sedgwick Co.	Kans.	
Chr'nd		Methodist Madison	Greenwood	Kans.	
Death					
Burial					

Places of Residence:
Occupation: Nurse-Housewife   Church Affiliation: Methodist   Military Rec:
Other husbands: #2 Alan Steinback June 1982
Her Father: Merle D. Harlan   Mother's Maiden Name: Opal Marian Moore

Sex	Children's Names in Full		Day Month Year	City, Town or Place	County or Province, etc.	State or Country	Add. Info on Children
F	1 Michelle Rene Sheets	Birth	27-2-1964	Council Grove	Morris Co.	Ks.	
		Marr.	3-8-1985	Emporia	Lyons Co.	Kans.	
	Full Name of Spouse: Harry Gifford	Death					
		Burial					
M	2 John Michael Sheets	Birth	27-2-1964	Council Grove	Morris Co.	Ks.	
		Marr.					
	Full Name of Spouse:	Death					
		Burial					
M	3 Stephen Ray Sheets	Birth	28-9-1965	Lindsburg	McPhearson Co.	Kans.	divorced 1988
		Marr.	10-11-1986	Neodesha	Wilson Co.	Kans.	
	Full Name of Spouse: Kim Green/Denys Musih	Death					
		Burial					

STATE OF KANSAS, CENTRAL DIVISION OF VITAL STATISTICS

MARRIAGE LICENSE

State No. 76906
P.J. No. 3500

IN THE PROBATE COURT OF LYON COUNTY, KANSAS

February 15th, 1963

TO ANY PERSON IN THE STATE OF KANSAS AUTHORIZED TO PERFORM THE MARRIAGE CEREMONY,

Greeting:

You are hereby authorized to join in marriage

RONALD SHEETS (Groom) of EMPORIA, KANSAS, age 22
JANICE HARLAN (Bride) of EMPORIA, KANSAS, age 19

with the consent of _____ (Name of parent or guardian consenting), and of this license, duly endorsed by you, you will make return to my office at Emporia, Kansas, within ten (10) days after performing the ceremony.

/s/ William J. Dick
Probate Judge

(Seal)

ENDORSEMENT

To Whom It May Concern:

I hereby certify that I performed the Ceremony joining in marriage the above named couple on the 17th day of February, 1963, at Madison, Kansas.

Signed /s/ Arthur L. Hardy
Title Pastor of Methodist Church
Address Madison, Kansas

Janice's daughter, Michelle Sheets Gifford, Harry Gifford, Ryan-5yrs., and Kendra-3yrs.

Family Group Sheet

Husband's Full Name: Harry Gifford
Chart No.:

	Day	Month	Year	City, Town or Place	County or Province, etc.	State or Country	Add. Info on Husband
Birth							
Chr'nd							
Marr	3	8	1985	Emporia Congregational	Lyons	Kansas	
Death							
Burial							

Places of Residence:
Occupation: Church Affiliation: Military Rec:
His Father: Mother's Maiden Name:

Wife's Full Maiden Name: Michelle Rene Sheets

	Day	Month	Year	City, Town or Place	County or Province, etc.	State or Country	Add. Info on Wife
Birth	27	2	1964	Council Grove	Morris Co.	Kansas	
Chr'nd							
Death							
Burial							

Places of Residence:
Occupation: Public Relations   Church Affiliation: Military Rec:
Her Father: Ronald Hiram Sheets   Mother's Maiden Name: Janice Kay Harlan

Sex	Children's Names in Full		Day	Month	Year	City, Town or Place	County or Province, etc.	State or Country	Add. Info on Children
M	1. Ryan Michael Gifford	Birth	15	7	1987	Emporia	Lyons	Kans.	
		Marr							
		Death							
		Burial							
F	2. Kendra Elyse Gifford	Birth	24	9	1992	Emporia	Lyons	Kans.	
		Marr							
		Death							
		Burial							
	3.	Birth							
		Marr							

No. 106426 — STATE OF KANSAS — THE KANSAS STATE DEPARTMENT OF HEALTH AND ENVIRONMENT — Bureau of Vital Statistics

Marriage License — 85 M 217

District Court of Lyon County. July 31, 1985.

To any Person in the State of Kansas Authorized by Law to Perform the Marriage Ceremony, Greetings:

Harry YOU ARE HEREBY AUTHORIZED TO JOIN IN MARRIAGE

Harry Edward Gifford of Waverly, Kansas, Age 21
Michelle Rene Sheets of Emporia, Kansas, Age 21

with the consent of _____ and with this license duly endorsed, you will make return to my office at Emporia, Kansas, within ten days after performing the ceremony.

Clerk of District Court - Jeanne S. Turner
by Deputy Clerk

ENDORSEMENT

TO WHOM IT MAY CONCERN:
I hereby certify that I, the undersigned, performed the ceremony joining in marriage the above named couple on the 3rd day of August 1985 at Emporia, Kansas, in Lyon County. My credentials are recorded in the D.C.'s office of Lyon Co., Ks.

Signed: Rev. Bill Carlson
Title: Family Life Minister
Address: 1118 Rural St. Emporia, Ks. 217-

License No. 052290 — STATE OF KANSAS — DEPARTMENT OF HEALTH AND ENVIRONMENT — Office of Vital Statistics

Marriage License

GROOM:
1. Groom's Name: Stephen Ray Sheets
2. Residence — City, Town, or Location: Madison
3. County: Greenwood
4. State: Kansas
5. Birthplace: Kansas
6. Date of Birth: September 28, 1965
7. Father's Name: Ronald Hiram Sheets — Kansas
9. Mother's Name / Maiden Surname: Janice Kay Harlan — Kansas

BRIDE:
11. Bride's Name: Denys Suzanne Musch
13. Residence — City, Town, or Location: Emporia
14. County: Lyon
15. State: Kansas
16. Birthplace: Kansas
17. Date of Birth: October 23, 1968
18. Father's Name: Dennis Keith Musch — Kansas
20. Mother's Name: Kathleen Ann Mount — Kansas

22. Date License Issued: March 25, 1991
24. Expiration Date: September 25, 1991
28. Title of Issuing Official: Clerk Of District Court
27. Certify date: March 30, 1991
30. Where Married — City, Town, or Location: Madison, KS.
31. County Where Credentials Are Filed: Greenwood — Coffey
33. Name of Person Performing Ceremony: William H. Winter
34. Address: 322 Sherman Ave. Madison, Ks 66860
35. Groom's Signature: Stephen Sheets
36. Bride's Signature: Denys Musch
37. Signature of Witness: Todd G. Harris

District Court of Issuance: Lyon County District Court
Date Received by Court Official: 4/2/91

191

Family Group Sheet

Husband's Full Name: John Michael Sheets

Chart No. -

	Day Month Year	City, Town or Place	County or Province, etc.	State or Country	Add. Info on Husband
Birth	27- 2-1964	Council Grove	Harris Co.	Kansas	
Chr'nd					
Marr					
Death					
Burial					

Places of Residence

Occupation: Computer Pgm.   **Church Affiliation:**   **Military Rec:**

His Father: Ronald Hiram Sheets   **Mother's Maiden Name:** Janice Kay Harlan

Wife's Full Maiden Name:

	Day Month Year	City, Town or Place	County or Province, etc.	State or Country	Add. Info on Wife
Birth					
Chr'nd					
Death					
Burial					

Places of Residence

Occupation: **Church Affiliation:**   **Military Rec:**

Her Father: **Mother's Maiden Name:**

Family Group Sheet

Husband's Full Name: Stephen Ray Sheets

Chart No. -

	Day Month Year	City, Town or Place	County or Province, etc.	State or Country	Add. Info on Husband
Birth	28- 9-1965	Lindsborg	McPherson Co.	Kansas	Divorced 1988
Chr'nd					
Marr	10-11-1986	Neodesha	Wilson Co.	Kansas	
Death					
Burial					

Places of Residence

Occupation: Iron Worker   **Church Affiliation:**   **Military Rec:**

Other wives: #2 Deny Musch (M) 31 April, 1991 Madison, Ks. Divorced 1992

His Father: Ronald Hiram Sheets   **Mother's Maiden Name:** Janice Kay Harlan

Wife's Full Maiden Name: #1 Kim Green

	Day Month Year	City, Town or Place	County or Province, etc.	State or Country	Add. Info on Wife
Birth					
Chr'nd					
Death					
Burial					

Places of Residence

Occupation: **Church Affiliation:**   **Military Rec:**

Her Father: **Mother's Maiden Name:**

Sex	Children's Names in Full		Day Month Year	City, Town or Place	County or Province, etc.	State or Country	Add. Info on Children
F	1 Sheets Kayla Michelle	Birth Marr. Death Burial	28- 3-1987	Neodasha	Wilson Co.	Kans.	1st. wife
F	2 Sheets Rachelle Nicole	Birth Marr. Death Burial	15-10-1991	Emporia	Lyon	Kans.	2nd. wife

City, State, Zip:

Date:

Family Group Sheet

Husband's Full Name Mervin Jay Harlan   **Chart No.**

	Day Month Year	City, Town or Place	County or Province, etc.	State or Country	Add Info on Husband
Birth	21-8-1946	Wichita Wesley hospital	Sedgwick Co.	Kansas	
Chr'nd					
Marr					
Death					
Burial					

Places of Residence

Occupation Brakeman-Santa Fe   **Church Affiliation** Methodist   **Military Rec**

His Father Merle Dean Harlan   **Mother's Maiden Name** Opal Marian Moore

Family Group Sheet

Husband's Full Name Duane Thomas Schroeder   **Chart No.**

	Day Month Year	City, Town or Place	County or Province, etc.	State or Country	Add Info on Husb
Birth					
Chr'nd					
Marr	18-11-1976	Madison Methodist church	Greenwood Co.	Kansas	
Death					
Burial					

Places of Residence

Occupation   **Church Affiliation**   **Military Rec**

His Father   **Mother's Maiden Name**

Wife's Full Maiden Name Barbara Louise Harlan

	Day Month Year	City, Town or Place	County or Province, etc.	State or Country	Add Info on Wife
Birth	24-7-1953	Emporia Newman	Lyons	Kansas	
Chr'nd		Methodist	Madison Greenwood Co.	Kansas	
Death					
Burial					

Places of Residence

Occupation Worker Hopkins Inc.   **Church Affiliation** Methodist   **Military Rec**

Her Father Merle Dean Harlan   **Mother's Maiden Name** Opal Marian Moore

Sex	Children's Names in Full		Day Month Year	City, Town or Place	County or Province, etc.	State or Country	Add Info on Child
M	1 Schroeder Matthew Thomas	Birth	4-4-1981	Emporia	Lyons Co.	Kansas	
	Full Name of Spouse	Marr.					
		Death					
		Burial					
F	2 Schroeder Melanie Rene	Birth	4-4-1981	Emporia	Lyons Co.	Kansas	
	Full Name of Spouse Jarrod Fell	Marr.	23-6-1998	Emporia	Lyons Co.	Kansas	
		Death					
		Burial					
F	3 Schroeder Shawna Marie	Birth	28-11-1993	Emporia	Lyons Co.	Kansas	
	Full Name of Spouse	Marr.					
		Death					
		Burial					
	8 Full Name of Spouse	Birth					
		Marr.					
		Death					
		Burial					

Compiler

Address

City, State, Zip

Date

Notes:

Family Group Sheet

Husband's Full Name Alva Daniel Moore SS-513-26-4336 **Chart No.**

	Day Month Year	City, Town or Place	County or Province, etc.	State or Country	Add Info on Hus
Birth	28-11-1927	Potwin	Butler Co.	Kansas	
Chr'nd					
Marr	23-10-1946	ElDorado	Butler Co.	Kansas	
Death					
Burial					

Places of Residence Benton-Rosalia -Okla.- Independence, Ks.
Occupation Farmer-Real Estate-car salesman **Church Affiliation** Christian **Military Rec.**
#2 Donna Lea Hinthorn-21 Oct. 1982 Independence, Ks.
His Father Reuben Moore **Mother's Maiden Name** Edith Grace Taylor

Wife's Full Maiden Name Lois Valetta Bachelder

	Day Month Year	City, Town or Place	County or Province, etc.	State or Country	Add. Info on W
Birth	13-10-1927	Benton	Butler Co.	Kansas	
Chr'nd					
Death					
Burial					

Places of Residence
Occupation Housewife-Restate **Church Affiliation** Christian **Military Rec.**
Her Father Theodore N. Bachelder **Mother's Maiden Name** Edith Blanche Pheres

Sex	Children's names in Full		Day Month Year	City, Town or Place	County or Province, etc.	State or Country	Add. Info on Chil
F	1 Edith Valetta Moore	Birth	26- 6-1948	Wichita	Sedgwick Co.	Kans.	
	Full Name of Spouse	Marr.	16-9-1966	Eureka	Greenwood Co.	Kans.	divorce
	Wayne Arthur Austin	Death					
		Burial					
F	2 Sue Ann Moore	Birth	26- 1-1951	Wichita	Sedgwick Co.	Kans.	
		Marr.					
	Full Name of Spouse	Death	15- 2-1974	Winfield	Cowly Co.	Kans.	
		Burial	2-1974	Winfield	Cowley Co.	Kans.	
M	3 Allen Dee Moore	Birth	26- 5-1953	Wichita	Sedgwick Co.	Kans.	
		Marr.	13- 9-1973	Eureka	Greenwood Co.	Kans.	
	Full Name of Spouse	Death					
	Kathleen Kay George	Burial					
F	4 Ava Lynne Moore	Birth	23-10-1954	Wichita	Sedgwick Co.	Kans.	divorce 1996
		Marr.	4- 1-1975	ElDorado	Butler Co.	Kans.	
	Full Name of Spouse	Death					
	Victor L. Vogts	Burial					
F	5 Rose Annette Moore	Birth	24- 9-1960	Wichita	Sedgwick Co.	Kans.	divorce 1996
		Marr.	28-10-1978	ElDorado	Butler Co.	Kans.	
	Full Name of Spouse	Death					
	Martin G. Brenton	Burial					
M	6 Thomas Herbert Moore	Birth	22- 7-1962	Eureka	Greenwood Co.	Kans.	
		Marr.	28- 6-1997	ElDorado	Butler Co.	Kans.	
	Full Name of Spouse	Death					
	Faye Ann Younke	Burial					
	7	Birth					
		Marr.					
	Full Name of Spouse	Death					
		Burial					
	8	Birth					
		Marr.					
	Full Name of Spouse	Death					
		Burial					

Comp'er
Address
City, State, Zip
Date

Notes.

STATE OF KANSAS
THE KANSAS STATE DEPARTMENT OF HEALTH
DIVISION OF VITAL STATISTICS

Marriage License

License No. 90790
P. J. No. 1558

IN THE PROBATE COURT OF LYON COUNTY.   November 4, 1976

To Any Person in the State of Kansas Authorized by Law to Perform the Marriage Ceremony, Greetings: You are hereby authorized to join in Marriage:

Duane Thomas Schroeder — Name of Groom — of Madison, Kansas — Residence—City & State — age 28

and Barbara Louise Harlan — Name of Bride — of Madison, Kansas — Residence—City & State — age 23

with the consent of _____ Name of Parent or Guardian Consenting _____ and with this License duly endorsed, you will make

(SEAL) return to my office at Emporia, Kansas, within ten days after performing the ceremony.

/s/ Darrell D. Meyer, Probate Judge.

ENDORSEMENT

Credentials Recorded in P. J. Office _____ Lyon _____ County, Kansas

Signatures of Witnesses:
Jan Sheets
Art D. Altis

DATE RECEIVED BY PROBATE JUDGE 11-22- 1976
DATE RECORDED BY PROBATE JUDGE 11-22- 1976

TO WHOM IT MAY CONCERN:
I hereby certify that I, the undersigned, performed the ceremony joining in marriage the above named couple on the 19 day of November, 1976 at Madison, Kansas, in Greenwood County.

Signed P. Eugene Riley
Title United Methodist Minister
Address Box 265 Madison, Kansas

NOTE.—After recording, the probate judge shall forward this original marriage license to the State Registrar, Topeka, Kansas, not later than the third day of following month.

STANDARD CERTIFICATE OF BIRTH.
PLACE OF BIRTH.   STATE BOARD OF HEALTH,
County of Butler   DIVISION OF VITAL STATISTICS.
Township of Murdock   STATE OF KANSAS.
City of _____ No. _____ street. Reg. No. 17

DO NOT WRITE IN THIS SPACE
8   8403

Full Name of Child: Alva Daniel Moore
Sex of Child: Male
Twin, triplet, or other?:
Number in order of birth: 1
Legitimate: Yes
Date of birth: Nov 28 1927

FATHER. Full Name: Rudy H. Moore
Residence: Murdock Township
Color: White   Age at last birthday: 41
Birthplace: Butler Co. Kansas
Occupation: Farmer

MOTHER. Full Maiden Name: Edith Taylor
Residence: Murdock Township
Color: White   Age at last birthday: 39
Birthplace: Danville Ill.
Occupation: Housewife

Number of children born to this mother, including present birth: 7
Number of children of this mother now living: 7

CERTIFICATE OF ATTENDING PHYSICIAN OR MIDWIFE.
I hereby certify that I attended the birth of this child, who was born alive at 7:30 A.M. on the date above stated.
Signature: W. J. _____
Address: Benton, Kans
Filed Dec 1st 1927

Given name added from supplemental report _____ 191__

Barbara Harlan Schroeder's children: Melanie and Matthew - 14 yrs. and Shawna Marie - 1 yr.

Alva D. Moore, graduation picture.

Alva D. Moore, 1980

No. 49261
P. J. No. 9761

STATE OF KANSAS
STATE OF KANSAS, CENTRAL DIVISION OF VITAL STATISTICS
THE KANSAS STATE BOARD OF HEALTH
DIVISION OF VITAL STATISTICS

MARRIAGE LICENSE

IN THE PROBATE COURT OF BUTLER COUNTY.   October 23, 1946

To any Person in the State of Kansas Authorized by Law to Perform the Marriage Ceremony, Greeting:

YOU ARE HEREBY AUTHORIZED TO JOIN IN MARRIAGE

Alva Daniel Moore (Groom) of Benton, Kansas Age 23
Lois V. Bachelder (Bride) of Benton, Kansas Age 19

with the consent of _____ (Name of parent or guardian consenting)

(SEAL) and of this license, duly endorsed, you will make return to my office at El Dorado, Kansas, within ten days after performing the ceremony.

Ralph B. Ralston, Probate Judge.

ENDORSEMENT

TO WHOM IT MAY CONCERN:

I hereby certify that I performed the ceremony joining in marriage the above named couple, on the 30th day of November, 1946, at (Home) in Benton, Kansas.

Signed Rev. Howard S. Millspaugh
Title Baptist Minister
Address 528 1/2 West Douglas
Wichita 12, Kansas

License No. 49642
D.C. No. 28884

STATE OF KANSAS
THE KANSAS STATE DEPARTMENT OF HEALTH AND ENVIRONMENT
Bureau of Vital Statistics

Marriage License

In the District Court of Montgomery County, October 21, 1982

To Any Person in the State of Kansas Authorized by Law to Perform the Marriage Ceremony, Greetings:

YOU ARE HEREBY AUTHORIZED TO JOIN IN MARRIAGE

Alva Daniel Moore of Little River, Kansas Age 54
Donna Lea Hinthorn of Independence, Kansas Age 51

with the consent of _____

and with this license duly endorsed, you will make return to my office at Independence, Kansas, within ten days after performing the ceremony.

Laura Faye Fellers, Deputy Clerk

ENDORSEMENT

TO WHOM IT MAY CONCERN:

I hereby certify that I, the undersigned, performed the ceremony joining in marriage the above named couple on the 23 day of October, 1982, at Independence, Kansas, in M.G. County.

Lois Bachelder and Alva Moore

Alan Moore, Ava Moore Vogts, Thomas Moore, Valetta Moore Austin and Annette Moore Brenton

Alva Moore, 1996

196

Family Group Sheet

Husband's Full Name: Wayne Arthur Austin
Chart No.:

	Day Month Year	City, Town or Place	County or Province, etc.	State or Country	Add. Info on Hus.
Birth	27- 8-1943				
Chr'nd					
Marr.	16- 9-1966	Eureka	Greenwood Co.	Kans.	divorced
Death					30 June
Burial					1988

Places of Residence: Severy, Ks.
Occupation: Hay Hauler **Church Affiliation:** Baptist **Military Rec.:**

His Father: Neil Austin **Mother's Maiden Name:** Betty

Wife's Full Maiden Name: Edith Valetta Moore

	Day Month Year	City, Town or Place	County or Province, etc.	State or Country	Add. Info on W.
Birth	26- 6-1948	Wichita	Sedgwick Co.	Kansas	
Chr'nd					
Death					
Burial					

Places of Residence: Benton, Kansas
Occupation: Housewife **Church Affiliation:** Baptist **Military Rec.:**

Her Father: Alva Daniel Moore **Mother's Maiden Name:** Lois Valetta Bachelder

Sex	Children's names in full		Day Month Year	City, Town or Place	County or Province, etc.	State or Country	Add Info on Chil.
M	1 Heath Wayne Austin	Birth	23- 4-1967	Wichita	Sedgwick Co.	Kans.	
		Marr.	4- 4-1987	ElDorado	Butler Co.	Kans.	
	Full Name of Spouse	Death					
	Michael Maureen Coats	Burial					
M	2 Michael Daniel Austin	Birth	1- 4-1969	Wichita	Sedgwick Co.	Kans.	
		Marr.	12-3-1994	Augusta	Butler Co.	Kans.	
	Full Name of Spouse	Death					
	Tracie Deann Ball	Burial					

STATE OF KANSAS
THE KANSAS STATE BOARD OF HEALTH
Division of Vital Statistics

No. 31263
P. J. No. _____

MARRIAGE LICENSE

IN THE PROBATE COURT OF GREENWOOD COUNTY September 12th, 1966

To Any Person in the State of Kansas Authorized by Law to Perform the Marriage Ceremony, GREETINGS:

YOU ARE HEREBY AUTHORIZED TO JOIN IN MARRIAGE

Wayne A. Austin (Groom) of Severy, Kansas Age 23
Edith Valetta Moore (Bride) of Eureka, Kansas Age 18

(SEAL) with the consent of _____ (Name of Parent or Guardian Consenting)
and of this license, duly endorsed, you will make return to my office at Eureka, Kansas, within ten days after performing the ceremony.

B M Beyer, Probate Judge.

ENDORSEMENT

TO WHOM IT MAY CONCERN:
I hereby certify that I performed the ceremony joining in marriage the above-named couple on the 16th day of September, 1966, at Eureka, Kansas.

Signed: Rev. Floyd L. Roberts
Title: Minister First Baptist Church
Address: Eureka, Kansas

G.S. 1949, 23-109—Every person who shall perform any marriage ceremony under the provisions of this act, shall, within ten days after such marriage, return the said license to the Probate Judge who issued the same with his certificate of such marriage endorsed thereon, etc.

NOTE—After recording, the probate judge shall forward this original marriage license to the State Registrar, Topeka, Kan., not later than the third day of the following month.

Filed Sept 19, 1966

Valetta Moore

Family Group Sheet

Husband's Full Name: Heath Wayne Austin

Chart No.:

	Day	Month	Year	City, Town or Place	County or Province, etc.	State or Country	Add. Info on Husband
Birth	23	4	1967	Wichita	Sedgwick Co.	Kans.	
Chr'nd							
Marr	4	4	1987	ElDorado	Butler Co.	Kans.	
Death							
Burial							

Places of Residence: Potwin, Kansas
Occupation: State Reformatory
Church Affiliation:
Military Rec.:

His Father: Wayne Arthur Austin
Mother's Maiden Name: Edith Valetta Moore

Wife's Full Maiden Name: Michael Maureen Coates

	Day	Month	Year	City, Town or Place	County or Province, etc.	State or Country	Add. Info on Wife
Birth	11	10	1964	Burbank	Los Angeles Co.	California	
Chr'nd							
Death							
Burial							

Places of Residence: Potwin, Kansas
Occupation: Teacher
Church Affiliation:
Military Rec.:

Her Father: Alvin Garst
Mother's Maiden Name: Joy Camp

Sex	Children's Names in Full		Day	Month	Year	City, Town or Place	County or Province, etc.	State or Country	Add. Info on Child
F	1. Audie Austin	Birth	17	11	1982	Torcorteb		Colorado	
	Full Name of Spouse	Marr.							
		Death							
		Burial							
M	2. Cody Austin	Birth	23	10	1987	Wichita	Sedgwick Co.	Kans.	
	Full Name of Spouse	Marr.							
		Death							
		Burial							
	3.	Birth							
	Full Name of Spouse	Marr.							
		Death							
		Burial							
	4.	Birth							
	Full Name of Spouse	Marr.							
		Death							
		Burial							

Michael, Heath, Wayne and Valetta Austin, 1985

Compiler:
Address:
City, State, Zip:
Date:

License No. 162262

STATE OF KANSAS
THE KANSAS STATE DEPARTMENT OF HEALTH AND ENVIRONMENT
Office of Vital Statistics

D.C. No. 8750

Marriage License

In the District Court of _Butler_ County, _April 3_ 19_87_

To Any Person in the State of Kansas Authorized by Law to Perform the Marriage Ceremony, Greetings:

YOU ARE HEREBY AUTHORIZED TO JOIN IN MARRIAGE

Heath Wayne Austin of Whitewater, Kansas Age 19
Michal Maureen Coates of El Dorado, Kansas Age 22

with the consent of _____

and with this license duly endorsed, you will make return to my office at El Dorado, Kansas, within ten days after performing the ceremony.

John M. Jowarsky, District Judge

ENDORSEMENT

Signatures of Witnesses:
Jean Messing
Michael Austin

DATE RECEIVED BY DISTRICT COURT: Apr. 16, 1987
DATE RECORDED BY DISTRICT COURT: Apr. 16, 1987

TO WHOM IT MAY CONCERN:
I hereby certify that I, the undersigned, performed the ceremony joining in marriage the above named couple on the 4th day of April, 1987, at El Dorado, Kansas, in Butler County. My credentials are recorded in the D.C.'s office of Butler Co., Ks

Signed: Wayne Hoy
Title: Pastor, Trinity United Methodist Church
Address: 439 Eunice, El Dorado, Ks. 67042

Family Group Sheet

Husband's Full Name: Michael Daniel Austin — Chart No. _____

	Day Month Year	City, Town or Place	County or Province, etc.	State or Country	Add Info on Husb
Birth	1-4-1969	Wichita	Sedgwick Co.	Kansas	
Chr'nd					
Marr	12-4-1994	Augusta	Butler Co.	Kansas	
Death					
Burial					

Places of Residence: Augusta, Kansas
Occupation: Northcut Trailer **Church Affiliation:** _____ **Military Rec:** _____

His Father: Wayne Arthur Austin **Mother's Maiden Name:** Edith Valetta Moore

Wife's Full Maiden Name: Tracie Deann Ball

	Day Month Year	City, Town or Place	County or Province, etc.	State or Country	Add Info on Wife
Birth	17-12-1969	Wichita	Sedgwick Co.	Kansas	
Chr'nd					
Death					
Burial					

Places of Residence: _____
Occupation: Housewife **Church Affiliation:** _____ **Military Rec:** _____

Her Father: Gary Lee Ball **Mother's Maiden Name:** Neva Jannie Jones

Sex	Children's Names in Full		Day Month Year	City, Town or Place	County or Province, etc.	State or Country	Add Info on Child
M	1 Jared L. Austin	Birth	20-5-1995	ElDorado	Butler Co.	Kansas	
	Full Name of Spouse	Marr.					
		Death					
		Burial					
M	2 Joshua L. Austin	Birth	9-4-1997	Wichita	Sedgwick Co.	Kans.	
	Full Name of Spouse	Marr.					
		Death					

Mr. and Mrs. Gary Ball

invite you to share in the joy

of the marriage uniting their daughter

Tracie Deann

to

Michael Daniel Austin

This celebration of love will be

Saturday, the twelfth of March

Nineteen hundred and ninety-four

at six o'clock in the evening

First Baptist Church

1501 State Street

Augusta, Kansas

Reception and Dance
following ceremony
Lehr's Restaurant
212 West Seventh Street

License No. 109240

STATE OF KANSAS
DEPARTMENT OF HEALTH AND ENVIRONMENT
Office of Vital Statistics

Marriage License

1. GROOM'S NAME: MICHAEL DANIEL AUSTIN
2. RESIDENCE—CITY, TOWN, OR LOCATION: Wichita 3. COUNTY: Sedgwick
4. STATE: Kansas 5. BIRTHPLACE: Kansas 6. DATE OF BIRTH: April 1, 1969
7. FATHER'S NAME: Wayne Arthur Austin BIRTHPLACE: Kansas MOTHER'S NAME: Edith Valetta Moore BIRTHPLACE: Kansas

11. BRIDE'S NAME: TRACIE DEANN BALL 12. MAIDEN SURNAME: _____
13. RESIDENCE—CITY, TOWN, OR LOCATION: Wichita 14. COUNTY: Sedgwick
15. STATE: Kansas 16. BIRTHPLACE: Kansas 17. DATE OF BIRTH: December 12, 1969
18. FATHER'S NAME: Gary Lee Ball BIRTHPLACE: Kansas MOTHER'S NAME: Nelva Janean Jones BIRTHPLACE: Kansas

DATE LICENSE ISSUED: January 24, 1994
EXPIRATION DATE: July 24, 1994
TITLE OF ISSUING OFFICIAL: Deputy Clerk

WHERE MARRIED—CITY, TOWN, OR LOCATION: Augusta, Kansas COUNTY: Butler
DATE MARRIED: March 12, 1994
TITLE: Senior Pastor
NAME OF PERSON PERFORMING CEREMONY: Dr. Robert A. Box
ADDRESS: 1501 State Street, Augusta, KS 67010

DISTRICT COURT: Butler County District Court
DATE RECEIVED: MAR 15 1994

Family Group Sheet

Husband's Full Name:

Chart No.:

	Day	Month	Year	City, Town or Place	County or Province, etc.	State or Country	Add. Info on Husband
Birth							
Chr'nd							
Marr							
Death							
Burial							

Places of Residence:

Occupation: **Church Affiliation:** **Military Rec:**

His Father: **Mother's Maiden Name:**

Wife's Full Maiden Name: Sue Ann Moore

	Day	Month	Year	City, Town or Place	County or Province, etc.	State or Country	Add. Info on Wife
Birth	26	1	1951	Wichita	Sedgwick Co.	Kansas	
Chr'nd							
Death	15	2	1974	Winfield	Cowley Co.	Kansas	
Burial	19	2	1974	State Hospital	Winfield Cowley Co.	Kansas	

Places of Residence:

Occupation: **Church Affiliation:** Christian **Military Rec:**

Her Father: Alva Daniel Moore **Mother's Maiden Name:** Lois Valetta Batchelder

Sex	Children's Names in Full		Day	Month	Year	City, Town or Place	County or Province, etc.	State or Country	Add. Info on Children
1		Birth							
		Marr.							

CERTIFICATE OF LIVE BIRTH — BOARD OF HEALTH / Vital Statistics

CITY FEB 14 1951 Registrar's No. 474 BIRTH NUMBER 51 002616

Sedgwick 872 — Kansas — Butler — Wichita — Benton 80 — Wesley Hospital — Murdock Township

Sue Ann Moore — Twin — DATE OF BIRTH 1 26 51

FATHER OF CHILD: Alva Daniel Moore — White — Kansas — Farmer

MOTHER OF CHILD: Lois Valetta Batchelder — White — Kansas

Children Previously Born to Mother: Father one / None / None

SIGNATURE: W.C. Siebert M.D. — ADDRESS: Wichita, Ks. — DATE SIGNED Jan. 31, 1951

KANSAS STATE DEPARTMENT OF HEALTH — Division of Vital Statistics — **CERTIFICATE OF DEATH**

FEB 24 1975 — 75-002452

Sue Ann Moore — Female — February 15, 1975

White — 24 — No — January 26, 1951 — Cowley

Winfield — No — Winfield State Hospital and Training Center

Kansas — U.S.A. — Never married

515-70-9645 — None

Kansas — Butler — Benton 67017 — None

FATHER: Alva Moore MOTHER: Lois Bachelder

INFORMANT: Medical Records, Winfield State Hospital and Training Center

9314 — Cardiac arrest — Immediate
Hepatic coma — Two days
Serum Hepatitis — One week

Mongolism, profound mental retardation

5:30 A. — 2/15/75

Winfield, Kansas 67158

SUE ANN MOORE
1951 — 1975

Full Name of Spouse (7):
Full Name of Spouse (8):

Compiler:
Address:
City, State, Zip:
Date:

Family Group Sheet

Husband's Full Name: Allen Dee Moore

Chart No.:

	Day Month Year	City, Town or Place	County or Province, etc.	State or Country	Add. Info on Husband
Birth	26- 5-1953	Wichita	Sedgwick Co.	Kansas	
Chr'nd					
Marr	13- 9-1973	Eureka	Greenwood Co.	Kansas	
Death					
Burial					

Places of Residence: 11826 SE 30th. Rosalia, Kansas
Occupation: Maintenance -hospital- ~~Farmer~~
Military Rec:

His Father: Alva Daniel Moore
Mother's Maiden Name: Lois Valetta Bachelder

Wife's Full Maiden Name: Kathleen Kay George

	Day Month Year	City, Town or Place	County or Province, etc.	State or Country	Add. Info on Wife
Birth	30- 7-1954	Arkansas City	Cowley Co.	Kansas	
Chr'nd					
Death					
Burial					

Places of Residence: 11826 SE 30th. Rosalia, Kansas
Occupation: Doctor Office
Church Affiliation:
Military Rec:

Her Father: Ross E. George
Mother's Maiden Name: Dorathea E. Peterson

Children

Sex	Children's Names in Full		Day Month Year	City, Town or Place	County or Province, etc.	State or Country	Add. Info on Children
F	1. Amanda Elaine Moore	Birth	11- 3-1974	ElDorado	Butler Co.	Kansas	
	Full Name of Spouse	Marr.					
		Death					
		Burial					
F	2. Alana Deann Moore	Birth	1-12-1976	ElDorado	Butler Co.	Kansas	
	Full Name of Spouse	Marr.					
		Death					
		Burial					
	3.	Birth					
	Full Name of Spouse	Marr.					
		Death					

License No. 7838

STATE OF KANSAS
THE KANSAS STATE DEPARTMENT OF HEALTH
P. J. No. 2038
Division of Vital Statistics

MARRIAGE LICENSE

IN THE PROBATE COURT OF BUTLER COUNTY, ...September 10.......... 19 73
To Any Person in the State of Kansas Authorized by Law to Perform the Marriage Ceremony, Greetings:
YOU ARE HEREBY AUTHORIZED TO JOIN IN MARRIAGE

Alan Dee Moore (Name of Groom) of Cassoday, Kansas (Residence-City & State) Age 20
Kathleen Kay George (Name of Bride) of El Dorado, Kansas (Residence-City & State) Age 19

with the consent of .... (Name of parent or guardian consenting)
and with this license duly endorsed, you will make return to my office at El Dorado, Kansas, within ten days after performing the ceremony.

[SEAL]

G. le Moss, Probate Judge

ENDORSEMENT
TO WHOM IT MAY CONCERN:

Signature of Witnesses:
Sandy Glenn
James Unruh

Date Received By Probate Judge Sept. 14, 19 73
Date Recorded By Probate Judge Sept. 14, 19 73

I hereby certify that I, the undersigned, performed the ceremony joining in marriage the above named couple on the 13th day of September 19 73 at Eureka, Kansas, in Greenwood County.
My credentials are recorded in the PJ's office of .... Co. Ks.

Signed: Harriet Shumard
Title: Probate Judge
Address: Eureka, Kansas

Kathy, Allen, Amanda and Alana Moore

Family Group Sheet

Husband's Full Name: Victor L. Vogts SS-510-60-3113 **Chart No.**

	Day Month Year	City, Town or Place	County or Province, etc.	State or Country	Add. Info. on Husband
Birth	18-10-1954	ElDorado	Butler Co.	Kansas	Divorced 1996
Chr'nd					
Marr	4-1-1975	ElDorado	Butler Co.	Kansas	
Death					
Burial					

Places of Residence: Rosalia, Ks. 67132
Occupation: **Church Affiliation:** Catholic **Military Rec.**

His Father: **Mother's Maiden Name:**

Wife's Full Maiden Name: Ava Lynne Moore SS-510-60-2802

	Day Month Year	City, Town or Place	County or Province, etc.	State or Country	Add. Info. on Wife
Birth	23-10-1954	Wichita	Sedgwick Co.	Kansas	
Chr'nd					
Death					
Burial					

Places of Residence: Rosalia, Ks. 67123
Occupation: **Church Affiliation:** Catholic **Military Rec.**

Her Father: Alva Daniel Moore **Mother's Maiden Name:** Lois Valetta Bachelder

Sex	Children's Names in Full		Day Month Year	City, Town or Place	County or Province, etc.	State or Country
F	Valecia Lynne Vogts	Birth	25-5-1979	Wesley hospital Wichita		Kans.
		Marr.				
	Full Name of Spouse	Death				
		Burial				
M	2 SS-513-86-6050 Wesley Vogts	Birth	24-9-1981	Susan Allen ElDorado		Kans.
		Marr.				
	Full Name of Spouse	Death				
		Burial				
M	3 SS-510-60-3113 Nathan Daniel Vogts	Birth	26-2-1991	Wesley Wichita Sedgwick		Kans.
		Marr.				
	Full Name of Spouse	Death				
		Burial				
	4	Birth				
		Marr.				
	Full Name of Spouse	Death				

License No. 43088
STATE OF KANSAS
THE KANSAS STATE DEPARTMENT OF HEALTH
Division of Vital Statistics
MARRIAGE LICENSE
J. No. 2588

IN THE PROBATE COURT OF BUTLER COUNTY, January 2, 1975
To Any Person in the State of Kansas Authorized by Law to Perform the Marriage Ceremony, Greetings:
YOU ARE HEREBY AUTHORIZED TO JOIN IN MARRIAGE

Victor Leroy Vogts (Name of Groom) of Rosalia, Kansas (Residence—City & State) Age 20
Ava Lynne Moore (Name of Bride) of Augusta, Kansas (Residence—City & State) Age 20

with the consent of _____ (Name of parent or guardian consenting)
and with this license duly endorsed, you will make return to my office at El Dorado, Kansas, within ten days after performing the ceremony.

Gale Moss, Probate Judge
[SEAL]

ENDORSEMENT
TO WHOM IT MAY CONCERN:
I hereby certify that I, the undersigned, performed the ceremony joining in marriage the above named couple on the 4th day of January 1975 at El Dorado, Kansas, in Butler County.
My credentials are recorded in the PJ's office of Butler Co. Ks.
Signed: Michael R. Blackledge
Title: Catholic Priest
Address: El Dorado, Kansas

Signature of Witnesses:
Alan D. Moore
Edith Valetta Austin
Date Received By Probate Judge January 7, 19 75
Date Recorded By Probate Judge January 7, 19 75
NOTE—After recording, the probate judge shall forward the original marriage license to the State Registrar, Topeka, Kansas, not later than the third day of following month.

Ava Moore Vogts, Valecia, Wesley and Nathan Vogts

Compiler:
Address:
City, State, Zip:
Date:
Notes:

Family Group Sheet

Husband's Full Name: Thomas Herbert Moore
Chart No.:

	Day Month Year	City, Town or Place	County or Province, etc.	State or Country	Add. Info on Husband
Birth	22-7-1962	Eureka	Greenwood Co.	Kansas	
Chr'nd					
Marr.	28-6-1997	ElDorado Community College	Butler Co.	Kansas	
Death					
Burial					

Places of Residence:
Occupation: Farmer Church Affiliation: Military Rec.:

His Father: Alva Daniel Moore
Mother's Maiden Name: Lois Valetta Bachelder

Wife's Full Maiden Name: Faye Ann Wickhom Younker

	Day Month Year	City, Town or Place	County or Province, etc.	State or Country	Add. Info on Wife
Birth	25-2-1955	Hays		Kansas	
Chr'nd					
Death					
Burial					

Places of Residence:
Occupation: Church Affiliation: Military Rec.:

Other husbands: 1st. Gerald Younker married July 23, 1978 divorced Nov. 10, 1994

Her Father: Ora Emmett Wickhom
Mother's Maiden Name: Josephine Marie Pulee

Sex	Children's Names in Full		Day Month Year	City, Town or Place	County or Province, etc.	State or Country	Add. Info on Children
M	1. Younker, Matthew Scott	Birth	16-2-1975				
	Full Name of Spouse	Marr.					
		Death					
		Burial					
M	2. Younker, Jeremy Tyler	Birth	25-1-1979				
	Full Name of Spouse	Marr.					
		Death					
		Burial					

Thomas and Faye Moore — Thomas Moore, 1980

Marriage License No. 192211 — State of Kansas, Department of Health and Environment, Office of Vital Statistics

- Groom: Thomas Herbert Moore
- Residence: Rosalia, Butler, Kansas
- Date of Birth: July 22, 1962
- Father: Alva Daniel Moore (Kansas)
- Mother: Lois Valetta Bachelder (Kansas)
- Bride: Faye Ann Younker (Wickham)
- Residence: Cassoday, Butler, Kansas
- Date of Birth: February 25, 1955
- Father: Ora Emmett Wickham (Kansas)
- Mother: Josephine Marie Pulee (Kansas)
- Date License Issued: June 16, 1997
- Expiration Date: December 16, 1997
- Signature of Issuing Official: Rachel M. Kelley, Deputy Clerk
- Married: June 28, 1997, El Dorado, Kansas, Butler County
- Officiant: Rev. Mack R. Ferren, Ordained Baptist Pastor, 97 SE Cole Creek rd, El Dorado, Kans. 67042-8545
- Groom's Signature: Thomas H. Moore
- Bride's Signature: Faye Younker
- Witnesses: Alan D. Moore, Carla Holland

203

Family Group Sheet

Husband's Full Name Martin G. Brenton
Chart No.

	Day Month Year	City, Town or Place	County or Province, etc.	State or Country	Add. Info. on Husband
Birth	18-10-1956	Eureka	Butler Co.	Kans.	
Chr'nd					
Marr	28-10-1978	ElDorado	Butler Co.	Kans.	divorced 1996
Death					
Burial					

Places of Residence
Occupation Rancher **Church Affiliation** **Military Rec**

His Father George Wilber Brenton **Mother's Maiden Name** Rosalie Pauline Storey

Wife's Full Maiden Name Rose Annette Moore

	Day Month Year	City, Town or Place	County or Province, etc.	State or Country	Add. Info. on Wife
Birth	24-9-1960	Wichita	Sedgwick Co.	Kansas	
Chr'nd					
Death					
Burial					

Places of Residence
Occupation Cashier **Church Affiliation** **Military Rec.**

Her Father Alva Daniel Moore **Mother's Maiden Name** Lois Valetta Bachelder

Sex	Children's Names in Full		Day Month Year	City, Town or Place	County or Province, etc.	State or Country	Add. Info. on Children
M	1 Brenton, Tyson George	Birth	29-8-1981	ElDorado	Butler Co.	Kans.	
	Full Name of Spouse	Marr. / Death / Burial					
F	2 Brenton, Shelly Renae	Birth	9-5-1984	ElDorado	Butler Co.	Kans.	
	Full Name of Spouse	Marr. / Death / Burial					
	3	Birth / Marr. / Death					

License No. 16663
STATE OF KANSAS
THE KANSAS STATE DEPARTMENT OF HEALTH AND ENVIRONMENT
D.C. No. 79201 Bureau of Vital Statistics
MARRIAGE LICENSE
IN THE DISTRICT COURT OF BUTLER COUNTY. October 26, 1978
To Any Person in the State of Kansas Authorized by Law to Perform the Marriage Ceremony, Greetings:
YOU ARE HEREBY AUTHORIZED TO JOIN IN MARRIAGE

Martin Greg Brenton (Name of Groom) of El Dorado, Kansas (Residence—City & State), Age 22
Rose Annette Moore (Name of Bride) of Rosalia, Kansas (Residence—City & State), Age 18
with the consent of _____ (Name of parent or guardian consenting)

and with this license duly endorsed, you will make return to my office at El Dorado, Kansas, within ten days after performing the ceremony.

s/John M. Jaworsky, Associate District Judge

[SEAL]

ENDORSEMENT
TO WHOM IT MAY CONCERN:
Signature of Witnesses:
Michael C. Brenton
Ava L. Vogts
Date Received by District Judge Oct. 31, 1978
Date Recorded by District Judge Oct. 31, 1978

I hereby certify that I, the undersigned, performed the ceremony joining in marriage the above named couple on the 28th day of October 1978 at El Dorado, Kansas, in Butler County. My credentials are recorded in the D.C.'s office at Butler Co. Ks.
Signed Donald McCracken
Title Pastor First Baptist
Address 315 W. Central

Filed October 31, 1978
s/John M. Jaworsky, Associate District Judge

Annette Moore and Alva Moore
Oct. 28, 1978

Compiler
Address
City, State, Zip
Date

Tyson and Shelly Brenton

Alva Moore, Ava Vogts, Valetta Austin, Thomas Moore, Faye Wickham, Alan Moore, Kathleen Moore, Annette Brenton, June 28, 1997

Jeremy Younker, October 1997

Lloyd Moore, Emily Moore, Opal Harlen, Glenn Moore and Alva Moore

Glenn Moore

Family Group Sheet

Husband's Full Name Howard Milton Balzer Chart No.

	Day Month Year	City, Town or Place	County or Province, etc.	State or Country	Add Info on Husb
Birth	15-4-1930	Newton	Harvey Co.	Kansas	
Chr'nd					
Marr.	29-12-1950	Potwin	Butler Co.	Kansas	
Death					
Burial					

Places of Residence: Potwin, Kansas
Occupation: Owner-operator trucking   Church Affiliation: Christian church   Military Rec.

His Father: Abraham Balzer   Mother's Maiden Name: Ida Gaede

Wife's Full Maiden Name Veda Mae Moore

	Day Month Year	City, Town or Place	County or Province, etc.	State or Country	Add Info on Wife
Birth	22-7-1930	Potwin	Butler Co.	Kansas	
Chr'nd					
Death					
Burial					

Places of Residence: 317 West Violet Potwin, Kansas 67123
Occupation: Homemaker   Church Affiliation: Christian church   Military Rec.

Her Father: Reuben Moore   Mother's Maiden Name: Edith Taylor

Sex	Children's names in Full		Day Month Year	City, Town or Place	County or Province, etc.	State or Country
F	1 Balzer, LaVonn Elaine	Birth	20-6-1952	Newton	Harvey Co.	Kans.
		Marr.	12-8-1972	Potwin	Butler Co.	Kans.
	Full Name of Spouse: Charles Roland Baker	Death				
		Burial				
F	2 JoAnn Balzer	Birth	17-2-1956	Newton	Harvey Co.	Kans.
		Marr.	20-10-1980	Potwin	Butler Co.	Kans.
	Full Name of Spouse: David Cecil Denny	Death				
		Burial				
F	3 Balzer, Sarah Katherine	Birth	16-11-1961	Newton	Harvey Co.	Kans.
		Marr.				
	Full Name of Spouse:	Death				
		Burial				
M	4 Milton Lee Balzer	Birth	27-2-1964	Newton	Harvey Co.	Kans.
		Marr.	3-8-1991	Arkansas City		Kans.
	Full Name of Spouse: Jennifer Lynn Carr	Death				
		Burial				
M	5 Morey Howard Balzer	Birth	27-2-1964	Newton	Harvey Co.	Kans.
		Marr.	7-1-1989	Newton	Harvey Co.	Kans.
	Full Name of Spouse: Lori Ann Bean	Death				
		Burial				

Howard and Veda, 1981

STATE OF KANSAS, CENTRAL DIVISION OF VITAL STATISTICS

No. 30497   MARRIAGE LICENSE

IN THE PROBATE COURT OF HARVEY COUNTY, December 23, 1950

To Any Person in the State of Kansas Authorized by Law to Perform the Marriage Ceremony, Greeting:

YOU ARE HEREBY AUTHORIZED To Join in Marriage

Howard Milton Balzer of Sedgwick, Kansas, Age 20
Veda Mae Moore of Curtis, Kansas, Age 20

with the consent of A. Balzer, father of groom, and of this license, duly endorsed, you will make return to my office at Newton, Kansas, within ten days after performing the ceremony.

(SEAL)   Alfred G. Schroeder, Probate Judge

ENDORSEMENT

To Whom It May Concern:

I HEREBY CERTIFY That I performed the ceremony joining in marriage the above named couple on the 29th day of December, 1950, at Potwin, Kansas.

Signed: Clyde C. Mosher
Title: Christian Minister
Address: Box 152, Potwin, Kansas

Family Group Sheet

Husband's Full Name: Charles Roland Baker — Chart No.

	Day Month Year	City, Town or Place	County or Province, etc.	State or Country	Add. Info on Husb.
Birth	16-11-1952	ElDorado	Butler Co.	Kansas	
Chr'nd					
Marr	12-8-1972	Potwin-Christian Church	Butler Co.	Kansas	
Death					
Burial					

Places of Residence: 121 E. Violet, Potwin, Ks. 67123
Occupation: School Custodian **Church Affiliation:** Potwin Christian church

His Father: Ellsworth Roland Baker **Mother's Maiden Name:** Esther Christine Elmore

Wife's Full Maiden Name: LaVonne Elaine Balzer

	Day Month Year	City, Town or Place	County or Province, etc.	State or Country	Add. Info on Wife
Birth	20-6-1952	Newton	Harvey Co.	Kansas	
Chr'nd					
Death					
Burial					

Places of Residence: 121 E. Violet, Potwin, Kansas
Occupation: KDG Teacher **Church Affiliation:** Potwin Christian church

Her Father: Howard Milton Balzer **Mother's Maiden Name:** Veda Mae Moore

Sex	Children's names		Day Month Year	City, Town or Place	County or Province	State or Country
F	Charla Jean Baker	Birth	8-8-1976	Newton	Harvey Co.	Kans.
F	Chanda Mae Baker	Birth	26-5-1980	Newton	Harvey Co.	Kans.
M	Jarret Roland Baker	Birth	26-5-1980	Newton	Harvey Co.	Kans.

Compiler: LaVonne, Charles, Charla, Chanda and Jarret Baker

August 1988

Chanda and Jarret, 1998

Family Group Sheet

Husband's Full Name: David Cecil Denny **Chart No.**

	Day Month Year	City, Town or Place	County or Province, etc.	State or Country	Add Info on Husb
Birth	5-9-1953	ElPaso	ElPaso Co.	Texas	
Chr'nd					
Marr	20-10-1979	Potwin	Butler Co.	Kansas	
Death					
Burial					

Places of Residence:
Occupation: Safety Administrator **Church Affiliation:** Christian **Military Rec:** ROTC

His Father: Marvin C. Denny **Mother's Maiden Name:** Aurelia McGee

Wife's Full Maiden Name: Jo Ann Balzer

	Day Month Year	City, Town or Place	County or Province, etc.	State or Country	Add Info on Wife
Birth	17-2-1956	Newton	Harvey Co.	Kansas	
Chr'nd					
Death					
Burial					

Places of Residence:
Occupation: Expedites Beach Aircraft **Church Affiliation:** Christian **Military Rec:**

Her Father: Howard Milton Balzer **Mother's Maiden Name:** Veda Mae Moore

Children

Sex	Children's Names	Event	Day Month Year	City, Town or Place	County or Province, etc.	State or Country
F	1. Katrina Ann Denny	Birth	17-4-1985	Newton	Harvey Co.	Kansas
	Full Name of Spouse:	Marr. / Death / Burial				
F	2. Rebecca Jo Denny	Birth	12-9-1990	Newton	Harvey Co.	Kans.
	Full Name of Spouse:	Marr. / Death / Burial				

Address: Box 158
City, State, Zip: Potwin, Kansas

Family Group Sheet

Husband's Full Name _____ **Chart No.** _____

	Day Month Year	City, Town or Place	County or Province, etc.	State or Country	Add Info on Husband
Birth					
Chrnd					
Marr					
Death					
Burial					

Places of Residence _____

Occupation _____ Church Affiliation _____ Military Rec. _____

Other wives, if any, No. (1), (2), etc. Make separate sheet for each marr.

His Father _____ Mother's Maiden Name _____

Wife's Full Maiden Name Sarah Katherine Balzer

	Day Month Year	City, Town or Place	County or Province, etc.	State or Country	Add Info on Wife
Birth	16-11-1961	Newton	Harvey Co.	Kansas	
Chrnd					
Death					
Burial					

Places of Residence Towanda, Kansas

Occupation Sales   Church Affiliation Christian   Military Rec.

Her Father Howard Milton Balzer   Mother's Maiden Name Veda Mae Moore

Sex	Children's Names in Full		Day Month Year	City, Town or Place	County or Province, etc.	State or Country	Add Info on Child
	1	Birth					
		Marr.					
	Full Name of Spouse	Death					
		Burial					
	2	Birth					
		Marr.					
	Full Name of Spouse	Death					
		Burial					
	3	Birth					
		Marr.					
	Full Name of Spouse	Death					
		Burial					
	4	Birth					
		Marr.					
		Death					
		Burial					

Sarah Balzer

Moore Twins

Co _____
Address _____
City, State, Zip _____
Date _____

Family Group Sheet

Husband's Full Name: Milton Lee Balzer
Chart No.:

	Day Month Year	City, Town or Place	County or Province, etc.	State or Country	Add Info on Husband
Birth	27- 2-1964	Newton	Harvey Co.	Kansas	
Chr'nd		Potwin	Butler Co.	Kansas	
Marr	3- 8-1991	Arkansas City	Cawley Co.	Kansas	
Death					
Burial					

Places of Residence: 300 E. Locust   Independence, Kansas   67301
Occupation: Finance   **Church Affiliation:** Protestant   **Military Rec:**

His Father: Howard Milton Balzer   **Mother's Maiden Name:** Veda Mae Moore

Wife's Full Maiden Name: Jennifer Lynn Carr

	Day Month Year	City, Town or Place	County or Province, etc.	State or Country	Add Info on Wife
Birth	19- 3-1970	Arkansas City	Cowley Co.	Kansas	
Chr'nd	1978	Arkansas City	Cowley Co.	Kansas	
Death					
Burial					

Places of Residence: 300 E. Locust   Independence, Kansas   67301
Occupation: Homemaker   **Church Affiliation:** Protestant   **Military Rec:**

Her Father: Thomas Edwin Carr   **Mother's Maiden Name:** Marsha Lynn Nelson

Sex	Children's names in Full		Day Month Year	City, Town or Place	County or Province, etc.	State or Country	Add Info on Child
F	1 Abby Marie Balzer	Birth	23- 3-1992	Wichita	Sedgwick Co.	Kans.	
	Full Name of Spouse	Marr.					
		Death					
		Burial					
M	2 Thomas Lee Balzer	Birth	21- 7-1994	Wichita	Sedgwick Co.	Kans.	
	Full Name of Spouse	Marr.					
		Death					
		Burial					
M	3 Ethan Cole Balzer	Birth	21-10-1998	Bartlesville	Washington, Co.	Oklahoma	
	Full Name of Spouse	Marr.					
		Death					
		Burial					
	4	Birth					
	Full Name of Spouse	Marr.					
		Death					

Milton, Jennifer and Abby Balzer   Abby Balzer   Thomas Balzer   Abby 5 1/2 and Thomas 3 1/2

Compiler		Notes:
Address		
City, State, Zip		
Date		

Family Group Sheet

Husband's Full Name: Morey Howard Balzer
Chart No.:

	Day Month Year	City, Town or Place	County or Province, etc.	State or Country	Add. Info on Husb.
Birth	27- 2-1964	Newton	Harvey Co.	Kansas	
Chr'nd					
Marr	7- 1-1989	Newton	Harvey Co.	Kansas	
Death					
Burial					

Places of Residence: 220 S. Lincoln Belle Plains, Ks.
Occupation: School Teacher   **Church Affiliation:** Christian   **Military Rec:**

His Father: Howard Milton Balzer   **Mother's Maiden Name:** Veda Mae Moore

Wife's Full Maiden Name: Lori Ann Bean

	Day Month Year	City, Town or Place	County or Province, etc.	State or Country	Add. Info on Wife
Birth	11-11-1963	Wichita	Sedgwick Co.	Kansas	
Chr'nd					
Death					
Burial					

Places of Residence: 220 S. Lincoln Belle Plains, Kansas
Occupation: **Church Affiliation:** Christian   **Military Rec.**

Her Father: Waymann Bean   **Mother's Maiden Name:** Imelda Fagan

Sex	Children's names in Full		Day Month Year	City, Town or Place	County or Province, etc.	State or Country
M	1 Balzer, Jordan Matthew	Birth	2- 8-1990	Wichita	Sedgwick Co.	Kans.
		Marr.				
	Full Name of Spouse	Death				
		Burial				
M	2 Dereck Morey Balzer	Birth	10- 5-1993	Wichita	Sedgwick Co.	Kansas
		Marr.				
	Full Name of Spouse	Death				
		Burial				
F	3 Balzer, Danielle Marie	Birth	12- 1-1995	Wichita	Sedgwick Co.	Kansas
		Marr.				
	Full Name of Spouse	Death				
		Burial				
F	4	Birth	30-10-1996	Wichita	Sedgwick Co.	Kansas

Milton and Morey Baker

Danielle

Jordan-7, Derek-4, Danielle-2, Bethany-1

211

Family Group Sheet

Husband's Full Name Orin E. Moore SS 509-40-5865 — Chart No.

	Day Month Year	City, Town or Place	County or Province, etc.	State or Country	Add Info on Hus
Birth	29-11-1888	near Potwin	Butler Co.	Kansas	
Chr'nd	8-1903	Potwin	Butler Co.	Kansas	
Marr	5-3-1913	Potwin	Butler Co.	Kansas	
Death	9-8-1982	Newton	Harvey Co.	Kansas	
Burial		Whitewater cem.	Butler Co.	Kansas	

Places of Residence: Butler Co., Kansas
Occupation: Farmer   Church Affiliation: Federated Church   Military Rec.

His Father: William Oscar Moore   Mother's Maiden Name: Lovisa May Adams

Wife's Full Maiden Name Susie May Keys SS 510-68-1338

	Day Month Year	City, Town or Place	County or Province, etc.	State or Country	Add Info on W
Birth	3-9-1892	Beason		Illinois	
Chr'nd					
Death	18-1-1975	Newton	Harvey Co.	Kansas	
Burial	21-1-1975	Whitewater	Butler Co.	Kansas	

Places of Residence: Benton, Kansas   Benson, Illinois   503 E. Elm Whitewater, Ks.
Occupation: Housewife   Church Affiliation: Federated Church   Military Rec.

Her Father: John J. Keys   Mother's Maiden Name: Eva Sullivan

Sex	Children's names in Full		Day Month Year	City, Town or Place	County or Province, etc.	State or Country
M	1 Elwood Orin Moore	Birth	12-11-1913	Whitewater	Butler Co.	Kans.
	Full Name of Spouse: Maxine D. Baxter	Marr.	10-6-1959	Wichita	Sedgwick Co.	Ks.
		Death				
		Burial				
F	2 Helen Mae Moore	Birth	2-3-1916	Milton township	Butler Co.	Kans
	Full Name of Spouse: E. Jay Mayhew	Marr.	3-8-1938	Hutchinson	Reno Co.	Kans.
		Death				
		Burial				
M	3 Melvin Moore	Birth				
	Full Name of Spouse:	Marr.				
		Death				
		Burial				

State of Kansas, Butler County, ss.
Office of Probate Judge of said County.

BE IT REMEMBERED, That on the 3 day of March A.D. 1913, there was issued from the office of said Probate Judge, a marriage license of which the following is a true copy:

Marriage License.

El Dorado, Butler County, State of Kansas, March 3ᵈ 1913

To Any Person Authorized by Law to Perform the Marriage Ceremony, Greeting:
You are hereby authorized to Join in marriage Orin Edgar Moore of Butler County Kansas aged ___ and Susie May Keys of Butler County Kansas aged ___ the ___ consenting ___ and of this License you will make due return to my office within thirty days.

(Seal.)   C E Hunt Probate Judge.

And which said Marriage License was afterwards, to-wit, on the 7 day of March A.D. 1913, returned to said Probate Judge with the following Certificate endorsed thereon, to-wit:

STATE OF KANSAS, Butler County, ss.
I, Homer E Moore do hereby certify that, in accordance with the authorization of the within License, I did, on the 5ᵗʰ day of March A.D. 1913, at home of Brides parents in said county, Join and unite in marriage the within named Orin Edgar Moore Susie May Keys

Witness my hand the day and year above written. Homer E Moore
C E Hunt Probate Judge.

p. 233

Susie, Orin, Elwood, Melvin and Helen Moore

Melvin, Jane, Elwood, Maxine, Susie, Mike, Jack, Orin, John and Helen

Susie and Orin

Orin Moore

Orin Moore

Orin Moore and Susie Keys' Wedding picture, 1913.

The El Dorado Times
Monday, January 20, 1975

Mrs. O. E. Moore of Whitewater dies at 82

Mrs. O. E. (Susan M.) Moore, 82, died Saturday. She was born Sept. 3, 1892, in Illinois, and was married March 5, 1913, to Orin Moore in Potwin. They had lived in the Whitewater area since 1917.

Surviving are her widower of the home; three sons, Elwood O. Moore, El Dorado; John W. Moore, Ranier, Minn., and Melvin E. Moore, Albuquerque, N. M.; a daughter, Mrs. Helen M. Mayhew, Denver, Colo.; a step-brother, William Hawes, Benton; a step-sister, Mrs. Alma McCann, Ontario, Calif., and seven grandchildren.

Services will be at 2 p.m., Tuesday in the Federated Church at Whitewater, of which she was a member. Lamb Mortuary is in charge, and the Rev. Kenneth Tubbesing will officiate. Burial will be in Whitewater Cemetery.

A memorial has been established with Wheat State Manor nursing home at Whitewater.

CERTIFICATE OF DEATH

- Deceased: Susan May Moore
- Sex: F
- Date of Death: January 18, 1975
- Race: White
- Age: 82
- Date of Birth: Sept. 3, 1892
- County of Death: Harvey
- City of Death: Newton
- Hospital: Axtell Christian Hospital
- State of Birth: Illinois
- Citizen of: U.S.A.
- Married
- Surviving Spouse: Orin E. Moore
- Social Security Number: 510-68-1338
- Occupation: Housewife
- Industry: Homemaker
- Residence: Kansas, Butler, Whitewater, 67154, 503 S. Elm
- Father: John J. Keys
- Mother: Eva Sullivan
- Informant: Orin E. Moore, 503 S. Elm, Whitewater, Kansas 67154

Cause of Death:
(a) Cerebral vascular hemorrhage — 2 weeks
(b) Hypertensive cardiovascular disease — 10 years

- Physician attended from Feb. 13, 1950 to Jan. 18, 1975; last saw alive Jan. 18, 1975; did not view body after death; death occurred at 4:25 PM
- Certifier: Dr. Charles T. Sills, 203 E. Broadway, Newton, Kansas 67114
- Date Signed: Jan. 21, 1975
- Burial: Whitewater Cemetery, Whitewater, Kansas 67154
- Date: January 21, 1975
- Funeral Home: Lamb Mortuary, P.O. Box 57, Whitewater, Kansas 67154
- Date Received by Local Registrar: 1-21-75

THIS INFORMATION FOR DEATH CERTIFICATE & NEWSPAPER

- Full Name: Susan M. (May) (Keys) Moore — Maiden Name
- Residence: 503 S. Elm, W.W.
- Date & Time of Death: 1-18-75, 3:30 - 4:00?
- Place of Death: Axtel Hospital, Newton, Harvey, Kans.
- Length of Stay at Place of Death: Dec. 26
- Age: 82
- Date & Place of Birth: Sept. 3, 1892, Beason Ill. (Logan Co.)
- Date & Place of Marriage: March 5, 1913, Potwin, at the Home
- How Long Ill?
- How Long Lived Here? Good many years. He lived... Orin E. Moore
- Since 1917 in Whitewater

```
   1975   1 18
   1892   9  3
    82    4 15  1974
```

- Occupation: House Wife
- Employer: Self
- Social Security Number: 510-68-1338
- Father's Name: John J. Keys
- Mother's Maiden Name: Eva Sullivan
- If Veteran: No

- Cause of Death: Cerebral Vascular Hemorrhage
- Due to: Hypertensive Cardiovascular hemorrhage
- Physician & Address: Dr. Sills — Dr. Bill
- Church Membership: Federated Church
- Fraternal Orders: Mite Society

SERVICES

- Date, Hour, Day: Tuesday Jan 21, 1975, 2:00
- Place of Funeral: Federated Church
- Minister: Ken Tubbesing
- Place of Burial: Whitewater, Kans.
- Bearers: "B" Rao Grundy, Red the Graham, Art Newman, Bernie Long, Elden Mission, Henry Wm
- Singers: Rosie Cowan 799-2664
- Songs: "Whispering Hope", "A Perfect Day"
- Organist: Gertrud Brondard 777-2377

The Information for Death Certificates & Newspapers

1. Name: Moore, Orin Edgar 93yr
2. Residence: 503 S. Elm, Whitewater, K
3. Date of Death: Aug 9, 1982 at 1 p.m.?
4. Place of Death: Axtell Hosp., Newton, Ks
5. Date & Place of Birth: Nov. 29, 1888, at Potwin
6. Date & Place of Marriage: Mar 5, 1913 at Potwin
7. Married to: Susan M Keys (deceased 1-18-75)
8. How Long Ill?: 1½ yrs
9. How Long Lived Here?: At Whitewater since 1917 —

Occupation: Ret. Farmer
Employer: Self
Father's Name: William O. Moore
Mother's Maiden Name: Louisa M. Adams
Social Security Number: 509-40-5865-A
Veteran, Specify War & Unit: WWI
Entered Service: ____ Service No. ____
Discharged: ____ Rank or Rating: ____
Cause of Death: Renal Failure due to ureteral Obstruction
Physician & Address: Dr. Ivan Cooper
Church Membership: Federated Church
Fraternal Orders, Boards, &ct: Charter member Am. Legion at W.W.

The Newton Kansan,
Orin C. Moore

WHITEWATER — Orin C. Moore, 93, retired farmer and a lifetime Whitewater area resident, died Monday, Aug. 9, at Axtell Christian Hospital in Newton.

Services will be conducted at 10 a.m. Thursday at the Federated Church in Whitewater, of which he was a member. Pastor Bill Glenn will officiate and burial will be in the Whitewater Cemetery.

He was born Nov. 29, 1888, at Potwin. On March 5, 1913, he married Susan M. Keys at Potwin. They moved to Whitewater in 1917. Mrs. Moore died Jan. 18, 1975.

Mr. Moore was a veteran of World War I and he was a charter member of the Whitewater American Legion Post.

Survivors include three sons, Melvin of Bullhead City, Ariz., and Elwood and John, both of Potwin; one daughter, Helen Mayhew of Denver, Colo.; seven grandchildren and 13 great-grandchildren.

Friends may call at the Lamb Mortuary in Whitewater from 9 a.m. to 9 p.m. Wednesday. Memorials have been established for the church or the Wheat State Manor at Whitewater.

On March 5, 1913 she was united in marriage to Orin E. Moore, also of the Whitewater area. For a brief time after their marriage, Mr. and Mrs. Moore lived on the farm before moving into town. To their union four children were born.

Mrs. Moore was preceded in death by her parents, two sisters and one brother. She is survived by her husband, Orin of Whitewater; three sons, Melvin, Albuquerque, New Mexico, Elwood of El Dorado, and John, of Ranier, Minnesota; one daughter, Mrs. Helen Mayhew of Denver, Colorado; a step-sister, Alma McCann of Ontario, California; and a step-brother, William Hawes of rural Whitewater; seven grandchildren; seven great-grandchildren, and many other relatives and friends.

Susan Moore was a loving wife, a devoted mother and a loyal friends. Those who knew her will miss her quiet warmth.

Services were held at the Federated Church Tuesday, January 21, with the Rev. Ken Tubbesing officiating. Mrs. Wayne Brainerd, organist, acccompanied Mrs. Wendell Cowan, who sang "Whispering Hope" and "A Perfect Day."

Bearers were Leo Gronau, Art Neuman, Eldon Mosiman, Keith Graham, Bernie Long and Henry Ulmer.

Interment was in the Whitewater Cemetery with

CERTIFICATE OF DEATH

1. Deceased Name: Susan May Moore
2. Sex: F
3. Date of Death: January 18, 1975
4. Race: White
5. Age: 82
7. Date of Birth: Sept. 3, 1892
8. County of Death: Harvey
9. City, Town, or Location of Death: Newton
10. Inside City Limits: Yes
11. Hospital or Other Institution: Axtell Christian Hospital
12. State of Birth: Illinois
13. Citizen of What Country: U.S.A.
14. Married, Never Married, Widowed, Divorced: Married
15. Surviving Spouse: Orin E. Moore
16. Social Security Number: 510-68-1338
17. Usual Occupation: Housewife
18. Kind of Business or Industry: Homemaker
19. Residence — State: Kansas
20. County: Butler
21. City, Town, or Location: Whitewater 67154
22. Inside City Limits: Yes
23. Street and Number: 503 S. Elm
24. Father — Name: John J. Keys
25. Mother — Maiden Name: Eva Sullivan
26. Informant's Name: Orin E. Moore
27. Mailing Address: 503 S. Elm, Whitewater, Kansas 67154

PART I. Death was caused by:
(a) Cerebral vascular hemorrhage — 2 weeks
(b) Hypertensive cardiovascular disease — 10 years

Autopsy: No

Certification — Physician: I attended the deceased from Feb. 13, 1950 to Jan. 18, 1975; last saw him/her alive on Jan. 18, 1975; Did Not view body after death; Death occurred at 4:25PM

Certifier Name: Dr. Charles T. Sills
Signature: Charles T. Sills
Date Signed: Jan. 21, 1975
Mailing Address: 203 E. Broadway, Newton, Kansas 67114

Burial, Cremation, Removal: Burial
Cemetery or Crematory Name: Whitewater Cemetery
Location: Whitewater, Kansas 67154
Date: January 21, 1975
Funeral Home: Lamb Mortuary, P.O. Box 57, Whitewater, Kansas 67154
Date Received by Local Registrar: 1-21-75

Family Group Sheet

Husband's Full Name: Elwood Orin Moore   **Chart No.**

	Day Month Year	City, Town or Place	County or Province, etc.	State or Country	Add. Info on Hus
Birth	12-11-1913	6 mi. S. of Whitewater	Butler Co.	Kansas	
Chrnd					
Marr	10-6-1939	Wichita	Sedgwick Co.	Kansas	
Death					
Burial					

Places of Residence:
Occupation: Farming   **Church Affiliation:**   **Military Rec:** US Navy

#1 Rose Margaret Andrew married July 1935

His Father: Orin Edgar Moore   **Mother's Maiden Name:** Susan May Keys

Wife's Full Maiden Name: Maxine D. Baxter

	Day Month Year	City, Town or Place	County or Province, etc.	State or Country	Add. Info on W
Birth	31-8-1920	Wichita	Sedgwick Co.	Kansas	
Chrnd					
Death					
Burial					

Places of Residence: Newton, Kansas
Occupation: Airplane Factory   **Church Affiliation:**   **Military Rec:**

Her Father: Otto Baxter   **Mother's Maiden Name:** Floy Piercy

Sex	Children's Names in Full		Day Month Year	City, Town or Place	County or Province, etc.	State or Country	Add. Info on Chil
M 1	Larry J. Moore	Birth	13-12-1940	Wichita	Sedgwick Co.	Kans.	
		Marr.					
	Full Name of Spouse: Dalton Evelyn Groun/Linda	Death					
		Burial					
2		Birth					
		Marr.					

216

NOTICE OF SEPARATION FROM U. S. NAVAL SERVICE
NAVPERS-553 (Rev. 5-45)

1245 306

MOORE, Elwood Orin
Radarman, Third Class (T)
USNR. (SV).
White Water, Butler Co., Kansas

PSC-Norman, Okla.

Honorable Discharge

White Water, Butler Co., Kans.

M | Married | Yes

12/11/13 White Water, Butler Co., Tex.

LB #1 El Dorado, Kans.

White Water, Kans.

[X] Inducted

4/14/44

4/18/44

1yr. 8mos 0days

LB #1 El Dorado, Kans.

See Rating Description Booklet for Radarman, Third Class

AS; S2c(RdM); S1c(RdM); RdM3c(T)

(Radar Operators), Point Loma, San Diego, Calif. 4

NavTraSta, Farragut, Idaho
USS Lenawee, APA 195

12/45 | 1/46 | 7.10 | No

91.00 | 11.35 | 100.00 | A.W.JOHNSON,Lt.(SC)USN

System

Frank E. Couch
FRANK E. COUCH
Lieut., USNR.
Ass't. Personnel Officer.

Farming for Self

From 3/37 To 4/44

Farming

Undecided

Undecided

Gen. Ed.

12/21/45

C963119

Honorable Discharge
from the
United States Navy

This is to certify that

Elwood Orin MOORE, Radarman Third Class (T) SV6 USNR

is Honorably Discharged from the U.S. NAVAL PERSONNEL SEPARATION CENTER Norman, Oklahoma and from the Naval Service of the United States this 21st day of December 1945.

This certificate is awarded as a Testimonial of Fidelity and Obedience.

D. CARLSON
Captain, U.S. Navy
Commanding

ATTEST:

Pollan K. Eberhard
Pollan K. Eberhard, City Clerk

THE CITY WHITEWATER

By Pete Klassen
Pete Klassen, Mayor

(SEAL)

Elwood Moore

STATE OF KANSAS.
STATE BOARD OF HEALTH—DIV. OF VITAL STATISTICS.
STANDARD CERTIFICATE OF BIRTH.

PLACE OF BIRTH.
County of Butler
Township of Murdock
City of 1771-1
Registered No. 8W
No. ______ street.

Full Name of Child: Orin Elwood Moore

Sex of Child: Male
Twin, triplet, or other? (To be answered only in event of plural births.)
Number in order of birth
Legitimate: Yes
Date of birth: Dec 11 1913

FATHER.
Full Name: Orin Moore
Residence: Benton
Color: White
Age at last birthday: 25
Birthplace: Kans
Occupation: Farmer

MOTHER.
Full Maiden Name: Susan Kays
Residence: Benton
Color: White
Age at last birthday: 21
Birthplace: Ill
Occupation: Housewife

Number of children born to this mother, including present birth: 1
Number of children of this mother now living: 1

CERTIFICATE OF ATTENDING PHYSICIAN OR MIDWIFE.

I hereby certify that I attended the birth of this child, who was born alive at 3 P.M. on the date above stated.

(Signature) H. H. Norris
, Physician
Address: Whitewater, Kas.

Given name added from supplemental report 1914
L. C. Glass, Registrar

Filed Jan 2 1914 L. C. Glass, Registrar

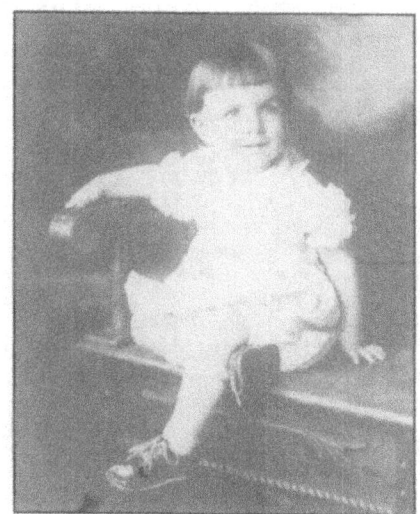

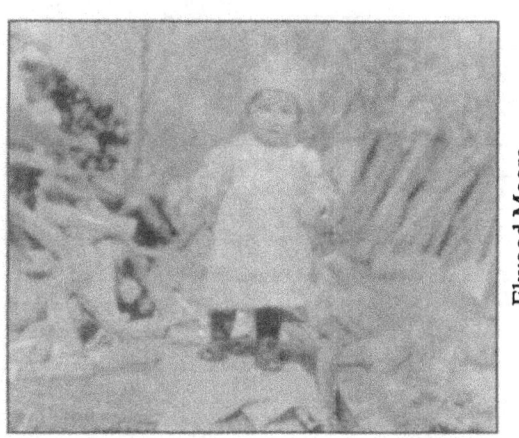

Elwood Moore

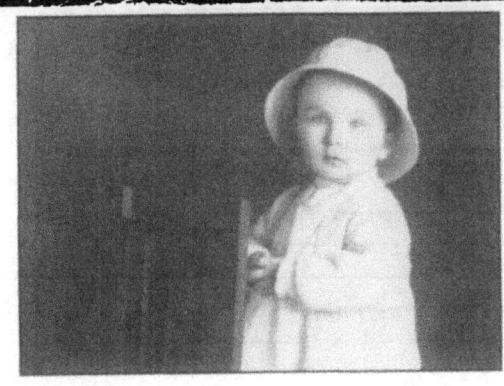

Elwood Moore

Family Group Sheet

Husband's Full Name Larry Joe Moore SS 513-40-2036 Chart No.

	Day Month Year	City, Town or Place	County or Province, etc.	State or Country	Add. Info on Husband
Birth	13-12-1940	Wichita	Sedgwick Co.	Kansas	
Chr'nd					divorced
Marr					
Death					
Burial					

Places of Residence: Moab, Utah – Wichita, Kansas
Occupation: Telephone installation repairman   Military Rec: US Army

His Father: Elwood Oren Moore   Mother's Maiden Name: Maxine D. Baxter

Wife's Full Maiden Name Evelyn Gronau

	Day Month Year	City, Town or Place	County or Province, etc.	State or Country	Add. Info on Wife
Birth					
Chr'nd					
Death					
Burial					

Places of Residence:
Occupation: Church Affiliation: Military Rec:

Her Father: Leo Gronau   Mother's Maiden Name:

Sex	Children's Names in Full		Day Month Year	City, Town or Place	County or Province, etc.	State or Country	Add. Info on Children
M	1 Jeffery Dean Moore	Birth	1-9-1960	Newton	Harvey Co.	Kans.	
	Full Name of Spouse	Marr.					
		Death					
		Burial					
M	2 Randy Ray Moore	Birth	23-5-1959	Newton	Harvey Co.	Kans.	still-born
		Marr.					
	Full Name of Spouse	Death	23-5-1959	Newton	Harvey Co.	Kans.	
		Burial	23-5-1959	Whitewater cem.	Butler Co.	Ks.	
	3	Birth					
		Marr.					

Hope you'll plan on being there!

It's for *Evelyn & Larry Moore*
Date *November 14*
Time *7:30*
Place *Potwin Christian Church*
Hostess *Lola Moss,*
Doris McLain & Wilma Bremner

JEFFREY DEAN MOORE BORN SEPTEMBER 1

Mr. and Mrs. Larry Moore (Evelyn Gronau) announce the birth of their son, Jeffrey Dean, weight six pounds and two ounces in the Axtell Hospital Thursday, September 1.

Mr. and Mrs. Leo Gronau are the maternal grandparents, and Mr. and Mrs. Elwood Moore are the young man's paternal grandparents.

Larry completes his basic training at Ft. Leonard Wood, Mo., September 8.

1ST CAV. DIV. Korea (AHTNC) —Army Pvt Larry J. Moore, whose wife, Evelyn, lives in Whitewater, Kan., recently arrived in Korea and is now serving with the 1st Cavalry Division's 13th Signal Battalion.

The 1st is the only U.S. division presently manning a front line in Korea.

Moore, a telephone installation repairman in the battalion's Company B, entered the Army in June 1960 and completed basic training at Fort Leonard Wood, Mo.

The son of Mr. and Mrs. Elwood O. Moore, Route 1, Potwin, he is a 1958 graduate of Potwin High School.

	8	Birth					
		Marr.					
	Full Name of Spouse	Death					
		Burial					

Compiler:
Address:
City, State, Zip:
Date:

Notes:

Family Group Sheet

Husband's Full Name: Larry Joe Moore

Chart No.:

	Day Month Year	City, Town or Place	County or Province, etc.	State or Country	Add. Info on Husband
Birth	13-12-1940	Wichita	Sedgwick Co.	Kans.	divorced 7-2-1982
Chr'nd					
Marr.	11-4-1968				
Death					
Burial					

Places of Residence:

Occupation: Church Affiliation: Military Rec:

His Father: Elwood Oren Moore   **Mother's Maiden Name:** Maxine D. Baxter

Wife's Full Maiden Name: Lynda Lee Dalton

	Day Month Year	City, Town or Place	County or Province, etc.	State or Country	Add. Info on Wife
Birth	9-5-1945				
Chr'nd					
Death					
Burial					

Places of Residence:

Occupation: Church Affiliation: Military Rec:

Her Father: **Mother's Maiden Name:**

Sex	Children's Names in Full		Day Month Year	City, Town or Place	County or Province, etc.	State or Country	Add. Info on Children
F	1 Angela Dawn Moore	Birth	17-10-1970				
		Marr.	7-1-1991				divorced Dec. 17, 1997
	Full Name of Spouse: George Amasa Larsen	Death					
		Burial					
M	2 Shawn Dean Moore	Birth	28-8-1974				
		Marr.					
	Full Name of Spouse:	Death					
		Burial					
	3	Birth					
		Marr.					
	Full Name of Spouse:	Death					
		Burial					
	4	Birth					
		Marr.					
	Full Name of Spouse:	Death					
		Burial					
	5	Birth					
		Marr.					
	Full Name of Spouse:	Death					
		Burial					
	6	Birth					
		Marr.					
	Full Name of Spouse:	Death					
		Burial					
	7	Birth					
		Marr.					
	Full Name of Spouse:	Death					
		Burial					
	8	Birth					
		Marr.					
	Full Name of Spouse:	Death					
		Burial					

Compiler: Notes:

Address:

City, State, Zip:

Date:

Family Group Sheet

Husband's Full Name: George Amasa Larsen

Chart No.

Husband's Data	Day Month Year	City, Town or Place	County or Province, etc.	State or Country	Add. Info on Husband
Birth	22- 2-1965				Divorced Dec. 17, 1997
Chr'nd					
Marr	7- 1-1991				
Death					
Burial					

Places of Residence:

Occupation: **Church Affiliation:** **Military Rec:**

His Father: **Mother's Maiden Name:**

Wife's Full Maiden Name: Angela Dawn Moore

Wife's Data	Day Month Year	City, Town or Place	County or Province, etc.	State or Country	Add. Info on Wife
Birth	17-10-1970				
Chr'nd					
Death					
Burial					

Places of Residence: Utah

Occupation: **Church Affiliation:** **Military Rec:**

Her Father: Larry Joe Moore **Mother's Maiden Name:** Lynda Lee Dalton

Sex	Children's Names in Full	Children's Data	Day Month Year	City, Town or Place	County or Province, etc.	State or Country	Add. Info on Children
F	1 Moore, Shayla Michalle	Birth	8- 8-1988				
		Marr.					
	Full Name of Spouse	Death					
		Burial					
F	2 Larsen, Jessica Darlene	Birth	10-12-1989				
		Marr.					
	Full Name of Spouse	Death					
		Burial					
M	3 Larsen, Raymon Amasa	Birth	30- 1-1993				
		Marr.					
	Full Name of Spouse	Death					
		Burial					

Shayla-9yrs., Jessie-8 yrs, Ray-4 yrs., 1997

Compiler:
Address:
City, State, Zip:
Date:

Notes:

General Discharge

Under Honorable Conditions
from the Armed Forces of the United States of America

This is to certify that

LARRY JOE MOORE RA 17 574 641 PRIVATE REGULAR ARMY

was Discharged from the

United States Army

on the 10TH *day of* JUNE 1963 *under honorable conditions*

ROBERT S. YOUNG
BRIGADIER GENERAL, USA

DD FORM 257A
1 MAY 50

THIS IS AN IMPORTANT RECORD
SAFEGUARD IT.

1. LAST NAME - FIRST NAME - MIDDLE NAME	2. SEX	3. SOCIAL SECURITY NUMBER	4. DATE OF BIRTH YEAR	MONTH	DAY
MOORE LARRY JOE	M	513 40 2036	40	12	13

5. DEPARTMENT, COMPONENT AND BRANCH OR CLASS	6a. GRADE, RATE OR RANK	6b. PAY GRADE	7. DATE OF RANK YEAR	MONTH	DAY
ARMY RA	PVT	E1	63	02	21

8a. SELECTIVE SERVICE NUMBER	8b. SELECTIVE SERVICE LOCAL BOARD NUMBER, CITY, STATE AND ZIP CODE	8c. HOME OF RECORD AT TIME OF ENTRY INTO ACTIVE SERVICE (Street, RFD, City, State and ZIP Code)
NA	NA	RR #1 POTWIN KS

9a. TYPE OF SEPARATION	9b. STATION OR INSTALLATION AT WHICH EFFECTED
DISCHARGE	FT BLISS TX

9c. AUTHORITY AND REASON	9d. EFFECTIVE DATE YEAR	MONTH	DAY
------------	63	06	10

9e. CHARACTER OF SERVICE	9f. TYPE OF CERTIFICATE ISSUED	10. REENLISTMENT CODE
UNDER HONORABLE CONDITIONS	DD FORM 257A	----------

11. LAST DUTY ASSIGNMENT AND MAJOR COMMAND	12. COMMAND TO WHICH TRANSFERRED
CO A USA GAR WSMR NM	NA

13. TERMINAL DATE OF RESERVE / MSS OBLIGATION			14. PLACE OF ENTRY INTO CURRENT ACTIVE SERVICE (City, State and ZIP Code)	15. DATE ENTERED ACTIVE DUTY THIS PERIOD		
YEAR	MONTH	DAY		YEAR	MONTH	DAY
NA			KANSAS CITY MO	60	06	30

16a. PRIMARY SPECIALTY NUMBER AND TITLE	16b. RELATED CIVILIAN OCCUPATION AND D.O.T. NUMBER	18. RECORD OF SERVICE	YEARS	MONTHS	DAYS
NA	NA	(a) NET ACTIVE SERVICE THIS PERIOD	2	9	12
		(b) PRIOR ACTIVE SERVICE	0	0	0
17a. SECONDARY SPECIALTY NUMBER AND TITLE	17b. RELATED CIVILIAN OCCUPATION AND D.O.T. NUMBER	(c) TOTAL ACTIVE SERVICE (a + b)	2	9	12
		(d) PRIOR INACTIVE SERVICE	0	0	0
NA	NA	(e) TOTAL SERVICE FOR PAY (c + d)	2	9	12
		(f) FOREIGN AND/OR SEA SERVICE THIS PERIOD	1	3	29

19. INDOCHINA OR KOREA SERVICE SINCE AUGUST 5, 1964	20. HIGHEST EDUCATION LEVEL SUCCESSFULLY COMPLETED (In Years)
☒ YES ☐ NO	SECONDARY/HIGH SCHOOL 12 YRS (1-12 grades) COLLEGE 0 YRS

21. TIME LOST (Preceding Two Yrs)	22. DAYS ACCRUED LEAVE PAID	23. SERVICEMEN'S GROUP LIFE INSURANCE COVERAGE	24. DISABILITY SEVERANCE PAY	25. PERSONNEL SECURITY INVESTIGATION	
		☐ $15,000 ☐ $5,000	☐ NO ☐ YES	a. TYPE	b. DATE COMPLETED
59 DAYS	NONE	☐ $10,000 ☒ NONE	DNA AMOUNT	NONE	NA

26. DECORATIONS, MEDALS, BADGES, COMMENDATIONS, CITATIONS AND CAMPAIGN RIBBONS AWARDED OR AUTHORIZED
SHARPSHOOTER QUALIFICATION BADGE WITH RIFLE BAR

27. REMARKS
MSN: RA 17 574 641   US CITIZEN: YES   PLACE OF BIRTH: WICHITA KS
MARITAL STATUS: DIVORCED   SIGNAL SCH: NOV 60 - FEB 61   TELEPHONE INSTALLER RPMN
61 DAYS LOST UNDER 10 USC 972 FROM: 13-14 AUG 60; 15 NOV - 6 DEC 62; 17-18 JAN 63;
21 FEB - 14 MAR 63; 12-16 APR 63; 14-14 MAY 63; 28 MAY - 1 JUN 63; 5-6 JUN 63

28. MAILING ADDRESS AFTER SEPARATION (Street, RFD, City, County, State and ZIP Code)	29. SIGNATURE OF PERSON BEING SEPARATED
477 GRAND CIRCLE DR MOAB UT	
30. TYPED NAME, GRADE AND TITLE OF AUTHORIZING OFFICER	31. SIGNATURE OF OFFICER AUTHORIZED TO SIGN
SUSAN E. BARNICK, 1LT, AGC	*(signature)*

PREVIOUS EDITIONS OF THIS   THIS IS AN IMPORTANT RECORD   REPORT OF SEPARATION FROM ACTIVE DUTY

LAMB MORTUARY

This Information for Death Certificates and Newspapers

Name: Infant of Mr & Mrs Larry Moore
Residence: Whitewater, Kansas
Date of Death: May 23, 1959   Time: 6:30 AM
Place of Death: Axtell Hospital at Newton, Kansas
Date and Place of Birth: Axtell Hospital (Stillbirth) 5-23-59
Date and Place of Marriage: none
How Long Ill? none
How Long Lived Here? none

Occupation: none
Employer:
Father's Name: Larry Moore
Mother's Maiden Name: Evlyn Sue Gronau
Social Security Number: none
If Veteran, Specify War and Unit: none
Entered Service: none   Service No.: none
Discharged: none   Rank or Rating: none
Cause of Death: stillbirth
Physician: Dr. Grizwold
Address: Newton, Kansas
Was a Member of What Church? none
What Fraternal Orders? none

Names and Addresses of Surviving Relatives

Husband or Wife:
Father: Mr & Mrs Larry Moore----Whitewater, Kansas
Mother:
Daughters: none
Maternal Grandparents---Mr & Mrs Leo Gronau--Whitewater
Paternal " " " Elwood Moore--Potwin
Sons: none
Paternal Great Grandparents--Mr & Mrs Oren Moore--Whitewater
Maternal Great Grandfather--Albert Gronau--Whitewater
Sisters: none
Brothers: none

Services

Date, Hour, Place: Whitewater Cemetery 4:00PM May 23, 1959
Minister: Rev. Louis Poppe
Place of Burial: Whitewater Cemetery
Bearers: none
Music Singer:- none
Songs:- none
Organist:- none
Organizations Attending in a Body: none

Family Group Sheet

Husband's Full Name: Eldon Jay Mayhew
Chart No.:

	Day Month Year	City, Town or Place	County or Province, etc.	State or Country	Add. Info. on Husband
Birth	1-11-1916	Edwards Co. Lincoln Township		Kansas	
Chr'nd					
Marr	3-8-1938	Hutchinson	Reno Co.	Kansas	
Death					
Burial					

Places of Residence: Belpre, Kansas before marriage (Colo.-Utah-Ky., Calif.-New Mex.)
Occupation: Geologist **Church Affiliation:** Christian **Military Rec.:**

His Father: Allen A. Mayhew **Mother's Maiden Name:** Mary Woods

Wife's Full Maiden Name: Helen May Moore

	Day Month Year	City, Town or Place	County or Province, etc.	State or Country	Add. Info. on Wife
Birth	2-3-1916	Butler Co., Milton Township		Kansas	
Chr'nd					
Death					
Burial					

Places of Residence: Whitewater, Ks. (before marriage)
Occupation: Housewife **Church Affiliation:** Christian **Military Rec.:**

Her Father: Orin Edgar Moore **Mother's Maiden Name:** Susan May Keyes

Sex	Children's Names in Full		Day Month Year	City, Town or Place	County or Province, etc.	State or Country	Add. Info. on Children
M	1 John Daryl Mayhew	Birth	13-1-1943	Moab	Gund Co.	Utah	
	Full Name of Spouse: Carol Ann Curfman	Marr	13-8				
		Death					
		Burial					
M	2 Robert Jay Mayhew	Birth	14-7-1947	Pasadena	Los Angeles Co.	Ca.	
	Full Name of Spouse: Julie	Marr	24-7				
		Death					
		Burial					
M	3 Allen Edward Mayhew	Birth	30-9-1949	Pasadena	LosAngeles	Calif.	
	Full Name of Spouse: Donna Michelle Borg	Marr	21-8-				
		Death					
		Burial					
	4	Birth					
		Marr					

State of Kansas, Central Division of Vital Statistics

P. J. No. 296

MARRIAGE LICENSE

In the Probate Court of Reno County. Aug. 3rd 1938

To Any Person in the State of Kansas Authorized by Law to Perform the Marriage Ceremony, Greeting:

YOU ARE HEREBY AUTHORIZED TO JOIN IN MARRIAGE

E. J. Mayhew (Groom) of Belpre, Kansas Age 21
Helen Moore (Bride) of Whitewater, Kansas Age 22

With the consent of _____ (Name of Parent or Guardian Consenting)

and of this license, duly endorsed, you will make return to my office at Hutchinson, Kansas, within ten days after performing ceremony.

(SEAL) A. B. Leigh, Probate Judge

INDORSEMENT

TO WHOM IT MAY CONCERN:

I hereby certify that I performed the ceremony joining in marriage the above-named couple, on the 3 day of August 1938 at Hutchinson, Kans.

Signed: W. O. Mulvaney
Title: Pastor Trinity Meth. Epis. C.
Address: Hutchinson, Ks.

Helen Moore

Bob and wife, Julie, in back. Jennifer Mayhew, Sarah Johnson, Melanie Mayhew, Aaron Johnson.

Left to right: Bob Mayhew, Lisa Mayhew. Standing - Allen, Carol, Donna, Jennifer, Michael, Melanie, Jack, Matthew. All Mayhews II. Jamie sitting in front with Bart the dog. Everyone relaxing at the cabin.

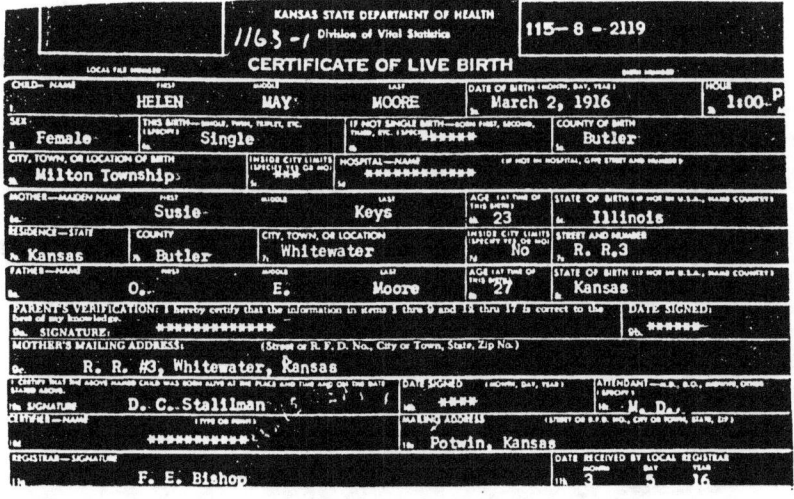

Mayhew Family Project Represents Much Work, Payoff Comes Soon

Some people like Christmas carols played by a philharmonic orchestra—others like a nostalgic combo. But Rep. and Mrs. Jay Mayhew are dreaming of hearing Jingle Bells a-la-honky tonk.

Several years ago when old player pianos were once again becoming interesting, Helen told her husband she wanted one for an anniversary present. Jay started looking, but every time he followed a tip on an old player piano for sale, it was sold before he could reach it.

Then one day luck was with him. Jay was in Scofield at an old mining camp looking for some warehouse space. The owner of an abandoned dance hall suggested he might rent the building for storage. When Jay walked in to look the hall over he couldn't believe his eyes. There, pushed back in a corner with the floor caved in all about it was the most intriguing ancient player piano he had ever seen.

Jay immediately lost interest in the building and started dealing for the piano. In the end he was allowed to purchase it for a nominal sum if he rented the building. The deal was closed.

The Mayhews moved the piano to their home in Moab. They soon realized they had more than they had bargained for. At one time the old piano, built around the turn of the century, had been equipped with base drums, snare drums, a triangle, 96 wooden whistles and a player attachment. In its heyday it had been a coin operated instrument, and there was even a magnet attachment that atracted "slugs" to prevent the cusomer from getting a free tune. A selection button on the outside gave them their favorite number.

But the loveliest portion of the ancient instrument was its stained glass front—each piece of gothic glass was outlined with a blackened metal, which after many hours of polishing proved to be copper dividers.

Of course there is a catch to every bargain. The piano wouldn't work. Mr. Mayhew and his mechanically minded son, Jack, tore it down and went to work on it. All the tubing, they found, was deteriorated with age and had to be replaced. They have used over 400 feet of rubber tubing to date. The bellows were in excellent repair, but still facing them is the replacement of 96 air valves which activate the whistles and drums.

The piano used a shorter piano roll than average and the Mayhews scoured the country for one that would work. Finally in Boston they found one roll to fit the instrument.

The finish on the piano was badly deteriorated. Helen wanted to paint it red—but friends insisted she should antique the wood. She worked for weeks applying paint and varnish. When it was finished she still didn't like it. This, she said, was a fun piano and it should be a fun color—red. So once again she went to work and today the beautiful stained glass sits in a frame of the gayest holiday red.

Little did the Mayhews realize what a treasure they had bought when the old piano was first unloaded into their home. Shortly after, even before repairs had started, an antique collector called on them. He had been to Scofield to search for the piano; he heard had once been in the old dance hall and traced it to the Mayhew's Moab home. He offered them $1300 for it. They didn't sell—after all it was an anniversary present and they still hadn't heard it play.

They still haven't heard it, but they are getting closer. By next year they hope the old piano can sound out their Christmas carols in real honky tonk style—just like it did those many years ago in the old dance hall in the Scofield mining camyp.

Rep. E. J. Mayhew, left, and Sen. Samuel J. Taylor, study pre-legislative literature as biennial session nears opening.

Legislators Face Major Issues In Coming State Session

By Don Robinson

Educational financing and reapportionment are viewed as the major issues facing the Utah State Legislature starting Monday by Senator Samuel J. Taylor and Representative E. J. Mayhew.

Both men will depart Sunday for the opening of the legislative session. They are to be sworn in Monday at noon in the respective state chambers along with eight new senators and 32 representatives.

Mr. Taylor, a 1962 senatorial appointee, won the right to represent the 12th senatorial district of Emery, San Juan and Grand counties in November. The Times-Independent editor will be attending his first legislature in that office.

Representative E. J. Mayhew also will be attending for the first time. Prominent here as a consulting geologist, he too won his first political office in November.

Both stated a desire to hear from constituents during their stay in the state capitol and urged people to write when they had opinions on pending legislation.

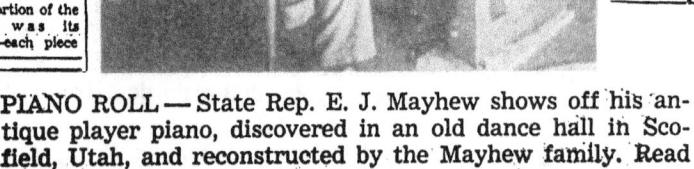

PIANO ROLL — State Rep. E. J. Mayhew shows off his antique player piano, discovered in an old dance hall in Scofield, Utah, and reconstructed by the Mayhew family. Read the story on the restoration project on Page B-8.

WONDERFUL ONE-HOSS SHAY—A 1907 Studebaker limousine owned by O. O. Ediger broke down Friday, as Ediger was driving the antique auto west on Douglas Avenue. The front axle disintegrated as the car was cruising along the 800 block on East Douglas and the limousine lost its right front wheel. Ediger sensed something was wrong just before the wheel dropped off and headed the machine toward the curb. The mishap puts the car out of the antique auto show to be held at Joyland Sunday, but Ediger has another antique—a 1901 Oldsmobile—which he will have in the show.

Jay and Helen Mayhew

Family Group Sheet

Husband's Full Name: Melvin E. Moore
Chart No.:

	Day Month Year	City, Town or Place	County or Province, etc.	State or Country	Add. Info. on Husband
Birth					
Chr'nd					
Marr					
Death	14-10-1993	Albuquerque	Bernandillo Co.	New Mexico	
Burial					

Places of Residence:
Occupation: **Church Affiliation:** **Military Rec:** Army
His Father: Orin E. Moore **Mother's Maiden Name:** Susan May Keys

Wife's Full Maiden Name: Jayne

	Day Month Year	City, Town or Place	County or Province, etc.	State or Country	Add. Info. on Wife
Birth					
Chr'nd					
Death					
Burial					

Places of Residence:
Occupation: **Church Affiliation:** **Military Rec:**
Her Father: **Mother's Maiden Name:**

Sex	Children's Names in Full		Day Month Year	City, Town or Place	County or Province, etc	State or Country
M	1 Michael Orin Moore	Birth	22-7-1958	Durango	LaPlata Co.	Colo.
		Marr.	12-12-1980	Austin	Clark Co.	Minnesota
	Spouse: Joyce Ann Troester	Death / Burial				
F	2 Sally Kay Moore	Birth	26-2-1956	Farmington	San Juan Co.	New Mex.
		Marr.	1981	Albuquerque	Bernandillo	New Mex.
	Spouse: Darrel Collins	Death / Burial				
F	3 Susan Ann Moore	Birth				
		Marr.				
	Spouse: Henry	Death / Burial				
	4	Birth				

Whitewater

Moore, Melvin E., 75, of Albuquerque, formerly of Whitewater, died Thursday, Oct. 14, 1993. Service 1 p.m. Monday, French Mortuary.

Survivors: wife, Jayne; son, Mike of Las Vegas; daughters, Susanne Henry of Albuquerque, Sally Collins of Chesapeake, Va.; brothers, Elwood of Newton, John of Wichita; sister, Helen Mayhew of Denver; two grandchildren.

Jayne and Melvin Moore

Jayne and Melvin

John W. Moore, 70

Former Falls High School teacher John W. Moore, 70, of Wichita, Kan., died Thursday, Nov. 10, 1994, in Wichita.

He was born in Whitewater, Kan., on Dec. 15, 1923. He graduated from Whitewater High School and from Wichita State University with a major in music. He also earned a master of art degree from Northwestern University specializing in voice and flute.

During World War II, Moore served in the Army and participated in the Battle of the Bulge.

Moore was hired to teach music and direct the senior high school choir in International Falls in 1951 and retired from teaching in 1978.

He was preceded in death by his parents and one brother.

JOHN W. MOORE

Survivors include his sister Helen and her husband Jay Mayhew of Lakewood, Colo.; a brother, Elwood of Newton, Kansas; five nephews and two nieces.

Services are being held in Whitewater, Kan., today, Nov. 14. Lamb-Nutter Mortuary is in charge of arrangements.

The family would prefer memorials to The Federated Church of Whitewater, Kan. of Wellington. Pvt. Moore entered the army at Leavenworth on December 5, 1944. He attended Whitewater high school and Kansas State College.

Recp Cen No. 1773
Ft. Leavenworth, Kansas

Property of:

Pvt. Melvin E Moore

Serial No. 37726265

TO: O. E. Moore
Whitewater
Kans.

John Moore

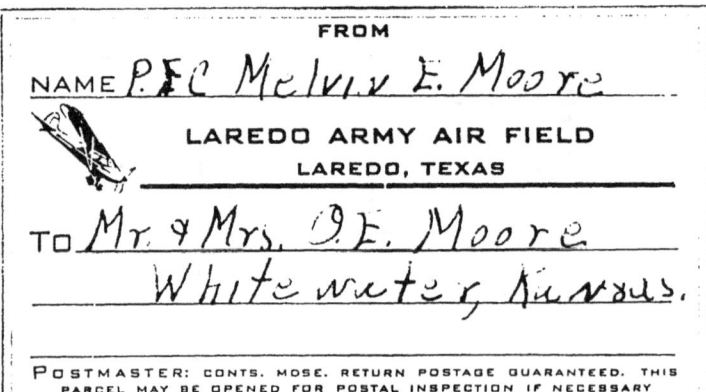

Jayne, Sally and Melvin Moore

Family Group Sheet

Husband's Full Name Michael Orin Moore   **Chart No.**

	Day Month Year	City, Town or Place	County or Province, etc	State or Country	Add. Info on Husband
Birth	22-7-1958	Durango	La Plata Co.	Colorado	
Chr'nd					
Marr	12-12-1980	Austin	Clark Co.	Minnesota	
Death					
Burial					

Places of Residence 4359 Wendy Ln. Las Vegas, Nevada 89115

Occupation Schwans Sales   **Church Affiliation** Christian   **Military Rec** US Army

His Father Melvin E. Moore   **Mother's Maiden Name** F. Jayne Jones

Wife's Full Maiden Name Joyce Ann Troester

	Day Month Year	City, Town or Place	County or Province, etc	State or Country	Add. Info on Wife
Birth	5-4-1961	Austin	Clark Co.	Minnesota	
Chr'nd					
Death					
Burial					

Places of Residence same as above

Occupation   **Church Affiliation** Christian   **Military Rec.**

Her Father Robert Lamar Troester   **Mother's Maiden Name** Evon Fay Downs

Sex	Children's Names in Full		Day Month Year	City, Town or Place	County or Province, etc	State or Country	Add. Info on Children
M	1 Moore Robert Fredrick	Birth	4-2-1977	Austin	Clark Co.	Minn.	
		Marr.					

Family Group Sheet

Husband's Full Name Darl Garrel Collin, Jr.   **Chart No.**

	Day Month Year	City, Town or Place	County or Province, etc	State or Country	Add. Info on Husband
Birth	1-7-1959	Frankfurt,		Germany	Father stnd in Germany when born Husband's family from Calhoun Co. W.
Chr'nd					
Marr	4-6-1991	Virginia Beach	Princess Ann Co.	Virginia	
Death					
Burial					

Places of Residence

Occupation American GFM Software Eng.   **Church Affiliation** Presbyterian   **Military Rec** US Army

His Father Darl Garrel Collins, Sr.   **Mother's Maiden Name** Margaret Findling

Wife's Full Maiden Name Sally Kay Moore

	Day Month Year	City, Town or Place	County or Province, etc	State or Country	Add. Info on Wife
Birth	2-26-1956	Farmington	San Juan Co.	New Mexico	
Chr'nd	1981	Albuquerque	Bernandito Co.	New Mexico	
Death					
Burial					

Places of Residence 1317 Bramblewood Crt. Chesapeake, Va.

Occupation X-Ray Technician   **Church Affiliation** Presbyterian   **Military Rec.**

Her Father Melvin E. Moore   **Mother's Maiden Name** F. Jayne Jones

Sex	Children's Names in Full		Day Month Year	City, Town or Place	County or Province, etc	State or Country	Add. Info on Children
M	1 Collins Christopher Orin	Birth	3-16-1991	Norfolk	Norfolk Co.	Va.	Adopted by Sally and Darl Collin
	Full Name of Spouse	Marr.					
		Death					
		Burial					
	2	Birth					
		Marr.					
	Full Name of Spouse	Death					
		Burial					

E. Military Service Record

Name of Veteran: Moore (last) Mike (first) Orin (middle)

State from Which Served: New Mexico

War in Which, or Dates between Which, He Served: November 1982 -- May 1987

If Service Was Civil War:

Union _____ Confederate _____

Unit in Which He Served:

Name or Number of Regiment: H H C IIth Sig. BN

Company: Headquarters

Name of Ship: _____

Branch in Which He Served:

Infantry __X__ Cavalry _____ Artillery _____ Navy _____ Other __Signal__

Kind of Service: Volunteers __X__ Regulars _____

Pension File Number: N/A

Bounty Land File Number (for Service before 1856 Only): _____

Military Record Number: _____

Date of Birth: July 22, 1958

Place of Birth: Durango (city) La Plata (county) Colorado (state)

Name of Widow or Other Claimant: _____

Date of Death: _____

Place of Death: _____ (city) _____ (county) _____ (state)

Places Lived after Service: Albuquerque, New Mexico   Las Vegas, Nevada

If Veteran Lived in a Home for Soldiers:

Location: _____ (city) _____ (state)

Family Group Sheet

Husband's Full Name: John William Moore **Chart No.**

	Day Month Year	City, Town or Place	County or Province, etc.	State or Country	Add Info on Husband
Birth	15-12-1923	Whitewater	Butler Co.	Kansas	
Chr'nd					
Marr					
Death	10-11-1994	Wichita	Sedgwick Co.	Kansas	
Burial	14-11-1994	Whitewater cem.	Butler Co.	Kansas	

Places of Residence:
Occupation: Musician and Teacher **Church Affiliation:** **Military Rec:** US Army

His Father: Orin Edgar Moore **Mother's Maiden Name:** Susan May Keyes

John Moore

John Moore

231

Family Group Sheet

Husband's Full Name Elmer Moore SS 513-38-1567   **Chart No.**

Husband's Date	Day Month Year	City, Town or Place	County or Province, etc.	State or Country	Add. Info on Husband
Birth	5-10-1891	Potwin	Butler Co.	Kansas	
Chrند					
Marr					
Death	7-1973	Satanta	Haskell Co.	Kansas	
Burial		Shaffer cem Potwin	Butler Co.	Kansas	

Places of Residence
Occupation   Church Affiliation   Military Rec
Other wives, etc.

His Father William Oscar Moore   Mother's Maiden Name Louisa M. Adams

---

NAME: MOORE, Elmer

Birth Date
05 Oct 1891

Social Security
513-38-1567

State of Issuance of Social Security Number
Kansas

Death Date
Jul 1973

Death Residence Localities
67870
Satanta, Haskell, Kansas

Ruth and Elmer Moore

Family Group Sheet

Husband's Full Name Ruth Moore   **Chart No.**

Husband's Date	Day Month Year	City, Town or Place	County or Province, etc.	State or Country	Add. Info on Husband
Birth					
Chrند					
Marr					died of Diptheria
Death					
Burial					

Places of Residence
Occupation   Church Affiliation   Military Rec

His Father William Oscar Moore   Mother's Maiden Name Louvisa M. Adams

Date

Family Group Sheet

Husband's Full Name: Ray I. Moore   SS 515-20-2386   **Chart No.**

	Day Month Year	City, Town or Place	County or Province, etc.	State or Country	Add. Info on Husband
Birth	3- 4-1896	Potwin	Butler Co.	Kansas	
Chr'nd					
Marr	10-1-1917	ElDorado	Butler Co.	Kansas	
Death	18-12-1979	Newton	Harvey Co.	Kansas	
Burial	21-12-1979	McGill cem. Potwin	Butler Co.	Kansas	

Places of Residence:
Occupation: Farmer-Retired carpenter   **Church Affiliation:** Christian   **Military Rec:**

His Father: William Oscar Moore   **Mother's Maiden Name:** M. Louvisa Adams

Wife's Full Maiden Name: Vida M Maxwell   SS 509-4-6787

	Day Month Year	City, Town or Place	County or Province, etc.	State or Country	Add. Info on Wife
Birth	23- 1-1897	Potwin	Butler Co.	Kansas	
Chr'nd					
Death	19- 4-1975	Newton	Harvey Co.	Kansas	
Burial	4-1975	McGill cem. Potwin	Butler Co.	Kansas	

Places of Residence:
Occupation: Housewife/SalesClerk   **Church Affiliation:** Christian   **Military Rec:**

Her Father: Guy V. Maxwell   **Mother's Maiden Name:** Nina McGill

Sex	Children's Names in Full		Day Month Year	City, Town or Place	County or Province, etc.	State or Country	Add. Info on Children
F	1 Dorothy Moore	Birth					
		Marr.					
	Full Name of Spouse	Death	1953				
		Burial					

Ray I. Moore, June 1913

Ray Moore and Gladys Taylor

Vida, Ray, Veva and Bill

NAME: MOORE, Ray

Birth Date Social Security Number
03 Apr 1896 515-20-2386

State of Issuance of Social Security Number
Kansas

Death Date
Dec 1979

Death Residence Localities
67114
Newton, Harvey, Kansas
Zimmerdale, Harvey, Kansas

Death Benefit Localities
67114
Newton, Harvey, Kansas
Zimmerdale, Harvey, Kansas

VITAL INFORMATION BLANK

All residents of Newton Presbyterian Manor are requested to file with the Administrator the following information which is frequently needed.

Name: Mrs. Vida M. Moore Date of Entrance Feb. 19, 1975
(Please include middle name or initial)

Date of Birth Jan. 23, 1897 Place of Birth Potwin, Kansas
Place of residence before retirement (Street & Town) 573 W. First, Valley Center, Kansas
Occupation before retirement: Sales-clerk

To whom married Ray I. Moore Date and Place of Marriage Jan. 10, 1917 - Potwin, Kansas
Maiden Name (If married or widowed) Vida M. Maxwell
Father's Name Guy V. Maxwell Place of Birth Xenia, Ohio
Mother's Maiden Name Mima McGill Place of Birth Potwin, Kansas

Names and residence of living relatives:
Sister - Mrs. Vera M. Lewis, 708 South Kansas, Newton, Kansas -Ph. 283-1323
Nephews - to contact for assistance
Warren McClain, Potwin, Kansas - Ph. SK1-3330
Husband - Ray Moore - 715 Olive, Newton, Kansas - Ph. 283-4905
(If deceased at night, call Richard or Nancy Parsons -716 Olive-283-0694
To be notified - Lucile Anderson - 1115 E. 7th St., Newton, Kansas - Ph. 283-4401

Social Security # 509-14-6787 Medicare # 509-24-6787 A
Blue Cross & Blue Shield? Yes X No ___ Number 145167000 Group 8028 over 65
Other Health Insurance
If Veteran, what war?
Church of which a member First Christian Church, Newton, Kansas
Where do you wish to be buried? McGill Cemetery, Potwin, Kansas Rev. Gerald Hough to have service, Prayer by Rev. John Frakes
(Unless otherwise specified, burial will be in Manor lot, Greenwood Cem.Newton
Do you have a lot? Yes, adjoins Wm. Lewis lot.
(Please file deed or legal description with this blank)
Where do you wish your service to be held? Petersen Mortuary- Ph. 283-2525
Undertaker preferred Petersen
What Songs do you wish sung? How Great Thou Art, and I Won't Cross Jordan Alone.
Singer - Rev. Gerald Hough
Other requests:
If you want an obituary printed or read, write it and place it in our files.

Name of Deceased	Ray I. Moore	Yrs.		Date of Death	Dec. 18, 1929	Time
Place of Death	715 Olive		Funeral from	Chapel		
	Presbyterian Manor		Day	Friday	Date Dec. 21, 1979 Time 2:00 P.M.
Sex Male	Color White	Widowed	Burial	McGill Cemetery, Potwin, Ks.		
Husband or Wife of	Vida (Maxwell)		Clergyman	Darryl Godinez & Rev. Herb Kieller		
			Singers	Mr. Gene Price		
Date of Birth	April 3, 1896	Yrs Months Days	Pallbearers	Wayne Austin, David McLain Elwood Moore		
	83			Alan Moore, Lloyd M. Moore, Howard R. Moore		
Birthplace	Potwin, Kansas			Survived		
Business or Industry	Retired		1-Brother: Mr. O.E. Moore Whitewater, Ks.			
Last worked		Years of work				
Trade or Profession	Carpenter					
Name of Father	Oscar Moore		at Bel.Bud+Bud			
Birthplace of father			Eldorado,ks			
Maiden name of mother	Lavisa Wait					
Birthplace						
Physician	Dr.					

MARRIAGE LICENSE.

El Dorado, Butler County, State of Kansas,
OFFICE OF PROBATE JUDGE OF SAID COUNTY.

State of Kansas, Butler County, ss.

BE IT REMEMBERED, That on the 6 day of July, A.D. 1917 there was issued from the office of said Probate Judge, a marriage license of which the following is a true copy:

To Any Person Authorized by Law to Perform the Marriage Ceremony, Greeting:
You are hereby authorized to join in Marriage Ray Moore
of _____, aged 20 and Vida Maxwell
of _____, aged 19 the following day of _____ ... concerning and of this License you will make due return to my office within thirty days.

And which said Marriage License was afterwards, to-wit, on the ____ day of _____, A.D. 19__ returned to said Probate Judge with the following Certificate endorsed thereon, to-wit:

State Of Kansas, Butler County, ss.

I, _____, do hereby certify that, in accordance with the authorization of the within License, I did, on the 10th day of January, A.D. 1917, at Whitewater, Kansas join in marriage Ray Moore in said county, join and unite in marriage the within named _____ and Vida Maxwell

Witness my hand the day and year above written.

Attest: _____ Probate Judge.

_____ Minister of the Gospel
Potwin, Kansas

Family Group Sheet

Husband's Full Name   **Chart No.**

	Day	Month	Year	City, Town or Place	County or Province, etc.	State or Country	Add. Info. on Husband
Birth							
Chr'nd							
Marr							
Death							
Burial							

Places of Residence

Occupation   Church Affiliation   Military Rec.

Other wives, if any...
Make separate sheet for each man.

His Father   Mother's Maiden Name

Wife's Full Maiden Name   INFANTE   MOORE

	Day	Month	Year	City, Town or Place	County or Province, etc.	State or Country	Add. Info. on Wife
Birth							
Chr'nd							
Death							
Burial							

Places of Residence

Occupation   Church Affiliation   Military Rec.

Other husbands, if any...
Make separate sheet for each man.

Her Father William Cres Moore   Mother's Maiden Name Louisa M.

Sex	Children's Names in Full (arranged in order of birth)		Day	Month	Year	City, Town or Place	County or Province, etc.	State or Country	Add. Info on Child

INFANT

RAY L. MOORE
APR 3, 1896 — DEC 13, 1979

VIDA M. MOORE
JAN 23, 1897 — APR 19, 1975

Dorothy Moore

Ray Moore and Hazel Newcom

235

Family Group Sheet

Husband's Full Name: Richard Edgar Moore **Chart No.**

Husband's Data	Day Month Year	City, Town or Place	County or Province, etc.	State or Country	Add. Info on Husband
Birth	3-7-1854	Chautauqua	Chautauqua Co.	Kansas	
Chr'nd					
Marr	1-1-1882	ElDorado	Butler Co.	Kansas	
Death	21-1-1934				
Burial	1-1934				

Places of Residence
Occupation: Farmer **Church Affiliation:**   **Military Rec:**
Other wives: May Flint married 29 Dec., 1885 Greenwood Co., Kansas
His Father: Reuben Moore **Mother's Maiden Name:** Melvina Barbara Paul

Wife's Full Maiden Name: Eunice E. Adams

Wife's Data	Day Month Year	City, Town or Place	County or Province, etc.	State or Country	Add. Info on Wife
Birth	1883				
Chr'nd					
Death	13-1-1883		Butler Co.	Kansas	age 49 yrs.
Burial	1-1883	Shaffer cem. Potwin	Butler Co.	Kansas	& 9 mo.

Places of Residence

Military Rec.

STATE OF KANSAS,
Butler County. Office of Probate Judge of said County.

BE IT REMEMBERED, That on the 24th day of December, A. D. 1882, there was issued from the office of said Probate Judge, a Marriage License, of which the following is a true copy:

Marriage License.

El Dorado, Butler County, State of Kansas, Dec 24th A. D. 1882

To any person authorized by law to perform the Marriage Ceremony—Greeting:

You are hereby authorized to join in Marriage R. E. Moore of Butler Co Kansas aged 27 and Eunice Electa Adams of Butler Co Kansas aged 17, and of this License you will make due return to my office within thirty days.

(SEAL) E D Stratford Probate Judge.

And which said Marriage License was afterwards, to-wit: on the 1st day of January A. D. 1882, returned to said Probate Judge, with the following Certificate endorsed thereon, to-wit:

STATE OF KANSAS, Butler County, ss.

I, I Mooney, do hereby certify, that in accordance with the authorisation of the within License, I did, on the 1st day of January, A. D. 1882, at Cairbou in said County, join and unite in Marriage the within named R. E. Moore and Eunice Electa Adams

WITNESS my hand and seal the day and year above written.

Family Group Sheet

Husband's Full Name: Jimmie E. Moore

Chart No.:

	Day Month Year	City, Town or Place	County or Province, etc.	State or Country	Add. Info. on Husband
Birth	1-8-1857		Butler Co.	Kansas	
Chr'nd					
Marr					
Death	22-9-1869				12 yrs. old
Burial					

Places of Residence:

Occupation: **Church Affiliation:** **Military Rec:**

His Father: Reuben Moore **Mother's Maiden Name:** Melvina Barbara Paul

Wife's Full Maiden Name:

	Day Month Year	City, Town or Place			
Birth					
Chr'nd					
Death					
Burial					

Places of Residence:

Occupation: **Church Affiliation:**

Her Father:

Sex	Children's Names in Full		Day Month Year
1		Birth	
		Marr.	
	Full Name of Spouse	Death	
		Burial	
2		Birth	

Gravestone: **J. M. MOORE / OCT. 26, 1859 / JULY 20, 1954**

STATE OF KANSAS, CHAUTAUQUA COUNTY. Office of Probate Judge of said County.

Be it Remembered, That on the 13 day of August A.D. 1884, there was issued from the office of said Probate Judge, a Marriage License, of which the following is a true copy:

MARRIAGE LICENSE.

Chautauqua County, State of Kansas, August 13, A.D. 1884.

To any Person authorized by Law to perform the Marriage Ceremony, Greeting:

You are hereby authorized to join in Marriage James M. Moore of Chautauqua County, aged 25 years, and Julie B. Smith of Chautauqua County, aged 16 years; and of this License you will make due return to my office within thirty days.

E. V. Bale, Probate Judge.

And which said Marriage License was afterwards, to wit, on the 15 day of September A.D. 1884, returned to said Probate Judge, with the following Certificate endorsed thereon, to wit:

STATE OF KANSAS, CHAUTAUQUA COUNTY, ss.

I, William Magee, do hereby certify, that in accordance with the authorization of the within License, I did, on the 16 day of August A.D. 1884, at the residence of J. M. Smith, in said County, join and unite in Marriage the within-named James M. Moore and Miss Julie B. Smith.

Wm Magee, Justice of the Peace

WITNESS my hand and seal, the day and year above written.

Attest: E. V. Bale, Probate Judge.

Husband's Full Name

Family Group Sheet

Husband's Full Name: James Monroe Moore
Chart No.:

	Day Month Year	City, Town or Place	County or Province, etc.	State or Country	Add. Info on Husband
Birth	26-10-1859	near Lawrence	Douglas Co.	Kansas	
Chr'nd					
Marr.	16-8-1884	Elgin	Chatauqua Co.	Kansas	
Death	20-7-1954		Chautauqua Co.	Kansas	
Burial	7-1954	Oak Grove cem.	Chautauqua Co.	Kansas	

Places of Residence: Elgin
Occupation: Farmer-Santa Fe
Church Affiliation:
Military Rec:

His Father: Reuben Moore
Mother's Maiden Name: Melvina Barbara Paul

Wife's Full Maiden Name: Julia Belle Smith

	Day Month Year	City, Town or Place	County or Province, etc.	State or Country	Add. Info on Wife
Birth	27-12-1869				
Chr'nd					
Death	16-6-1900				
Burial	6-1900	Oak Grove cem. Elgin	Chautauqua Co.	Kansas	

Places of Residence: Elgin
Occupation: Housewife
Church Affiliation:
Military Rec:

Her Father: Thomas W. Smith (Todd)
Mother's Maiden Name: Mary Frances Dale

Sex	Children's Names in Full		Day Month Year	City, Town or Place	County or Province, etc.	State or Country	Add. Info on Children
F	1. Della M. Moore	Birth	15-4-1885	Chautauqua	Chatauqua Co.	Ks.	with flu
		Marr.	6-3-1904	Sedan	Chautauqua Co.	Ks.	
	Full Name of Spouse: George Hafeker/Ernest Fitts	Death	1918				
		Burial					
F	2. Infant twin Moore	Birth	15-4-1885	Chautauqua	Chautauqua	Ks.	died at birth
		Marr.					
	Full Name of Spouse	Death	15-4-1885	Chautauqua	Chautauqua	Ks.	
		Burial					
F	3. Rosa L. Moore	Birth	8-9-1887	Chautauqua	Chautauqua	Ks.	Pneumonia
		Marr.	1903	Sedan	Chautauqua	Ks	
	Full Name of Spouse: Marsh Ecker/Jess Crawford	Death	1927				
		Burial					
F	4. Eva V. Moore	Birth	14-11-1889		Osage Co.	Okla.	
		Marr.					
	Full Name of Spouse: Harve Riley	Death	1967				
		Burial	1967	Moore cem.	Chautauqua	Kans.	
F	5. Clara S. Moore	Birth	20-2-1892		Chautauqua	Kans.	
		Marr.	1912				
	Full Name of Spouse: Virge Rector/Guy Johnson	Death	9-9-1926			Okla.	
		Burial	9-1926			Okla.	
M	6. Lester Leroy Moore	Birth	30-1-1895	Elgin	Chautauqua Co.	Kans.	killed by a horse kicking him
		Marr.	25-2-1920	SEdan	Chautauqua Co.	Kans.	
	Full Name of Spouse: Lydia Carricker	Death	25-6-1920	Sedan	Chautauqua Co.	Kans.	
		Burial	27-6-1920	Oak Grove cem	Chau. Co.	Kans.	
M	7. Clydes Earl Moore	Birth	3-7-1896	Oolagah	Rogers Co.	Okla.	
		Marr.	27-12-1922	Sedan	Chautauqua Co.	Kans.	
	Full Name of Spouse: Rhoda Carricker	Death	26-8-1981	Sedan	Chautauqua Co.	Kans.	
		Burial	28-8-1981	Oak Grove cem	Chau. Co.	Ks.	
F	8. Gladys Moore	Birth	1897				TB death
		Marr.					
	Full Name of Spouse	Death					
		Burial					

Compiler:
Address:
City, State, Zip:
Date:
Notes:

Family Group Sheet

Husband's Full Name: George Hafeker   **Chart No.**

Husband's Data	Day Month Year	City, Town or Place	County or Province, etc.	State or Country	Add. Info on Husband
Birth					
Chr'nd					
Marr	6-3-1904	Sedan	Chautauqua Co.	Kansas	
Death					
Burial					

Places of Residence: Chautauqua Co.- Arkansas City-Peru, Kansas
Occupation: Church Affiliation: Military Rec:
Other wives:
His Father: Mother's Maiden Name:

Wife's Full Maiden Name: Della M. Moore

Wife's Data	Day Month Year	City, Town or Place	County or Province, etc.	State or Country	Add. Info on Wife
Birth	15-4-1885		Chautauqua Co.	Kansas	
Chr'nd					
Death	1918				Flu
Burial					

Places of Residence: Chautauqua Co.-Arkansas City-Peru, Kansas
Occupation: Church Affiliation: Military Rec:
Other husbands: Ernest Fittro
Her Father: James Monroe Moore   Mother's Maiden Name: Julia Belle Smith

Sex	Children's Names in Full	Children's Data	Day Month Year	City, Town or Place	County or Province, etc.	State or Country	Add. Info on Children
F	1 Hazel Hafeker	Birth	1905				death 4 yrs. old
	Full Name of Spouse	Marr.					
		Death	1909				
		Burial					
F	2 Gladys Hafeker	Birth					
	Full Name of Spouse	Marr.					
		Death					
		Burial					
M	3 Lawrence Hafeker	Birth					
	Full Name of Spouse	Marr.					
		Death					
		Burial					
M	4 Otis Fittro	Birth					
		Marr.					

MARRIAGE LICENSE.

State of Kansas, Chautauqua County, ss.

Sedan, Kansas, March 6th A.D. 1904

To any Person Authorized by Law to Perform the Marriage Ceremony, Greeting:

YOU ARE HEREBY AUTHORIZED TO JOIN IN MARRIAGE

(Seal) George Hafeker of Elgin Kans, aged 21 years,
and Della M Moore of Elgin Kans, aged 19 years,
and of this License you will make due return to my office within thirty days.

W T Studey, Probate Judge

State of Kansas, Chautauqua County, ss.

I, W T Studey, do hereby certify, that in accordance with the authorization of the within License, I did, on the 6 day of March A.D. 1904 at Sedan in said County, join and unite in Marriage the above named George Hafeker and Della M Moore

Witness my Hand and Seal, the day and year above written.

W T Studey, Probate Judge

Filed 6 day of March 1904.
W T Studey, Probate Judge

IN THE MATTER OF THE ESTATE OF
T.W. Smith, DECEASED.

State of Kansas, Chautauqua County, ss.

J.E. Moore being sworn says: That he was the husband of Julia B. Moore, deceased, formerly Julia B. Smith. That said Julia B. Moore died on or about the 17 day of June 1902. That the following and no other children were born to said Julia B. Moore, to-wit:

Name	Age	Place of Residence
Della Moore	28	Bartles, Okla
Rosa Moore	26	Elgin, Kans
Eva Moore	24	Elgin, Ks
Clara Moore	20	Elgin, Ks
Lester Moore	18	Elgin, Ks
Clyde Moore	16	Elgin, Ks

and further affiant saith not.

J M Moore

Subscribed in my presence and sworn to before me this 26 day of July, 1913.

Notary Public

January 22 1914

Family Group Sheet

Husband's Full Name: Marsh Ecker

Chart No.:

Husband's Data	Day Month Year	City, Town or Place	County or Province, etc.	State or Country	Add. Info on Husband
Birth					
Chr'nd					
Marr	1903	Sedan	Chautauqua Co.	Kans.	
Death					
Burial					

Places of Residence: Chautauqua County
Occupation: **Church Affiliation:**   **Military Rec:**

His Father: **Mother's Maiden Name:**

Wife's Full Maiden Name: Rosa Moore

Wife's Data	Day Month Year	City, Town or Place	County or Province, etc.	State or Country	Add. Info on Wife
Birth	8-9-1887				
Chr'nd					
Death	2-1927				Pneumonia
Burial					

Places of Residence: Chautauqua Co.
Occupation: **Church Affiliation:**   **Military Rec:**

Other husbands: Jess Crawford
Her Father: James Monroe Moore   **Mother's Maiden Name:** Julia Belle Smith

Sex	Children's Names in Full	Children's Data	Day Month Year	City, Town or Place	County or Province, etc.	State or Country	Add. Info on Children
F	1 Minnie Ecker	Birth/Marr./Death/Burial					
M	2 George Ecker	Birth/Marr./Death/Burial					
M	3 Leroy Crawford	Birth/Marr./Death/Burial					
F	4 Lillie Crawford	Birth/Marr./Death/Burial					
	5 Infant Crawford	Birth/Marr./Death/Burial					
F	6 Julia Bell Crawford	Birth/Marr./Death/Burial					
M	7 Jerry Crawford	Birth/Marr./Death/Burial					
M	8 Jo Crawford	Birth/Marr./Death/Burial					

Compiler: **Notes:**
Address:
City, State, Zip:
Date:

Family Group Sheet

Husband's Full Name: E. Harve Riley — **Chart No.**

	Day Month Year	City, Town or Place	County or Province, etc.	State or Country	Add. Info on Husband
Birth	1878				
Chr'nd					
Marr.					
Death	1964				
Burial					

Places of Residence:
Occupation: **Church Affiliation:** **Military Rec:**

His Father: **Mother's Maiden Name:**

Wife's Full Maiden Name: Eva V. Moore

	Day Month Year	City, Town or Place	County or Province, etc.	State or Country	Add. Info on Wife
Birth	14-11-1889		Osage Co.	Oklahoma	
Chr'nd					
Death	1967				
Burial					

Places of Residence:
Occupation: **Church Affiliation:** **Military Rec:**

Her Father: James Monroe Moore **Mother's Maiden Name:** Julia Belle Smith

Sex	Children's Names / Spouse		Day Month Year	City, Town or Place	County or Province, etc.	State or Country	Add. Info on Children
F	1. Stella Riley	Birth	4-2-1906	Sedan	Chautauqua Co.	Kans.	
	Spouse: L. Newton Mayo	Marr.	23-6-1924	Winfield		Kans.	
		Death					
		Burial					
F	2. Cora Riley	Birth					
	Spouse:	Marr.					
		Death					
		Burial					
M	3. Edward Monroe Riley	Birth	4-8-1883	Louisville		Kentucky	
	Spouse: Mary Verlynn Kelley	Marr.	22-8-1936	Sedan		Kansas	
		Death	29-1-1963				
		Burial	1-2-1963				
F	4. Nila Riley	Birth					
	Spouse:	Marr.					
		Death					
		Burial					
M	5. Ralph Riley	Birth					
	Spouse:	Marr.					
		Death					
		Burial					
M	6. Gilbert Riley	Birth					
	Spouse:	Marr.					
		Death					
		Burial					

MARRIAGE AFFIDAVIT.

State of Kansas, Chautauqua County, ss.

In the Probate Court of said County and State.

E H Riley, who now here makes application for MARRIAGE LICENSE, addressed to any person authorized by law to join in Marriage the said E H Riley, aged 24 years, and Eva V Moore, aged 14 years, being by me first duly sworn, doth say, that they have the unqualified consent of their parents to their marriage, and that neither of said parties has been divorced by the decree of any Court in this State within six months last past.

And that they, the said E H Riley and Eva V Moore are not related to each other in the degrees prohibited by law, to wit: Parent and child, grandparent and grandchild of any degree, brother and sister of either of the one-half or of the whole blood, uncle and niece aunt and nephew, nor first cousins; and that there exists no legal impediment to said marriage.

E. H. Riley

IN TESTIMONY WHEREOF, I, the undersigned, Judge of the Probate Court in and for Chautauqua County, and ex-officio Clerk thereof, have hereunto subscribed my name and affixed the seal of said Court, at my office, this 28 day of Sept 1904

(Seal)

No. 365

W H Study

Filed 28 day of Sept 1904

W H Study, Probate Judge

MARRIAGE LICENSE.

State of Kansas, Chautauqua County, ss.

Sedan, Kansas, Sept 28, A. D. 1904.

To any Person Authorized by Law to Perform the Marriage Ceremony, Greeting:

YOU ARE HEREBY AUTHORIZED TO JOIN IN MARRIAGE

(Seal) E H Riley of Chautauqua, aged 24 years, and Eva V Moore of " , aged 14 years, and of this License you will make due return to my office within thirty days.

W H Study, Probate Judge

State of Kansas, Chautauqua County, ss.

I, W H Study, do hereby certify, that in accordance with the authorization of the within License, I did, on the 28 day of Sept A.D. 1904 at Sedan in said County, join and unite in Marriage the above named E H Riley and Eva V Moore

Witness my Hand and Seal, the day and year above written.

Filed 28 day of Sept 1904

W H Study, Probate Judge
W H Study, Probate Judge

Family Group Sheet

Husband's Full Name: L. Newton Mayo SS 511-03-3565 Chart No.

Husband's Data	Day Month Year	City, Town or Place	County or Province, etc.	State or Country	Add. Info on Husband
Birth	7-4-1902				
Chr'nd					
Marr	23-6-1924	Winfield		Kansas	
Death	7-1979	Belmond	Kingman Co.	Kansas	
Burial	7-1979				

Places of Residence:

Occupation: Church Affiliation: Military Rec:

Other wives if any:

His Father: Mother's Maiden Name:

Wife's Full Maiden Name: Stella Riley SS 514-10-7143

Wife's Data	Day Month Year	City, Town or Place	County or Province, etc.	State or Country	Add. Info on Wife
Birth	4-2-1906	New Sedan	Chautauqua Co.	Kansas	
Chr'nd					
Death	1-1993	New Salem	Cowley Co.	Kansas	
Burial	1-1993	New Salem	Cowley Co.	Kansas	

Places of Residence:

Occupation: Church Affiliation: Military Rec:

Other husbands: Frank Schisler (b) 20 May, 1906 (M) 1947 died 30 Dec. 1988

Her Father: Harve Riley Mother's Maiden Name: Eva Moore

Sex	Children's Names in Full	Children's Data	Day Month Year	City, Town or Place	County or Province, etc.	State or Country	Add. Info on Children
M	1 Roy Mayo	Birth	4-4-1925	Winfield		Kans.	
		Marr.	1-1943				
	Full Name of Spouse: Norma Lee Chaplin	Death					
		Burial					
M	2 Richard Dean Mayo	Birth	4-4-1928	Winfield		Kansas	
		Marr.	13-10-1945				
	Full Name of Spouse: Irene Edmonds	Death					
		Burial					
F	3 Emogene Ethel Mayo	Birth	12-5-1929	Winfield		Kansas	
		Marr.	22-10-1946	Winfield		Kansas	
	Full Name of Spouse: Melvin O. Bear	Death					
		Burial					
M	4 Charles Leo Mayo	Birth	28-8-1934				
		Marr.	23-5-1953				
	Full Name of Spouse: Wretha Van Fossen	Death					
		Burial					
	5	Birth					
		Marr.					
	Full Name of Spouse	Death					
		Burial					
	6	Birth					
		Marr.					
	Full Name of Spouse	Death					
		Burial					
	7	Birth					
		Marr.					
	Full Name of Spouse	Death					
		Burial					
	8	Birth					
		Marr.					
	Full Name of Spouse	Death					
		Burial					

Compiler: Notes:

Address:

City, State, Zip:

Date:

Family Group Sheet

Husband's Full Name William Roy Mayo — **Chart No.**

	Day Month Year	City, Town or Place	County or Province, etc.	State or Country	Add. Info on Husband
Birth	4-4-1925	Winfield	Cowley Co.	Kansas	
Chr'nd					
Marr	8-1-1944	Winfield	Cowley Co.	Kansas	
Death					
Burial					

Places of Residence

Occupation — **Church Affiliation** — **Military Rec**

His Father L Newton Mayo — **Mother's Maiden Name** Stella Riley

Wife's Full Maiden Name Norma Lee Chaplin

	Day Month Year	City, Town or Place	County or Province, etc.	State or Country	Add. Info on Wife
Birth					
Chr'nd					
Death					
Burial					

Places of Residence

Occupation — **Church Affiliation** — **Military Rec**

Her Father — **Mother's Maiden Name**

Sex	Children's Names in Full		Day Month Year	City, Town or Place	County or Province, etc.	State or Country	Add. Info on Children
F 1	Judy Mayo	Birth					
	Full Name of Spouse	Marr.					
		Death					
		Burial					
F 2	Janice Mayo	Birth					
		Marr.					

IN THE PROBATE COURT OF COWLEY COUNTY, KANSAS

MARRIAGE AFFIDAVIT — LICENSE NO. N6881

STATE OF KANSAS, COUNTY OF COWLEY, SS.

The undersigned hereby applies to the above named court that a marriage license shall issue authorizing the joining in marriage of: William Roy Mayo, aged 21 years, of Winfield, Kansas, and Norma Lee Chaplin, aged 19 years, of Winfield, Kansas, and being first duly sworn, states:

That each of the above named parties is of the age set opposite his name; is unmarried; and has not been divorced within six months last past.

That the contracting parties are not related to each other in any of the degrees prohibited by law.

That neither of the parties is or has been epileptic, feeble minded, imbecile, or insane; and that neither party was born subsequent to the insanity of his or her parents or either of them.

That no legal impediment to the marriage of the above named parties exists to the knowledge of the undersigned applicant.

William Roy Mayo, Applicant

Subscribed and sworn to before me this 8th day of January, 1944.

Sallie O. Atherton, Notary Public—Probate Judge

My commission expires _____

GROOM: Color White — Married before No — Divorced No — Birthplace Kansas

BRIDE: Color White — Married before No — Divorced No — Birthplace Kansas

State of Kansas, Central Division of Vital Statistics

MARRIAGE LICENSE No. N6881

In the Probate Court of Cowley County, January 8th, 1944.

To Any Person in the State of Kansas Authorized by Law to Perform the Marriage Ceremony, Greeting:

YOU ARE HEREBY AUTHORIZED TO JOIN IN MARRIAGE William Roy Mayo, of Winfield, Kansas, Age 21, and Norma Lee Chaplin, of Winfield, Kansas, Age 19, With the consent of _____ and of this license, duly indorsed, you will make return to my office at Winfield, Kansas, within ten days after performing the ceremony.

Sallie O. Atherton, Probate Judge

ENDORSEMENT

TO WHOM IT MAY CONCERN: I hereby certify that I performed the ceremony joining in marriage the above-named couple, on the 8 day of January, 1944, at Arkansas City, Kansas.

Signed Edwin G. Michael
Title Pastor Central Christian Church
Address Arkansas City, Kansas

Family Group Sheet

Husband's Full Name: Richard Dean Mayo — **Chart No.**

	Day Month Year	City, Town or Place	County or Province, etc.	State or Country	Add. Info on Husband
Birth	4- 4-1928	Winfield	Cowley Co.	Kans.	
Chr'nd					
Marr	13-10-1945	Winfield	Cowley Co.	Kans.	
Death					
Burial					

Places of Residence:
Occupation: Santa Fe R.R. **Church Affiliation:** **Military Rec:**

His Father: L. Newton Mayo **Mother's Maiden Name:** Stella Riley

Wife's Full Maiden Name: Irene Edmonds

	Day Month Year	City, Town or Place	County or Province, etc.	State or Country	Add. Info on Wife
Birth					
Chr'nd					
Death					
Burial					

Places of Residence:
Occupation: **Church Affiliation:** **Military Rec:**

Her Father: **Mother's Maiden Name:**

Children

Sex	Children's Names in Full		Day Month Year	City, Town or Place	County or Province, etc	State or Country	Add. Info on Children
F	1	Mayo Virginia Louise	Birth / Marr. / Death / Burial				
F	2	Mayo Kathryn Irene	Birth / Marr. / Death / Burial				
M	3	John Michael Mayo	Birth / Marr. / Death / Burial				
M	4	Richard Dean Mayo, Jr.	Birth / Marr. / Death / Burial				
M	5	Mayo William Joseph	Birth / Marr. / Death / Burial				

IN THE PROBATE COURT OF COWLEY COUNTY, KANSAS

MARRIAGE AFFIDAVIT

STATE OF KANSAS, COUNTY OF COWLEY } SS.   LICENSE NO. 18268

The undersigned hereby applies to the above named court that a marriage license shall issue authorizing the joining in marriage of:

Richard Dean Mayo, aged 17 years, of Winfield, Kansas
and Georgia Irene Edmonds, aged 17 years, of Winfield, Kansas
and being first duly sworn, states:

That each of the above named parties is of the age set opposite his name; is unmarried; and has not been divorced within six months last past.

That the contracting parties are not related to each other in any of the degrees prohibited by law.

That neither of the parties is or has been epileptic, feeble minded, imbecile, or insane; and that neither party was born subsequent to the insanity of his or her parents or either of them.

That no legal impediment to the marriage of the above named parties exist to the knowledge of the undersigned applicant.

Richard Dean Mayo, Applicant

Subscribed and sworn to before me this 13th day of October 1945.

(SEAL)   Sallie O. Atkinson, Notary Public—Probate Judge

My commission expires ____

GROOM: Color White, Married before No, Divorced No, Birthplace Kansas
BRIDE: Color White, Married before No, Divorced No, Birthplace Kansas

---

State of Kansas, Central Division of Vital Statistics

MARRIAGE LICENSE

In the Probate Court of Cowley County, October 13, 1945

To Any Person in the State of Kansas Authorized by Law to Perform the Marriage Ceremony, Greeting:

YOU ARE HEREBY AUTHORIZED TO JOIN IN MARRIAGE

Richard Dean Mayo, of Winfield, Kansas, Age 17 (Groom)
Georgia Irene Edmonds, of Winfield, Kansas, Age 17 (Bride)

With the consent of L.N. Mayo, Father of groom / Ellen Edmonds, Mother of bride

and of this license, duly endorsed, you will make return to my office at Winfield, Kansas, within ten days after performing the ceremony.

(SEAL)   Sallie O. Atkinson, Probate Judge

ENDORSEMENT

TO WHOM IT MAY CONCERN:
I hereby certify that I performed the ceremony joining in marriage the above-named couple, on the 13th day of October, 1945, at Winfield, Kansas.

Signed: Lloyd E. Griffith
Title: Pastor First Baptist Church
Address: Winfield, Kans.

Family Group Sheet

Husband's Full Name Melvin O. Bear — **Chart No.**

	Day Month Year	City, Town or Place	County or Province, etc.	State or Country	Add. Info. on Husband
Birth					
Chr'nd					
Marr.	22-10-1946	Winfield	Cowley Co.	Kansas	
Death					
Burial					

Places of Residence

Occupation — Church Affiliation — Military Rec.

His Father — Mother's Maiden Name

Wife's Full Maiden Name Emogene Ethel Mayo

	Day Month Year	City, Town or Place	County or Province, etc.	State or Country	Add. Info. on Wife
Birth	12-5-1929	Winfield	Cowley Co.	Kansas	
Chr'nd					
Death					
Burial					

Places of Residence

Occupation — Church Affiliation — Military Rec.

Her Father L. Newton Mayo — Mother's Maiden Name Stella Riley

Sex	Children's Names in Full		Day Month Year	City, Town or Place	County or Province, etc.	State or Country	Add. Info. on Children
M	1. Melvin David Bear	Birth	22-10-1947				
		Marr.					
	Full Name of Spouse	Death					
		Burial					
	2.	Birth					
		Marr.					
	Full Name of Spouse	Death					
		Burial					
	3.	Birth					
		Marr.					
	Full Name of Spouse	Death					
		Burial					
	4.	Birth					
		Marr.					
	Full Name of Spouse	Death					
		Burial					
	5.	Birth					
		Marr.					
	Full Name of Spouse	Death					
		Burial					
	6.	Birth					
		Marr.					
	Full Name of Spouse	Death					
		Burial					
	7.	Birth					
		Marr.					
	Full Name of Spouse	Death					
		Burial					
	8.	Birth					
		Marr.					
	Full Name of Spouse	Death					
		Burial					

Compiler — Notes:

Address

City, State, Zip

Date

Family Group Sheet

Husband's Full Name: Charles Lee Mayo — Chart No. _____

Husband's Data	Day Month Year	City, Town or Place	County or Province, etc.	State or Country	Add. Info. on Husband
Birth	28-8-1934				
Chr'nd					
Marr	23-5-1953				
Death					
Burial					

Places of Residence:

Occupation: **Church Affiliation:**   **Military Rec:**

Other wives: Doris Dudeck from Atlanta Ks. married May 1955

His Father: L. Newton Mayo   **Mother's Maiden Name:** Stella Riley

Wife's Full Maiden Name: Wretha Van Fossen

Wife's Data	Day Month Year	City, Town or Place	County or Province, etc.	State or Country	Add. Info. on Wife
Birth		Council Grove	Morris Co.	Kansas	
Chr'nd					
Death					
Burial					

Places of Residence:

Occupation: **Church Affiliation:**   **Military Rec:**

Her Father: **Mother's Maiden Name:**

Sex	#	Children's Names in Full	Children's Data	Day Month Year	City, Town or Place	County or Province, etc.	State or Country	Add. Info. on Children
M	1	Randy Charles Mayo	Birth	20-4-1956				
		Full Name of Spouse	Marr. / Death / Burial					
M	2	Robin Keith Mayo	Birth	29-6-1957				
		Full Name of Spouse	Marr. / Death / Burial					
F	3	Keri Judith Mayo	Birth	25-12-1962				
		Full Name of Spouse	Marr. / Death / Burial					
F	4	Kelly Beth Mayo	Birth	26-7-1970				
		Full Name of Spouse	Marr. / Death / Burial					

Compiler: _____
Address: _____
City, State, Zip: _____
Date: _____
Notes: _____

Family Group Sheet

Husband's Full Name Collins — Chart No.

Husband's Data	Day	Month	Year	City, Town or Place	County or Province, etc.	State or Country	Add. Info. on Husband
Birth							
Chr'nd							
Marr.							
Death							
Burial							

Places of Residence

Occupation | Church Affiliation | Military Rec

Other wives, if any, No. (1)(2) etc. Make separate sheet for each marr.

His Father | Mother's Maiden Name

Wife's Full Maiden Name Cora Riley

Wife's Data	Day	Month	Year	City, Town or Place	County or Province, etc.	State or Country	Add. Info. on Wife
Birth							
Chr'nd							
Death							
Burial							

Places of Residence

Occupation | Church Affiliation | Military Rec

Other husbands, if any, No. (1)(2) etc. Make separate sheet for each marr.

Her Father E. Harve Riley | Mother's Maiden Name Eva V. Moore

Sex	#	Children's Names in Full (arranged in order of birth)	Children's Data	Day	Month	Year	City, Town or Place	County or Province, etc.	State or Country	Add. Info. on Children
M	1	William Bill Collins	Birth							
		Full Name of Spouse	Marr.							
			Death							
			Burial							
M	2	Lee Wayne Collins	Birth							
		Full Name of Spouse	Marr.							
			Death							
			Burial							
F	3	Mary Collins	Birth							
		Full Name of Spouse	Marr.							
			Death							
			Burial							
F	4	Helen Collins	Birth							
		Full Name of Spouse	Marr.							
			Death							
			Burial							
	5		Birth							
		Full Name of Spouse	Marr.							
			Death							
			Burial							
	6		Birth							
		Full Name of Spouse	Marr.							
			Death							
			Burial							
	7		Birth							
		Full Name of Spouse	Marr.							
			Death							
			Burial							
	8		Birth							
		Full Name of Spouse	Marr.							
			Death							
			Burial							

Compiler:
Address:
City, State, Zip:
Date:

Notes:

Family Group Sheet

Husband's Full Name Edward M. Riley SS-512-03-4780   Chart No.

Husband's Data	Day Month Year	City, Town or Place	County or Province, etc.	State or Country	Add. Info on Husband
Birth	2-2-1908	Near Sedan	Chautauqua Co.	Kansas	
Chr'nd					
Marr.	22-8-1936	Sedan	Chautauqua Co.	Kansas	
Death	23-3-1988	Bartlesville	Wash. Co.	Okla.	
Burial		Greenwood Cem. Sedan	Chautauqua Co.	Kansas	

Places of Residence: Elgin and Peru, Kansas
Occupation: Farmer-Oil Field-Rancher   Church Affiliation: Military Rec.
Other wives, if any: June Miller-Oct. 20, 1971 at Winfield, Kansas
His Father: E. Harve Riley   Mother's Maiden Name: Eva V. Moore

Wife's Full Maiden Name Mary Verlynn Kelly

Wife's Data	Day Month Year	City, Town or Place	County or Province, etc.	State or Country	Add. Info on Wife
Birth					
Chr'nd					
Death	6-1971				
Burial					

Places of Residence:
Occupation: Church Affiliation: Military Rec.
Other husbands, if any:
Her Father: Mother's Maiden Name:

Sex	Children's Names in Full	Children's Data	Day Month Year	City, Town or Place	County or Province, etc.	State or Country	Add. Info on Child
M	1 Carl Floyd Riley	Birth	9-5-1933				
		Marr.	9-7-1955				
	Full Name of Spouse: Wanda Finney	Death					
		Burial					
M	2 Claude Eugene R.	Birth	21-8-1937				
		Marr.	5-7-1956				
	Full Name of Spouse: Jerry Collins	Death					
		Burial					
F	3 Edna Arlene Riley	Birth	8-2-1939	E. of Chautauqua	Chau. Co.	Ks.	
		Marr.	12-11-1955				
	Full Name of Spouse: Roy Stephens	Death					
		Burial					
M	4 Curtis Armined R.	Birth	18-7-1941	Cherryville	Chaug. Co.	Ks.	
		Marr.					
	Full Name of Spouse	Death					
		Burial					
M	5 Adrian Monroe R.	Birth	8-10-1945	Cherryvale	Mont. Co.	Ks.	
		Marr.					
	Full Name of Spouse	Death					
		Burial					
M	6 Kenneth Armine R.	Birth	30-1-1948	Between Sedan-Peru	Chau. Co.	Ks.	
		Marr.					
	Full Name of Spouse	Death					
		Burial					
M	7 Steve William R.	Birth	18-8-1950	Pawhuska	Osage Co.	Okla.	
		Marr.					
	Full Name of Spouse	Death					
		Burial					
	8	Birth					
		Marr.					
	Full Name of Spouse	Death					
		Burial					

Compiler: Notes:
Address:
City, State, Zip:
Date:

Verlyn and Ed, Steve and son, Travis Riley. (Three generations)

Ed Riley, 21 years old.

Adrian Riley and his two children.

Edward M. Riley

CANEY — Edward M. Riley, 80, of rural Peru, died Wednesday at Jane Phillips Medical Center in Bartlesville, Okla.

Services will be held at 2 p.m. Friday at the Graves Memorial Chapel, with the Rev. Andy Daniels of the First Southern Baptist Church officiating. Burial will be in the Greenwood Cemetery at Sedan.

Friends may call at the funeral home tonight from 7 to 8 o'clock.

Mr. Riley was born Feb. 2, 1908, near Sedan, to Harvey and Eva (Moore) Riley.

On Aug. 22, 1936, he married Mary Verlynn Kelly at Sedan. She died in June 1971. He then married June Miller on Oct. 20, 1971, at Winfield. She survives at the home.

Mr. Riley worked as an oil field pumper, farmer and rancher. He was employed with the Rigdon-Bruen Oil Co. and the Phoenix Oil Co. He lived in the Elgin-Peru area all his life.

Other survivors include six sons, Carl Riley, Sedan, Steve Riley, Paola, Adrian Riley, Coffeyville, Gene Riley, Pleasant City, Ohio, Curtis Riley, Sheridan, Wyo., and Kenneth Riley, Adamsville, Tenn.; one daughter, Edna Stephens, Caney; one stepson, Calvin Miller, Wichita; one stepdaughter, Avanelle Walker, Wichita; one brother, Gilbert Riley, McCook, Neb.; and three sisters, Stella Schisler, Winfield, Cora Collins, Oklahoma City, Okla., and Nila Tackitt, Berthoud, Colo.; and 20 grandchildren and 23 great-grandchildren.

One brother is deceased.

The family has suggested memorials to the Leukemia Society or the American Heart Association.

Ed and Verlyn, Carl, Gene, Edna, Curtis, Adrian, Ken and Steve Riley. Easter 1956

Family Group Sheet

Husband's Full Name: Lois Virge Rector   **Chart No.**

Husband's Data	Day Month Year	City, Town or Place	County or Province, etc.	State or Country	Add. Info on Husband
Birth	30-1-1882			Kansas	
Chr'nd					
Marr	26-2-1913	Sedan	Chautauqua Co.	Kansas	
Death	5-2-1916				
Burial					

Places of Residence: Kansas
Occupation: **Church Affiliation:**   **Military Rec:**

His Father: Mack C. Rector   **Mother's Maiden Name:** Nancy Jane

Wife's Full Maiden Name: Clara S. Moore

Wife's Data	Day Month Year	City, Town or Place	County or Province, etc.	State or Country	Add. Info on Wife
Birth	20-2-1892	Elgin	Chautauqua Co.	Kansas	
Chr'nd					
Death	9-9-1926				
Burial	9-1926				

Places of Residence: Kansas - Oklahoma
Occupation: **Church Affiliation:**   **Military Rec:**

Other husbands: Guy Johnson
Her Father: James Monroe Moore   **Mother's Maiden Name:** Julia Belle Smith

Sex	Children's Names in Full	Children's Data	Day Month Year	City, Town or Place	County or Province, etc.	State or Country	Add. Info on Children
F	1. Louise Rector	Birth					lived short time
	Full Name of Spouse	Marr.					
		Death					
		Burial					
F	2. L. Marie Rector	Birth					
	Full Name of Spouse	Marr.					
		Death					
		Burial					
F	3. Virgie Bell Rector	Birth	21-8-1902			Kansas	
	Full Name of Spouse	Marr.					
		Death	1-1970	Wichita	Sedgwick Co.	Kans.	
		Burial					
F	4. Maxine Johnson	Birth					
	Full Name of Spouse	Marr.					
		Death					
		Burial					

251

Family Group Sheet

Husband's Full Name: Lester L. Moore **Chart No.**

	Day Month Year	City, Town or Place	County or Province, etc	State or Country	Add. Info on Husband
Birth	30-1-1895	Elgin	Chautauqua Co.	Kansas	
Chr'nd					
Marr	25-2-1920	Sedan	Chautauqua Co.	Kansas	Killed by a horse kicking him
Death	25-6-1920	Elgin	Chautauqua Co.	Kansas	
Burial	6-1920	Oak Grove cem.	Elgin Chautauqua Co.	Kansas	

Places of Residence:
Occupation: Farmer-Oil Field **Church Affiliation:** **Military Rec:** Army in 1918
His Father: James Monroe Moore **Mother's Maiden Name:** Julia Belle Smith

Wife's Full Maiden Name: Lida L. Carriker

	Day Month Year	City, Town or Place	County or Province, etc.	State or Country	Add. Info on Wife
Birth					
Chr'nd					
Death					
Burial					

Places of Residence:
Occupation: **Church Affiliation:** **Military Rec:**
Her Father: **Mother's Maiden Name:**

Sex	Children's Names in Full		Day Month Year	City, Town or Place	County or Province, etc	State or Country	Add. Info on Children
F	1 Moore Lessie Louise	Birth	12-1920	Sedan	Chautauqua Co.	Kans.	7yrs old died of Indigestion
	Full Name of Spouse	Marr.					
		Death	1927	Sedan	Chautauqua Co.	Kans.	
		Burial	1927	Oak Grove cem.	Elgin	Kans.	

Marriage Affidavit.

State of Kansas, Chautauqua County, ss. In the Probate Court in and for said County and State

Lester L. Moore hereby applies for a MARRIAGE LICENSE...

That said Lester L. Moore is 25 years of age
and that said Lida L. Carriker is aged 26 years.

IN WITNESS WHEREOF... Lester Moore
in Sedan this 25 day of February 1920.
E.E. Conner, Probate Judge

Marriage License.

State of Kansas, Chautauqua County, ss.
Sedan, Kansas, February 25, A.D. 1920

To any Person Authorized by Law to Perform the Marriage Ceremony, Greeting:
You are Hereby Authorized to Join in Marriage
Lester L. Moore of Elgin Kans. aged 25 years.
and Lida L. Carriker Chautauqua Kans. aged 26 years.

E.E. Conner, Probate Judge

State of Kansas, Chautauqua County, ss.
I, E.E. Conner, hereby certify... 25 day of February A.D. 1920 at Sedan Kansas... Lester L. Moore and Lida L. Carriker
E.E. Conner Probate Judge

MOORE
In memory of our son
LESTER LEROY
JAN 30 1895
JUNE 25 1920

Family Group Sheet

Husband's Full Name: Clyde Earl Moore SS-511-22-7414A   Chart No.

	Day Month Year	City, Town or Place	County or Province, etc.	State or Country	Add. Info. on Husband
Birth	31-7-1896	Oolagah	Rogers Co.	Okla.	
Chr'nd					
Marr	27-12-1922	Sedan	Chautauqua Co.	Kans.	
Death	26-8-1981	Sedan	Chautauqua Co.	Kansas	
Burial	8-1981	Oak Hill cem. Elgin	Chautauqua Co.	Kansas	

Places of Residence: Kansas
Occupation: Farmer-Oil Field   **Church Affiliation:**   **Military Rec:**

His Father: James Munroe Moore   **Mother's Maiden Name:** Julia Belle Smith

Wife's Full Maiden Name: Rhoda Ruth Carriker SS-510-68-7368

	Day Month Year	City, Town or Place	County or Province, etc.	State or Country	Add. Info. on Wife
Birth	13-12-1902	Oolagah	Rogers Co.	Okla.	
Chr'nd					
Death	12-6-1982	Bartlesville	Washington Co.	Okla.	
Burial	6-1982	Oak Hill cem. Elgin	Chautauqua Co.	Kansas	

Places of Residence:
Occupation: Housewife   **Church Affiliation:**   **Military Rec:**

Her Father: Paul Ruffin Carrikier   **Mother's Maiden Name:** Lucinda Knoth

Children

Sex	Children's Names / Spouse		Day Month Year	City, Town or Place	County or Province, etc.	State or Country
M	1 Paul Monroe Moore	Birth	9-12-1927	Elgin	Chautauqua Co.	Kansas
	Spouse: Margaret E. Kirchner	Marr.	18-5-1946	Chautauqua	Chau. Co.	Kansas
		Death				
		Burial				
F	2 Moore, Velda Pauline	Birth	6-11-1933	Elgin	Chautauqua Co.	Kansas
	Spouse: Woodrow Lee Talley	Marr.	5-5-1953		Lancaster Co.	Nebr.
		Death				
		Burial				
M	3 Allen Dale Moore	Birth	22-2-1940	Elgin	Chautauqua Co.	Kans.
	Spouse: Marilyn Stanley	Marr.	27-12-1976			
		Death				
		Burial				

Grave markers:
- RHODA R. MOORE DEC. 13 1902 — JUNE 12 1982
- CLYDE E. MOORE JULY 31 1896 — AUG. 26 1981

Attending Physician Certificate of Death — State of Oklahoma, Department of Health:
Rhoda R. Moore, died June 12, 1982, Bartlesville, Washington Co., Oklahoma. Jane Phillips Medical Center. Born Dec. 13, 1902. Homemaker. SS 510-68-7368. Father: Paul Ruffin Carriker. Mother: Lucinda Knott. Informant: Allen Moore, PO Box 303, Chautauqua, KS 67334. Burial: June 15, 1982, Oak Hill Cemetery, Chautauqua, KS. Neekamp F.H., Bartlesville, OK 74003 — Alan Graham. Physician: Daniel J. Houtman, M.D., 224 SE DeBell, Bartlesville, Okla. 74003.

Family Group Sheet

Husband's Full Name: Paul Moore
Chart No.:

	Day Month Year	City, Town or Place	County or Province, etc.	State or Country	Add. Info on Husband
Birth	9-12-1927	Elgin	Chautauqua Co.	Kansas	
Chr'nd					
Marr	18-5-1946	Chautauqua	Chautauqua Co.	Kansas	
Death					
Burial					

Places of Residence:
Occupation: Church Affiliation: Military Rec:

His Father: Clyde Earl Moore   **Mother's Maiden Name:** Rhoda Ruth Carrikier

Wife's Full Maiden Name: Margaret Kirchmer

	Day Month Year	City, Town or Place	County or Province, etc.	State or Country	Add. Info on Wife
Birth					
Chr'nd					
Death					
Burial					

Places of Residence:
Occupation: Church Affiliation: Military Rec:

Her Father: **Mother's Maiden Name:**

MARRIAGE AFFIDAVIT

The State of Kansas, Chautauqua County, ss.

IN THE PROBATE COURT OF SAID COUNTY AND STATE

Paul Moore hereby applies for a MARRIAGE LICENSE addressed to any minister or magistrate authorized by law to unite in matrimony Paul Moore and Margaret Kirchner and being duly sworn, deposes: That said Paul Moore is aged 18 years of age, and that said Margaret Kirchner is aged 19 years; that they have their parents' consent to said union and that neither has been divorced within six months last past.

That said contracting parties are not related to each other in any of the degrees prohibited by law, namely: Parent and child, grandparent and grandchild in any degree, brother and sister of the whole or the half blood, uncle or niece, aunt or nephew, nor first cousins.

That neither of said parties is or has been epileptic, imbecile, feeble minded or insane; or, if either or any have ever been so afflicted then that the woman is more than forty-five years of age.

And that neither party was born subsequent to the insanity of either of his or her parents, or, if so, that the one woman about to be married is more than forty-five years of age.

Signed: Paul Moore

Subscribed and sworn to before me, this 18 day of May, 1946.
(Seal)   Rathbun, Probate Judge

Filed May 18, 1946.
No. 4148   Rathbun, Probate Judge

Marriage License Record, Q
H. No. 12285
P. J. No. 4148
STATE OF KANSAS
CENTRAL DIVISION OF VITAL STATISTICS

MARRIAGE LICENSE

IN THE PROBATE COURT OF CHAUTAUQUA COUNTY   Sedan, Kansas, May 18, 1946

To Any Person Authorized by Law to Perform the Marriage Ceremony, GREETING:

YOU ARE HEREBY AUTHORIZED TO JOIN IN MARRIAGE

Paul Moore (Bridegroom) of Elgin, Kansas, age 18
Margaret Kirchner (Bride) of Elgin, Kansas, age 19

(SEAL) with the consent of Rhoda Moore (Name of Parent or Guardian Consenting)

and of this license, duly endorsed, you will make return to my office at Sedan, Kansas, within ten days after performing the ceremony.

Rathbun, Probate Judge

ENDORSEMENT

TO WHOM IT MAY CONCERN

I hereby certify that I performed the ceremony joining in marriage the above-named couple, on the 18th day of May, 1946, at Chautauqua, Kansas.

Signed: J. H. Ray
Title: Minister of the Gospel
Address: Chautauqua, Kansas

P 419

Compiler:
Address:
City, State, Zip:
Date:
Notes:

Family Group Sheet

Husband's Full Name: Woodrow Lee Talley SS-486-36-7457   Chart No.

Husband's Data	Day Month Year	City, Town or Place	County or Province, etc.	State or Country	Add. Info on Husband
Birth	22-2-1935	Western Grove		Ark.	
Chr'nd					
Marr	5-5-1953	Lincoln	Lancaster Co.	Nebraska	
Death	18-6-1993	Joplin	Jasper Co.	Mo.	
Burial	23-6-1993	Oak Hill cem. Elgin	Chautauqua Co.	Kansas	

Places of Residence: Elgin, Kansas
Occupation: **Church Affiliation:**   **Military Rec:**

His Father: William Franklin Talley   **Mother's Maiden Name:** Esther Ellen Boring

Wife's Full Maiden Name: Velda Pauline Moore

Wife's Data	Day Month Year	City, Town or Place	County or Province, etc.	State or Country	Add. Info on Wife
Birth	6-11-1933	Elgin	Chautauqua Co.	Kansas	
Chr'nd					
Death					
Burial					

Places of Residence: Elgin, Kansas
Occupation: **Church Affiliation:**   **Military Rec:**

Her Father: Clyde Earl Moore   **Mother's Maiden Name:** Rhonda Ruth Carrikier

Sex	Children's Names in Full		Day Month Year	City, Town or Place	County or Province, etc. State or Country	Add. Info on Children
M	1 James Lee Talley	Birth	21-1-1956	Cedarvale	Chautauqua Co. Ks.	
		Marr.	13-1-1984	Sedan	Chautauqua Co. Ks.	
	Full Name of Spouse	Death				
		Burial				
M	2 Leslie Dale Talley	Birth	9-1-1959	Sedan	Chautauqua Co. Ks.	
		Marr.				
	Full Name of Spouse	Death				
		Burial				
M	3 Larry Dean Talley	Birth	26-7-1960	Sedan	Chautauqua Co. Ks.	
		Marr.				
	Full Name of Spouse	Death				
		Burial				

WHEN THIS COPY CARRIES THE RAISED SEAL OF THE NEBRASKA HEALTH AND HUMAN SERVICES SYSTEM, IT CERTIFIES THE BELOW TO BE A TRUE COPY OF THE ORIGINAL RECORD ON FILE WITH THE NEBRASKA HEALTH AND HUMAN SERVICES SYSTEM, VITAL STATISTICS SECTION, WHICH IS THE LEGAL DEPOSITORY FOR VITAL RECORDS.

Stanley S. Cooper
STANLEY S. COOPER
ASSISTANT STATE REGISTRAR
HEALTH AND HUMAN SERVICES SYSTEM

DATE OF ISSUANCE
MAY 2 1997
LINCOLN, NEBRASKA

STATE OF NEBRASKA
DEPARTMENT OF HEALTH
BUREAU OF VITAL STATISTICS

Record of Marriage
Personal and Statistical Particulars

1. PLACE OF MARRIAGE
County of Lancaster
Township of ___
or
Village of ___
City of ___

2. State File No. 53 007223

Herbert A. Ronin
County Judge
Lancaster
County of ___

GROOM T-400 BRIDE M-600

	GROOM	BRIDE
3/4. Full Name	Woodrow Talley	Pauline Moore
5/6. Residence	Route #1 Anderson, Missouri	Route #1 Elgin, Kansas
7/8. Color or Race	White	White
9/10. Age at Last Birthday	22	19
11/12. Single, Widowed or Divorced	Single	Single
13/14. Number of Previous Marriages	None	Single
15/16. Birthplace	Missouri	Kansas
17/18. Occupation	Filling Station Attendant	None
19/20. Name of Father	William Talley	Clyde Moore
21/22. Birthplace of Father	Arkansas	Kansas
23/24. Maiden Name of Mother	Esther Borning	Rhoda Carriker
25/26. Birthplace of Mother	Kansas	North Carolina
27/28. If a minor, name of person consenting		Mother

29. Maiden Name of Bride if she were previously married ___ BLOOD RELATION, WHAT DEGREE None
30. Date of License May 5, 1953
31. License Record Number 96-73
32. Date of Marriage May 5, 1953
33. By Whom the Marriage Ceremony was Performed and Official Title
Herbert A. Ronin, County Judge
Witness: Jeane E. Shankland Address: Lancaster County, Nebraska
Witness: Virginia Tate Address: Lancaster County, Nebraska

CERTIFICATE OF DEATH — KANSAS STATE DEPARTMENT OF HEALTH AND ENVIRONMENT, VITAL STATISTICS

File No. 134-3 SEP 8 1981

CLYDE E. MOORE — Male — Aug. 26, 1981 — Age 85
Born: July 31, 1896 — White — American
Place of Death: Chautauqua, Sedan, Sedan City Hosp. — DOA
Oklahoma, USA — Married — Rhoda Carriker — NO
SSN: 511-22-7414-A — Farmer — Farm
Kansas — Chautauqua — Chautauqua — P.O. Box 233 — 67334 — No
Father: James M. Moore Mother: Julia B. Smith
Mrs. Rhoda Moore — P.O. Box 233 Chautauqua, KS, 67334
Burial: Oak Hill Cemetery, Chautauqua, KS.
Del Huggins 2898 Graves-Baird Sedan, KS, 6736
08-28-81 1:00 pm
Elmer W. Taylor, M.D., P.O. Box 8, Sedan, KS 67361
9-3-1981
Cardio Vascular Accident — minutes
Hypertension; Emphysema

WOODROW L. "WOODY" TALLEY
FEB. 22 1935 — JUNE 18 1993

CERTIFICATE OF DEATH — STATE FILE NUMBER 124-

TALLEY — MALE — JUNE 18, 1993
Age 50 — Date of Birth: FEBRUARY 22, 1935 — Birthplace: WESTERN GROVE, ARKANSAS
Place of Death: REGIONAL MEDICAL CENTER — JOPLIN — JASPER — ER/Outpatient
Surviving Spouse: PAULINE MOORE
Usual Occupation: FOREMAN — FLORIST GREENHOUSE
City: SEDAN — County: CHAUTAUQUA — Zip: 67371
Race: WHITE — Education: 12
Father: FRANKLIN TALLEY Mother: ESTHER ELLEN BORING
Mailing Address: RT 1 BOX 121 SEDAN, KANSAS 67361
Date of Disposition: JUNE 23, 1993 — OAK HILL CEMETERY — CHAUTAUQUA, KANSAS
Funeral: THORNHILL-DILLON MORTUARY — P.O. BOX 134 JOPLIN, MISSOURI 64802 — License 28
Cause: Acute Myocardial Infarction
Due to: Arteriosclerotic heart disease

Certifier: Robert H. Ball — July 7, 1993 — 4:47 P
Carthage, Mo. — Jasper Co. — Coroner
Registrar: Monica Canfield/Public Health — July 9, 1993

THIS IS A CERTIFIED COPY OF AN ORIGINAL DOCUMENT.
REPRODUCTION OF THIS DOCUMENT IS PROHIBITED BY LAW (section 193.315, RSMo Supp. 1984)

STATE OF MISSOURI — I HEREBY CERTIFY that this is an exact reproduction of the certificate for the person named therein as it now appears in the permanent records of the Bureau of Vital Records of the Missouri Department of Health. Witness my hand as County Registrar of Vital Statistics and the Seal of the Missouri Department of Health.
Date: July 9, 1993
William Gary, William Gary

Name of Deceased: CLYDE E. MOORE
Died: 1:10 P.M., Date 26 August, 1981, Age 85 Years 0 Months 21 Days
Place of Residence: P.O. Box 233—Chautauqua, KS. 67334 Place of Death: DOA Sedan City Hosp.
Cause of Death: ___
Name of Doctor: Dr. Taylor
Father's Name: James M. Moore
Mother's Maiden Name: Julia B. Smith
Name Before Marriage: ___
Date of Birth: 31 July 1896 Place of Birth: Oblagah, OK.
Places of Residence from Birth to Present with Dates: Lived in Chautauqua Co. Since a Small Child
Social Security No.: 511-22-7414-A Veteran: No
Length of Residence in City Where Death Occurred: ___
Wife's or Husband's Birthdate: 13 December 1902 Social Security No.: 511-22-7414-A
Wife's or Husband's Birthplace: Oblagah, OK.
Informant: Mrs. Rhoda Moore
Married, Date: 12/27/1922 Place: Sedan, KS. To: Rhoda Carriker Is he or she still living? Yes
Occupation, War Service, Activity in Church, School or Public Affairs: Farmer
Membership in Church and Fraternal Organizations: ___

Children Living: 1 Daughter, 2 Sons
Mrs. Woodrow (Pauline) Talley — Chautauqua, KS.
Paul Moore — Chautauqua, KS.
Allen Moore — Elgin, KS.

Children Who Have Passed Away: Daughter — Sons
Grandchildren: 13 Great-Grandchildren: 10
Sisters and Brothers Living: ___

Parents Surviving and Address: ___
Date and Hour of Funeral: Saturday 8/29/81 10:00 A.M.
Place: GRAVES-BAIRD CHAPEL
Name of Minister: Rev. Dale Nix
Interment in: Oak Hill Cemetery of: Chautauqua, KS.
Body Resting at: ___

MOORE, Clyde E.
26 August 1981 Sidman, OK
8133 Oak Hill

Family Group Sheet

Husband's Full Name: James Lee Talley — Chart No. _____

	Day Month Year	City, Town or Place	County or Province, etc.	State or Country	Add. Info. on Husband
Birth	21-1-1956	Cedarvale	Chautauqua Co.	Kansas	
Chr'nd					
Marr	13-1-1984	Sedan	Chautauqua Co.	Kansas	
Death					
Burial					

Places of Residence:
Occupation: ___ Church Affiliation: ___ Military Rec: ___

His Father: Woodrow Lee Talley **Mother's Maiden Name:** Velda Pauline Moore

Wife's Full Maiden Name: Melissa Jean Gilmore

	Day Month Year	City, Town or Place	County or Province, etc.	State or Country	Add. Info. on Wife
Birth					
Chr'nd					
Death					
Burial					

Places of Residence:
Occupation: ___ Church Affiliation: ___ Military Rec: ___

Her Father: ___ **Mother's Maiden Name:** ___

License No. 60783

STATE OF KANSAS
THE KANSAS STATE DEPARTMENT OF HEALTH AND ENVIRONMENT
Bureau of Vital Statistics

Marriage License

D.C. No. 84-M-2

In the District Court of Chautauqua County, January 13th 1984

To Any Person in the State of Kansas Authorized by Law to Perform the Marriage Ceremony, Greetings:

YOU ARE HEREBY AUTHORIZED TO JOIN IN MARRIAGE

James Lee Talley (Name of Groom) of Chautauqua, Kansas (Residence—City & State) Age 27

Melissa Jean Gilmore of Sedan, Kansas (Residence—City & State) Age 21

with the consent of ___ (Name of parent or guardian consenting)

and with this license duly endorsed, you will make return to my office at Sedan, Kansas, within ten days after performing the ceremony.

Name and Title of Court Official: Judge

ENDORSEMENT

TO WHOM IT MAY CONCERN:

I hereby certify that I, the undersigned, performed the ceremony joining in marriage the above named couple on the 13 day of January, 1984, at Sedan, Kansas, in Chautauqua County. My credentials are recorded in the D.C.'s office of ___ Co., Ks.

Signed: ___
Title: District Magistrate Judge
Address: Sedan, Kansas

Signatures of Witnesses:
Lynn Sanders
Donna Dunnigan

DATE RECEIVED BY DISTRICT COURT: 1/13 1984
DATE RECORDED BY DISTRICT COURT: 1/13 1984

NOTE.—After recording, the judge shall forward this original marriage license to the State Registrar, Topeka, Kansas, not later than the third day of following month.

257

Family Group Sheet

Husband's Full Name Allen Dale Moore — **Chart No.**

	Day Month Year	City, Town or Place	County or Province, etc.	State or Country	Add. Info on Husband
Birth	22-2-1940	Elgin	Chautauqua Co.	Kansas	
Chr'nd					
Marr	10-9-1963	Peru	Chautauqua Co	Kansas	
Death					
Burial					

Places of Residence

Occupation — Church Affiliation — Military Rec

Other wives: Janet Palmer married March 7, 1963

His Father Clyde Earl Moore — **Mother's Maiden Name** Rhoda Ruth Carrikier

Wife's Full Maiden Name Marilyn Stanley

	Day Month Year	City, Town or Place	County or Province, etc.	State or Country	Add. Info on Wife
Birth	28-8-				
Chr'nd					
Death					
Burial					

Places of Residence

Occupation — Church Affiliation — Military Rec

Her Father — **Mother's Maiden Name**

Sex	Children's Names in Full		Day Month Year	City, Town or Place	County or Province, etc.	State or Country	Add. Info on Children
F	1 Vickie Jan Moore	Birth	13-12-	Cedarvale	Chautauqua Co.	Ks.	
	Full Name of Spouse	Marr.					
		Death					
		Burial					
M	2 Jayen Dale Moore	Birth	8-1979	Independence	Mont. Co.	Ks.	
	Full Name of Spouse	Marr.					
		Death					
		Burial					
F	3 Moore Marla Darlene	Birth	27-8-1981	Independence	Mont. Co.	Kans.	
		Marr.					

MARRIAGE APPLICATION AND AFFIDAVIT

The State of Kansas, Chautauqua County, ss. No. 68258 P.J. No. 620

IN THE PROBATE COURT IN AND FOR SAID COUNTY AND STATE

Allen D. Moore of Elgin, State of Kansas, hereby makes application to marry Janet Sherril Palmer of Peru, State of Kansas, and further applies for a marriage license addressed to any person authorized by law to unite said parties in marriage; being duly sworn deposes:

That said Allen D. Moore is 23 years of age and that he has no living wife and that the said Janet Sherril Palmer is 18 years of age and that she has no living husband; and that neither party has been divorced within the past six months.

That said contracting parties are not related to each other in any of the degrees prohibited by law to-wit: Parent or Child, grandparent and grandchild in any degree, brother and sister of the whole or the half blood, uncle or niece, aunt or nephew, nor first cousins.

That the following questions are truthfully answered

(1) Have you or has the person you are expecting to marry ever been adjudicated insane or afflicted with feeble mindedness? No
(2) If your answer to question number (1) is yes, have all the persons adjudicated been discharged or restored? ___
That there is no legal impediment to such marriage, to the best of the affiant's knowledge and belief.

Further affiant saith not. (Signed) Allen D. Moore / Janet Palmer

Subscribed and sworn to before me this 9th day of March, 1963.
Elizabeth A. Dunn, Probate Judge

Application Filed 3-7 1963

Health Cert'f: File 2210 No. 2211
Vol. ___ Page ___ Vol. ___ Page ___
Name of Parent or Guardian Consenting (Groom)
Name of Parent or Guardian Consenting (Bride)

No. 68258
P.J. No. 620

THE KANSAS STATE BOARD OF HEALTH
DIVISION OF VITAL STATISTICS

MARRIAGE LICENSE

IN THE PROBATE COURT OF CHAUTAUQUA COUNTY, March 9, 1963

To Any Person in the State of Kansas Authorized by Law to Perform the Marriage Ceremony, GREETING:

YOU ARE HEREBY AUTHORIZED TO JOIN IN MARRIAGE

Allen D. Moore of Elgin, Kansas, Age 23 (Groom)
Janet Sherril Palmer of Peru, Kansas, Age 18 (Bride)

with the consent of ___ (Name of Parent or Guardian Consenting)

and of this license, duly endorsed, you will make return to my office at Sedan, Kansas, within ten days after performing the ceremony.

(SEAL) Elizabeth A. Dunn, Probate Judge

ENDORSEMENT

TO WHOM IT MAY CONCERN:
I hereby certify that I have performed the ceremony joining in marriage the above-named couple, on the 10th day of March, 1963, at Peru, Kansas.

Signed Robert M. Craig
Title Methodist Minister
Address Sedan, Kansas

Filed 3-20 1963 Elizabeth A. Dunn

UNITED STATES OF AMERICA (SEAL)   Dated September 26, 1877
R. B. Hayes, President

                                 Filed for record November 3, 1877
      To   and recorded in Volume P of Deeds
                                 at page 332 of the records of
Robert L. Taylor   Butler County, Kansas

Patent

Consideration-Homestead

Description- North East ¼ of section 10, Township 25, Range 3 East
160 acres.

STATE OF KANSAS)
COUNTY OF BUTLER) SS   IN THE PROBATE COURT IN AND FOR SAID COUNTY

On this 18th day of February, A. D. 1878 personally appeared in
open court before me the undersigned Judge of the said court Jane
Taylor of lawful age who being by me first duly sworn according to
law, doth upon her oath depose and say that Robert L. Taylor, died
on the 25th day of January A. D. 1878, in the County of Butler and
State aforesaid, that to the best of her knowledge and belief the names
and places of residence of the heirs of the said deceased are as
follows, to-wit:
Jane Taylor, widow of deceased
Mary E. Taylor,
John Taylor
James Taylor
David F. Taylor
Harvey T. Taylor
Grace J. Taylor, Caribou Butler County, Kansas and
Harriet Casebeer, Elgin Kansas.
William H. Taylor Pilate, Illinois
and that deceased died without a will as affiant verily believes
and affiant further states that the said Robert L. Taylor died siezed
and possessed of certain real and personal estate consisting chiefly
of Real estate all of said Estate being estimated to be worth about
$2,385. Dollars.
                                 Jane Taylor

    Sworn to and subscribed before me the day and year above written.
(SEAL)   S. E. Black, Probate Judge
    Your petitioner would therefore respectfully pray that your
Honorable court will grant letters of Administration on the Estate of
Robert L. Taylor deceased to Jane Taylor and giving bonds as the law
directs.
    Dated this 18th day of February, A. D. 1878.
                           Jane Taylor

STATE OF KANSAS, Butler County, ss
    Upon examination and no person appearing to object it appearing
to this court that the facts alledged in the foregoing petition are
true it is therefore ordered and adjudged that the prayers thereof be
granted and that administration on the estate of said deceased be
granted to Jane Taylor she giving bonds as the law directs.
    In Testimony Thereof I do hereunto sign my name and affix the seal

Family Group Sheet

Husband's Full Name: John Ira Taylor **Chart No.**

	Day Month Year	City, Town or Place	County or Province, etc.	State or Country	Add. Info on Husband
Birth	29- 3-1857	Milton	Jefferson Co.	Indiana	
Chr'nd					
Marr.	4- 7-1881		Butler Co.	Kansas	
Death	4- 2-1949	Axtell	Marshall Co.	Kansas	
Burial	2-1949	Altoona	Wilson Co.	Kansas	

Places of Residence:
Occupation: Blacksmith Church Affiliation: Military Rec:

His Father: Robert Lackey Taylor **Mother's Maiden Name:** Jenny (Jane) Weir

Wife's Full Maiden Name: Melissa Rebecca Moore

	Day Month Year	City, Town or Place	County or Province, etc.	State or Country	Add. Info. on Wife
Birth	19-12-1862	Lawrence	Douglas Co.	Kansas	
Chr'nd					
Death	30- 4-1923	Berryville	Carroll Co.	Ark.	
Burial	4-1923	Altoona	Wilson Co.	Kansas	

Places of Residence:
Occupation: Housewife Church Affiliation: Military Rec:

Her Father: Reuben Moore **Mother's Maiden Name:** Melvina Barbara Paul

Sex	Children's Names in Full		Day Month Year	City, Town or Place	County or Province, etc.	State or Country	Add. Info. on Children
F	1 Taylor, Melvina (Vina)	Birth	10- 5-1882	Elgin	Chautauqua Co.	Ks.	
		Marr.	31- 8-1907	Fredonia	Wilson Co.	Ks.	
	Full Name of Spouse: Bernard Hagstrom	Death	6- 2-1945				
		Burial					
M	2 Carl William Taylor	Birth	16- 6-1884		Butler Co.	Ks.	
		Marr.	2- 5-1906	Fredonia	Wilson Co.	Ks.	
	Full Name of Spouse: Elizabeth Johnson	Death	22- 2-1972	Mesa	Maricopa Co.	Ariz.	
		Burial	24- 2-1972	East Resthaven Phoenix		Ariz.	
F	3 Taylor, Mabel Blanche	Birth	1-12-1886		Butler Co.	Kans.	
		Marr.	6- 4-1906	Altoona	Wilson Co.	Kans.	
	Full Name of Spouse: John Ira Crossfield	Death	23- 4-1960	Eureka	Greenwood Co.		
		Burial	26- 4-1960	Altoona	Wilson Co.	Kans.	
M	4 James Orcen Taylor	Birth	19-10-1890	Altoona	Wilson Co.	Kans.	
		Marr.					
	Full Name of Spouse:	Death	5-1964	Newkirk	Kay co.	Okla.	
		Burial					
F	5 Gladys Hazel Taylor	Birth	14-11-1895	Newkirk	Kay Co.	Okla.	
		Marr.	25- 8-1959	Toronto	Woodson Co.	Kans.	
	Full Name of Spouse: Azel C. Sharrits	Death	20- 2-1977	Pratt	Stafford Co.	Kans.	
		Burial	22- 2-1977	Stafford	Stafford Co.	Kans.	
M	6 John Harold Taylor	Birth	20- 3-1898	Chanute	Neosha Co.	Kans.	
		Marr.					
	Full Name of Spouse: Opal J.	Death	4- 2-1949				
		Burial					
M	7 Taylor, George Lackey	Birth	8-12-1901		Butler Co.	Kans.	
		Marr.					
	Full Name of Spouse: Faye	Death	2-1957				
		Burial	2-1957				

Notes: Etta Ellen Moore stayed with them when her parents died within a year of each other.

('Altoona Paper')
('Died Apr. 30, 1923')

Death of Mrs. John Taylor

Melissa Rebecca Moore was born December 19th, 1862, in Douglas county, Kansas. She later moved with her parents to Butler county, Kansas, where she grew to womanhood. She was married to John Taylor July 4th, 1881, at Elgin, Kansas. To this union seven children were born. She leaves to mourn her death, her husband, John Taylor, and Mrs. Bernard Hagstrom, of Utica, Kansas; Carl Taylor and Mable Crossfield, of Toronto, Kansas. Orcen Taylor, of Holley. Colorado; Gladys Sharrits, of Conway Springs, Kansas; Harold Taylor, of Glen Elder, Kansas, and George Taylor, who is in the U. S. navy; a sister, Mrs. Geo. Wiley, of Dewey, Oklahoma; two brothers, R. E. Moore of Herring, Oklahoma; and J. M. Moore, of Elgin, Kansas.

Mrs. Taylor united with the Christian church when sixteen years old and had lived a faithful Christian life being a member of the church at Berryville, Arkansas, at the time of her death. She suffered six weeks but was at all times patient and never complained. She was a faithful and loving wife and a devoted Mother already to help any one in need. She will be sadly missed by her family and her memory will ever be shared in their lives.

Mrs. Taylor and her husband lived at Berryville, Arkansas, at the time of her sickness and death. Her age was sixty years, four months, and eleven days.

Funeral services will be held this afternoon at the Christian church in Altoona, conducted by Elder G.W. Leonard, the pastor. The Taylor family lived in Altoona for several years, leaving here about six years ago. The body arrived yesterday, accompanied by Mr. Taylor, Mr. and Mrs. Sharrits and Mrs. Geo. Wiley. Mr. Wiley arrived here Tuesday night to make arrangements for the funeral.

John Taylor, son of Robert and Jane Taylor, was born near Madison in Jefferson county, Indiana, March 29, 1857, and passed away Friday evening, Feb. 4, 1949, at the home of his son, Harold Taylor, in Axtell, following a illness of severall weeks.

When a boy of 14 he came to Kansas with his parents, who settled in Butler county. On July 4, 1881, he was married to Melissa Moore; to this union were born seven children. His wife passed away in 1923 and his eldest daughter, Vina, Mrs. Bernard Hagstrom, died in 1944. He leaves to mourn his passing two daughters, Mabel, Mrs. John Crossfield, Toronto, and Gladys, Mrs. A. C. Sharits, Iuka. Also four sons, Carl, of Chandler, Ariz., Orcen of Shawnee, Okla.; Harold of Axtell, and George of Bethel, Maine; one sister, Mrs. Grace Bossler, Stafford, Kansas. 26 grandchildren; 35 great-grandchildren; two great-great-grandchildren and a host of relatives and friends.

Mr. Taylor would have been 92 years old had he lived until March 29. He was a member of the Christian church; he had a cheerful disposition and his jovial sense of humor kept him enjoying his later years which he divided with his family. During his stay in Axtell he gained the admiration and respect of many friends for his busy and happy life.

Until a few years ago Mr. Taylor was a wizard on the loom. There are countless rugs, the products of his weaving, in and around Axtell, many of them finding their way to distant districts for his weaving was the exceptional fine quality. He continued to weave rugs of all sizes and colors until age and accompanying infirmities called a halt. He had a most pleasant disposition and a cheerful greeting for all.

Funeral services were held Sunday afternoon, Feb. 6, at the Christiam church in Altoona where interment was made in the family lot. Pall bearers were six of his grandsons. The Smith Funeral Home of Axtell was in charge.

JOHN TAYTLOR RITES HELD HERE SUNDAY

Elderly Man Had Been Residing at Home of Son Near Topeka

Funeral services for John Taylor, 92, who had made his home with his son and family near Topeka for some years, were held here at the Christian church last Sunday, February 6. The rites, which began at 2:30 p. m., were conducted by Elder S.F. Scott of the local church. Interment was made in the Altoona cemetery.

Singers at the services were Miss Dorothy Gentry and Mrs. Clifford Cranor, accompanied by Mrs. Ben Cranor.

The deceased was a former blacksmith in Altoona, having left this immediate community in 1906.

DIED

Mrs. Melissa Rebecca Taylor, wife of John Taylor, died at her home in Berryville, Ark., Monday, April 30th, 1923, aged 60 years and 5 months.

Funeral Services will be held at the Altoona Christian Church, Thursday afternoon, May 3rd, 1923, conducted by Elder Leonard.

Interment in the Altoona cemetery.

Family Group Sheet

Husband's Full Name: Bernard N. Hagstrom — Chart No.

	Day Month Year	City, Town or Place	County or Province, etc.	State or Country	Add. Info. on Husband
Birth					
Chr'nd					
Marr	31-8-1907	Fredonia	Wilson Co.	Kansas	
Death					
Burial					

Places of Residence:
Occupation: Church Affiliation: Military Rec.:

His Father: Mother's Maiden Name:

Wife's Full Maiden Name: Melvina Jane Taylor (Vina)

	Day Month Year	City, Town or Place	County or Province, etc.	State or Country	Add. Info. on Wife
Birth	10-5-1882	Elgin	Chautauqua Co.	Kansas	
Chr'nd					
Death	6-2-1945	Ransom Hospital			
Burial					

Places of Residence:
Occupation: Church Affiliation: Military Rec.:

Her Father: John Taylor   Mother's Maiden Name: Melissa Rebecca Moore

Sex	Children's Names in Full		Day Month Year	City, Town or Place	County or Province, etc.	State or Country	Add. Info. on Children
	1 Gladys	Birth					
		Marr.					
	Full Name of Spouse	Death	1910 2 mo. 1 day				
		Burial					
	2 Bessie	Birth					
		Marr.					
	Full Name of Spouse	Death	1921 4 yrs. 4 mo. 28 days				
		Burial					
	3 Oscar	Birth					
		Marr.	1929 21 yrs. 17 days				
	Full Name of Spouse	Death					
		Burial					
	4 Bertha Hagstrom	Birth					
		Marr.					
	Full Name of Spouse Pinkston	Death					
		Burial					
	5 Orville	Birth					
		Marr.					
	Full Name of Spouse	Death					
		Burial					
	6 Theodore	Birth					
		Marr.					
	Full Name of Spouse	Death					
		Burial					
	7 Permelia	Birth					
		Marr.					
	Full Name of Spouse Carter	Death					
		Burial					
	8 Emanuel	Birth					
		Marr.					
	Full Name of Spouse	Death					
		Burial					

Compiler:
Address: 9- Beulah married Donovan
City, State: 10- Marjie
Date:

John and Melissa Taylor

This is one of the places that John Taylor horse-shoed and Leland Crossfield was born in this place.

Family Group Sheet

Husband's Full Name: Carl William Taylor SS 512-07-2249 Chart No.

	Day Month Year	City, Town or Place	County or Province, etc.	State or Country	Add. Info on Husband
Birth	16-6-1884		Butler Co.	Kansas	
Chr'nd					
Marr	2-5-1906	Fredonia	Wilson Co.	Kansas	
Death	22-2-1972	Chandler	Maricopa Co.	Arizona	
Burial	24-2-1972	East Resthaven	Chandler Maricopa Co.	Arizona	

Places of Residence: 337½ N. Dakota
Occupation: Farmer   **Church Affiliation:**   **Military Rec.:**

His Father: John Taylor   **Mother's Maiden Name:** Rebecca Melissa Moore

Wife's Full Maiden Name: Elizabeth Johnson (Lizzie)

	Day Month Year	City, Town or Place	County or Province, etc.	State or Country	Add. Info. on Wife
Birth	2-9-1884	Fredonia		Kansas	
Chr'nd					
Death	23-5-1962	Chandler		Arizona	
Burial	26-5-1962	East Resthaven Cem. Chandler,		Arizona	

Places of Residence: Toronto, Ks.-Chandler, Arizona
Occupation: **Church Affiliation:** First Christian   **Military Rec.:**

Her Father: Henry Johnson   **Mother's Maiden Name:** Eveline Turner

Sex	#	Children's Names in Full		Day Month Year	City, Town or Place	County or Province, etc.	State or Country	Add. Info on Children
M	1	Cleo Taylor	Birth					
			Marr.					
		Full Name of Spouse	Death					
			Burial					
F	2	Nellie Taylor	Birth					
			Marr.					
		Full Name of Spouse: Merle Adams	Death					
			Burial					
M	3	Gerald William Taylor	Birth					
			Marr.					
		Full Name of Spouse	Death					
			Burial					
F	4	Fern Taylor	Birth					
			Marr.					
		Full Name of Spouse: Wesley Livingston	Death					
			Burial					
M	5	Harvey Taylor	Birth					
			Marr.					
		Full Name of Spouse	Death					
			Burial					
M	6	Cecil Taylor	Birth					
			Marr.					
		Full Name of Spouse	Death					
			Burial					
M	7	Glen Taylor	Birth					
			Marr.					
		Full Name of Spouse	Death					
			Burial					
	8		Birth					
			Marr.					
		Full Name of Spouse	Death					
			Burial					

Compiler: **Notes:**
Address:
City, State, Zip:
Date:

Melvina Jane Taylor

A precious one from us has gone, a voice we loved is stilled;
a place is vacant in our home which never can be filled. God in His
wisdom has recalled the boon His love had given; and though the body
peacefully slumbers here, Her soul is safe in heaven.

Melvina Jane Taylor, eldest daughter of John and Melissa R. Taylor,
was born May 10, 1882, at Elgin, Kansas, and died February 6, 1945, at the
Ransom Hospital, at the age of 62 years, 8 months and 26 days.

She was married August 31, 1907, to Bernard M. Hagstrom at Fredonia,
Kansas. To this union were born ten children, three of whom preceded her
in death:

Gladys - in 1910 at the age of 2 months and 1 day.
Bessie - in 1921 at the age of 4 years, 4 months, and 26 days.
Oscar - in 1929 at the age of 21 years and 17 days.

She leaves to mourn their loss, her husband - Bernard Hagstrom, of
the home, and seven children --:

Bertha Pinkston, of Arriba, Colorado.
Orvilla, of San Diego, California.
Theodora, of Tulsa, Oklahoma.
Parmelia Carter, of De Ridder, Louisiana.
Emanuel, of United States Army. - Overseas.
Lucien Eunovna, of Horace, Kansas.
Marcia of the home.

Seven Grandchildren
Father, John Taylor - Age 86 - of Axtel, Kansas.
Sisters and four Brothers:
Maude Crossfield, of Toronto, Kansas.
Lady Marcia, of Luka, Kansas.
Earl Taylor, of Chandler, Arizona.
Lee Taylor, of Shawnee, Oklahoma.
Harold Taylor, of Axtel, Kansas.
Lieut. George Taylor, of the Coast Guard, New London, Connecticut.

They moved to Ness County in 1911, living on farms in Gove and Ness
Counties, then moving to Utica, where they have resided for 25 years.

She joined the Christian Church early in life and transferred her
membership to Utica in April 1936.

God called and the sound of His voice,
Called our loved one away,
To a world of beauty and of peace
Where love alone holds sway.

Though we'll miss her voice, her lips are still,
Her memories linger on,
And as He calls us, one by one,
We'll meet her there at dawn.

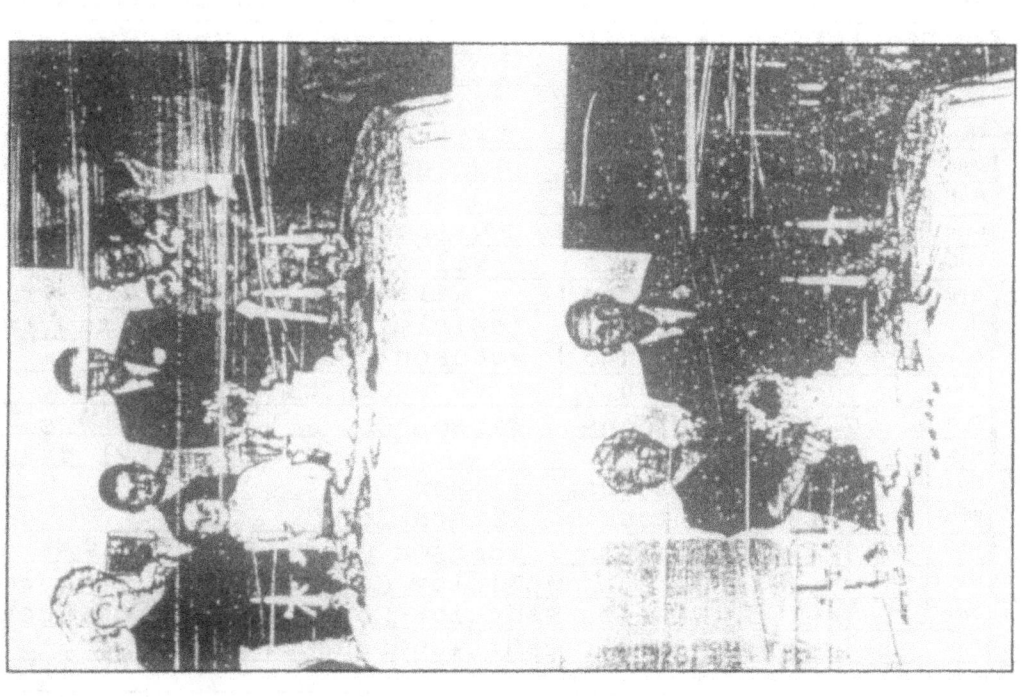

Golden Wedding Congratulations
To Mr. and Mrs. John Crossfield

It's been fifty years since you
  started out
To walk life's road together,
And to face the storms that came
  along
And enjoy the pleasant weather.

How young you were on that wed-
  ding day
And how very free from care
The way ahead looked very bright
And the days seemed very fair.

Time passed by and a small son
  came
To fill your heart with joy
Your happiness was almost comp'e
When there came another little
  boy.

You watched them grow and as
  time rolled on
To school they trudged away
They soon grew up and for each
  of them
There came a wedding day.

Then you were alone but happy
  still
And some way you didn't mind
Your family had grown larger
And the new daughters sweet and
  kind.

Now your home is gay once more
When the grandchildren come to
  see you.
They drive away the cares of life
And bring the sunshine to you.

You've reached the golden pinacle
Now you're travelling toward the
  west.
We earnestly hope these later years
Will be the very best.

May the golden glow of the ev'ning
  sun
Shine on your path each day
And keep you safe and happy
All the rest of the way.
      — Alberta Ireland

Family Group Sheet

Husband's Full Name: John Ira Crossfield SS-514-09-9784   Chart No.

	Day Month Year	City, Town or Place	County or Province, etc.	State or Country	Add. Info on Husband
Birth	13-7-1885	Elk City	Montgomery Co.	Kansas	
Chr'nd					
Marr.	11-4-1906	Altoona	Wilson Co.	Kansas	
Death	11-9-1964	Yates Center	Woodson Co.	Kansas	
Burial	14-9-1964	Altoona	Wilson Co.	Kansas	

Places of Residence:
Occupation: Butcher   Church Affiliation: Christian   Military Rec:
Other wives: #2-Vivian Neilson August 18, 1979
His Father: Francis Marlon Crossfield   Mother's Maiden Name: Margaret Alice Stark

Wife's Full Maiden Name: Mabel Blanche Taylor SS-511-01-4038

	Day Month Year	City, Town or Place	County or Province, etc.	State or Country	Add. Info on Wife
Birth	1-12-1886		Butler Co.	Kansas	
Chr'nd					
Death	23-4-1960	Eureka	Greenwood Co.	Kansas	
Burial	26-4-1960	Altoona	Wilson Co.	Kansas	

Places of Residence:
Occupation: Housewife   Church Affiliation: Christian   Military Rec:
Her Father: John Taylor   Mother's Maiden Name: Rebecca Melissa Moore

Sex	Children's Names in Full		Day Month Year	City, Town or Place	County or Province, etc.	State or Country	Add. Info on Children
F	1 Edith Marie C.	Birth	26-1-1907	Altoona	Wilson Co.	Ks.	8 mo. 1 wk.
		Marr.					
	Full Name of Spouse	Death	9-10-1907	Altoona	Wilson Co.	Ks.	
		Burial	10-1907	Altoona	Wilson Co.	Ks.	
M	2 Infant Crossfield	Birth	3-2-1908	Altoona	Wilson Co.	Ks.	still-born
		Marr.					
	Full Name of Spouse	Death	3-2-1908	Altoona	Wilson Co.	Ks.	
		Burial	2-1908	Altoona	Wilson Co.	Ks.	
M	3 Lewis Ira Crossfield	Birth	22-1-1909	Altoona	Wilson Co.	Ks.	63 yrs. 6mo. 3days
		Marr.	17-4-1941	Gallup	McKinley Co.	New M.	
	Full Name of Spouse	Death	25-7-1972	Toronto	Woodson Co.	Ks.	
		Burial	7-1972	Toronto Cem	Woodson Co.	Ks.	
F	4 Hazel Louise C.	Birth	2-7-1912	Altoona	Wilson Co.	Ks.	5 yrs. 2mo. 21 days
		Marr.					
	Full Name of Spouse	Death	11-4-1918	Altoona	Wilson Co.	Ks.	
		Burial	4-1918	Altoona	Wilson Co.	Ks.	
M	5 Leland Francis C.	Birth	19-8-1917	Toronto	Woodson Co.	Ks.	63 yrs. 8mo. 9days
		Marr.	27-5-1941	Gallup	McKinley Co.	New Mex.	
	Full Name of Spouse	Death	29-4-1981	Wichita	Sedgwick Co.	Ks.	
		Burial	1-5-1981	Toronto cem.	Woodson Co.	Ks.	

State of Kansas, County of Wilson.
OFFICE OF THE PROBATE JUDGE OF SAID COUNTY.

BE IT REMEMBERED, That on the 4th day of April A. D. 1906, there was issued from the office of said Probate Judge, a Marriage License, of which the following is a true copy:

MARRIAGE LICENSE.
WILSON COUNTY, STATE OF KANSAS.

Fredonia, Kan. April 9, 1906.

To any Person Authorized by Law to Perform the Marriage Ceremony, Greeting:

You are hereby authorized to join in Marriage John I Crossfield of Altoona Kan. aged 20 years, and Miss Mabel Taylor of Altoona Kan. aged 19 years; and of this License you will make due return to my office within thirty days.

F Jno Crossfield father John I. Crossfield consenting   (Seal) B H Lindel, Probate Judge.

And which said Marriage License was afterwards, to wit, on the 16th day of April A. D. 1906, returned to said Probate Judge, with the following certificate endorsed thereon, to wit:

State of Kansas, County of Wilson, ss.

I, Thomas Miller, do hereby certify, that in accordance with the authorization of the within License, I did, on the 11 day of April A. D. 1906, at Altoona, in said county, join and unite in Marriage the within-named John I Crossfield and Miss Mabel Taylor

RECORD OF FUNERAL

Total No. 308 • Yearly No. 7 • Date of Entry April 25, 1960
Name of Deceased: Mabel Blanche Crossfield
Residence: Toronto
(Married • Husband: John Crossfield)

Complete Funeral (except outlays):
- Casket: $590.00
- Embalming Body: $25.00
- Opening of Grave or Tomb: $20.00
- Clergymen: $20.00
- Sales Tax: $1.60

Occupation: Housewife
Date of Death: April 23, 1960, 1:40 PM
Date of Birth: December 1, 1886, Age 73y 4m 22d
Name of Father: John Taylor
Maiden Name of Mother: Melissa Moore
Date of Funeral: April 26, Tuesday, 2:30 PM
Services at: Christian Church
Clergyman: Rev. R.F. Schaechtele
Birthplace: Kansas
Place of Death: Greenwood Co. Hosp.
Size of Casket: 6/6 #890 White Gold Master
Cemetery: Altoona Cemetery

ELIZABETH TAYLOR

FULL NAME: Elizabeth Taylor
PLACE OF DEATH: Comm. Hosp - Chandler
DATE OF DEATH: Yr 1962 Mo 5 Day 23 Hour 3 PM
DATE OF BIRTH: Yr 1884 Mo 9 Day 2
AGE: Yrs 77 Mos 8 Days 21
BIRTHPLACE: Fredonia, Kansas
FATHER'S NAME: Henry Johnson — BIRTHPLACE: Ill.
MOTHER'S MAIDEN NAME: Eveline Turner — BIRTHPLACE: Ill.
INFORMANT'S NAME: Carl W. Taylor
INFORMANT'S ADDRESS: Rt 1 Box 230 Chandler
BURIAL PLACE: East Resthaven — DATE: 5/26/62
SECTION C • BLOCK 18 • LOT 2 • GRAVE 4
SEND CAR TO: Carl Taylor — May 2, 1906
CAME TO ARIZONA FROM: Toronto, Kansas — WHEN: 1938
Occupation: Housewife at home
CHURCH AND LODGES: First Christian Church

SURVIVORS:
- Husb: Carl W. Taylor, Chandler
- Daus: Mrs. Fern Livingston, Chandler; Mrs. Merle Adams, Chandler
- Sons: Harvey Taylor, Chandler; Clea Taylor; Larry; Glen
- Bro: Herbert Johnson, Tulsa
- Sis: Mollie Olinger, Houston
- 12 gc

Mrs. J. Crossfield Dies Following Short Illness

Mrs. John Crossfield became suddenly ill last Thursday and was taken to the Greenwood County Hospital, Eureka, where she passed away Saturday evening, April 23, 1960.

Mable Blanche Taylor, daughter of John and Melissa Taylor, was born December 1, 1886, in Butler County, Kas. She grew up in Altoona and united with the Christian Church at an early age.

She was united in marriage to John Crossfield April 11, 1906. To this union were born five children, three preceding her in death.

Mrs. Crossfield moved with her husband from Altoona to Toronto and lived on a farm in the Big Sandy community, then to Toronto in 1923.

She leaves to mourn her passing her husband, and two sons, Lewis and Lee, and their wives, Bernice and Frances; five grandchildren; one sister, Mrs. Gladys Sharits of Stafford; and three brothers, Carl Taylor, Chandler Ariz., Orcen Taylor, ____, and Harold Taylor, Axtell, Kas.

Her father, mother, one sister and one brother preceded her in death.

Mrs. Crossfield was interested in her grandchildren and they visited her most every day. She was most helpful in homes where there was sickness, cheerfully lending a helping hand. She will be sadly missed by relatives and friends.

Funeral services were held in her memory Tuesday afternoon at 2:30 o'clock from the Toronto Christian Church with the pastor Rev. R. F. Schaechtele officiating. Amy Rogers and Lorene LaRue sang "Going Down the Valley," and Rev. Schaechtele sang "Beyond The Sunset." Phyllis Gustin was the accompanist. Blake Hibbard, Ivan Gustin, Edwin Dyer, Art Ireland, Mahlon Marhofer and Harold Williams were casketbearers. Interment was in the Altoona Cemetery.

In Memory Of
ELIZABETH TAYLOR

September 2, 1884 — May 23, 1962
Fredonia, Kansas — Chandler, Arizona

Memorial Services
May 26, 1962 — 2:30 P.M.
Chapel of Bueler Mortuary
Rev. Aurel Mayson & Irwin N. Son
Officiating
Interment at East Resthaven

Bearers:
Dean Nelson — John Mathias
B. D. Dory — Boyd Mowery
Calvin Toon — Francis Adams

John Crossfield Rites Monday

John Crossfield, long-time resident of Toronto, passed away Friday evening September 11, 1964, at the home of Mr. and Mrs. Fred Warren in Yates Center, where he had been cared for during the past few months.

John Ira Crossfield, son of Francis Marion and Alice (Stark) Crossfield, was born July 13, 1885 near Elk City, Kansas. He was the eldest of seven children: Martha, Iva, Charley, Dora, Lucy, and Dollie. The family moved to Altoona in 1897 where he grew to manhood. He was united in marriage to Mable Blanche Taylor, April 11, 1906. To this union were born five children: Lewis Ira and Leland Francis, both of Toronto; Hazel Louise, age six, Edith Marie, age nine months, and an infant son, preceded him in death.

During the early years of their married life they, with their family, moved to the Big Sandy community where they lived until 1923 when they moved to Toronto. The remaining years of his life were spent in and around Toronto, where he engaged in farming, operated several butcher shops, and managed the Toronto Locker Plant.

When a young man, he joined the Christian Church and remained a member the rest of his life. He was an active member of the Toronto Christian Church for many years which he served as a member of the board and as a deacon.

He leaves to mourn his passing his two sons, Lew and Lee of Toronto; five grandchildren: Carroll Crossfield of Lawrence, Larry Crossfield of Fort Ord, Calif., Helen Crossfield, Ann Crossfield, and Kay Crossfield, all of Toronto; two daughters-in-law, Bernice and Frances; and one granddaughter-in-law, JoAnne of Lawrence; one brother, Charley Crossfield of Elk City; three sisters, Mrs. Dora Crowder, Mrs. Dollie McDonald, both of Bartlesville, Okla.; Mrs. Lucy Moffatt of Altoona, and other relatives and friends.

He was preceded in death by his wife Mable in April of 1960, three children, his father and mother, two sisters, Mrs. Martha Bowie and Mrs. Iva Ragan.

John will long be remembered for his helpfulness to others which gained him a host of friends. He was never too busy to help others in their times of need.

During the last four years of his life, he endured a great deal of pain which he bore with patience and cheerfulness. His sunny disposition was an inspiration to all his friends.

Funeral services were held from the Toronto Christian Church, Monday afternoon with Rev. R. F. Schaechtele, officiating. Soloist, Mrs. Jeanette Swilley, accompanied by Mrs. Evelyn Baker, sang "Ivory Palaces" and "Beyond The Sunset."

Casketbearers were Arthur Ireland, Harold Williams, Norman

Family Group Sheet

Husband's Full Name Infant Crossfield   **Chart No.**

Husband's Data	Day	Month	Year	City, Town or Place	County or Province, etc.	State or Country	Add. Info. on Husband
Birth	02	02	1908	Altoona	Wilson County	Kansas	still
Chr'nd							born
Marr							
Death	02	02	1908	Altoona	Wilson County	Kansas	
Burial		02	1908	Altoona	Wilson County	Kansas	

Places of Residence

Occupation   Church Affiliation   Military Rec

His Father John I. Crossfield   **Mother's Maiden Name** Mabel B. Taylor

Wife's Full Maiden Name Edith Marie Crossfield

Wife's Data	Day	Month	Year	City, Town or Place	County or Province, etc.	State or Country	Add. Info. on Wife
Birth	26	01	1907	Altoona	Wilson County	Kansas	8 month
Chr'nd							1 week
Death	17	10	1907	Altoona	Wilson County	Kansas	
Burial		10	1907	Altoona	Wilson County	Kansas	

Places of Residence

Occupation   Church Affiliation   Military Rec

Her Father John I. Crossfield   **Mother's Maiden Name** Mabel B. Taylor

Sex	Children's Names in Full	Children's Data	Day	Month	Year	City, Town or Place	County or Province, etc.	State or Country	Add. Info. on Children
1		Birth							
		Marr.							
	Full Name of Spouse	Death							
		Burial							

Gravestones:
- INFANT SON CROSSFIELD FEB. 2, 1908
- EDITH MARIE CROSSFIELD JAN. 26, 1907 OCT. 17, 1907
- JOHN I. CROSSFIELD 1885—1964
- MABEL B. CROSSFIELD 1886—1960

Compiler:
Address:
City, State, Zip:
Date:

Notes:

Family Group Sheet

Husband's Full Name

Chart No.

Husband's Data	Day	Month	Year	City, Town or Place	County or Province, etc.	State or Country	Add. Info. on Husband
Birth							
Chr'nd							
Marr							
Death							
Burial							

Places of Residence

Occupation — Church Affiliation — Military Rec

Other wives, if any, No. (1) (2) etc. Make separate sheet for each marr.

His Father — Mother's Maiden Name

Wife's Full Maiden Name Hazel Louise Crossfield

Wife's Data	Day	Month	Year	City, Town or Place	County or Province, etc.	State or Country	Add. Info. on Wife
Birth	02	07	1912	Altoona	Wilson County	Kansas	5 yrs.
Chr'nd							2 mo.
Death	11	04	1918	Altoona	Wilson County	Kansas	21 days
Burial		04	1918	Altoona	Wilson County	Kansas	

Places of Residence

Occupation — Church Affiliation — Military Rec

Her Father John I. Crossfield — Mother's Maiden Name Mabel B. Taylor

Sex	Children's Names in Full	Children's Data	Day	Month	Year	City, Town or Place	County or Province, etc.	State or Country	Add. Info. on Children
1		Birth							
		Marr.							
	Full Name of Spouse	Death							
		Burial							
2									
3									
4									
5									
6									
7									
8									

Headstones shown:
- HAZEL LOU CROSSFIELD, JULY 2, 1912, APR 11, 1918
- LEWIS I. CROSSFIELD, 1909 — 1972

Compiler:
Address:
City, State, Zip:
Date:

Notes:

Family Group Sheet

Husband's Full Name: Lewis Ira Crossfield — Chart No. _____

	Day Month Year	City, Town or Place	County or Province, etc.	State or Country	Add. Info. on Husband
Birth	22-1-1909	Altoona	Wilson Co.	Kansas	
Chr'nd					
Marr.	17-4-1941	Gallup	McKinley Co.	New Mex.	
Death	25-7-1972	Toronto	Woodson Co.	Kansas	
Burial	27-7-1972	Toronto Cem.	Woodson Co.	Kansas	

Places of Residence: Gun dealer-Farming
Occupation: Heavy Equip. Operator **Church Affiliation:** Christian **Military Rec:**

His Father: John Ira Crossfield **Mother's Maiden Name:** Mable Blanche Taylor

Wife's Full Maiden Name: Bernice E. Schlinloff

	Day Month Year	City, Town or Place	County or Province, etc.	State or Country	Add. Info. on Wife
Birth					
Chr'nd					
Death					
Burial					

Places of Residence:
Occupation: **Church Affiliation:** **Military Rec:**

Her Father: **Mother's Maiden Name:**

Sex	Children's Names in Full		Day Month Year	City, Town or Place	County or Province, etc.	State or Country	Add. Info on Children
M	1 Carrol Lew Crossfield	Birth / Marr. / Death / Burial					
F	2 Helen Crossfield — Spouse: Gordon Webb	Birth / Marr. / Death / Burial					
F	3 Kay Crossfield — Spouse: Teddy Banks	Birth / Marr. / Death / Burial					
	4	Birth / Marr. / Death / Burial					
	5	Birth					

Lewis I. Crossfield

Lewis I. Crossfield, second child of John I. Crossfield and Mable Blanche Taylor, was born January 22, 1909 at Altoona, Kans. and died July 25, 1972 at Toronto.

He was preceded in death by his parents, two sisters, one brother, and one son-in-law, Robert Gumke.

He leaves to mourn his passing his widow, Bernice, of Toronto: one son Carrol, of Lawrence; two daughters, Mrs. Helen Webb and Mrs. Kay Banks; one brother, Leland, all of Toronto; five grandchildren, one daughter-in-law, Judy, two sons-in-law, Gordon Webb and Teddy Banks, and many other relatives and friends.

Lew, with his family, moved to the Big Sandy neighborhood when he was about 7 years old. Later they moved to Toronto.

He was united in marriage to Bernice E. Schlinloff, April 17, 1941. They moved to Gallup, N.Mex., where he was a heavy equipment operator. They returned to Toronto in 1943, where he engaged in farming until his health forced him to quit. He became a gun dealer, specializing in custom finished gun stocks.

He was a member of the First Christian Church of Toronto. He was a Past Master of Woodson Lodge No. 121 A.F.&A.M., and a Past Patron of Golden Star Chapter No. 173, O.E.S. Funeral services were held at 1:30 p.m. July 27, from the United Methodist Church with Rev. William Atchley officiating. Mrs. Evelyn Baker was the organist and Mrs. Hazel Leathman was the soloist. Pallbearers were Leslie Sherman, Vic Dyer, Howard LaRue, Ed Sherman, Floyd Sowder and Gale Webb. Honorary pallbearers were Edwin Dyer, Frank McCurdy, Lloyd Hartman, Alfred Sowder, Floyd Swilley and Howard Jones. Interment in the Toronto Cemetery.

Compiler:
Address:
City, State, Zip:
Date:

Family Group Sheet

Husband's Full Name: Leland F. Crossfield **Chart No.**

	Day Month Year	City, Town or Place	County or Province, etc.	State or Country	Add. Info on Husband
Birth	19-8-1917	Toronto Co.	Woodson Co.	Kansas	
Chr'nd					
Marr	27-5-1941	Gallup	McKinley Co.	New Mexico	
Death	29-4-1981	Wichita	Sedgwick Co.	Kansas	
Burial	1-5-1981	Toronto	Woodson Co.	Kansas	

Places of Residence: Correctional Superviser
Occupation: Heavy Construction **Church Affiliation:** United Methodist **Military Rec:** US Army WW 2
Other wives: Vivian Lee Neilson (M) Aug. 18, 1979 Yates Center, Ks.
His Father: John Ira Crossfield **Mother's Maiden Name:** Mable Blanche Taylor

Wife's Full Maiden Name: Beulah Frances Sowder

	Day Month Year	City, Town or Place	County or Province, etc.	State or Country	Add. Info on Wife
Birth	22-3-1913	Toronto	Woodson Co.	Kansas	
Chr'nd					
Death	12-6-1978	Fredonia	Wilson Co.	Kansas	
Burial	15-6-1978	Toronto cem.	Woodson Co.	Kansas	

Places of Residence:
Occupation: Teacher **Church Affiliation:** Methodist **Military Rec:**
Her Father: Franklin L. Sowder **Mother's Maiden Name:** Addie Faye Kaltenbach

Sex	Children's Names in Full		Day Month Year	City, Town or Place	County or Province, etc.	State or Country	Add. Info on Children
M	1 Larry Lee Crossfield	Birth	25-5-1943	Eureka	Greenwood Co.	Ks.	
		Marr.	30-3-1968				
	Full Name of Spouse: Cherly Sue Hilyard	Death					
		Burial					
F	2 Crossfield Ann Elizabeth	Birth	7-3-1948	Eureka	Greenwood Co.	Ks.	Divorced
		Marr.	4-6-1966				
	Full Name of Spouse: Robert Henry Oehlert	Death					
		Burial					
	3	Birth					
		Marr.					

Leland F. Crossfield — Funeral services were held Friday, May 1, 1981 for Leland F. Crossfield at the Toronto United Methodist Church with the Rev. Paul Waters officiating. He died April 29 at the Wesley Medical Center in Wichita. Leland F. Crossfield was born Aug. 19, 1917 near Toronto. His parents were John Ira and Mable Blanche (Taylor) Crossfield. He grew up in and around Toronto. He was a Toronto High School graduate, a member of the Toronto United Methodist Church, a 25 year member of Woodson Lodge 121 AF&AM, a member of Golden Star Chapter 173, a member of the American Legion Post 325 and a member of the Kansas Peace Officers Association.

He was united in marriage to Frances Sowder on May 27, 1941 at Gallup, New Mexico. Two children were born to this marriage. They are Larry Lee Crossfield and Ann Elizabeth Oehlert. His wife died June 12, 1978.

In March of 1943, Leland enlisted in the United States Army and served for three years during World War II in Burma and India where he was a construction foreman, building the Burma Road. When he returned home he worked in heavy construction work until he took a position in 1965 at the Toronto Honor Camp. He was employed there by the Kansas Department of Corrections as a Correctional Supervisor at the time of his death.

He was united in marriage to Vivian Lee Nielsen, Aug. 18, 1979, at the United Methodist Church in Yates Center. They made their home in Toronto.

Preceding him in death, were his parents, two sisters and two brothers. He is survived by his wife Vivian of the home, Larry of Olathe; Ann Oehlert and her husband Robert of Yates Center; two grandsons, Aaron and Jordon Crossfield; four step children, Mr. and Mrs. Herbert Shores of Chanute, Mr. and Mrs. Ralph Shores of Plattsville, Missouri, Mr. and Mrs. Thad Marshall of Comroe, Texas, and Mr. and Mrs. Bill McMichael of Tulsa, Oklahoma. Interment for Leland F. Crossfield was in the Toronto cemetery with Woodson Lodge 121 AF&AM in charge of the service there.

A memorial to the Toronto United Methodist Scholarship Fund has been established.

TORONTO -- Leland F. Crossfield, 63, Toronto Honor Camp correctional superviser, died Wednesday. Service 2 p.m. Friday, Toronto United Methodist Church.

Survivors: wife, Vivian; son, Larry of Olathe; daughter, Mrs. Ann Oehlert of Yates Center; Campbell Funeral Home, Eureka.

FRANCES CROSSFIELD

Beulah Frances Crossfield, Toronto, died June 12, at St. Margaret's Mercy Hospital, Fredonia. She was 65.

She was born the daughter of Addie Faye Sowder Kaltenbach and Franklin L. Sowder, on March 22, 1913, in Toronto. She grew up in Toronto and attended grade school and high school there. She received her Bachelor of Science degree from Emporia State Teacher's College.

She was united in marriage to Leland F. Crossfield, May 27, 1941, in Gallup, N.M. They lived their entire life in Toronto. To this union, two children were born, Larry Lee Crossfield and Ann Elizabeth Crossfield. She joined the United Methodist Church at an early age. She taught a Sunday school class and was an active member of the church. For a number of years, until her retirement in 1967, she taught English and French in the Toronto and Fredonia high schools.

Survivors include her widower, Lee, of the home; one son, Larry, of Gardner; one daughter, Mrs. Ann Oehlert, of Yates Center; her mother, Mrs. Faye Kaltenbach, Toronto; and two grandsons. She was preceded in death by her father and grandmother.

Funeral services were held at the Toronto United Methodist Church, June 15, with the Reverends Jack and Marilyn Gregory officiating. Interment was in Toronto Cemetery. Campbell Funeral Home, Eureka, was in charge.

Family Group Sheet   SS-702-16-7381

Husband's Full Name: Azel Coffland Sharrits — Chart No.

Husband's Data	Day Month Year	City, Town or Place	County or Province, etc.	State or Country	Add. Info on Husband
Birth	30-5-1895	Independence	Mont. Co.	Kansas	
Chr'nd					
Marr	25-8-1915	Toronto	Woodson Co.	Kansas	
Death	16-11-1978	Pratt Co. hospital	Pratt Co.	Kansas	
Burial	18-11-1978	Stafford cem.	Stafford Co.	Kansas	

Places of Residence:

Occupation: Railroad agent   Church Affiliation: First Christian   Military Rec.

His Father: Charles Joseph Braford Sharrits   **Mother's Maiden Name:** Mary Jane Coffland

Wife's Full Maiden Name: Gladys Hazel Taylor   SS 509-22-2385

Wife's Data	Day Month Year	City, Town or Place	County or Province, etc.	State or Country	Add. Info. on Wife
Birth	14-11-1895	Newkirk	Kay Co.	Oklahoma	
Chr'nd					
Death	20-2-1977	St. John hospital	Stafford Co.	Kansas	
Burial	2-1977	Stafford cem.	Stafford Co.	Kansas	

Places of Residence:

Occupation: Church Affiliation: Christian church   Military Rec.

Her Father: John Taylor   **Mother's Maiden Name:** Rebecca Melissa Moore

Sex	Children's Names in Full	Children's Data	Day Month Year	City, Town or Place	County or Province, etc.	State or Country	Add. Info on Children
F	1. Yvonne Eloise S.	Birth					
		Marr.					
	Full Name of Spouse: Bill Amerine	Death					
		Burial					
	2.	Birth					
		Marr.					

272

STAFFORD COURIER

23 Feb 1977   Pg. 1 Col 5

MRS. SHARITS DIED SUNDAY

Mrs. A. C. (Gladys H.) Sharits, 81, died Sunday 20 Feb, at St. John District Hospital. She was born 14 Nov, 1895 at Newkirk, OK., and was married to A. C. Sharits 25 Aug 1915, at Toronto, she lived here since 1950, moving here from Iuka.

She was a member of the Christian Church, OES, EHU, Mothers Club, all of Stafford.

Survivors include the widower, daughter, Mrs. W. B. Amerine, Turon; three grandchildren, five great-grandchildren.

Funeral was at 2 P.M. Tuesday at Peacock-Milton Chapel.

In Memory Of

Azel Caffland Sharits

May 30, 1895   November 16, 1978

Services
Peacock — Milton Chapel
Stafford, Kansas
November 18, 1978

Conducted By
Rev. Ernest Marsh

Casket Bearers
George Ellis   Alva Minnis
Lee Paulsen   George Evans
Edgar Wright   Merlyn Hoskinson

Soloist
Bob Minks

Organist
Mrs. Rex Milton

Interment
Stafford Cemetery

Cemetery Services Conducted By
Stafford Lodge No. 252   A. J. & A. M

STAFFORD COURIER
16 November 1978

A.C. Sharits, 83, died thursday, Nov. 16 at Pratt County Hospital. Born May 30, 1895 at Independence, Kansas, he married Gladys Paylor Aug. 25, 1915 at Toronto, Kansas. She died Feb. 20, 1977. He was a retired Missouri pacific Railroad Agent. He lived here since 1950 He was a member of the Firest Christian Church, O.E.S., both of Stafford; Masonic Lodge of Pratt, Ks. Survivors: daughter: Mrs. Eloise Amerine of Turon, Ks. three grandchildren; five great-grandchildren. Funeral was P.M. Saturday at Peacock-Milton Funeral Chapel, Stafford, Ks. Rev. Ernest Marsh officiated. Burial at Stafford Cemetery, Stafford, Ks

Family Group Sheet

Husband's Full Name W. Brownie Amerine — Chart No.

Husband's Data	Day	Month	Year	City, Town or Place	County or Province, etc.	State or Country	Add. Info on Husband
Birth							
Chr'nd							
Marr.							
Death							
Burial							

Places of Residence:

Occupation: Farmer Church Affiliation: Military Rec:

Other wives, if any (1) (2) etc. Make separate sheet for each marr.

His Father: Mother's Maiden Name:

Wife's Full Maiden Name Yvonne Eloise Sharrits

Wife's Data	Day	Month	Year	City, Town or Place	County or Province, etc.	State or Country	Add. Info on Wife
Birth							
Chr'nd							
Death							
Burial							

Places of Residence:

Occupation: Church Affiliation: Military Rec:

Other Husbands, if any (1)(2) etc. Make separate sheet for each marr.

Her Father: Azel Cofford Sharrits Mother's Maiden Name: Gladys Hazel Taylor

Sex	Children's Names in Full (arranged in order of birth)	Children's Data	Day	Month	Year	City, Town or Place	County or Province, etc.	State or Country	Add. Info on Children
F	1 Vickie Amerine	Birth							
	Full Name of Spouse: Ronnie Wells	Marr.							
		Death							
		Burial							
M	2 Bill Amerine	Birth							
	Full Name of Spouse	Marr.							
		Death							
		Burial							
	3	Birth							
	Full Name of Spouse	Marr.							
		Death							
		Burial							
	4	Birth							
	Full Name of Spouse	Marr.							
		Death							

Gladys and Azel Sharits, Aug. 25, 1965
50th Anniversary

60th Wedding Anniversay — Mr. and Mrs. A.C. Sharits of Stafford are celebrating their wedding anniversary, August 24th, with a basket dinner at the Stafford Park. Relatives and friends are welcome. Please, no gifts.

Hosts are Mr. and Mrs. Brownie Amerine, their daughter and her husband, also their grandchildren, Mr. and Mrs. Dennis Nitzsche, Mr. and Mrs. Ronnie Wells, Mr. and Mrs. Bill Amerine.

Family Group Sheet

Husband's Full Name: Ronnie Wells — Chart No.

	Day Month Year	City, Town or Place	County or Province, etc.	State or Country	Add. Info. on Husband
Birth					
Chr'nd					
Marr					
Death					
Burial					

Places of Residence

Occupation — Church Affiliation — Military Rec.

His Father: — Mother's Maiden Name:

Wife's Full Maiden Name: Vickie Amerine

	Day Month Year	City, Town or Place	County or Province, etc.	State or Country	Add. Info. on Wife
Birth					
Chr'nd					
Death					
Burial					

Places of Residence

Occupation — Church Affiliation — Military Rec.

Her Father: W. Brownie Amerine — Mother's Maiden Name: Yvonne Eloise Sharrits

Sex	Children's Names	Data	Day Month Year	City, Town or Place	County or Province, etc.	State or Country	Add. Info. on Children
M	1 Scottie	Birth / Marr. / Death / Burial					
	Full Name of Spouse						
	2 Terri	Birth / Marr. / Death / Burial					
	Full Name of Spouse						
	3 Sharon Amerine — Nitzsche	Birth / Marr. / Death / Burial					
	Full Name of Spouse						
	4 John Albert Lea	Birth / Marr.					

Husband's Full Name: John Harold Taylor — Chart No.

	Day Month Year	City, Town or Place	County or Province, etc.	State or Country	Add. Info. on H
Birth	20-3-1898	Chanute	Neosha Co.	Kansas	
Chr'nd					
Marr					
Death	4-2--1949				
Burial					

Places of Residence

Occupation — Church Affiliation — Military Rec.

His Father: John Ira Taylor — Mother's Maiden Name: Melissa Rebecca Moore

Wife's Full Maiden Name: Opal J.

	Day Month Year	City, Town or Place	County or Province, etc.	State or Country	Add. Info. on
Birth					
Chr'nd					
Death					
Burial					

Places of Residence

Occupation — Church Affiliation — Military Rec.

Date

Family Group Sheet

Husband's Full Name: George Lackey Taylor Chart No.

	Day Month Year	City, Town or Place	County or Province, etc.	State or Country	Add. Info on Husband
Birth	8-12-1901		Butler Co.	Kansas	
Chr'nd					
Marr					
Death	2-1957	Bethel	Offord Co.	Maine	
Burial					

Places of Residence: Bethel, Maine
Occupation: **Church Affiliation:** **Military Rec:** Coast Guard-Marines

His Father: John Ira Taylor **Mother's Maiden Name:** Melissa Rebecca Moore

Wife's Full Maiden Name: Faye

	Day Month Year	City, Town or Place	County or Province, etc.	State or Country	Add. Info on Wife
Birth					
Chr'nd					
Death					
Burial					

Her Father:

Sex	Children's Names in Full		
M 1	Kent Taylor	Birth / Marr / Death / Burial	
M 2	Bruce Taylor	Birth / Marr / Death / Burial	

Cruising about the Pacific and visiting various ports along the west coast, George Lackey Taylor, son of Mrs. Melissa Taylor, of Berryville, Arkansas, is now a member of the U. S. Marine guard of the U. S. S. New York, one of the battleships of the Pacific fleet. His name appears on a list of Marine attached to that vessel. George joined the marines at their recruiting station, in Kansas City, Missouri, November 23, 1922 and for several months was stationed at Mare Island, California. Later he was assigned to duty on the New York, where the Marines are trained to man certain typed of guns and to perform guard duties. The New York, recently returned from maneuvers in the vicinity of the Panama Canal, and is now cruising along the west coast, frequently dropping anchor near Los Angeles or San Francisco, affording the marines an opportunity to go ashore. The vessel was recently reported at San Pedro, the harbor of Los Angeles. No doubt this Berryville boy will have many interesting experiences to recount when he returns home.

GEORGE L. TAYLOR

George L. Taylor, age 56, died Friday at his home after a short illness. The son of John and Melissa Moore Taylor, he was born December 8, 1901, in Butler, Kansas. He received his early education in public schools of that city after which he entered the armed forces and served as a career man in the Marine Corps and as a Lieutenant in the Coast Guard.

Mr. Taylor was a veteran of World War II retiring in December 1948, to come to Bethel to make his home. He was the commander of the American Legion Mundt Allen Post #81, a member of Bethel Lodge #97 F. and A.M. the Chamber of Commerce, and Bethel Health Council. He had a deep love for the young people of the community and founded as well as served as Cub Master of Pack #165 of the Bethel Cub Scouts.

Besides his widow, Faye, he is survived by two sons, Kent and Bruce, two sisters, Mrs. Gladys Sharits of Stafford, Kansas, and Mrs. Maole Crossfield of Toronto, Kansas; and three brothers, Carl of Chandler, Arizona, Harold of Axtell, Kansas, and Orson of Shawnee, Oklahoma.

Funeral services were held at the Greenleaf Funeral Homes in Bethel, Sunday, at 2 p. m. with Rev. Clifford Laws officiating.

A few short months after coming with his family to live in Bethel, George's value as a citizen was established. Forthrightness and loyalty were dominant features in his sincere and fine character.

Strong convictions and courage to take a stand for the right won lasting friends for him and he valued and returned the confidence and friendship of his adopted townsmen.

He sponsored many camping trips and outings for neighborhood children and his long leadership in the Cub Scouts has been popular and fruitful.

To dozens of civic activities and patriotic efforts he has given unsparingly of his time. As an artist and a decorator he has done much to beautify our village and neat appearing private homes and public buildings testify to his fine work.

The Bethel Public Library owes its attractive interior to his craftsmanship. The American Legion Hall, the Community Room, the Manse and the handsome auditorium of the West Parish Congregational Church are examples of his artistic skill. His time and labor for community and church projects were always donated.

Sympathy for his bereaved family and a sense of personal loss is felt by us all.

There is no better heritage to leave than the courage of truth and strength.

Family Group Sheet

Husband's Full Name: William Thompson Smith   **Chart No.**

Husband's Data	Day Month Year	City, Town or Place	County or Province, etc.	State or Country	Add. Info. on Husband
Birth	22-9-1865			Illinois	injuries from Auto accident
Chr'nd					
Marr.	6-2-1885				
Death	4-12-1946	ElDorado	Butler Co.	Kansas	
Burial	8-12-1946	McGill cem. Potwin	Butler Co.	Kansas	

Places of Residence:
Occupation: Farmer   **Church Affiliation:** Methodist   **Military Rec.**

Other wives: #2 wife-Mary Ann Motter

His Father: Thomas W. Smith (Todd)   **Mother's Maiden Name:** Mary Frances Dale

Wife's Full Maiden Name: Sarah Louise Moore

Wife's Data	Day Month Year	City, Town or Place	County or Province, etc.	State or Country	Add. Info. on Wife
Birth	6-7-1867	Chautauqua	Chautauqua Co.	Kansas	died in child birth
Chr'nd					
Death	12-1-1889	Elgin	Chautauqua Co.	Kansas	
Burial	1-1889	Oak Grove cem.	Elgin Chautauqua Co.	Kansas	

Places of Residence:
Occupation: Housewife   **Church Affiliation:**   **Military Rec.**

Her Father: Reuben Moore   **Mother's Maiden Name:** Melvina Barbara Paul

Sex	Children's Names in Full	Children's Data	Day Month Year	City, Town or Place	County or Province, etc.	State or Country	Add. Info. on Children
M	1 Oscar L. Smith Full Name of Spouse Mary Catherine	Birth Marr. Death Burial	2-1886 1963			Kansas	
F	2 Bertha M. Smith Full Name of Spouse Fred Petty	Birth Marr. Death Burial	3-1888 29-12-1904		Chautauqua Co. Ks.		

Family Group Sheet

Husband's Full Name: Oscar L. Smith

Chart No. —

	Day Month Year	City, Town or Place	County or Province, etc.	State or Country	Add. Info. on Husband
Birth	2-1886			Kansas	
Chr'nd					
Marr.					
Death	1963				
Burial					

Places of Residence:

Occupation: | Church Affiliation: | Military Rec:

Other wives, if any, No. (1)(2) etc. Make separate sheet for each marr.

His Father: William Thompson Smith **Mother's Maiden Name:** Sarah Louise Moore

Wife's Full Maiden Name: Mary Catharine Stevens

	Day Month Year	City, Town or Place	County or Province, etc.	State or Country	Add. Info. on Wife
Birth					
Chr'nd					
Death					
Burial					

Places of Residence:

Occupation: | Church Affiliation: | Military Rec:

Other husbands, if any, No. (1)(2) etc.: #1-Baker

Her Father: | **Mother's Maiden Name:**

Sex	Children's Names in Full		Day Month Year	City, Town or Place	County or Province, etc.	State or Country	Add. Info. on Children
F	1. Laverna Smith	Birth					
	Full Name of Spouse	Marr.					
		Death					
		Burial					
	2.	Birth					
	Full Name of Spouse	Marr.					
		Death					
		Burial					

FRED PETTY 1879 — 1959

BERTHA M. PETTY 1888 — 1966

JUNE LEOTA FERN PETTY 1918 — 1922

	6.	Birth					
	Full Name of Spouse	Marr.					
		Death					
		Burial					
	7.	Birth					
	Full Name of Spouse	Marr.					
		Death					
		Burial					
	8.	Birth					
	Full Name of Spouse	Marr.					
		Death					
		Burial					

Compiler:
Address:
City, State, Zip:
Date:

Family Group Sheet

Husband's Full Name: Fred Petty
Chart No.:

	Day Month Year	City, Town or Place	County or Province, etc	State or Country	Add. Info on Husband
Birth	1879				
Chr'nd					
Marr	29-12-1904				
Death	1959				
Burial		Oak Grove cem. Elgin	Chautauqua Co.	Kansas	

Places of Residence:
Occupation: Church Affiliation: Military Rec:
His Father: Mother's Maiden Name:

Wife's Full Maiden Name: Bertha M. Smith

	Day Month Year	City, Town or Place	County or Province, etc.	State or Country	Add. Info. on Wife
Birth	3-1888			Kansas	
Chr'nd					
Death	1966				
Burial		Oak Grove cem. Elgin	Chautauqua Co.	Kansas	

Places of Residence:
Occupation: Church Affiliation: Military Rec:
Her Father: William Thompson Smith   Mother's Maiden Name: Sarah Louise Moore

Sex	#	Children's Names in Full	Children's Data	Day Month Year	City, Town or Place	County or Province, etc	State or Country	Add. Info on Children
M	1	Fred Petty	Birth / Marr / Death / Burial					
M	2	Roy Petty	Birth / Marr / Death / Burial					
M	3	Dean Petty	Birth / Marr / Death / Burial					
M	4	Alvin Petty	Birth / Marr / Death / Burial					
F	5	Ola Petty	Birth / Marr / Death / Burial					
F	6	Nora Petty	Birth / Marr / Death / Burial					
F	7	Eula Petty	Birth / Marr / Death / Burial					
F	8	June Leota Fern P	Birth	1918				
			Marr.					
			Death	1922				
			Burial	1922	Oak Grove cem. Elgin Chau. Ks.			

Notes: #9 Gladys Irene born 1924
Ralph Omer Bohannah d. 1996 Ks.

The Eleven Months the George Wileys spent in Arkansas.

Mr. and Mr. Geo. Wiley and 3 children bought a 40 acre farm in Harrison Co., Ark. and moved there in Sept. 1903. As soon as my mother learned that they just had 4 mo. of school in Ark. she said "Let's move back to Kansas". That event took place sooner than expected on account of the death of my brother Reuben, Ruby, for short. We children thought it was a great treat to live on the farm where we had cows, horses, hogs, geese, ducks and chickens. At Christmas time we had a big Christmas tree and had Uncle John Taylors family as our guests. We had few gifts but there was popcorn and apples and everyone had a good time. My father was the Santa Claus and I knew who it was but the other kids didn't.

At Easter time we had company (the Taylors) who lived one-half mile from us. They had to come down a big hill to get to our house and my uncle John named it Mt. Sinai. At the base of the hill there was an everlasting spring of the clearest water you ever saw. Ozarka Water, if you please! The best ever.

On our Easter Sunday afternoon picnic we kids boiled eggs in an old gallon bucket. We had salt shakers of course and I slipped in the kitchen and got a big loaf of home made bread and what more could you want for Easter lunch. Of course we had a bucket of that good Old Ozarka water!

My cousin Orcen Taylor had a little bird with a string tied on its feet and it would fly away as far as it could and then he would pull it back with the string. I thought the bird should be loose so I ran up and broke the string. Orcen said now the poor little bird will die and I felt bad about it. Some things you never forget.

My Father had gotten the use of a vacant house in Blue Eye, Mo. which was our post office., as we lived 2½ miles from there. The building was to be used for a Sunday School and we went there every Sunday. We had Bibles and   lesson leaves and it was better than no church at all. We had 3 classes, Adults, Youth and children. I've often wondered if the people kept it going after we moved away. Probably not as my Father was the Supt. and kept it going.

My brother Walter and I rode to the Grocery store on one of the horses one day. The trip was to take a bucket of eggs to market. The trip was to take a bucket of eggs to market. On the way we met my cousin Orcen coming back from the store riding on his little burro. He had bought a sack of flour and put it on the burros back and can you imagine what a picture that made with the burros long ears wagging every step of the way and the white flour sack showing on both sides. No wonder our horse got scared and jumped and threw us off--eggs and all. Well there were less eggs to take to the store, for sure.

Sadness-

In May we had lots of rain and we all went out to the field where the rail fences were washed out. My father was repairing them and we kids waded in the ditches of water. My brother Reuby took sick right away and they said it was rheumatic fever that killed him. He died on May 27-1904. and we took him back to Altoona, Kansas for burial. The folks and Uncle John Taylors family decided to move back to Altoona and they had a sale and sold the stock and we moved back in August 1904. Walter and I started school in Sept., in the same grades we would have been in the year before.

When my Father and Mother lived on a farm in Harrison Co. Ark., my father went to the little store in Blue Eye, Mo. It was 3   or 4 miles from our house. His plan was to get a sack of flour but they were out of flour. Imagine a store being out of flour when everyone made their own bread. Well, he came home and my mother made Cornbread that noon and again that evening. Myself and brother's Walter and Ruby thought that was plenty of cornbread. The next morning my father rode a horse to Green Forest, a town 15 miles away to get a sack of flour. So we ate cornbread again at noon. Then in the afternoon my father came home with the flour and my mother made biscuits for supper. She said we kids were as happy as if he had brought candy.

Grandpa and Grandma Wiley then lived on a farm six miles south and east of Altoona and one spring Grandma Wiley put garden in at a small fenced in plot close to the house and then she put in several rows of beans about a block from the house in a plowed field and it wasn't fenced in. One morning after the beans had come up. Grandma Wiley looked out and saw an old Gander (they had a bunch of geese) and he was just walking down the bean row snipping off every bean and eating it. Grandma was really mad at him. Grandpa said we will get some wire and fence in a larger place for a garden next year.

I met and married John Eller in 1911 and as the Altoona Cement plant shut down he went to Dewey, Okla. and got work in the plant there. Before Glen was born I went back to stay with the folks a few weeks. Again before Everett was born I went back up there so the two of them were both born in Kansas and are Kansas Jay-hawkers. The other four children were all born in Oklahoma and are Sooners.

John and our six children were all baptized in the Dewey First Christian Church. I was baptized in the Verdigris River in Altoona, Kans. Several of our grandchildren were baptized here, too. Larry and Gerald Case, Rita Jo Eller, Barbara (Jones) and Sonya and Alice Marie Eller, Eileen Brockhouse, were their names. John Bartlett has his membership here too. Also, Wayneta Eller and Durena Case were baptized here. Helens 4 children were baptized in the Memorial Christian Church in Bartlesville when they lived there. Wayne, Stella, John and Norma Bartlett. Betty's son Michael was baptized in the Christian Church in Kansas City where they lived for a time. Bobbies children were baptized in the Christian Church in Champaign, Ill. They are Donna, Darlene, Diane, Debra and Ronnie Butts. All 17 grand-children are in the Christian Church. There is not a nicer church anywhere than the one in Dewey and I went into the church here in 1912 and John later in 1912.

In 1912 John had a sick spell. The Dr. sent him on the train to Independence, Kansas to the hospital. His father went up there on the train with him and stayed till he was over the operations. He had peritonitis and couldn't work for six months. Luckily we had insurance to take care of the expenses. I took Helen and went to his mothers in Collinsville, and stayed there a month and then went to my folks and stayed till he was able to work again.

Walter Wiley, Stella and John Eller, Etta Ellen, John and George Alan Wiley

Walter, Etta Ellen and John

Family Group Sheet

Husband's Full Name: GEORGE ALAN WILEY — Chart No.

Husband's Data	Day Month Year	City, Town or Place	County or Province, etc.	State or Country	Add. Info. on Husband
Birth	22-12-1863		Marion Co.	Ind.	Married by H.H. Brundridge
Chr'd					
Marr	19-3-1893	Altoona	Wilson Co.	Kansas	
Death	3-1-1949	Dewey	Washington Co.	Okla.	
Burial	1-1949	Altoona	Wilson Co.	Kansas	

Places of Residence: Altoona, Ks. Dewey, Okla.
Occupation: Bank clerk-Post Office **Church Affiliation:** Christian church **Military Rec:**

His Father: John Harvey Wiley **Mother's Maiden Name:** Harriet Adaline Cooper

Wife's Full Maiden Name: Etta Ellen Moore

Wife's Data	Day Month Year	City, Town or Place	County or Province, etc.	State or Country	Add. Info. on Wife
Birth	27-10-1874		Butler Co.	Kansas	
Chr'd					
Death	3-10-1945	Dewey	Washington Co.	Okla.	
Burial	6-10-1945	Altoona	Wilson Co.	Kansas	

Places of Residence: 3rd. St. Dewey, Okla. Altoona, Kans.
Occupation: Housewife **Church Affiliation:** Christian Church **Military Rec:** (Charter member in Altoona Christian church

Her Father: Reuben Moore **Mother's Maiden Name:** Melvina Barbara Paul

Sex	Children's Names in Full	Children's Data	Day Month Year	City, Town or Place	County or Province, etc.	State or Country	Add. Info. on Children
F	1 Stella Adaline W.	Birth	13-1-1894	Altoona	Wilson Co.	Kans.	
		Marr.	22-4-1911	Altoona	Wilson Co.	Kans.	
	Full Name of Spouse: John Everett Eller	Death	1-11-1986	Dewey	Wash. Co.	Okla.	
		Burial	4-11-1986	Dewey cem.	Wash. Co.	Okla.	
M	2 Walter George W.	Birth	27-5-1895	Altoona	Wilson Co.	Kans.	Killed in car wreck
		Marr.					
	Full Name of Spouse: Irene Sullivan	Death	18-6-1941	Newton	Harvey Co.	Kans.	
		Burial	6-1941	Altoona	Wilson Co.	Kans.	
M	3 Reuben William W.	Birth	4-3-1899	Altoona	Wilson Co.	Kans.	Rheumatic Fever
		Marr.					
	Full Name of Spouse:	Death	28-5-1904	Harrison		Ark.	
		Burial	1904	Altoona	Wilson Co.	Kans.	
M	4 John Moore Wiley	Birth	23-10-1904	Altoona	Wilson Co.	Kans.	Killed at work-Oil Co.
		Marr.					
	Full Name of Spouse: Irma Rogers	Death	14-3-1934	near Okla. City, Okla.		Okla.	
		Burial	3-1934				

Etta Moore and George Wiley

State of Kansas, County of Wilson.
BE IT REMEMBERED That on the 1. day of March A.D. 1873, there was issued from office of said Probate Judge, a Marriage License, of which the following is a true copy:

MARRIAGE LICENSE.
WILSON COUNTY, STATE OF KANSAS.

To any Person Authorized by Law to Perform the Marriage Ceremony, Greeting:
You are hereby authorized to join in Marriage George A Wiley of Altoona Kans aged 29 years, and Miss Etta E. Moore of Altoona Kans aged 18 years, and of this License you will make due return to my office within thirty days.

(SEAL) B.F. McPherson Probate Judge

And which said Marriage License was afterwards, to wit, on the 19th day of April A.D.
returned to said Probate Judge, with the following certificate endorsed thereon, to wit:

STATE OF KANSAS, COUNTY OF WILSON

I, H A Brundidge do hereby certify, that in accordance with the authorization of the within License I did, on the 19 day of March A.D. 1873, at Altoona, in said County join and unite in Marriage the within named George A Wiley and Etta E Moore
Witness my hand and seal the day and year above written.

ATTEST: J B F McPherson Probate Judge
H A Brundidge minister of Gospel

MRS. ETTA WILEY DIES

Another Dewey mother has been called to her reward when Mrs. Etta Wiley passed away at her home in Dewey on Wednesday, October 3rd, following a lingering illness. Mrs. Wiley fell at her home about three years ago, breaking her leg which has caused her to be an invalid ever since. Mrs. Wiley came to Dewey with her husband, George W. Wiley and their 3 children in 1917 from Altoona, Kansas and have made their home here since.

And since their arrival, their two sons have passed away and are buried in the Altoona cemetery.

Mrs. Wiley is survived by her husband, George Wiley, one daughter, Mrs. John E. Eller, 7 grandchildren and 8 great grandchildren.

Funeral services were held last Saturday afternoon at the Dewey Christian Church with the pastor J. T. Foust officiating and burial was in the cemetery at Altoona, Kansas with the Burt Funeral Home in Bartlesville.

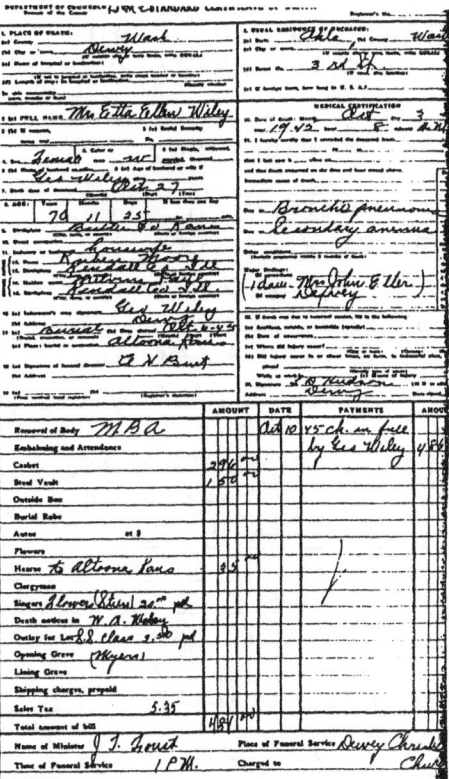

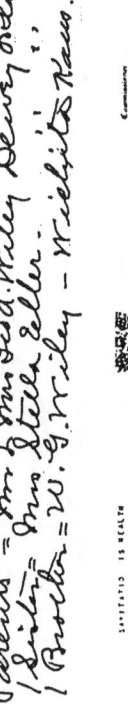

Family Group Sheet

Husband's Full Name John Everett Eller SS-487-07-7840 Chart No.

	Day Month Year	City, Town or Place	County or Province, etc.	State or Country	Add. Info on Husband
Birth	2-9-1893	Nevada	Vernon Co.	Mo.	
Chr'nd					
Marr	22-4-1911	Altoona	Wilson Co.	Kans.	
Death	25-11-1975	Bartlesville hospital	Wash. Co.	Okla.	
Burial	28-11-1975	Dewey cem.	Wash. Co.	Okla.	

Places of Residence Mo., Kansas and Okla.
Occupation Electrician-Farmer   Church Affiliation Christian Church   Military Rec

His Father John Wilkerson Eller   Mother's Maiden Name Eliza Ellen Routh

Wife's Full Maiden Name Stella Adaline Wiley

	Day Month Year	City, Town or Place	County or Province, etc.	State or Country	Add. Info on Wife
Birth	13-1-1894	Altoona	Wilson Co.	Kans.	
Chr'nd					
Death	1-11-1986	Dewey	Wash. Co.	Okla.	
Burial	5-11-1986	Dewey cem.	Wash. Co.	Okla.	

Places of Residence
Occupation Housewife   Church Affiliation Christian Church   Military Rec

Her Father George Alan Wiley   Mother's Maiden Name Etta Ellen Moore

Sex	Children's Names in Full		Day Month Year	City, Town or Place	County or Province, etc.	State or Country	Add. Info on Children
F	1 Helen Louise Eller	Birth	8-11-1911	Altoona	Wilson Co.	Kans.	
		Marr.	3-2-1931	Bartlesville	Wash. Co.	Okla.	
	Full Name of Spouse Bartlett Glen Clifford	Death	9-9-1991	Okla. City hosp.		Okla.	
		Burial	12-9-1991	Pauls Valley cem.	Garvin co.	Okla.	
M	2 George Everett E.	Birth	29-1-1915	Altoona	Wilson Co.	Kans.	
		Marr.	15-8-1936	Bartlesville	Wash. Co.	Okla.	
	Full Name of Spouse Wayneta O. Woody	Death	10-4-1998	Bartlesville hosp.	Wash.	Okla.	
		Burial	13-4-1998	Dewey cem.	Wash. Co.	Okla.	
M	3 James Wilkerson E.	Birth	8-7-1918	Dewey	Wash. Co.	Okla.	
		Marr.	12-1940	Ind.	Mont. Co.	Kans.	
	Full Name of Spouse Margaret Montgomery	Death	12-9-1995	Ochelata	Wash. Co.	Okla.	
		Burial	15-9-1995	Ramona	Wash. Co.	Okla.	
F	4 Willa Mae Eller	Birth	19-11-1922	Dewey	Wash. Co.	Okla.	
		Marr.	29-6-1940	Dewey	Wash. Co.	Okla.	
	Full Name of Spouse Bernal L. (Bud) Case	Death					
		Burial					
F	5 (Betty) Elizabeth Irene E.	Birth	12-4-1926	Dewey	Wash. Co.	Okla.	
		Marr.	31-10-1949	Kansas City	Wyandotte Co.	Ks.	
	Full Name of Spouse Bob A. Brockhouse	Death					
		Burial					
F	6 Barbara Ledora E.	Birth	20-3-1929	Dewey	Wash. Co.	Okla.	
		Marr.	1-6-1947	Dewey	Wash. Co.	Okla.	
	Full Name of Spouse Ronald Deane Butts	Death					
		Burial					

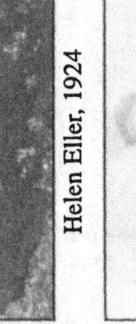
Helen Eller, 1924

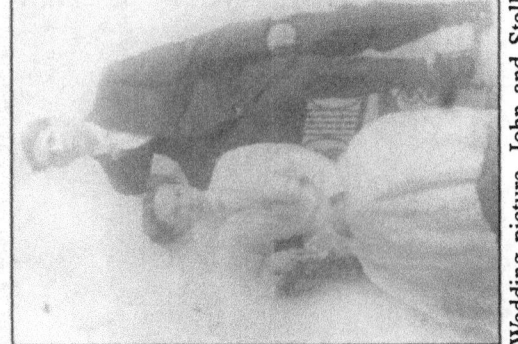
Wedding picture, John and Stella Eller

Examiner-Enterprise NOV 26 '75

John Eller Dies Tuesday; Rites Friday

John Everett Eller, 82, retired employe of the Dewey Portland Cement Co. and resident of Dewey since 1911, died at 1:10 p.m. Tuesday in the Jane Phillips Building of the local Medical Center, where he had been a patient since Nov. 22.

Funeral services will be held at 4 p.m. Friday in the sanctuary of the Dewey First Christian Church of which he had been an active member for over 63 years. Mr. Paul J. Enabnit Sr., his pastor, and Mr. B.J. Vernon, former pastor, will officiate and interment will be in the Dewey Cemetery by the Dewey Funeral Service. His body will lie in state where friends may call for their visitation until the service hour on Friday.

A native of Missouri, Eller was born on Sept. 2, 1893 at Nevada, and during his early boyhood moved with his family members to Altoona, Kan. He was united in marriage on April 22, 1911 at Altoona to the former Miss Stella Adaline Wiley and they established their first home at Dewey when he became employed with the Dewey Portland Cement Company's electrical department. He remained associated with Dewey Portland for over forty-five years and retired in 1956 and since that time Mr. and Mrs. Eller have remained residents of Dewey. They celebrated their sixty-fourth wedding anniversary in April of this year. In addition to his church membership, Mr. Eller was a 32 degree Mason and 50-year member of the Dewey Masonic Lodge No. 466 A.F. & A.M., a member and past president of the Local A.F.L. Union, Dewey and a member of the Central Trades and Labor Council, Bartlesville.

Survivors, in addition to his wife of the home in Dewey, include two sons, George Everett Eller, College Station, Texas and James W. Eller, Hominy; four daughters, Mrs. Glen (Helen) Bartlett, Pauls Valley; Mrs. Bob Brockhouse, Independence, Mo.; Mrs. Barbara Butts, Champaign, Ill.; and Mrs. Bud (Willa Mae) Case of Dewey; 17 grandchildren; 27 great-grandchildren and three great-great-grandchildren.

Stella Eller to celebrate birthday

The children of Stella Eller invite her friends to help celebrate Mrs. Eller's 90th Birthday Jan. 14. A reception will be held 2 to 4 p.m. at her home, 713 East Third Street, Dewey.

A scrapbook is being made including letters and pictures from friends and relatives, recalling memories of yesterday. Anyone wishing to contribute to the scrapbook may do so.

All of Mrs. Eller's children will be present for this happy occasion: Helen Bartlett of Pauls Valley; Everett and Jim Eller of Bartlesville; Mae Case of Dewey; Betty Brockhouse of Independence, Mo.; and Bobbie Butts of Denver, Colo.

John and Stella Eller, 50th Wedding Anniversary

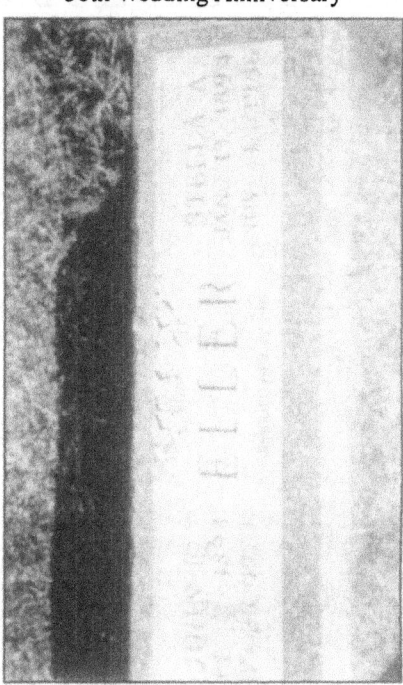

The John E. Eller Family

John grew up in Altoona, Kansas and went to work at the Cement Plant until they closed because of shortage of gas. He then came to Dewey and got work at the Dewey Portland Cement Plant in 1911.

Stella transferred membership to Dewey First Christian Church from the Altoona Christian Church. and John was Baptised here in 1912. Stella and her parents and Grandmother were Charter members of the Altoona Christian Church and Stella played the piano some there. Our two older children, Helen and Everett were born in Altoona, Kansas and our four other children, Jim, Willa Mae, Betty and Bobby were born in Dewey. We lived in Dewey when all of them were born but I went to Altoona to be with my parents when the two were born. Helen went to school at the Tuxedo school her first year and then to Dewey until she graduated. The others all graduated from Blue Mound school except Jim and he went to Wayside his last year so he could play basketball for them. Everett was the Valedictorian of his 8th. Grade class. Betty and Bobby went all 8 years to Blue Mound. Willa Mae went two years to Dewey Grade School and then to Blue Mound 6 years before going back to High School in Dewey. The boys went several years of Grade School in Dewey before going to the country school. All attended High School in Dewey and the girls all graduated from High School there. Betty went on and Graduated from the Phillips University in Enid, Okla. A Christian University at that time. Both boys played Football in High School. They both were in Tract Meets and did good in them in Grade School.

In 1926 we bought 40 acres east of Dewey and moved out there to a 5 room not modern house. It was a quiet life on the farm, no telephone, no gas, electric or running water. We did have electricity after the REA came in our last two years in the country. They all had horses to ride to school and had fun riding the horses to school no matter what the weather.

Grandma Wiley fell and broke her hip and I went to her house and stayed nights with her for 9 months till she died. Also, took care of her in the daytime when she needed me. Then moved to town to be closer to them and lived first on 3rd. St. and moved across the Alley to 4th. St. Then Grandpa Wiley said for us to move down and live with him so John built another room on his house and we moved to help see about him. Grandma Wiley died Oct. 3, 1945 and Grandpa Wiley died Jan. 3, 1949. He died when he was 85 yrs. and 12 days old. Grandma was 71 when she died.

Life on the Farm

When we moved to the the farm John worked nights every other month so we had to be quiet, so he could sleep in the day-time. He also farmed during the day. Growing cattle, cows, horses, calves and hay-baling and wheat threshing, etc. in his spare time. We owned some cows and sold milk and cream at different times. Also sold eggs. We had a well drilled close to the house and it had Alkali water that we couldn't drink so still had to haul water from town for cooking and drinking but could do the washing in it. The boys each had a big dog but we never bought them food. If the table scraps were not enough for them they could run down a rabbit. A neighbor once said he killed a coyote and Everett's dog disappeared at the same time so we always thought he killed the dog instead. I can't remember what became of Jim's dog. Willa Mae had a black and white dog named Bounce a cousin in Kansas had given her. We moved him to town with us but he was hit by a car and never lived very long after that. She also had a pony named Muggins to ride and one time when our nephew Billy Eller

Family Group Sheet

SS-441-05-8787

Husband's Full Name: Glenn Clifford Bartlett   Chart No.

	Day Month Year	City, Town or Place	County or Province, etc.	State or Country	Add. Info on Husband
Birth	1-7-1906	Bartlett		Ohio	
Chr'nd					
Marr	3-2-1931	Bartlesville	Washington Co.	Okla.	
Death	23-11-1988	Pauls Valley	Garvin Co.	Okla.	
Burial	26-11-1988	Mt. Olivet cem.	Pauls Valley-Garvin Co. Okla.		

Places of Residence: Dewey, Bartlesville, Caney, Ks., Ramona, Pauls Valley Okla.
Occupation: Telegraph- Engineer Sinclair-Arco Oil Co.   Military Rec

His Father: Don Carlos Bartlett   **Mother's Maiden Name:** Bessie Jane Heald

Wife's Full Maiden Name: Helen Louise Eller SS-443-36-4447

	Day Month Year	City, Town or Place	County or Province, etc.	State or Country	Add. Info on Wife
Birth	8-11-1911	Altoona	Wilson Co.	Kansas	
Chr'nd					
Death	9-9-1991	Okla. City hospital	Oklahoma Co.	Oklahoma	
Burial	12-9-1991	Mt. Olivet cem. Pauls Valley	Garvin Co.	Okla.	

Places of Residence: same as above
Occupation: Bookeeper-housewife   Church Affiliation   Military Rec

Her Father: John Everett Eller   **Mother's Maiden Name:** Stella Adaline Wiley

Sex	Children's Names in Full		Day Month Year	City, Town or Place	County or Province, etc.	State or Country	Add. Info on Children
M 1	Wayne Irvin Bartlett	Birth	4-9-1931	Dewey	Wash. Co.	Okla.	
		Marr	8-7-1951	Bartlesville	Wash. Co.	Okla.	
	Full Name of Spouse	Death					
	Rose Bond	Burial					
F 2	Stella Mae Bartlett	Birth	28-2-1934	Dewey	Wash. Co.	Okla.	
		Marr	22-5-1953	Leiphiem		Germany	
	Full Name of Spouse	Death					
	Calvin Hoover Pfeiff	Burial					
M 3	John Carl Bartlett	Birth	4-12-1936	Dewey	Wash. Co.	Okla.	
		Marr	3-6-1963	Pawhuska	Osage Co.	Okla.	
	Full Name of Spouse	Death					
	Carol Stephenson	Burial					
F 4	Norma Jean Bartlett	Birth	23-8-1938	Dewey	Wash. Co.	Okla.	
		Marr	12-19-1959	Pauls Valley	Garvin Co.	Okla.	
	Full Name of Spouse	Death					
	Jerry Lehman	Burial					
	5	Birth					

Helen and Glen Bartlett's children: Stella Mae Patterson, Wayne, John and Norma Lehman.

Helen and family, 1990.

Family Group Sheet

Husband's Full Name: Wayne Irvin Bartlett — Chart No.

	Day Month Year	City, Town or Place	County or Province, etc.	State or Country	Add. Info. on Husband
Birth	4-9-1931	Dewey	Wash. Co.	Okla.	
Chr'nd					
Marr	8-7-1951	Bartlesville	Wash. Co.	Okla.	
Death					
Burial					

Places of Residence: Kansas-Oklahoma-Colorado
Occupation: Enforcement officer City of Colorado **Church Affiliation:** Christian **Military Rec:** US Army--Korea
His Father: Glenn Clifford Bartlett **Mother's Maiden Name:** Rose Bond

Wife's Full Maiden Name: Rose Marie Bond

	Day Month Year	City, Town or Place	County or Province, etc.	State or Country	Add. Info. on Wife
Birth	14-11-1933		Osage Co.	Okla.	
Chr'nd					
Death					
Burial					

Places of Residence: Oklahoma-Colorado
Occupation: Nurse **Church Affiliation:** Christian **Military Rec:**
Her Father: Charles Bond **Mother's Maiden Name:** Wren

Sex	Children's Names in Full		Day Month Year	City, Town or Place	County or Province, etc.	State or Country	Add. Info. on Children
F	1 Alice Fay Bartlett	Birth	12-1-1953	Bartlesville	Wash. Co.	Okla.	
		Marr.	20-4-1973	Colo. Springs	ElPaso Co.	Colo.	
	Full Name of Spouse: John Eugene Orcutt	Death					
		Burial					
M	2 Johnny Wayne Bartlett	Birth	9-7-1957	Pawhuska	Osage Co.	Okla.	
		Marr.	12-1978	Fountain	ElPaso Co.	Colo.	
	Full Name of Spouse: Susan (Div)	Death					
		Burial					
M	3 Charles Clifford	Birth	6-11-1958	Pawhuska	Osage Co.	Okla.	
		Marr.	25-9-1982	Fountain	ElPaso Co.	Colo.	
	Full Name of Spouse: Judy Taylor	Death					
		Burial					

Wayne Irvin Bartlett, 1994

1931 — 1981

The children and grandchildren of Mr. and Mrs. Glen Bartlett request the honour of your presence at their

Fiftieth Wedding Anniversary

on Sunday, the first of February Nineteen hundred and eighty-one

from two to four o'clock

at the Pauls Valley Library
215 North Walnut
Pauls Valley, Oklahoma

IN LOVING MEMORY OF

Helen L. Bartlett

BORN
November 8, 1911
Altoona, Kansas

PASSED THIS LIFE
September 9, 1991
Oklahoma City, Oklahoma

SERVICES
2:00 P.M., September 12, 1991
Stufflebean Chapel

CLERGY
Rev. Van Alan Grubbs

INTERMENT
Mt. Olivet Cemetery
Pauls Valley, Oklahoma

SERVICES DIRECTED BY
Stufflebean Funeral Home
Pauls Valley, Oklahoma

Page 8 Friday, November 25, 1988

Obituaries
Glen C. Bartlett

July 1 1906
Nov. 23 1988

Funeral services for Glen C. Bartlett, of Pauls Valley, Oklahoma, who died Wednesday, Nov. 23, at Pauls Valley General Hospital, will be held at 1:00 p.m. Saturday, Nov. 26, at Stufflebean Funeral Home Chapel. Rev. Wayne Ashlock will officiate and burial will be in Mt. Olivet Cemetery, under the direction of Stufflebean Funeral Home.

Bartlett had lived in the Pauls Valley community for the past 37 years. He married Helen Louise Eller on Feb. 3, 1931, in Bartlesville, Okla. He retired after 30 years with Arco Pipe Line Co.

Surviving are his wife, Helen, of the home, two sons, Wayne Bartlett, of Fountain, Colo., and John Bartlett, of Elk City, Okla., two daughters, Stella Patterson, of Bartlesville and Norma Lehman, of Pauls Valley, one brother, James Bartlett, of Pawhuska, Okla., one sister, Clara Pendleton, of Coffeyville, Kan., 11 grandchildren and 22 great grandchildren.

Mr. & Mrs. Glenn Bartlett
Sunday January 25, 1981
Couple to celebrate Golden Anniversary

Mr. and Mrs. Glenn Bartlett of Pauls Valley will be celebrating their 50th Wedding Anniversary Feb. 3.

In honor of this special occasion, their children and grandchildren will be hosting a reception to honor Mr. and Mrs. Bartlett at the Pauls Valley Library Feb. 1. Friends and relatives are cordially invited to attend the reception from 2 to 4 p.m.

Glenn and Helen Bartlett were married in Bartlesville Feb. 3, 1931. They have four children: Wayne Bartlett of Fountain, Colo., Stella Patterson of Bartlesville, Johnny Bartlett of Burns Flat and Norma Lehman of Pauls Valley. They also have 11 grandchildren and 1 great grandchildren.

Glenn Bartlett retired from Arco Oil Co. in 1971 after 30 years of service. Before that he had worked 13 years for the Home Service Station in Dewey, where the couple were raised.

Charles and Judy, Johnie and Darlene, Johnny and Alice

Johnathon, Jason, Heather, Jacob (Jake), Alissa, Travis, Amanda (Mandy)

Charles, Wayne, Rose, Johnie, Alice

Charles Clifford, Alice Fay and Johnie Wayne

Family Group Sheet

Husband's Full Name: John Eugene Orcutt **Chart No.**

Husband's Data	Day Month Year	City, Town or Place	County or Province, etc.	State or Country	Add. Info. on Husband
Birth	27- 8-1947	Colo. Springs	ElPaso Co.	Colo.	
Chr'nd					
Marr	20- 4-1973	Fountain	ElPaso Co.	Colo.	
Death					
Burial					

Places of Residence:
Occupation: Electric Co.   Church Affiliation: Military Rec: Navy 1966-1970

His Father: Mother's Maiden Name:

Wife's Full Maiden Name: Alice Faye Bartlett

Wife's Data	Day Month Year	City, Town or Place	County or Province, etc.	State or Country	Add. Info. on Wife
Birth	12- 1-1953	Bartlesville	Wash. Co.	Okla.	
Chr'nd					
Death					
Burial					

Places of Residence:
Occupation: Secretary-Housewife   Church Affiliation: Christian   Military Rec:

Her Father: Wayne Irvin Bartlett   Mother's Maiden Name: Rose Bond

Sex	Children's Names in Full	Children's Data	Day Month Year	City, Town or Place	County or Province, etc.	State or Country	Add. Info. on Children
M	1 Travis Eugene O.	Birth	23- 7-1974	Colo. Springs	ElPaso Co.	Colo.	
	Full Name of Spouse: Carmen Bartels	Marr	19- 4-1997				
		Death					
		Burial					
F	2 Amanda Michelle O.	Birth	22- 5-1977	Colo. Springs	ElPaso Co.	Colo.	
		Marr					

Family Group Sheet

Husband's Full Name: Travis Eugene Orcutt   **Chart No.**

Husband's Data	Day Month Year	City, Town or Place	County or Province, etc.	State or Country	Add. Info. on Husband
Birth	23- 7-1974	Colo. Springs	ElPaso Co.	Colo.	
Chr'nd					
Marr	19- 4-1997	Fountain	ElPaso Co.	Colo.	
Death					
Burial					

Places of Residence:
Occupation: Church Affiliation: Military Rec:

His Father: John Eugene Orcutt   Mother's Maiden Name: Alice Faye Bartlett

Wife's Full Maiden Name: Carmen Bartels

Wife's Data	Day Month Year	City, Town or Place	County or Province, etc.	State or Country	Add. Info. on Wife
Birth					
Chr'nd					
Death					
Burial					

Places of Residence:
Occupation: Church Affiliation: Military Rec:

Her Father: John Bartels   Mother's Maiden Name: Joanne

Sex	Children's Names in Full	Children's Data	Day Month Year	City, Town or Place	County or Province, etc.	State or Country	Add. Info. on Children
F	1 Carly Savannah O.	Birth	25-7-1996	Fountain	ElPaso Co.	Colo.	
	Full Name of Spouse:	Marr					
		Death					
		Burial					

Family Group Sheet

Husband's Full Name _____ **Chart No.** _____

	Day Month Year	City, Town or Place	County or Province, etc.	State or Country	Add. Info on Husband
Birth					
Chr'nd					
Marr.					
Death					
Burial					

Places of Residence: _____

Occupation: _____ Church Affiliation: _____ Military Rec: _____

His Father: **David Williwm McDonner, Sr.**   Mother's Maiden Name: **Andrea Santos (Fadden)**

Wife's Full Maiden Name: Amanda Michelle Orcutt

	Day Month Year	City, Town or Place	County or Province, etc.	State or Country	Add. Info on Wife
Birth	22-5-1977	Fountain	ElPaso Co.	Colo.	
Chr'nd					
Death					
Burial					

Places of Residence: Colorado

Occupation: _____ Church Affiliation: _____ Military Rec: _____

Her Father: **John E. Orcutt**   Mother's Maiden Name: **Alice Faye Bartlett**

Sex	Children's Names in Full		Day Month Year	City, Town or Place	County or Province, etc.	State or Country	Add. Info on Children
M	1. Alexander Chance O	Birth	22-7-1996	Fountain	ElPaso Co.	Colo.	
		Marr.					
	Full Name of Spouse	Death					
		Burial					
	2.	Birth					
		Marr.					
	Full Name of Spouse	Death					

Carly Savannah Orcutt, 46 days old.

Alexander Chance Orcutt, 1 day old.

Family Group Sheet

Husband's Full Name: Johnny Wayne Bartlett

Chart No.

	Day Month Year	City, Town or Place	County or Province, etc.	State or Country	Add. Info on Husband
Birth	9-7-1957	Pawhuska	Osage Co.	Okla.	#2 wife Darlene
Chr'nd					
Marr	12-1978	Fountain	ElPaso Co.	Colo.	
Death					
Burial					

Places of Residence:

Occupation: City of Fountain **Church Affiliation:** **Military Rec:**

His Father: Wayne Irvin Bartlett **Mother's Maiden Name:** Rose Bond

Wife's Full Maiden Name: Susan

	Day Month Year	City, Town or Place	County or Province, etc.	State or Country	Add. Info on Wife
Birth					
Chr'nd					
Death					
Burial					

Places of Residence:

Occupation: **Church Affiliation:** **Military Rec:**

Her Father: **Mother's Maiden Name:**

Sex	Children's Names in Full	Children's Data	Day Month Year	City, Town or Place	County or Province, etc.	State or Country	Add. Info on Children
F	1 Alissa Christina B	Birth	7-12-1979	Colo. Springs	ElPaso Co.	Colo.	
	Full Name of Spouse	Marr.					
		Death					
		Burial					
	2	Birth					
	Full Name of Spouse	Death					
		Burial					

MARCH 23, 1943

50TH WEDDING ANNIVERSARY

Mr. and Mrs. Geo. A. Wiley observed their 50th wedding anniversary at their home at 715 East 3rd Street in Dewey last Friday the 19th day of March.

George A. Wiley was born in Marion County Indiana, 10 miles north of Indianapolis 79 years ago and moved to Altoona, Kansas when he was 5 years old. Etta E. Moore was born in Butler County Kansas 69 years ago and they were married on March 19th, at 1893 at Altoona, Kansas.

They farmed for a few years then Mr. Wiley entered the mercantile field then, had some experience as a clerk in a Bank then, was assistant postmaster and worked on a small newspaper so he has had a varied experience in the business world.

To them, were born four children, one daughter who is now Mrs. J. E. Eller of Dewey and three sons who have all passed on. One of the sons died a natural death at the age of 5 years but accidents took the other two, as one was killed in an automobile accident near Newton, Kansas in 1941 at the age of 46 while the other was killed in a plant where he was working in Oklahoma in 1934 at the age of 30.

Tragedy oft times plays a part in the mysteries of life and it is not for us to understand why things of this sort happen to such worthy people but it is not for us to judge.

Mr. and Mrs. Wiley have most always been blessed with good health, through all the fifty years of their married life until recently Mrs. Wiley had the misfortune to suffer a broken limb in June of 1942 and has not been able to get around as had been her custom before.

We congratulate you Mr. and Mrs. Wiley on your having attained your 50th wedding anniversary as we believe the percentage of those who reach the 50th mark is small.

Husband's Full Name

Stella A. Eller

Mrs. Stella Adaline (Wiley) Eller, 92, 713 E. 3rd in Dewey and area resident for the past 75 years, died at 3 p.m. Saturday at the home of her daughter and son-in-law, Mr. and Mrs. Bud (Willa Mae) Case, Dewey.

Funeral services for Mrs. Eller will be held at 2 p.m. Wednesday in the sanctuary of the Dewey First Christian Church. Leon Martin, her pastor, will be the officiant. Committal prayers and interment will be directed in the Dewey Cemetery by the Arnold Moore Funeral Service.

A native of Kansas, Mrs. Eller was born at Altoona on Jan. 13, 1894 and was the daughter of George A. and Etta Ellen Moore Wiley. She was reared and educated in Altoona graduating with the senior class of 1911.

She married Everett Eller on April 22, 1911 at Altoona and the couple came to Dewey that same year.

Mr. Eller was an employee of the Dewey Portland Cement Co. and served at the president of the local A.F. of L. Union for several years. He preceded her in death on Nob. 25, 1975.

Mrs. Eller was a charter member of the Altoona First Christian Church and was a member of the Dewey First Christian Church and taught the Fidelis Sunday School class for 17 years.

Mrs. Eller will lie in state at the Dewey Funeral Home where friends may call for visitation until the service hour on Wednesday.

Surviving Mrs. Eller are two sons, George Everett Eller of Bartlesville and James W. Eller of Ramona; four daughters, Mrs. Glen (Helen) Bartlett of Pauls Valley, Okla., Mrs. Bud (Willa Mae) Case of rural Dewey, Mrs. B.A. (Betty) Brockhouse of Independence, Mo., and Mrs. Barbara Butts of Champaign, Ill.; 17 grandchildren; 39 great grandchildren; six step-grandchildren and 10 great step-grandchildren.

Nov. 1, 1986

Compiler	Notes:
Address	
City, State, Zip	
Date	

Family Group Sheet

Husband's Full Name Charles Clifford Bartlett — **Chart No.**

Husband's Data	Day Month Year	City, Town or Place	County or Province, etc.	State or Country	Add. Info on Husband
Birth	6-11-1958	Pawhuska	Osage Co.	Okla.	
Chr'nd					
Marr	25-9-1982	Fountain	ElPaso Co.	Colo.	
Death					
Burial					

Places of Residence

Occupation: Heavy Equip. operator Church Affiliation Military Rec

His Father: Wayne Irvin Bartlett Mother's Maiden Name: Rose Bond

Wife's Full Maiden Name Judy Taylor

Wife's Data	Day Month Year	City, Town or Place	County or Province, etc.	State or Country	Add. Info on Wife
Birth					
Chr'nd					
Death					
Burial					

Places of Residence

Occupation Church Affiliation Military Rec

Her Father: Mother's Maiden Name:

Sex	Children's Names in Full	Children's Data	Day Month Year	City, Town or Place	County or Province, etc.	State or Country	Add. Info on Children
F	1 Heather Bartlett	Birth	15-6-1980	Colo. Springs	ElPaso Co.	Colo.	
	Full Name of Spouse	Marr.					
		Death					
		Burial					
M	2 Jacob Brian Bartlett	Birth	31-10-1986	Colo. Springs	ElPaso Co.	Colo.	
	Full Name of Spouse	Marr.					
		Death					
		Burial					
	3	Birth					
		Marr.					
	Full Name of Spouse	Death					
		Burial					
	4	Birth					
		Marr.					
	Full Name of Spouse	Death					
		Burial					
	5	Birth					
		Marr.					
	Full Name of Spouse	Death					
		Burial					
	6	Birth					
		Marr.					
	Full Name of Spouse	Death					
		Burial					
	7	Birth					
		Marr.					
	Full Name of Spouse	Death					
		Burial					
	8	Birth					
		Marr.					
	Full Name of Spouse	Death					
		Burial					

Compiler: Notes:
Address:
City, State, Zip:
Date:

Family Group Sheet

Husband's Full Name: Calvin Hoover Pfeiff   **Chart No.**

	Day Month Year	City, Town or Place	County or Province, etc.	State or Country	Add. Info. on Husband
Birth	3-11-1928	Olney Springs		Colo.	
Chr'nd					
Marr	22-5-1953	Leipheim	Augsburg Co.	Germany	
Death	14-2-1963	Ft. Hood		Texas	
Burial	19-2-1963	Ft. Gibson		Okla.	

Places of Residence: Germany, Texas, Colorado
Occupation: Career-Army   **Church Affiliation:** Christian   **Military Rec:** Armored Div. US Army Korea-Germany Occ Forces
His Father: Otto L. Pfeiff   **Mother's Maiden Name:**

Wife's Full Maiden Name: Stella Mae Bartlett

	Day Month Year	City, Town or Place	County or Province, etc.	State or Country	Add. Info. on Wife
Birth	28-2-1934	Dewey	Wash. Co.	Okla.	
Chr'nd					
Death					
Burial					

Places of Residence: Oklahoma-Kansas-Texas-Germany
Occupation: Nursing at State School   **Church Affiliation:** Christian   **Military Rec:**
Other husbands: #3 Elmer Patterson
Her Father: Glenn C. Bartlett   **Mother's Maiden Name:** Helen Louise Eller

Sex	Children's Names in Full	Children's Data	Day Month Year	City, Town or Place	County or Province, etc.	State or Country	Add. Info. on Children
F	1 Emma Jean Pfeiff	Birth	8-1-1956	Ft. Polk		La.	#2 Sam Reece husband
	Spouse: Mike Nicholson (div)	Marr	7-11-1973	Pauls Valley	Garvin Co.	Okla.	
		Death					
		Burial					
F	2 Cynthia Louise P.	Birth	16-2-1957	Ft. Hood		Texas	#2 husband Paget Loper
	Spouse: Bill Sherrell (div)	Marr	13-2-1976	Pauls Valley	Garvin Co.	Okla.	
		Death					
		Burial					
M	3 Glen Stephen Pfieff	Birth	18-6-1959	Leipheim	Augsburg	Germany	
		Marr					

295

Dewey News

Mrs. Elise Still   Phone 807

The Bartlesville Examiner-Enterprise is as near as your Telephone. Have Your paper started today. CALL

L. C. JONES   DEWEY 262

Former Dewey Girl Is Wed In Germany

Marriage vows were read for Miss Stella Mae Bartlett, daughter of Mr. and Mrs. Glen Bartlett, formerly of Dewey, but now residing in Pauls Valley, and Sgt. Calvin Herbert Pfieff of Fowler, Colo., on May 22 at the army base chapel at Lepheim, Germany, following a civil ceremony earlier in the day at Ulm, Germany.

The bridal gown was of white slipper satin and she wore a veil of silk illusion. Her bouquet was of pink and white carnations, with a shower of white satin streamers, and she carried a white Bible.

Miss Esther Bell of Los Angeles was the bridesmaid and the best man was Sgt. Simmon. Chaplain Mobley of San Antonio read the vows for the young couple.

A reception followed the ceremony, and they will make their home in Leipheim. Mrs. Pfieff is a granddaughter of Mr. and Mrs. John Eller of Dewey.

Mrs. Dave Haymes has just returned from a week's visit in Dallas, with her son, Dr. Carl Haymes and family.

Mr. and Mrs. Glenn Bartlet Pauls Valley have returned after a visit here with their ents, Mr. and Mrs. D. C. Bar and Mr. and Mrs. John Elle

MRS. CALVIN H. PFIEFF

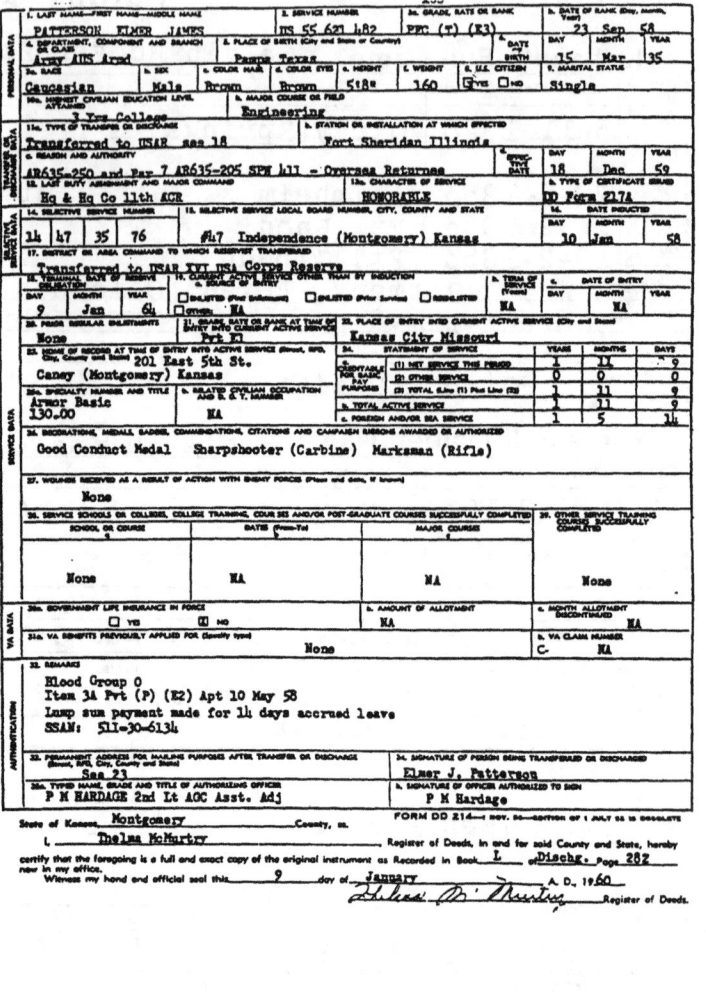

Stella Mae Pfieff and Emer Patterson (2nd husband)

Alissa Bartlett, 1998

LAST NAME - FIRST NAME - MIDDLE NAME	GRADE	SERVICE NUMBER	NAME OF CEMETERY
Pfeiff, Calvin Hoover	SFC(E6)	RA 17192061	Fort Gibson National Cemetery, Oklahoma

DATES OF SERVICE
ENLISTMENT	SEPARATION	RETIRED / ☒ DIED ON AD	SERVICE DATA	CHECK IF REMAINS CREMATED
	14 Feb 1963	☒ DIED ON AD	Ft. Hood, Texas HQ. & HQ. Co. 2nd Armored Division	

☐ WW I ☐ WW II ☒ KOREA ☐ OTHER (Specify)

STATE	EMBLEM	
Colorado	☒ CHRISTIAN ☐ HEBREW ☐ NONE ☐ OTHER (Specify)	

DATE OF BIRTH	DATE OF DEATH	DATE OF INTERMENT	GRAVE LOCATION	DEPTH OF GRAVE	CASKET IN	DB, RE, SR
Nov 3 1928	Feb 14 1963	Feb 19 1963	SECTION 10 GRAVE NO. 18	7FtCL	☒ BOX ☐ VAULT ☐ NONE	☒ VERIFIED NOK ☐ NOT VERIFIED

NAME AND ADDRESS OF NEXT OF KIN OR OTHER RESPONSIBLE PERSON (Include postal zone and relationship)
Mrs Stella Mae Pfeiff (Widow)
404 Robins Circle, Killeen, Texas

HEADSTONE OR MARKER ORDERED

REMARKS (Authority for interment, disinterment)
Auth: MSG CG, FT. HOOD, TEXAS DTD 16 FEB 1963.
NOK desires burial in same gravesite with
serviceman. DB of NOK: 28 Feb. 1934.

SHIPPING POINT FOR HEADSTONE (Nearest freight station)
Fort Gibson, Oklahoma

PERTINENT BURIAL DATA

PLACE OF DEATH	RELIGIOUS DENOMINATION OF DECEDENT
Ft. Hood, Texas	Christian Church
NAME OF FUNERAL DIRECTOR	NAME OF CHAPLAIN OFFICIATING AT BURIAL SERVICE
Lescher F.H., Muskogee, Oklahoma	Lt. Col. William C. Taggart Jr.

TYPED NAME OF SUPERINTENDENT	SIGNATURE OF SUPERINTENDENT
Clifton Cockrell	

DA FORM 2122 1 OCT 61 PREVIOUS EDITION IS OBSOLETE. RECORD OF INTERMENT (TM 10-287) 2

```
VID          VETERAN IDENTIFICATION DATA    SEQ NO 2600552490129639      09-17-1997
FILE NO 22-101-546    PN 00    BR           NAME
SSN                   INS NO                SVC NO 17192061         STUB NAME


FILE NO 22-101-546    PAYEE NO 00           NAME PFEIFF,CALVIN,H
ASSIGN FILE NO AS     CLAIM OR    SSN       CLAIM FOLDER LOCATION   070 FTW
SOCIAL SECURITY NO                          DATE OF DEATH           02-14-1963
INSURANCE FILE NO                           CAUSE OF DEATH          UNKNOWN
INSURANCE POLICY NO                         DEATH IN SVC
DATE OF BIRTH                               POSITIVE INDICATION
SEX                                         POWER OF ATTORNEY
SERVICE NO(S)         17192061                                      PG IN-THEATER
EOD                   10-25-1962                                    START
RAD                   02-14-1963                                    END
BRANCH OF SVC         ARMY                                          DAYS
CHARACTER OF SVC      UNK
SEP REASON CODE
PAY GRADE
NON-PAY DAYS


CONTESTED DATA        DELETE RECORD         VADS        VERIFIED U
                                                                    NEXT SCREEN
```

Family Group Sheet

Husband's Full Name Mike Nicholson   **Chart No.**

Husband's Data	Day	Month	Year	City, Town or Place	County or Province, etc.	State or Country	Add. Info. on Husband
Birth							
Chr'nd							
Marr	07	10	1973	Pauls Valley	Garvin County	Oklahoma	
Death							
Burial							

Places of Residence

Occupation   Church Affiliation   Military Rec.

Other wives, if any No. (1) (2) etc. Make separate sheet for each marr.

His Father   Mother's Maiden Name

Wife's Full Maiden Name Emma Jean Pfieff

Wife's Data	Day	Month	Year	City, Town or Place	County or Province, etc.	State or Country	Add. Info. on Wife
Birth	09	01	1956	Ft. Polk		Louisianna	
Chr'nd	Christian						
Death							
Burial							

Places of Residence

Occupation Waitress-Manager   Church Affiliation Christian   Military Rec.

Other husbands, if any No. (1) (2) etc. Sam Reece married 28, 1978

Her Father Calvin Hoover Pfieff   Mother's Maiden Name Stella Mae Bartlett

Sex	Children's Names in Full (arranged in order of birth)	Children's Data	Day	Month	Year	City, Town or Place	County or Province, etc. State or Country	Add. Info. on Children
M	1 Robert Allen Nickolson	Birth	31	10	1974	Pauls Valley, Garvin Co. OK		Army
		Marr.						
	Full Name of Spouse	Death						
		Burial						
	2	Birth						
		Marr.						
	Full Name of Spouse	Death						
		Burial						
	3	Birth						
		Marr.						
	Full Name of Spouse	Death						
		Burial						
	4	Birth						
		Marr.						
	Full Name of Spouse	Death						
		Burial						
	5	Birth						
		Marr.						

Cynthia, Stella, Calvin, Glen and Jean Pfieff

Emma Pfieff Reece, Tommy Reece, and Stella Mae Patterson

Family Group Sheet

Husband's Full Name: Sam Reece
Chart No.:

	Day Month Year	City, Town or Place	County or Province, etc.	State or Country	Add. Info on Husband
Birth					
Chr'nd					
Marr	28-11-1978	Pauls Valley	Garvin Co.	Okla.	
Death					
Burial					

Places of Residence:
Occupation: Works for City-Trucker **Church Affiliation:** **Military Rec:**
His Father: **Mother's Maiden Name:**

Wife's Full Maiden Name: Emma Jean Pfeiff

	Day Month Year	City, Town or Place	County or Province, etc.	State or Country	Add. Info on Wife
Birth	9-1-1956	Ft. Polk		La.	
Chr'nd					
Death					
Burial					

Places of Residence: Oklahoma-La.-Germany
Occupation: Manager-food store **Church Affiliation:** Christian **Military Rec:**
Other husbands: #1 husband Mike Nicholson (M) Oct. 1, 1973
Her Father: Calvin Hoover Pfeiff **Mother's Maiden Name:** Stella Mae Bartlett

Sex	Children's Names		Day Month Year	City, Town or Place	County or Province, etc.	State or Country	Add. Info on Children
M	1 Nicholson Robert Allen	Birth	31-10-1974	Pauls Valley	Garvin Co.	Okla.	US Army
	Full Name of Spouse	Marr. Death Burial					
M	2 Nathan Edward Reece	Birth	1-11-1979	Pauls Valley	Garvin Co.	Okla.	
	Full Name of Spouse	Marr. Death Burial					
M	3 Reece Jonathan Adrian	Birth	2-11-1980	Pauls Valley	Garvin Co.	Okla.	
	Full Name of Spouse	Marr. Death Burial					
M	4 Thomas Ray Reece	Birth	24-10-1982	Pauls Valley	Garvin Co.	Okla.	
	Full Name of Spouse	Marr. Death Burial					
F	5 Alisha Dawn Reece	Birth	21-9-1985	Pauls Valley	Garvin Co.	Okla.	
	Full Name of Spouse	Marr. Death Burial					
F	6 Reece Christina Elizabeth	Birth	5-11-1992	Pauls Valley	Garvin Co.	Okla.	
	Full Name of Spouse	Marr. Death Burial					
	7	Birth Marr. Death Burial					
	8	Birth Marr. Death Burial					

Compiler:
Address:
City, State, Zip:
Date:
Notes:

Family Group Sheet

Husband's Full Name: Paget Loper **Chart No.**

	Day Month Year	City, Town or Place	County or Province, etc.	State or Country	Add. Info on Husband
Birth					
Chr'nd					
Marr.	22-7-1994	Pauls Valley	Garvin Co.	Okla.	
Death					
Burial					

Places of Residence:
Occupation: Trucker   **Church Affiliation:**   **Military Rec:**
His Father: **Mother's Maiden Name:**

Wife's Full Maiden Name: Cynthia (Cindy) Louise Pfeiff

	Day Month Year	City, Town or Place	County or Province, etc.	State or Country	Add. Info on Wife
Birth	16-2-1957	Ft. Hood		Texas	
Chr'nd					
Death					
Burial					

Places of Residence:
Occupation: Waitress   **Church Affiliation:**   **Military Rec:**
Other husbands: #1 husband-Bill Sherrell (M) Feb. 13, 1976
Her Father: Calvin H. Pfeiff   **Mother's Maiden Name:** Stella Mae Bartlett

Sex	Children's Names in Full		Day Month Year	City, Town or Place	County or Province, etc.	State or Country	Add. Info on Children
M	1 Sherrell Billy Don	Birth	25-8-1978	Pauls Valley	Garvin Co.	Okla.	
	Full Name of Spouse	Marr.					
		Death					
		Burial					
F	2 Patricia Lee Loper	Birth	9-8-1995	Pauls Valley	Garvin Co.	Ok.	
	Full Name of Spouse	Marr.					
		Death					
		Burial					
	3	Birth					
		Marr.					
	Full Name of Spouse	Death					

Cynthia Pfeiff and Stella Mae Patterson, Don Sherrell (Cindy's son), Paget and Patricia.

Cynthia, Stella Mae and Calvin, Glen and Jean Pfeiff.

Compiler:
Address:
City, State, Zip:
Date:

Family Group Sheet

Husband's Full Name Glen Stephen Pfeiff **Chart No.**

	Day Month Year	City, Town or Place	County or Province, etc.	State or Country	Add. Info. on Husb
Birth	18-6-1959	Leipheim		Germany	
Chr'nd					
Marr					
Death					
Burial					

Places of Residence Oklahoma-Oregon-Germany
Occupation Welder **Church Affiliation** **Military Rec.**

His Father Calvin H. Pfeiff **Mother's Maiden Name** Stella Mae Bartlett

Wife's Full Maiden Name

	Day Month Year	City, Town or Place	County or Province, etc.	State or Country	Add. Info. on Wife
Birth					
Chr'nd					
Death					
Burial					

Places of Residence
Occupation **Church Affiliation** **Military Rec.**

Her Father **Mother's Maiden Name**

Sex	Children's Names		Day Month Year	City, Town or Place	County or Province, etc.	State or Country	Add Info on Child
	1	Birth					
		Marr.					
	Full Name of Spouse	Death					
		Burial					
	2	Birth					
		Marr.					

GEBURTSURKUNDE

(Standesamt Augsburg — — — — — — — — Nr 2808/1959)

— — — — Glen Stephen P f e i f f — — — — —

ist am 18. Juni 1959

in Augsburg — — — — — — — — — — geboren.

Eltern: Calvin Hoover Pfeiff, protestantisch und Stella Mae Pfeiff, geborene Bartlett, protestantisch, beide wohnhaft in Leipheim, Landkreis Günzburg.

Änderungen des Geburtseintrags:

Augsburg, den 25. Juni 1959
Der Standesbeamte
In Vertretung:
Scherer

Glen Pfieff, 1997

301

Family Group Sheet

Husband's Full Name: John Carl Bartlett — **Chart No.**

	Day Month Year	City, Town or Place	County or Province, etc.	State or Country	Add. Info on Husband
Birth	4-12-	Dewey	Wash. Co.	Okla.	
Chr'nd					
Marr.	3-6-1963	Pawhuska	Osage Co.	Okla.	
Death					
Burial					

Places of Residence: Oklahoma-Kansas-Germany-Lebanon
Occupation: Rancher-Trucker **Church Affiliation:** Christian **Military Rec:** Green Beret-Special Forces
His Father: Glen Clifford Bartlett **Mother's Maiden Name:** Helen Louise Eller

Wife's Full Maiden Name: Carol Stephenson

	Day Month Year	City, Town or Place	County or Province, etc.	State or Country	Add. Info on Wife
Birth	25 -1-				
Chr'nd					
Death					
Burial					

Places of Residence:
Occupation: **Church Affiliation:** **Military Rec:**
Her Father: **Mother's Maiden Name:**

Men Serving Country From Bartlesville Area

TAKES BASIC TRAINING — Taking his basic training at Ft. Meade, Maryland, is Pvt. John Carl Bartlett, son of Mr. and Mrs. Glenn Bartlett, of Pauls Valley, Okla.

Bartlett enlisted in the army in January of 1956 while attending Edmond State College. He graduated from the Pauls Valley High School in 1954.

The army private spent the past three summers in Dewey, Okla., with his grandparents, Mr. and Mrs. John Eller and was employed at the Rex Sharpton Service station and the Alfalfa Mill north of town. His address is R. A. 13496859, Co. F. (Tng) 2nd. Bn. 2nd a-c, 3rd Platoon 3rd Squadron, Ft. George E. Meade, Md.

John and Carol Bartlett

Family Group Sheet

Husband's Full Name: Jerry Lehman   **Chart No.**

	Day Month Year	City, Town or Place	County or Province, etc.	State or Country	Add. Info on Husband
Birth	28-7-1940				
Chr'nd					
Marr	19-12-1959	Pauls Valley	Garvin Co.	Okla.	
Death					
Burial					

Places of Residence:
Occupation: **Church Affiliation:** Catholic   **Military Rec:**
Other wives:
His Father: **Mother's Maiden Name:** Lucena

Wife's Full Maiden Name: Norma Jean Bartlett

	Day Month Year	City, Town or Place	County or Province, etc.	State or Country	Add. Info on Wife
Birth	23-8-1938	Dewey	Washington Co.	Okla.	
Chr'nd					
Death					
Burial					

Places of Residence:
Occupation: domestic work   **Church Affiliation:** Christaan   **Military Rec:**
Other husbands: #1husband-J.D. Cottrell(M) 3-23-1955 #2 Riley Oliver(M) 7-17-1956
Her Father: Glenn C. Bartlett   **Mother's Maiden Name:** Helen Louise Eller

Sex	Children's Names in Full		Day Month Year	City, Town or Place	County or Province, etc.	State or Country	Add. Info on Children
F	1. Dixie Louise Cottrell	Birth	16-5-1955	Pawhuska	Osage Co.	Okla.	#2 husband Danny Williams
	Spouse: J.D. Blevins	Marr	8-6-1973	Pauls Valley	Garvin Co.	Okla.	
		Death/Burial					
M	2. Oliver Johnnie Eugene (J.O.)	Birth	5-7-1957	Memphis	Shelly Co.	Tenn.	
	Spouse:	Marr/Death/Burial					
F	3. Brenda Lehman	Birth	18-6-1960	Pauls Valley	Garvin Co.	Okla.	
	Spouse: Jimmy Sherrell	Marr	18-6-1984	Pauls Valley	Garvin Co.	Okla.	
F	4. Jeri Ann Lehman	Birth	21-4-1961	Pauls Valley	Garvin Co.	Okla.	#2 husband John Towler #3 Bill Sherrell
	Spouse: Larry Sherrell (div.)	Marr	1-1979	Pauls Valley	Garvin Co.	Okla.	
F	5. Lucena Ruth Lehman	Birth	13-8-1962	Pauls Valley	Garvin Co.	Okla.	#2 husband Mike Hockersmith
	Spouse: Danny Williams (div.)	Marr	2-6-1978	Pauls Valley	Garvin Co.	Okla.	

Norma Lehman, Willa Mae Case and Jerry Lehman, July 6, 1996.

Dixie (Norma's daughter) and children.

Family Group Sheet

Husband's Full Name Jimmy Sherrell   **Chart No.**

Husband's Data	Day	Month	Year	City, Town or Place	County or Province, etc.	State or Country	Add. Info. on Husband
Birth	12	10	1966				
Chr'nd							
Marr	18	06	1984	Pauls Valley	Garvin county	Oklahoma	
Death							
Burial							

Places of Residence

Occupation   Church Affiliation   Military Rec.

Other wives, if any, No. (1)(2) etc. Make separate sheet for each man.

His Father   Mother's Maiden Name

Wife's Full Maiden Name Brenda Lehman

Wife's Data	Day	Month	Year	City, Town or Place	County or Province, etc.	State or Country	Add. Info. on Wife
Birth	18	06	1960	Pauls Valley	Garvin county	Oklahoma	
Chr'nd							
Death							
Burial							

Places of Residence

Occupation **Housewife waitress**   Church Affiliation **Catholic**   Military Rec.

Her Father **Jerry Lehman**   Mother's Maiden Name **Norma Jean Bartlett**

Sex	Children's Names in Full	Children's Data	Day	Month	Year	City, Town or Place	County or Province, etc. State or Country	Add. Info. on Children
F	1 Angel Marie Lehman	Birth	04	12	1978	Pauls Valley Garvin Co. OK		
	Full Name of Spouse: Billy Fetgatter	Marr.	27	03	1998	Pauls Valley Garvin Co. OK		
		Death						
		Burial						
F	2 Jeri Sue Sherrell	Birth	06	08	1985	Pauls Valley GArvin Co. OK		
	Full Name of Spouse	Marr.						
		Death						
		Burial						
M	3 Gary Don Sherrell	Birth	05	01	1988	Pauls Valley Garvin Co. OK		
	Full Name of Spouse	Marr.						
		Death						
		Burial						

Billy Fetgatter and Angel Marie Lehman (Norma Jean Bartlett's granddaughter) taken in Pauls Valley, OK. March 27, 1998

Compiler
Address
City, State, Zip
Date

304

Family Group Sheet

Husband's Full Name J.D. Cottrell   **Chart No.**

Husband's Data	Day	Month	Year	City, Town or Place	County or Province, etc.	State or Country	Add. Info. on Husband
Birth							
Chr'nd							
Marr	23	08	1955	Pauls Valley	Garvin Co.	Oklahoma	
Death							
Burial							

Places of Residence

Occupation   Church Affiliation   Military Rec.

Other wives if any No. (1) (2) etc. Make separate sheet for each marr.

His Father   Mother's Maiden Name

Wife's Full Maiden Name Norma Jean Bartlett

Wife's Data	Day	Month	Year	City, Town or Place	County or Province, etc.	State or Country	Add. Info. on Wife
Birth	23	08	1938	Dewey	Washington	Oklahoma	
Chr'nd							
Death							
Burial							

Places of Residence

Occupation   Church Affiliation Christian   Military Rec.

Other husbands if any No. (1) (2) etc. Make separate sheet for each marr.

Her Father Glen Clifford Bartlett   Mother's Maiden Name Helen Louise Eller

Sex	Children's Names in Full (Arranged in order of birth)	Children's Data	Day	Month	Year	City, Town or Place	County or Province, etc.	State or Country	Add. Info. on Children
F	1 Dixie Louise Cottrell	Birth	16	05	1955	Pawhuska	Orange Co.	Oklahoma	
	Full Name of Spouse J.D. Danny Blevins / Williams	Marr.	08	06	1973	Pauls Valley	Garvin Co.	OK	
		Death							
		Burial							
	2	Birth							
	Full Name of Spouse	Marr.							
		Death							
		Burial							
	3	Birth							
	Full Name of Spouse	Marr.							
		Death							
		Burial							
	4	Birth							
	Full Name of Spouse	Marr.							
		Death							
		Burial							
	5	Birth							
	Full Name of Spouse	Marr.							
		Death							
		Burial							
	6	Birth							
	Full Name of Spouse	Marr.							
		Death							
		Burial							
	7	Birth							
	Full Name of Spouse	Marr.							
		Death							
		Burial							
	8	Birth							
	Full Name of Spouse	Marr.							
		Death							
		Burial							

Compiler   Notes:

Address

City, State, Zip

Date

Family Group Sheet

Husband's Full Name: J.D. Blevins
Chart No.

	Day Month Year	City, Town or Place	County or Province, etc.	State or Country	Add. Info on Husband
Birth	8-10--1950	Pauls Valley	Garvin Co.	Okla.	
Chr'nd					
Marr	8-6-1973				
Death					
Burial					

Places of Residence:
Occupation: | Church Affiliation: | Military Rec: Spec. 4th. Tanks Viet Nam
His Father: | Mother's Maiden Name:

Wife's Full Maiden Name: Dixie Louise Cottrell

	Day Month Year	City, Town or Place	County or Province, etc.	State or Country	Add. Info on Wife
Birth	16-5-1955	Pawhuska	Osage Co.	Okla.	#2 husband Danny Williams
Chr'nd					
Death					
Burial					

Places of Residence:
Occupation: Housewife | Church Affiliation: | Military Rec:
Her Father: J.D. Cottrell | Mother's Maiden Name: Norma Jean Bartlett

Sex	Children's Names in Full		Day Month Year	City, Town or Place	County or Province, etc.	State or Country	Add. Info on Children
F	1 Blevins, Melinda Dawn	Birth	27-1-1975	Pauls Valley	Garvin Co.	Ok.	Divorced
	Full Name of Spouse: Glen Reiser	Marr. / Death / Burial					
M	2 James David Blevins	Birth	15-7-1980	Pauls Valley	Garvin Co.	Okla.	
	Full Name of Spouse:	Marr. / Death					

APPLICATION FOR MARRIAGE LICENSE
STATE OF OKLAHOMA, COUNTY OF GARVIN, ss.
IN DISTRICT COURT

We, the undersigned, hereby apply for the issuance of a Marriage License and certify as to our ages and places of residence as follows:

Name: Jimmy D. Blevins of Pauls Valley, County of Garvin, State of Oklahoma, Age 22
Name: Dixie L. Cottrell of Pauls Valley, County of Garvin, State of Oklahoma, Age 18

and for the purpose of procuring same, we do solemnly swear that the names, ages and places of residence as set out above are true and correct, as evidenced by documents described in particular as follows:

(First Party) Okla. Drivers Lic. Born. 10-8-50 (Second Party) Okla. Drivers Lic. Born. 5-16-55

and that we are not disqualified or incapable under law of entering into the marriage relation, nor are we related to each other within the degree prohibited by law.

Applicant: Jimmy D. Blevins
Applicant: Dixie L. Cottrell

Subscribed and sworn to before me this 5th day of June A.D. 1973
Judge / Elden L. Michael, Court Clerk
By Thelma King, Deputy

MARRIAGE LICENSE — THIS LICENSE VALID ONLY IN GARVIN COUNTY, OKLAHOMA
STATE OF OKLAHOMA, COUNTY OF GARVIN, ss.
IN DISTRICT COURT

TO ANY PERSON AUTHORIZED TO PERFORM OR SOLEMNIZE THE MARRIAGE CEREMONY — GREETINGS:

You are hereby authorized, upon delivery of this marriage license within ten days from the date of its issue to you, to join in marriage Mr. Jimmy D. Blevins of Pauls Valley, County of Garvin, State of Oklahoma, Age 22 years, and Dixie L. Cottrell of Pauls Valley, County of Garvin, State of Oklahoma, Age 18 years; and by the command of the statute you shall make due return of this license to my office within five days succeeding the performance of the marriage herein authorized.

Issued under my hand and official seal, in my Marriage Record before delivery, at Pauls Valley, Oklahoma, this 5th day of June, 1973.
Elden L. Michael, Court Clerk
By Thelma King, Deputy
(SEAL)

Filed...

Witness my hand and official seal this 5th day of June, 1973.
Elden L. Michael, Court Clerk
By Thelma King, Deputy

All the above and foregoing recorded on this 5th day of June, A.D. 1973, and thereafter said License delivered according to Law.
By Thelma King, Deputy / Elden L. Michael, Court Clerk

CERTIFICATE OF MARRIAGE
STATE OF OKLAHOMA, COUNTY OF GARVIN, ss.

I, Robert L. Siebs, Catholic Priest, St. Catherine's Catholic Church, Pauls Valley, in Garvin County, State of Oklahoma, do hereby certify that I joined in marriage the persons named in and authorized by this License to be married on the eighth day of June, A.D. 1973, at Pauls Valley, in Garvin County, State of Oklahoma, in the presence of Robert W. Blevins of Pauls Valley, Ok., and Lahoma Tompkins of Pauls Valley, Ok.

My credentials of authority are recorded in Minister's Credentials Book 1 at page 288 of Washington County, Oklahoma.
R. L. Siebs, Catholic Priest

License returned, and Certificate of Marriage record subjoining the record of License issued and recorded in Marriage Record Book 37 at page 363, on this 11th day of June, 1973.
Elden L. Michael, Court Clerk
By Linda McMahan, Deputy

Notes: Jonathan, Danny and Dixie Williams

Family Group Sheet

Husband's Full Name: Glen Reiser
Chart No.: —

	Day Month Year	City, Town or Place	County or Province, etc.	State or Country	Add. Info. on Husband
Birth					
Chr'nd					
Marr.	1992	Pauls Valley	Garvin Co.	Okla.	
Death					
Burial					

Places of Residence:
Occupation: Church Affiliation: Military Rec:

His Father:
Mother's Maiden Name:

Wife's Full Maiden Name: Melinda Dawn Blevins

	Day Month Year	City, Town or Place	County or Province, etc.	State or Country	Add. Info. on Wife
Birth	27-1-1975	Pauls Valley	Garvin Co.	Okla.	(divorced)
Chr'nd					
Death					
Burial					

Places of Residence:
Occupation: Church Affiliation: Military Rec:

Her Father: J.D. Blevins
Mother's Maiden Name: Dixie Louise Cottrell

Sex	Children's Names in Full		Day Month Year	City, Town or Place	County or Province, etc.	State or Country	Add. Info. on Children
F	1 Reiser, Tiffany Renee	Birth	6-6-1993	Pauls Valley	Garvin Co.	Ok.	
	Full Name of Spouse	Marr.					
		Death					
		Burial					
F	2 Reiser, Brittany Nicole	Birth	28-11-1994	Pauls Valley	Garvin Co.	Okla.	
	Full Name of Spouse	Marr.					
		Death					

James David Blevins, Melinda Dawn Blevins Reiser and daughters, Tiffany and Brittany Reiser.

Family Group Sheet

Husband's Full Name Riley Oliver **Chart No.**

Husband's Data	Day	Month	Year	City, Town or Place	County or Province, etc.	State or Country	Add. Info. on Husband
Birth							Divorciced
Chr'nd							02 12 1959
Marr	17	07	1956				
Death							
Burial							

Places of Residence
Occupation Church Affiliation Military Rec
Other wives if any No (1)(2) etc. Make separate sheet for each marr.
His Father Mother's Maiden Name

Wife's Full Maiden Name Norma Jean Bartlett

Wife's Data	Day	Month	Year	City, Town or Place	County or Province, etc.	State or Country	Add. Info. on Wife
Birth	23	08	1948	Dewey	Washington County	Oklahoma	
Chr'nd							
Death							
Burial							

Places of Residence Oklahoma and Kansas
Occupation Church Affiliation Military Rec
Other husbands if any No (1)(2) etc. Make separate sheet for each marr. Jerry Lehman D.O.B. 28 07 1940 Married 19 12 1959
Her Father Glen Bartlett **Mother's Maiden Name** Helen Louise Eller

Sex	Children's Names in Full (Arranged in order of birth)	Children's Data	Day Month Year	City, Town or Place	County or Province, etc	State or Country	Add. Info. on Children
M	1 Johnnie Eugene Oliver	Birth	05 07 1957	Memphis	Shelby Co.	Tennesse	
	Full Name of Spouse	Marr. Death Burial					
	2	Birth Marr. Death Burial					
	3	Birth Marr. Death Burial					
	4	Birth Marr. Death Burial					
	5	Birth Marr. Death Burial					
	6	Birth Marr. Death Burial					
	7	Birth Marr. Death Burial					
	8	Birth Marr. Death Burial					

Compiler
Address
City, State, Zip
Date

Notes:

Family Group Sheet

Husband's Full Name Larry Sherrell — **Chart No.**

	Day Month Year	City, Town or Place	County or Province, etc.	State or Country	Add. Info on Husband
Birth					
Chr'nd					
Marr	1-1979	Pauls Valley	Garvin Co.	Okla.	(divorced)
Death					
Burial					

Places of Residence:
Occupation: Church Affiliation: Military Rec:
Other wives, if any
His Father: Mother's Maiden Name:

Wife's Full Maiden Name Jeri Ann Lehman

	Day Month Year	City, Town or Place	County or Province, etc.	State or Country	Add. Info. on Wife
Birth	21-4-1961	Pauls Valley	Garvin Co.	Okla.	
Chr'nd					
Death					
Burial					

Places of Residence:
Occupation: Church Affiliation: Military Rec:
Other husbands: #2 husband John Towler, Jr. (M) June 18, 1984   #3 Dom. Part. Billy Sherrel
Her Father: Jerry Lehman   Mother's Maiden Name: Norma Jean Bartlett

Sex	Children's Names in Full		Day Month Year	City, Town or Place	County or Province, etc.	State or Country	Add. Info on Children
M	1. Jerry Ray Sherrell	Birth	14-2-1980	Pauls Valley	Garvin Co.	Okla.	
	Full Name of Spouse	Marr./Death/Burial					
F	2. Rebecca Ann Sherrell	Birth	11-8-1981	Pauls Valley	Garvin Co.	Okla.	
	Full Name of Spouse	Marr./Death/Burial					
F	3. Carol Jean Towler	Birth	8-7-1984	Pauls Valley	Garvin Co.	Okla.	
	Full Name of Spouse	Marr./Death/Burial					
F	4. Savanna ~~Sherrell~~ Towler	Birth	30-10-1989	Pauls Valley	Garvin Co.	Ok.	(Father is Billy Sherrell)
	Full Name of Spouse	Marr./Death/Burial					
	5.	Birth					

Family Group Sheet

Husband's Full Name Johnnie Eugene Oliver — **Chart No.**

	Day Month Year	City, Town or Place	County or Province, etc.	State or Country	Add. Info on Husband
Birth	05 07 1957	Memphis	Shelby Co.	Tennesse	
Chr'nd					
Marr					
Death					
Burial					

Places of Residence: Pauls Valley, Florida, and Tennesse
Occupation: Police Dispatcher   Church Affiliation: Military Rec:
Other wives:
His Father: Riley Oliver   Mother's Maiden Name: Norma Jean Bartlett
Compiler: Notes:
Address:
City, State, Zip:
Date:

Family Group Sheet

Husband's Full Name: Danny Williams
Chart No.:

	Day Month Year	City, Town or Place	County or Province, etc.	State or Country	Add. Info on Husband
Birth					
Chr'nd					
Marr	2-6-1978	Pauls Valley	Garvin Co.	Okla.	(divorced)
Death					
Burial					

Places of Residence:
Occupation: Church Affiliation: Military Rec:
His Father: Mother's Maiden Name:

Wife's Full Maiden Name: Lucena (Lucy) Ruth Lehman

	Day Month Year	City, Town or Place	County or Province, etc.	State or Country	Add. Info on Wife
Birth	13-8-1962	Pauls Valley	Garvin Co.	Okla.	
Chr'nd					
Death					
Burial					

Places of Residence:
Occupation: Housewife   Church Affiliation: Military Rec:

#2 Husband-Mike Hockersmith (M) July 1, 1985 (Manager Fast Food Store)

Her Father: Jerry Lehman   Mother's Maiden Name: Norma Jean Bartlett

Sex	Children's Names in Full		Day Month Year	City, Town or Place	County or Province, etc.	State or Country	Add. Info on Children
F	1 Kristi Gail Williams	Birth	30-1-1979	Pauls Valley	Garvin Co.	Okla.	
	Full Name of Spouse	Marr. / Death / Burial					
M	2 Jonathan Paul W.	Birth	21-2-1980	Pauls Valley	Garvin Co.	Okla.	
	Full Name of Spouse	Marr. / Death / Burial					
M	3 Williwms Kenneth Wayne	Birth	14-12-1982	Pauls Valley	Garvin Co.	Okla.	
	Full Name of Spouse	Marr. / Death / Burial					
M	4 Hockersmith Brandon M.	Birth	5-9-1984	Pauls Valley	Garvin Co.	Okla.	(Adopted)
	Full Name of Spouse	Marr. / Death / Burial					
M	5 Hockersmith Stephen Nicholas	Birth	17-11-1997	Pauls Valley	Garvin Co.	Okla.	(twin)
	Full Name of Spouse	Marr. / Death / Burial					
F	6 Hockersmith Stephanie Nichole	Birth	17-11-1997	Pauls Valley	Garvin Co.	Okla.	(Twin)
	Full Name of Spouse	Marr. / Death / Burial					
	7	Birth / Marr. / Death / Burial					
	Full Name of Spouse						
	8	Birth / Marr. / Death / Burial					
	Full Name of Spouse						

Compiler:
Address:
City, State, Zip:
Date:
Notes:

Family Group Sheet

George Everett Eller SS-441-10-4851 — Chart No. ___

Husband's Full Name

	Day Month Year	City, Town or Place	County or Province, etc.	State or Country	Add. Info. on Husband
Birth	29-1-1915	Altoona	Wilson Co.	Kansas	
Chr'nd					
Marr	15-8-1936	Dewey	Washington Co.	Okla.	
Death	10-4-1998	Bartlesville	Wash. Co.	Okla.	
Burial	13-4-1998	Dewey cem.	Wash. Co.	Okla.	

Places of Residence: Okla.-Texas-La.-Montana-Idaho-Utah-Wyoming-Calif.-Arizona-West Va.
Occupation: Welder - Terminal Supervisor   Church Affiliation: Christian   Military Rec: Navy-See-Bees WW2
#2 wife-Genia (Katie) Anderson (M) June 30, 1994 Ark. born-12-30-1919

His Father: **John Everett Eller**   Mother's Maiden Name: **Stella Adaline Wiley**

Wife's Full Maiden Name: Wayneta (Neta) Orpha Woody SS-443-14-2848

	Day Month Year	City, Town or Place	County or Province, etc.	State or Country	Add. Info. on Wife
Birth	12-7-1919	Dewey	Washington Co.	Okla.	
Chr'nd					
Death	13-8-1990	Bartlesville	Wash. Co.	Okla.	
Burial	15-8-1990	Dewey cem.	Wash. Co.	Okla.	

Occupation: housewife   Church Affiliation: Christian

Her Father: **James Homer Woody**   Mother's Maiden Name: **Rosie Bell Coke**

Children

Sex	Name	Event	Day Month Year	City, Town or Place	County or Province, etc.	State or Country
M 1	George Kenneth E.	Birth	29-11-1938	Dewey	Wash. Co.	Okla.
		Marr.				
	Full Name of Spouse	Death	29-11-1938	Dewey	Wash. Co.	Okla.
		Burial		Dewey cem.	Wash. Co.	Okla.
F 2	Nita Jo Eller	Birth	21-11-1947	McAllen	Hidelgo Co.	Texas
		Marr.	7-6-1969	Rock Springs	Sweetwater Co.	Wyo.
	Full Name of Spouse: Ronald A. Rushton	Death				
		Burial				

Rock Springs, WY, Golden Wedding Anniversary for Everett and Wayneta.
Pictured: Everett and Wayneta, Jody, Craig and Ron Rushton, Tracy and Brett.

311

C960439 Honorable Discharge from the United States Navy Series C

This is to certify that George Everett ELLER, a Shipfitter First Class (CB) USNR

is HONORABLY DISCHARGED from the U.S. NAVAL PERSONNEL SEPARATION CENTER Norman, Okla

and from the Naval Service of the United States this 17th day of November 1945

This certificate is awarded as a Testimonial of Fidelity and Obedience.

D. Carlson
D. CARLSON, Captain, U.S. Navy, Command

Recorded this 11th day of Oct. A.D. 1946 at 1:55 o'clock P.M.

Enriqueta Garcia, Deputy. Lauro Garza, Clerk, County Court, Starr County, Texas.

NOTICE OF SEPARATION FROM U.S. NAVAL SERVICE 1145 163
NAVPERS-553 (REV. 8-45)

- Serial/File No.: 849-76-77
- Name: ELLER, George Everett
- Rate: Shipfitter, first class (CB)
- V-6 USNR (SV)
- Permanent address: Box 285, Dewey, Washington Co., Oklahoma
- Place of separation: PSC-Norman, Okla.
- Character of separation: Honorable Discharge
- Address from which employment will be sought: Box 285, Dewey, Washington Co., Okla.
- Race: W, Sex: M, Marital Status: Married, U.S. Citizen: Yes
- Date and place of birth: 1-29-15 Altoona, Kansas
- Registered: Yes, L.B. #1, Bartlesville, Okla.
- Home address at time of entry: Dewey, Oklahoma
- Date of entry into active service: 5-27-43
- Net service: 2 yrs. 5 mos. 28 days
- Means of entry: Inducted 5-20-43
- Place of entry into active service: L.B. #1, Bartlesville, Oklahoma
- Qualifications: See Rating Description Booklet, Shipfitter, first class (CB), (Welder)
- Ratings held: SF2c (CB); SF1c (CB)
- Foreign and/or sea service: 23 1/2 month
- Service schools completed: Torpedo Air Compressor, Davisville, R.I. — 1 week
- Service/vessels/stations: USNCTC., Williamsburg, Va.; 109th Naval Const. Batt.
- Insurance: NSI, Effective 11-45, Next premium 12-45, Amount $6.90, Continue: Undecided
- Total payment upon discharge: 170.21
- Travel/mileage allowance: 8.20
- Initial mustering out payment: 100.00
- Disbursing officer: A.W. Johnson, Lt.(jg)(SC)USN
- Signature: Frank E. Couch, FRANK E. COUCH, Lieut., USNR, Ass't. Personnel Officer
- Last employer: Continental Oil Co., Valley Pipe Line, McAllen, Texas
- Dates: From 1-41 to 5-43
- Main civilian occupation: Welder
- Preference for additional training: Continental Oil Co., Valley Pipe Line, McAllen, Texas
- Education: Gram. 8, H.S. 4, Coll. — , Major: General
- Date of separation: 11-17-45
- Signature of person being separated: George Everett Eller

Recorded this 11th day of Oct. A.D. 1946 at 2:20 o'clock P.M.
By Enriqueta Garcia, Deputy. Lauro Garza, Clerk, County Court, STARR County, Texas.

MR. AND MRS. G.E. ELLER

Ellers Celebrate Golden Wedding Anniversary

ROCK SPRINGS — Mr. and Mrs. G.E. Eller of Bartlesville, Okla., and former residents of Rock Springs celebrated their 50th wedding anniversary Aug. 15 at the Holiday Inn in Rock Springs.

The dinner was hosted by their son-in-law and daughter, Mr. and Mrs. Ron (Jody) Rushton of Spokane, Wash., and their children, Brett, Craig and Tracy.

Eller retired from Conoco Oil Company in 1978 and is in Rock Springs on routine inspections for the company. He is a member of the Elk's Club and the Moose Club.

Mrs. Eller is a housewife and has participated in numerous Duplicate Bridge clubs in Rock Springs.

Mr. and Mrs. Ralph Lamb, long-time friends of the Ellers, were guests at the celebration.

Seabees. He received honorable discharge on November 17, 1945. Mr. Eller was a member of the First Christian Church in Dewey, the Senior Advantage Center in Bartlesville and the Elks Lodge in Rock Springs, Wyoming.

Survivors include his wife, Geraia, of the home and a daughter, Jody

---

George F. Eller

George Everett Eller, 83, of Bartlesville, died at 2:35 p.m. Friday at the Jane Phillips Medical Center.

Services will be 11 a.m. Tuesday at the Dewey Cemetery with the Rev. Joe Fowler of the First Baptist Church officiating with interment in the Dewey Cemetery under the direction of the Stumpff Funeral Home.

Memorials have been established to the First Christian Church in Dewey, 900 N. Wyandotte, Dewey, Oklahoma, 74029 or to the First Baptist Church, P.O. Box 1080, Bartlesville, Oklahoma 74005.

Mr. Eller was born on January 29, 1915 at Altoona, Kan., to John Everett and Stella Adaline (Wiley) Eller and he came to Dewey with his family as an infant. He grew up in Dewey and received his education there graduating from Dewey High School. He married Wayneta Orpha Woody in Bartlesville on Aug. 15, 1936. They made their home in Dewey until 1938 when Mr. Eller joined Conoco and they moved to McAllen, Texas, to make their home. They also lived in Utah, Wyoming and Idaho. Following Mr. Eller's retirement in 1978, the Ellers came to Bartlesville to make their home. Mrs. Eller preceded him in death on Aug. 13, 1990. Mr. Eller married Geria (Katie) Atudel son on June 30, 1994 at Eureka Springs, Ark. They made their home in Bartlesville since that time. Mr. Eller entered the United States Navy on May 20, 1943 serving in the Pacific Theatre with the

Family Group Sheet

Husband's Full Name Ronald A. Rushton — **Chart No.**

	Day Month Year	City, Town or Place	County or Province, etc	State or Country	Add. Info. on Husband
Birth					
Chr'nd					
Marr	7-6-1969	Rock Springs	Sweetwater Co.	Wyo.	
Death					
Burial					

Places of Residence Wis.-Montana-Calif.-Colo.-Okla.-Mo.-Wash.-Texas
Occupation V.Pres.Oil Co./ Yellowstone Pipe Line Co. **Church Affiliation** Latter Day Sts. **Military Rec**

His Father — **Mother's Maiden Name**

Wife's Full Maiden Name Nita Jo Eller

	Day Month Year	City, Town or Place	County or Province, etc.	State or Country	Add. Info. on Wife
Birth	21-11-1947	McAllen	Hidelgo Co.	Texas	
Chr'nd					
Death					
Burial					

Places of Residence
Occupation Sec.Space Center Housewife **Church Affiliation** Latter Day Saints **Military Rec**

Her Father George Everett Eller — **Mother's Maiden Name** Wayneta O. Woody

Sex	Children's Names		Day Month Year	City, Town or Place	County or Province, etc	State or Country	Add. Info. on Children
M	1 Rushton Craig Allen Spouse: Sandy Anderson	Birth Marr Death Burial	7-2-1970 14-2-1998	Bountiful Houston	Davis Co. Harris Co.	Utah Texas	
M	2 Rushton Michael Brett Spouse: Jannelle Lynn Cottrell	Birth Marr Death Burial	14-11-1972 23-7-1994	Madison Houston	Dane Co. Harris Co.	Wisc. Texas	
F	3 Rushton Tracy Noelle Spouse:	Birth Marr Death Burial	11-12-1974 23-3-1996	Billings Houston	Yellowstone Co. Harris Co.	Montana Texas	

City County State
SURVIVORS—NAME AND ADDRESS

Husband: * George Everett "Red" Eller   333 5989
4100 Lester
Bartlesville, Oklahoma 74006
(DOB: January 29, 19
Altoona, Kansas: SS# 441 10 4851)

One Daughter: Mrs. Ronald A. (Nita Jo) Rushton   713 482 2
1710 Valero
Friendswood, Texas

Two Brothers: John L. Woody   534 3276
354 S. Oak
Dewey, Oklahoma

Cecil G. Woody
701 East 4th
Dewey, Oklahoma

Preceded in death by one son, George Kenneth Eller, November, 1939
one sister, Mrs. Ellen Fair
one brother, James Woody

3 Grandchildren: Craig Allen Rushton
Michael Brett Rushton
Tracy Noelle Rushton

Family Group Sheet

Husband's Full Name: Craig Allen Rushton

Chart No.

	Day Month Year	City, Town or Place	County or Province, etc.	State or Country	Add. Info on Husband
Birth	7-2-1970	Bountiful	Davis Co.	Utah	
Chr'nd					
Marr	14-2-1998	Houston	Harris Co.	Texas	
Death					
Burial					

Places of Residence:

Occupation: Tower operator **Church Affiliation:** **Military Rec:**

His Father: Ronald A. Rushton **Mother's Maiden Name:** Nita Jo Eller

Wife's Full Maiden Name: Sandy Anderson

	Day Month Year	City, Town or Place	County or Province, etc.	State or Country	Add. Info on Wife
Birth					
Chr'nd					
Death					
Burial					

Places of Residence:

Occupation: **Church Affiliation:** **Military Rec:**

Her Father: **Mother's Maiden Name:**

Family Group Sheet

Husband's Full Name: Michael Brett Rushton
Chart No.:

	Day Month Year	City, Town or Place	County or Province, etc.	State or Country	Add. Info. on Husband
Birth	14-11-1972	Madison	Dane Co.	Wisconsin	
Chr'nd					
Marr	23-7-1994	Houston	Harris Co.	Texas	
Death					
Burial					

Places of Residence:
Occupation: Oil Co. Superviser   **Church Affiliation:**   **Military Rec:**

His Father: Ronald A. Rushton   **Mother's Maiden Name:** Nita Jo Eller

Wife's Full Maiden Name: Janelle Lynn Cottrell

	Day Month Year	City, Town or Place	County or Province, etc.	State or Country	Add. Info. on Wife
Birth					
Chr'nd					
Death					
Burial					

Places of Residence:
Occupation: **Church Affiliation:**   **Military Rec:**

Her Father: **Mother's Maiden Name:**

Sex	Children's Names in Full		Day Month Year	City, Town or Place	County or Province, etc.	State or Country	Add. Info. on Children
M	1 Rushton, Hunter Austin	Birth	28-9-1994	Augusta	Richmond Co.	Ga.	
		Marr.					
	Full Name of Spouse	Death					
		Burial					
M	2 Rushton, Tyler Michael	Birth	14-4-1996	Augusta	Richmond Co.	Ga.	
		Marr.					
	Full Name of Spouse	Death					
		Burial					

Marriage License

The State of Texas, County of Harris

490-08-2199

To any person authorized by the laws of the State of Texas to celebrate the Rites of Matrimony in the State of Texas

Greeting:
You are hereby authorized to conduct the Rites of Matrimony between

MICHAEL BRETT RUSHTON   and
JANELLE LYNN COTTRELL

and make due return to the County Clerk of Harris County, Texas, within thirty days of performing the marriage, certifying your action under this license.

Witness my official signature and seal of office in Harris County, Texas at 1:10 P.M. on JULY 5, 1994.

Beverly B. Kaufman
County Clerk, Harris County, Texas

Deputy ROBERTA CHAN

Officer's Return

This certifies that I have united in marriage the parties named above on this 23rd day of July 19 94.

14439

315

Family Group Sheet

Husband's Full Name: Loren Culley Staton — **Chart No.**

Husband's Data	Day Month Year	City, Town or Place	County or Province, etc.	State or Country	Add. Info on Husband
Birth					
Chr'nd					
Marr.	23-3-1996	Houston	Harris Co.	Texas	
Death					
Burial					

Places of Residence:

Occupation: Church Affiliation: Military Rec:

Other wives, if any, No. (1), (2), etc. Make separate sheet for each marr.

His Father: David H. Staton   **Mother's Maiden Name:** Sharon

Wife's Full Maiden Name: Tracy Noelle Rushton

Wife's Data	Day Month Year	City, Town or Place	County or Province, etc.	State or Country	Add. Info on Wife
Birth	11-12-1974	Billings	Yellowstone Co.	Montana	
Chr'nd					
Death					
Burial					

Places of Residence:

Occupation: Nurse   Church Affiliation: Military Rec:

Her Father: Ronald A. Rushton   **Mother's Maiden Name:** Nita Jo Eller

Sex	Children's Names in Full	Children's Data	Day Month Year	City, Town or Place	County or Province, etc.	State or Country	Add. Info on Children
F	1 Haley Loren Staton	Birth	19-11-1997	Houston	Harris Co.	Texas	
	Full Name of Spouse	Marr.					
		Death					
		Burial					
	2	Birth					
		Marr.					
	Full Name of Spouse	Death					
		Burial					
	3	Birth					
		Marr.					
	Full Name of Spouse	Death					

Three Generations: Tracy Staton, Jody Rushton, and Haley Staton, Nov. 19, 1997.

MARRIAGE LICENSE — The State of Texas, County of Harris

493-19-0849

To any person authorized by the laws of the State of Texas to celebrate the Rites of Matrimony in the State of Texas
Greeting:
You are hereby authorized to conduct the Rites of Matrimony between

LOREN CULLEY STATON and TRACY NOELLE RUSHTON

and make due return to the County Clerk of Harris County, Texas, within thirty days of performing the marriage, certifying your action under this license.
Witness my official signature and seal of office in Harris County, Texas at 10:10 A.M. on MARCH 12, 1996.

Beverly B. Kaufman
County Clerk, Harris County, Texas

Deputy LISA A. SCHEWITZ

Officer's Return:
This certifies that I have united in marriage the parties named above on this 23rd day of MARCH 19 96.

	8	Birth					
		Marr.					
	Full Name of Spouse	Death					
		Burial					

Compiler:

Address:

City, State, Zip:

Date:

Notes:

Family Group Sheet

Husband's Full Name George Everett Eller — Chart No.

Husband's Data	Day	Month	Year	City, Town or Place	County or Province, etc.	State or Country	Add. Info. on Husband
Birth	29	01	1915	Altoona	Wilson County	Kansas	
Chr'nd							
Marr	30	6	1994				
Death							
Burial							

Places of Residence

Occupation — Church Affiliation — Military Rec.

Other wives, if any. No. (1)(2) etc. Make separate sheet for each man.

His Father John Everett Eller **Mother's Maiden Name** Stella Adaline Wiley

Wife's Full Maiden Name Katie (Anderson)

Wife's Data	Day	Month	Year	City, Town or Place	County or Province, etc.	State or Country	Add. Info. on Wife
Birth	30	12					
Chr'nd							
Death							
Burial							

Places of Residence

Occupation — Church Affiliation

Her Father

Sex	Children's Names in Full	Children's Data	Day	Month
1		Birth / Marr. / Death / Burial		
	Full Name of Spouse			
2		Birth / Marr. / Death / Burial		
	Full Name of Spouse			
3		Birth / Marr. / Death / Burial		
	Full Name of Spouse			
4		Birth / Marr. / Death / Burial		
	Full Name of Spouse			
5		Birth / Marr. / Death / Burial		
	Full Name of Spouse			
6		Birth / Marr.		

Everette and Katie Eller, Jody and Ron Rushton, Brett and family, Tracy and Culley Staton, Craig and Sandy, and daughter. Houston, Texas, December 25, 1996.

Washington County in the War

ANOTHER BROTHER TEAM

Everett — James

Another brother team representing Dewey includes Everett Eller, petty officer, second class, who has recently returned to Davisville, R.I., after a visit with his wife and parents, at 503 East Third street in Dewey, and Corporal James Eller, who is now stationed at Alexandria, La.

Both attended Dewey high school. Everett also attended a school for welding at Augusta, Kan. He enlisted in the Seabees in Houston, Texas, May 1, 1943, and had his boot training at Williamsburg, Va. Prior to his enlistment he was employed by the Continental Oil company as welder at McAllen, Texas. His wife is employed at the Reda Pump company plant here.

Corporal Eller attended the Blue Mound and Wayside schools before entering the Dewey high school. He was working for the Continental Oil company at Villa Platte, La. when he enlisted in the air corps in September of the past year. He has been stationed at Leavenworth, Kan., Tucson, Ariz., Coffeyville, Amarillo, and was at Salt Lake City before being transferred to Louisiana. His wife and two daughters make their home with his grandparents, Mr. and Mrs. George Wiley, 715 East Third, Dewey.

Family Group Sheet

Husband's Full Name: James Wilkerson Eller
Chart No.

	Day Month Year	City, Town or Place	County or Province, etc.	State or Country	Add. Info. on Husband
Birth	8-7-1918	Dewey	Wash. Co.	Okla.	
Chr'nd					
Marr	14-11-1952	Nowata	Nowata Co.	Okla.	
Death	12-9-1995	Ochelata	Wash. Co.	Okla.	died from
Burial	15-9-1995	Ramona cem.	Wash. Co.	Okla.	gun shot

Places of Residence:
Occupation: Mechanic **Church Affiliation:** Christian **Military Rec:** WW2 (Germany-Europe)
Other: #1 wife Margaret Montgomery
His Father: John E. Eller **Mother's Maiden Name:** Stella Adaline Wiley

Wife's Full Maiden Name: Alice Luster Sagel

	Day Month Year	City, Town or Place	County or Province, etc.	State or Country	Add. Info. on Wife
Birth	25-10-1922				
Chr'nd					
Death	5-1-1996	Ochelata	Wash. Co.	Okla.	
Burial	8-1-1996	Ramona	Wash. Co.	Okla.	

Places of Residence:
Occupation: **Church Affiliation:** **Military Rec:**
Her Father: Charles Bryon Luster **Mother's Maiden Name:** Goldie Mae St. Clair

Sex	Children's Names in Full		Day Month Year	City, Town or Place	County or Province, etc.	State or Country	Add. Info. on Children
F	1 Alma Mae Eller	Birth	25-7-1953	Bartlesville	Wash. Co.	Okla.	
	Full Name of Spouse	Marr.					
		Death	28-7-1953	Hospital B'ville	Wash. Co.	Ok.	
		Burial	30-7-1953	Dewey cem.	Wash. Co.	Okla.	
F	2 Alice Marie Eller	Birth	25-7-1953	Bartlesville	Wash. Co.	Okla.	Twin
	Full Name of Spouse	Marr.	28-12-1970	Dewey	Wash. Co.	Okla.	
	Bill Jones	Death					
		Burial					

Hominy Society News
Nov. 13, 1977

Mr. And Mrs. James Eller To Celebrate 25th Wedding Anniversary

Mr. and Mrs. James W. Eller will celebrate their 25 Anniversary Sunday.

Friends and relatives are invited to a reception hosted by the Eller children from 1 to 5 p.m. at the Eller home. home is located five miles n one mile west and a quarter mile north again of Hominy

Jim Eller and Alice Lu Sagel were married Nov. 14, at Nowata. They moved to Hominy and Wynona area 1966. They previously lived Ramona and Ochelata.

The Ellers have children. They are: Bar Jones, Frances McGuire, K Sagel, Vivian Alexander George Sagel all of Bartlesv Sonya Allison, Oklahoma Howard Emerson Sa Hawaiian Gardens, Calif.; Alice Jones, Manhattan, Ka They also have 15 gr children.

James W. Eller

318

Eller-Allison Vows

DEWEY--Miss Sonya Eller and William Allison were married in a pre-Christmas wedding Saturday afternoon in the auditorium of the First Christina church with the pastor, E. E. Butts, reading the impressive double-ring service. The bride is the daughter of Mrs. Margaret Eller, 215 S. Sante Fe, Bartlesville, and James Eller of Ramona. The groom is the son of Mr. and Mrs. W. A. Allison, 4919 E. 38th Place, Tulsa.

Mrs. Dale Pitman sang "I Love You Truly" and "Whither Thou Goest," with Mrs. Sam Watt as organist, who also played a group of appropriate numbers preceeding the ceremony.

The bride was given in marriage by her grandfather, John Eller. She was attended by her sister, Mrs. Loren Jones, as matron of honor. Her other attendants were Nancy Allison, Patti Houseman and Linda Baker, all of Tulsa.

Little Becky Sue Jones, niece of the bride, was the flower girl and Mary Beth Allison served as candlelighter. Jim Allison, brother of the groom, was best man. Groomsmen were Loren Jones of Bartlesville and Jim Tuggle and Dave Allison of Tulsa. Ushers were Frank Bryant and Bob Leslie, both of Tulsa. Jolene Allison was in charge of the guest book.

The refreshment table in Fellowship Hall was lovely with the bride's bouquet and a three-tiered wedding cake as the centerpiece. Hostesses were Mrs. John Eller, grandmother of the bride, and Mrs. Bud Case, aunt of the bride.

The bride was lovely in a gown of organza over white taffeta with a short train and her shoulder length veil was held in place with a crown of lace and pearls. Her attendants all wore identical dresses of emerald green with matching flower hats and carried white mums.

James Eller's daughters: Loran and Barbara Jones, Sonya Smith, Becky Jones. Lonnie and Ronnie Jones, Clifford Jones and Sonya's daughters Jill and Kristin.

James W. Eller, Alice (second wife), granddaughters, Sandi and children, Randi, Cody and Casey.

Melrose (Luster) (Sagel) Eller, 73, widow of James Wilkerson "Jim" Eller and longtime Washington County resident, died Friday morning at her family residence in Ochelata.

Graveside services for Mrs. Eller will be held at 10 a.m. Tuesday in the Ramona Cemetery with Roman Ward Jr. officiating. Committal prayers and interment will be directed in the Ramona Cemetery by the Arnold Moore Funeral Service.

Alice Melrose Luster was born on Oct. 25, 1922, at Sunnyside, near Broken Arrow. She was the daughter of the late Charlie Bryan and Goldie Mae (St. Clair) Luster. She began her education in the Sunnyside community school and completed her education at Broken Arrow.

She and Howard E. Sagel were married on Jan. 7, 1940 in Broken Arrow, and they established their first home in Broken Arrow. Mr. and Mrs. Sagel moved to Walnut Grove, Mo., and Mr. Sagel preceded her in death there on Feb. 17, 1950.

The Sagel family moved to Ochelata and on Nov. 14, 1952, she and James Wilkerson "Jim" Eller were married at Nowata and they made their home in Ochelata. Mr. and Mrs. Eller had a brief residence at Hominy, prior to returning to the Ramona-Ochelata community. Mr. Eller was employed as a mechanic and Mrs. Eller was employed by Phillips Petroleum Co. General Maintenance Dept. and the Saddoris Laundry. Mr. Eller preceded her in death on Sept. 12, 1995, and since that time, Mrs. Eller lived in the Ochelata community in retirement.

Mrs. Eller will lie in state in the Drawing Rooms of The Arnold Moore Funeral Residence where friends may call for their visitation until she is removed for graveside rites on Tuesday morning.

Surviving Mrs. Eller are three daughters: Mrs. Charles (Frances) (Sagel) McGuire and Mrs. James (Vivian) (Sagel) King, both of Bartlesville and Alice Marie Eller, Kansas City Mo.; three sons: Keith Sagel, rural Nowata, Emmerson Sagel, Cutoff, La., and George Sagel, Bartlesville; two stepdaughters: Mrs. Loren (Barbara Elouise) (Eller) Jones, Bartlesville, and Mrs. Harry (Sonya Lou) (Eller) Smith, Norman; 19 grandchildren; 12 great-grandchildren; one brother, Billy Joe Luster, Bartlesville; and one sister, Thelma Ruth Reed, Bartlesville.

She was preceded in death by her parents; one son, John Charles Sagel; one daughter

Family Group Sheet

Husband's Full Name: James Wilkerson Eller SS-442-20-9954 Chart No.

	Day Month Year	City, Town or Place	County or Province, etc.	State or Country	Add. Info on Husband
Birth	8-7-1918	Dewey	Wash. Co.	Okla.	
Chr'nd					
Marr	12-1940	Independence	Mont. Co.	Kansas	
Death	12-9-1995	Ochelata	Wash. Co.	Okla.	
Burial	15-9-1995	Ramona	Wash. Co.	Okla.	

Places of Residence:

Occupation: Mechanic **Church Affiliation:** **Military Rec:** WW2 Army

Other wives: #2 wife Alice Sagel

His Father: John Everett Eller **Mother's Maiden Name:** Stella Adaline Wiley

Wife's Full Maiden Name: Margaret Montgomery

	Day Month Year	City, Town or Place	County or Province, etc.	State or Country	Add. Info on Wife
Birth	1922				
Chr'nd					
Death					
Burial					

Places of Residence:

Occupation: **Church Affiliation:** **Military Rec:**

Her Father: **Mother's Maiden Name:**

Sex	Children's Names in Full		Day Month Year	City, Town or Place	County or Province, etc.	State or Country	Add. Info on Children
F	1 Eller Barbara Elouise	Birth	24-9-1941	Dewey	Wash. Co.	Okla.	
		Marr.	1958	Dewey	Wash. Co.	Okla.	
	Full Name of Spouse: Loren Jones	Death					
		Burial					
F	2 Sonya Lou Eller	Birth	26-5-1943	Dewey	Wash. Co.	Okla.	#2 husband
		Marr.	22-12-1962	Dewey	Wash. Co.	Okla.	Harry Smith
	Full Name of Spouse: Bill Allison	Death					
		Burial					
	3	Birth					
		Marr.					
	Full Name of Spouse:	Death					

No. H-13443
J. No. 5440

STATE OF KANSAS
CENTRAL DIVISION OF VITAL STATISTICS

MARRIAGE LICENSE

To the Probate Court of Montgomery County. December 13, 1939

TO ANY PERSON AUTHORIZED BY LAW TO PERFORM THE MARRIAGE CEREMONY, GREETING:

You Are Hereby Authorized to Join in Marriage James Eller of Dewey Oklahoma age 21 and Margaret Montgomery of Dewey Oklahoma age 19

...with the consent of...

...of this license, duly endorsed, you will make return to my office at Independence, Kansas, within ten days after performing the ceremony.

(SEAL) Ross E. Borders, Probate Judge

And which said Marriage License was afterwards, to-wit, on the 21st day of December A.D. 1939 returned to said Probate Court with the following certificate endorsed thereon, to-wit:

ENDORSEMENT

TO WHOM IT MAY CONCERN:

I hereby certify that I performed the ceremony joining in marriage the above named couple on the 21st day of December 1939 at Independence, Kansas 3:45 P.M.

Signed: Harold H. Humbert
Title: Christian Minister
Address: 614 N. 10th, Independence, Kansas

James and Margaret (first wife) and Barbara and Sonya.

ENLISTED RECORD AND REPORT OF SEPARATION
HONORABLE DISCHARGE

1. Last name - First name - Middle initial: Eller James W
2. Army serial no.: AF17 060 405
3. Grade: 1Feb46 S Sgt
4. Arm or service: AF
5. Comp. & term of enl.: RA 3 yrs
6. Organization: 353rd Bomb Sq 301st Bomb Gp(M)
7. Date of separation: 26 Mar 49
8. Place of separation: SHAFB Salina Kansas
9. Permanent address for mailing purposes: 715 E 3rd St Dewey Okla
10. Date of birth: 8 Jul 18
11. Place of birth: Dewey Okla
12. Address from which employment will be sought: See 9
13. Color eyes: Blue
14. Color hair: Brown
15. Height: 64
16. Weight: 160 lbs.
17. No. depend.: 3
18. Race: White X
19. Marital status: Married X
20. U. S. citizen: Yes X
21. Civilian occupation and no.: Auto Mech

MILITARY HISTORY

22. Date of induction:
23. Date of enlistment: 25 Mar 46
24. Date of entry into active service: 25 Mar 46
25. Place of entry into service: Kaufbeuren Germany
26. Selective service data – Registered: Yes X
27. Local S.S. board no.: unk
28. County and state: Washington Okla
29. Home address at time of entry into service: See 9
30. Military occupational specialty and no.: AP Maint Tech(750-D)
31. Military qualification and date (i.e., infantry, aviation and marksmanship badges, etc.): Carbine(exp)
32. Battles and campaigns: None
33. Decorations and citations: American Campaign Medal WW II Victory Medal
34. Wounds received in action: None
35. Latest immunization dates – Smallpox: unk; Typhoid: unk; Tetanus: unk; Other (specify): unk
36. Service outside continental U. S. and return:

Date of departure	Destination	Date of arrival
	Reenlisted ETO	25 Mar 46
24 May 46	USA	12 Jun 46
3 Jul 47	ETO	5 Jul 47
15 Jul 47	USA	17 Jul 47

37. Total length of service:

Continental service			Foreign service		
Years	Months	Days	Years	Months	Days
2	3	10	0	8	22

38. Highest grade held: S Sgt
39. Prior service: 2 yrs 11 mos 8 days
40. Reason and authority for separation: AR 615-360 ETS
41. Service schools attended: None
42. Education (Years): Grammar 8; High School 3; College 0

PAY DATA

43. Longevity for pay purposes: Years 5; Months 11; Days 10
44. Mustering out pay: Total None
45. Soldiers deposits: None
46. Travel pay: 75.75
47. Total amount, name of disbursing officer: $215.40 S.B. HENDREN, Captain, USAF

INSURANCE NOTICE

Important: ... Make Checks or Money Orders Payable to the Treasurer of the U. S. ... Veterans Administration, Washington 25, D. C.

48. Kind of insurance: U.S. Govt. None X

55. Remarks (This space for completion of above items or entry of other items specified in W. D. Directives)

Right thumb print

Blood Type(O)
AGCT II(112)

Retained in service(2 days)
CofG

Item 36			
13 Apr 48	ETO	18 Apr 48	
25 Apr 48	USA	26 Apr 48	
6 Jun 48	ETO	9 Jun 48	
5 Aug 48	USA	7 Aug 48	
19 Oct 48	ETO	20 Oct 48	
		21 Jan 49	

56. Signature of person being separated:
57. Personnel officer (Type name, grade and organization - signature): FREDERICK L BUTLER 1st Lt, USAF [signature]

WD AGO FORM 53 1 JUL 47
Previous editions of this form are obsolete.

SERVICE RECORD COPY
(Affixed to Service Record in accordance with instructions in TM 12-230 A.)

2

U. S. GOVERNMENT PRINTING OFFICE: 1948 - 785078

ENLISTED RECORD AND REPORT OF SEPARATION
HONORABLE DISCHARGE

1. Last name - First name - Middle initial: Eller James W
2. Army serial no.: 17060405
3. Grade: S/Sgt.
4. Arm or service: Air Corps
5. Component: AUS
6. Organization: 5?? Fighter Sqdn. 55th Ftr. Gp.
7. Date of separation: 24 March 1946
8. Place of separation: AAF Station Kaufbeuren, Germany
9. Permanent address for mailing purposes: Dewey, Oklahoma
10. Date of birth: 3 July 1918
11. Place of birth: Dewey, Oklahoma
12. Address from which employment will be sought: Dewey, Oklahoma
13. Color eyes: Blue
14. Color hair: Brown
15. Height: 65 in.
16. Weight: 145 lbs.
17. No. depend.: Three
18. Race: White X
19. Marital status:
20. U.S. citizen: Yes X
21. Civilian occupation and no.: Auto Mechanic

MILITARY HISTORY

22. Date of induction:
23. Date of enlistment: 5 October 1942
24. Date of entry into active service: 5 October 1942
25. Place of entry into service: Fort Leavenworth, Kansas
26. Selective service data – Registered: Yes X
27. Local S.S. board no.:
28. County and state: Dewey, Oklahoma
29. Home address at time of entry into service: Dewey, Oklahoma
30. Military occupational specialty and no.: Aircraft Mechanic 750
31. Military qualification and date (i.e., infantry, aviation and marksmanship badges, etc.): Marksmanship Badge
32. Battles and campaigns: None
33. Decorations and citations: Good Conduct Medal EAME Ribbon American Theater Ribbon.
34. Wounds received in action: None
35. Latest immunization dates – Smallpox: 11-12-45; Typhoid: 23-3-45; Tetanus: 23-3-45
36. Service outside continental U.S. and return:

Date of departure	Destination	Date of arrival
23 April 1945	Scotland	1 May 1945

37. Total length of service:

Continental service			Foreign service		
Years	Months	Days	Years	Months	Days
2		10	0	11	2

38. Highest grade held: S/Sgt.
39. Prior service: None
40. Reason and authority for separation: Convenience of Government to enlist in the Regular Army AR 615-365 and WD Cir 310.
41. Service schools attended: Aviation Mechanic School, Amarillo, Texas
42. Education (Years): Grammar 8; High School 3; College 0

PAY DATA

43. Longevity for pay purposes: Years 3; Months 11; Days 11
44. Mustering out pay: Total $300.; This payment $300.
45. Soldier deposits: None
46. Travel pay: $ 4.75
47. Total amount, name of disbursing officer: $??? P.L. ??? 1st Lt FD

INSURANCE NOTICE

Important: If premium is not paid when due or within thirty-one days thereafter, insurance will lapse. Make checks or money orders payable to the Treasurer of the U. S. and forward to Collections Subdivision, Veterans Administration, Washington 25, D. C.

48. Kind of insurance: Nat. Serv. U.S. Govt. None
49. How paid: Allotment; Direct to V.A.
50. Effective Date of Allotment Discontinuance
51. Date of Next Premium Due (One month after 50)
52. Premium due each month
53. Intention of veteran to: Continue; Continue Only; Discontinue

55. Remarks (This space for completion of above items or entry of other items specified in W. D. Directives)

Right thumb print

Honorably Discharged to enlist in the Regular Army at Convenience of Government AR 615-365 and WD Cir 310, 1945
Discharged as Temporary Staff Sergeant

56. Signature of person being separated: [signature]
57. Personnel officer (Type name, grade and organization - signature): [signature] Frederick C. Wirth Jr. 1st Lt. AC ??? Ftr Sq 55 F Gp.

WD AGO Form 53-55
1 November 1944

This form supersedes all previous editions of WD AGO Forms 53 and 55 for enlisted persons entitled to an Honorable Discharge, which will not be used after receipt of this revision.

1. FINAL INDORSEMENT COPY (Affixed to final indorsement page of Service Record)

Family Group Sheet

Husband's Full Name: Loran Jones — **Chart No.**

	Day Month Year	City, Town or Place	County or Province, etc.	State or Country	Add. Info on Husband
Birth					
Chr'nd					
Marr	15-6-1958	Mountain View	Kiowa Co.	Okla,	
Death					
Burial					

Places of Residence:
Occupation: Trucker-B and B   **Church Affiliation:**   **Military Rec:**

His Father: **Mother's Maiden Name:**

Wife's Full Maiden Name: Barbara Elouise Eller

	Day Month Year	City, Town or Place	County or Province, etc.	State or Country	Add. Info on Wife
Birth	29-9-1941	Dewey	Wash. Co.	Okla.	
Chr'nd					
Death					
Burial					

Places of Residence:
Occupation: Tulsa-World Carrier   **Church Affiliation:** Christian   **Military Rec:**

Her Father: James W. Eller   **Mother's Maiden Name:** Margaret Montgomery

Sex	Children's Names in Full	Event	Day Month Year	City, Town or Place	County or Province, etc.	State or Country	Add. Info on Children
F	1 Becky Sue Jones	Birth	14-8-1959	Bartlesville	Wash. Co.	Okla.	
	Full Name of Spouse: Kent Barnes	Marr.	9-6-1984	Bartlesville	Wash. Co.	Okla.	
		Death					
		Burial					
M	2 Lonnie Lee Jones	Birth	12-4-1960	Bartlesville	Wash. Co.	Okla.	
	Full Name of Spouse:	Marr.					
		Death					
		Burial					
M	3 Ronnie Jones	Birth	21-11-1963	Bartlesville	Wash. Co.	Okla.	
	Full Name of Spouse:	Marr.					
		Death	5-4-1981	Bartlesville	Wash. Co.	Okla.	Car Wreck
		Burial	8-4-1981	Dewey cem.	Wash. Co.	Okla.	
M	4 Clifford Jones	Birth	28-9-1967	Bartlesville	Wash. Co.	Okla.	
	Full Name of Spouse: Karen Griggs	Marr.	-3-1-1986	Bartlesville	Wash. Co.	Okla.	
		Death					
		Burial					

Compiler:
Address:
City, State, Zip:
Date:
Notes:

Family Group Sheet

Husband's Full Name: Kent Barnes **Chart No.**

	Day Month Year	City, Town or Place	County or Province, etc	State or Country	Add. Info on Husband
Birth					
Chr'nd					
Marr	9-6-1984	Bartlesville	Wash. Co.	Okla.	
Death					
Burial					

Places of Residence:
Occupation: Church Affiliation: Military Rec:
His Father: Mother's Maiden Name:

Wife's Full Maiden Name: Becky Sue Jones

	Day Month Year	City, Town or Place	County or Province, etc	State or Country	Add. Info on Wife
Birth	14-8-1959	Bartlesville	Wash. Co.	Okla.	
Chr'nd					
Death					
Burial					

Places of Residence: Okla.-Texas-Korea
Occupation: Church Affiliation: Military Rec: US Army
Her Father: Loren Jones   Mother's Maiden Name: Barbara Elouise Eller

Sex	Children's Names in Full		Day Month Year	City, Town or Place	County or Province, etc	State or Country	Add. Info on Children
M	1. Michael Jones	Birth	9-5-1980	Bartlesville	Wash.Co.	Okla.	
	Full Name of Spouse	Marr.					
		Death					
		Burial					
F	2. Barnes, Shannon Renee	Birth	3-2-1987	Bartlesville	Wash.Co.	Okla.	
	Full Name of Spouse	Marr.					
		Death					
		Burial					

Compiler: Notes:
Address:
City, State, Zip:
Date:

Family Group Sheet

Husband's Full Name: Clifford Jones
Chart No.

	Day Month Year	City, Town or Place	County or Province, etc.	State or Country	Add. Info on Husband
Birth	28-9-1967	Bartlesville	Wash. Co.	Okla.	
Chr'nd					
Marr	3-7-1986				
Death					
Burial					

Places of Residence:
Occupation: Church Affiliation: Military Rec:

His Father: Loren Jones   **Mother's Maiden Name:** Barbara Elouise Eller

Wife's Full Maiden Name: Karen Griggs

	Day Month Year	City, Town or Place	County or Province, etc.	State or Country	Add. Info. on Wife
Birth					
Chr'nd					
Death					
Burial					

Places of Residence:
Occupation: Church Affiliation: Military Rec:

Her Father: **Mother's Maiden Name:**

Sex	Children's Names in Full		Day Month Year	City, Town or Place	County or Province, etc.	State or Country	Add. Info on Children
F	1. Cliffa Jones	Birth					
		Marr.					
	Full Name of Spouse	Death					
		Burial					
F	2. Kara Dawn Jones	Birth	16-10-1987	Bartlesville	Wash. Co.	Okla.	
		Marr.					
	Full Name of Spouse	Death					
		Burial					
	3.	Birth					
		Marr.					
	Full Name of Spouse	Death					
		Burial					
	4.	Birth					
		Marr.					
	Full Name of Spouse	Death					
		Burial					
	5.	Birth					
		Marr.					
	Full Name of Spouse	Death					
		Burial					
	6.	Birth					
		Marr.					
	Full Name of Spouse	Death					
		Burial					
	7.	Birth					
		Marr.					
	Full Name of Spouse	Death					
		Burial					
	8.	Birth					
		Marr.					
	Full Name of Spouse	Death					
		Burial					

Compiler:
Address:
City, State, Zip:
Date:

Notes:

Family Group Sheet

Husband's Full Name: William (Bill) Allison — **Chart No.**

	Day Month Year	City, Town or Place	County or Province, etc.	State or Country	Add. Info on Husband
Birth	3-8-1943				
Chr'nd					
Marr	22-12-1962	Christian Church Dewey	Wash. Co.	Okla.	
Death					
Burial					

Places of Residence:
Occupation: Architect   Church Affiliation: Military Rec:

His Father: W.A. Allison   Mother's Maiden Name:

Wife's Full Maiden Name: Sonya Lou Eller

	Day Month Year	City, Town or Place	County or Province, etc.	State or Country	Add. Info. on Wife
Birth	26-5-1943	Bartlesville	Wash. Co.	Okla.	#2 husband Harry Smith
Chr'nd					
Death					
Burial					

Places of Residence: Oklahoma-California-Kansas
Occupation: Grade School Principal   Church Affiliation: Christian Church   Military Rec:

Her Father: James W. Eller   Mother's Maiden Name: Margaret Montgomery

Sex	Children's Names in Full		Day Month Year	City, Town or Place	County or Province, etc. State or Country	Add. Info on Children
F	1 Kristin Kay A.	Birth	31-7-1961	Tracy	San Joaquin Co. Calif.	
	Full Name of Spouse	Marr.				
		Death				
		Burial				
F	2 Jill Annette A.	Birth	13-10-1968	Tracy	San Joaquin Co. Calif.	
	Full Name of Spouse	Marr.				
		Death				

325

Family Group Sheet

Husband's Full Name: William James Phillips — **Chart No.**

	Day Month Year	City, Town or Place	County or Province, etc.	State or Country	Add Info on Husband
Birth	1-3-1955				
Chr'nd					
Marr	2-4-1979	Edwardsville	Madison Co.	Ill.	(div.)
Death					
Burial					

Places of Residence:
Occupation: Church Affiliation: Military Rec:
His Father: Mother's Maiden Name:

Wife's Full Maiden Name: Alice Marie Eller

	Day Month Year	City, Town or Place	County or Province, etc.	State or Country	Add Info on Wife
Birth	25-7-1953	Bartlesville	Wash. Co.	Okla.	
Chr'nd					
Death					
Burial					

Places of Residence:
Occupation: Nurse aide   Church Affiliation: Christian   Military Rec:
#1 husband-Bill Jones   #3 husband Clair Enabinent
Her Father: Mother's Maiden Name:

Sex	Children's Names in Full	Children's Data	Day Month Year	City, Town or Place	County or Province, etc.	State or Country	Add Info on Children
F	1 Sandra Lynn Jones	Birth	2-12-1972	Ft. Carson Larimer Co.		Colo.	
	Full Name of Spouse: Mike Schapansky	Marr	13-2-1991	Bartlesville	Wash. Co.	Okla.	
		Death					
		Burial					
F	2 Virginia Rose Phillips	Birth	6-3-1981	Bartlesville	Wash. Co.	Okla.	
	Full Name of Spouse:	Marr					
		Death					
		Burial					
F	3 Randie Renee Phillips	Birth	25-1-1989	Bartlesville	Wash. Co.	Okla.	
	Full Name of Spouse:	Marr					
		Death					
		Burial					
	4	Birth					
	Full Name of Spouse:	Marr					
		Death					
		Burial					
	5	Birth					
	Full Name of Spouse:	Marr					
		Death					
		Burial					
	6	Birth					
	Full Name of Spouse:	Marr					
		Death					
		Burial					
	7	Birth					
	Full Name of Spouse:	Marr					
		Death					
		Burial					
	8	Birth					
	Full Name of Spouse:	Marr					
		Death					
		Burial					

Comp'er: Notes:
Address:
City, State, Zip:
Date:

Family Group Sheet

Husband's Full Name Mike Schapansky — **Chart No.**

	Day Month Year	City, Town or Place	County or Province, etc.	State or Country	Add. Info on Husband
Birth	10-1-1970				
Chr'nd					
Marr	13-2-1991				
Death					
Burial					

Places of Residence:
Occupation: — Church Affiliation: — Military Rec:
His Father: — Mother's Maiden Name:

Wife's Full Maiden Name Sandra Lynn Jones

	Day Month Year	City, Town or Place	County or Province, etc.	State or Country	Add. Info on Wife
Birth	4-12-1973	Ft. Carson	Larimer Co.	Colo.	
Chr'nd					
Death					
Burial					

Places of Residence: Colorado-Oklahoma
Occupation: — Church Affiliation: — Military Rec:
Her Father: Bill Jones — Mother's Maiden Name: Alice Marie Eller

Sex	Children's Names in Full		Day Month Year	City, Town or Place	County or Province, etc.	State or Country
M	1. William Cody S.	Birth	15-10-1991	Bartlesville	Wash. Co.	Okla.
	Full Name of Spouse	Marr. Death Burial				
M	2. James Allen S.	Birth	4-10-1993	Bartlesville	Wash. Co.	Okla.
	Full Name of Spouse	Marr. Death Burial				
	3.	Birth Marr. Death Burial				

Walter and John Wiley

Walter Wiley, WWI, 1917

Walter and Irene Wiley

Family Group Sheet

Husband's Full Name: Walter George Wiley
Chart No.

Husband's Data	Day	Month	Year	City, Town or Place	County or Province, etc.	State or Country	Add. Info. on Husband
Birth	27	05	1895	Altoona	Wilson County	Kansas	
Chr'nd	Age 12 yrs.			Christian Church	Altoona Wilson Co.	Kansas	
Marr							
Death	18	06	1941	5 miles South of Newton	Harvey Co.	Kansas	car accident
Burial	22	06	1941	Altoona Cem.	Wilson County	Kansas	

Places of Residence:
Occupation: Continental Oil   **Church Affiliation:** Christian   **Military Rec:** WWI in Germany
His Father: George Allen Wiley   **Mother's Maiden Name:** Etta Ellen Moore

Wife's Full Maiden Name: Irene Sullivan

Wife's Data	Day	Month	Year	City, Town or Place	County or Province, etc.	State or Country	Add. Info. on Wife
Birth			1898				
Chr'nd							
Death	18	08	1940				
Burial	21	08	1940	Dewey Cem.	Washington County	Oklahoma	

Places of Residence:
Occupation: **Church Affiliation:**   **Military Rec:**
Her Father: **Mother's Maiden Name:**

Walter G. Wiley Dies In Car Accident

Son of Mr. and Mrs. Geo. Wiley of Geneseo Killed June 18 Near Newton, Kas.

Walter G. Wiley of Geneseo, Kas., son of Mr. and Mrs. George Wiley, passed away in a car accident four miles west and five miles south of Newton, Kas., June 18, 1941.

Walter had been an employee of the Continental Oil company for more than twenty years and was a faithful and efficient employee.

Deceased was born in Altoona, Kas., May 27, 1895, where he lived until he was grown. At the time of his death, he was 46 years and 22 days of age. His wife died August 18, 1940, and was buried in Dewey, Okla.

Funeral for the deceased was held in the Christian church in Dewey, Okla., Sunday, June 22, 1941, and was largely attended by relatives and friends. The pastor, Rev. C. E. Venable, officiated, and burial was in the Altoona cemetery beside his brother, John, who was killed in an accident March 14, 1934.

The following relatives from a distance attended the last sad rites: Mr. and Mrs. Chas. Land of Kansas City, Kas.; Mr. and Mrs. J. D. Whitaker of Thayer, Kas.; Mrs. L. V. Moore and three sons, of Butler county, Kas.; Mr. and Mrs. Ray Moore and daughter, of Maize, Kas.; Mr. and Mrs. Garner Bailey and son of Cleveland, Okla.; Mr. and Mrs. Wm. Green of Seminole, Okla.; Mrs. Pearl Gordon of Tulsa, Okla., and Miss Shirley Jean Wiley and mother, Mrs. Erma Rogers, of Kiowa, Kas.

Pallbearers were his associates of the oil company.

Deceased joined the Christian church in Altoona when 12 years old and lived a conscientious life, was kind and generous to all, and will live in the lives of relatives and friends always.

Family Group Sheet

Husband's Full Name: John Moore Wiley   **Chart No.** —

Husband's Data	Day	Month	Year	City, Town or Place	County or Province, etc.	State or Country	Add. Info. on Husband
Birth	23	10	1905	Altoona	Wilson County	Kansas	killed in an accident at work
Chr'nd							
Marr							
Death	14	03	1934	Close to Oklahoma City	Oklahoma Co.	Oklahoma	
Burial	16	03	1934	Altoona	Wilson Co.	Kansas	divorced

Places of Residence:
Occupation: Portland Cement/control — oil   **Church Affiliation:**   **Military Rec:**

His Father: George Alan Wiley   **Mother's Maiden Name:** Etta Ellen Moore

Wife's Full Maiden Name: Irma Rogers

Wife's Data	Day	Month	Year	City, Town or Place	County or Province, etc.	State or Country	Add. Info. on Wife
Birth							
Chr'nd							
Death							
Burial							

Places of Residence:
Occupation: **Church Affiliation:**

Her Father: **Mother's Maiden Name:**

Sex	Children's Names in Full	Children's Data	Day	Month	Year	City, Town
F	1 Shirley Jean Wiley	Birth				
	Full Name of Spouse: Mullholand	Marr.				
		Death				
		Burial				

Rites Today for Dewey Woman

Dewey, Aug. 21 — (Special) — Funeral services for the late Mrs. Irene Wiley will be held Thursday afternoon at 2 o'clock at the Christian church with Rev. C. E. Venable in charge. Out of town relatives now at the Wiley home include her sisters and families, Mr. and Mrs. Bill Green and son, Winston Russell, of Seminole, and Mr. and Mrs. Garner Bailey and son of Cleveland. Other relatives will arrive Thursday morning. Casket-bearers will be nephews of the deceased or her husband and will include Everett and Jimmy Eller, Bernal Case, Glen Bartlett, Winston Russell Green and Jay Stead. The body was removed from the Burt chapel Wednesday afternoon, to the home of Mr. and Mrs. George Wiley on East Third street where it will remain until time for the services. Burial will be in the Dewey cemetery.

FUNERAL REGISTER — Mar 14, 1934
STANDARD CERTIFICATE OF DEATH

1. **Place of Death:** Ponca City, County: ____, State: ____
2. **Full Name:** John M. Wiley
   - Residence: Dewey

PERSONAL AND STATISTICAL PARTICULARS

3. Sex: M   Color: W   Single/Married/Widowed/Divorced: Divorced
5. **Date of Birth:** Oct 23, 1905
7. **Age:** Years 29, Months 4, Days 21
8. **Occupation:** Oil field worker
9. **Birthplace:** Altoona, Kansas
10. **Name of Father:** Geo. A.
11. **Birthplace of Father:** Ind.
12. **Maiden Name of Mother:** Etta Moore
13. **Birthplace of Mother:** Kansas
14. **Informant:** Mr. & Mrs. Geo. Wiley, Dewey

MEDICAL CERTIFICATE OF DEATH

16. **Date of Death:** May 14, 1934
17. I HEREBY CERTIFY, That I attended deceased...
   - **Cause of Death:** Accident — caught in machinery
   - Contributory: at the Hartford pool
19. **Place of Burial:** Altoona, Kansas   **Date of Burial:** Mar 16
   - Undertaker: C. H. Burt, Altoona city

	AMOUNT	DATE	PAYMENTS	AMOUNT
Removal of Body		Apr 12	by check Mrs. Geo. Wiley	145.00
Embalming and Attendance				
Casket				
Steel Vault OE	100.00			
Outside Box				
Burial Robe	30.00			
Autos to Altoona Kans				
Flowers + Funeral at Ch.	1.00			
Hearse	Prof Services			
Clergyman	Skipped in			
Singers				
Death notices in Papers				
Outlay for Lot				
Opening Grave				
Lining Grave				
Shipping charges, prepaid				
Sales Tax	1.00			
Total amount of bill	135.00			

Name of Minister: Saladin + Wagoner
Time of Funeral Service: 2 PM   Place of Funeral Service: ____
REMARKS: 10 am at Dewey

JOHN M. WILEY
1904-1934

Compiler:
Address:
City, State, Zip:
Date:

Family Group Sheet

Husband's Full Name: Bernal Laverne (Bud) Case — Chart No.

	Day Month Year	City, Town or Place	County or Province, etc.	State or Country	Add. Info. on Husband
Birth	8-1-1914	Dewey	Wash. Co.	Okla.	
Chr'nd					
Marr	29-6-1940	Dewey	Wash. Co.	Okla.	
Death	2-10-1991	Dewey	Wash. Co.	Okla.	
Burial	4-10-1991	Dewey cem.	Wash. Co.	Okla.	

Places of Residence:
Occupation: Mechanic-Owner Auto Repair   **Church Affiliation:** Christian   **Military Rec:**

His Father: Ervin H. Case   **Mother's Maiden Name:** Rickie Ruth Schere

Wife's Full Maiden Name: Willa Mae Eller

	Day Month Year	City, Town or Place	County or Province, etc.	State or Country	Add. Info. on Wife
Birth	19-11-1922	Dewey	Wash. Co.	Okla.	
Chr'nd					
Death					
Burial					

Places of Residence:
Occupation: **Church Affiliation:** Christian   **Military Rec:**

Her Father: John Everett Eller   **Mother's Maiden Name:** Stella Adaline Wiley

Sex	Children's Names in Full		Day Month Year	City, Town or Place	County or Province, etc.	State or Country	Add. Info on Children
M	1 Larry Ervin Case	Birth	8-12-1941	Dewey	Wash. Co.	Okla.	
		Marr.	5-10-1968	Ardmore	Carter Co.	Okla.	
	Spouse: Durena Dale Elkins	Death					
		Burial					
M	2 Davie Laverne Case	Birth	1-5-1946	Bartlesville	Wash. Co.	Okla.	
		Marr.					
	Spouse:	Death	8-7-1946	Bartlesville	Wash. Co.	Okla.	
		Burial	10-7-1946	Dewey cem.	Wash. Co.	Okla.	
M	3 Gerald Allen Case	Birth	26-8-1948	Bartlesville	Wash. Co.	Okla.	
		Marr.	16-6-1972	Bartlesville	Wash. Co.	Okla.	
	Spouse: Janet Lee Ward	Death					
		Burial					
	4	Birth					
		Marr.					
	Spouse:	Death					

Barbara Anderson, Helen Bartlett, Betty Brockhause, James Eller, Willa Mae and Bud Case, July 1, 1990.

Bud and Willa Case, 1990, 50th Wedding Anniversary

Compiler:
Address:
City, State, Zip:
Date:
Notes:

Cases to celebrate 50th

Mr. and Mrs. B.L. Case of Dewey will celebrate their 50th wedding anniversary July 1. A reception, hosted by their children and grandchildren, will be held from 2 p.m. to 4 p.m. in the Fellowship Hall of First Presbyterian Church, Ninth and Wyandotte, Dewey.

B.L. "Bud" Case and Willa Mae Eller were married June 29, 1940, in the First Christian Church, Dewey. Mr. Case retired after 36 years ownership of Case Auto Repair, south of Dewey. He now is a crosswalk guard for Dewey schools. His hobby is restoring old cars and tractors. Mrs. Case is active in church work, and has been director of Friday School for 17 years and a Bible School teacher for 49 years. Mr. Case is a church elder.

Mr. and Mrs. B.L. Case

Their children are Larry E. and Durena Case of Delaware; Gerald A. and Janet Case of Wann; and Davie Laverne Case, deceased. They also have four grandchildren.

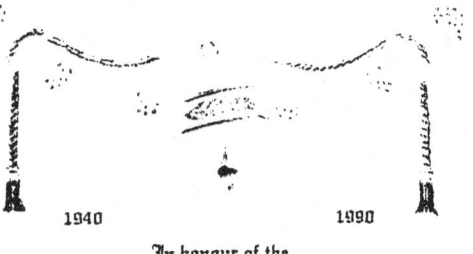

1940 1990

In honour of the
Fiftieth Wedding Anniversary of
Mr. and Mrs. B. L. Case
their children and grandchildren
request the pleasure of your company
at a Reception
on Sunday, the first of July
Nineteen hundred and ninety
from two until four o'clock in the afternoon
First Christian Church
Ninth and Wyandotte
Dewey, Oklahoma

Please no gifts
except the cherished gift of your presence

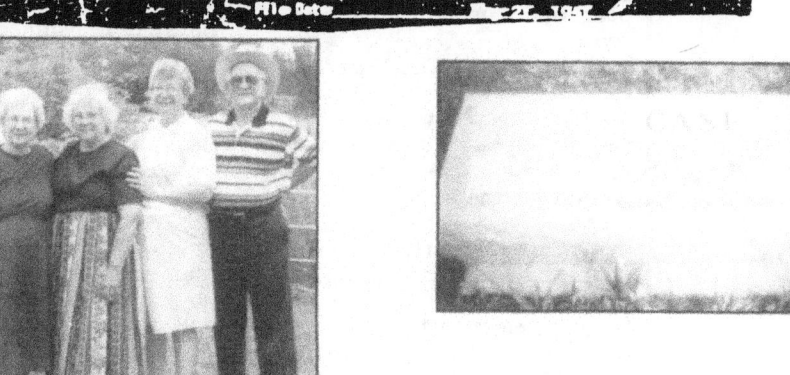

Jim, Willa Mae, Betty, Bobby, Everette, 1995.

ER-ENTERPRISE

Sunday, May 3, 1992 — 242 Pages, 11 Sections, 50 Cents

This tornado took our home. We lived north of the Dewey Cemetery. Larry was 5 months old. He & I were in the cellar & the roof of our house landed on the cellar door & had to be taken off before we could get out. Bud was at work & ran over telephone poles in our lane to get to us.

50 YEARS AGO. This tornado dropped out of the sky east of Pawhuska on May 2, 1942, and did not retreat into the clouds until it had blown through Dewey where it killed one person and destroyed numerous homes.

Photo courtesy of Virgil Miller

Spring showers mean potential for twisters

By Andy Williams
E-E Staff Reporter

The old saying goes, "April showers bring may flowers." But as last year proved, spring can bring something much more destructive.

Twisters, funnels, wind devils — they are all slang for one of nature's most destructive forces, tornados.

It's that time of year again. The time when Oklahomans keep an eye on the western sky, watching for a dark gloomy cloud that might appear ominously on the horizon.

In the movie "The Wizard of Oz," one whisked Dorothy away to the yellow brick road. But in Green Country, it is more likely to send residents running to the cellar.

Over the years, area residents have experienced their share of the deadly storms. Some clouds spawn several funnels, each swirling out of the towering black image hanging in the sky.

Others give birth to a single twister that skips aimlessly for miles, growing as it rips across the landscape.

On May 2, 1942, a single funnel dropped out of the sky east of Pawhuska. It didn't stop until it blew through Dewey.

Virgil Miller of Dewey witnessed the storm's mass destruction as he sat on top of his cellar.

"It passed about a mile in front of my house and just NORTH of the Dewey Cemetery," Miller recalled. "There were 16 people and three dogs cramped in my cellar at the time."

He said it claimed one life and destroyed several homes in Dewey before it returned to the clouds.

Dewey was hit again in May of 1986 and again several homes were destroyed.

Last April, a tornado ripped through the Copan area. One person was killed while driving in a car, and several other people were injured. The tornado destroyed several homes and businesses in the quiet town, however, most have rebuilt and things appear back to normal.

Gerald, Larry, Bud and Willa Mae Case, 1963.

Wed. Oct 2, 1991

Deaths

B.L. 'Bud' Case

B.L. "Bud" Case, 77, native Washington County resident and former owner-operator of Case Auto Repair Service, died Wednesday at 8:23 a.m. at his home.

Funeral services will be Friday at 2 p.m. in the sanctuary of the Dewey First Christian Church. Leon Martin will officiate. Committal prayers and interment will be directed in the Dewey Cemetery by The Arnold Moore-Dewey Funeral Service.

Case

B.L. Case was born Jan. 8, 1914, at Dewey. He was the son of Ervin H. and Rickie Ruth (Schere) Case. He was reared and received his education in the Dewey community schools, graduating with the Senior Class of 1933 from Dewey High School.

He married Willa Mae Eller on June 29, 1940, at Dewey, and they lived there. Mr. Case was the owner-operator of Case Auto Repair Service and was a crossing guard for the Dewey Public School System.

"Bud" Case was a member of the Dewey First Christian Church, for which he had served as an elder and chairman of the elders.

Mr. Case will lie in state in the Arnold Moore-Dewey Funeral Home where friends may call for visitation until he is removed to the church for Friday's services.

Survivors include his wife, Willa Mae (Eller) Case of the home in Dewey; two sons: Larry E. Case of Delaware and Gerald A. Case of Wann; four grandchildren; a sister, Mrs. Robert "Bob" (Murna) Parks of Enid; and an aunt, Mrs. Dora Todd of Great Falls, Mont. He was preceded in death by a daughter, Davie Laverne Case, and a sister, Mrs. Doris Thurman.

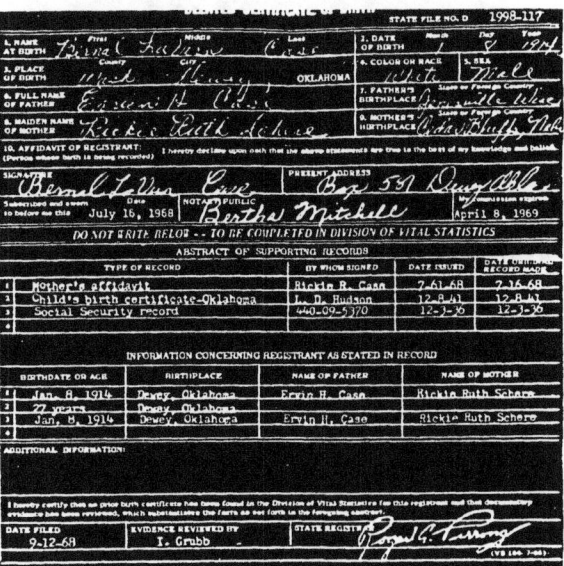

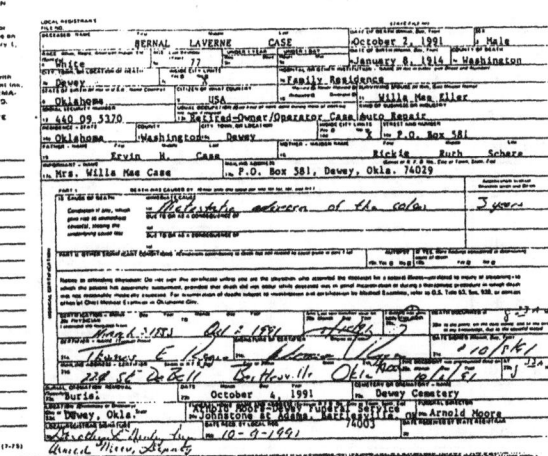

Willa Mae (Eller) Case

Bud Case family: Brett, Gerald, Larry, Scott, Janet, Bud, Caleb, Desiree, Durena, Willa Mae, August 1990.

Glenn and Helen Bartlett, Stella Wiley Elder, Stella Mae (Bartlett) Patterson, Elmer Patterson, Mrs. Patterson.

Family Group Sheet

Husband's Full Name: Larry Ervin Case
Chart No.

	Day Month Year	City, Town or Place	County or Province, etc.	State or Country	Add. Info. on Husband
Birth	8-12-1941	Dewey	Wash. Co.	Okla.	
Chr'nd					
Marr	5-10-1968	Ardmore	Carter Co.	Okla.	
Death					
Burial					

Places of Residence: Okla.-Ga.-Japan-Korea-Thailand-Texas-Kansas
Occupation: Mechanic-Rancher **Church Affiliation:** Christian **Military Rec:** USAF 1961-1969

His Father: Bernal L. Case **Mother's Maiden Name:** Willa Mae Eller

Wife's Full Maiden Name: Durena Dale Elkins

	Day Month Year	City, Town or Place	County or Province, etc.	State or Country	Add. Info. on Wife
Birth	28-5-1946				
Chr'nd					
Death					
Burial					

Places of Residence:
Occupation: RN Nurse **Church Affiliation:** Christian **Military Rec:**

Her Father: Carno Elkins **Mother's Maiden Name:** Stella

Sex	Children's Names in Full		Day Month Year	City, Town or Place	County or Province, etc.	State or Country	Add. Info. on Children
M	1. Brett Michael Case	Birth	6-7-1969	Tinker AFB Okla. City		Okla.	
		Marr.	21-1-1998	Bartlesville	Wash. Co.	Okla.	
	Full Name of Spouse: Heather Ballard	Death					
		Burial					
F	2. Desiree Dale Case	Birth	16-2-1971	Marietta	Cobb Co.	Ga.	
		Marr.	6-7-1996	Okla. City	Okla. Co.	Okla.	
	Full Name of Spouse: Mason Scott Thomas 11	Death					
		Burial					
M	3. Scott Allen Case	Birth	15-2-1975	Bartlesville	Wash. Co.	Okla.	
		Marr.					
	Full Name of Spouse	Death					
		Burial					

Jan. 17-1963

Larry Case has returned to Lubbock, Texas, after spending the Christmas vacation with his parents Mr. and Mrs. Bud Case in Dewey. Larry is serving in the Air Force and is stationed at Reese Air Force Base in Lubbock.

 **dL Cattle Co.**

Larry E. or Durena Case
Rt.1 Box 195-1
Delaware, Okla. 74027
Ph#. 918-467-3358/918-337-7157
Fax: 918-467-4051
le Case@ msn.com.

Bud Case family: Gerald, Caleb, Desiree and Scott Thomas, Larry, Brett, Janet, Durena, Willa Mae and Scott, July 6, 1996.

Durena and Larry Case, July 6, 1996.

Family Group Sheet

Husband's Full Name: Brett Michael Case **Chart No.**

	Day Month Year	City, Town or Place	County or Province, etc.	State or Country	Add. Info on Husband
Birth	6- 7-1963	Tinker AFB	Oklahoma City	Okla.	
Chr'nd					
Marr	21- 1-1998	Bartlesville	Wash. Co.	Okla.	
Death					
Burial					

Places of Residence: Oklahoma-Ga.-
Occupation: Welder-Mechanic   **Church Affiliation:** Christian   **Military Rec:**

His Father: Larry E. Case   **Mother's Maiden Name:** Durena Dale Elkins

Wife's Full Maiden Name: Heather Ballard

	Day Month Year	City, Town or Place	County or Province, etc.	State or Country	Add. Info on Wife
Birth					
Chr'nd					
Death					
Burial					

Places of Residence:
Occupation: **Church Affiliation:**   **Military Rec:**
Her Father: **Mother's Maiden Name:**

Larry Case family: Scott and Durena, Desiree and Scott Thomas, Larry and Brett.

Brett and Heather Case, Jan. 21, 1998.

336

Family Group Sheet

Husband's Full Name: Mason Scott Thomas ll **Chart No.** -

	Day Month Year	City, Town or Place	County or Province, etc.	State or Country	Add. Info on Husband
Birth	24-5-1969				
Chr'nd					
Marr	6- 7-1996	Oklahoma City	Okla. Co.	Okla.	
Death					
Burial					

Places of Residence:

Occupation: Mechanical Engineer **Church Affiliation**: **Military Rec**:

His Father: **Mother's Maiden Name**:

Wife's Full Maiden Name: Desiree Dale Case

	Day Month Year	City, Town or Place	County or Province, etc.	State or Country	Add. Info. on Wife
Birth	16- 2-1971	Kennestone hospital Marietta	Cobb Co.	Ga.	
Chr'nd					
Death					
Burial					

Places of Residence:

Occupation: Manager store **Church Affiliation**: Christian **Military Rec**:

Her Father: Larry E. Case **Mother's Maiden Name**: Durena Dale Elkins

Sex	Children's Names in Full		Day Month Year	City, Town or Place	County or Province, etc.	State or Country	Add. Info on Children
1		Birth					
		Marr.					
	Full Name of Spouse	Death					
		Burial					

337

Family Group Sheet

Husband's Full Name	Scott Allen Case	Chart No.	
	Day Month Year	City, Town or Place	County or Province, etc.	State or Country	Add Info on Husband
Birth	15-2-1975	Bartlesville	Wash. Co.	Okla.	
Chr'nd					
Marr					
Death					
Burial					

Places of Residence

Occupation: **Rancher** Church Affiliation: **Christian** Military Rec

His Father: **Larry E. Case** Mother's Maiden Name: **Durena Dale Elkins**

Stella Eller holding "Sandy," Dec.25, 1982.

Desiree Case and pig, "Sandy," 1983.

The Tale of a Pig – A true story

One time in December of 1982 my Great Granddaughter, Desiree Case, was given a two weeks old pig to raise as a pet. Now Desiree lived 20 miles east of Dewey, Oklahoma on a farm with her parents, Larry and Durena Case and her two brothers, Brett and Scott.

Desiree named her pig, Sandy and fed her milk from a baby bottle. She grew and grew. After awhile when she got strong enough to push the top off the carton where she lived on the back porch, Desiree's Daddy said, "I think Sandy should stay in the barn now, especially at night. So Desiree said, "Daddy, can Sandy have a blanket to keep her warm?" Of course, Larry didn't want Sandy to get cold. About that time they started giving Sandy real pig feed and she grew and grew. One day soon after that Larry decided to build a pen with a little house in it so Sandy was happy in her new house, and Desiree never forgot to feed her. She even taught Sandy to lie down in her pen so Desiree could scratch her stomach with a stick or corn cob. After a few minutes of that Desiree would say, "Sandy hold your leg up" and Sandy would put up her front leg so she could scratch her leg. When Desiree said, "Sandy kiss me", she would put her snout up to Desiree to be kissed, dirt and all. Now Sandy is over a year old and weighs over 300 lbs. and is still Sandy the pet pig!

(She weighed over 600 lbs. and finally Desiree sold her because she was opening the gate and let the horses out. She was afraid the young colts would get out on the road and get hit by a car. When she got out of her pen Desiree was the only one who could call her and she would come running. She still tried to sit on Desiree's lap when she weighed 600 lbs.!)

Written by Stella A. Eller in 1985.

Standard Certificate of Live Birth — State of Oklahoma

State File No. 7-14395

1. Place of Birth:
- (a) County: Washington
- (b) City or town: Bartlesville
- (c) Name of hospital or institution: Washington County Hospital
- (d) Mother's stay before delivery: In hospital or institution — In this community: life

2. Usual Residence of Mother:
- (a) State: Oklahoma
- (b) County: Washington
- (c) City or town: Dewey
- (d) Street No.:

3. Full name of child: Davie Laverne Case
4. Date of birth: 5/1/46
5. Sex: Male
6. Twin or triplet: —
7. No. months of pregnancy: 9
8. Is mother married? Yes

Father of Child
- 9. Full name: Bernal Laverne Case
- 10. Color or race: White
- 11. Age at time of this birth: 32 yrs
- 12. Birthplace: Dewey, Oklahoma
- 13. Usual occupation: Mechanic
- 14. Industry or business: Mechanic

Mother of Child
- 15. Full maiden name: Willa Mae Eller
- 16. Color or race: White
- 17. Age at time of this birth: 23 yrs
- 18. Birthplace: Dewey, Oklahoma
- 19. Usual occupation: Housewife
- 20. Industry or business:

21. Children born to this mother:
- (a) How many other children of this mother now living? 1
- (b) How many other children born alive but now dead?
- (c) How many children were born dead?

22. Mother's mailing address: Mrs. Bernal Case, Dewey, Oklahoma

23. (a) Silver Nitrate used in eyes? Yes
(b) Blood test for syphilis made? Yes

24. I hereby certify that I attended the birth of this child who was born alive at the hour of 9:00 p.m., on the date above stated and that the information given was furnished by Willa Mae Case, related to this child as mother.

25. Date received by local registrar: May 11, 1946
26. Registrar's own signature: —
27. Date given name added: —

Attendant's signature / M.D. / Date signed / Address: Dewey

Date: 8 July 1946
Funeral Of: Davie Laverne Case
Address: Dewey, Oklahoma
Funeral Authorized By: Bernal L. Case
Relationship to Deceased: father
Address: Dewey
Phone:
Place of Death: Memorial Hospital
Time: 10:45 P.M. 8 July 1946
Cause of Death:
Single: Yes Married: Widow: Widower:
Sex: Male Occupation: none
Date of Birth: 1 May 1946
Age: 0 Years 2 Months 7 Days
Birthplace: Memorial Hospital, Bartlesville
Father's Name: Bernal L. Case
Birthplace: Dewey
Mother's Name: Willa Mae Eller
Birthplace: Dewey
Physician: Dr. L. D. Hudson
Social Security Number:

July 8, 1946

A grave-side service will be held this afternoon at 2 o'clock for little Davie LaVerne Case, six weeks old son of Mr. and Mrs. Bernal Case. Mr. Sidney Hawkins of the Christian church will conduct the service in the Dewey cemetery and burial will be under the direction of the Neekamps. The baby died at Memorial hospital about 11 o'clock Monday night where he had been since birth. He leaves the parents, Mr. and Mrs. Bernal Case, and a four year old brother, Larry and grandparents, Mr. and Mrs. E. H. Case of Dewey and Mr. and Mrs. John Eller also of Dewey and a great-grandfather, Mr. George Wiley.

Announce:—
Davie Laverne Case

Graveside services for Davie Leverne Case, infant son of Mr. and Mrs. Bernal L. Case of Dewey, will be held at 2:00 p. m., Wednesday afternoon at the Dewey Cemetery with the Reverend Sidney Hawkins, Pastor of the Dewey Christian Church officiating. Davie was born May 1, 1946 at the Washington County Memorial Hospital and had been under their care until his death Monday evening at 10:45 p. m. Services will be under direction of the Neekamps.

Family Group Sheet

Husband's Full Name: Gerald Allen Case

Chart No.:

Husband's Data	Day Month Year	City, Town or Place	County or Province, etc.	State or Country	Add Info on Husband
Birth	26-8-1948	Bartlesville	Wash. Co.	Okla.	
Chr'nd					
Marr	16-6-1972	Bartlesville	Wash. Co.	Okla.	
Death					
Burial					

Places of Residence: Oklahoma-Washington
Occupation: Painter Rancher **Church Affiliation:** Christian **Military Rec:**

His Father: Bernal L. Case **Mother's Maiden Name:** Willa Mae Eller

Wife's Full Maiden Name: Janet Lee Ward

Wife's Data	Day Month Year	City, Town or Place	County or Province, etc.	State or Country	Add. Info. on Wife
Birth	1-9-1952	Bartlesville	Wash. Co.	Okla.	
Chr'nd					
Death					
Burial					

Places of Residence:
Occupation: Dr's Office Manager **Church Affiliation:** Church of God **Military Rec:**

Her Father: Ward **Mother's Maiden Name:** Lois

Sex	Children's Names in Full	Children's Data	Day Month Year	City, Town or Place	County or Province, etc.	State or Country	Add Info on Children
M	1. Caleb Levi Case	Birth	15-2-1981				
	Full Name of Spouse	Marr.					
		Death					
		Burial					

Gerald and Janet Case, July 6, 1996.

LITTLE CALAB CASE enjoying the 100 year old antique carriage while his mother works.

Antique Crib Put To Use

Little Caleb Case naps in the same carriage occupied by his great-grandmother in her baby days.

Caleb's mother, Janet (Mrs. Gerald) Case, operates The Rope Garden in Dewey, making custom dry and silk flower arrangements, macrame hangers, and sells macrame supplies and unusual gifts.

She has been in business two years. Eight months ago when Caleb was born she closed the shop for six weeks. At that time she felt the baby was old enough to accompany her to work.

Explaining her decision to take Caleb to the shop with her, Mrs. Case said, "That first year is really important, they learn so many things then, I wanted to be with him all the time. I wanted it to be me, not a baby sitter, that discovered his first tooth. I just didn't want to miss any of his cute little baby actions."

When she was considering how to care for Caleb in a place of business, his grandfather, B.L. "Bud" Case, remembered the old buggy and offered its use.

The exact age of the carriage is unknown. It was purchased in Cedar Bluff, NB. almost 100 years ago when Caleb's great-grandmother was a baby, but it was second hand then. The buggy was used for many years by a large number of babies, passed from one family of relatives to another as the need arose.

Bud Case explained the carriage had been stored over a corn crib in the barn of relatives. While visiting in Nebraska about 20 years ago he became interested in it, and it was given to him. He brought it home and refinished it.

The buggy has 24 inch iron spoke rear wheels with front wheels of the same type but slightly smaller. All wheels show a blacksmith weld. There are no rubber tires, but leaf steel springs provide ample bounce for an easy ride.

Square iron nails, bentwood, and wicker were used in its construction.

Caleb will soon outgrow the carriage for naps, but for the first eight months of his life it has made it easier for his mother to care for him while at her work.

Wednesday, October 28, 1981

Family Group Sheet

Husband's Full Name: Bobby Arno Brockhouse
Chart No.:

	Day Month Year	City, Town or Place	County or Province, etc	State or Country	Add. Info on Husband
Birth	7-8-1922	Kansas City	Jackson Co.	Mo.	Twin- Betty Ann
Chr'nd					
Marr	31-10-1949	Kansas City	Jackson Co.	Mo.	
Death	9-12-1997	Kansas City Veteran's hospital		Mo.	
Burial	15-12-1997	Kansas City	Jackson Co.	Mo.	

Places of Residence: Kansas City, Mo.-Jacksonville, Florida
Occupation: Electrician **Church Affiliation:** Christian **Military Rec:** WW2-Korean conflict
His Father: Cecil Allen Brockhouse **Mother's Maiden Name:** Irma Montaldo Roach

Wife's Full Maiden Name: Elizabeth Irene (Betty) Eller

	Day Month Year	City, Town or Place	County or Province, etc.	State or Country	Add. Info. on Wife
Birth	12-4-1926	Dewey	Wash. Co.	Okla.	
Chr'nd					
Death					
Burial					

Places of Residence: Country East of Dewey, Okla. Enid, Okla. Kansas City
Occupation: Secretary-Child Care **Church Affiliation:** Christian **Military Rec.:**
Her Father: John Everett Eller **Mother's Maiden Name:** Stella Adaline Wiley

Sex	Children's Names in Full		Day Month Year	City, Town or Place	County or Province, etc.	State or Country	Add. Info on Children
M	1 Brockhouse Michael Wayne	Birth	12-11-1951	Jacksonville	Duval	Florida	Naval Air Station
		Marr.	6-5-1978	Kansas City	Jackson	Mo.	
	Full Name of Spouse: Darcy Ann O'Brien	Death					
		Burial					
F	2 Brockhouse Madeline Eileen	Birth	30-7-1953	Kansas City	Jackson Co.	Mo.	
		Marr.	8-7-1970	Kansas City	Jackson Co.	Mo.	#2 husband Jeff Garman
	Full Name of Spouse: William W. Ashurst	Death					
		Burial					
	3	Birth					
		Marr.					

Marriage Certificate

I, Nile A. Sessions, Jr., a Minister hereby certify that on the 31st day of October in the year of our Lord one thousand nine hundred and forty nine Mr. Bobby Arno Brockhouse of Kansas City in the County of Jackson and State of Missouri and Miss Elizabeth Irene Eller of Kansas City in the County of Jackson and State of Missouri were by me united in marriage at Kansas City in the County of Jackson and State of Missouri according to the laws of said state. I further certify that the marriage license was issued in the County of Jackson, State of Missouri on the 28th day of October A.D. 1949.

Mrs. Willie Mae Cone, Witness
Clifford N. _____, Witness
Thos. A. Sessions, Jr., Minister
Independence Boulevard
Christian Church
Kansas City, Missouri

Betty and Bob Brockhouse

Notes: #2 Jeff Garman (M) K.C. Mo. 1995 born 10-12-1957

Army of the United States

Honorable Discharge

This is to certify that

BOBBY A BROCKHOUSE 17 129 109 PRIVATE FIRST CLASS
461ST BOMB SQ 346 BOMB GP 2 AF

Army of the United States

is hereby Honorably Discharged from the military service of the United States of America.

This certificate is awarded as a testimonial of Honest and Faithful Service to this country.

Given at SEPARATION CENTER
JEFFERSON BARRACKS MISSOURI

Date 22 FEBRUARY 1946

THOMAS B. HENLEY
MAJOR FA

ENLISTED RECORD AND REPORT OF SEPARATION
HONORABLE DISCHARGE

1. Last Name - First Name - Middle Initial	Brockhouse Bobby A
2. Army Serial No.	17 129 109
3. Grade	PFC
4. Arm or Service	AAF
5. Component	AUS
6. Organization	461st Bomb Sq 346 Bomb Gp 2 AF
7. Date of Separation	22 Feb 1946
8. Place of Separation	Jefferson Barracks Mo Separation Center
9. Permanent Address for Mailing Purposes	3003 E 6th St Kansas City 1 Mo
10. Date of Birth	7 Aug 1922
11. Place of Birth	Kansas City Mo
12. Address from which employment will be sought	See #9
13. Color Eyes	Blue
14. Color Hair	Brn
15. Height	5'8"
16. Weight	137 lbs
17. No. Depend.	0
18. Race	X (White)
19. Marital Status	Single
20. U.S. Citizen	Yes
21. Civilian Occupation	Student Trade School X-02

MILITARY HISTORY

22. Date of Induction	—
23. Date of Enlistment	7 Nov 1942
24. Date of Entry into Active Service	7 Nov 42
25. Place of Entry into Service	Ft Leavenworth Kansas
26. Home Address at Time of Entry into Service	3003 E 6th Kansas City 1 Mo
30. Military Occupational Specialty	Airplane & Engine Mech 747
31. Military Qualification	not eval

Latest Immunization Dates: Smallpox 9 Nov 1942; Typhoid 8 Nov 42; Other 20 Jun 45 28 Apr 44; Blood Type "B"; Current Grade PFC

Total Length of Service: Continental Service 3 yrs 3 mos 16 days; Foreign Service 0

33. Decorations and Citations: Victory Ribbon American Theatre Ribbon Good Conduct Medal

34. Wounds Received in Action: None

35. Battles and Campaigns: None

40. Reason and Authority for Separation: AR 615-365 Convenience of the Govt RR 1-1 Per 1D SPKM 210.8 16 Jan 46

41. Service Schools Attended: AAFTS Sheppard Fld Tex Ap & Engine Mech Chanute Fld Ill Power Plant

44	Mustering Out Pay	Soldier Deposits	Travel Pay	Total Amount Name of Disbursing Officer
Total $200	$100	—	$14.60	160.40 J W MC MANUS 1T COL F.D

45. Longevity for Pay Purposes: 3 yrs 3 mos

Insurance Notice: 31 Mar 46

46. Date of this Payment: 28 Feb 46 $6.50

55. Remarks: Lapel Button Issued ASR Score 34

56. Signature of Person Being Separated: Bobby A Brockhouse

57. Personnel Officer: J J DEMLAND 1ST LT AC

ARMY LAPEL BUTTON
READJUSTMENT ALLOWANCE
PUBLIC LAW #346
MADE THROUGH
STATE OF MISSOURI
DATE 3-12-46

E. Military Service Record

Name of Veteran BROCKHOUSE   BOBBY   ARNO
                 last   first   middle

State from Which Served Missouri

War in Which, or Dates between Which, He Served WWI-USAF (11/07/42-02/22/45) (Navy) KOREAN CONFLICT (08/50), Retired Air Force 02-52, Reserves 1967.

If Service Was Civil War:

   Union _____ Confederate _____

Unit in Which He Served:

   Name or Number of Regiment WWI 461st Bomb Sq. 346 Bomb Gp.2AF, 442nd Military Airlift Wing Navy 442nd Troop Carrier Wing

   Company _____

   Name of Ship _____

Branch in Which He Served:

   Infantry _____ Cavalry _____ Artillery _____ Navy X Other USAF

Kind of Service: Volunteers _____ Regulars _____

Pension File Number _____

Bounty Land File Number (for Service before 1856 Only) _____

Military Record Number USAF 17-129-109; USN 326-67-78

Date of Birth 07/08/1922

Place of Birth Kansas City Jackson   Jackson   Missouri
                city   county   state

Name of Widow or Other Claimant Elizabeth (Betty) I. Brockhouse

Date of Death _____

Place of Death _____
               city   county   state

Places Lived after Service 3205 S. Vermont-815 Queen Rd. Drive Independence MO
3006 E. 6th, Kansas City, MO

If Veteran Lived in a Home for Soldiers:

   Location _____
                    city   state

Retired March 6, 1967 Staff Sgt. E6

Honorable Discharge

from the Armed Forces of the United States of America

This is to certify that

BROCKHOUSE, Bobby Arno, 326 67 78, BMP3, USNR-R

was Honorably Discharged from the

United States Navy

on the 2nd day of March 1953. *This certificate is awarded as a testimonial of Honest and Faithful Service*

John B. Cameron
JOHN B. CAMERON, LCDR., USNR-R
COMMANDING OFFICER NR SURF DIV 9-123

Place of discharge U.S. Naval Reserve Training Center, 801 Walnut St., Kansas City, Missouri

Authority for discharge Article H-6206 BuPers Manual

Serial or file number 326 67 78

Date and place of birth 7 August 1922   Kansas City, Missouri

Date of entry into active service 3 March 1948 (USNR O-1)

Highest rank or rating held BMP3

Service (vessels and stations served on) U.S. Naval Reserve Training Center, Kansas City, Missouri

Sub Group ONE, Florida Group ATLANTIC RESERVE Fleet, Green Cove Springs, Florida

U.S. Naval Reserve Training Center, OrgSurf Div 6-42, Jacksonville, Florida

Remarks Recommended for Re-Enlistment.

John B. Cameron
JOHN B. CAMERON, LCDR.,   U.S.N.(9.

Honorable Discharge

from the Armed Forces of the United States of America

This is to certify that

STAFF SERGEANT BOBBY ARNO BROCKHOUSE, AF17129109

was Honorably Discharged from the

United States Air Force

on the 6TH *day of* MARCH 1967 *This certificate is awarded as a testimonial of Honest and Faithful Service*

BEN J. MANGINO, COLONEL, AFRes
Commander

DD FORM 256 AF   PREVIOUS EDITIONS OF THIS FORM MAY BE USED.
1 NOV 51
THIS IS AN IMPORTANT RECORD — SAFEGUARD IT!

B-No. 4161   DEPARTMENT OF HEALTH
Bureau of Vital Statistics
CERTIFIED COPY OF BIRTH RECORD

Registration District No. 309   Primary Registration District No. 1002   Registrar's No. 4342

1. PLACE OF BIRTH:
 (a) County: Jackson
 (b) City or town: Kansas City
 (c) Name of hospital or institution: Christian Church Hospital

2. USUAL RESIDENCE OF MOTHER:
 (a) State: Missouri   (b) County: Jackson
 (c) City or town: Kansas City
 Street No.: 3008 East 7th St.

3. Full name of child: Bobby Arno Brockhouse
4. Date of birth: August 7 1922
5. Sex: Male   6. Twin or triplet: twin   1st   7. Number months of pregnancy: 9   8. Is mother married? Yes

FATHER OF CHILD
9. Full name: Cecil Allen Brockhouse
10. Color or race: White   11. Age at time of this birth: 37
12. Birthplace: Peculiar, Missouri
13. Usual occupation: Cashier in Bank

MOTHER OF CHILD
14. Full maiden name: Irma Koach
15. Color or race: White   17. Age at time of this birth: 28
16. Birthplace: Lamar, Mo.
18. Usual occupation: Housewife

21. I hereby certify that I attended the birth of this child who was born alive at the hour of 7:10 A on the date above stated...
22. Date received by local registrar: 8-27-1922
Attendant's own signature: Geo. C. Mosher, M.D.
Address: 605 Bryant Bldg.

State of Missouri, City of Kansas City

I hereby certify that the above is a true and correct copy of the certificate of birth of Bobby Arno Brockhouse filed in the office of Vital Statistics of Kansas City, Missouri...

Witness my hand as Director of Health, Kansas City, Missouri this 27th day of July, 1942.

Fee 50c

Hugh L. Dwyer, M.D.
DIRECTOR OF HEALTH

4	Burial	
	Birth	
	Marr.	
Full Name of Spouse	Death	
	Burial	
5	Birth	
	Marr.	
Full Name of Spouse	Death	
	Burial	
6	Birth	
	Marr.	
Full Name of Spouse	Death	
	Burial	
7	Birth	
	Marr.	
Full Name of Spouse	Death	
	Burial	
8	Birth	
	Marr.	
Full Name of Spouse	Death	
	Burial	

Compiler
Address
City, State, Zip
Date

Add. Info. on Husband

Add. Info. on Wife

Add. Info on Children

United States Air Force

Retired Reserve

This is to certify that,

by authority of the Secretary of the Air Force,

STAFF SERGEANT BOBBY A. BROCKHOUSE AF 1712 91 09

has been transferred to the Retired Reserve in recognition of honorable service and continued interest in the defense of our Nation, on the SIXTH *day of* MARCH 1967.

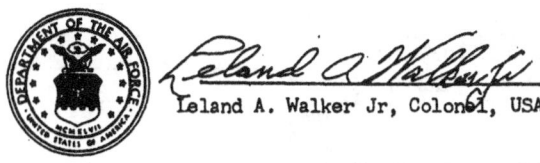

Leland A. Walker Jr, Colonel, USAF

AF FORM 951, AUG 65

DEPARTMENT OF THE AIR FORCE
HEADQUARTERS 442D MILITARY AIRLIFT WING (H) (RESERVE) (CONAC)
RICHARDS-GEBAUR AIR FORCE BASE, MISSOURI 64030

DATE OF ENLISTMENT: 7 March 1967

REASON & AUTHORITY FOR DISCHARGE: ETS, AFR 45-43

PRIMARY AF SPECIALTY CODE: 42350, Acft Elect Repairman
ADDITIONAL AFSCs: 54530, Apr Refrig Specl

PRIOR ACTIVE MILITARY SERVICE: 04 YEARS, 10 MONTHS, 16 DAYS

TOTAL SERVICE COMPLETED FOR PAY PURPOSES: 22 YEARS

GRADE AND DATE OF RANK: SSGT, 1 NOVEMBER 1954

RECOMMENDED FOR REENLISTMENT: YES X   NO

ELI M. OLBIN, Major, AFRes
Director Personnel Management

Bobby and Betty Brockhouse and Elizabeth, Sept. 28, 1997.

Family Group Sheet

Husband's Full Name: Michael Wayne Brockhouse — Chart No.

Husband's Data	Day Month Year	City, Town or Place	County or Province, etc.	State or Country	Add. Info. on Husband
Birth	12-11-1951	Jacksonville Naval Air Station	Duval Co.	Florida	
Chrd					
Marr	6-5-1978	Kansas City	Jackson Co.	Mo.	
Death					
Burial					

Places of Residence: Florida-Independence, Mo. ---Kansas
Occupation: Chef **Church Affiliation:** Christian **Military Rec:**

His Father: Bobby Arno Brockhouse **Mother's Maiden Name:** Elizabeth Irene Eller

Wife's Full Maiden Name: Darcy Ann O'Brien

Wife's Data	Day Month Year	City, Town or Place	County or Province, etc.	State or Country	Add. Info. on Wife
Birth	26-6-1955	Kansas City	Jackson Co.	Mo.	
Chrd					
Death					
Burial					

Places of Residence: Raytown, Mo-Kansas
Occupation: Housewife **Church Affiliation:** Pentecostal **Military Rec:**

Her Father: Richard Francis O'Brien **Mother's Maiden Name:** Edith Ann Padley

Sex	Children's Names in Full	Children's Data	Day Month Year	City, Town or Place	County or Province, etc.	State or Country	Add. Info. on Children
F	1 Brockhouse Michelle Jenette	Birth	30-12-1978	Kansas City	Jackson Co.	Mo.	
	Full Name of Spouse	Marr. Death Burial					
M	2 Brockhouse Michael Lee O'Brien	Birth	6-7-1982	Overland Park	Johnson Co.	Kan.	
	Full Name of Spouse	Marr. Death Burial					
M	3 Brockhouse Luke Wayne Richard	Birth	26-1-1988	Salina	Salina Co.	Ks.	
	Full Name of Spouse	Marr. Death					

Darcy, Betty, Bob Brockhouse, Michael, Michele, Michael Lee, Luke Brockhouse, 1990.

CERTIFIED COPY

I HEREBY CERTIFY THE COPY REPRODUCED BELOW TO BE A TRUE AND CORRECT COPY OF THE ORIGINAL RECORD ON FILE IN THE BUREAU OF VITAL STATISTICS OF THE STATE OF FLORIDA, DEPARTMENT OF HEALTH AND REHABILITATIVE SERVICES, AT JACKSONVILLE, FLORIDA.

(NOT VALID UNLESS THE SEAL OF THE STATE OF FLORIDA, DEPARTMENT OF HEALTH AND REHABILITATIVE SERVICES, IS AFFIXED.)

JAN 13 1983

Everett H. Williams, Jr.
STATE REGISTRAR FOR VITAL STATISTICS
DEPARTMENT OF HEALTH AND REHABILITATIVE SERVICES

CERTIFICATE OF LIVE BIRTH — FLORIDA
Birth No. 109-51-058182

- Place of Birth: Duval County, Florida
- Usual Residence of Mother: Duval County, Florida, Jacksonville, 4719 Post St.
- Full Name of Hospital or Institution: Dependents Hospital USN
- Child's Name: Michael Wayne Brockhouse
- Sex: Male; Single; Date of Birth: Nov. 12, 1951
- Father: Bobby Arno Brockhouse; Age 29; Birthplace Mo.; Usual Occupation EMPFN; Kind of Business U.S.N.R.; Color White
- Mother: Elizabeth Irene Eller; Age 25; Birthplace Okla.; Color White
- Children previously born to this mother: 0 / 0 / 0
- Informant: Mother
- Signature: Everett M. Clayton
- Address: 2570 Hospital J, Jacksonville, Fla.
- Attendant at Birth: M.D.; Date Signed: NOV 13 1951
- Date Rec'd by Local Reg: NOV 14 1951

Family Group Sheet

Husband's Full Name: William Wallace Ashurst
Chart No.: —

Husband's Data	Day Month Year	City, Town or Place	County or Province, etc.	State or Country	Add. Info on Husband
Birth	30-6-1950	Fulton	Callaway Co.	Mo.	divorced 1979
Chr'nd					
Marr	7-8-1970	Kansas City	Jackson Co.	Mo.	
Death					
Burial					

Places of Residence: Indep., Mo.-Fulton, Mo.
Occupation: Electrician **Church Affiliation:**   **Military Rec:**
His Father: Robert Craig Ashurst, Jr. **Mother's Maiden Name:** Sara Sue Stevinson

Wife's Full Maiden Name: Madeline Eileen Brockhouse

Wife's Data	Day Month Year	City, Town or Place	County or Province, etc.	State or Country	Add. Info on Wife
Birth	30-7-1953	Kansas City	Jackson Co.	Mo.	
Chr'nd					
Death					
Burial					

Places of Residence: Independence, Mo.
Occupation: Maintenance **Church Affiliation:** Pentecostal **Military Rec:**
Other Husbands: #2 Jeff Garman (M) 7-7-1995 Kansas City, Mo. in USAF (Korea)(80-88)
Her Father: Bobby Arno Brockhouse **Mother's Maiden Name:** Elizabeth (Betty) Eller

Sex	Children's Names in Full		Day Month Year	City, Town or Place	County or Province, etc.	State or Country	Add. Info on Children
M	1 Ashurst, Robert Craig	Birth	27-1-1971	Indep.	Jackson Co.	Mo.	twin
	Full Name of Spouse	Marr.					
		Death					
		Burial					
M	2 Ashurst, William Brandy	Birth	27-1-1971	Indep.	Jackson Co.	Mo.	twin
	Full Name of Spouse: Bertrand Stahr Denise	Marr.	13-7-1996	Indep.	Jackson Co.	Mo.	
		Death					
		Burial					
F	3 Ashurst, Cherry Sherie	Birth	16-2-1977	Indep.	Jackson Co.	Mo.	(divorced)
	Full Name of Spouse: James (Alex) Williams	Marr.	30-11-1992	Lee Summit	Jackson Co.	Mo.	
		Death					
		Burial					

Betty and Bob with Eileen and Jeff Gorman.

Eileen, daughter of Betty and Bob with Bill Ashurst (first husband), Cherry, Craig and Brandy.

Family Group Sheet

Husband's Full Name Jeffery Earl Garman — **Chart No.**

Husband's Data	Day	Month	Year	City, Town or Place	County or Province, etc.	State or Country	Add. Info. on Husband
Birth	12	10	1962				
Chr'nd							
Marr	07	07	1995	Kansas City	Jackson County	Missouri	
Death							
Burial							

Places of Residence	Kansas City, Kansas		
Occupation		Church Affiliation	Military Rec. 2/25/80 - 05/15/88
Other wives, if any. No. (1)(2) etc. Make separate sheet for each marr.			
His Father	James W. Garman	Mother's Maiden Name	Joanne Wall

Wife's Full Maiden Name Madeline Eileen Brockhouse

Wife's Data	Day	Month	Year	City, Town or Place	County or Province, etc.	State or Country	Add. Info. on Wife
Birth	30	07	1953	Kansas City	Jackson County	Missouri	
Chr'nd							
Death							
Burial							

Places of Residence	3205 S. Vermont Independence, MO		
Occupation	Maintenance	Church Affiliation Pentecostal	Military Rec.
Other husbands, if any. No. (1)(2) etc. Make separate sheet for each marr.	1st-William Wallace Ashurst		
Her Father	Bobby Arno Brockhouse	Mother's Maiden Name	Elizabeth Irene Eller

Sex	Children's Names in Full (Arranged in order of birth)	Children's Data	Day	Month	Year	City, Town or Place	County or Province, etc.	State or Country	Add. Info. on Children
	1	Birth							

KANSAS CITY MISSOURI
A 30220
DEPARTMENT OF HEALTH
Bureau of Vital Statistics

Certified Copy of Birth Record

NAME: MADELINE E BROCKHOUSE
FILE # 53-07907

DATE OF BIRTH: JULY 30, 1953
PLACE OF BIRTH: KANSAS CITY, MISSOURI
YEAR OF FILING: 1953

STATE OF MISSOURI, CITY OF KANSAS CITY

I HEREBY CERTIFY THAT THE ABOVE IS A TRUE AND CORRECT COPY OF THE CERTIFICATE OF BIRTH OF MADELINE E BROCKHOUSE FILED IN THE OFFICE OF VITAL STATISTICS OF KANSAS CITY, MISSOURI; THAT THE ABOVE CERTIFICATE IS FILED IN SAID OFFICE AND IS A PART OF THE PERMANENT RECORDS OF THE BUREAU OF VITAL STATISTICS OF KANSAS CITY, MISSOURI. WITNESS MY HAND AS DIRECTOR OF HEALTH, KANSAS CITY, MISSOURI THIS 13TH DAY OF JANUARY, 1983.

RICHARD M. BIERY, HEALTH DIRECTOR   LUTHER O. BOYT, REGISTRAR

WARNING: This document is not valid if it has been altered in any manner whatsoever, including photographic reproduction. Do not accept it if seal of THE BUREAU OF VITAL STATISTICS is missing

E. Military Service Record

Name of Veteran Garman   Jeffrey   Earl
                 last   first   middle

State from Which Served Kansas

War in Which, or Dates between Which, He Served 8 yrs. Peacetime Korea, 02/25/80-03/15/88

If Service Was Civil War:

    Union _____ Confederate _____

Unit in Which He Served:

    Name or Number of Regiment _____

    Company _____

    Name of Ship _____

Branch in Which He Served:

    Infantry _____ Cavalry _____ Artillery _____ Navy _____ Other USAF

Kind of Service: Volunteers _____ Regulars _____

Pension File Number _____

Bounty Land File Number (for Service before 1856 Only) _____

Military Record Number _____

Date of Birth 12/10/1962

Place of Birth _____
    city   county   state

Name of Widow or Other Claimant _____

Date of Death _____

Place of Death Kansas City, Kansas- 1209 W. 27th Independence, MO
    city   county   state

Places Lived after Service _____

If Veteran Lived in a Home for Soldiers:

    Location _____
    city   state

Family Group Sheet

Husband's Full Name Robert Craig Ashurst

Chart No. —

	Day Month Year	City, Town or Place	County or Province, etc.	State or Country	Add. Info. on Husband
Birth	27-1-1971	Indep.	Jackson Co.	Mo.	twin
Chr'nd					
Marr					
Death					
Burial					

Places of Residence Indep., Mo.
Occupation Printer **Church Affiliation** Pentecostal **Military Rec.**

His Father William Wallace Ashurst **Mother's Maiden Name** Madeline Eileen Brockhouse

Wife's Full Maiden Name (Domestic Partner) Rhonda Lynne Baldwin

	Day Month Year	City, Town or Place	County or Province, etc.	State or Country	Add. Info. on Wife
Birth	19-11-1973	Kansas City	Jackson Co.	Mo.	
Chr'nd					
Death					
Burial					

Places of Residence Indep., Mo.
Occupation Medical **Church Affiliation** Pentecostal **Military Rec.**

Her Father Joseph Ambrose Baldwin **Mother's Maiden Name** Deborah Diane Tippett

Sex	Children's Names in Full		Day Month Year	City, Town or Place	County or Province, etc. State or Country	Add. Info. on Children
F	1 Ashurst, Chelsey Lynne	Birth	21-4-1992	Kansas City	Jackson Co. Mo.	
		Marr.				
	Full Name of Spouse	Death				
		Burial				
M	2 Ashurst, Joseph Timothy	Birth	18-12-1993	Kansas City	Jackson Co. Mo.	
		Marr.				
	Full Name of Spouse	Death				
		Burial				
	3	Birth				
		Marr.				
	Full Name of Spouse	Death				
		Burial				

Alex and Cherry Williams and Haley, Bob and Betty Brockhouse, Eileen (Ashurst) Gorman, Stahr and Brandy Ashurst, Virginia Rose Phillips, Alice Marie Enabinett, and Randi Phillips.

Chelsey Baldwin, 3 yrs. 1 mo., May 8, 1995

Joseph Baldwin, 1 yr. 5 mo., May 8, 1995

Family Group Sheet

Husband's Full Name: William Brandy Ashurst — **Chart No.**

	Day Month Year	City, Town or Place	County or Province, etc.	State or Country	Add. Info. on Husband
Birth	27-1-1971	Indep.	Jackson Co.	Mo.	twin
Chr'nd					
Marr	13-7-1996	Kansas City	Jackson Co.	Mo.	
Death					
Burial					

Places of Residence: Missouri
Occupation: Construction **Church Affiliation:** Pentecostal **Military Rec.:**

His Father: William W. Ashurst   **Mother's Maiden Name:** Madeline Eileen Brockhouse

Wife's Full Maiden Name: Stahr Denyse Bertrand

	Day Month Year	City, Town or Place	County or Province, etc.	State or Country	Add. Info. on Wife
Birth	6-8				
Chr'nd					
Death					
Burial					

Places of Residence: Canada
Occupation: Insurance **Church Affiliation:** Catholic **Military Rec.:**

Her Father: Phillippe J. Bertrand   **Mother's Maiden Name:** Gertrude

Sex	Children's names in Full		Day Month Year	City, Town or Place	County or Province, etc.	State or Country	Add. Info. on Children
1		Birth					
		Marr.					
	Full Name of Spouse	Death					
		Burial					
2		Birth					
		Marr.					
	Full Name of Spouse	Death					
		Burial					
3		Birth					
		Marr.					
	Full Name of Spouse	Death					
		Burial					
4		Birth					
		Marr.					
	Full Name of Spouse	Death					
		Burial					
5		Birth					
		Marr.					
	Full Name of Spouse	Death					
		Burial					
6		Birth					
		Marr.					
	Full Name of Spouse	Death					
		Burial					
7		Birth					
		Marr.					
	Full Name of Spouse	Death					
		Burial					
8		Birth					
		Marr.					
	Full Name of Spouse	Death					
		Burial					

Compiler:
Address:
City, State, Zip:
Date:

Notes:

353

Family Group Sheet

Husband's Full Name James Edward Alexander Williams   **Chart No.**

Husband's Data	Day Month Year	City, Town or Place	County or Province, etc.	State or Country	Add. Info. on Husband
Birth	1-9-1970				
Chr'nd					
Marr	30-11-1992	Lee Summit	Jackson Co.	Mo.	
Death					
Burial					

Places of Residence Oak Grove and Kansas City, Mo
Occupation   **Church Affiliation** RLDS   **Military Rec.**

His Father James Williams   **Mother's Maiden Name** Retha Seward

Wife's Full Maiden Name Cherry Sherie Ashurst

Wife's Data	Day Month Year	City, Town or Place	County or Province, etc.	State or Country	Add. Info. on Wife
Birth	16-2-1977	Indep.	Jackson Co.	Mo.	
Chr'nd					
Death					
Burial					

Places of Residence Kansas City, Mo.
Occupation   **Church Affiliation** Pentecostal   **Military Rec.**

Her Father William Wallace Ashurst   **Mother's Maiden Name** Madeline Eileen Brockhouse

Sex	Children's Names in Full	Children's Data	Day Month Year	City, Town or Place	County or Province, etc.	State or Country	Add. Info. on Children
F	1 Williams, Haley Nichole	Birth	14-3-1993				
	Full Name of Spouse	Marr.					
		Death					
		Burial					
	2	Birth					
		Marr.					
	Full Name of Spouse	Death					
		Burial					
	3	Birth					
		Marr.					
	Full Name of Spouse	Death					
		Burial					
	4	Birth					
		Marr.					
	Full Name of Spouse	Death					
		Burial					
	5	Birth					
		Marr.					
	Full Name of Spouse	Death					
		Burial					
	6	Birth					
		Marr.					
	Full Name of Spouse	Death					
		Burial					
	7	Birth					
		Marr.					
	Full Name of Spouse	Death					
		Burial					
	8	Birth					
		Marr.					
	Full Name of Spouse	Death					
		Burial					

Compiler   **Notes:**
Address
City, State, Zip
Date

Family Group Sheet

Husband's Full Name: Ronald Deane Butts — **Chart No.**

Husband's Data	Day Month Year	City, Town or Place	County or Province, etc	State or Country	Add. Info. on Husband
Birth					
Chr'nd					
Marr	1-6-1947	Dewey	Wash. Co.	Okla.	
Death					
Burial					

Places of Residence: Illinois
Occupation: **Church Affiliation:** Christian **Military Rec:** WW2 Navy

His Father: **Mother's Maiden Name:**

Wife's Full Maiden Name: Barbara Ledora Eller

Wife's Data	Day Month Year	City, Town or Place	County or Province, etc	State or Country	Add. Info. on Wife
Birth	20-3-1929	Dewey	Wash. Co.	Okla.	
Chr'nd					
Death					
Burial					

Places of Residence:
Occupation: Legal Secretary **Church Affiliation:** Christian **Military Rec:**
#2 husband Joe Anderson (M) June 27, 1992
Her Father: John E. Eller **Mother's Maiden Name:** Stella Adaline Wiley

Sex	Children's Names in Full	Children's Data	Day Month Year	City, Town or Place	County or Province, etc.	State or Country	Add. Info. on Children
F	1 Janet Louise Butts	Birth	23-4-1942	Champaign	Champaign	Ill.	
		Marr.	22-12-1962	Spokane	Maryville	Wash.	
	Full Name of Spouse: Allen Thompson	Death					
		Burial					
F	2 Donna Sue Butts	Birth	5-1-1952	Champaign	Champaign	Ill.	
		Marr.	9-1972				
	Full Name of Spouse: Roger Skinner	Death					
		Burial					
F	3 Darlene Sue Butts	Birth	4-12-1954	Champaign	Champaign	Ill.	
		Marr.	28-7-1973	Champaign	Champaign	Ill.	
	Full Name of Spouse: John Lynn	Death					
		Burial					
F	4 Diane Sue Butts	Birth	1-11-1956	Champaign	Champaign	Ill.	
		Marr.	22-11-1974	Champaign	Champaign	Ill.	
	Full Name of Spouse: John Robert Hemrich	Death					
		Burial					
F	5 Debra Sue Butts	Birth	27-11-1958	Champaign	Champaign	Ill.	
		Marr.	5-10-1976	Gulfport	Harrison	Miss.	
	Full Name of Spouse: John Miller	Death					
		Burial					
M	6 Ronald Eugene Butts	Birth	11-7-1960	Champaign	Champaign	Ill.	
		Marr.	7-1-1984	Chicago	Champaign	Ill.	
	Full Name of Spouse	Death					
		Burial					
	7	Birth					
		Marr.					
	Full Name of Spouse	Death					
		Burial					
	8	Birth					
		Marr.					
	Full Name of Spouse	Death					
		Burial					

Compiler: **Notes:**
Address:
City, State, Zip:
Date:

Family Group Sheet

Husband's Full Name: Allen Thompson — **Chart No.**

Husband's Data	Day Month Year	City, Town or Place	County or Province, etc.	State or Country	Add. Info. on Husband
Birth					
Chr'nd					
Marr	22-12-1962				
Death					
Burial					

Places of Residence:

Occupation: School Teacher **Church Affiliation:** **Military Rec:**

His Father: **Mother's Maiden Name:**

Wife's Full Maiden Name: Janet Louise Butts

Wife's Data	Day Month Year	City, Town or Place	County or Province, etc.	State or Country	Add. Info. on Wife
Birth	23-4-1942	Champaign	Champaign	Ill.	
Chr'nd					
Death					
Burial					

Places of Residence:

Occupation: School Teacher **Church Affiliation:** **Military Rec:**

Her Father: Ronald Deane Butts **Mother's Maiden Name:** Stella Adaline Wiley

Sex	Children's Names in Full		Day Month Year	City, Town or Place	County or Province, etc.	State or Country	Add. Info. on Children
F	1. Jennifer Thompson	Birth	24-6-1970	Marysville	Snohomish	Wash.	
		Marr.	18-7-1998	Seattle	King Co.	Wash.	
	Full Name of Spouse: Scott Seven	Death					
		Burial					
M	2. Thompson Eric Allen	Birth	6-11-1974	Marysville	Snohomish	Wash.	
		Marr.					
	Full Name of Spouse:	Death					
		Burial					

July 4, 1993, Barbara Anderson and family and Joe.

Family Group Sheet

Husband's Full Name: Roger Skinner
Chart No.

Husband's Data	Day Month Year	City, Town or Place	County or Province, etc	State or Country	Add Info on Husband
Birth					
Chr'nd					
Marr	9-1972				
Death					
Burial					

Places of Residence:
Occupation: Computers-RN nurse **Church Affiliation:** **Military Rec:**

His Father: **Mother's Maiden Name:**

Wife's Full Maiden Name: Donna Sue Butts

Wife's Data	Day Month Year	City, Town or Place	County or Province, etc.	State or Country	Add. Info. on Wife
Birth	5-1-1952	Champaign	Champaign	Ill.	
Chr'nd					
Death					
Burial					

Places of Residence: Illinois-New Mexico
Occupation: Nurse RN **Church Affiliation:** **Military Rec:**
Other husbands: #1 husband-Max Brewer (M) Aug. 23, 1952 div.
Her Father: Ronald Deane Butts **Mother's Maiden Name:** Barbara Ledora Eller

Sex	Children's Names in Full	Children's Data	Day Month Year	City, Town or Place	County or Province, etc.	State or Country	Add. Info on Children
1		Birth					
		Marr.					
	Full Name of Spouse	Death					
		Burial					
2		Birth					
		Marr.					
	Full Name of Spouse	Death					
		Burial					
3		Birth					
		Marr.					
	Full Name of Spouse	Death					
		Burial					
4		Birth					
		Marr.					
	Full Name of Spouse	Death					
		Burial					

Roger and Donna Sue Skinner

MARRIAGE LICENSE 1069
THE PEOPLE OF THE STATE OF ILLINOIS
CHAMPAIGN COUNTY
TO ANY PERSON LEGALLY AUTHORIZED TO SOLEMNIZE MARRIAGE
GREETING
MARRIAGE MAY BE CELEBRATED

Between Mr. Max Eugene Brewer, Jr. of Champaign in the County of Champaign and State of Illinois of the age of 24 years, and M. Donna Sue Butts of Champaign in the County of Champaign and State of Illinois of the age of 17 years, and with written consent of Barbara L. Butts, mother of Donna Sue Butts, a minor.

Witness John P. Hill, County Clerk, and the seal of said County at his Office in Urbana in said County, the 20th day of August A.D. 1969.

I, MARK SHELDEN, duly elected, qualified, and acting County Clerk of Champaign County, Illinois, and keeper of the records thereof, do hereby certify that the foregoing is a true and correct copy of the original MARRIAGE LICENSE issued to MAX EUGENE BREWER, JR. and DONNA SUE BUTTS issued on AUGUST 20, 1969.

IN WITNESS WHEREOF, I have hereunto set my hand and affixed my seal this 12th Day of MAY, A.D. 1997.

(NOT OFFICIAL WITHOUT RAISED SEAL)
Mark Shelden, County Clerk
Rosalee Bell, Deputy County Clerk

Address:
City, State, Zip:
Date:

Family Group Sheet

Husband's Full Name: John Lynn
Chart No.: —

	Day Month Year	City, Town or Place	County or Province, etc.	State or Country	Add. Info on Husband
Birth					
Chr'nd					
Marr	28-7-1973	Champaign	Champaign	Ill.	
Death					
Burial					

Places of Residence:
Occupation: Dry Wall Oper. **Church Affiliation:** Christian **Military Rec:**
His Father: **Mother's Maiden Name:**

Wife's Full Maiden Name: Darlene Sue Butts

	Day Month Year	City, Town or Place	County or Province, etc.	State or Country	Add. Info. on Wife
Birth	4-12-1954	Champaign	Champaign	Ill.	
Chr'nd					
Death					
Burial					

Places of Residence:
Occupation: Secretary **Church Affiliation:** Christian **Military Rec:**
Her Father: Ronald Deane Butts   **Mother's Maiden Name:** Barbara Ledora Eller

Sex	Children's Names in Full		Day Month Year	City, Town or Place	County or Province, etc.	State or Country	Add. Info on Children
F	1 Kimberly Diane Lynn	Birth	13-11-1975	Denver	Denver Co.	Colo.	
		Marr.	23-8-1997	Mahomat	Champaign	Ill.	
	Spouse: Jason Edward Harden	Death / Burial					
M	2 Benjamine John Lynn	Birth	29-4-1977	Champaign	Champaign Co.	Ill.	3-27-1999 in Japan
		Marr.	24-6-1998			Okinawa	
	Spouse: Katura Naka	Death / Burial					
F	3 Alexis Ann Lynn	Birth	8-12-1980	Champaign	Champaign	Ill.	
		Marr.					
	Spouse:	Death / Burial					

Darlene and John Lynn and family, John, Alexis, Benjamin, Darlene, 1974.

Benjamin Lynn

Family Group Sheet

Husband's Full Name: Jason Edward Harden

Chart No.

	Day Month Year	City, Town or Place	County or Province, etc.	State or Country	Add. Info on Husb.
Birth					
Chr'nd					
Marr	23-8-1997	Mahomet	Champaign	Ill.	
Death					
Burial					

Places of Residence:

Occupation: **Church Affiliation:**   **Military Rec.**

His Father: **Mother's Maiden Name:**

Wife's Full Maiden Name: Kimberly Diane Lynn

	Day Month Year	City, Town or Place	County or Province, etc.	State or Country	Add. Info on Wife
Birth	13-11-1975	Denver	Denver Co.	Colo.	
Chr'nd					
Death					
Burial					

Places of Residence:

Occupation: Secretary   **Church Affiliation:** Christian   **Military Rec.**

Her Father: John Lynn   **Mother's Maiden Name:** Darlene Sue Butts

Sex	Children's names in Full		Day Month Year	City, Town or Place	County or Province, etc.	State or Country	Add. Info on Child
1		Birth					
		Marr.					
	Full Name of Spouse	Death					
		Burial					
2		Birth					
		Marr.					

Kimberly Diane Lynn

and

Jason Edward Harden

along with their parents

request the honour of your presence

at their marriage

on Saturday, the twenty-third of August

Nineteen hundred and ninety-seven

at four-thirty in the afternoon

Grace Baptist Church

800 West Oak Street

Mahomet, Illinois

Kimberly Lynn

Family Group Sheet

Husband's Full Name Benjamine Lynn — Chart No.

	Day Month Year	City, Town or Place	County or Province, etc.	State or Country	Add Info on Husb.
Birth	29-4-1977	Champaign	Champaign	Ill.	
Chr'nd					
Marr	24-6-1998	Okinawa			
Death					
Burial					

Places of Residence Colorado-Illinois
Occupation — **Church Affiliation** — **Military Rec.** US Marines

His Father John Lynn — **Mother's Maiden Name** Darlene Sue Butts

Wife's Full Maiden Name Katura Naka

	Day Month Year	City, Town or Place	County or Province, etc.	State or Country	Add Info on Wife
Birth				Japan	
Chr'nd					
Death					
Burial					

Places of Residence
Occupation — **Church Affiliation** — **Military Rec.**

Her Father — **Mother's Maiden Name**

Sex	Children's names in Full		Day Month Year	City, Town or Place	County or Province, etc.	State or Country	Add Info on Child
M	1. Koki Lynn	Birth	17-1-1998			Japan	
		Marr.					
	Full Name of Spouse	Death					
		Burial					
	2.	Birth					
		Marr.					
	Full Name of Spouse	Death					
		Burial					
	3.	Birth					
		Marr.					
	Full Name of Spouse	Death					
		Burial					
	4.	Birth					
		Marr.					
	Full Name of Spouse	Death					
		Burial					
	5.	Birth					
		Marr.					
	Full Name of Spouse	Death					
		Burial					
	6.	Birth					
		Marr.					
	Full Name of Spouse	Death					
		Burial					
	7.	Birth					
		Marr.					
	Full Name of Spouse	Death					
		Burial					
	8.	Birth					
		Marr.					
	Full Name of Spouse	Death					
		Burial					

Notes: Married in Okinawa June 24, 1998
Marry in Japan March 3, 1999

Family Group Sheet

Husband's Full Name: John Robert Hemrich **Chart No.**

	Day Month Year	City, Town or Place	County or Province, etc.	State or Country	Add. Info on Husb.
Birth		Champaign	Champaign	Ill.	
Chr'nd					
Marr	22-11-1974	Champaign	Champaign	Ill.	
Death					
Burial					

Places of Residence:
Occupation: Truck Driver **Church Affiliation:** Christian **Military Rec:** Viet Nam - Navy

His Father: John V. Hemrich **Mother's Maiden Name:** Betty Lou Benneth

Wife's Full Maiden Name: Diane Sue Butts

	Day Month Year	City, Town or Place	County or Province, etc.	State or Country	Add. Info on Wife
Birth	1-11-1956	Champaign	Champaign	Ill.	
Chr'nd					
Death					
Burial					

Places of Residence:
Occupation: Sec.-Business manager **Church Affiliation:** Christian **Military Rec.:**

Her Father: Ronald Deane Butts **Mother's Maiden Name:** Barbara Ledora Eller

Sex	Children's Names in Full		Day Month Year	City, Town or Place	County or Province, etc.	State or Country	Add. Info on Child
F	1 Christina Diane Hemrich	Birth	27-1-1980	Champaign	Champaign	Ill.	
	Full Name of Spouse	Marr.					
		Death					
		Burial					
F	2 Chrystal Michelle Hemrich	Birth	11-4-1985	Champaign	Champaign	Ill.	
	Full Name of Spouse	Marr.					
		Death					
		Burial					
	3	Birth					
		Marr.					
	Full Name of Spouse	Death					
		Burial					
	4	Birth					
		Marr.					
	Full Name of Spouse	Death					
		Burial					
	5	Birth					
		Marr.					
	Full Name of Spouse	Death					
		Burial					
	6	Birth					
		Marr.					
	Full Name of Spouse	Death					
		Burial					
	7	Birth					
		Marr.					
	Full Name of Spouse	Death					
		Burial					
	8	Birth					
		Marr.					
	Full Name of Spouse	Death					
		Burial					

Compiler: **Notes:**
Address:
City, State, Zip:
Date:

Honorable Discharge

from the Armed Forces of the United States of America

This is to certify that

HEMRICH JOHN ROBERT   318-52-7641   SP4   USAR

was Honorably Discharged from the **United States Army**

on the 24TH *day of* MAY 1982

This certificate is awarded as a testimonial of Honest and Faithful Service

C. F. BRIGGS
BRIGADIER GENERAL, USA

DD FORM NO. 256A 1 MAY 50

Diane and John Hemrich, Crystal and Christine, 1994.

Charlie, Debra and John Miller, Hannah, Katie, Johnsey, Ashley.

Diane Hemrich, Bobbie Anderson, Debra Miller, Ronnie Butts, Donna Skinner, Darlene Lynn

Family Group Sheet

Husband's Full Name: John Miller — **Chart No.**

	Day Month Year	City, Town or Place	County or Province, etc.	State or Country	Add Info on Husband
Birth					
Chr'nd					
Marr	5-10-1976	Gulfport	Harrison Co.	Miss.	
Death					
Burial					

Places of Residence:
Occupation: Warehouse Manager **Church Affiliation:** Christian **Military Rec:** US Navy

His Father: **Mother's Maiden Name:**

Wife's Full Maiden Name: Debra Sue Butts

	Day Month Year	City, Town or Place	County or Province, etc.	State or Country	Add Info on Wife
Birth	27-11-1958	Champaign	Champaign	Ill.	
Chr'nd					
Death					
Burial					

Places of Residence:
Occupation: Day Care **Church Affiliation:** Christian **Military Rec.**

Her Father: Ronald Deane Butts **Mother's Maiden Name:** Barbara Ledora Eller

Sex	#	Children's Names in Full	Event	Day Month Year	City, Town or Place	County or Province, etc.	State or Country	Add Info on Child
M	1	Miller Charles Lawrence	Birth	4-9-1979	Champaign	Champaign	Ill.	
		Full Name of Spouse	Marr. / Death / Burial					
F	2	Miller Katherine Diane	Birth	17-10-1981	Champaign	Champaign	Ill.	
		Full Name of Spouse	Marr. / Death / Burial					
F	3	Miller Ashely Nicole	Birth	1-7-1985	Champaign	Champaign	Ill.	
		Full Name of Spouse	Marr. / Death / Burial					
M	4	John Andrew Miller	Birth	4-3-1989	Champaign	Champaign	Ill.	
		Full Name of Spouse	Marr. / Death / Burial					
F	5	Miller Hannah Elizabeth	Birth	13-9-1990	Champaign	Champaign	Ill.	
		Full Name of Spouse	Marr. / Death / Burial					
M	6	Eric James Miller	Birth	30-6-1995	Champaign	Champaign	Ill.	
		Full Name of Spouse	Marr. / Death / Burial					
	7							
	8							

Compiler:
Address:
City, State, Zip:
Date:
Notes:

Family Group Sheet

Husband's Full Name: Ronald Eugene Butts — Chart No.

	Day Month Year	City, Town or Place	County or Province, etc.	State or Country	Add Info on Husb
Birth	11-7-1960	Champaign	Champaign	Ill.	
Chr'nd					
Marr	7-1-1984	Chicago	Cook Co.	Ill.	
Death					
Burial					

Places of Residence:
Occupation: Manager Health Clinic Church Affiliation: Christian Military Rec:

His Father: Ronald Deane Butts   Mother's Maiden Name: Barbara Ledora Eller

Wife's Full Maiden Name: Leanne Renae Mache

	Day Month Year	City, Town or Place	County or Province, etc.	State or Country	Add Info on Wife
Birth					
Chr'nd					
Death					
Burial					

Places of Residence:
Occupation: Real Estate Church Affiliation: Christian Military Rec:

Her Father: Mother's Maiden Name:

Sex	Children's names in Full		Day Month Year	City, Town or Place	County or Province, etc.	State or Country	Add Info on Child
F	1 Casi Renae Butts	Birth	1-2-1988	Denver	Denver Co.	Colo.	
	Full Name of Spouse	Marr.					
		Death					
		Burial					
F	2 Courtney Anne Butts	Birth	27-7-1990	Denver	Denver Co.	Colo.	
	Full Name of Spouse						

Family Group Sheet

Husband's Full Name: Mullholland — Chart No.

	Day Month Year	City, Town or Place	County or Province, etc.	State or Country	Add Info on Husb
Birth					
Chr'nd					
Marr					
Death					
Burial					

Places of Residence:
Occupation: Church Affiliation: Military Rec:

His Father: Mother's Maiden Name:

Wife's Full Maiden Name: Shirley Jean Wiley

	Day Month Year	City, Town or Place	County or Province, etc.	State or Country	Add Info on Wife
Birth					
Chr'nd					
Death					
Burial					

Places of Residence:
Occupation: Church Affiliation: Military Rec:

Her Father: John Moore Wiley   Mother's Maiden Name: Irma Rogers

Sex	Children's names in Full		Day Month Year	City, Town or Place	County or Province, etc.	State or Country	Add Info on Child
M	1 Buddy Mullholland	Birth					
	Full Name of Spouse	Marr.					
		Death					
		Burial					
M	2 Roger Mullholland	Birth					
		Marr.					

Family Group Sheet

Husband's Full Name: Edmond Hall   **Chart No.**

Husband's Data	Day Month Year	City, Town or Place	County or Province, etc.	State or Country	Add. Info. on Husband
Birth	9-12-1828	London		England	
Chr'nd					
Marr	7-5-1857	Plano	Kendall Co.	Illinois	
Death	27-8-1888	Potwin	Butler Co.	Kansas	
Burial	29-8-1888	Shaffer cem. Potwin	Butler Co.	Kansas	

Places of Residence

Occupation: Farmer   **Church Affiliation:**   **Military Rec.:**

Other wives, if any No. (1)(2) etc. #1 wife Lovina Westgate

His Father: David Hall   **Mother's Maiden Name:** Sarah Jenner

Wife's Full Maiden Name: #2 Seny Moore

Wife's Data	Day Month Year	City, Town or Place	County or Province, etc.	State or Country	Add. Info. on Wife
Birth	17-8-1836	Plano	Kendall Co.	Illinois	
Chr'nd					
Death	5-11-1908	Inglewood	Los Angeles Co.	California	
Burial	11-1908	Shaffer cem. Potwin	Butler Co.	Kansas	

Places of Residence

Occupation: Housewife   **Church Affiliation:**   **Military Rec.:**

Her Father: Richard S. Moore   **Mother's Maiden Name:** Rebecca Owens

Sex	Children's Names in Full	Children's Data	Day Month Year	City, Town or Place	County or Province, etc.	State or Country	Add. Info. on Children
F	1 Harriet ElNora Hall	Birth	15-12-1857	Plano	Kendall Co.	Ill.	
		Marr.	20-10-1890	ElDorado	Butler Co.	Kans.	
	Full Name of Spouse	Death	29-5-1947	ElDorado	Butler Co.	Kans.	
	Robert E. Kelley	Burial	5-1947	McGill cem. Potwin		Kans.	
M	2 Frances Leaton Hall	Birth	18-5-1859	Plano	Kendall Co.	Kans.	
		Marr.	6-1-1880	ElDorado	Butler Co.	Kans.	
	Full Name of Spouse	Death	24-1-1936	Kaw City		Okla.	
	Rachel Caroline Paul	Burial	1-1936	Shaffer cem. Potwin		Kansas	
M	3 Owen Archibald Hall	Birth	9-7-1862	Plano	Kendall Co.	Illinois	
		Marr.	21--10-1896	ElDorado	Butler Co.	Kansas	
	Full Name of Spouse	Death	14-7-1950	ElDorado	Butler Co.	Kansas	
	Frances Emma Litzkes	Burial	7-1950	McGill cem. Potwin		Kansas	
M	4 Elmer E. Hall	Birth	14-11-1863	Chicago	Cook Co.	Illinois	
		Marr.	28-11-1885	ElDorado	Butler Co.	Kansas	
	Full Name of Spouse	Death	6-6-1942	ElDorado	Butler Co.	Kansas	
	Sarah Frances Maxwell	Burial	8--6-1942	Towanda	Butler Co.	Kansas	
F	5 Sena Americas Hall	Birth	17-1-1865	Aurora	Kane Co.	Illinois	
		Marr.	1-8-1881	Augusta	Butler Co.	Kansas	
	Full Name of Spouse #2	Death	15-3-1909	Long Beach	Los Angeles	Calif.	
	James Riley Kelley	Burial	17-3-1909	Sunnyside cem. Long Beach-Calif.			
M	6 David R. Hall	Birth	29-1-1866			Iowa	
		Marr.					
	Full Name of Spouse	Death	5-2-1879		Butler Co.	Kansas	
		Burial	7-2-1879	Shaffer cem	Butler Co.	Kansas	
M	7 Verne Reuben Hall	Birth	15-12-1868	Potwin	Butler Co.	Kansas	
		Marr.	30-11-1897	ElDorado	Butler Co.	Kansas	
	Full Name of Spouse	Death	19-1-1939	ElDorado	Butler Co.	Kansas	
	Ella	Burial	22-1-1939	Shaffer cem.	Butler Co.	Kansas	
F	8 Florence Ann Hall	Birth	2-2-1873	Potwin	Butler Co.	Kansas	
		Marr.	13-11-1893	ElDorado	Butler Co.	Kansas	
	Full Name of Spouse	Death	22-5-1947	Potwin	Butler Co.	Kansas	
	Charles Ruben Jacobs	Burial	25-5-1947	Shaffer cem.	Butler Co.	Kansas	

Notes: (over)

Compiler:
Address:
City, State, Zip:
Date:

Additional Children and Sources:

Husband's name: Edmund Hall   Wife's name: Seny Moore

Sex	Children's Names in Full (Arranged in order of birth)	Children's Data	Day Month Year	City Town or Place	County or Province, etc.	State or Country	Add. Info on Children
M	9 Robert E. Hall	Birth	23-1-1874			Kansas	
	Full Name of Spouse	Marr					
		Death	1-1906	Potwin	Butler Co.	Kansas	
		Burial	1-1906	Shaffer cem.	Butler Co.	Kansas	
F	10 Euaela Elmira Hall	Birth	23-4-1877			Kansas	#1 husband Broadhurst
	Full Name of Spouse Soward	Marr	8-1-1910				
	#2 Charles Benjamine	Death	4-5-1954	Port Angeles		Wisconsin	
		Burial	5-1954	Wichita	Sedgwick Co.	Kansas	
F	11 Almeda Maude Hall	Birth	17-8-1880	Potwin	Butler Co.	Kansas	
	Full Name of Spouse	Marr	26-12-1896	Eldorado	Butler Co.	Kansas	
	George Ray Maxwell	Death	26-12-1969	Eldorado	Butler Co.	Kansas	
		Burial	12-1969				
F	12 (Molly) Mary Elmira Hall	Birth	5-5-1883			Kansas	
	Full Name of Spouse	Marr					
	Miller	Death	1963				
		Burial	1963	Winfield		Kansas	
	13	Birth					
	Full Name of Spouse	Marr					
		Death					
		Burial					
	14	Birth					
	Full Name of Spouse	Marr					
		Death					
		Burial					

Seny Moore

Rachel Caroline Paul and Frances Leaton Hall

MATILDA JANE (MOORE) -

1837 - Matilda Jane born 11 Mar 1837 @ Plano, Kendall Co. IL

1850 - Harvey liv/Oswego, Kendall Co.IL
1856 - Jane (m) Harvey Greenfield @ Kendall Co.IL (have certificate)

1858 - Sara born Milbrook, IL.

1860 - Emma Jane born - d.infant,bur. @ Plano, IL.

1862 - Geo.E.born Plano, IL.

1863 - James Ira b. Milbrook, IL.

1869 - (Nov)Jane's Fa. died 'Archibald Owens' Kendall Co.IL

1870 - (May) Jane's Mo. died ' Nancy Judd' Kendall Co. IL.

1870 - (March) Lilly May b. IA
1870 - Massilon, Cedar Co.IA (census)

1880 - Sara (m) B.Thornburg - Mad.Co.IA
1880 - Mad.Co.IA (census) Scott twp

1885 - Geo. (m) Effie - Mad.Co.IA

1887 - (March) Harvey's father 'Thos.Greenfield' (b.1810 NY) died visiting Winterset, bur. Oak Grove Cem., Bristol, Kendall Co. IL.

1887 - (July) Lilly (m) Atcheson - Mad.Co.IA

1887 - (November) James (m) M.Wilson - Mad.Co.IA

1891 - Petitioned to pay for rental property (since Mar 1888) in Mad.Co.IA.
1900 - Webster twp HArvey & Jane (Dist.7,Enum.37, pg 5)
1906 To Greene Co. IA
1918 - Harvey died - (1835) bur.@ Pleasant Hill Cem.(no marker)

1926 - Matilda Jane died Jefferson, Greene Co. IA., bur @ Pleasant Hill - apparently no markers or destroyed. (have certificate)

Harvey Greenfield - M. Jane (Moore)
1835 PA - 1918 IA   1837 IL - 1926 IA

① NO RECORD FOR HARVEY GREENFIELD - 1918.

② MATILDA JANE MOORE GREENFIELD - 1926
DATE OF FUNERAL - MONDAY, APRIL 26, 1926, 2:00 P.M.
PLACE OF FUNERAL - PLEASANT HILL CHURCH
DATE OF DEATH - APRIL 24, 1926
PLACE OF DEATH - JACKSON TWP, GREENE CO., IA.
PLACE OF BURIAL - PLEASANT HILL CEMETERY
AGE - 89 YEARS
OCCUPATION - HOMEMAKER
WIDOWED
BIRTHPLACE - ILLINOIS
LAST PLACE OF RESIDENCE - JACKSON TWP.
HUSBAND - HARVEY GREENFIELD
FATHERS NAME - RICHARD MOORE
BIRTHPLACE - N. CAROLINA
MOTHERS NAME - REBECCA OWENS
BIRTH PLACE - N. CAROLINA
PHYSICIAN - DR. JAMES H. JACKSON
CAUSE OF DEATH - PNEUMONIA

③ GEORGE ELMER GREENFIELD - 1941
DATE OF FUNERAL - MARCH 30, 1941 - 2:00 P.M.
PLACE OF FUNERAL - UNION CHURCH - JAMAICA, IA.
DATE OF DEATH - MARCH 28, 1941
PLACE OF DEATH - JAMAICA, IA.
PLACE OF BURIAL - FRANKLIN TWP. CEMETERY - COOPER
AGE - 79
OCCUPATION - FARMER
MARRIED
BIRTHPLACE - KENDALL CO., ILLINOIS
WIFES NAME - EFFIE LACETTA FOSHER
FATHERS NAME - HARVEY GREENFIELD
BIRTHPLACE - PENNSYLVANIA
MOTHERS NAME - JANE MOORE
BIRTHPLACE - ILLINOIS
PHYSICIAN - DR. JEAN JONGEWAARD
CAUSE OF DEATH - STROKE

HOLD SERVICES FOR MRS. GREENFIELD ON MONDAY
Had Been Resident of this County For 20 Years
Passed Away at the Home of Her Daughter Mrs.
Atchison, Saturday, April 24th

Mrs. Harvey Greenfield, for twenty years, a resident of Greene county, passed away in Jefferson on Saturday, April 24th at the home of her daughter here Mrs May Atchison of Jefferson. Services for Mrs Greenfied were conducted in the church at Pleasant Hill on Monday afternoon of this week, by the Rev. C. V. Pence of this city. The body was laid to rest beside that of her husband in the Pleasant Hill cemetery.

Mr. Greenfield preceded his wife in death eight years ago. Mrs. Greenfield united with the United Brethern church in 1880 and continued to be a member of that church until the end.

Matilda Jane Moore was born on March 11th, 1837 in Kendall County, Illinois and passed away, April 24th at the age of 80 years. She grew to womanhood in Illinos and was married to Harvey Greenfield in 1856. The Greenfields had five children, one dying in infancy. The four living are Sarah Thornburg of Martinsdale, Iowa; George Greenfield, Jamaica; James I. Greenfield, Oskaloosa and Mrs. Atchinson of this city.

She is also survived by sixteen grandchildren and thirty great grandchildren, all of whom mourn her passing.

Chautuaqua Co., Kansas

Sedan, Kansas

Elgin, Kansas

Family Group Sheet

Husband's Full Name: Harvey Ira Greenfield — Chart No.

	Day Month Year	City, Town or Place	County or Province, etc.	State or Country	Add. Info on Husb.
Birth	23-10-1835		Erie	Pa.	
Chr'nd					
Marr	23-10-1856		Kendall Co.	Ill.	
Death	1918	Jefferson		Iowa	
Burial		Pleasant Hill Cem.			

Places of Residence: Pa.-Ill.-Iowa
Occupation: Farmer   Church Affiliation: Military Rec:
His Father: Thomas C. Greenfield   Mother's Maiden Name: Edyth

Wife's Full Maiden Name: Matilda Jane Moore

	Day Month Year	City, Town or Place	County or Province, etc.	State or Country	Add. Info on Wife
Birth	11-3-1837	Plano	Kendall Co.	Ill.	
Chr'nd					
Death	24-4-1926	Jefferson	Greene Co.	Iowa	
Burial	26-4-1926	Pleasant Hill cem.		Iowa	

Places of Residence: Ill.-Iowa
Occupation: housewife   Church Affiliation: United Brethren 1880   Military Rec:
Her Father: Richard S. Moore   Mother's Maiden Name: Rebecca Owens

Sex	Children's Names in Full		Day Month Year	City, Town or Place	County or Province, etc.	State or Country	Add. Info on Child
F	1 Sara Rebecca (Getty) Greenfield	Birth	29-9-1858	Milbrook		Ill.	
		Marr.	4-1-1880		Madison Co.	Iowa	
		Death	3-1-1937	Martensdale	Warren Co.	Iowa	
	Spouse: Benjamine Thornburg	Burial		Wick cem.			
F	2 Emma Jane Greenfield	Birth	16-1-1860	Plano	Kendall Co.	Ill.	
		Marr.					
		Death	Infant	Plano	Kendall Co.	Ill.	
	Spouse:	Burial					
M	3 George Elmer G.	Birth	11-3-1862	Plano	Kendall Co.	Ill.	
		Marr.	30-9-1885		Madison	Iowa	
		Death	28-3-1941	Jefferson	Greene Co.	Iowa	
	Spouse: Effie Lucetta Fosher	Burial		Cooper	Greene Co.	Iowa	
M	4 James Ira G.	Birth	20-12-1863	Milbrook	Kendall Co.	Ill.	
		Marr.	24-11-1887	Winterset	Madison Co.	Iowa	
		Death	18-4-1947	Univ. Park	Mahaska Co.	Iowa	
	Spouse: Mary Ellen Wilson	Burial	20-4-1947	Univ. Park	Mahaska Co.	Iowa	
F	5 Lilly Mae (Mary) G.	Birth	13-3-1870		Cedar Co.	Iowa	
		Marr.	4-7-1887		Madison Co.	Iowa	
		Death					
	Spouse: Will Atchison	Burial					
	6	Birth					

Family Group Sheet

Husband's Full Name: Benjamine A. Thornburg — Chart No.

	Day Month Year	City, Town or Place	County or Province, etc.	State or Country	Add Info on Husb.
Birth	18-9-1855		Madison Co.	Iowa	
Chr'nd					
Marr.	4-1-1880		Madison Co.	Iowa	
Death	22-5-1922	Martinsdale	Warren Co.	Iowa	
Burial	5-1922	Wick cemetery	Warren Co.	Iowa	

Places of Residence:
Occupation: Church Affiliation: Military Rec.:

His Father: Absolem Thornburg   **Mother's Maiden Name:** Delilah Miller

Wife's Full Maiden Name: Sarah Rebecca "Getta" Greenfield

	Day Month Year	City, Town or Place	County or Province, etc.	State or Country	Add Info on Wife
Birth	29-1-1858	Plano	Kendall Co.	Ill.	
Chr'nd					
Death	3-1-1937	Martensdale	Warren Co.	Iowa	
Burial		Wick Cem.	Warren Co.	Iowa	

Places of Residence:
Occupation: Church Affiliation: Military Rec.:

Her Father: Harvey Ira Greenfield   **Mother's Maiden Name:** Matilda Jane Moore

Sex	Children's names in full		Day Month Year	City, Town or Place	County or Province, etc.	State or Country	Add Info on Child
F	1. Alma Delilah T.	Birth	27-10-1880	Winterset	Madison Co.	Iowa	
		Marr.	5-10-1898	Lincoln Twn.	Madison Co.	Iowa	
	Full Name of Spouse: David Nicholl 1875 Ill.	Death	31-10-1974	Indianola	Warren Co.	Iowa	David- 1875-Ill. 1964-Ia.
		Burial		Wick/Wallace cem.			

SARAH R. GREENFIELD

Sarah Rebecca Greenfield, daughter of Harvey and Matelda Greenfield, was born Sept. 20, 1857, in Plano, Kendall county, Illinois, and died at Martensdale, Iowa, Jan. 3, 1937, at the age of 79 years, 3 months and 19 days.

On Jan. 4, 1880, she was united in marriage to Benjamin Thornburg of Madison county, Iowa.

To this union one daughter was born, Mrs. Alma Nichols, of Wick.

Since her marriage she had made her home in Warren and Madison counties.

In the spring of 1915 they moved to Martensdale where she had since made her home. Mr. Thornburg preceded her in death May 22, 1922.

She leaves to mourn their loss one daughter, Mrs. Alma Nichols; three grandchildren, Don Nichols of Martensdale, Carl Nichols of Wick and Hazel Lamb of Liberty Center; five great-grandchildren; two brothers, James of Oskaloosa and George of Jamaica, and one sister, Mrs. Mae Allison of Long Beach, Calif. Funeral services were held at the Wick Methodist Episcopal church ... Jan. ... at 2 p.m. conduc... ... N. D. Gordon of Indian... ... by the Rev. Mr. Menden... Martensdale. Interment was ... Wick cemetery.

Family Group Sheet

Husband's Full Name: David Nicholl — Chart No.

	Day Month Year	City, Town or Place	County or Province, etc.	State or Country	Add. Info on Husb.
Birth	18-4-1875	Mammouth	Knox Co.	Iowa	
Chr'nd					
Marr	5-10-1898	Lincoln Twp.	Madison Co.	Iowa	
Death	15-10-1964	Indianola	Warren Co.	Iowa	
Burial		Wallace-Wick cem.	Warren Co.	Iowa	

Places of Residence: Ill.-Iowa
Occupation: Farming **Church Affiliation:** Presbyterian **Military Rec.:**
Div. 4-7-1955
His Father: James Nicholl **Mother's Maiden Name:** Margaret Picken

Wife's Full Maiden Name: Alma Delilah Thornburg

	Day Month Year	City, Town or Place	County or Province, etc.	State or Country	Add. Info. on Wife
Birth	27-10-1880	Winterset	Madison Co.	Iowa	
Chr'nd					
Death	31-10-1974	Indianola	Warren Co.	Iowa	
Burial		Wallace-Wick cem.		Iowa	

Places of Residence:
Occupation: **Church Affiliation:** **Military Rec.:**
Her Father: Ben A. Thornburg **Mother's Maiden Name:** Sara Rebecca Greenfield

Sex	Children's names in Full		Day Month Year	City, Town or Place	County or Province, etc.	State or Country	Add. Info on Child
F	1 Ruby Nicholl	Birth	3-1-1901			Iowa	
	Full Name of Spouse	Marr.					
		Death	9-2-1913	St. Mary's	Warren Co.	Iowa	
		Burial					
M	2 Claude Nicholl	Birth	2-5-1903				
	Full Name of Spouse	Marr.					
		Death	29-10-1914	St Mary's	Warren Co.	Iowa	
		Burial					
M	3 Don Merle Nicholl	Birth	23-4-1908	Indianola	Warren Co.	Iowa	
	Full Name of Spouse	Marr.	2-10-1928	Osceola	Warren Co.	Iowa	
	Opal Gertrude Lamb	Death	6-4-1979	Des Moines		Iowa	
		Burial					
F	4 Hazel Leota Nicholl	Birth	23-11-1910	St. Mary's	Warren Co.	Iowa	
	Full Name of Spouse	Marr.	12-12-1928				#1 husband Floyd Lamb
	Orville Wagner	Death					
		Burial					
M	5 Carl Russell Nicholl	Birth	11-4-1916	Wick	Warren Co.	Iowa	
	Full Name of Spouse	Marr.	8-6-1939			Mo.	#1 wife Edith Hathaway
	Evelyn Nicolle	Death	12-2-1971	Denver		Colo.	
		Burial		Fairmont (Denver)			

Compiler:
Address:
City, State, Zip:
Date:

Family Group Sheet

Husband's Full Name: Carl Russell Nicholl — Chart No.

	Day Month Year	City, Town or Place	County or Province, etc.	State or Country	Add Info on Husb.
Birth	11-4-1916	Wick	Warren	Iowa	
Chr'nd					
Marr	8-6-1939			Mo.	
Death	12-2-1971	Denver	Denver	Colo.	
Burial	16-2-1971	Fairmont Cem.	Denver	Colo.	

Places of Residence: Iowa, Colorado
Occupation: Auto Supply   **Church Affiliation:**   **Military Rec.:**
Other wives: #1 Edith Hathaway
His Father: Dave Nicholl   **Mother's Maiden Name:** Alma Thornburg

Wife's Full Maiden Name: Evelyn Ellen Nicolle

	Day Month Year	City, Town or Place	County or Province, etc.	State or Country	Add Info on Wife
Birth	5-9-1921	Norwalk		Iowa	
Chr'nd					
Death					
Burial					

Places of Residence: Iowa, Colorado, Arizona
Occupation: telephone operator   **Church Affiliation:**   **Military Rec.:**
Her Father: Earle Nicolle   **Mother's Maiden Name:** Ruth Clarke

Sex	Children's names in Full		Day Month Year	City, Town or Place	County or Province, etc.	State or Country	Add Info on Child
F	1. R. June Nicholl Gerbode	Birth	26-11-1939	Martendale	Warren Co.	Iowa	
	Full Name of Spouse: Kenneth David	Marr.	14-2-1959	Aurora		Colo.	
		Death					
		Burial					
M	2. Jimmie Duane N.	Birth	20-1-1941	Martendale		Iowa	
	Full Name of Spouse: Mrs. Delores Goode	Marr.	29-12-1969	Denver		Colo.	
		Death					
		Burial					
F	3. Dorothy Kay N.	Birth	13-6-1949	Osceola		Iowa	
	Full Name of Spouse: Robert Osborn	Marr.	16-2-1968				Div.
		Death					#2 husband Dean Knowles
		Burial					#3 husband Terry Kelly

373

Family Group Sheet

Husband's Full Name: Thomas Moore — **Chart No.** ___

	Day Month Year	City, Town or Place	County or Province, etc.	State or Country	Add. Info on Husb.
Birth	1840	Plano	Kendall Co.	Ill.	
Chr'nd					
Marr	8-1-1863		Kendall Co.	Ill.	
Death					
Burial					

Places of Residence: ___
Occupation: ___ **Church Affiliation:** ___ **Military Rec:** ___

His Father: Richard S. Moore **Mother's Maiden Name:** Rebecca Owens

Wife's Full Maiden Name: Lucinda Adeline Isabell

	Day Month Year	City, Town or Place	County or Province, etc.	State or Country	Add. Info on Wife
Birth					
Chr'nd					
Death					
Burial					

Places of Residence: ___
Occupation: Housewife **Church Affil:** ___

Her Father: ___

Sex	Children's Names in Full		Children's Date	Day Mo
1		Birth		
	Full Name of Spouse	Marr.		
		Death		
		Burial		
2		Birth		
		Marr.		

Marriage Record
Madison Co.

Issued January 8 1863
To
Thomas D. Moore
and
Adeline Isbell

Married by
E.N. Nestell
January 8 A.D. 1863
Returned,
Jan'y 16 A.D. 1863
J.K. Cole Clerk

MARRIAGE LICENSE No. 951
STATE OF ILLINOIS, COUNTY OF KENDALL.
THE PEOPLE OF THE STATE OF ILLINOIS,
TO ANY PERSON LEGALLY AUTHORIZED TO SOLEMNIZE MARRIAGE, GREETING:
You are hereby authorized to join in the Holy Bands of Matrimony... between Mr. Thomas D. Moore and Miss Adeline Isbell of Kendall County...
In Witness Whereof... this eighth day of January A.D. 1863.
___ County Clerk.
Kendall County, Ill., ___ 1863.

Affidavit by John Shearer
Consent given ___
Full name of Groom James F. Moore
Place of residence ___ Occupation ___
Grooms age next birthday ___ Color & Race ___
# of Grooms marriage ___ Grooms place of birth ___
Grooms fathers name ___
Grooms mothers full maiden name ___
Full name of Bride Martha W. Shearer
Bride's maiden name, if widow ___
Brides place of residence ___
Brides age next birthday ___ Color & Race ___
# of Brides Marriage ___
Brides place of Birth ___
Brides fathers full name ___
Brides mothers full maiden name ___
Where and when married 31 Dec 1869
Witness ___
By whom married & office John Haston, M.G.

Bk B
Pg 107
Date of search ___

Family Group Sheet

Husband's Full Name: James C. Moore
Chart No.

	Day Month Year	City, Town or Place	County or Province, etc.	State or Country	Add. Info on Hus.
Birth	4-3-1844		Kendall Co.	Ill.	
Chr'nd					
Marr	31-12-1868		Madison Co.	Iowa	
Death	18-11-1915				
Burial		Peru			

Places of Residence:
Occupation: Church Affiliation: Military Rec:

His Father: Richard S. Moore **Mother's Maiden Name:** Rebecca Owens

Wife's Full Maiden Name: Martha M. Shearer

	Day Month Year	City, Town or Place	County or Province, etc.	State or Country	Add Info on Wife
Birth	12-4-1847			In.	
Chr'nd					
Death	1821		Madison Co.	Ia.	
Burial		Peru			

Places of Residence:
Occupation: Church Affiliation: Military Rec:

Her Father: John **Mother's Maiden Name:** Mary

Sex	Children's Names in Full		Day Month Year	City, Town or Place	County or Province, etc.	State or Country	Add. Info on Chil.
M	1. Ira Austin Moore	Birth	1-10-1869			Iowa	
		Marr.	4-9-1894		Madison Co.	Iowa	
	Full Name of Spouse: Applegate	Death	7-6-1938			Iowa	
	Mary/Minnie Rose	Burial		Winterset (Catholic)			
M	2. Wm. H. Moore	Birth	1-2-1871			Iowa	
		Marr.	8-10-1902		Madison Co.	Iowa	
	Full Name of Spouse:	Death	2-11-1938			Iowa	
	Delilah M. Hoyt	Burial	-11-1938	Peru			
F	3. Nettie M. Moore	Birth	12-4-1872			Iowa	
		Marr.	2-10-1892		Madison Co.	Iowa	
	Full Name of Spouse:	Death	28-6-1937		Madison Co.	Iowa	6 child.
	Elwood C. Hiskey	Burial	2-7-1937	Barney			
F	4. Mary	Birth	1875			Iowa	
		Marr.					
	Full Name of Spouse:	Death	1890				
		Burial					
F	5. Myrtle E. Moore	Birth	12-12-1877			Iowa	
		Marr.					
	Full Name of Spouse:	Death	12-6-1946		Madison Co.	Iowa	
		Burial	14-6-1946	Peru		Iowa	
M	6. James Clarence M.	Birth	21-1-1879			Iowa	
		Marr.					
	Full Name of Spouse:	Death	16-9-1936			Iowa	
		Burial	19-9-1936	Peru			teacher
M	7. Herbert T. Moore	Birth	28-5-1881			Iowa	
		Marr.	13-8-1906		Madison Co.	Iowa	
	Full Name of Spouse:	Death	21-11-1950			Iowa	
	Edith Beecroft	Burial		Peru		Iowa	
F	8. Elizabeth Ann M.	Birth	31-8-1886	Peru	Madison Co.	Iowa	
		Marr.	15-11-1903	Winterset	Madison Co.	Iowa	
	Full Name of Spouse:	Death	12-11-1938	Murray	Clarke Co.	Iowa	
	George Clifton	Burial	14-11-1938	Murray		Iowa	

Compiler:
Address:
City, State, Zip:
Date:
Notes:

Herbert L.
1881-1948

Jas. C.
1879-1936

Ira
1869-1946

Myrtle
1877-1946

Eliz. Ann
1885-1938
(m)Clifton

Wm. H.
1871-1938

James E. MOORE
1844-1915

Martha M. (Shearer)
1847-1922

Mattie
1872-1937 (m)Hiskey

Family Group Sheet

Husband's Full Name: Calvin W. Moore   **Chart No.**

	Day Month Year	City, Town or Place	County or Province, etc.	State or Country	Add. Info on Husb.
Birth	2-1845			Ill.	
Chr'nd					
Marr	1873				
Death					
Burial					

Places of Residence:
Occupation: Church Affiliation: Military Rec:

His Father: Richard S. Moore   **Mother's Maiden Name:** Rebecca Judd

Wife's Full Maiden Name: Carinda

	Day Month Year	City, Town or Place	County or Province, etc.	State or Country	Add. Info on Wife
Birth	1855			Iowa	
Chr'nd					
Death					1/??
Burial					by 1900

Places of Residence:
Occupation: Church Affiliation: Military Rec:

Her Father: **Mother's Maiden Name:**

Sex	Children's Names in Full		Day Month Year	City, Town or Place	County or Province, etc.	State or Country	Add. Info on Child
F	1. Ada Moore	Birth	5-1872			Kans.	March 12 1912
	Full Name of Spouse: Lewis Bryan / J E Wolf (1870 Ks.)	Marr.	1894 ca.				2nd marr
		Death					
		Burial					
F	2. Minnie Moore	Birth	1876			Iowa	
	Full Name of Spouse	Marr.					
		Death					
		Burial					
M	3. George Moore	Birth	10-1884			Kansas	
	Full Name of Spouse	Marr.					
		Death					
		Burial					

377

Family Group Sheet

Husband's Full Name Thomas Garrity — **Chart No.**

	Day Month Year	City, Town or Place	County or Province, etc	State or Country	Add Info on Husb.
Birth	1947 ca.			NJ	
Chr'nd					
Marr	1-3-1876		Madison Co.	Ia.	
Death					
Burial					

Places of Residence

Occupation — Church Affiliation — Military Rec

His Father — Mother's Maiden Name

Wife's Full Maiden Name Charlotte M. Moore

	Day Month Year	City, Town or Place	County or Province, etc.	State or Country	Add Info on Wife
Birth	1850 ca.			Ill.	
Chr'nd					
Death					
Burial					

Places of Residence

Occupation — Church Affiliation — Military Rec.

Her Father: Richard S. Moore — Mother's Maiden Name: Rebecca Owens

Sex	Children's Names in Full		Day Month Year	City, Town or Place	County or Province, etc.	State or Country	Add Info on Child
F	1 Julie E. Garrity	Birth	1877 ca.			Ia.	
		Marr.					
	Full Name of Spouse	Death					
		Burial					
F	2 Sarah Garrity	Birth	1879 ca.			Ia.	
		Marr.					
	Full Name of Spouse	Death					

To The District Court of Madison Co., Iowa.

The undersigned Administrator of the Estate of J.C. Moore Deceased, would respectfully report as follows; to-wit:

NAMES OF WIDOW AND HEIRS.	DATE of BIRTH	RESIDENCE of Heirs
Martha M. Moore (widow)	4/1/47	
Ira C. Moore	10/1/69	
W.H. Moore	2/ /71	
Nellie M. Hiskey	4/12/72	
Myrtle E. Moore	12/12/77	
James C. Moore	1/21/79	
Herbert E. Moore	5/28/81	
Elizabeth A. Clifton	6/31/86	

STATE OF IOWA, Madison County, SS

I, James C. Moore do solemnly swear that the foregoing is a true and correct list of the names, ages and residences of the heirs of the estate of J.C. Moore, deceased, late of said county.

James C. Moore

Sworn to before me and subscribed in my presence, this 8th day of Dec 1915.

Clerk
Notary Public Deputy

Date

Marriage Record Madison Co.

Affidavit by Silicious Moore
Consent given
Full name of Groom Thomas Garity
Place of residence — Occupation
Grooms age next birthday full age Color & Race
# of Grooms marriage — Grooms place of birth
Grooms fathers name
Grooms mothers full maiden name
Full name of Bride Charlotte Moore
Bride's maiden name, if widow
Brides place of residence
Brides age next birthday full age Color & Race
# of Brides Marriage
Brides place of Birth
Brides fathers full name
Brides mothers full maiden name
Where and when married 1 Mar 1876
Witness
By whom married & office John Read, M.J.
Bk B
Pg 188
Date of search

Family Group Sheet

Husband's Full Name: Tom Bascom — Chart No.

	Day	Month	Year	City, Town or Place	County or Province, etc.	State or Country	Add. Info on Husband
Birth							
Chr'nd							
Marr							
Death							
Burial							

Places of Residence:

Occupation: | Church Affiliation: | Military Rec:

His Father: | Mother's Maiden Name:

Wife's Full Maiden Name: Martha Moore

	Day	Month	Year	City, Town or Place	County or Province, etc.	State or Country	Add. Info on Wife
Birth			1846	Plano	Kendall Co.	Ill.	
Chr'nd							
Death							
Burial							

Places of Residence:

Occupation: Housewife | Church Affiliation: | Military Rec:

Her Father: Richard S. Moore | Mother's Maiden Name: Rebecca Owens

Children

1.
2.
3.
4.
5.
6.
7.
8.

Marriage License

State of Kansas, Butler County — To any Person qualified by law to perform the Marriage Ceremony, Greeting:

You are hereby authorized to join in marriage Mr. James H. Colley aged 25 years and Miss Phebe C. Moon aged 18 years and of this license make due return to my office at Eldorado within thirty days.

Eldorado October 8th A.D. 1869
Wm Harrison Probate Judge

This certifies that I have this day joined in marriage Mr. James H. Colley and Miss Phebe C. Moon at the residence of Mr. John Fulk in Towanda Township Butler County Kansas October 12th A.D. 1869.
Wm A Sallee Justice of the Peace

I hereby certify that the above is a true copy of license issued and return made.
Wm Harrison Probate Judge

Family Group Sheet

Husband's Full Name: James H. Colley
Chart No.

	Day Month Year	City, Town or Place	County or Province, etc.	State or Country	Add. Info on Husband
Birth	1845		Sciota Co.	Ohio	
Chr'nd					
Marr	12-10-1869		Butler Co.	Kansas	
Death					
Burial					

Places of Residence:
Occupation: Farmer
Church Affiliation:
Military Rec: War-Rebellion

His Father: Robert Colley
Mother's Maiden Name: Emeline Hurt

Wife's Full Maiden Name: Phoebe C. Moore

	Day Month Year	City, Town or Place	County or Province, etc.	State or Country	Add. Info on Wife
Birth	1850			Illinois	
Chr'nd					
Death					
Burial					

Places of Residence:
Occupation:
Church Affiliation:
Military Rec.:

Her Father: Richard S. Moore
Mother's Maiden Name: Rebecca Owens

Sex	Children's Names in Full		Day Month Year	City, Town or Place	County or Province, etc.	State or Country	Add. Info on Child
F	1 Laura F. Colley	Birth	1870 ca.			Kansas	
		Marr.	6-1892		Sedgwick Co. Ks.		
	Full Name of Spouse: John W. Suelthaus	Death					
		Burial					
F	2 Maud Colley	Birth	1872 ca.			Ks.	
		Marr.					
	Full Name of Spouse	Death					
		Burial					
F	3 Lelia Colley	Birth	1874 ca.			Ks.	
		Marr.					
	Full Name of Spouse	Death					
		Burial					
F	4 Emma Colley	Birth	1878 ca.			Ks.	
		Marr.					
	Full Name of Spouse	Death					
		Burial					
M	5 Walter Colley	Birth	27-3-1881			Ks.	
		Marr.					
	Full Name of Spouse	Death	29-11-1884				
		Burial		Greenwood Cem.			
M	6 George Colley	Birth	1885			Ks.	1885 5 mos.
		Marr.					
	Full Name of Spouse	Death					
		Burial					
	7	Birth					
		Marr.					
	Full Name of Spouse	Death					
		Burial					
	8	Birth					
		Marr.					
	Full Name of Spouse	Death					
		Burial					

KANSAS COLLECTION BOOKS

William G. Cutler's History of the State of Kansas

SEDGWICK COUNTY, Part 27

WACO TOWNSHIP.

JAMES H. COLLEY, farmer, Section 25, P. O. Wichita, was born in Sciota County, Ohio, in 1843; son of Robert and Emeline Hurt Colley; was married in 1869, to Miss Phoebe Moore, daughter of Richard and Rebecca Moore; has five children - Laura, Maud, Lelia, Emma and Walter. Mr. Colley came to Kansas in 1865, located in Shawnee County, and engaged in coal-mining; remained two years; in 1867 engaged with William Greiffinstein at his trading-post, on the Cow Skin Creek, eight miles from where Wichita now is. He remained at this post for two years, then moved to Wichita and engaged in farming. In 1872, located in Waco Township, where no (sic) now resides; was in the War of the Rebellion; enlisted in 1862, in the Ninety-first Ohio Regiment, Company F; was in the battles of Lynchburg, Winchester, July 19 and 24, and September 19, Fisher's Hill, Cedar Creek, and other engagements of his command; was mustered out in 1865.

Family Group Sheet

Husband's Full Name: Marion Moore   Chart No.

	Day Month Year	City, Town or Place	County or Province, etc.	State or Country	Add Info on Husb
Birth	1856	Plano	Kendall Co.	Illinois	
Chr'nd					
Marr	20-12-1884	Eldorado	Butler Co.	Kansas	
Death					
Burial					

Places of Residence:
Occupation: **Church Affiliation:**   **Military Rec:**

His Father: Richard S. Moore   **Mother's Maiden Name:** Rebecca Owens

Wife's Full Maiden Name: Mary A. Hunter

	Day Month Year	City, Town or Place	County or Province, etc.	State or Country	Add Info on Wife
Birth					
Chr'nd					
Death					
Burial					

Places of Residence:
Occupation: **Church Affiliation:**   **Military Rec:**

Her Father: **Mother's Maiden Name:**

Sex	Children's Names in Full		Day Month Year	City, Town or Place	County or Province, etc.	State or Country	Add Info on Child
M	1. Will Moore	Birth					
		Marr.					
	Full Name of Spouse	Death					
		Burial					
F	2. Helen Moore	Birth					
		Marr.					
	Full Name of Spouse	Death					
		Burial					

381

Family Group Sheet

Husband's Full Name: Samuel R. Atkinson — **Chart No.**

	Day Month Year	City, Town or Place	County or Province, etc.	State or Country	Add. Info on Hust.
Birth	27-4-1847		Monroe Co.	Ohio	
Chr'nd					
Marr	26-10-1872	Eldorado	Butler Co.	Ks.	
Death	16-9-1927	Independence	Montgomery Co.	Ks.	
Burial		Mt. Hope Cem.	Montgomery Co.	Ks.	

Places of Residence

Occupation: Farmer **Church Affiliation:** **Military Rec:** Civil War Co. "F" Regt. Kans. Vol.

His Father: Wm. Nathaniel Atkinson **Mother's Maiden Name:** Cath. Eliz. Faulk

Wife's Full Maiden Name: Susan Nancy Moore

	Day Month Year	City, Town or Place	County or Province, etc.	State or Country	Add. Info on Wife
Birth	3-10-1855		Putnam Co.	Ill.	
Chr'nd					
Death	31-8-1939	Independence	Montgomery Co.	Kansas	
Burial		Mt. Hope Cem.	Montgomery Co.	Kansas	

Places of Residence

Occupation: **Church Affiliation:** **Military Rec.:**

Her Father: Richard S. Moore **Mother's Maiden Name:** Rebecca Owens

Sex	Children's Names in Full		Day Month Year	City, Town or Place	County or Province, etc.	State or Country	Add. Info on Child
M	1 Charles Atkinson	Birth	10-17-1873	Potwin	Butler Co.	Ks.	
	Full Name of Spouse	Marr.					
		Death	16-9-1873	Potwin	Butler Co.	Ks.	
		Burial		Shaffer Cem.	Butler Co.	Ks.	
M	2 Robert A. Atkinson	Birth	13-9-1875	Potwin	Butler Co.	Ks.	
	Full Name of Spouse	Marr.					
		Death	7-11-1875	Potwin	Butler Co.	Ks.	
		Burial		Shaffer Cem.	Butler Co.	Ks.	
F	3 Atkinson Ada Francis	Birth	12-2-1876	Potwin	Butler Co.	Ks.	
	#1 Jacob M. Copeland	Marr.	28-10-1894	Howard	Elk Co.	Ks.	
	#2 Will Copeland	Death	24-7-1959		Drumcreek Co.	Okla.	
		Burial					
M	4 William R. Atkinson	Birth	20-8-1878		Butler Co.	Ks.	Span. Am War
	Full Name of Spouse	Marr.	6-8-1902	Howard	Elk Co.	Ks.	
	Clemmie Jennings	Death					
		Burial					
M	5 Alphard M. Atkinson	Birth	28-12-1880	Potwin	Butler Co.	Ks.	
	Full Name of Spouse	Marr.	5-11-1902	Howard	Elk Co.	Ks.	
	Anna Blair	Death	3-7-1966	Longton	Elk Co.	Ks.	
		Burial					
F	6 Effie E. Atkinson	Birth	24-2-1883	Potwin	Butler Co.	Ks.	
	Full Name of Spouse	Marr.	14-7-1900	Howard	Elk	Co.	Ks.
	Joe Garrison	Death	8-1948				
		Burial					
M	7 Fred L. Atkinson	Birth	22-5-1887		Butler Co.	Ks.	
	Full Name of Spouse	Marr.					
		Death	1893				
		Burial					
F	8 Minnie M. Atkinson	Birth	29-6-1891		Butler Co.	Ks.	
	Full Name of Spouse	Marr.					
	Earl Wells	Death	5-3-1967			Ca.	
		Burial					

#9 M-John C. Atkinson (b)12-3-1899 Butler Co. Ks.
Josephine Lovelace (m)12-12-1920 (D) 17-3-1967 Havana, Ks.

DEATH RECORD

Name: Samuel R. Atkinson
Sex: Male   Color: White
Age: 80 Yr.   4 Mo.   19 Days
Date of Death: Sept 16, 1927
Place of Death: 400 S 14 St, Independence, Kans
Cause of Death: Prostate Hypertophy
Single or Married: Married
Physician: Dr. F. W. Shelton
Undertaker: Jackson Und Co

I, G. H. Krienhagen, duly appointed, qualified, and acting Clerk of the City of Independence, Kansas and ex-officio registrar of vital statistics in and for said City of Independence, Independence Township and Drum Creek Township, do hereby certify that the above and foregoing is a true and correct copy of the record of the Death of Samuel R. Atkinson as shown by the Record of Deaths in my office.

IN WITNESS WHEREOF, I have hereunto subscribed my name and affixed the seal of said city this 19th day of Nov A. D. 1927.

G. H. Krienhagen
(City Clerk)

STATE OF KANSAS, Butler County.   Office of Probate Judge of said County.

BE IT REMEMBERED, That on the 26th day of October, 1872,

there was issued from the office of said Probate Judge, a Marriage License, of which the following is a true copy:

MARRIAGE LICENSE

El Dorado, Butler County, State of Kansas, October 26th, 1872

To Any Person Authorized by Law to Perform the Marriage Ceremony, Greeting:

You Are Hereby Authorized to Join in Marriage Samuel Atkison of Butler County, Kansas.   aged 25 years
and Susan N. Moore of Butler County, Kansas.   aged 17 years

the end of this License you will make due return to my office within thirty days.

(SEAL)   Wm. Harrison   Probate Judge.

And said Marriage License was afterwards, to-wit: the 26th day of October, 1872, A. D. returned to said Probate Judge, with the following Certificate endorsed thereon, to-wit:

STATE OF KANSAS, Butler County. } ss.

I, do hereby certify that, in pursuance of the authorization of the within License, I did, on the 26th day of October, 1872 A. D., in ElDorado Township, Butler County, Kansas, join in marriage the within named Samuel Atkison and Susan N. Moore.

Witness my hand the day and year above written.

W. A. Salles

Attest: Wm. Harrison   Probate Judge.   Official Title: Justice of the Peace.

STATE OF Kansas   COUNTY OF Elk

Sworn to and subscribed before me this day by the above named affiant, and I certify that I read said affidavit to said affiants, including the words Notary Public erased, and the words added, and acquainted them with its contents before they executed the same. I further certify that I am in nowise interested in said case, nor am I concerned in its prosecution; and that said affiants are personally known to me and that they are credible persons.

J. P. Holmes
Justice of the Peace

I, , Clerk of the County Court in and for aforesaid County and State, do certify that , Esq., who hath signed his name to the foregoing declaration and affidavit was at the time of so doing in and for said County and State, duly commissioned and sworn; that all his official acts are entitled to full faith and credit, and that his signature thereto is genuine.

Witness my hand and seal of office, this day of 18

(L. S.)   Clerk of the

Note.—This should be sworn to before a CLERK OF COURT, NOTARY PUBLIC or JUSTICE OF THE PEACE. If before a JUSTICE or NOTARY, then CLERK OF COUNTY COURT must add his certificate of character hereto, and not on a separate slip of paper.

STATE OF IOWA,   COUNTY REGISTRAR Vital Statistics
County of Greene

CERTIFICATION OF DEATH

Soc. Sec. No. -------

NAME OF DECEASED: Matilda J. Greenfield   Sex: Female
Date of Death: April 24, 1926   Place of Death: Jefferson, Iowa
Date of Birth or Age of Deceased: 89-1-13   Date Filed: Year of 1926
Cause of Death: Broncho Pneumonia

I HEREBY CERTIFY that the above information was taken from the Record of Death on file in this office in accordance with the law of Iowa requiring filing of vital records. Recorded in Book 4 Page 50.

Date: November 13, 1991

County Registrar and Clerk of District Court.
By Designee

STATE OF KANSAS — STANDARD CERTIFICATE OF DEATH
State Board of Health—Division of Vital Statistics

1 PLACE OF DEATH: County Montgomery
Township or City: Independence   Registered No.
No. 400   South Fourteenth St.   Ward
(If death occurred in a hospital or institution, give its NAME instead of street and number.)

2 FULL NAME: Samuel R. Atkinson
(a) Residence: No. 400 South Fourteenth St. Ward
Length of residence in city or town where death occurred yrs. mos. ds. How long in U. S., if of foreign birth? yrs. mos. ds.

PERSONAL AND STATISTICAL PARTICULARS

3 SEX: M   4 COLOR OR RACE: W   5 Single, Married, Widowed, or Divorced: Married
5a If married, widowed, or divorced HUSBAND of (or) WIFE of: Susan Atkinson
6 DATE OF BIRTH: Apr. 27, 1847
7 AGE: Years 80   Months 4   Days 19   If LESS than 1 day, hrs. or min.
8 OCCUPATION OF DECEASED:
(a) Trade, profession, or particular kind of work: Retired
(b) General nature of industry, business, or establishment in which employed (or employer): Laborer
(c) Name of employer:
9 BIRTHPLACE (city or town): Monroe Co.
(State or country): Ohio
10 NAME OF FATHER: Wm Atkinson
11 BIRTHPLACE OF FATHER (city or town): Unknown
12 MAIDEN NAME OF MOTHER: Katherine Folk
13 BIRTHPLACE OF MOTHER (city or town): Unknown

14 Informant: Mrs. Susan Atkinson
(Address): Independence, Kansas.

15 Filed Sept 21, 27   G. H. Krienhagen   Registrar.

MEDICAL CERTIFICATE OF DEATH

16 DATE OF DEATH (month, day, and year): Sept. 16, 1927
17 I HEREBY CERTIFY, That I attended deceased from May 22, 1927 to Sept. 16, 1927 that I last saw h.. alive on Sept. 16, 1927 that death occurred, on the date stated above, at 5:00 P.M.
The CAUSE OF DEATH was as follows:
Prostatic Hepertrophr. (duration) Several yrs. mos. ds.
Nephritis
CONTRIBUTORY (Secondary) (duration) Not Known
18 Where was disease contracted if not at place of death?
Did an operation precede death? No
Was there an autopsy? No
What test confirmed diagnosis?
(Signed) F. W. Shelton M.D.
9-20-1927   (Address) Independence, Kan.
*State the Disease Causing Death, or in deaths from VIOLENT CAUSES, state (1) MEANS and NATURE OF INJURY, and (2) whether ACCIDENTAL, SUICIDAL, or HOMICIDAL. (See reverse side for additional space.)

19 PLACE OF BURIAL, CREMATION OR REMOVAL: Mt. Hope Cemetery   DATE OF BURIAL: 9-18-27
20 UNDERTAKER: Jackson Und. Co.   ADDRESS: Independence, Kan.

383

Family Group Sheet

Son
Husband's Full Name Charles A. Atkinson — Chart No.

	Day Month Year	City, Town or Place	County or Province, etc.	State or Country	Add. Info. on Husband
Birth	21-07-1879	Potwin	Buther, Co.	Kansas	1 Month
Chr'nd					2o Days
Marr					Old
Death	10-09-1879	Potwin	Buther, Co.	Kansas	
Burial	-09-1879	Shaffer Cem.	Buther, Co.	Kansas	

Places of Residence
Occupation — Church Affiliation — Military Rec.

His Father Samuel R. Atkinson **Mother's Maiden Name** Susan Nancy Moore

Son
Full Name Robert A. Atkinson

	Day Month Year	City, Town or Place	County or Province, etc.	State or Country	Add. Info. on Wife
Birth	13-09-1874	Potwin	Butler, Co.	Kansas	1 Month
Chr'nd					24 Days
Death	7-11-1874	Potwin	Butler, Co.	Kansas	Old
Burial	-11-1874	Shaffer Cem.	Butler, Co.	Kansas	

Places of Residence
Occupation — Church Affiliation — Military Rec.

Her Father Samuel R. Atkinson **Mother's Maiden Name** Susan Nancy Moore

Family Group Sheet

Husband's Full Name: Jacob M. Copeland (Jake) — **Chart No.**

	Day Month Year	City, Town or Place	County or Province, etc.	State or Country	Add. Info on Husb.
Birth	19-2-1869		Reynolds Co.	Mo.	
Chr'nd					
Marr	28-10-1894	Howard	Elk Co.	Ks.	
Death	25-12-1949	Kilgore	Rush Co.	Texas	
Burial					

Places of Residence:
Occupation: Carpenter-Fiddler **Church Affiliation:** **Military Rec:**
Other wives:
His Father: Jacob Wesley Copeland   **Mother's Maiden Name:** Savina Coil

Wife's Full Maiden Name: Ada Frances Atkinson

	Day Month Year	City, Town or Place	County or Province, etc.	State or Country	Add. Info on Wife
Birth	12-2-1876		Butler Co.	Ks.	
Chr'nd					
Death	24-7-1959	Drumright	Creek Co.	Okla.	
Burial					

Places of Residence: Independence, Ks.—Bartlesville, Okla., Shidler, Okla.
Occupation: Housewife **Church Affiliation:** **Military Rec:**
Other husbands: #2 William Copeland #3 J.E. Wolfe March 25, 1912
Her Father: Samuel R. Atkinson   **Mother's Maiden Name:** Susan Nancy Moore

Sex	Children's names in Full		Day Month Year	City, Town or Place	County or Province, etc.	State or Country	Add. Info on Child
F	1. Ivie Gladys Copeland	Birth	17-8-1895	Independence	Mont. Co.	Ks.	
	Full Name of Spouse	Marr.					
		Death	23-4-1897				
		Burial					
M	2. William Carl C.	Birth	7-12-1897	Independence	Mont. Co.	Ks.	
	Full Name of Spouse	Marr.					
		Death	16-6-1898				
		Burial					
F	3. Vera Beatrice C.	Birth	7-3-1903	Independence	Mont. Co.	Ks.	2 child.
		Marr.	28-10-1920	Bartlesville	Wash. Co.	Okla.	Robert
	Full Name of Spouse	Death	2-1-1983	Drumright	Creek Co.	Okla.	Leland
	Joe Kilpatrick	Burial		Drumright	Creek Co.	Okla.	& Joy
F	4. Yseba Mae (Phyllis)	Birth	27-1-1906	Independence	Mont. Co.	Ks.	#2 husband
		Marr.	1922				Gibson
	Full Name of Spouse	Death	8-10-1979	Bartlesville	Wash. Co.	Ok.	Arthur
	Gerald O. Sears, Sr.	Burial	10-10-1979	Dewey Cem.	Wash. Co.	Ok.	
F	5. Leona Belle C.	Birth	14-11-1915	Independence	Mont. Co.	Ks.	1 child
		Marr.	25-1-1931	Independence	Mont. Co.	Ks.	Janice
	Full Name of Spouse	Death	20-10-1992				2 g-ch.
	Dave Smithhisler	Burial	23-10-1992	Pampa		Texas	Debra & Judy

Ada and Joseph Copeland, Oct. 28, 1894.

Family Group Sheet

#2 child

Husband's Full Name William Carl Copeland — **Chart No.**

Husband's Data	Day	Month	Year	City, Town or Place	County or Province, etc.	State or Country	Add. Info. on Husband
Birth	07	12	1897			Kansas	1 yr. old
Chr'nd							
Marr							
Death	16	01	1898			Kansas	
Burial		01	1898			Kansas	

Places of Residence

Occupation — Church Affiliation — Military Rec.

His Father Jacob H. Copeland — **Mother's Maiden Name** Ada Frances Atkinson

1st child

Wife's Full Maiden Name Ivie Gladys Copeland

Wife's Data	Day	Month	Year	City, Town or Place	County or Province, etc.	State or Country	Add. Info. on Wife
Birth	17	08	1895			Kansas	2 yrs. old
Chr'nd							
Death	23	04	1897			Kansas	
Burial		04	1897				

Places of Residence

Occupation — Church Affiliation — Military Rec.

Her Father Jacob H. Copeland — **Mother's Maiden Name** Ada Frances Atkinson

Sex	Children's Names in Full	Children's Data	Day	Month	Year	City, Town or Place	County or Province, etc.	State or Country	Add. Info on Children

Family Group Sheet

Husband's Full Name Joe Kilpatrick — **Chart No.**

Husband's Data	Day	Month	Year	City, Town or Place	County or Province, etc.	State or Country	Add. Info. on Husband
Birth							
Chr'nd							
Marr							
Death							
Burial							

Places of Residence

Occupation — Church Affiliation — Military Rec.

His Father — **Mother's Maiden Name**

#3 child

Wife's Full Maiden Name Vera Copeland

Wife's Data	Day	Month	Year	City, Town or Place	County or Province, etc.	State or Country	Add. Info. on Wife
Birth	07	03	1903	Independence	Montgomery Co.	Kansas	
Chr'nd							
Death	02	01	1983	Drumright	Creek Co.	Oklahoma	
Burial							

Places of Residence

Occupation — Church Affiliation — Military Rec.

Her Father Jacob H. Cpeland — **Mother's Maiden Name** Ada Frances Atkinson

Sex	Children's Names in Full	Children's Data	Day	Month	Year	City, Town or Place	County or Province, etc.	State or Country	Add. Info on Children
	1	Birth							
		Marr.							
	Full Name of Spouse	Death							
		Burial							
	2	Birth							
		Marr.							
	Full Name of Spouse	Death							
		Burial							

Date

RADER FUNERAL HOME
Kilgore, Texas

Date: December 25th 1949.
Name of Deceased: Jacob Henry Copeland.
Address: Magnolia Street, Kilgore, Texas.
Length of Residence: 20 years.
Came from: Okla.
Date of Death: 12/25/49 Time: ___ m.
Place of Death: Kilgore Texas. Residence.
Cause of Death: Burned to death - House fire.
Length of Illness: —
Doctor in Charge: Coak Wilkins, Justice of Peace
Informant: Mrs. Joe Kilpatrick Phone: 196
Address: Cornright, Oklahoma
Date of Birth: Feb. 9, 1868 Age: 81
Place of Birth: Missouri
Single ___ Married ___ Widowed ___ Divorced ___
Husband or Wife of: ___
Occupation: Carpenter Time Spent: Retired
Employer: ___ Address: ___
Social Security No.: ___
Name of Father: ___
Birth Place: Missouri
Name of Mother: Dawson
Birth Place: ___
Lodges: ___

Church Affiliations: Methodist
Place of Service: Graveside Time: 1:30
Date of Service: Dec. 26 Burial: Same
Minister in Charge: D. Brown
Name of Cemetery: Kilgore
Sec. H Lot 110 Block 7
Music: ___
Arrange Music ___ Yes ___ No
Body to Repose Funeral Home ___ Res.
Remove Body to Church ___
No. in Family Group ___ Family Car ___
Meet Family ___
Casket Piece ___ Yes ___ No
Door Badge ___ Chairs ___ Register ___
Military Service ___ Branch ___
W. War I ___ No ___ W. War II
Serial No. ___ Years of Service ___
Newspapers to Notify: Kilgore

1868

387

ONE DEATH MARS WEEK-END HERE

Kilgore's Christmas week-end was marred by one violent death early Sunday morning when Jacobs Henry Copeland, 81, was burned to death in a one-room house.

A 13-year-old Kilgore Junior High School girl student suffered burns on more than 50 per cent of her body about noon Saturday when her dress caught fire.

Several other Kilgore residents suffered injuries in two accidents on nearby highways.

Mr. Copeland, a retired carpenter and partially paralyzed, died about 7:26 a.m. Sunday when the house in which he lived caught fire. The house was located on Magnolia Street, just off North Longview.

Firemen believe the fire originated from a wood stove. The house was destroyed.

Funeral services were held Monday morning for Mr. Copeland in Rader Funeral Home Chapel. Rev. Deckert Anderson, pastor of Eastview Baptist Church, officiated. Interment was in Kilgore Cemetery.

Mr. Copeland was born on Feb. 9, 1868, in Missouri. He moved to Kilgore about 20 years ago and had been retired for many years. He was a member of the Methodist Church.

Survivors include three daughters, Mrs. Joe Kilpatrick, Dwight, Okla., Mrs. Gibson Arthur, Bartlesville, Okla., and Mrs. David Smithisler, Pampa; two sisters, Mrs. J. A. Pratt and Mrs. A. H. Bass, both of California, four grandchildren and four great-grandchildren.

RELATIVES

3 Daughters —
Mrs. Joe Kilpatrick, Okla.
Mrs. Gibson Arthur, Bartlesville Okla.
Mrs. David Smithisler, Pampa Texas
4 G. Children
4 G. G. Children
2 Sisters
Mrs. J. A. Pratt — Calif.
Mrs. A H Bass — "

Mrs Joe Kilpatrick — Bx-728
Cornright Okla.
Mail her a Kilgore paper of the event.

Family Group Sheet

Husband's Full Name: Gerald Orlando Sears — Chart No.

	Day Month Year	City, Town or Place	County or Province, etc.	State or Country	Add. Info on Husb.
Birth	30-1-1904	Elk City	Mont. Co.	Kansas	
Chr'nd					
Marr	5-4-1922	Bartlesville	Wash. Co.	Okla.	
Death	27-1-1975	Bartlesville	Wash. Co.	Okla.	
Burial		Memorial Park	Wash. Co.	Okla.	

Places of Residence: Kansas-Mo.-Okla.
Occupation: Machinist-Reda Pump   Church Affiliation: Military Rec: US Army (1931-32)
Other wives: #2 Mary LeClair (step-daughter, Sally) #3 Mary Thompson
His Father: William Thomas Sears   Mother's Maiden Name: Jessie Louisa Brown

Wife's Full Maiden Name: Phyllis (Useba Mae) Copeland

	Day Month Year	City, Town or Place	County or Province, etc.	State or Country	Add. Info on Wife
Birth	26-1-1906	Independence	Mont. Co.	Kansas	
Chr'nd					
Death	8-10-1979	Bartlesville	Wash. Co.	Okla.	
Burial		Dewey Cem.	Wash. Co.	Okla.	

Places of Residence: Okla.-Ks.-Mo.
Occupation: Saleslady   Church Affiliation: Methodist   Military Rec.
Other husbands: #1-Frances Gibson Arthur-March 1935
Her Father: Jacob H. Copeland   Mother's Maiden Name: Ada Frances Atkinson

Sex	Children's names in Full		Day Month Year	City, Town or Place	County or Province, etc.	State or Country	Add. Info on Child
M	1 Gerald O. Sears, Jr.	Birth	28-3-1923	Bartlesville	Wash. Co.	Okla.	Michael
		Marr.	14-5-1945	Vinita	Craig Co.	Okla.	Patrick
	Full Name of Spouse	Death					Janet Su
	Neva Marie Fields	Burial					
	2	Birth					
		Marr.					

Phyllis Mae, Leona and Vera Copeland

Phyllis Arthur dies Monday

Funeral services for Phyllis M. Arthur, 73, 221 S.E. Myers, who died early Monday morning in the Memorial Building of the local medical center, will be held at the graveside in the Dewey Cemetery at 11 a.m. on Wednesday.

The Rev. Carl Lawson, minister of the East Cross United Methodist Church, of which she was a member, will be the officiant and committal prayers will be said, interment will be directed by Arnold Moore Funeral Service.

A native of Kansas, Mrs. Arthur was born on Jan. 26, 1906 at Independence and during her early childhood she moved with her family members to Bartlesville where her father was engaged in the building construction of early day Bartlesville. She was reared and received her education in the local schools. She was united in marriage to Mr. G.O. Sears, Sr. in January 1922 and they established their home here. He preceded her in death.

She was later married to Mr. F. Gibson Arthur at Springfield, Mo., on Jan. 20, 1935 and they made their home first in Joplin, Mo. before moving to Vinita in 1943. Following a four year residence in Vinita, Mr. and Mrs. Arthur moved to Tulsa in 1947 coming to Bartlesville in 1949. Mr. Arthur had been in sales for the Yeager Wholesale Company in Oklahoma until 1961. During that same year, the Arthur's established "Mr. Chicken", a broasted chicken eating facility in Comanche Center which they owned and operated until 1969. Mrs. Arthur was also employed for several years as sewing instructor at the Singer Sewing Center. She had been in failing health for the past year.

Deaths   Jan. 8-1985

Frances Gibson "Gib" Arthur

Mr. Frances Gibson "Gib" Arthur, 79, of 221 S.E. Myers, was found dead at his residence Tuesday.

Mr. Arthur was born June 19, 1905 in Jasper County, Mo. to Loren and Lela Lee (Gibson) Arthur. He grew up and received his education in the Carthage, Missouri area, where he graduated from high school. Mr. Arthur made his home in the Joplin, Mo. area as a young man where he was active as a salesman. He married Phyllis Mae Copeland on Jan. 20, 1935 at Springfield, Mo. They made their home in the Joplin area, Baxter Springs, Kan., and Vinita until coming to the Bartlesville area in 1949 where Mr. Yeager was active in sales with the Yeager Company. Mrs. Arthur preceded him in death in 1979. Mr. Arthur operated the Mr. Chicken in Comanche Center until 1970, at which time he became active in furniture refinishing at his home. Mr. Arthur was a member of the East Cross United Methodist Church and a former member and past president of the Dewey Kiwanis.

Mr. Arthur is survived by one son, Gerald Sears, Bartlesville; one sister, Arnata Paul, Morro Bay, Calif.; three grandchildren; and six great grandchildren.

Funeral services for Mr. Arthur will be held at 11 a.m. Thursday in the Dewey Cemetery with Dr. Robert VanHouse of the East Cross United Methodist Church officiating. Funeral services and interment will be under the direction of the Stumpff Funeral Home.

A memorial has been established to the East Cross United Methodist Church, 820 S.E. Madison, Bartlesville, Okla. 74006.

Jan. 8, 1985

G. O. Sears Dies; Services Set Wednesday

Gerald O. Sears, 70, father of G. O. Sears Jr., 3515 Sheridan Road, died at 4:45 p.m. Monday in the Jane Phillips Episcopal Memorial Medical Center following a long illness.

Mr. Sears was born Jan. 30, 1904 at Independence, Kan. He moved to Bartlesville in 1917 where he worked as a carpenter and went to work for Reda Pump in 1935 until his retirement in 1969. He served with the U.S. Army.

Graveside services will be held at 2 p.m. Wednesday in the Memorial Park Cemetery with Dr. M. O. Smith, minister of the First Methodist Church, officiating. Friends may gather at the cemetery about 1:45 p.m. for the services.

He is survived by his mother, Mrs. Jennie Sears of Bartlesville; one son, G. O. Sears Jr., Bartlesville; one stepdaughter, Mrs. Sally Vargas of Miami, Florida; two brothers, Thomas E. Sears of Dewey and Paul Sears of St. Louis; one sister, Mrs. Esper Brown of Bartlesville; eight grandchildren and five great grandchildren.

Services and interment will be under the direction of the Stumpff Funeral Home.

IN MEMORY OF
MRS. PHYLLIS MAE ARTHUR

DATE OF BIRTH
January 26, 1906
Independence, Kansas

ENTERED INTO REST
October 8, 1979
Bartlesville, Oklahoma

SERVICES
Graveside
11:00 A.M. Wednesday
October 10, 1979

OFFICIANT
Rev. Carl Lawson
East Cross United Methodist Church

INTERMENT
Dewey Cemetery

Mae and Gibson Arthur, Verl and Sue.

Sue

Family Group Sheet

Husband's Full Name: Gerald Orlando Sears, Jr. (Jerry)   **Chart No.**

	Day Month Year	City, Town or Place	County or Province, etc.	State or Country	Add. Info on Husb.
Birth	28-3-1923	Bartlesville	Wash. Co.	Okla.	
Chr'nd					
Marr	14-5-1945	Vinita	Craig Co.	Okla.	
Death					
Burial					

Places of Residence: Mo.-Kansas-Okla.
Occupation: Research-Phillips   **Church Affiliation:**   **Military Rec:** Marine Corps (42-45)
His Father: Gerald O. Sears, Sr.   **Mother's Maiden Name:** Phyllis (Useba) Mae Copeland

Wife's Full Maiden Name: Neva Marie Fields

	Day Month Year	City, Town or Place	County or Province, etc.	State or Country	Add. Info on Wife
Birth	31-1-1923	Bartlesville	Wash. Co.	Okla.	
Chr'nd					
Death					
Burial					

Places of Residence: Vinita, Okla.-Bartlesville, Okla.
Occupation: Legal Sec.-Homemaker   **Church Affiliation:** Methodist   **Military Rec:**
Her Father: Vernon Earl Fields, Sr.   **Mother's Maiden Name:** Tillie Marie Leonard

Sex	Children's Names in Full		Day Month Year	City, Town or Place	County or Province, etc.	State or Country	Add. Info on Child
M	1. Michael Ernest S.	Birth	28-3-1946	Vinita	Craig Co.	Okla.	#1 Kim
	Full Name of Spouse: Claudia	Marr	3-9-1965	Bartles.	Wash. Co.	Okla.	twin boys
	1) Cheryl 2) Rene #3)	Death					Stacy and
		Burial					Tracy
M	2. Patrick Thomas S.	Birth	28-12-1948	Vinita	Craig Co.	Ok.	/#3-Danielle
	Full Name of Spouse:	Marr	21-8-1976	Krebs	Pittsburg Co.	Ok	/& Christine
	Diane Marie Stanbeck	Death					
		Burial					
F	3. Janet Sue Sears	Birth	24-12-1955	Bartlesville	Wash. Co.	Okla.	2-Jill
	Full Name of Spouse:	Marr	3-1-1976	Bartlesville	Wash. Co.	Okla.	3-Amanda
	Marshall Newman #3	Death					
	#1 Brent Moyer	Burial					
	#2 Blake Stanfield deceased	Birth					

Gerald O. Sears Jr.

Oklahoma State Health Department
State of Oklahoma
OKLAHOMA CITY

I, Mary Hill, State Registrar of Vital Statistics, do hereby certify the following to be a true and correct copy of the CERTIFICATE OF BIRTH as the same appears of record in the office of the BUREAU OF VITAL STATISTICS of Oklahoma, to-wit:

PLACE OF BIRTH
County of Washington   Volume 1048
Township   Page 30
City or town of Bartlesville

FULL NAME OF CHILD: GERALD ORLANDO SEARS JR.

Sex of Child: Male   Legitimate: yes   Twin, Triplet, or other: Date of birth: March 28, 1923

FATHER	MOTHER
Full Name: G.O. Sears	Full Maiden Name: Useba May Copeland
Residence: Bartlesville, Okla.	Residence: Bartlesville, Okla.
Color or Race: white Age at last Birthday: 19	Color or Race: white Age at last Birthday: 17
Birthplace: Kansas	Birthplace: Kansas
Occupation: Carpenter	Occupation: Housewife

Number of child of this mother: 1   Number of child of this mother, now living: 1

CERTIFICATE OF ATTENDING PHYSICIAN OR MIDWIFE
I hereby certify that I attended the birth of this child and that it occurred on 3-28 19 23 at 3 p.m.
Signature: W.H. Shipman M.D.
Bartlesville, Okla.

Family Group Sheet

Husband's Full Name: Michael Ernest Sears
Chart No.:

	Day Month Year	City, Town or Place	County or Province, etc.	State or Country	Add Info on Husb
Birth	28-3-1946	Vinita	Craig Co.	Okla.	
Chr'nd					
Marr	3-9-1965	Bartlesville	Wash. Co.	Okla.	(Div.)
Death					
Burial					

Places of Residence:
Occupation: **Church Affiliation:** **Military Rec:**

His Father: Gerald Orlando Sears, Jr.
Mother's Maiden Name: Neva Marie Fields

Wife's Full Maiden Name: Cheryl Kitchell

	Day Month Year	City, Town or Place	County or Province, etc.	State or Country	Add Info on Wife
Birth	16-7-1947				
Chr'nd					
Death					
Burial					

Places of Residence:
Occupation: **Church Affiliation:** **Military Rec:**

Her Father: **Mother's Maiden Name:**

Sex	Children's names in Full		Day Month Year	City, Town or Place	County or Province, etc.	State or Country	Add Info on Child
F	1 Kimberli Marie S.	Birth	24-5-1967	Talequah	Cherokee Co.	Okla.	
		Marr.	2-4-1988	Bartlesville	Wash. Co.	Okla.	
	Full Name of Spouse	Death					
	Terrance Hyche	Burial					
M	2 Stacy Brock Sears	Birth	3-7-1969	Bartlesville	Wash. Co.	Okla.	
		Marr.					
	Full Name of Spouse	Death					
		Burial					
M	3 Tracy Lance Sears	Birth	3-7-1969	Bartlesville	Wash. Co.	Okla.	
		Marr.	28-4-1990	Bartlesville	Wash. Co.	Okla.	
	Full Name of Spouse	Death					
	Dawn Marie Limpert	Burial					

Family Group Sheet

Husband's Full Name: Terrance Hyche   **Chart No.**

	Day Month Year	City, Town or Place	County or Province, etc.	State or Country	Add. Info on Husband
Birth	29-10-1969				
Chr'nd					
Marr	2-4-1988	Bartlesville	Wash. Co.	Okla.	
Death					
Burial					

Places of Residence:

Occupation: Church Affiliation: Military Rec:

His Father: Mother's Maiden Name:

Wife's Full Maiden Name: Kimberli Marie Sears

	Day Month Year	City, Town or Place	County or Province, etc.	State or Country	Add. Info on Wife
Birth	24-5-1967	Tahlequah	Cherokee Co.	Okla.	
Chr'nd					
Death					
Burial					

Places of Residence:

Occupation: Church Affiliation: Military Rec:

Her Father: Michael Ernest Sears   Mother's Maiden Name: Cheryl Kitchell

Sex	Children's Names in Full		Day Month Year	City, Town or Place	County or Province, etc.	State or Country	Add. Info on Child
F	1 Hyche, Breanne Machelle	Birth	7-8-1988	Bartlesville	Wash. Co.	Ok.	
		Marr.					
	Full Name of Spouse	Death					
		Burial					
	2	Birth					
		Marr.					
	Full Name of Spouse	Death					
		Burial					
	3	Birth					
		Marr.					
	Full Name of Spouse	Death					
		Burial					
	4	Birth					
		Marr.					
	Full Name of Spouse	Death					
		Burial					
	5	Birth					
		Marr.					
	Full Name of Spouse	Death					
		Burial					
	6	Birth					
		Marr.					
	Full Name of Spouse	Death					
		Burial					
	7	Birth					
		Marr.					
	Full Name of Spouse	Death					
		Burial					
	8	Birth					
		Marr.					
	Full Name of Spouse	Death					
		Burial					

Compiler: Notes:
Address:
City, State, Zip:
Date:

Family Group Sheet

Husband's Full Name: Stacy Brock Sears — **Chart No.**

	Day Month Year	City, Town or Place	County or Province, etc.	State or Country	Add Info on Husb.
Birth	3-7-1969	Bartlesville	Wash. Co.	Okla.	
Chr'nd					
Marr.					
Death					
Burial					

Places of Residence:
Occupation: Church Affiliation: Military Rec.

His Father: Michael Ernest Sears **Mother's Maiden Name:** Cheryl Kitchell

Wife's Full Maiden Name: Felicia

	Day Month Year	City, Town or Place	County or Province, etc.	State or Country	Add Info on Wife
Birth					
Chr'nd					
Death					
Burial					

Places of Residence:
Occupation: Church Affiliation: Military Rec.

Her Father: Mother's Maiden Name:

Sex	Children's Names in Full		Day Month Year	City, Town or Place	County or Province, etc.	State or Country	Add Info on Child
M	1 Justin Brock Sears	Birth	5-4-1997	Waco	McLennon Co.	Texas	
		Marr.					
	Full Name of Spouse	Death					
		Burial					
	2	Birth					
		Marr.					
	Full Name of Spouse	Death					
		Burial					
	3	Birth					
		Marr.					
	Full Name of Spouse	Death					
		Burial					
	4	Birth					
		Marr.					
	Full Name of Spouse	Death					
		Burial					
	5	Birth					
		Marr.					
	Full Name of Spouse	Death					
		Burial					
	6	Birth					
		Marr.					
	Full Name of Spouse	Death					
		Burial					
	7	Birth					
		Marr.					
	Full Name of Spouse	Death					
		Burial					
	8	Birth					
		Marr.					
	Full Name of Spouse	Death					
		Burial					

Comp'er:
Address:
City, State, Zip:
Date:

Family Group Sheet

Husband's Full Name: Tracy Lance Sears
Chart No.: —

	Day Month Year	City, Town or Place	County or Province, etc.	State or Country	Add Info on Husb
Birth	3-7-1969	Bartlesville	Wash. Co.	Okla.	
Chr'nd					
Marr	28-4-1990	Bartlesville	Wash. Co.	Okla.	
Death					
Burial					

Places of Residence:
Occupation: Church Affiliation: Military Rec.:

His Father: Michael Ernest Sears **Mother's Maiden Name:** Cheryl Kitchell

Wife's Full Maiden Name: Dawn Marie Limpert

	Day Month Year	City, Town or Place	County or Province, etc.	State or Country	Add Info on Wife
Birth	28-5-1968				
Chr'nd					
Death					
Burial					

Places of Residence:
Occupation: Church Affiliation: Military Rec.:

Her Father: Leo Joseph Limpert **Mother's Maiden Name:** Lucille Lorene Luck

Sex	Children's Names in Full		Day Month Year	City, Town or Place	County or Province, etc.	State or Country	Add Info on Child
M	1 Cameron Jacob Sears	Birth	31-7-1991	St. Louis	St. Louis	Mo.	
		Marr.					
	Full Name of Spouse	Death					
		Burial					
M	2 Alec Tanner Sears	Birth	13-7-1993	St. Louis	St. Louis	Mo.
		Marr.					
	Full Name of Spouse	Death					
		Burial					

394

Family Group Sheet

Husband's Full Name: Patrick Thoman Sears — Chart No.

	Day Month Year	City, Town or Place	County or Province, etc	State or Country	Add Info on Husb.
Birth	28-12-1948	Vinita	Craig Co.	Okla.	
Chr'nd					
Marr	21-8-1976	Krebbs	Pittsburg Co.	Okla.	
Death					
Burial					

Places of Residence

Occupation — Church Affiliation — Military Rec

His Father: Gerald Orlando Sears **Mother's Maiden Name:** Neva Marie Fields

Wife's Full Maiden Name: Diane Maris Stambeck

	Day Month Year	City, Town or Place	County or Province, etc.	State or Country	Add. Info on Wife
Birth	13-10-1953	McAlester	Pittsburg Co.	Okla.	
Chr'nd					
Death					
Burial					

Places of Residence

Occupation — Church Affiliation — Military Rec.

Her Father: Louis Bartholmew Stambeck **Mother's Maiden Name:** Cecelia Dorothy Zavoina

---

Family Group Sheet

Husband's Full Name: Marshall Richard Newman — Chart No.

	Day Month Year	City, Town or Place	County or Province, etc	State or Country	Add Info on Husb.
Birth	7-12-1950	San Diego	San Diego	Calif.	
Chr'nd					
Marr	16-3-1985	Hobbs	Lea Co.	New Mexico	
Death					
Burial					

Places of Residence

Occupation — Church Affiliation — Military Rec

His Father: Marshall Rudolph Newman **Mother's Maiden Name:** Evelyn Mae Weaver

Wife's Full Maiden Name: Janet Sue Sears

	Day Month Year	City, Town or Place	County or Province, etc.	State or Country	Add Info on Wife
Birth	24-12-1955	Bartlesville	Wash. Co.	Okla.	
Chr'nd					
Death					
Burial					

Places of Residence

Occupation — Church Affiliation — Military Rec.

#1 husband Brent Moyer (b.3-1-1976) #2 Blake Stanfield (d) 1990

Her Father: Gerald Orlando Sears Jr **Mother's Maiden Name:** Neva Marie Fields

Sex	Children's Names in Full		Day Month Year	City, Town or Place	County or Province, etc.	State or Country	Add Info on Child
F	1 Jill Stanfield Newman	Birth	19-8-1981	Hobbs	Lee Co.	NM	Adopted by M.R. Newman
	Full Name of Spouse	Marr.					
		Death					
		Burial					
F	2 Amanda Newman	Birth	21-7-1986	Hobbs	Lee Co.	NM	
	Full Name of Spouse	Marr.					
		Death					
		Burial					

Family Group Sheet

Husband's Full Name: Michael Ernest Sears

	Day Month Year	City, Town or Place	County or Province, etc.	State or Country	Add. Info on Husb.
Birth	28-3-1946	Vinita	Craig Co.	Okla.	
Chr'nd					
Marr	28-3-1982	Carson City		Nev.	(Div.)
Death					
Burial					

Places of Residence:
Occupation: Church Affiliation: Military Rec.:

His Father: Gerald Orlando Sears   **Mother's Maiden Name:** Neva Marie Fields

Wife's Full Maiden Name: Claudia Openshaw

	Day Month Year	City, Town or Place	County or Province, etc.	State or Country	Add. Info on Wife
Birth	27-5-1955	Copenhagen		Denmark	
Chr'nd					
Death					
Burial					

Places of Residence:
Occupation: Church Affiliation: Military Rec.:

Her Father: **Mother's Maiden Name:**

Sex	Children's Names in Full		Day Month Year	City, Town or Place	County or Province, etc.	State or Country	Add. Info on Child
F	1 Sears, Danielle Elizabeth	Birth	7-3-1983	Modesto	Stanislaus	Calif.	
		Marr.					
	Full Name of Spouse	Death					
		Burial					
F	2 Sears, Christina Michelle	Birth	7-1-1985	Thousand Oaks	Ventura	Calif.	
		Marr.					
	Full Name of Spouse	Death					
		Burial					

396

Family Group Sheet

Husband's Full Name: David Pious Smithhisler SS-441-01-2666 Chart No. _____

	Day Month Year	City, Town or Place	County or Province, etc.	State or Country	Add Info on Husb
Birth	20-11-1912	Danville		Kansas	
Chr'nd					
Marr	25-1-1931	Shidler	Osage Co.	Oklahoma	
Death	3-6-1995	Coronado Hosp. Pampa	Gray Co.	Texas	
Burial	5-6-1995	Memory Gardens	Gray Co.	Texas	

Places of Residence:
Occupation: Pumper   Church Affiliation: Catholic   Military Rec:

His Father: Charles E. Smithhisler   Mother's Maiden Name: Jennie Bradley

Wife's Full Maiden Name: Leona Bernice Copeland SS-443-14-6629

	Day Month Year	City, Town or Place	County or Province, etc.	State or Country	Add Info on Wife
Birth	14-11-1915	Independence	Mont. Co.	Kansas	
Chr'nd					
Death	20-10-1992	Pampa	Gray Co.	Texas	
Burial	23-10-1992	Memory Gardens	Gray Co.	Texas	

Places of Residence:
Occupation: J.C. Pennys sale clerk   Church Affiliation: Catholic   Military Rec:

Her Father: Jacob H. Copeland   Mother's Maiden Name: Ada Frances Atkinson

Sex	Children's Names in Full		Day Month Year	City, Town or Place	County or Province, etc.	State or Country	Add Info on Child
F	1. Jan Smithhisler — Birth						
	Marr.						
	Full Name of Spouse: Jim Hawkins — Death						
	Burial						
	2. — Birth						
	Marr.						
	Full Name of Spouse: — Death						

City of _____ County of _____ Reg. District No. _____

Reg. No.	Name of Child	Sex	Color	Date of Birth (Day Month Year)	Place of Birth	Father's Name	Mother's Maiden Name	Date of Supplemental Report	Reported By
193		M	W	25 Sept 1915	W Main	Joseph Hall			J.C. Chaney
194		F	W	1 Nov 1915	516 So 6th	Robt Hildebrand	Flora Kufman		W.C. Chaney
195	Mary Louise Riley	F	W	28 Oct "	409 W Myrtle	Ewing J Riley	Jessie Carter		C.C. Auber
196	Mildred Alice Hilyard	F	W	2 Nov "	Indep Twp	Jesse Hilyard	Lizzie Henderson	18 June '94	J.C. Long
197	Elmer Leland Vaughn	M	W	8 " "	Indep City	Ernest A Vaughn	Ethel M Downing	12 June '94	Do
198	Clarence Earl McBride	M	W	31 Oct "	211 So 9th	Andrew Clarence McBride	Bessie Barnett		M.J. Tanguary
199	Mildred Snider	F	W	5 Nov "	WV 31 W Main	Albert R Snider	Vera E Frazier		Do
200		F	W	8 " "	Indep Twp	Geo F Magee	Georgie Zimmer		J.T. Davis
201	Dorothy Blanche Smith	F	W	9 " "	601 So 12th	Thos. S Smith	Mary Ellen Dodson		E.C. Wickersham
202	Arline Rose Shaddey	F	W	4 " "	401 So 6th	Roy N Shaddey	Genevieve Ava Higgins		F.B. Taggart
203	Leona Copeland	F	W	14 " "	611 So 15th	Jacob H Copeland	Ada F Atkinson		J.A. Alford
204	Guy Walton Arey Jr	M	W	21 Sept "	709 So 10th	Guy Walton Arey	Ruth Agnes Yoe		C.W. DeMott

	Marr.			
Full Name of Spouse	Death			
	Burial			

Comp'er: _____   Notes: _____
Address: _____
City, State, Zip: _____
Date: _____

Family Group Sheet

Husband's Full Name: William R. Atkinson — Chart No.

	Day Month Year	City, Town or Place	County or Province, etc.	State or Country	Add. Info on Husband
Birth	20 8-1878		Butler Co.	KS.	
Chr'nd					
Marr	6-8-1902	Howard	Elk Co.	KS.	
Death					
Burial					

Places of Residence:
Occupation: Church Affiliation: Military Rec:

His Father: Samuel R. Atkinson   Mother's Maiden Name: Susan Nancy Moore

Wife's Full Maiden Name: Clemmie Jennings

	Day Month Year	City, Town or Place	County or Province, etc.	State or Country	Add. Info on Wife
Birth		Longton	Elk Co.	Kansas	
Chr'nd					
Death					
Burial					

Places of Residence:
Occupation: housewife

Family Group Sheet

Husband's Full Name: Alphard M. Atkinson — Chart No.

	Day Month Year	City, Town or Place	County or Province, etc.	State or Country	Add. Info on Husband
Birth	28-12-1880	Potwin	Butler Co.	Kansas	
Chr'nd					
Marr	5-11-1902	Howard	Elk Co.	Kansas	
Death	3-7-1966				
Burial	7-1966				

Places of Residence: Elk Co. Longton
Occupation: Church Affiliation: Military Rec:

His Father: Mother's Maiden Name:

Wife's Full Maiden Name: Anna Blair

	Day Month Year	City, Town or Place	County or Province, etc.	State or Country	Add. Info on Wife
Birth	2-3-1885		Neosho Co.	Kansas	
Chr'nd					
Death					
Burial					

Places of Residence: Longton, Kansas
Occupation: Church Affiliation: Military Rec:

Her Father: James C. Blair   Mother's Maiden Name: Jennie Robinson

Sex	Children's Names in Full		Day Month Year	City, Town or Place	County or Province, etc.	State or Country	Add. Info on Child
F	1 Ruby Atkinson	Birth					
		Marr.					
	Full Name of Spouse	Death					
		Burial					
F	2 Pearl Atkinson	Birth					
		Marr.					
	Full Name of Spouse	Death					
		Burial					
F	3 Grace Atkinson	Birth					
		Marr.					
	Full Name of Spouse	Death					
		Burial					
F	4 Treva Atkinson	Birth					
		Marr.					

Family Group Sheet

Husband's Full Name Joseph Garrison — Chart No.

	Day Month Year	City, Town or Place	County or Province, etc.	State or Country	Add Info on Husb
Birth					
Chr'nd					
Marr	14-7-1900	Howard	Elk Co.	KS.	
Death					
Burial					

Places of Residence

Occupation — Church Affiliation — Military Rec

His Father — Mother's Maiden Name

Wife's Full Maiden Name Effie E. Atkinson

	Day Month Year	City, Town or Place	County or Province, etc.	State or Country	Add Info on Wife
Birth	24-2-1885	Potwin	Butler Co.	Kansas	
Chr'nd					
Death	8-1948				
Burial	8-1948				

Places of Residence

Occupation — Church Affiliation — Military Rec

Her Father: Samuel Moore — Mother's Maiden Name: Susan Nancy Moore

---

Marriage License Record.

State of Kansas, Elk County, OCT 29 1902 A.D. 190_

To any Person authorized by law to perform the Marriage Ceremony, Greeting:

YOU ARE HEREBY AUTHORIZED TO JOIN IN MARRIAGE Alfred Atkinson of Howard Kansas aged 21 years, and Miss Anna Blair of Junction Kansas aged 17 years, and of this License you will make due return to my office thirty days.

(Seal) D.W. Jackson Probate

State of Kansas, Elk County, ss.

I, D.W. Jackson, do hereby certify, that in accordance with the authorization of the within License I did, on the 5th day of November A.D. 1902, at Howard in said County, join and unite in Marriage the above named Alfred Atkinson and Miss Anna Blair.

Witness my hand and seal, the day and year above written.

No 88
D.W. Jackson Probate Judge

State of Kansas, Elk County, JUL 14 1900 A.D. 188_

To any person authorized by law to perform the marriage ceremony—Greeting: YOU ARE HEREBY AUTHORIZED TO JOIN IN MARRIAGE Joseph Garrison of Howard Kansas aged 19 years, and Miss Effie Atkinson of _____ aged 17 years and of this License you will make due return to my office within thirty days.

D.W. Jackson Probate Judge.

State of Kansas, Elk County, ss:

I, D.W. Jackson, do hereby certify, that in accordance with the authorization of the within License, I did, on the 18th day of July A.D. 1900 at Howard in said County, join and unite in Marriage the above named Joseph Garrison and Miss Effie Atkinson.

WITNESS my hand and seal the day and year above written.

D.W. Jackson Probate Judge
ATTEST: D.W. Jackson Probate Judge

56

Marriage License Record. A.D. 190_

State of Kansas, Elk County, AUG 6 1902

To any Person authorized by law to perform the Marriage Ceremony, Greeting:

YOU ARE HEREBY AUTHORIZED TO JOIN IN MARRIAGE William R. Atkinson of Howard Kansas aged 23 years, and Miss Clemmie Jennings of Junction Kansas aged 18 years, and of this License you will make due return to my office within thirty days.

(Seal) D.W. Jackson Probate Judge

State of Kansas, Elk County, ss.

I, D.W. Jackson, do hereby certify, that in accordance with the authorization of the within License, I did, on the 6th day of August A.D. 1902, at Riverland in said County, join and unite in Marriage the above named William R. Atkinson and Miss Clemmie Jennings.

Witness my hand and seal, the day and year above written.

(Seal) No 62
D.W. Jackson Probate Judge
Attest: D.W. Jackson Probate Judge

Family Group Sheet

Husband's Full Name: Freddie T. Atkinson — **Chart No.**

	Day Month Year	City, Town or Place	County or Province, etc.	State or Country	Add Info on Husb.
Birth	22-5-1884	Potwin	Butler Co.	Kansas	
Chr'nd					
Marr					
Death	1893				
Burial					

Places of Residence:
Occupation: — Church Affiliation: — Military Rec:

His Father: Samuel R. Atkinson — **Mother's Maiden Name:** Susan Nancy Moore

---

Family Group Sheet

Husband's Full Name: Earl Wells — **Chart No.**

	Day Month Year	City, Town or Place	County or Province, etc.	State or Country	Add Info on Husb.
Birth					
Chr'nd					
Marr					
Death					
Burial					

Places of Residence:
Occupation: — Church Affiliation: — Military Rec:

His Father: — **Mother's Maiden Name:**

Wife's Full Maiden Name: Minnie M. Atkinson

	Day Month Year	City, Town or Place	County or Province, etc.	State or Country	Add Info on Wife
Birth	29-1-1891	Potwin	Butler Co.	Kansas	
Chr'nd					
Death	5-3-1967			Calif.	
Burial					

Places of Residence:
Occupation: — Church Affiliation: — Military Rec:

Her Father: Samuel R. Atkinson — **Mother's Maiden Name:** Susan Nancy Moore

400

Family Group Sheet

Husband's Full Name John C. Atkinson — Chart No.

	Day Month Year	City, Town or Place	County or Province, etc.	State or Country	Add Info on Husb
Birth	12- 3-1899		Butler Co.	Kansas	
Chr'nd					
Marr	12-12-1920				
Death	17- 3-1967	Independence	Mont. Co.	Kansas	
Burial	3-1967	Mt. Hope Cem.	Mont. Co.	Kansas	

Places of Residence

Occupation   Church Affiliation   Military Rec

His Father: Samuel R. Atkinson   Mother's Maiden Name: Susan Nancy Moore

Wife's Full Maiden Name Josephine

	Day Month Year	City, Town or Place	County or Province, etc.	State or Country	Add Info on Wife
Birth	18- 5-1900				
Chr'nd					
Death	10- 7-1987				
Burial	7-1987	Mt. Hope Cem. Ind.	Mont. Co.	Kansas	

Places of Residence

Occupation   Church Affiliation   Military Rec

Her Father: Mother's Maiden Name:

Sex	Children's Names in Full		Day Month Year	City, Town or Place	County or Province, etc.	State or Country	Add Info on Child
M	1 Gerald Atkinson	Birth					
	Full Name of Spouse	Marr.					
		Death					
		Burial					
M	2 Wilbur Atkinson	Birth					
	Full Name of Spouse	Marr.					
		Death					
		Burial					
M	3 Walter Atkinson	Birth					
	Full Name of Spouse	Marr.					
		Death					
		Burial					
M	4 Claude Atkinson	Birth					
	Full Name of Spouse	Marr.					
		Death					
		Burial					

ATKINSON

JOSEPHINE   MARRIED   JOHN C.
MAY 18, 1900   DEC 12   MAR. 12, 1899
JULY 10, 1987   1920   MAR. 17, 1967

Family Group Sheet

Husband's Full Name Andrew J. Moore
Chart No.

	Day Month Year	City, Town or Place	County or Province, etc.	State or Country	Add Info on Husb
Birth	1858	Plano	Kendell Co.	Illinois	
Chr'nd					
Marr	17-9-1880	Eldorado	Butler Co.	Kansas	
Death					
Burial					

Places of Residence

Occupation | **Church Affiliation** | **Military Rec**

His Father Richard S. Moore **Mother's Maiden Name** Rebecca Owens

Wife's Full Maiden Name Amanda Paul

	Day Month Year	City, Town or Place	County or Province, etc.	State or Country	Add Info on Wife
Birth	1858				
Chr'nd					
Death					
Burial					

Places of Residence

Occupation | **Church Affiliation** | **Military Rec.**

Her Father | **Mother's Maiden Name**

Marriage License transcription:

STATE OF KANSAS, Butler County. Office Probate Judge of Said County.

That on the 17th day of Sept A.D. 1880 there was issued from the office of said Probate Judge, a Marriage License of which the following is a true copy:

Marriage License

ElDorado Butler County, State of Kansas, Sept 17th A.D. 1880

To any Person Authorized by Law to Perform the Marriage Ceremony—GREETING:

You are hereby authorized to join in Marriage Andrew J Moore of Butler County aged 22 and Amanda Paul of Butler County aged 22 and of this License you will make due return to my office within thirty days.

S.A. Black, Probate Judge

And which said Marriage License was afterwards, to-wit: on the 17th day of Sept, A.D. 1880, returned to said Probate Judge, with the following Certificate endorsed thereon, to-wit:

STATE OF KANSAS, Butler COUNTY, SS.

I, C.B. Daughters, do hereby certify, that in accordance with the authorization of the within License, I did, on the 17 day of September A.D. 1880, at ElDorado, in said County, join and unite in Marriage the within named Andrew J. Moore and Amanda Paul.

Witness my hand and seal the day and year above written.

Attest:
C.B. Daughters, Justice of the Peace of Butler County

402

Kinship of Richard S Moore

Name	Relationship with Richard Moore	Civil	Canon
???, Carinda	Daughter-in-law		
???, Cecil	Wife of the great-grandson		
???, Chris	Wife of the 3rd great-grandson		
???, Darlene	Wife of the 4th great-grandson		
???, Esta	Wife of the 2nd great-grandson		
???, Faye	Wife of the great-grandson		
???, Jan	Ex-wife of the 3rd great-grandson		
???, Jan	Wife of the 3rd great-grandson		
???, Jayne	Wife of the 2nd great-grandson		
???, Joan	Partner of the 4th great-grandson		
???, Julie	Wife of the 3rd great-grandson		
???, Maria Kathlien	Wife of the 2nd great-grandson		
???, Pamuela	Wife of the 3rd great-grandson		
???, Rebecca	Wife of the 3rd great-grandson		
???, Rita	Ex-wife of the 3rd great-grandson		
???, Susan	Wife of the 4th great-grandson		
???, Terry L	Wife of the 4th great-grandson		
???, Unknown	Wife of the great-grandson		
???, Virgilene	Wife of the great-grandson		
Abbelfazi, ???	Husband of the 4th great-granddaughter		
Abbott, Valerie	Wife of the 3rd great-grandson		
Adams, Eunice Electa	Wife of the grandson		
Adams, Louisa M	Wife of the grandson		
Adamson, Billy Lee	3rd great-grandson	V	5
Adamson, Bobby Jo	3rd great-grandson	V	5
Adamson, William V	Husband of the 2nd great-granddaughter		
Aemisegger, Treva Sue	Wife of the 3rd great-grandson		
Albert, Christine Marie	4th great-granddaughter	VI	6
Albert, Jennifer Dawn	4th great-granddaughter	VI	6
Albert, Victor Lee	Ex-husband of the 3rd great-granddaughter		
Allison, Bill	Husband of the 3rd great-granddaughter		
Allison, Jill Annette	4th great-granddaughter	VI	6
Allison, Kristin Kay	4th great-granddaughter	VI	6
Allison, Megan Leigh	5th great-granddaughter	VII	7
Allison, Renee' Maria	5th great-granddaughter	VII	7
Allison, Richard Nheil	Ex-husband of the 3rd great-granddaughter		
Allison, Richard Nheil	4th great-grandson	VI	6
Allison, Ronald Ray	4th great-grandson	VI	6
Allison, Stephanie Renee	5th great-granddaughter	VII	7
Alvarez, Dennis Vince	Husband of the 3rd great-granddaughter		
Alvarez, Guy Eldon	4th great-grandson	VI	6
Alvarez, Kaylene Lynn	4th great-granddaughter	VI	6
Alvarez, Scott Allen	4th great-grandson	VI	6
Amerine, Vicki	3rd great-granddaughter	V	5
Amerine, W B	Husband of the 2nd great-granddaughter		
Amerine, William	3rd great-grandson	V	5
Amerine, Yvonne Eloise	3rd great-granddaughter	V	5
Anderson, Charlette Maxine	4th great-granddaughter	VI	6
Anderson, Joe	Husband of the 2nd great-granddaughter		
Anderson, Joshua Justin	4th great-grandson	VI	6
Anderson, Katie	Wife of the 2nd great-grandson		

Name	Relationship with Richard Moore	Civil	Canon
Anderson, Lindsey Renee	4th great-granddaughter	VI	6
Anderson, Lyle Lynn	5th great-grandson	VII	7
Anderson, Stephen Craig	Husband of the 3rd great-granddaughter		
Anderson, Thomas Grant	Ex-husband of the 3rd great-granddaughter		
Anderson, Thomas Grant, Jr	4th great-grandson	VI	6
Anderson, Tony Grant	4th great-grandson	VI	6
Andrews, Rose Margaret	Wife of the 2nd great-grandson		
Antel, Richelle Lynn	Wife of the 4th great-grandson		
Applegate, Mary Rose	Wife of the grandson		
Archer, Aaron James	5th great-grandson	VII	7
Archer, Amanda Rae	5th great-granddaughter	VII	7
Archer, Raymond Lee	Husband of the 4th great-granddaughter		
Arnold, ???	Husband of the great-granddaughter		
Arthur, Frances Gibson	Husband of the great-granddaughter		
Ashurst, Chelsey Lynne	5th great-granddaughter	VII	7
Ashurst, Cherry Sherie	4th great-granddaughter	VI	6
Ashurst, Joseph Timothy	5th great-grandson	VII	7
Ashurst, Robert Craig	4th great-grandson	VI	6
Ashurst, William Brandy	4th great-grandson	VI	6
Ashurst, William Wallace	Ex-husband of the 3rd great-granddaughter		
Atchison, William E	Husband of the granddaughter		
Atkinson, Ada Francis	Granddaughter	II	2
Atkinson, Alphard M	Grandson	II	2
Atkinson, Charles A	Grandson	II	2
Atkinson, Claude	Great-grandson	III	3
Atkinson, Effie E	Granddaughter	II	2
Atkinson, Fred L	Grandson	II	2
Atkinson, Gerald	Great-grandson	III	3
Atkinson, John C	Grandson	II	2
Atkinson, Minnie M	Granddaughter	II	2
Atkinson, Robert	Grandson	II	2
Atkinson, Samuel R	Son-in-law		
Atkinson, Walter	Great-grandson	III	3
Atkinson, Wilbur	Great-grandson	III	3
Atkinson, William R	Grandson	II	2
Austin, Audie	5th great-grandson	VII	7
Austin, Cody	5th great-grandson	VII	7
Austin, Heath Wayne	4th great-grandson	VI	6
Austin, Michael Daniel	4th great-grandson	VI	6
Austin, Wayne Arthur	Husband of the 3rd great-granddaughter		
Bachelder, Lois Valette	Ex-wife of the 2nd great-grandson		
Bair, Orval Alton, Jr	Husband of the 2nd great-granddaughter		
Bair, Rhonda Leigh	3rd great-granddaughter	V	5
Bair, Roy William	3rd great-grandson	V	5
Bair, Teresa Renea'	3rd great-granddaughter	V	5
Baker, Angela Margaret	4th great-granddaughter	VI	6
Baker, Carla Jean	4th great-granddaughter	VI	6
Baker, Chanda Mae	4th great-granddaughter	VI	6
Baker, Charles Roland	Husband of the 3rd great-granddaughter		
Baker, Craig	Husband of the 3rd great-granddaughter		
Baker, Heather Renee	4th great-granddaughter	VI	6
Baker, Jarret Roland	4th great-grandson	VI	6
Baldwin, Rhonda Lynne	Partner of the 4th great-grandson		

Name	Relationship with Richard Moore	Civil	Canon
Ball, Tracie Deann	Wife of the 4th great-grandson		
Balzer, Abbey Marie	4th great-granddaughter	VI	6
Balzer, Bethamy	4th great-granddaughter	VI	6
Balzer, Danielle Marie	4th great-granddaughter	VI	6
Balzer, Derck	4th great-grandson	VI	6
Balzer, Howard Milton	Husband of the 2nd great-granddaughter		
Balzer, Jo Ann	3rd great-granddaughter	V	5
Balzer, Jordan	4th great-grandson	VI	6
Balzer, LaVonne Elaine	3rd great-granddaughter	V	5
Balzer, Milton Lee	3rd great-grandson	V	5
Balzer, Morey Howard	3rd great-grandson	V	5
Balzer, Sarah Katherine	3rd great-granddaughter	V	5
Balzer, Thomas Lee	4th great-grandson	VI	6
Banks, Theodore	Husband of the 3rd great-granddaughter		
Barg, Allen	Husband of the 4th great-granddaughter		
Barnes, Ella	Wife of the grandson		
Barnes, Kent	Husband of the 4th great-granddaughter		
Barnes, Shannon Renee	5th great-granddaughter	VII	7
Bartels, Carmen	Wife of the 5th great-grandson		
Bartlett, Alice Fay	4th great-granddaughter	VI	6
Bartlett, Alissa Christina	5th great-granddaughter	VII	7
Bartlett, Charles Clifford	4th great-grandson	VI	6
Bartlett, Glen Clifford	Husband of the 2nd great-granddaughter		
Bartlett, Heather	5th great-granddaughter	VII	7
Bartlett, Jacob Brian	5th great-grandson	VII	7
Bartlett, John Carl	3rd great-grandson	V	5
Bartlett, Johnny Wayne	4th great-grandson	VI	6
Bartlett, Norma Jean	3rd great-granddaughter	V	5
Bartlett, Stella Mae	3rd great-granddaughter	V	5
Bartlett, Wayne Irvin	3rd great-grandson	V	5
Bascom, Thomas	Son-in-law		
Baxter, Delphia Maxine	Wife of the 2nd great-grandson		
Bean, Lori Ann	Wife of the 3rd great-grandson		
Beasley, Kenneth Eugene	Ex-husband of the 3rd great-granddaughter		
Beasley, Kristine Renee	4th great-granddaughter	VI	6
Beecroft, Edith	Wife of the grandson		
Beer, Orlie Eugene	Ex-husband of the 2nd great-granddaughter		
Beiter, Kathy Annette	3rd great-granddaughter	V	5
Beiter, Rodney Earl	3rd great-grandson	V	5
Beiter, Terry Lynn	3rd great-grandson	V	5
Beiter, Willie Earl	Ex-husband of the 2nd great-granddaughter		
Benoit, Colleen	5th great-granddaughter	VII	7
Benoit, Linda	Partner of the 4th great-grandson		
Bertrand, Stahr Denyse	Wife of the 4th great-grandson		
Biewener, Emily Hope	Wife of the 2nd great-grandson		
Bishop, Brenda Kay	Wife of the 3rd great-grandson		
Bitting, Misty Dawn	4th great-granddaughter	VI	6
Bitting, Monte	Ex-husband of the 3rd great-granddaughter		
Blake, Robert	Husband of the 4th great-granddaughter		
Blevins, J D	Ex-husband of the 4th great-granddaughter		
Blevins, James David	5th great-grandson	VII	7
Blevins, Melinda Dawn	5th great-granddaughter	VII	7
Bond, Rose Marie	Wife of the 3rd great-grandson		

Name	Relationship with Richard Moore	Civil	Canon
Borg, Donna Michelle	Wife of the 3rd great-grandson		
Bowling, Cordelia Lynn	Wife of the 3rd great-grandson		
Brace, Betty Vero	Wife of the 2nd great-grandson		
Brace, Elmer Evertt	Husband of the great-granddaughter		
Brahier, Raymond Golightly	Husband of the 3rd great-granddaughter		
Brahier, Raymond Golightly, Jr	4th great-grandson	VI	6
Brandel, Roger Jermo	Ex-husband of the 3rd great-granddaughter		
Brandel, Vivian Maxine	4th great-granddaughter	VI	6
Brandt, Duke	Husband of the 4th great-granddaughter		
Brenner, Charles Martin	Husband of the great-granddaughter		
Brenner, George LeRoy	2nd great-grandson	IV	4
Brenner, Gwin Lee	3rd great-granddaughter	V	5
Brenner, Harold F	2nd great-grandson	IV	4
Brenner, Iva Jo	3rd great-granddaughter	V	5
Brenner, Rodonna Sue	3rd great-granddaughter	V	5
Brenner, Verl W	2nd great-grandson	IV	4
Brenner, Virginia	3rd great-granddaughter	V	5
Brenton, Martin Greg	Ex-husband of the 3rd great-granddaughter		
Brenton, Shelly Renae	4th great-granddaughter	VI	6
Brenton, Tyson George	4th great-grandson	VI	6
Brewer, Max Eugene, Jr	Husband of the 3rd great-granddaughter		
Brindle, Deborah Ann Fudger	Ex-wife of the 4th great-grandson		
Briscoe, Abigail Denise	5th great-granddaughter	VII	7
Briscoe, Lee Charles	Husband of the 4th great-granddaughter		
Broadhurst, ???	Husband of the granddaughter		
Broadhurst, Dewey Bryant	Great-grandson	III	3
Broadhurst, Haley	Great-granddaughter	III	3
Broadhurst, Hope	Great-granddaughter	III	3
Broadhurst, Ruth	Great-granddaughter	III	3
Brockhouse, Bobby Arno	Husband of the 2nd great-granddaughter		
Brockhouse, Luke Wayne Richard	4th great-grandson	VI	6
Brockhouse, Madeline Eileen	3rd great-granddaughter	V	5
Brockhouse, Michael Wayne	3rd great-grandson	V	5
Brockhouse, Michael-Lee O'Brien	4th great-grandson	VI	6
Brockhouse, Michelle Jenette	4th great-granddaughter	VI	6
Brown, Blance LaVon	Wife of the great-grandson		
Brown, William	Husband of the great-granddaughter		
Bryant, Dewey	Husband of the great-granddaughter		
Buchanan, David	Husband of the 4th great-granddaughter		
Butts, Casi Renae	4th great-granddaughter	VI	6
Butts, Courtney Anne	4th great-granddaughter	VI	6
Butts, Darlene Sue	3rd great-granddaughter	V	5
Butts, Debra Sue	3rd great-granddaughter	V	5
Butts, Diane Sue	3rd great-granddaughter	V	5
Butts, Donna Sue	3rd great-granddaughter	V	5
Butts, Ronald Deane	Husband of the 2nd great-granddaughter		
Butts, Ronald Eugene	3rd great-grandson	V	5
Byran, Lewis	Husband of the granddaughter		
Cain, Bonnie Lou	4th great-granddaughter	VI	6
Cain, Cindy D	4th great-granddaughter	VI	6
Cain, Danny J	4th great-grandson	VI	6
Cain, Harry	4th great-grandson	VI	6
Cain, Harry Russell	Husband of the 3rd great-granddaughter		

Name	Relationship with Richard Moore	Civil	Canon
Cain, Jerry D	4th great-grandson	VI	6
Cain, Michael	5th great-grandson	VII	7
Cain, Sheldon	5th great-grandson	VII	7
Cain, Thelma Rozella	Wife of the 3rd great-grandson		
Campbell, Daisy Berryline	Wife of the great-grandson		
Cannon, Rita Sue	Wife of the 3rd great-grandson		
Carr, Jennifer Lynn	Wife of the 3rd great-grandson		
Carrikier, Lida L	Wife of the great-grandson		
Carrikier, Rhoda R	Wife of the great-grandson		
Carter, ???	Husband of the 2nd great-granddaughter		
Case, Bernal Lavern	Husband of the 2nd great-granddaughter		
Case, Brett Michael	4th great-grandson	VI	6
Case, Caleb Levi	4th great-grandson	VI	6
Case, Davie Laverne	3rd great-grandson	V	5
Case, Desiree' Dale	4th great-granddaughter	VI	6
Case, Gerald Allen	3rd great-grandson	V	5
Case, Larry Ervin	3rd great-grandson	V	5
Case, Scott Allen	4th great-grandson	VI	6
Chaplin, Norma Lee	Wife of the 3rd great-grandson		
Clifton, George	Husband of the granddaughter		
Coates, Michal Maureen	Wife of the 4th great-grandson		
Cole, Charles John	Husband of the 3rd great-granddaughter		
Cole, Elizabeth Maxine	Wife of the 4th great-grandson		
Coleman, James D	Husband of the 4th great-granddaughter		
Colley, Emma	Granddaughter	II	2
Colley, George	Grandson	II	2
Colley, James H	Son-in-law		
Colley, Laura F	Granddaughter	II	2
Colley, Lelia	Granddaughter	II	2
Colley, Maude	Granddaughter	II	2
Colley, Walter	Grandson	II	2
Collins, ???	Husband of the 3rd great-granddaughter		
Cook, Amy	Wife of the 4th great-grandson		
Copeland, Ivil Gladys	Great-granddaughter	III	3
Copeland, Jacob Henry	Ex-husband of the granddaughter		
Copeland, Leona Belle	Great-granddaughter	III	3
Copeland, Phyllis Useba Mae	Great-granddaughter	III	3
Copeland, Vera Beatrice	Great-granddaughter	III	3
Copeland, Will	Husband of the granddaughter		
Copeland, William Carl	Great-grandson	III	3
Corl, Danielle Dawn	5th great-granddaughter	VII	7
Corl, Derik Eugene	5th great-grandson	VII	7
Corl, Eugene Thomas	Husband of the 4th great-granddaughter		
Corl, Heather Lynn	5th great-granddaughter	VII	7
Cosentino, Amy Lorraine	4th great-granddaughter	VI	6
Cosentino, Angela Domenica Lynn	4th great-granddaughter	VI	6
Cosentino, Christina	4th great-granddaughter	VI	6
Cosentino, Guy Vincent	3rd great-grandson	V	5
Cosentino, James Hall	3rd great-grandson	V	5
Cosentino, James Hall II	4th great-grandson	VI	6
Cosentino, Julie Alexis	4th great-granddaughter	VI	6
Cosentino, Marllena' Renee	4th great-granddaughter	VI	6
Cosentino, Vernon Leroy	3rd great-grandson	V	5

Name	Relationship with Richard Moore	Civil	Canon
Cosentino, Victor Herbert	Husband of the 2nd great-granddaughter		
Cosentino, Victoria Alexandra	4th great-granddaughter	VI	6
Cottrell, Dixie Louise	4th great-granddaughter	VI	6
Cottrell, J D	Husband of the 3rd great-granddaughter		
Cottrell, Janelle Lynn	Wife of the 4th great-grandson		
Courter, Cecil	2nd great-grandson	IV	4
Courter, Clarence	2nd great-grandson	IV	4
Courter, Denise	4th great-granddaughter	VI	6
Courter, Doris Lea	3rd great-granddaughter	V	5
Courter, Freda	2nd great-granddaughter	IV	4
Courter, Kenneth	2nd great-grandson	IV	4
Courter, Max	3rd great-grandson	V	5
Courter, Robert	Husband of the great-granddaughter		
Courter, Ross	4th great-grandson	VI	6
Courter, Susan	4th great-granddaughter	VI	6
Covert, Joan Mae	Wife of the 4th great-grandson		
Craig, Cody James	5th great-grandson	VII	7
Craig, Dylan Reese	5th great-grandson	VII	7
Craig, George Arthur	Husband of the 4th great-granddaughter		
Craig, Wyatt Willam	5th great-grandson	VII	7
Crain, Cecil G	Husband of the 2nd great-granddaughter		
Crain, Dewey Ben	3rd great-grandson	V	5
Crawford, Infant	2nd great-granddaughter	IV	4
Crawford, J O	2nd great-grandson	IV	4
Crawford, Jerry	2nd great-grandson	IV	4
Crawford, Jess	Husband of the great-granddaughter		
Crawford, Julia Bell	2nd great-granddaughter	IV	4
Crawford, Larry D	Ex-husband of the 3rd great-granddaughter		
Crawford, Leroy	2nd great-grandson	IV	4
Crawford, Lillie	2nd great-granddaughter	IV	4
Crossfield, Ann Elizabeth	3rd great-granddaughter	V	5
Crossfield, Carrol Lew	3rd great-grandson	V	5
Crossfield, Edith Marie	2nd great-granddaughter	IV	4
Crossfield, Hazel Louise	2nd great-granddaughter	IV	4
Crossfield, Helen	3rd great-granddaughter	V	5
Crossfield, Infant Son	2nd great-grandson	IV	4
Crossfield, John Ira	Husband of the great-granddaughter		
Crossfield, Kay	3rd great-granddaughter	V	5
Crossfield, Larry Lee	3rd great-grandson	V	5
Crossfield, Leland Francis	2nd great-grandson	IV	4
Crossfield, Lewis Ira	2nd great-grandson	IV	4
Curfman, Carol Ann	Wife of the 3rd great-grandson		
Daines, Michael	Partner of the 4th great-granddaughter		
Daines, William Michael	5th great-grandson	VII	7
Dalton, Linda Lee	Ex-wife of the 3rd great-grandson		
Dane, ???	Daughter-in-law		
Darnell, Alfred	Nephew of the wife		
Darnell, Benjamin	Nephew of the wife		
Darnell, Elizabeth	Niece of the wife		
Darnell, Enoch	Nephew of the wife		
Darnell, Fannie	Niece of the wife		
Darnell, James	Nephew of the wife		
Darnell, Mary	Niece of the wife		

Name	Relationship with Richard Moore	Civil	Canon
Darnell, Ruben	Nephew of the wife		
Darnell, Thomas	Nephew of the wife		
Darnell, William	Nephew of the wife		
DeHaven, Donald Keith	Husband of the 2nd great-granddaughter		
DeHaven, Jeffrey Lynn	3rd great-grandson	V	5
DeHaven, Kimberly Sue	3rd great-granddaughter	V	5
DeHaven, Tiffany M	4th great-granddaughter	VI	6
DeHaven, Zachery D	4th great-grandson	VI	6
Delahanty, Meg Ann	Wife of the 3rd great-grandson		
Dennett, Carl Leland	4th great-grandson	VI	6
Dennett, Diana LeeAnn	4th great-granddaughter	VI	6
Dennett, Robert Lee	Ex-husband of the 3rd great-granddaughter		
Denny, David Cecil	Husband of the 3rd great-granddaughter		
Denny, Katrina Ann	4th great-granddaughter	VI	6
Dexter, John Isaac	Husband of the great-granddaughter		
Dexter, Juanita Faye	2nd great-granddaughter	IV	4
Dexter, Viola G	2nd great-granddaughter	IV	4
Dexter, Zora Douthard	2nd great-granddaughter	IV	4
Donovan, ???	Husband of the 2nd great-granddaughter		
Dorise, Connie Sue	Wife of the 3rd great-grandson		
Doty, Jack Eugene	Partner of the 3rd great-granddaughter		
Dugan, Edward W	4th great-grandson	VI	6
Dugan, William Russell	Husband of the 3rd great-granddaughter		
Dugan, Winifred Tabor	Wife of the 2nd great-grandson		
Duke, Cory	Ex-husband of the 4th great-granddaughter		
Dunbin, Maxine	Wife of the 2nd great-grandson		
Duncan, Bryon	4th great-grandson	VI	6
Duncan, Christine	4th great-granddaughter	VI	6
Duncan, David Robert	3rd great-grandson	V	5
Duncan, Ennis Claude	Husband of the 2nd great-granddaughter		
Duncan, Faith Eileen	3rd great-granddaughter	V	5
Duncan, Joyce Ann	3rd great-granddaughter	V	5
Durfey, Vienna	Wife of the 2nd great-grandson		
Durham, Heidi Jean	Wife of the 5th great-grandson		
Easum, Dewey Allen	Husband of the 3rd great-granddaughter		
Ebejer, Renee'	Wife of the 4th great-grandson		
Ecker, George	2nd great-grandson	IV	4
Ecker, Margarie	2nd great-granddaughter	IV	4
Ecker, Marsh	Husband of the great-granddaughter		
Edminster, Peggy Charline	Wife of the 3rd great-grandson		
Edmonds, Georgia Irene	Wife of the 3rd great-grandson		
Edris, Bruce Leon	4th great-grandson	VI	6
Edris, Charles Richard	4th great-grandson	VI	6
Edris, Dennis Lee	4th great-grandson	VI	6
Edris, Harry L	4th great-grandson	VI	6
Edris, Jacob Logan	5th great-grandson	VII	7
Edris, Joshua Nathaniel	5th great-grandson	VII	7
Edris, Kristain Dale	5th great-grandson	VII	7
Edris, Richard Dale	Husband of the 3rd great-granddaughter		
Edris, Sue Charlene	4th great-granddaughter	VI	6
Edris, Tawnya Christine	5th great-granddaughter	VII	7
Edris, Tiffany Crystal	5th great-granddaughter	VII	7
Edris, Tina Marie	4th great-granddaughter	VI	6

Name	Relationship with Richard Moore	Civil	Canon
Edris, Travis Charles	5th great-grandson	VII	7
Edwards, Nancy Lou	Wife of the 3rd great-grandson		
Eldenburg, Mike	4th great-grandson	VI	6
Eldenburg, Robert	Husband of the 3rd great-granddaughter		
Eldenburg, Robin	4th great-granddaughter	VI	6
Elkins, Durena Dale	Wife of the 3rd great-grandson		
Eller, Alice Marie	3rd great-granddaughter	V	5
Eller, Alma Mae	3rd great-granddaughter	V	5
Eller, Barbara Elouise	3rd great-granddaughter	V	5
Eller, Barbara Ledora	2nd great-granddaughter	IV	4
Eller, Elizabeth Irene	2nd great-granddaughter	IV	4
Eller, George Everett	2nd great-grandson	IV	4
Eller, George Kenneth	3rd great-grandson	V	5
Eller, Helen Louise	2nd great-granddaughter	IV	4
Eller, James Wilkerson	2nd great-grandson	IV	4
Eller, John Everett	Husband of the great-granddaughter		
Eller, Nita Jo	3rd great-granddaughter	V	5
Eller, Sonya Lou	3rd great-granddaughter	V	5
Eller, Willa Mae	2nd great-granddaughter	IV	4
Ellis, Melba Marie	Wife of the 2nd great-grandson		
Enabinett, Claire	Husband of the 3rd great-granddaughter		
Farley, John K	Husband of the 3rd great-granddaughter		
Farley, Seth Kelly	4th great-grandson	VI	6
Farley, Tessa Jane	4th great-granddaughter	VI	6
Fetgatter, Billy	Husband of the 5th great-granddaughter		
Fields, Neva Marie	Wife of the 2nd great-grandson		
Fittro, Ernest	Husband of the great-granddaughter		
Fittro, Otis	2nd great-grandson	IV	4
Foelke, Joe	Husband of the 4th great-granddaughter		
Fosher, Effie	Wife of the grandson		
Foster, William T	Husband of the great-granddaughter		
Fowler, Brian Carl	4th great-grandson	VI	6
Fowler, Kevin Lee	4th great-grandson	VI	6
Fowler, Maude Della	Wife of the great-grandson		
Fowler, Ralph Vestel, Jr	Husband of the 3rd great-granddaughter		
Foyle, Charlotte Jean	4th great-granddaughter	VI	6
Foyle, William Neil	Ex-husband of the 3rd great-granddaughter		
Frye, Kimberly	Wife of the 4th great-grandson		
Gaines, Naomi Estellee	Wife of the great-grandson		
Gardner, Janice Ann Holt	Wife of the 3rd great-grandson		
Garman, Jeffery Earl	Husband of the 3rd great-granddaughter		
Garrison, Joseph	Husband of the granddaughter		
Garrity, Julie E	Granddaughter	II	2
Garrity, Sarah W	Granddaughter	II	2
Garrity, Thomas	Son-in-law		
George, Kathleen Kay	Wife of the 3rd great-grandson		
Gerbode, Kenneth David	Husband of the 3rd great-granddaughter		
Gifford, Harry Edward	Husband of the 4th great-granddaughter		
Goebel, Mary Teresa	Wife of the 3rd great-grandson		
Goode, Delores	Wife of the 3rd great-grandson		
Greenfield, Charlotte	Granddaughter	II	2
Greenfield, Emma Jane	Granddaughter	II	2
Greenfield, George Elmer	Grandson	II	2

Name	Relationship with Richard Moore	Civil	Canon
Greenfield, Harvey I	Son-in-law		
Greenfield, James Ira	Grandson	II	2
Greenfield, Lilly Mae	Granddaughter	II	2
Greenfield, Sarah Rebecca	Granddaughter	II	2
Griggs, Karen	Wife of the 4th great-grandson		
Grimmet, Margaret Louise	Wife of the 2nd great-grandson		
Gronau, Evelyn Sue	Ex-wife of the 3rd great-grandson		
Guajardo, Jacqueline Nicole	Wife of the 4th great-grandson		
Gumpke, ???	Husband of the 4th great-granddaughter		
Haffaker, Gladys	2nd great-granddaughter	IV	4
Haffaker, Goerge	Husband of the great-granddaughter		
Haffaker, Hazel	2nd great-granddaughter	IV	4
Haffaker, Lawrence	2nd great-grandson	IV	4
Hagstrom, Bernard N	Husband of the great-granddaughter		
Hagstrom, Bertha	2nd great-granddaughter	IV	4
Hagstrom, Bessie	2nd great-granddaughter	IV	4
Hagstrom, Beulah	2nd great-granddaughter	IV	4
Hagstrom, Emanuel	2nd great-grandson	IV	4
Hagstrom, Gladys	2nd great-granddaughter	IV	4
Hagstrom, Marjie	2nd great-granddaughter	IV	4
Hagstrom, Orville	2nd great-grandson	IV	4
Hagstrom, Oscar	2nd great-grandson	IV	4
Hagstrom, Permelia	2nd great-granddaughter	IV	4
Hagstrom, Theodore	2nd great-grandson	IV	4
Hague, Douglas L	Husband of the 3rd great-granddaughter		
Hague, Matthew D	4th great-grandson	VI	6
Hague, Molly A	4th great-granddaughter	VI	6
Hague, Morgan Ashley	4th great-granddaughter	VI	6
Hall, Alice Eliza	Great-granddaughter	III	3
Hall, Almeda Maude	Granddaughter	II	2
Hall, America Seny	Granddaughter	II	2
Hall, Art	Great-grandson	III	3
Hall, Audrey Faye	2nd great-granddaughter	IV	4
Hall, Baby Boy	Great-grandson	III	3
Hall, Blanche	Great-granddaughter	III	3
Hall, Brian	3rd great-grandson	V	5
Hall, Buell	2nd great-grandson	IV	4
Hall, Calvin	2nd great-grandson	IV	4
Hall, Catherine Ann	3rd great-granddaughter	V	5
Hall, Cecil Lorne	2nd great-grandson	IV	4
Hall, Celia Laverna	Great-granddaughter	III	3
Hall, Cindy	3rd great-granddaughter	V	5
Hall, Clara May	2nd great-granddaughter	IV	4
Hall, Clarene	Great-granddaughter	III	3
Hall, Clayton Oakley	2nd great-grandson	IV	4
Hall, Clifford Gaines	2nd great-grandson	IV	4
Hall, David R	Grandson	II	2
Hall, Diana Kay	3rd great-granddaughter	V	5
Hall, Doris Maxine	2nd great-granddaughter	IV	4
Hall, Duane Deloise	2nd great-grandson	IV	4
Hall, Edmund	Son-in-law		
Hall, Edwina	Great-granddaughter	III	3
Hall, Elmer Elwood	Grandson	II	2

Name	Relationship with Richard Moore	Civil	Canon
Hall, Euseba Elmira	Granddaughter	II	2
Hall, Florence Ann	Granddaughter	II	2
Hall, Francis Leaton	Grandson	II	2
Hall, Grace Maude	Great-granddaughter	III	3
Hall, Guy Christian	Great-grandson	III	3
Hall, Harriett El Nora	Granddaughter	II	2
Hall, Ines	Great-granddaughter	III	3
Hall, Ira Emmutt	Great-grandson	III	3
Hall, James Edmund	Great-grandson	III	3
Hall, Janice De Lois	2nd great-granddaughter	IV	4
Hall, Joan Ann	3rd great-granddaughter	V	5
Hall, Kenneth J	2nd great-grandson	IV	4
Hall, Laurie	3rd great-granddaughter	V	5
Hall, Lester Milton	2nd great-grandson	IV	4
Hall, Lois	2nd great-granddaughter	IV	4
Hall, Lulu Seny	Great-granddaughter	III	3
Hall, Lynn Merle	Great-grandson	III	3
Hall, Mabel Inez	Great-granddaughter	III	3
Hall, Mary Elmira	Granddaughter	II	2
Hall, Milo	Great-grandson	III	3
Hall, Nancy Ann	2nd great-granddaughter	IV	4
Hall, Naomi Lee	3rd great-granddaughter	V	5
Hall, Nell	Great-granddaughter	III	3
Hall, Newell VIvian	2nd great-granddaughter	IV	4
Hall, Owen Archebald	Grandson	II	2
Hall, Robert E	Grandson	II	2
Hall, Roy Lutrell	Great-grandson	III	3
Hall, Sheila L	3rd great-granddaughter	V	5
Hall, Sheldon	3rd great-grandson	V	5
Hall, Sherry L	3rd great-granddaughter	V	5
Hall, Terry Jean	3rd great-grandson	V	5
Hall, Tim	3rd great-grandson	V	5
Hall, Verne Reuben	Grandson	II	2
Hall, Virgil H	Great-grandson	III	3
Hall, Wanda Marlene	2nd great-granddaughter	IV	4
Hall, Zachary Hurshel	Great-grandson	III	3
Harden, Jason Edward	Husband of the 4th great-granddaughter		
Harlan, Barbara Louise	3rd great-granddaughter	V	5
Harlan, Janice Kay	3rd great-granddaughter	V	5
Harlan, Merle Dean	Husband of the 2nd great-granddaughter		
Harlan, Mervin Jay	3rd great-grandson	V	5
Harper, Charles	2nd great-grandson	IV	4
Harper, Monroe	Husband of the great-granddaughter		
Hastings, Amos Leland III	Husband of the 4th great-granddaughter		
Hataway, Edith	Wife of the 2nd great-grandson		
Hatch, Allen Scott	4th great-grandson	VI	6
Hatch, Naomi LuElla	4th great-granddaughter	VI	6
Hatch, Thomas Henry	Husband of the 3rd great-granddaughter		
Hawkins, Debbie	3rd great-granddaughter	V	5
Hawkins, Jim	Husband of the 2nd great-granddaughter		
Hayes, Judy Arlene	Wife of the 3rd great-grandson		
Hayes, Phillip	Partner of the 3rd great-granddaughter		
Hemrich, Christina Diane	4th great-granddaughter	VI	6

Name	Relationship with Richard Moore	Civil	Canon
Hemrich, Crystal Michelle	4th great-granddaughter	VI	6
Hemrich, John Robert	Ex-husband of the 3rd great-granddaughter		
Henry, ???	Husband of the 3rd great-granddaughter		
Herman, ???	Husband of the 4th great-granddaughter		
Herman, Jordan	5th great-grandson	VII	7
Herman, Joshua	5th great-grandson	VII	7
Herman, Kayci	5th great-granddaughter	VII	7
Herman, Michael D	Ex-husband of the 3rd great-granddaughter		
Herman, Shawn	5th great-grandson	VII	7
Herrman, ???	Husband of the 4th great-granddaughter		
Herrman, Jordan	5th great-grandson	VII	7
Herrman, Joshua	5th great-grandson	VII	7
Herrman, Kayci	5th great-granddaughter	VII	7
Herrman, Shawn	5th great-grandson	VII	7
Hill, Andy	Husband of the 3rd great-granddaughter		
Hoagland, Raymond	Husband of the 3rd great-granddaughter		
Hockersmith, Brandon M	5th great-grandson	VII	7
Hockersmith, David	5th great-grandson	VII	7
Hockersmith, Mike L	Husband of the 4th great-granddaughter		
Hockersmith, Stephanie Nichole	5th great-granddaughter	VII	7
Hockersmith, Stephen Nicholas	5th great-grandson	VII	7
Holliday, Paul Richard	Husband of the 3rd great-granddaughter		
Holliday, Seth Myron	4th great-grandson	VI	6
Hopkins, Amanda Christine	4th great-granddaughter	VI	6
Hopkins, Brenda Jo	3rd great-granddaughter	V	5
Hopkins, Bruce Lynn	3rd great-grandson	V	5
Hopkins, Deborah Sue	Wife of the 4th great-grandson		
Hopkins, Mariah Marie	4th great-granddaughter	VI	6
Hopkins, Pamela Kay	3rd great-granddaughter	V	5
Hopkins, Sondra Sue	3rd great-granddaughter	V	5
Hopkins, Theodore, Jr	Ex-husband of the 2nd great-granddaughter		
Hopkins, Veda Lou	3rd great-granddaughter	V	5
Hornecker, Margaret Ann	Wife of the 3rd great-grandson		
Howe, Edrie	Husband of the 3rd great-granddaughter		
Hoyt, Delilah M	Wife of the grandson		
Hummel, Irving James II	Ex-husband of the 3rd great-granddaughter		
Hunt, Ruth Porter	Wife of the great-grandson		
Huskey, Elwood C	Husband of the granddaughter		
Hyche, Breanne Michelle	5th great-granddaughter	VII	7
Hyche, Terrance Leon	Husband of the 4th great-granddaughter		
Isabell, Adeline	Daughter-in-law		
Jackson, Jeffrey	Husband of the 3rd great-granddaughter		
Jacobs, Angela Rae	3rd great-granddaughter	V	5
Jacobs, Baby Unknown	Great-granddaughter	III	3
Jacobs, Charles Forrest	2nd great-grandson	IV	4
Jacobs, Charles Ray	2nd great-grandson	IV	4
Jacobs, Charles Reuben	Husband of the granddaughter		
Jacobs, Christian Forrest	4th great-grandson	VI	6
Jacobs, Clarice	Great-granddaughter	III	3
Jacobs, Curtis	2nd great-grandson	IV	4
Jacobs, Elizabeth Ellen	4th great-granddaughter	VI	6
Jacobs, Enuice Marjorie	Great-granddaughter	III	3
Jacobs, Erica Lynn	4th great-granddaughter	VI	6

Name	Relationship with Richard Moore	Civil	Canon
Jacobs, Gary Forrest	3rd great-grandson	V	5
Jacobs, Hannah Marie	4th great-granddaughter	VI	6
Jacobs, Homer	Great-grandson	III	3
Jacobs, Janice Allene	3rd great-granddaughter	V	5
Jacobs, Jeffrey Homer	3rd great-grandson	V	5
Jacobs, Jim Laird	2nd great-grandson	IV	4
Jacobs, Joan	2nd great-granddaughter	IV	4
Jacobs, John Eric	3rd great-grandson	V	5
Jacobs, Jonathon Wade	4th great-grandson	VI	6
Jacobs, Joy Sue	3rd great-granddaughter	V	5
Jacobs, Julia Ann	4th great-granddaughter	VI	6
Jacobs, Kenneth Lyle	3rd great-grandson	V	5
Jacobs, Lane	2nd great-granddaughter	IV	4
Jacobs, Leston Lyle	Great-grandson	III	3
Jacobs, Lucy Susanne	3rd great-granddaughter	V	5
Jacobs, Melanie Dawn	3rd great-granddaughter	V	5
Jacobs, Monica	3rd great-granddaughter	V	5
Jacobs, Nita F	Great-granddaughter	III	3
Jacobs, Patrick Marty	3rd great-grandson	V	5
Jacobs, Thomas Carl	3rd great-grandson	V	5
Jennings, Clemmie	Wife of the grandson		
Jesseph, Chastity Dawn Hopkins	4th great-granddaughter	VI	6
Jesseph, Dennis Lynn	Husband of the 3rd great-granddaughter		
Jesseph, Kelly Tanner	4th great-grandson	VI	6
Johnson, Edmond Jack	Husband of the 3rd great-granddaughter		
Johnson, Elizabeth	Wife of the great-grandson		
Johnson, Guy	Husband of the great-granddaughter		
Johnson, Maxine	2nd great-granddaughter	IV	4
Johnston, Christine Nicole	4th great-granddaughter	VI	6
Johnston, Michelle Annette	4th great-granddaughter	VI	6
Johnston, Richard Lee	Husband of the 3rd great-granddaughter		
Jones, Becky Sue	4th great-granddaughter	VI	6
Jones, Cliffa	5th great-granddaughter	VII	7
Jones, Clifford	4th great-grandson	VI	6
Jones, Kara Dawn	5th great-granddaughter	VII	7
Jones, Lonnie Lee	4th great-grandson	VI	6
Jones, Loren	Husband of the 3rd great-granddaughter		
Jones, Michael	5th great-grandson	VII	7
Jones, Ronnie	4th great-grandson	VI	6
Jones, Sandra Lynn	4th great-granddaughter	VI	6
Jones, Sandy Lee	Ex-wife of the 4th great-grandson		
Jones, William E	Husband of the 3rd great-granddaughter		
Jorns, Burke Jacobs	4th great-grandson	VI	6
Jorns, Kenneth D	Husband of the 3rd great-granddaughter		
Judd, Nancy	Mother-in-law		
Kaufman, Neva Belle	Wife of the 3rd great-grandson		
Keen, Terry	Ex-husband of the 3rd great-granddaughter		
Kehoe, Leslie Elmer	Husband of the 2nd great-granddaughter		
Keisel, Suzanne Prince	Wife of the 3rd great-grandson		
Kelley, Abeata Daisy	2nd great-granddaughter	IV	4
Kelley, Daphne K	Great-granddaughter	III	3
Kelley, Eugene Shelby	2nd great-grandson	IV	4
Kelley, Gladys Irene	Great-granddaughter	III	3

Name	Relationship with Richard Moore	Civil	Canon
Kelley, Helen Elizabeth	2nd great-granddaughter	IV	4
Kelley, Henry James	2nd great-grandson	IV	4
Kelley, James Riley	Husband of the granddaughter		
Kelley, Kathleen Sena	2nd great-granddaughter	IV	4
Kelley, Leota Seba	2nd great-granddaughter	IV	4
Kelley, Leslie Calvin	Great-grandson	III	3
Kelley, Marilyn Joan	2nd great-granddaughter	IV	4
Kelley, Patricia Ann	2nd great-granddaughter	IV	4
Kelley, Samuel Malcom	Great-grandson	III	3
Kelley, Seba Vera	Great-granddaughter	III	3
Kelley, Sidney Edmond, Jr	2nd great-grandson	IV	4
Kelley, Sidney Edmund	Great-grandson	III	3
Kelley, Thelma Doris	Great-granddaughter	III	3
Kelley, Woodest Marion	2nd great-grandson	IV	4
Kelly, Mose	Great-grandson	III	3
Kelly, Robert E	Great-grandson	III	3
Kelly, Robert J	Husband of the granddaughter		
Kelly, Romona	Great-granddaughter	III	3
Kelly, Terry	Ex-husband of the 3rd great-granddaughter		
Kennedy, Boy	3rd great-grandson	V	5
Kennedy, Charlene Wilma	3rd great-granddaughter	V	5
Kennedy, LeVerne Neil	Husband of the 2nd great-granddaughter		
Kennedy, LeVerne Paul	3rd great-grandson	V	5
Kennedy, Marcella Jean	3rd great-granddaughter	V	5
Kennedy, Mary Esther	3rd great-granddaughter	V	5
Keys, Susan May	Wife of the great-grandson		
Kibbe, Erma Lucile	Wife of the 2nd great-grandson		
Kilpatrick, Joe	Husband of the great-granddaughter		
Kirchmer, Galen	3rd great-grandson	V	5
Kirchmer, Larry Gene	3rd great-grandson	V	5
Kirchmer, Marion L	Husband of the 2nd great-granddaughter		
Kirchmer, Teresa	3rd great-granddaughter	V	5
Kirchner, Margaret	Wife of the 2nd great-grandson		
Kitchell, Cheryl Ann	Ex-wife of the 3rd great-grandson		
Knaak, Judith Bernadine	Wife of the 2nd great-grandson		
Knowles, Dean	Ex-husband of the 3rd great-granddaughter		
Krase, Jill Diane	4th great-granddaughter	VI	6
Krase, Lloyd Eugene	Husband of the 3rd great-granddaughter		
Krase, Shelley Anne	4th great-granddaughter	VI	6
Kropp, Erika Ruth	4th great-granddaughter	VI	6
Kropp, Kaitlyn Ann	4th great-granddaughter	VI	6
Kropp, Ronald David	Husband of the 3rd great-granddaughter		
Kropp, Trevor Charles	4th great-grandson	VI	6
Kropp, Tyler David	4th great-grandson	VI	6
Kuhns, Mark	Husband of the 4th great-granddaughter		
Lackey, Karen Jean	Wife of the 3rd great-grandson		
Laird, Lila Ellen	Wife of the great-grandson		
Lamb, Floyd William	Husband of the 2nd great-granddaughter		
Lamb, Opal Gertrude	Wife of the 2nd great-grandson		
Lantz, Bill	Husband of the 4th great-granddaughter		
Larsen, George Amasa	Ex-husband of the 4th great-granddaughter		
Larsen, Jessica Darlene	5th great-granddaughter	VII	7
Larsen, Raymon Amasa	5th great-grandson	VII	7

Name	Relationship with Richard Moore	Civil	Canon
Larsen, Shayla Michalle	5th great-granddaughter	VII	7
Lawton, Jessie Geneva	Wife of the 2nd great-grandson		
Lea, John Albert	Husband of the 4th great-granddaughter		
Lehman, Angel Marie	5th great-granddaughter	VII	7
Lehman, Brenda	4th great-granddaughter	VI	6
Lehman, Jeri Ann	4th great-granddaughter	VI	6
Lehman, Jerry	Husband of the 3rd great-granddaughter		
Lehman, Lucina Ruth	4th great-granddaughter	VI	6
Letzkus, Frances Emma	Wife of the grandson		
Lewis, Scott Carl	Ex-husband of the 3rd great-granddaughter		
Limpert, Dawn Marie	Wife of the 4th great-grandson		
Livingston, Wesley	Husband of the 2nd great-granddaughter		
Long, Anne E	3rd great-granddaughter	V	5
Long, Jim C	3rd great-grandson	V	5
Long, Kyle Jacobs	4th great-grandson	VI	6
Long, Rachell Ann	4th great-granddaughter	VI	6
Long, Sara Nell	4th great-granddaughter	VI	6
Long, Scott Jacobs	3rd great-grandson	V	5
Long, William Carl	Husband of the 2nd great-granddaughter		
Long, William Carl, Jr	3rd great-grandson	V	5
Loper, Paget	Husband of the 4th great-granddaughter		
Loper, Patricia Lee	5th great-granddaughter	VII	7
Lovelace, Josephine	Wife of the grandson		
Luekenga, Bill J R	Husband of the 2nd great-granddaughter		
Luster, Alice Melrose	Wife of the 2nd great-grandson		
Lynn, Alexis Ann	4th great-granddaughter	VI	6
Lynn, Benjamin John	4th great-grandson	VI	6
Lynn, Kimberly Diane	4th great-granddaughter	VI	6
Lynn, Melvin John	Husband of the 3rd great-granddaughter		
Mache, Leanne Renae	Wife of the 3rd great-grandson		
Macy, ???	Ex-husband of the 4th great-granddaughter		
Macy, Heather Kay	5th great-granddaughter	VII	7
Macy, Tatum Lyn	5th great-granddaughter	VII	7
Maxwell, Etna	Great-granddaughter	III	3
Maxwell, George Roy	Husband of the granddaughter		
Maxwell, Leonard Bill Baily	Great-grandson	III	3
Maxwell, Sarah Frances	Wife of the grandson		
Maxwell, Vida M	Wife of the great-grandson		
May, April Michelle	4th great-granddaughter	VI	6
May, Daniel Earl	4th great-grandson	VI	6
May, Earl Christopher	Ex-partner of the 3rd great-granddaughter		
Mayhew, Allen Edward	3rd great-grandson	V	5
Mayhew, Eldon Jay	Husband of the 2nd great-granddaughter		
Mayhew, John Daryl	3rd great-grandson	V	5
Mayhew, Robert Jay	3rd great-grandson	V	5
Mayo, Charles Leo	3rd great-grandson	V	5
Mayo, Emogene E	3rd great-granddaughter	V	5
Mayo, L Newton	Husband of the 2nd great-granddaughter		
Mayo, Richard D	3rd great-grandson	V	5
Mayo, William Roy	3rd great-grandson	V	5
Mays, ???	Son-in-law		
McConeghy, Arlene	3rd great-granddaughter	V	5
McConeghy, Becky	4th great-granddaughter	VI	6

Name	Relationship with Richard Moore	Civil	Canon
McConeghy, Cathy Lou	4th great-granddaughter	VI	6
McConeghy, Fred John	3rd great-grandson	V	5
McConeghy, Kim Dexter	4th great-grandson	VI	6
McConeghy, Randy	4th great-grandson	VI	6
McConeghy, Willard	Husband of the 2nd great-granddaughter		
McDoughall, Mellissa Jane	Wife of the 3rd great-grandson		
McGinn, Cynthia Lou	3rd great-granddaughter	V	5
McGinn, Duane Francis	Ex-husband of the 2nd great-granddaughter		
McGinn, Jill Marie	3rd great-granddaughter	V	5
McGinn, Karen Sue	3rd great-granddaughter	V	5
McGinn, Kurt Francis	3rd great-grandson	V	5
McLain, Darlene	3rd great-granddaughter	V	5
McLain, James W, Sr	3rd great-grandson	V	5
McLain, JoAnn	3rd great-granddaughter	V	5
McLain, Kenneth Wayne	Husband of the 2nd great-granddaughter		
McQueen, Vicki	Wife of the 4th great-grandson		
Mehling, Dorothy	Wife of the 3rd great-grandson		
Melton, Darren Robert	4th great-grandson	VI	6
Melton, Jason Walter	4th great-grandson	VI	6
Melton, Robert	Husband of the 3rd great-granddaughter		
Metz, Nellie Mae	Wife of the great-grandson		
Miller, ???	Husband of the 3rd great-granddaughter		
Miller, Annona	Great-granddaughter	III	3
Miller, Ashley Nicole	4th great-granddaughter	VI	6
Miller, Blendena Caroline	2nd great-granddaughter	IV	4
Miller, Bonnie Lou	2nd great-granddaughter	IV	4
Miller, Charles Lawrence	4th great-grandson	VI	6
Miller, Edmond	Great-grandson	III	3
Miller, Frank Joseph	Husband of the great-granddaughter		
Miller, Hannah Elizabeth	4th great-granddaughter	VI	6
Miller, Howard	Great-grandson	III	3
Miller, Iva	Great-granddaughter	III	3
Miller, John Andrew	4th great-grandson	VI	6
Miller, John Foster II	Husband of the 3rd great-granddaughter		
Miller, Joseph R	Husband of the granddaughter		
Miller, Kalley	Great-granddaughter	III	3
Miller, Katherine Diane	4th great-granddaughter	VI	6
Miller, Marian Frances	2nd great-grandson	IV	4
Miller, Peggy Jean	2nd great-granddaughter	IV	4
Montgomery, Margaret	Wife of the 2nd great-grandson		
Moore, Ada	Granddaughter	II	2
Moore, Alama Deann	4th great-granddaughter	VI	6
Moore, Alan Arthur	3rd great-grandson	V	5
Moore, Alan Dee	3rd great-grandson	V	5
Moore, Allen	2nd great-grandson	IV	4
Moore, Alva Daniel	2nd great-grandson	IV	4
Moore, Amanda Elaine	4th great-granddaughter	VI	6
Moore, Andrew J	Son	I	1
Moore, Angela Dawn	4th great-granddaughter	VI	6
Moore, Angela Denise	4th great-granddaughter	VI	6
Moore, Arlene	2nd great-granddaughter	IV	4
Moore, Arthur Leon	3rd great-grandson	V	5
Moore, Austin	Great-grandson	III	3

Name	Relationship with Richard Moore	Civil	Canon
Moore, Ava Lynne	3rd great-granddaughter	V	5
Moore, Beulah Ruth	2nd great-granddaughter	IV	4
Moore, Brenda Sue	4th great-granddaughter	VI	6
Moore, Cade	4th great-grandson	VI	6
Moore, Calvin W	Son	I	1
Moore, Charlotte M	Daughter	I	1
Moore, Chelacen	4th great-granddaughter	VI	6
Moore, Clara S	Great-granddaughter	III	3
Moore, Clarence	Grandson	II	2
Moore, Clyde Earl	Great-grandson	III	3
Moore, Della M	Great-granddaughter	III	3
Moore, Donald Jay	3rd great-grandson	V	5
Moore, Dorothy	2nd great-granddaughter	IV	4
Moore, E William	Great-grandson	III	3
Moore, Edith Valetta	3rd great-granddaughter	V	5
Moore, Effie Sarah	Great-granddaughter	III	3
Moore, Elizabeth Ann	Granddaughter	II	2
Moore, Elmer	Great-grandson	III	3
Moore, Elwood Orin	2nd great-grandson	IV	4
Moore, Etta Ellen	Granddaughter	II	2
Moore, Eva V	Great-granddaughter	III	3
Moore, Floyd Virgil	2nd great-grandson	IV	4
Moore, Gary Lloyd	3rd great-grandson	V	5
Moore, Gary Lloyd, Jr	4th great-grandson	VI	6
Moore, George	Son	I	1
Moore, George	Grandson	II	2
Moore, George Arthur	4th great-grandson	VI	6
Moore, Ginger	4th great-granddaughter	VI	6
Moore, Glenn Leon	2nd great-grandson	IV	4
Moore, Helen	Granddaughter	II	2
Moore, Helen Mae	2nd great-granddaughter	IV	4
Moore, Herbert L	Grandson	II	2
Moore, Howard Ray	3rd great-grandson	V	5
Moore, Infant	Great-granddaughter	III	3
Moore, Infant Twin	Great-granddaughter	III	3
Moore, Ira Austin	Grandson	II	2
Moore, James Clarence	Grandson	II	2
Moore, James F	Son	I	1
Moore, James Monroe	Grandson	II	2
Moore, James Reuben	3rd great-grandson	V	5
Moore, Jeffrey Dean	4th great-grandson	VI	6
Moore, John Edward	Grandson	II	2
Moore, John William	2nd great-grandson	IV	4
Moore, Jordan Jayne	5th great-grandson	VII	7
Moore, Josephine	Granddaughter	II	2
Moore, Joshua Shane	5th great-grandson	VII	7
Moore, Judith Diane	3rd great-granddaughter	V	5
Moore, Karen l	Wife of the 3rd great-grandson		
Moore, Karen Sue	3rd great-granddaughter	V	5
Moore, Kari Cozette	4th great-granddaughter	VI	6
Moore, Karin Ann	4th great-granddaughter	VI	6
Moore, Kirsten Lei	4th great-granddaughter	VI	6
Moore, Kyle William	4th great-grandson	VI	6

Name	Relationship with Richard Moore	Civil	Canon
Moore, Larry Jo	3rd great-grandson	V	5
Moore, LaVina Jean	4th great-granddaughter	VI	6
Moore, Leon Arthur	Great-grandson	III	3
Moore, Lester L	Great-grandson	III	3
Moore, Lloyd Merle	2nd great-grandson	IV	4
Moore, Marion M	Son	I	1
Moore, Marissa	4th great-granddaughter	VI	6
Moore, Martha	Daughter	I	1
Moore, Mary	Granddaughter	II	2
Moore, Matilda Jane	Daughter	I	1
Moore, Melissa Rebecca	Granddaughter	II	2
Moore, Melvin E	2nd great-grandson	IV	4
Moore, Michael B	4th great-grandson	VI	6
Moore, Michael Wayne	4th great-grandson	VI	6
Moore, Mike	3rd great-grandson	V	5
Moore, Minnie	Granddaughter	II	2
Moore, Minnie	Granddaughter	II	2
Moore, Miriam Ann	3rd great-granddaughter	V	5
Moore, Myrtle E	Granddaughter	II	2
Moore, Nancy Ann	3rd great-granddaughter	V	5
Moore, Nettie M	Granddaughter	II	2
Moore, Olive	Great-granddaughter	III	3
Moore, Opal Marian	2nd great-granddaughter	IV	4
Moore, Orin Egar	Great-grandson	III	3
Moore, Paul	2nd great-grandson	IV	4
Moore, Paula Lynn	4th great-granddaughter	VI	6
Moore, Pauline	2nd great-granddaughter	IV	4
Moore, Phoebe C	Daughter	I	1
Moore, Randy Ray	4th great-grandson	VI	6
Moore, Raymond	2nd great-grandson	IV	4
Moore, Raymond I	Great-grandson	III	3
Moore, Reuben	Son	I	1
Moore, Reuben David	Great-grandson	III	3
Moore, Richard Donald	2nd great-grandson	IV	4
Moore, Richard Edgar	Grandson	II	2
Moore, Richard S	Self		0
Moore, Rick Dean	4th great-grandson	VI	6
Moore, Rosa L	Great-granddaughter	III	3
Moore, Rose Annette	3rd great-granddaughter	V	5
Moore, Rosemary Emily	4th great-granddaughter	VI	6
Moore, Ruth	Great-granddaughter	III	3
Moore, Sally	3rd great-granddaughter	V	5
Moore, Samuel William	4th great-grandson	VI	6
Moore, Sarah Louise	Granddaughter	II	2
Moore, Seny	Daughter	I	1
Moore, Shawn Dean	4th great-grandson	VI	6
Moore, Sheryl Ann	4th great-granddaughter	VI	6
Moore, Stephen Scott	4th great-grandson	VI	6
Moore, Sue Ann	3rd great-granddaughter	V	5
Moore, Susan N	Daughter	I	1
Moore, Susanne	3rd great-granddaughter	V	5
Moore, Tammy Rae	4th great-granddaughter	VI	6
Moore, Thomas Herbert	3rd great-grandson	V	5

Name	Relationship with Richard Moore	Civil	Canon
Moore, Thomas S	Son	I	1
Moore, Tony Brent	3rd great-grandson	V	5
Moore, Troy Douglas	4th great-grandson	VI	6
Moore, Valerie Jean	4th great-granddaughter	VI	6
Moore, Veda Mae	2nd great-granddaughter	IV	4
Moore, Violet Marie	2nd great-granddaughter	IV	4
Moore, Wayne Virgil	3rd great-grandson	V	5
Moore, Wesley Wayne	4th great-grandson	VI	6
Moore, William	Grandson	II	2
Moore, William David	3rd great-grandson	V	5
Moore, William H	Son	I	1
Moore, William H	Grandson	II	2
Moore, William Oscar	Grandson	II	2
Moore, William Reuben	2nd great-grandson	IV	4
Moore, Wllia Pauline	3rd great-granddaughter	V	5
Moore, Zelma Elva	2nd great-granddaughter	IV	4
Morse, Connie Arlene	3rd great-granddaughter	V	5
Morse, Corrin Moonyeon	4th great-granddaughter	VI	6
Morse, Gordon Russell	3rd great-grandson	V	5
Morse, Ivan Robert	Husband of the 2nd great-granddaughter		
Morse, Mark Edwin	3rd great-grandson	V	5
Morse, Nickolas Leroy	4th great-grandson	VI	6
Morse, Phyllis Ann	4th great-granddaughter	VI	6
Morse, Rex Eldon	3rd great-grandson	V	5
Morse, Robert Steven	3rd great-grandson	V	5
Morse, Teresa Anne	3rd great-granddaughter	V	5
Morse, Vance Steven	4th great-grandson	VI	6
Mossman, Emma	Wife of the great-grandson		
Mossman, Winnifred	Wife of the great-grandson		
Munford, Debra Ann	Wife of the 3rd great-grandson		
Musch, Denys Suzanne	Wife of the 4th great-grandson		
Myers, Carolyn June	3rd great-granddaughter	V	5
Myers, Katheryn	Wife of the 3rd great-grandson		
Myers, Robert Glen	3rd great-grandson	V	5
Myers, William Harold	3rd great-grandson	V	5
Myers, William Henry	Husband of the 2nd great-granddaughter		
Necomb, ???	Husband of the great-granddaughter		
Necomb, Hazel	2nd great-granddaughter	IV	4
Newman, Amanda Rene	4th great-granddaughter	VI	6
Newman, Candice Jill Stanfield	4th great-granddaughter	VI	6
Newman, Marshall Richard	Husband of the 3rd great-granddaughter		
Newton, Carolyn Lee	Wife of the 3rd great-grandson		
Nicholl, Carl Russell	2nd great-grandson	IV	4
Nicholl, Claude	2nd great-grandson	IV	4
Nicholl, David	Husband of the great-granddaughter		
Nicholl, Donald Merle	2nd great-grandson	IV	4
Nicholl, Dorothy Kay	3rd great-granddaughter	V	5
Nicholl, Hazel Leota	2nd great-granddaughter	IV	4
Nicholl, Jimmie Duane	3rd great-grandson	V	5
Nicholl, R June	3rd great-granddaughter	V	5
Nicholl, Ruby	2nd great-granddaughter	IV	4
Nicholson, Mike	Ex-husband of the 4th great-granddaughter		
Nicholson, Robert Allen	5th great-grandson	VII	7

Name	Relationship with Richard Moore	Civil	Canon
Nicolle, Evelyn Ellen	Wife of the 2nd great-grandson		
Nielson, Vivian Lee	Wife of the 2nd great-grandson		
Nitzsche, ???	Husband of the 3rd great-granddaughter		
Oberst, Chris	4th great-grandson	VI	6
Oberst, Jack	Ex-husband of the 3rd great-granddaughter		
Oberst, Scott S	4th great-grandson	VI	6
O'Brien, Darcy Ann	Wife of the 3rd great-grandson		
Oehlert, Aaron Lee	4th great-grandson	VI	6
Oehlert, Jordon Glenn	4th great-grandson	VI	6
Oehlert, Robert	Husband of the 3rd great-granddaughter		
O'Lear, ???	Wife of the 2nd great-grandson		
Oliver, Johnnie Eugene	4th great-grandson	VI	6
Oliver, Riley	Ex-husband of the 3rd great-granddaughter		
Openshaw, Claudia	Ex-wife of the 3rd great-grandson		
Orcutt, Alexander Chance	6th great-grandson	VIII	8
Orcutt, Amanda Michelle	5th great-granddaughter	VII	7
Orcutt, Carly Savannah	6th great-granddaughter	VIII	8
Orcutt, John Eugene	Husband of the 4th great-granddaughter		
Orcutt, Travis Eugene	5th great-grandson	VII	7
Osborn, Robert	Ex-husband of the 3rd great-granddaughter		
Owen, Albert	Nephew of the wife		
Owen, Archibald	Father-in-law		
Owen, Charlotte	Sister-in-law		
Owen, George	Nephew of the wife		
Owen, Horace E	Nephew of the wife		
Owen, Rebecca	Wife		
Owen, Reuben	Brother-in-law		
Owen, Susannah	Sister-in-law		
Owen, William R	Nephew of the wife		
Owens, Betty Lou	Wife of the 3rd great-grandson		
Parker, Linda Lee	Ex-wife of the 3rd great-grandson		
Patterson, Elmer J	Husband of the 3rd great-granddaughter		
Paul, Amanda	Daughter-in-law		
Paul, Melvina Barbara	Daughter-in-law		
Paul, Rachel Caroline	Wife of the grandson		
Pederren, Elener	Wife of the great-grandson		
Penner, Baby Boy	2nd great-grandson	IV	4
Penner, Darrell Lee	3rd great-grandson	V	5
Penner, Edna Maxine	2nd great-granddaughter	IV	4
Penner, Elizabeth Anna	2nd great-granddaughter	IV	4
Penner, Evelyn Ruth	2nd great-granddaughter	IV	4
Penner, Gary Ivan	3rd great-grandson	V	5
Penner, George Roscue	2nd great-grandson	IV	4
Penner, Henry Carl, Jr	Husband of the great-granddaughter		
Penner, Ivan Dale	2nd great-grandson	IV	4
Penner, Margaret Elnora	2nd great-granddaughter	IV	4
Penner, Michael Dale	3rd great-grandson	V	5
Penner, Norma Frances	2nd great-granddaughter	IV	4
Penner, Ralph Carl	2nd great-grandson	IV	4
Penner, Richard Lee	2nd great-grandson	IV	4
Penner, Roger Thaine	2nd great-grandson	IV	4
Perkins, Lori	Wife of the 3rd great-grandson		
Peters, John	Husband of the 3rd great-granddaughter		

Name	Relationship with Richard Moore	Civil	Canon
Peters, Lucelle	4th great-granddaughter	VI	6
Pettergill, Jessie	Wife of the 2nd great-grandson		
Petty, Alvin	2nd great-grandson	IV	4
Petty, Dean	2nd great-grandson	IV	4
Petty, Eula	2nd great-granddaughter	IV	4
Petty, Fred	2nd great-grandson	IV	4
Petty, Fred	Husband of the great-granddaughter		
Petty, Irene	2nd great-granddaughter	IV	4
Petty, June Leota Fern	2nd great-granddaughter	IV	4
Petty, Nora	2nd great-granddaughter	IV	4
Petty, Ola	2nd great-granddaughter	IV	4
Petty, Roy	2nd great-grandson	IV	4
Pfieff, Cynthia Louise	4th great-granddaughter	VI	6
Pfieff, Emma Jean	4th great-granddaughter	VI	6
Pfieff, Glen Stephen	4th great-grandson	VI	6
Pfiefff, Calvin Hoover	Husband of the 3rd great-granddaughter		
Phillips, Randie Renee	4th great-granddaughter	VI	6
Phillips, Virginia Rose	4th great-granddaughter	VI	6
Phillips, William James	Husband of the 3rd great-granddaughter		
Pickens, Wanda Lucina	Wife of the 2nd great-grandson		
Pickrell, George	Husband of the great-granddaughter		
Pinkerton, Dorothy May	Wife of the great-grandson		
Pinkston, ???	Husband of the 2nd great-granddaughter		
Pitts, Elizabeth A	Daughter-in-law		
Poe, Cecil Harold	Husband of the great-granddaughter		
Powers, Oscar	Husband of the 2nd great-granddaughter		
Racicky, Joan Kay	Wife of the 3rd great-grandson		
Ratanamon, Craig Austin	4th great-grandson	VI	6
Ratanamon, Kimberly Beth	4th great-granddaughter	VI	6
Ratanamon, Skol	Husband of the 3rd great-granddaughter		
Ray, ???	Husband of the 3rd great-granddaughter		
Ray, Cindy D	4th great-granddaughter	VI	6
Reagan, Art	Husband of the 3rd great-granddaughter		
Rector, E Virge	Husband of the great-granddaughter		
Rector, Louise	2nd great-granddaughter	IV	4
Rector, T Marie	2nd great-granddaughter	IV	4
Rector, Virgie Bell	2nd great-grandson	IV	4
Reece, Alisha Dawn	5th great-granddaughter	VII	7
Reece, Christina Elizabeth	5th great-granddaughter	VII	7
Reece, Jonathan Adrian	5th great-grandson	VII	7
Reece, Nathan Edward	5th great-grandson	VII	7
Reece, Sam	Husband of the 4th great-granddaughter		
Reece, Thomas Ray	5th great-grandson	VII	7
Reeves, Dustin Dwight	5th great-grandson	VII	7
Reeves, Matthew Levi	5th great-grandson	VII	7
Reeves, Steve	Ex-husband of the 4th great-granddaughter		
Reiser, Brittany Nicole	6th great-granddaughter	VIII	8
Reiser, Glen	Husband of the 5th great-granddaughter		
Reiser, Tiffany Renee	6th great-granddaughter	VIII	8
Reves, Lois	Ex-wife of the 2nd great-grandson		
Riley, E Harvey	Husband of the great-granddaughter		
Riley, Stella	2nd great-granddaughter	IV	4
Roberts, Theresie	Wife of the great-grandson		

Name	Relationship with Richard Moore	Civil	Canon
Robinson, Mable	Wife of the great-grandson		
Rogers, Buster E	Ex-husband of the 3rd great-granddaughter		
Rushton, Craig All	4th great-grandson	VI	6
Rushton, Hunter Austin	5th great-grandson	VII	7
Rushton, Michael Brett	4th great-grandson	VI	6
Rushton, Ronald A	Husband of the 3rd great-granddaughter		
Rushton, Tracy Noelle	4th great-granddaughter	VI	6
Rushton, Tyler Michael	5th great-grandson	VII	7
Russell, Neva Iona	Wife of the 2nd great-grandson		
Rutherford, Ruth Dona	Wife of the great-grandson		
Sanner, Patricia Lynne	Ex-wife of the 4th great-grandson		
Savoy, Kenneth James	Husband of the 4th great-granddaughter		
Schabell, Suzanne Elizabeth	Wife of the 3rd great-grandson		
Schelling, Frank Albert	Husband of the great-granddaughter		
Schisler, Cora	3rd great-granddaughter	V	5
Schisler, Edward	3rd great-grandson	V	5
Schisler, Frank	Husband of the 2nd great-granddaughter		
Schisler, Gilbert	3rd great-grandson	V	5
Schisler, Nela	3rd great-granddaughter	V	5
Schisler, Raplh	3rd great-grandson	V	5
Schlinloff, Bernice E	Wife of the 2nd great-grandson		
Schopansky, James Allen	5th great-grandson	VII	7
Schopansky, Mike	Husband of the 4th great-granddaughter		
Schopansky, William Cody	5th great-grandson	VII	7
Schroeder, Duane T	Husband of the 3rd great-granddaughter		
Schroeder, Matthew	4th great-grandson	VI	6
Schroeder, Melanie	4th great-granddaughter	VI	6
Schroeder, Shawna Marie	4th great-granddaughter	VI	6
Schroll, Wilma Lorena	Wife of the 2nd great-grandson		
Schuessler, Mary Lou	Wife of the 2nd great-grandson		
Schwehr, Claudia Maria	Ex-wife of the 4th great-grandson		
Scott, Dennis	Husband of the 4th great-granddaughter		
Scribner, William W	Husband of the great-granddaughter		
Scrivner, Archie D	Ex-husband of the great-granddaughter		
Sears, Alec Tanner	5th great-grandson	VII	7
Sears, Cameron Jacob	5th great-grandson	VII	7
Sears, Christina Michelle	4th great-granddaughter	VI	6
Sears, Danielle Elizabeth	4th great-granddaughter	VI	6
Sears, Gerald Orlando	Ex-husband of the great-granddaughter		
Sears, Gerald Orlando, Jr	2nd great-grandson	IV	4
Sears, Janet Sue	3rd great-granddaughter	V	5
Sears, Justin Brock	5th great-grandson	VII	7
Sears, Kiaberli Marie	4th great-granddaughter	VI	6
Sears, Michael Ernest	3rd great-grandson	V	5
Sears, Patrick Thomas	3rd great-grandson	V	5
Sears, Stacy Brock	4th great-grandson	VI	6
Sears, Tracy Lance	4th great-grandson	VI	6
Seeds, Ronald Gene	Ex-husband of the 3rd great-granddaughter		
Sellers, Donna	Ex-wife of the 4th great-grandson		
Sexton, Leonard J	Husband of the great-granddaughter		
Sexton, Virginia	2nd great-granddaughter	IV	4
Sharits, Azel Coffland	Husband of the great-granddaughter		
Sharits, Eloise	2nd great-granddaughter	IV	4

Name	Relationship with Richard Moore	Civil	Canon
Shartzer, Pat	Husband of the 4th great-granddaughter		
Shay, Jerry Wayne	Ex-husband of the 3rd great-granddaughter		
Shearer, Martha M	Daughter-in-law		
Sheets, Michelle Rene'	4th great-granddaughter	VI	6
Sheets, Ronald Hiram	Ex-husband of the 3rd great-granddaughter		
Sheets, Stephen Ray	4th great-grandson	VI	6
Sherrell, Bill	Ex-husband of the 4th great-granddaughter		
Sherrell, Billy	Partner of the 4th great-granddaughter		
Sherrell, Billy Don	5th great-grandson	VII	7
Sherrell, Gary Don	5th great-grandson	VII	7
Sherrell, Jeri Sue	5th great-granddaughter	VII	7
Sherrell, Jerry Ray	5th great-grandson	VII	7
Sherrell, Jimmy	Husband of the 4th great-granddaughter		
Sherrell, Larry	Ex-husband of the 4th great-granddaughter		
Sherrell, Rebecca Ann	5th great-granddaughter	VII	7
Shrigley, Sharon Lee	Wife of the 3rd great-grandson		
Skinner, Roger	Husband of the 3rd great-granddaughter		
Smart, Edna G	Wife of the 2nd great-grandson		
Smith, Amber	5th great-granddaughter	VII	7
Smith, Bertha Alpha	Wife of the great-grandson		
Smith, Bertha M	Great-granddaughter	III	3
Smith, Harry	Husband of the 3rd great-granddaughter		
Smith, John	Husband of the 4th great-granddaughter		
Smith, Julia Bell	Wife of the grandson		
Smith, Laverna	2nd great-granddaughter	IV	4
Smith, Mark	Husband of the 4th great-granddaughter		
Smith, Oscar L	Great-grandson	III	3
Smith, William Thompson	Husband of the granddaughter		
Smithhisler, David Pious	Husband of the great-granddaughter		
Smithhisler, Jan	2nd great-granddaughter	IV	4
Snyder, Shawn Suzanne	Ex-wife of the 4th great-grandson		
Soward, Charles Benjamin	Husband of the granddaughter		
Soward, Gary	Great-grandson	III	3
Soward, Lucille	Great-granddaughter	III	3
Soward, Raymond Martin	Great-grandson	III	3
Soward, Richard	Great-grandson	III	3
Soward, Sondra	Great-granddaughter	III	3
Sowder, Beulah Frances	Wife of the 2nd great-grandson		
Spradlin, Scott Edward	Husband of the 4th great-granddaughter		
Sprinell, Ruben B	Husband of the great-granddaughter		
Spurlin, Hershel Patric	Ex-husband of the 3rd great-granddaughter		
Stambeck, Diane Marie	Wife of the 3rd great-grandson		
Staton, Haley Loren	5th great-grandson	VII	7
Staton, Loren Culley	Husband of the 4th great-granddaughter		
Steffen, Victor	Husband of the 2nd great-granddaughter		
Steinback, Alan	Husband of the 3rd great-granddaughter		
Stephens, Craig Lavan	Husband of the 4th great-granddaughter		
Stephenson, Carol	Wife of the 3rd great-grandson		
Stevens, Mary Catharine	Wife of the great-grandson		
Suelthaus, John E	Husband of the granddaughter		
Sullivan, Irene	Wife of the great-grandson		
Swanson, Axel C	Husband of the 2nd great-granddaughter		
Swanson, Becky Jo	3rd great-granddaughter	V	5

Name	Relationship with Richard Moore	Civil	Canon
Swanson, Patricia Hope	3rd great-granddaughter	V	5
Swanson, Susan LaVern	3rd great-granddaughter	V	5
Talley, Woodrow	Husband of the 2nd great-granddaughter		
Tallman, Charles Wesley	Husband of the 2nd great-granddaughter		
Tallman, Glenn Edward	3rd great-grandson	V	5
Tallman, Roger Dennie	3rd great-grandson	V	5
Tallman, Thelma Elizabeth	3rd great-granddaughter	V	5
Tallman, Velma Ruth	3rd great-granddaughter	V	5
Taylor, Bruce	2nd great-grandson	IV	4
Taylor, Carl William	Great-grandson	III	3
Taylor, Cecil	2nd great-grandson	IV	4
Taylor, Cleo Turner	2nd great-grandson	IV	4
Taylor, Edith Leona	Wife of the great-grandson		
Taylor, Fern	2nd great-granddaughter	IV	4
Taylor, George	2nd great-grandson	IV	4
Taylor, George Lackey	Great-grandson	III	3
Taylor, Geraldine	2nd great-granddaughter	IV	4
Taylor, Gladys Hazel	Great-granddaughter	III	3
Taylor, Glen	2nd great-grandson	IV	4
Taylor, Harvey	2nd great-grandson	IV	4
Taylor, James Orcen	Great-grandson	III	3
Taylor, John	2nd great-grandson	IV	4
Taylor, John Harold	Great-grandson	III	3
Taylor, John Ira	Husband of the granddaughter		
Taylor, Judy	Wife of the 4th great-grandson		
Taylor, Kent	2nd great-grandson	IV	4
Taylor, Mabel Blanche	Great-granddaughter	III	3
Taylor, Melvina Jane	Great-granddaughter	III	3
Taylor, Nellie	2nd great-granddaughter	IV	4
Taylor, Sherry	Ex-wife of the 3rd great-grandson		
Taylor, Wilda Mae	2nd great-granddaughter	IV	4
Thomas, Andee	Wife of the 4th great-grandson		
Thomas, Mason Scott II	Husband of the 4th great-granddaughter		
Thornburg, Alma Delilah	Great-granddaughter	III	3
Thornburg, Benjamin	Husband of the granddaughter		
Thurman, Claude M	Husband of the granddaughter		
Towler, Carol Jean	5th great-granddaughter	VII	7
Towler, John, Jr	Husband of the 4th great-granddaughter		
Towler, Savanna	5th great-granddaughter	VII	7
Turbor, ???	Husband of the 2nd great-granddaughter		
Turner, David	3rd great-grandson	V	5
Turner, John Harold, Jr	3rd great-grandson	V	5
Turner, John Harold, Sr	Husband of the 2nd great-granddaughter		
Turner, Suzanne Keisel	4th great-granddaughter	VI	6
Turpin, Della Jean	Wife of the 3rd great-grandson		
Tyler, Beverly	Wife of the 3rd great-grandson		
Ullum, Naomi Hazel	Wife of the 2nd great-grandson		
Unruh, Shawn Christian	4th great-grandson	VI	6
Unruh, Warren Lee	Ex-husband of the 3rd great-granddaughter		
Valle, Cathryn Kay	Wife of the 4th great-grandson		
Veal, Andrew Lawrence	Ex-husband of the 3rd great-granddaughter		
Vogelman, Mary Lou	Wife of the 2nd great-grandson		
Vogts, Nathan Daniel	4th great-grandson	VI	6

Name	Relationship with Richard Moore	Civil	Canon
Vogts, Valecia Lynne	4th great-granddaughter	VI	6
Vogts, Victor Leroy	Ex-husband of the 3rd great-granddaughter		
Vogts, Wesley	4th great-grandson	VI	6
Wagner, Orville	Husband of the 2nd great-granddaughter		
Wainscott, David Shawn	4th great-grandson	VI	6
Wainscott, Jodi Lynn	4th great-granddaughter	VI	6
Wainscott, Robert Gordon	Husband of the 3rd great-granddaughter		
Wainscott, Steve Lee	4th great-grandson	VI	6
Walker, Laura Lee Doty	4th great-granddaughter	VI	6
Ward, Janet Lee	Wife of the 3rd great-grandson		
Webb, Barbara Dawn	4th great-granddaughter	VI	6
Webb, Gordon T	Husband of the 3rd great-granddaughter		
Webb, Marie Alaine	4th great-granddaughter	VI	6
Weedman, Mary Alice	Wife of the 2nd great-grandson		
Weisker, Emily Frances	Wife of the 2nd great-grandson		
Wells, ???	Husband of the 3rd great-granddaughter		
Wells, Scottie	4th great-grandson	VI	6
Wells, Sharon	4th great-granddaughter	VI	6
Wells, Terri	4th great-granddaughter	VI	6
Werner, ???	Husband of the 3rd great-granddaughter		
Werner, Judy	4th great-granddaughter	VI	6
Wertz, John	Husband of the 4th great-granddaughter		
Wheeler, Elwood	Husband of the great-granddaughter		
Whiteside, Bandie	4th great-granddaughter	VI	6
Whiteside, Danny	Husband of the 3rd great-granddaughter		
Whitney, Frances Ethlyn	Wife of the 2nd great-grandson		
Wiard, Tenley	Wife of the 3rd great-grandson		
Wickham, Faye Ann	Wife of the 3rd great-grandson		
Wiley, George Allen	Husband of the granddaughter		
Wiley, John Moore	Great-grandson	III	3
Wiley, Reuben William	Great-grandson	III	3
Wiley, Stella Adaline	Great-granddaughter	III	3
Wiley, Walter George	Great-grandson	III	3
Willams, Haley Nicole Marie	5th great-granddaughter	VII	7
Willams, Irma Rogers	Wife of the great-grandson		
Willams, James Edward Alexander	Ex-husband of the 4th great-granddaughter		
Williams, ???	Husband of the 3rd great-granddaughter		
Williams, Danny	Ex-husband of the 4th great-granddaughter		
Williams, Jonathan Paul	5th great-grandson	VII	7
Williams, Kenneth Wayne	5th great-grandson	VII	7
Williams, Kristi Gail	5th great-granddaughter	VII	7
Wilson, Bruce	Husband of the 3rd great-granddaughter		
Wilson, Mary Ellen	Wife of the grandson		
Winsky, Dolli Ann	Ex-wife of the 4th great-grandson		
Witt, ???	Husband of the 2nd great-granddaughter		
Wolfe, J E	Husband of the granddaughter		
Wolfe, J E	Husband of the granddaughter		
Woods, Ronald Phillip	Husband of the 3rd great-granddaughter		
Woods, Tyler Christian Lorne	4th great-grandson	VI	6
Woody, Wayneta Orpha	Wife of the 2nd great-grandson		
Wulz, James Elvyn	Husband of the 3rd great-granddaughter		
Wulz, James Patrick Nheil	5th great-grandson	VII	7
Wulz, Richard Nheil Allison	4th great-grandson	VI	6

Name	Relationship with Richard Moore	Civil	Canon
Wulz, Ronald Ray Allison	4th great-grandson	VI	6
Wulz, Susan Rene	4th great-granddaughter	VI	6

Moore Family History Index

ABBOTT
  Valerie 45
ADAMS
  Eunice Electa 7, 80, 236
  Louise 12, 80, 84, 86
  Merle 264
ADAMSON
  Billy Lee 41
  Bobby Jo 41
  William V. 40, 41
AEMISEGGER
  Treva Sue 65
ALBERT
  Christine Marie 65
  Jennifer Dawn 65
  Victor Lee 65
ALLISON
  Jill Annette 56, 325
  Kristin Kay 56, 325
  Megan Leigh 68
  Renee Maria 68
  Richard Nheil 50
  Ronald Ray 50, 68
  William (Bill) 56, 320, 325
ALVAREZ
  Dennis Vince 61
  Guy Eldon 61, 62
  Kaylene Lynn 61
  Scott Allen 61
AMERINE
  Bill 274
  Vicki 38, 55, 274, 275
  W.B. 38, 274
  William 38, 274
  Yvonne Eloise 38, 274
ANDERSON
  Charles 73
  Charlette Maxine 60, 61
  Christina Marie 73
  Joe 40, 355
  Joshua Justin 62
  Katie 38, 317
  Lindsey Renee 62
  Lyle Lynn 73
  Michelle Lynn 73
  Stephen Craig 62
  Sandy 313, 314
  Thomas Grant 60
  Thomas Grant, Jr. 60, 61, 73
  Tony Grant 61
ANDREWS
  Rose Margaret 36, 216
ANTEL
  Richelle 69, 140, 142
APPLEGATE
  Mary Rose 9, 375
ARCHER
  Aaron James 70, 154
  Amanda Rae 70, 154
  Raymond Lee 69, 70, 150, 154
ARENAS
  Ruth 135
ARTHUR
  Frances Gibson 31
ASHURST
  Chelsey Lynne 73, 352, 354
  Cherry Sherie 58, 73, 349, 354
  Joseph Timothy 73, 352
  Robert Craig 58, 72, 73, 349, 352
  William 58, 342, 349
  William Brandy 58, 349, 353
ATCHISON
  William E. 9, 370
ATKINSON
  Ada Francis 11, 18, 19, 31, 382, 385

AUSTIN (continued)
  Alphard M. 11, 382, 398
  Charles A 11, 382, 384
  Claude 19, 401
  Effie E. 11, 382, 399
  Fred L. 11, 382, 400
  Gerald 19, 401
  Grace 398
  John C. 11, 19, 382, 401
  Minnie M. 11, 382, 400
  Pearl 398
  Robert A. 11, 382, 384
  Samuel R. 11, 78, 382, 383
  Treva 398
  Walter 19, 401
  Wilbur 19, 401
  Ruby 398
  William R. 11, 382, 398
AUSTIN
  Audie 70, 198
  Cody 70, 198
  Heath Wayne 53, 70, 197, 198
  Jared L. 199
  Joshua L. 199
  Michael Daniel 53, 70, 197, 198
  Wayne Arthur 53, 194, 197
BACHELDER
  Lois 36, 120, 194, 196
BAIR
  Orval Alton Jr. 44
  Rhonda Leigh 45, 64
  Roy William 45
  Teresa Renea 45, 64
BAKER
  Angela Margaret 65
  Carla Jean 54, 207
  Chanda Mae 54, 207
  Charles Roland 54, 206, 207
  Craig 65
  Heather Renee 65
  Jarret Roland 54, 207
BALDWIN
  Rhonda Lynne 72, 73, 352
BALL
  Tracie DeAnn 53, 197, 199
BALLARD
  Heather 334, 336
BALZER
  Abby Marie 54, 210
  Bethamy 54
  Danielle Marie 54, 211
  Derek 54, 211
  Ethan Cole 210
  Howard Milton 36, 120, 206
  JoAnn 36, 54, 206, 208
  Jordan 54, 211
  LaVonne Elaine 36, 54, 206, 207
  Milton Lee 36, 54, 206, 210
  Morey Howard 36, 54, 206, 211
  Sarah Katherine 36, 206, 209
  Thomas Lee 54, 210
BANKS
  Theodore 37, 270
BARG
  Allen 52, 175, 178
BARNES
  Kent 72, 322, 323
  Shannon Rene 72, 323
BARTELS
  Carmen 75, 291
BARTLETT
  Alice Faye 55, 288, 291
  Alissa Christina 70, 293

  Charles Clifford 55, 70, 288, 294
  Glen Clifford 38, 284, 287, 289
  Heather 70, 294
  Jacob Brian 70, 294
  John Carl 38, 287, 302
  Johnny Wayne 55, 70, 288, 293
  Norma Jean 38, 55, 56, 287, 303, 305, 308
  Stella Mae 38, 55, 287, 295
  Wayne Irvin 38, 55, 287, 288
BASCOM
  Thomas 6, 77, 379
BAXTER
  Delphia Maxine 36
  Maxine D. 212, 216
BEACH
  Victor 185
BEAN
  Lori Ann 54m 206, 211
BEAR
  Melvin David 246
  Melvin O. 243, 246
BEASLEY
  Kenneth 64
  Kristine Renee 64
BEECROFT
  Edith 10, 375
BEER
  Orlie Eugene 43, 44
BEITER
  Kathy Annette 46
  Rodney Earl 46
  Terry Lynn 46
  Willie 46
BENOIT
  Linda 68
BERTRAND
  Stahr Denise 58, 349, 353
BIEWENER
  Emily Hope 43
BISHOP
  Brenda Kay 64
BITTING
  Misty Dawn 64
  Monte 64
BLAIR
  ANNA 382, 398
BLAKE
  Robert Doyle 52, 175, 176
BLEVINS
  J.D. 71, 303, 305, 306
  James David 71, 306
  Melinda Dawn 71, 75, 306, 307
BOND
  Rose Marie 55, 287, 288
BORG
  Donna Michelle 37, 224
BOWLING
  Cordella 62
BRACE
  Betty Vero 29
  Elmer Everett 17
BRAHIER
  Daniel Joseph 61
  Raymond 61
  Raymond Eugene 61
  Raymond Golightly Jr. 61
  Richard Lawrence 61
BRAHTER
  Thomas 164
BRANDEL
  Roger Jermo 61
  Vivian Maxine 61

BRANDT
  Duke 52, 175
BRENNER
  Charles Martin 26, 27
  George Leroy 27, 41, 42
  Gwin Lee 42
  Harold F. 27
  Iva Jo 42, 60
  Rodonna Sue 42, 60
  Verl W. 27, 42
  Virginia 42
BRENTON
  Martin 53, 54, 204
  Shelly Renae 54, 204
  Tyson George 54, 204
BRiNDLE
  Deborah Ann 68, 133
BRISCOE
  Abigail Denise 74
  Lee Charles 74
BROADHURST
  Dewey Bryant 17
  Haley 17
  Hope 17
  Ruth 17
BROCKHOUSE
  Bobby Arno 40, 284, 342, 343, 344, 345, 346, 347
  Luke Wayne Richard 58, 348
  Madeline Eileen 40, 58, 342, 349, 350
  Michael Lee O'Brien 58, 348
  Michael Wayne 40, 58, 342, 348
  Michelle Jeanette 58, 348
BROWN
  Blance LaVon 29
  William 16
BROYLES
  Marilyn Sue 41, 60
BRYAN
  Lewis 10, 377
BUCHANAN
  David 48, 107, 109
  Lea Grace 109
BUTTS
  Casi Renae 59, 365
  Courtney Anne 59, 365
  Darlene Sue 40, 58, 355, 358
  Debra Sue 40, 59, 355, 364
  Diane Sue 40, 59, 355, 361
  Donna Sue 40, 355, 357
  Janet Louise 355, 356
  Ronald Deane 40, 284, 355
  Ronald Eugene 40, 59, 355, 365
CAIN
  Bonnie Lou 51, 145, 149
  Cecil 45
  Cindy D. 51, 69, 148
  Danny J. 51, 69, 145, 147
  Dewey Ben 45
  Harry 51, 145, 147
  Harry Russell 50, 51, 144, 145
  Jerry D. 51, 145, 148
  Michael 69, 148
  Sheldon 69, 148
  Thelma Roselle 41
CAMPBELL
  Daisy Berryline 29, 30
CANNON
  Rita 65

CARR
  Jennifer Lynn 54, 206, 210
CARRICKER
  Lydia 238, 252
  Rhoda R. 23, 238, 253
CASE
  Bernal LaVerne 39, 284, 330, 331, 333
  Caleb Levi 58, 340, 341
  Brett Michael 57, 334, 336
  Davie LaVerne 39, 330, 339
  Desiree Dale 57, 334, 337
  Gerald Allen 40, 57, 58, 330, 340
  Larry Ervin 39, 57, 330, 334, 335
  Scott Allen 57, 334, 338
CHAPLIN
  Norma Lee 37, 243, 244
CLARK
  Carla Jean 174
CLIFTON
  George 10, 375
COATS
  Charles Arthur 60
  Jacklyn N. 73
  Jacobs M. 73
  Michael K. 60, 73
  Michal Maureen 70, 197, 198
  Pamela A. 73, 75
COLE
  Charles John 61
  Elizabeth Maxine 73
COLEMAN
  James D. 61
COLLEY
  Emma 10, 380
  George 10, 380
  James H. 10, 78, 380
  Laura F. 10, 380
  Lelia 10, 380
  Maude 10, 380
  Walter 10. 380
COLLINS
  Christopher Orin 229
  Darrel Jr. 227, 229
  Helen 248
  Jerry 249
  Lee Wayne 248
  Mary 248
  William Bill 248
CONSTABLE
  Nannette 179, 186
COOK
  Amy 61m 62
COPELAND
  Ivil Gladys 19, 385, 386
  Jacob Henry 18, 19, 382, 385, 387
  Leona Belle 19, 31, 32, 385, 397
  Phyllis Useba Mae 19, 31, 385, 388
  Vera Beatrice 19, 385, 386
  William Carl 19, 385, 386
CORL
  Danielle Dawn 68, 128
  Derik Eugene 68, 128
  Eugene Thomas 68. 126. 128
  Heather Lynn 68, 128
COSENTINO
  Amy Lorraine 62
  Angela Domenica 62
  Christina 62
  Donald Lee 62
  Guy Vincent 43, 62
  James Hall 43, 62

James Hall II 62
Julie Alexis 62
Marelena Renee 62
Vernon Leroy 43, 62
Victoria Alexandra 62
Victor Herbert 43
COTTRELL
Dixie Louise 56, 71, 303, 305, 306
J.D. 56, 305
Janelle Lynn 72, 313, 315
COURTER
Cecil 20, 90, 92, 93
Clarence 20, 33, 90, 92
Denise 48, 91
Doris Lea 33, 90
Freda 20, 90, 92, 95
Kenneth 20, 90, 92, 94
Max 33, 47, 48, 90, 91
Robert 20, 90, 92
Ross 48, 91
Susan 48, 91
COVERT
Joni Mae 50, 136, 139
CRAIG
Cody James 68, 141
Dylan Reese 68, 141
George Arthur 68, 140, 141
Wyatt William 68, 141
CRAWFORD
Infant 22, 240
Jerry 22, 240
Jess 22
Juila Bell 22, 240
Jo 22, 240
Larry 63
LeRoy 22, 240
Lillie 22, 240
CROSSFIELD
Ann Elizabeth 38, 55, 271
Carrol Lew 37, 270
Edith Marie 24, 266, 268
Hazel Louise 24, 266, 269
Helen 37, 55, 270
Infant son 24, 266, 268
John Ira 24, 260, 265, 266, 267
Kay 37, 270
Larry Lee 38, 271
Leland Francis 24, 37, 38, 266, 271
Lewis Ira
CURFMAN
Carol Ann 37, 224

DAINES
Michael 73, 74
William Michael 74
DALTON
Linda 54, 55, 219
DARNELL
Abram 76
James 76
DeHAVEN
Donald Keith 44
Kimberely Sue 44, 64
Jeffrey Lynn 44, 64
Tiffany M. 64
Zachery D. 64
DELAHANTY
Meg Ann 51, 161, 163
DENNETT
Carl Leland 50, 126, 127
Diana LeeAnn 50, 68, 126, 128
Robert Lee 50, 124, 126
DENNY
David Cecil 54, 206, 208
Katrina Ann 54, 208
Rebecca Jo 208
DEXTER
John Isaac 26
Juanita Faye 26, 41
Viola G. 26, 40, 41
Zora Douthard 26, 40

DOTY
Jack Eugene 63
DUGAN
Edward W. 65
William 65
Winifred Tabor 46
DUKE
Cory 169, 173
DUNBIN
Maxine 46
DUNCAN
Bryon 65
Christine 65
David Robert 46, 65
Ennis 45
Faith Eileen 46, 65
Joyce Ann 46, 65
DURFEY
Vienna 29
DURHAM
Heidi Jean 153

EASUM
Dewey Allen 65
EBEJER
Renee 48, 91
ECKER
George 22, 240
Margarie 22
Marsh 22, 238, 240
Minnie 240
EDMINSTER
Peggy Charlene 48, 100, 103
EDMONDS
Irene 37, 243, 245
EDRIS
Brandie 151
Brianane 151
Bruce Leon 51, 69, 150, 154
Charles Richard 51, 69, 150, 152
Daniel R. 151
Dennis Lee 51, 69, 150, 153
Harry L. 51, 150, 151
Jacob Logan 69, 154
Kristain Dale 69, 154
Joshua Nathaniel 69, 153
Richard Dale 51, 144, 150, 153
Sue Charlene 51, 69, 70, 150, 154
Tawnya Christine 69, 152
Tiffany Crystal 69, 152
Tina Marie 51, 69, 70, 150, 155
Travis Charles 69, 152
Vineisa M. 151
EDWARDS
Nancy Lou 34, 144, 156
ELDENBURG
Mike E. 60
Robert 60
Robin 60, 73
ELKINS
Durena Dale 57, 330, 334
ELLER
Alice Marie 39, 56, 57, 318, 326
Alma Mae 39, 318
Barbara Eloise 39, 56, 320, 322
Barbara Ledora 26, 40, 284, 355
Elizabeth Irene 26, 40, 284, 342
George Everett 26, 38, 39, 284, 311, 312, 317
George Kenneth 39, 311
Helen Louise 26, 38, 284, 287
James Wilkerson 26, 39, 284, 318, 320, 321
John Everett 25, 26, 282, 284, 285, 286

Nita Jo 39, 56, 311, 313
Sonya Lou 39, 56, 320, 325
Terry 96, 97
Willa Mae 26, 39, 284, 330
ELLIS
Melba Marie 35, 167
ENABINETT
Clair 57, 326
FARLEY
John 66
Seth Kelly 66
Tessa Jane 66
FAUL
Catherine 11
FETGATTER
Billy 71, 304
FIELDS
Neva Marie 47, 388, 391
FINNEY
Wanda 249
FITTRO
Ernest 22, 239
Otis 22, 239
FOSHER
Effie Lucetla 9, 370
FOSSEN
Wretha Van 243, 247
FOSTER
William 20
FOWLER
Brian Carl 65
Kevin Lee 65
Maude Della 29
Ralph Vestel 65
FOYLE
Charlotte Jean 61, 73
William Neil 61
FRYE
Kimberly 61

GAINES
Naomi Estellee 27, 28
GARDNER
Janice Ann Holt 44
GARMAN
Jeffery Earl 58, 350, 351
GARRISON
Joe 382, 399
GARRITY
Julie E. 10, 378
Sarah W. 10, 378
Thomas 10, 78, 378
GAYFORD
George C. 78
GEORGE
Kathleen 53, 194, 201
GERBODE
Kenneth David 47, 373
GIFFORD
Harry 53, 190, 191
Kendra Elyse 190, 191
Ryan Michael 190, 191
GILMORE
Melissa Jean 257
GOEBEL
Mary Teresa 51, 161, 164
GOODE
Delores 47
GREEN
Kim 190, 192
GREENFIELD
Charlotte 9
Emma Jane 9, 370
George Elmer 9, 370
Harvey I. 9, 77, 369, 370
James Ira 9, 370
Lily Mae 9, 370
Sarah Rebecca 9, 18, 370, 371
GRIGGS
Karen 72, 322, 324
GRIMMET
Margaret Louise 42
GRONAU
Evelyn Sue 54, 218

GUAJARDO
Jacqueline Nicole 50, 136, 139
HAFFEKER
George 22, 238, 239
Gladys 22, 239
Hazel 22, 239
Lawrence 22, 239
HAGSTROM
Bernard 23, 260, 262
Bertha 23, 262
Bessie 24, 262
Beulah 23, 262
Emanuel 23, 262
Gladys 24, 262
Margie 23, 262
Orville 23, 262
Oscar 24, 262
Permelia 23, 262
Theodore 23, 262
HAGUE
Douglas 64
Matthew D. 64
Molly A. 64
Morgan Ashley 64
HALIBURTON
Janell M. 151
HALL
Alice Eliza 15, 26, 27
Almeda Maude 8, 17, 18, 367
American Seny 8, 16, 366
Art 16
Audrey Faye 28, 43, 44
Baby boy 16
Blanche 16
Brian 45
Buell 27
Calvin 29, 45
Catherine Ann 43, 62
Cecil Lorne 27, 42
Celia Laverna 15, 28, 29
Cindy 45
Clara May 28, 44
Clarence 17
Clayton Oakley 28, 43
Clifford Gaines 28
David R. 7, 8, 366
Diana Kay 43, 61
Doris Maxine 28, 42, 43
Duane Deloise 28, 43
Edmund 7, 8, 77, 366, 367
Edwina 17
Elmer Elwood 8, 16, 366
Euseba Elmira 8, 17, 367
Florence Ann 8, 17, 366
Frances Leaton 8, 14, 15, 366
Grace Maude 15, 26
Guy Christian 15, 27, 28
Harriet ElNora 8, 14, 366
Ines 16
Ira Emmett 15, 27
James Edmund 15
Janice DeLois 28, 44, 45
Joan Ann 60
Kenneth 26
Kenneth J. 26, 41
Laurie 45
Lester Milton 26
Lois 29, 45
Lulu Seny 15, 27
Lynn Merle 16
Mable Inez 15
Milo 17
Mary Elmira 8, 18, 367
Martha May 43, 62
Nancy Ann 28, 44
Naomi Lee 43, 62
Nell 16
Owen Archebald 8, 15, 366
Robert E. 8, 367
Roy Lutrell 15, 26
Sheila L. 41
Sheldon 45
Sherry L. 41

Terry Jean 41
Tim 42
Verne Reuben 8, 17, 366
Virgil H. 15
Wanda Marlene 28, 43
Zachary Hurshel 15, 29
HARDEN
Jason Edward 58, 59, 358, 359
HARLAN
Barbara Louise 35, 53, 189, 193
Janice Kay 35, 53, 189, 190
Merle Dean 35, 120, 189
Mervin Jay 35, 189, 193
HARPER
Charles 31
Monroe 30, 31
HARRIS
Brenna Samora 73
Charles 73
James Duane 73
HASTINGS
Amos Leland III 70, 150, 155
HATAWAY
Edith 47
HATCH
Allen Scott 61
Naomi Luella 61
Thomas 60
HATFIELD
Kim Leigh 150, 151
HAWKINS
Debbie 47, 67
Jim 47, 397
HAYES
Judy 50, 124, 140
Phillip 63m 64
HEMRICH
Christina Diane 59, 361
Crystal Michelle 59, 361
John Robert 59, 355, 361, 362, 363
HENNING
Megan Leigh 134
HERMAN
Michael D. 63
HERRMAN
Jordan 69, 147
Joshua 69, 147
Kayce 69, 147
Shawn 69, 147
HILL
Andy 47
HILYARD
Cherly Sue 271
HISKEY
Elwood C. 375
HOAGLAND
Raymond 161, 165
HOCKERSMITH
Brandon M.72, 310
David 72
Mike 72, 303, 310
Stephanie Nichole 72, 310
Stephen Nicholas 72, 310
HOLIDAY
Adam Blair 50, 117, 118
Emie Lea 50, 117, 118
Heath Ray 49, 117, 118
Paul Richard 49, 112, 117, 118
Seth Myron 50, 117, 118
HOPKINS
Amanda Christine 64
Brenda Jo 44, 63
Bruce Lynn 44, 63
Deborah Sue 69, 150, 153
Mariah Marie 63
Pamela Kay 44, 63
Sondra Sue 44, 62, 63
Theodore Jr. 43, 44
Veda Lou 44, 63, 64
HORNBECKER
Margaret 50, 124, 136

HOWE
  Edrie 40
HOYT
  Delilah M. 18, 375
HUMMEL
  James II 64
HUNT
  Ruth Porter 17
HUNTER
  Mary A. 381

ISABELL
  Lucinda Adeline 6, 77, 374

JACKSON
  Jeffery 45
JACOBS
  Angela Rae 47, 66
  Baby 17
  Clarice 17
  Charles Forrest 30, 46
  Charles Ray 30, 46, 47
  Charles Reuben 17, 366
  Christian Forrest 66
  Curtis Jacobs 30
  Elizabeth Ellen 66
  Erica Lynn 66
  Eunice Marjorie 17, 30
  Gary Forrest 46, 66
  Hannah Marie 66
  Homer 17, 30
  Janice Allene 46, 66
  Joy Sue 46, 65
  Jefferey Homer 47
  Jim Laird 30, 46, 47
  Joan 30, 46
  John Eric 46, 65, 66
  Jonathon Wade 66
  Julia Ann 66
  Kenneth Lyle 47
  Lane 30
  Lester Lyle 17, 30
  Lucy Susanne 47
  Melanie Dawn 47
  Monica 47
  Nita F. 17
  Patrick Marty 47
  Thomas Carl 47
JENNER
  Sarah 7
JENNINGS
  Clemmie 11, 382, 398
JESSEPH
  Chastity Dawn 63, 74
  Dennis Lynn 63
  Kelly Tanner 63
JOHNSON
  Edmond Jack 44
  Elizabeth 24, 260, 264
  Guy 23, 238
  Maxine 23, 251
JOHNSTON
  Christine Nicole 64
  Michelle Annette 64
  Richard Lee 64
JONES
  Becky Sue 56, 72, 322, 323
  Cliffa 72, 324
  Clifford 56, 72, 322, 324
  Kara Dawn 72, 324
  Lonnie Lee 56, 322
  Loren 56, 320, 322
  Sandra Lynn 57, 72, 326, 327
  Sandy Lee 69, 150, 152
  Michael 72, 323
  William 318, 326
  William E. 56, 57
JORDAN
  Donald P. 165
JORNS
  Burke Jacobs 66
  Kenneth D. 66
JUDD
  Nancy 6, 76

KAUFMAN
  Neva Belle 41
KEEN
  Terry 63
KEHOE
  Leslie Elmer 46
KEISEL
  Suzanne 52, 179, 181
KELLEY
  Abeata Daisy 30
  Daphne 16
  Eugene Shelby 29
  Gladys Irene 16
  Helen Elizabeth 30
  Henry James 29
  James Riley 16, 366
  Kathleen Sena 30
  Leota Seba 30
  Leslie Calvin 17
  Marilyn Joan 30
  Mary Verlynn 241, 249
  Patricia Ann 30
  Samuel Malcom 16, 29
  Sidney Edmond 16, 29, 30
  Seba Vera 17
  Thelma Doris 17
  Woodest Marion 30
KELLY
  Moses 14
  Robert E. 14, 366
  Robert J. 14
  Romona 14
  Terry 47, 373
KENNEDY
  Boy 43
  Charlene Wilma 43, 61
  LeVerne Neil 42, 43
  Marcella Jean 43, 61
  Mary Esther 43, 60, 61
KEYS
  Susan May 21, 84, 212, 214
KIBLE
  Erma Lucile 33, 34, 98, 112, 113
KILPATRICK
  Joe 19, 385, 386
KIRCHMER
  Galen 45
  Larry 45
  Marion L. 45
  Teresa 45
KIRCHNER
  Margaret E. 23, 253, 254
KITCHELL
  Cheryl Ann 66, 391
KITTEMASA
  Ginger 73
KNACK
  Judith 47
KNOWLES
  Dean 47, 373
KRASE
  Jill Diane 49, 114, 115, 116
  Lloyd Eugene 48, 49, 112, 114, 115
  Shelly Anne 49, 114, 115, 116
KROPP
  Erika Ruth 66
  Kaitlyn Ann 66
  Ronald David 66
  Trevor Charles 66
  Tyler David 66

LACKEY
  Karen Jean 52, 167, 175
LAIRD
  Lila 30
LAMB
  Floyd William 31
  Opal Gertrude 31, 372
LANTZ
  Bill 52, 169, 173
LARSEN
  Brett Richard 103, 105

George 70, 219, 220
  Jessica Darlene 70, 220
  Raymond Amasa 70, 220
  Shayla Michalle 70
LAWTON
  Geneva 42
LEA
  John Albert 55
LEHMAN
  Angel Marie 71, 304
  Brenda 56, 71, 303, 304
  Jeri Ann 56, 303, 309
  Jerry 56, 287
  Lucina Ruth 56, 72, 303, 310
LEWIS
  Scott Carl 64
LIMPERT
  Dawn Marie 74, 391, 394
LINDEN
  Ruth 92, 93
LITZKES
  Frances Emma 15, 366
LIVINGSTON
  Wesley 24, 264
LOVELACE
  Josephine 19, 382
LONG
  Anne E. 46, 66
  Jim C. 46, 66
  Kyle Jacobs 66
  Rachell Ann 66
  Sara Nell 66
  Scott Jacobs 46, 66
  William Carl 46
  William Carl Jr. 46
LOPER
  Paget 71, 300
  Patricia Lee 71, 300
LUEKENGA
  Bill J.R. 43, 44
LUSTER
  Alice Melrose 39
LYNN
  Alexis Ann 59, 358
  Benjamin John 59, 358, 360
  Kimberly Diane 58, 358, 359
  Koki 360
  Melvin John 58, 355, 358

MACHE
  Leanne Renae 59, 365
MACY
  Heather Kay 70, 155
  Tatum Lyn 70, 155
MAXWELL
  Etna 18
  George 18, 367
  Leonard Bill Bailey 18
  Sarah Frances 16, 366
  Vida 22, 84, 233, 234
MAY
  April Michelle 63, 73
  Daniel Earl 63
  Earl 62, 63
MAYHEW
  Allen Edward 37, 224
  Eldon 36, 37, 224, 225
  John Daryl 37, 224
  Robert Jay 37, 224
MAYO
  Charles Leo 37, 243, 247
  Emogene E. 37, 243, 246
  Janice 244
  John Michael 245
  Judy 244
  Kathryne Irene 245
  Kelly Beth 247
  Keri Judith 247
  L. Newton 37, 243
  Randy Charles 247
  Richard Dean 37, 243, 245

Robin Keith 247
  Virginia Louise 245
  William Joseph 245
  William Roy 37, 244
MCCONEGHY
  Arlene 40
  Becky 60
  Cathy Lou 60
  Fred 40, 60
  Kim Dexter 60
  Mical 60
  Randy 60
  Sharon Hop 60
  Willard 40
MCCURDY
  Marci Lynn 158
MCGINN
  Cynthia Lou 44, 64
  Duane Frances 44
  Jill Marie 44
  Karen Sue 44
  Kurt Frances 44
MCLAIN
  Darlene 41
  James W. 41
  JoAnn 41
  Kenneth Wayne 41
MCQUEEN
  Vickie 68, 129
MCQUISTON
  Brian 75
  Roger 75
MEHLING
  Dorothy 47, 90, 91
MELTON
  Darren Robert 65
  Jason Walter 65
  Robert 65
METZ
  Nellie Mae 20, 84, 98
MILLER
  Annona 18
  Ashley Nicole 59, 364
  Blendena Caroline 29, 45
  Bonnie Lou 29, 45
  Charles Lawrence 59, 364
  Edmond 18
  Eric James 364
  Frank Joseph 28, 29
  Hannah Elizabeth 59, 364
  Howard 18
  Iva 18
  John Andrew 59, 364
  John Foster II 59, 355, 364
  Joseph 18
  Kalley 18
  Katherine Diane 59. 364
  Marian Frances 29
  Peggy Jean 29
MONTGOMERY
  Margaret 39, 284, 320
MOORE
  Ada 10, 377
  Alan Arthur 33, 48, 100, 102
  Alan Dee 36, 53, 194, 201
  Alana Deann 53, 201
  Allen 23, 253, 258
  Alva Daniel 21, 36, 120, 122, 123, 194, 195, 196
  Amanda Elaine 53, 201
  Andrew 6, 102
  Andrew J. 402
  Angela Dawn 70, 219, 220
  Angela Denise 52, 169, 172
  Annie Jean 174
  Arlene 20, 98, 119
  Arthur Leon 35, 51, 161, 163
  Austin 18
  Ava Lynne 36, 53, 194, 202
  B. Thomas 164
  Brenda Sue 52, 169, 173
  Brian 51
  Cade 48, 102

Calvin 6, 10, 77, 377
  Charlotte M. 6, 10, 78, 378
  Chelacen 51
  Christopher Lee 52, 164
  Clara S. 13, 23, 238, 251
  Clarence 7, 79
  Clyde Earl 13, 23, 238, 253
  Della M. 12, 22, 238, 239
  Donald Jay 34, 112
  Dorothy 22, 233
  E. William 12, 84
  Edith Valetta 36, 53, 194, 197
  Effie Sarah 12, 20, 84, 92, 123
  Elizabeth Ann 10, 375, 376
  Elizabeth Tyler 174
  Elmer 12, 84, 232
  Elwood Orin 21, 36, 123, 212, 216, 217
  Etta Ellen 7, 13, 14, 80, 282
  Eva V. 13, 22, 23, 123, 238, 241
  Floyd Virgil 20, 33, 98, 100, 101
  Gary Lloyd 35, 169, 170
  Gary Lloyd Jr. 52, 167, 169, 170, 173
  George 6, 10, 78, 377
  George Arthur 51, 163
  Ginger 48, 102
  Gladys 238
  Glenn Leon 21, 35, 120, 122, 123, 161, 162, 166
  Helen 10, 381
  Helen Mae 21, 36, 37, 212, 224
  Herbert L. 10, 375, 376
  Howard Ray 34, 50, 124, 136, 137
  Infant 12, 86, 235
  Infant twin 12, 13, 238
  Ira Austin 9, 375, 376
  James C. 77, 375, 376
  James Clarence 10, 375
  James F. 6, 9, 376
  James Monroe 7, 12, 80, 237
  James Reuben 34, 50, 124, 140
  Jayen Dale 258
  Jeffrey Dean 54, 218
  Jimmie E. 237
  John Edward 7, 80
  John William 21, 22, 228, 231
  Jordan Wayne 69, 142
  Josephine 7, 79
  Joshua Scott 174
  Joshua Shane 69, 142
  Judith Diane 34, 48, 49, 112, 114, 115
  Karen Ann 52, 164
  Karen L. 63
  Karen Sue 34, 49, 112, 117, 118
  Kari Cozette 48, 103, 105
  Kirsten Lee 48, 103, 105
  Kyle William 52, 164
  Larry Joe 36, 54, 55, 218, 219, 221
  Lauren 102
  LaVina Jean 52, 175, 176
  Leon Arthur 12, 20, 84, 98, 99
  Lessie Louise 252
  Lester Leroy 13, 238, 252
  Lloyd Merle 21, 35, 120, 122, 123, 167, 168
  Marion M. 6, 10, 78, 381
  Marissa 48, 102
  Martha 6, 77, 376, 379
  Marla Darlene 258
  Mary 10, 375
  Matilda Jane 6, 9, 77, 368, 369, 370

Melissa Rebecca 7, 13, 80, 260
Melvin E. 21, 37, 212, 227, 228
Michael Alan 50, 139
Michael B. 52, 169
Michael Orin 37, 227, 229, 230
Minnie 7, 10, 377
Mirian Ann 34, 50, 124, 126
Myrtle E. 10, 375, 376
Nancy Ann 35, 161, 165
Nathan Trevor 174
Nettie M. 9, 375
Olive 12, 20, 88
Opal Marian 21, 35, 84, 120, 122, 123, 189
Orin Edgar 12, 21, 123, 212, 215
Paula Lynn 52, 175, 178
Paul 23, 253, 254
Pauline 23, 256
Phoebe C. 6, 10, 78, 380
Randy Ray 54, 218
Raymond 98, 119
Raymond I. 12, 20, 21, 84, 123, 233, 234
Reuben 6, 7, 77, 80, 82, 120
Reuben David 12, 21, 84, 120, 121, 122
Richard Donald 34, 98, 112, 113
Richard Edgar 7, 80, 236
Richard S. 6, 7, 76, 77, 78
Rick Dean 52, 175, 177
Robert Fredrick 229
Rosa L. 13, 22, 238, 240
Rose Annette 36, 53, 54, 194, 204
Rosemary Emily 51, 163
Ruth 84, 232
Ruth B. 12, 21, 35, 120, 123, 179, 180, 186, 187, 188
Sally Kay 37, 227, 229
Samuel William 51, 163
Sarah Louise 7, 13, 80, 277
Seny 6, 7, 8, 16, 77, 366, 367
Shawn Dean 54, 219
Shayle Michelle 220
Sheryl Ann 50, 136
Stephen Scott 52, 169, 174
Sue Ann 36, 194, 200
Susan N. 6, 11, 78, 123, 382
Susanne 37, 227
Tammy Rae 50, 68, 140, 141
Taylor Thomas 177
Thomas Herbert 36, 194, 203
Thomas S. 6, 77, 374
Tony Brent 35, 52, 167, 175
Troy Douglas 50, 136, 139
Valerie Jean 52, 169, 171
Veda Mae 21, 36, 120, 122, 206
Velda Pauline 253, 255
Vickie Jan 258
Violet Marie 21, 34, 120, 122, 143, 144
Wayne Virgil 33, 48, 100, 103, 104
Wesley Wayne 50, 69, 140, 142
Will 381
Willa Pauline 34, 50, 123, 129
William 10, 12, 77, 79
William David 35, 51, 161, 164
William H. 6, 7, 9, 18
William Oscar 7, 12, 20, 80, 84, 85, 86, 87
William Reuben 34, 120, 124, 126
Zelma Elva 20, 33, 98, 106

MORSE
Connie Arlene 46, 65
Corrin Moonyeon 65
Gordon Russell 46
Ivan Robert 46
Mark Edwin 46
Nickolas Leroy 65
Phyllis Ann 65
Rex Eldon 46, 65
Robert Steven 46, 65
Teresa Anne 46, 65
Vance Steven 65

MOSSMAN
Winnifred 26

MOYER
Brent 391, 395

MULLHOLLAND
Buddy 365
Roger 365

MUNFORD
Debra Ann 66

MUSCH
Deny 192

MUSIH
Deny 190

MYERS
Carolyn June 33, 48, 106, 107, 108
Robert Glen 33, 106, 110, 111
William Harold 33, 106, 107
William Henry 33, 98, 106

NAKA
Katsura 360

NEWCOMB
Boyd 86, 88
Hazel 20, 88, 89

NEWMAN
Amanda Renee 67, 395
Candice Jill Stanfield 67, 395
Marshall Richard 67, 395

NEWTON
Carolyn Lee 62

NICHOLL
Carl Russell 31, 47, 372, 373
Claude 31, 372
David 31, 371, 372
Donald Merle 31, 372
Dorothy Kay 47, 373
Evelyn Ellen 47, 372, 373
Hazel Leota 31, 372
Jimmie Duane 47, 373
R. June 47, 373
Ruby 31, 372

NICHOLSON
Mike 71, 295, 298, 299
(Reece) Robert Allen 71, 298, 299

NIELSON
Vivian Lee 37

OBERST
Chris 60
Jack 60
Scott S. 60

O'BRIEN
Darcy Ann 58, 342, 348

OEHLERT
Aaron Lee 55
Jordan Glenn 55
Robert Henry 55, 271

OLIVER
Johnnie Eugene 56, 303, 308, 309
Riley 56, 303, 308

OPENSHAW
Claudia 66, 396

ORCUTT
Alexander Chance 75, 292
Amanda Michelle 70, 75, 291, 292
Carly Savannah 75, 291
John Eugene 70, 288, 291
Travis Eugene 70, 75, 291

OSBORN
Robert 47, 373

OVERHOLT
Kellie Jay 95

OWENS
Archibald 6, 76, 77, 78
Betty Lou 60
Charlotte 76
Rebecca 6, 76, 77, 78
Reuben 76
Susannah 76

PARKER
Linda Lee 46

PATTERSON
Elmer 55

PAUL
Amanda 6, 402
Melvina Barbara 7, 77, 80
Rachel Caroline 14, 15, 366

PEDERREN
Elener 26

PENNER
Baby boy 30
Darrell Lee 45
Edna Maxine 30, 46
Elizabeth Anna 30
Evelyn Ruth 30
Gary Ivan 46
George Roscue 30
Henry 30
Ivan Dale 30, 46
Margaret Elnora 30, 45
Michael Dale 46
Norma Frances 30, 46
Ralph Carl 30
Richard Lee 30
Roger Thaine 30, 45

PERKINS
Lori 66

PETERS
John 60
Lucelle 60

PETTY
Alvin 25, 279
Dean 25, 279
Eula 25, 279
Fred 25, 277, 279
Irene 25, 279
June Leota 25, 279
Nora 25, 279
Ola 25, 279
Roy 25, 279

PFEIFF
Calvin Hoover 55, 287, 295, 296, 297
Cynthia Louise 55, 71, 295, 300
Emma Jean 55, 71, 295, 298, 299
Glen Stephen 55, 295, 301

PHILLIPS
Randi Renee 57, 326
Virginia Rose 57, 326
William James 51, 326

PICKENS
Wanda 34, 120, 124

PICKRELL 84

PINKERTON
Dorothy 29
Leslie 159, 160
Elizabeth A.

POE
Cecil 15

POWERS
Oscar 24

RACICKY
Joan Kay 66

RAINWATER
Edward 165
Robin 165

RATANAMON
Craig Austin 62
Kimberly Beth 62
Skol 62

RAY
Cindy D. 51, 69

REAGAN
Art 46

RECTOR
E. 23
Lois Virge 251
Louise 23, 251
Marie 23, 251
Virgie Bell 23, 238, 251

REECE
Alisha Dawn 71, 299
Christina Elizabeth 71, 299
Jonathan Adrian 71, 299
Nathan Edward 71, 299
Sam 71, 299
Thomas Ray 71, 299

REEVES
Dustin Dwight 73
Matthew Levi 73
Steve 73

REISER
Brittany Nicole 75, 307
Glen 75, 306, 307
Tiffany Renee 75, 307

REVES
Lois 42

RILEY
Adrian Monroe 249
Carl Floyd 249
Claude Eugene 249
Cora 241, 248
Curtis Armined 249
E. Harvey 22, 23, 238, 241
Edna Arlene 249
Edward Monroe 241, 249, 250
Gilbert 241
Kenneth Armine 249
Nila 241
Ralph 241
Stella 23, 37, 241, 243
Steve William 249

ROBERTS
Terisie 15, 16

ROBINSON
Mable 19

ROGERS
Buster E. 61
Carly Jae 177
Carody Baur 177
Charles Caleb 177
Irma 282, 329
Jodi Caitlin 177
Rhonda Lee 175, 177

ROSSITER
Rebecca Lynn 184
Stephanie Rachel 181, 184
Todd 181, 184

RUSHTON
Craig Allen 56, 313, 314
Hunter Austin 72, 315
Michael Brett 56, 72, 313, 315
Ronald A. 56, 311, 313
Tracy Noelle 56, 72, 313, 316
Tyler Michael 72, 315

RUSSELL
Neva Iona 41, 42

RUTHERFORD
Ruth 30

RYON
Lucinda 76

SAGEL
Alice Luster 318, 320

SANNER
Patricia 68, 131

SAVOY
Kenneth James 49, 114, 115, 116

SCOTT
Dennis 48, 91
Donna

SCHISLER
Cora 37
Edward 37
Frank 37, 243
Gilbert 37
Nela 37
Ralph 37

SCHLINLOFF
Bernice 37, 270

SCHROEDER
Duane T. 53, 189, 193, 195
Matthew 53, 193
Melanie 53, 193
Shawna Marie 53, 193

SCHROLL
Wilma Lorena 42

SCHUESSLER
Mary Lou 28

SCHWEHR
Claudia Marie 68, 129, 131

SCRIBNER
William W. 16

SEEDS
Ronald 61
Ronald Jr. 61

SELLERS
Donna 73

SEXTON
Leonard 27
Virginia 27

SEARS
Alec Tanner 74, 394
Cameron Jacob 74, 394
Christina Michelle 66, 396
Danielle Elizabeth 66, 396
Gerald Orlando 31, 47, 385, 388, 389
Gerald Orlando Jr. 31, 47, 388, 390
Janet Sue 47, 67, 390, 395
Justin Brock 74, 393
Kimberli Marie 66, 74, 391, 392
Michael Ernest 47, 66, 390, 391, 396
Patrick Thomas 47, 390, 395
Stacy Brock 66, 74, 391, 393
Tracy Lance 66, 74, 391, 394

SHABELL
Suzanne Elizabeth 34, 112

SHAPANSKY
James Allen 72, 327
Mike 72, 327
William Cody 72, 327

SHARITS
Azel Coffland 25, 260, 272, 273, 274
Eloise 25, 272, 274

SHARTZER
Pat 48

SHAY
Jerry Wayne 63

SHEARER
Martha M. 9, 375

SHEETS
John Michael 190, 192
Kayla Michelle 192
Michelle Rene 53, 190, 191
Rachelle Nicole 192
Ronald 53, 189, 190
Stephen Ray 53, 190, 191, 192

SHERRELL
  Bill 71, 295, 303, 309
  Billy Don 71, 300
  Gary Don 71, 304
  Jeri Sue 71, 304
  Jerry Ray 71, 309
  Jimmy 71, 303, 309
  Larry 71, 303, 309
  Rebecca Ann 71, 309
  Savanna Towler 309
SHRIGLEY
  Sharon 62
SKINNER
  Roger 40, 355, 357
SMART
  Edna G. 33, 90
SMITH
  Amber 73
  Bertha 25, 27
  Bertha M. 13, 277, 279
  Harry 56, 320
  John 73
  Julia Bell 12, 80, 238
  LaVerna 25, 278
  Mark Lindsey 169, 171
  Oscar L. 13, 25, 277, 278
  William L. 80
  William Thompson 13, 277
SMITHHISLER
  David Pious 31, 32, 385, 397
  Jan 32, 47, 397
SNYDER
  Shawn Suzann 68, 134
SOWARD
  Charles 17, 367
  Richard 17
  Gary 17
  Lucille 17, 30
  Sondra 17
SOWDER
  Beulah Frances 37, 38, 271
SPRADLIN
  Scott Edward 49, 114, 115, 116
SPRINELL
  Ruben B. 22
SPURLIN
  Hershel P. 47
STANBECK
  Diane Marie 47, 395
STANFIELD
  Blake 391
STANLEY
  Marilyn 253, 258
STATON
  Harley Loren 72, 316
  Loren 72, 316
STEFFEN
  Victor 44
STEINBACK
  Alan 53, 189
STEPHENS
  Craig Lavan 51, 149
  Roy 249

STEPHENSON
  Carol 38, 302
STEVENS
  Mary Catherine 25, 277, 278
SUELTHAUS
  John W. 10, 380
SULLIVAN
  Irene 14, 282, 328
SWANSON
  Axel 45
  Becky Jo 45
  Patricia Hope 45
  Susan LaVern 45

TALLEY
  James Lee 255, 257
  Larry Dean 255
  Leslie Dale 255
  Woodrow 23, 253, 255, 256
TALLMAN
  Charles Wesley 34, 120, 144
  Charles West 156, 158
  Clayton 160
  Elizabeth Blanche 158
  Glen Edward 34, 35, 144, 159
  Laura Ann 160
  Roger Dennie 34, 144, 156, 157
  Ryan Charles 158
  Thelma Elizabeth 34, 50, 51, 144, 145
  Velma Ruth 34, 50, 51, 144, 145
  Wesley Edward 159, 160
TAYLOR
  Bruce 25, 276
  Carl William 13, 24, 260, 264
  Cecil 24, 264
  Cleo Turner 24, 264
  Edith Leona 21, 84, 120, 122
  Fern 24, 264
  George 24, 25
  George Lackey 13, 25, 260, 276
  Glen 24, 264
  Gerald 264
  Geraldine 24
  Gladys Hazel 13, 25, 260, 272
  Harvey 24, 264
  James Orcen 13, 24, 260
  John 24, 80, 260, 263
  John Harold 13, 260, 275
  John Ira 13, 260
  Judy 70, 288, 294
  Kent 25, 276
  Mabel Blanche 13, 24, 260, 266

  Melvina Jane 13, 23, 260, 262
  Nellie 24, 264
  Sharon 159
  Sherry 34, 144
  Wilda Mae 24
THOMAS
  Mason Scott II 57, 334, 337
THOMPSON
  Eric Allen 356
  Allen 355, 356
  Jennifer 356
THORNBURG
  Alma Delilah 18, 31, 371, 372
  Benjamine 18, 370, 371
THURMAN
  Claude M. 13
TOWLER
  Carol Jean 71, 309
  John Jr. 71, 303, 309
  Savanna 71, 309
TROESTER
  Joyce Ann 227, 229
TURNER
  Blake 186, 187
  Claude
  David P. 35, 179, 186, 188
  Jeremy John 186, 187
  John Harold Sr. 35, 120, 179, 180, 188
  John Harold Jr. 35, 52, 179, 181, 183, 184, 185, 188
  Justin David 186, 187
  Suzanne Keisel 52, 181, 184
TURPIN
  Della Jean 48, 100, 102
TYLER
  Beverly 52, 169

ULLUM
  Naomi Hazel 35, 120, 167
UNRUH
  Shawn Christian 63
  Warren 62, 63

VALLE
  Cathryn Kay 52, 173
VEAL
  Andrew Lawrence 63, 64
VOGELMAN
  Mary 46, 47
VOGTS
  Nathan Daniel 53, 202
  Valecia Lynne 53, 202
  Victor 53, 194, 202
  Wesley 53, 202

WAGNER
  Orville 31, 372
WAINSCOTT
  David Shawn 48, 107, 108

  Jodi Lynn 48, 107, 109
  Robert Gordon 48, 106, 107, 108
  Steve Lee 48, 107
WALKER
  Laura Lee Doty 63
WARD
  Janet Lee 57, 58, 330, 340
WATHEN
  James C. 62
  Shawn Cehri 62, 73
  Sloan Courtney 73
  Vernon James 62, 73
WEBB
  Barbara Dawn 55
  Gordon 270
  Gordon T. 55
  Marie Alaine 55
WEEDMAN
  Mary Alice 55
WEISKER
  Emily Frances 35, 120, 161, 166
WELLS
  Earl 382, 400
  John Albert 275
  Ronnie 274, 275
  Scottie 55, 275
  Sharon 55, 275
  Terri 55, 275
WELTMER
  Todd 103, 105
WERNER
  Judy 67
WERTZ
  John 48, 91
WESTGATE
  Lovina 366
WHEELER
  Elwood 16
WHITNEY
  Frances Ethlyn 33, 98, 100
WHITESIDE
  Bandie 60
  Danny 60
WHYDE
  Edward V. 95, 96
  Gregory 96, 97
  Michael 96, 97
  Gracelynn 97
WIARD
  Tenley 66
WICKHAM
  Faye Ann 36
WILEY
  George Alan 13, 14, 80, 282, 328
  John Moore 14, 282, 329
  Reuben William 14, 282
  Stella Adaline 14, 25, 26, 282, 284
  Shirley Jean 329, 365
  Walter George 14, 282
WILLIAMS
  Danny 72, 303, 305, 310

  Haley Nicole-Marie 73, 354
  James Edward-Alexander 73, 349, 354
  Jonathan Paul 72, 310
  Kenneth Wayne 72, 310
  Kristi Gail 72, 310
WILSON
  Bruce 90
  Mary Ellen 9, 370
WINSKY
  Dollie 63
WITT
  Earl Chester 88, 89
WOLFE
  J.E. 10, 18, 377
WOODS
  Marie 96, 97
  Ronald Phillip 64
  Tyler Christian Lorne 64
WOODY
  Wayneta Orpha 38, 39, 284, 311
WULZ
  Colleen Benoit 68, 133
  James Elvyn 50, 124, 129, 130
  James Patrick Nheil 68, 131
  James Wyett 135
  Renee Marie 132
  Richard Nheil Allison 50, 68, 129, 131
  Ronald Ray Allison 50, 68, 129, 133, 134, 135
  Sophia 132
  Stephanie Renee Allison 68, 133
  Susan Rene 50, 129

YOUNKER
  Faye Ann 194, 200
  Jeremy Tyler 203
  Matthew Scott 203

ZIRKLE
  Forrest 92, 95
  Jay Robert 95
  Joyce Ellen 95, 96
  Suzanne 95

www.ingramcontent.com/pod-product-compliance
Lightning Source LLC
Chambersburg PA
CBHW082022300426
44117CB00015B/2315